Also by Jason King

Beyond the Phog: Untold Stories from Kansas Basketball's Most Dominant Decade

Kansas Jayhawks: A Year to Remember Inside the Greatest Season in KU Basketball History

Printed in the United States of America by Walsworth Publishing Company, Marceline, MO.
ISBN 978-0-692-96890-1

Cover photos by Steve Puppe.
Cover and inside design by Beau White.

BEYOND THE STREAK

Untold Stories from KANSAS BASKETBALL'S UNRIVALED BIG 12 REIGN

JASON KING

with C.J. Moore

@kansasbook on Twitter

CONTENTS

INTRODUCTION

Hands clasped in the center pocket of his blue Kansas hoodie as the wind chill dipped below 10 degrees, Darnell Jackson walked through the empty Allen Fieldhouse parking lot. Puffs of white air streamed from his mouth as he flung open the doors to college basketball's aging cathedral.

It was just before 9 a.m. on the first Saturday of March—more than two hours before the Kansas Jayhawks hosted Texas in the final game of the 2007 Big 12 season—and Jackson had arrived early for treatment on his sore ankle.

A food vendor stacked crates of water on a dolly. Metal shutters covered concession stand windows and ropes that would serve as a barricade between fans and players sat unfurled in a corner. Nothing out of the norm, thought Jackson, and the 6-8 forward reached for the door to the Jayhawks locker room. But then Jackson paused. He heard a familiar sound.

Someone was bouncing a ball.

Jackson strolled into the tunnel and peered toward the far end of the court. Alone on the hardwood, launching shot after shot, rebounding his own misses and makes, was Kevin Durant, the 19-year-old Texas freshman who was averaging more than 25 points per game.

"He was soaked in sweat," Jackson said. "Every stitch of clothes he had on was stuck to his body. I had never seen that before, an opponent showing up for a road game before the rest of his teammates, just to get in an extra workout."

For more than five minutes, Jackson lurked in the darkness of that tunnel, watching Durant swish mid-range jumpers, 3s and fall-aways.

"As I walked back to the locker room," Jackson said, "the main thing I remember thinking was 'Damn, this guy is about to go crazy on us. He's about to kill us.'"

Jackson was right—but only partially.

In one of the most memorable performances in the then-52-year-history of the storied building, Durant—who just months later would become the No. 2 pick in the NBA draft—scored 32 points in his lone appearance at Allen Fieldhouse. Twenty-five came in the first half.

"That's the baddest man to ever play here," KU assistant Danny Manning, the Jayhawks legend, said to no one in particular on the bench just before intermission, and as accurate as the comment may have been, an hour later, it didn't matter.

Trailing by as many as 16 before the break, Kansas clawed back and rallied for a 90-86 victory that resulted in a Big 12 title for Bill Self and the Jayhawks.

More than 10 years later, in July of 2017—only weeks removed from his first NBA championship—I spoke with Durant for 20 minutes in his sixth-floor suite at the Marriott Convention Center in Augusta, South Carolina and asked him to reflect on that 2007 loss to the Jayhawks.

"It was fun," Durant told me, "to look over and see Coach Self shaking his head and to hear the crowd get quiet when we built that lead. We were up by 16 at one point. To suck the air out of that historic arena, even for a half ... I'll take that."

The future Hall of Famer leaned against the marble countertop of the suite's bar and crossed his arms. Ten years and 809 NBA games later, the scouting report from that afternoon in Lawrence was still fresh on Durant's mind as he rattled off names from KU's 2007 loaded roster. Jackson and Julian Wright and Brandon Rush couldn't guard him that day, he said. But the Jayhawks still had Mario Chalmers, Sasha Kaun, Russell Robinson, Darrell Arthur, and Sherron Collins.

"Kansas was so good—and they were so *deep*," Durant said. "They eventually just wore us down. That was their third Big 12 title in a row and now the streak is at 13. It's unbelievable."

And also difficult to fathom.

For the past 13 years, no one in the Big 12 has been able to stop the Kansas Jayhawks.

Not Durant, who, it could be argued, was as good as any collegian in NCAA history.

Not the Texas Longhorns, who boast 13 NBA draft picks since the streak began in 2005.

And not Blake Griffin, LaMarcus Aldridge, Buddy Hield, Michael Beasley, Marcus Smart or any of the other stars who have come through the Big 12's conveyor belt of talent during the Jayhawks' reign.

"It's something we won't ever see again," ESPN's Jay Bilas said of the streak. "It's arguably the most remarkable achievement in the history of sport."

And the story behind it needed to be told.

That was my mission back in June of 2017, when I conducted the first of more than 100 interviews for this book.

I wanted the Jayhawks to explain why they flourished in tense moments while so many others floundered. I wanted opponents to describe the angst of frustration of battling a machine that has never shown signs of rust. And I wanted to get inside the mind of a coach whose consistency is unrivaled, even by the legends of his sport.

Self has won Big 12 titles with no returning starters. He captured one with a walk-on in the starting lineup. He's won them with All-Americans, lottery picks and conference players of the year. And in some seasons, he's won with none of the above.

Mike Krzyzewski, the winningest college basketball coach in history, has 12 ACC titles in 37 years at Duke. Bob Knight, who ranks third in all-time victories, captured 11 Big Ten crowns in 29 seasons with Indiana.

From 2005-17—the span of KU's streak—Kentucky, North Carolina, Florida, Texas, UCLA and Indiana have each missed the NCAA Tournament at least once. The Jayhawks, meanwhile, have been a No. 1 or a No. 2 seed 10 of the last 13 years, and they've never been lower than a No. 4.

"I didn't think we'd see something like this in the modern era," Baylor coach Scott Drew said,

Kansas' 13 straight league titles aren't unprecedented. UCLA won 13 in a row from 1967-79, but that was a different era, when athletes weren't leaving school early for the NBA draft or transferring at record-setting rates. Not to mention, players are simply better and more athletic than they were in the 60s, 70s, 80s and even 90s. Grassroots basketball has grown, coaching has improved and, instead of competing in multiple sports, kids more than ever are focused on basketball year-round.

Still, even with so many factors leveling the playing field, even with so many reasons for there to be slippage, the Jayhawks have maintained a level of dominance over their Big 12 counterparts that evokes awe, respect—and in my case, profound curiosity.

Whether it was over dinner with Mario Chalmers in Houston, or after a charity event with Marcus Morris in Philadelphia, or during a post-workout pow-wow with Thomas Robinson in Los Angeles, I spent the majority of my summer in 2017 conducting interviews with former players about the inner-workings of Bill Self's program. I wanted to hear the heartbeat of KU basketball.

I listened as Russell Robinson described how the shortcomings of one era influenced the success of the next. I learned how the program benefited more from the development of an unheralded four-year player such as Frank Mason than one-year wonder Andrew Wiggins. I was moved at how the sudden passing of Lisa Robinson spurned a brotherhood between her son, Thomas, and the Morris twins that has only strengthened since they left Lawrence. And I was inspired by players such as Sherron Collins, Darnell Jackson and Jamari Traylor, who came to realize that Kansas basketball not only changed their lives, but saved them.

Colleague C.J. Moore and I interviewed 107 people for this book. Forty of them either played for the Jayhawks or are on the current team. We also gained perspective from nearly every coach who has served on Self's staff along with plenty of others who battled against them. Rick Barnes, Fred Hoiberg and Frank Martin, to name a few.

Thirty-four players who competed against the Jayhawks also contributed to this project. The tales from Durant, Jacob Pullen, Georges Niang, Quincy Acy, Kim English, Marcus Denmon and others are sure to inform and entertain.

No one, though, cooperated with this endeavor as much as Self. Three weeks after a 90-minute interview in his office, Self spent another hour-and-a-half in a booth at Henry T's, answering more questions as he ate a grilled chicken sandwich with cheese and bacon.

"No bun," Self told the waitress, "and cottage cheese for the side."

Later that night, the Hall of Fame coach sent me a text.

"Three hour interview ... longer than the one I did for my own biography!"

I chuckled as I typed my response.

"It's your fault for winning so many damn titles!"

I feel lucky to have chronicled such an incredible run. Something tells me it's not over yet.

CAST OF CHARACTERS

(in order of appearance)

Bill Self: The eighth coach in KU history; was hired in 2003 following Roy Williams' departure to North Carolina; inducted into the Naismith Memorial Basketball Hall of Fame in 2017

Tim Jankovich: Came with Self from Illinois; assistant coach at Kansas from 2003-2007; current head coach at SMU

Norm Roberts: Has had two separate stints as an assistant at KU—from 2003-2004 and then 2012 to present; spent six seasons as head coach at St. John's

Michael Lee: Key reserve from 2002-2005; high school teammate and best friend of Aaron Miles; started six games as a senior

Jeff Hawkins: Part of the 2002 recruiting class; redshirted as a freshman and was on Self's first three KU teams; started over Mario Chalmers at beginning of his senior season in 2005-06

Aaron Miles: KU's all-time leader in assists (954) and ranks third in steals (264); four-year starter from 2001-2005; played in two Final Fours (2002 and 2003) and an Elite Eight (2004)

Keith Langford: Sixth man on KU's 2002 and 2003 Final Four teams; outspoken two-year starter who is eighth on school's all-time scoring list with 1,812 career points

Stephen Vinson: Walk-on from 2002-2006; Lawrence native was occasionally part of the backcourt rotation in 2005-06

Wayne Simien: Starter on Self's first two teams; first-team All-American and Big 12 MVP in 2005; jersey was retired in 2010

Christian Moody: Joined Roy WIlliams final team as a walk-on in 2002 and became a starter under Self as a junior two years later; Tabbed "the best walk-on" in college basketball history by Billy Packer

Isma'il Muhammad: Georgia Tech forward who drew key blocking foul on Keith Langford in 2005 Elite Eight game

Russell Robinson: Three-year starting point guard who graduated in 2008; was known for his toughness and defense; ranks fifth all-time in steals (247) and 10th in assists (500)

Daryl Dora: Texas Tech forward from 2003-2007; twice played role of surprise star in wins over Kansas

Pat Knight: Son of legendary coach Bob Knight; served as assistant under father at Texas Tech from 2001-2008 and then head coach from 2008-2011

Joey Graham: Oklahoma State forward from 2003-2005; finished as runner up to KU's Simien for 2005 Big 12 Player of the Year honors

John Lucas III: Oklahoma State point guard from 2003-2005; started his career at Baylor; son of former NBA player/coach John Lucas Sr.

Darnell Jackson: Physical, bruising forward was the first recruit to commit to KU after Self was hired in 2003; starter on the 2008 national title team

Kurtis Townsend: Assistant coach at Kansas since 2004; known as one of the nation's top recruiters and was key in landing stars such as Andrew Wiggins, Josh Jackson and others

Sasha Kaun: The 6-11 Russian started at center as a sophomore and junior; Self considered him a sixth starter his senior season in 2008

Matt Kleinmann: Spent five years in KU program as a walk-on from 2004-2009; Blue Valley West graduate was a star in the classroom

Jeremy Case: Deadeye shooter was signed by Roy Williams but never played for him; was part of Self's first five teams at KU, finishing his career in 2008; current video coordinator at KU

J.R. Giddens: Starter on Self's first two teams; forced to transfer to New Mexico after getting stabbed in an altercation at the Moon Bar in the summer of 2005

Joe Dooley: KU assistant from 2003-2013; left in 2013 to become the head coach at Florida Gulf Coast; ace recruiter who helped land the Morris twins, Thomas Robinson and others

Brandon Rush: Three-year starting wing from 2005-2008; led the Jayhawks in scoring each of his three seasons in Lawrence; three-time first-team All-Big 12; jersey was retired in 2017

Mario Chalmers: Combo guard who spent three seasons at KU; the 2008 Final Four Most Outstanding Player; made the greatest shot in KU history to send 2008 championship game against Memphis to overtime; jersey was retired in 2013

Clent Stewart: Kansas State guard from 2004-2008; starter on the 2005-06 team that won at Allen Fieldhouse and the 2007-08 team that ended KU's winning streak at Bramlage Coliseum

Jim Wooldridge: Kansas State head coach from 2000-2006

Julian Wright: Member of the stacked 2005 recruiting class that included Rush and Chalmers; third-team All-American in 2007; declared for the NBA following his sophomore season

Sherron Collins: Sixth man his first two years at KU and a starter the final two; first-team All-American as a senior in 2010; school's fifth-leading scorer (1,888 points); jersey retired in 2018

Brady Morningstar: Lawrence native who spent five years at KU from 2006-2011; glue guy who took pride in being an elite defender

Darrell Arthur: Third-leading scorer on the national title team who arrived at KU with Collins in 2006; had 20 points and 10 rebounds in 2008 title game; declared for the NBA draft after sophomore season

Joseph Jones: Rugged Texas A&M forward who helped spark a program turnaround under Billy Gillispie; starter on 2006-07 that won at Allen Fieldhouse

Andrea Hudy: Assistant Athletics Director for Sport Performance has been at KU since 2004; regarded as one of the top strength and conditioning coaches in the country

Jerrance Howard: Played for Self at Illinois and joined his staff at Kansas as an assistant coach in 2013; also was on Gillispie's staff at A&M when Aggies won at Allen Fieldhouse in 2007

Acie Law: Texas A&M star guard who hit the game-winning shot at Allen Fieldhouse in 2007

Kevin Durant: As a one-and-done freshman at Texas, scored 25 of his 32 points in the first half in one of the most legendary performances ever at Allen Fieldhouse; averaged 34.5 points in his two games against KU in 2007 but lost both

A.J. Abrams: Sharp-shooting Texas guard from 2005-2009; the Big 12's all-time leader in 3-pointers

Danny Manning: The Jayhawk great had multiple roles on Self's staff from 2003-2012; left in 2012 to become the head coach at Tulsa and is now the head coach at Wake Forest.

Rick Barnes: The current Tennessee coach was at Texas from 1998-2015; won three Big 12 regular season titles—including two shared titles with KU (2006 and 2008)

Justin Mason: Four-year starting guard at Texas who arrived in the same recruiting class as Durant in 2006

JaRon Rush: Oldest brother of Brandon Rush who was one of the best prep players ever in Kansas City; played collegiately at UCLA

Tyrel Reed: The Kansas native was a seldom-used freshman on the NCAA title team before earning a spot in the rotation the next three years.

Frank Martin: K-State assistant under Bob Huggins; became the head coach when Huggins left for West Virginia in the spring of 2007; left K-State in 2012 for South Carolina

Jacob Pullen: K-State guard from 2007 through 2012; Ranks sixth on the Big 12's all-time scoring list

Brad Underwood: K-State grad who served as an assistant under Huggins and Martin from 2006-2012; head coach at Oklahoma State in 2016-17; currently the head coach at Illinois

Rodrick Stewart: KU reserve guard from 2005-08 who started his career at USC; injured his knee while dunking during shootaround the day before the 2008 Final Four

Cole Aldrich: Two-year starter who left after three seasons at KU; second-team All-American and Big 12 Defensive Player of the Year in 2010; jersey was retired in 2018

Ed Hightower: Veteran official who worked the 2008 national title game

Scott Drew: Became the head coach at Baylor the same year Self was hired at Kansas; has led Baylor to two Elite Eights and two Sweet 16s

Marcus Morris: Three-year starter from 2008-2011; second-team All-American and Big 12 Player of the Year in 2011; left along with his brother Markieff for the NBA after three years at KU; No. 14 pick in the 2011 NBA draft

Tyshawn Taylor: Four-year starting guard at Kansas who helped lead KU to 2012 national title game in his senior season; All-Big 12 first team and third-team All-American in 2012

Conner Teahan: One of the best walk-ons to ever play at KU; sixth man on the 2012 national runner-up

Barry Hinson: Current Southern Illinois coach was on Self's staff from 2008-2012

Greg McDermott: Iowa State coach from 2006-2010; current Creighton coach

Elijah Johnson: Two-year starter who made several clutch shots on the way to 2012 title game; team member from 2009-2013

Thomas Robinson: First-team All-American and Big 12 Player of the Year in his only season (2011-12) as a starter; declared for NBA draft after breakout junior season; No. 5 pick in the 2012 NBA draft

Xavier Henry: Self's first one-and-done freshman; starter on the 2009-10 team

Quincy Acy: Baylor forward from 2008-2012

Ali Farokhmanesh: Buried the dagger 3-pointer for Northern Iowa in the 2010 second-round upset of the top-ranked Jayhawks

Ben Jacobson: Northern Iowa head coach since 2006

Travis Releford: Two-year starter who spent five years at Kansas (2008-2013), redshirting his sophomore season; one of the best perimeter defenders Self has coached

Melvin Ejim: Iowa State forward from 2010-2014; Big 12 Player of the Year in 2014; high school teammate of Thomas Robinson

Dan Brinkley: Longtime mentor/agent to the Morris twins

Joey Rodriguez: Starting point guard on the 2010-11 VCU team that upset KU in the Elite Eight

Shaka Smart: VCU coach from 2009-2015; current head coach at Texas

Kevin Young: Key reserve forward on 2011-12 team and a starter in 2012-13; started his career at Loyola Marymount

Naadir Tharpe: Spent three seasons at Kansas (2011-2014); starting point guard on the 2013-14 team

Ben McLemore: Sat out 2011-12 season as an NCAA partial qualifier; second-team All-American in 2012-13; declared for 2013 draft and was the No. 7 pick

Jamari Traylor: One of Self's all-time favorites, he was an energy guy off the bench from 2012-2016; had to sit out 2011-12 season as a partial qualifier along with McLemore

Pierre Jackson: A juco transfer who starred at point guard for two seasons at Baylor (2011-2013)

Kim English: Played the small-ball power forward spot for Missouri's 2011-12 squad; was a four-year starter for the Tigers (2008-2012)

Michael Dixon: Sixth man on Missouri's 2011-12 team; finished his career at Memphis

Marcus Denmon: Led Missouri in scoring his final two seasons; averaged 28.5 points against KU in the final two games of the Border War in 2012

Frank Haith: Went 30-5 in his first season as Missouri's head coach in 2011-12; left after three years to become the head coach at Tulsa

Jeff Withey: A seldom-used bench player his first few years at KU, Withey turned into the best shot-blocker in KU (and Big 12) history; two-year starter who won back-to-back Big 12 Defensive Player of the Year awards in 2012 and 2013

Thomas Gipson: K-State forward from 2011-2015; played for both Frank Martin and Bruce Weber

Doc Sadler: Former Nebraska head coach spent one season (2012-13) as KU's Director of Basketball Operations; currently the head coach at Southern Miss

Perry Ellis: Three-year starter ranks ninth among KU's all-time leading scorers (1,798 points); a second-team All-American as a senior in 2016; two-time first-team All-Big 12 selection

Tad Boyle: Former Jayhawk who is the head coach at Colorado; led the Buffaloes to an upset win over KU during the 2013-14 season

Georges Niang: A four-year starter (2012-2016) at Iowa State and the Big 12's fourth all-time leading scorer; two-time All-American

Fred Hoiberg: Known as "The Mayor" in Ames, he was a star guard for the Cyclones and then the head coach from 2010-2015; left Iowa State to coach the Chicago Bulls

Naz Mitrou-Long: One of the Big 12's best shooters when he starred at Iowa State from 2012-2017

Phil Forte: Arrived at Oklahoma State in 2012 along with high school teammate Marcus Smart; graduated as OSU's all-time leader in 3-point field goals

Travis Ford: Oklahoma State's head coach from 2008-2016; currently the head coach at Saint Louis

Bruce Weber: Replaced Self at Illinois and then Frank Martin at K-State; shared the Big 12 title (KSU's first since 1977) with KU in his first season in Manhattan in 2012-13

Gary Browne: West Virginia guard from 2011-2015

Wayne Selden: McDonald's All-American arrived as part of Self's deepest (and best) recruiting class in 2013; three-year starter who made All-Big 12 second team as a junior in 2015-16, his final season in Lawrence

Landen Lucas: Expected to be just a role player, Lucas started most of his final two-and-a-half seasons at KU; spent five years at Kansas (2012-2017) after redshirting as a freshman

Tarik Black: Three-year standout at Memphis who joined KU as a graduate transfer in 2013-14; a strong defensive presence who also served as a mentor to Joel Embiid

Kevin Boyle: Head coach at powerhouse Montverde Academy in Florida; coached Joel Embiid in high school

Joel Embiid: Arguably the most talented player Self has ever coached; made a huge impact in his one season at KU (2013-14) before a back injury forced him to miss the postseason; No. 3 pick in the 2014 NBA draft

Andrew Wiggins: The top-ranked player in the 2013 class was KU's leading scorer in 2013-14 and a second-team All-American; No. 1 pick in the 2014 NBA draft

Frank Mason: Arrived at KU as an afterthought in the loaded 2013 class; finished as the AP National Player of the Year and the sixth all-time leading scorer in school history

Rico Gathers: Baylor power forward from 2012-2016; the Big 12's third all-time leading rebounder; currently a tight end with the Dallas Cowboys

Jevon Carter: Starter at West Virginia his first three seasons; entered 2017-18 senior season ninth on the Big 12 all-time steals list

Chris Crutchfield: Assistant coach at Oklahoma who helped recruit Buddy Hield to Norman

Ryan Spangler: Three-year starter at Oklahoma and key member of the 2015-16 Final Four team

Fred VanVleet: One of the greatest players in Wichita State history; was the starting point guard for the Shockers when they upset KU in the second round of the 2015 NCAA Tournament

Gregg Marshall: Wichita State head coach since 2007

Evan Wessel: Made four 3-pointers in Wichita State's 2015 upset win over KU; high school teammate of Perry Ellis

Fran Fraschilla: Color commentator for ESPN who mostly calls Big 12 games

Devonte' Graham: Two-year starter who enters his senior season in 2017-18 as the Big 12 preseason Player of the Year

Jordan Woodard: Four-year starter at Oklahoma (2013-2017); second-leading scorer on OU's 2016 Final Four squad

Lon Kruger: Kansas State graduate who has been the head coach at Oklahoma since 2011

Josh Jackson: An All-Big 12 selection and third-team All-American in his one season at Kansas in 2016-17; No. 4 pick in the 2017 NBA draft

Lagerald Vick: Key reserve on the 2016-17 team; enters his junior season in 2017-18 expected to start

Luke Cooper: Basketball trainer in the Kansas City area who worked with Mason before his senior season

Udoka Azubuike: Promising young big man expected to make a big leap in his sophomore season in 2017-18

Dean Wade: Starter in his first two seasons at Kansas State; one of the key veterans on K-State's 2017-18 roster

Barry Brown: Became a starter midway through his freshman season at K-State; the Wildcats' third-leading scorer as a sophomore in 2017-17

Sviatoslav Mykhailiuk: Ukrainian guard arrived at KU as a 17-year-old; starter and 3-point specialist on the 2016-17 team

Manu Lecomte: A Miami transfer who was Baylor's second-leading scorer in 2016-17; expected to be the Bears' top player in 2017-18

Donovan Jackson: Key reserve for Iowa State in 2016-17 who scored 10 points in the Cyclones' upset win at Allen Fieldhouse

Steve Prohm: Iowa State head coach who took over veteran team when Hoiberg left in 2015

Bob Huggins: West Virginia coach since 2007; spent the 2006-07 year at Kansas State and helped ignite the program's turnaround

Daxter Miles: Starter in his first three seasons at West Virginia; expected to team with Carter to form one of the nation's best and most experienced backcourts in 2017-18

Jamie Dixon: Entering his second year as the head coach at TCU, which has emerged as a contender after years as the league's doormat

Kenrich Williams: TCU's starting power forward who led the Horned Frogs with 18 points in an upset win over KU in the 2017 Big 12 Tournament

Dwight Coleby: Backup big man on KU's 2016-17 team

Mike Brey: Head coach at Notre Dame since 2000; one of the most underrated coaches in college basketball

Tom Izzo: Hall of famer who has been the head coach at Michigan State since 1995

Jay Bilas: Former Duke forward who has become one of the most respected television analysts in the country for ESPN

PROLOGUE

When Bill Self arrived at the Holiday Inn and Conference Center for Illinois' postseason banquet in 2003, more than 100 fans lined the corridor leading to the ballroom. Some wore orange, freshly-printed t-shirts with a proclamation—"We Love Our Self!"—on the front.

And on the back, a plea: "Don't Go Bill!"

One night earlier, on April 14, Roy Williams had crushed fans in Kansas by announcing he was leaving the Jayhawks' program after 15 years to become the head coach at North Carolina, his alma mater. Before the plane carrying Williams to Chapel Hill ever took off that afternoon, Self—who'd just completed his third season with the Illini—had been identified as his likely successor.

If, of course, he wanted the job.

Bill Self: Accepting the Kansas head coaching position was the best decision of my career. But in April of 2003, when the offer was made, I was a total mess. Everyone thought it was a no-brainer to come to Kansas. It wasn't. I loved my job at Illinois.

Truthfully, I didn't want Roy Williams to leave Kansas, because I knew I'd be faced with a choice I didn't want to make. Kansas is a great place, but I thought what we had going at Illinois was going to be unbelievable, too. I actually thought I'd be leaving a slightly better team than the one I'd inherit. Not significantly better, but maybe a little bit. If you add Charlie Villanueva, who was committed, to a roster that included five future pros (Deron Williams, Dee Brown, Luther Head, Roger Powell and James Augustine) ... that'd have been a pretty good group.

I remember the morning after our banquet, on a Wednesday, my family and I flew to Fisher Island in Florida for some time away. A few minutes after the plane touched down, it was obvious it wasn't going to be much of a vacation. My phone was blowing up. Drue Jennings, John Hadl, boosters ... I was getting all sorts of calls. We ended up flying home the next day to figure out what we were going to do..

Assistant coach Tim Jankovich: We had just finished our third season at Illinois when Bill got offered the job at Kansas. For about a week, I watched from a front-row seat as he made a very, very difficult decision.

It was agonizing for him. No matter which choice he made, we were going to be in a good situation. We had an NCAA championship-caliber team coming back at Illinois. But Bill also had an opportunity to coach at Kansas, which is arguably the top college basketball program in America. It was a "win-win" scenario, but at the time it hardly felt that way.

Assistant coach Norm Roberts: It was the most grueling, gut-wrenching thing I've ever seen a coach do. For about a week, he kept going back and forth, back and forth. I know people on the outside were probably thinking, "He's not going to turn down Kansas." But that was a very real possibility. At times, I actually thought it might happen.

Tim Jankovich: I'll never forget the moment Bill made his decision. We'd been holed up in his basement all day and our wives were upstairs. You could see on his face and even in the way he walked that he was being tortured. You could totally feel it. Most coaches are good-hearted people. It's not a, *"It's 100 percent about me ... who cares about anyone else?"* mindset. Coaches care about everyone around them, and that's what made this situation amazingly difficult. Finally, he'd had enough. He sprung up off the couch and said, "We're going."

Bill Self: It was tough, because I knew I wouldn't be able to take my whole staff, particularly Wayne McClain, my assistant, and Jeff Guin, my administrative assistant. I said, "I'm sorry but I don't think there will be a place for you, so we need to make sure everything works out for you here."

At that point, I called our athletic director, Ron Guenther, and told him I was going to leave. He said, "That's fine. Everyone on your staff is fired. Everybody needs to have their stuff out of the office by 8 a.m. Monday morning. I don't want to see any of you guys ever again."

So then I came back and told the staff, "We're not leaving. We're going to stay. Guys are going to lose jobs over this. I'm not going to let that happen. We can't go." Then Wayne McClain said, "Coach, before I came here I was a high school coach my whole life. We won four straight state championships. I can get a job. Don't worry about me." Jeff was the same way. I called our associate AD, told him about my conversation with Ron, and said, "If Wayne McClain is not allowed to remain with this program, it's going to set Illinois basketball back further than it's ever been." He was that important. Everyone loved him. Guenther immediately made him the interim head coach and guaranteed him a spot on the staff. That's what held everything together.

Norm Roberts: As soon as Bill was firm with his decision, he secluded himself in a side room in his basement and called every player on the Illinois roster. He was able to get a hold of most of them. Then he called each and every parent. He'd say, "OK, take 10 minutes, 15 minutes—however long you need—and let me have it. Say whatever you want to say." Whether it was Dee Brown's mom ripping into him or a player expressing his disappointment, Bill got an earful. But almost every conversation ended with, "I understand. Thanks for everything you did. Best of luck to you."

When he walked out of the room after making that last call ... I've never seen a guy that drained before in my life. Just emotionally and physically drained.

Bill Self: Those were hard phone calls. Everything about it was painful. I ticked a lot of people off in Champaign. At that time, I wasn't a guy that was mentally tough enough to not care if I ticked off people, because it really bothered me. But I tried to pick the situation that would be the best over time, not just one or two years. And there's no question Kansas was the best situation over time.

Jason King: Kansas had reached out to a few other coaches—Tom Crean, Mark Turgeon and Ernie Kent—but that was just a formality. Everyone knew Self was getting the job. Still, *The Kansas City Star* was adamant I get the scoop. We had a reporter, Wright Thompson, staked out at the airport in Champaign while I waited to cover the news back in Kansas. On Easter Sunday, Wright called me in a panic around 10 a.m. and told me Self was on a plane headed for Lawrence. I dressed as quickly as I could, called our photographer and raced to the airport. There were three people there when I arrived: a woman running the control panel, the guy with the bright orange sticks landing the aircraft and KU chancellor Robert Hemenway. Five minutes later, Self's plane touched down and Hemenway was there to greet Bill and Cindy and their kids—as well as Norm Roberts—as they walked down the steps and onto the runway. Our photographer snapped a photo of Hemenway and Bill shaking hands, but instead of keeping it to herself, she hurried back to the office and put it on the Associated Press wire. The next day, newspapers across America (including the *Lawrence Journal-World*, our biggest competitor) ran our "exclusive" picture. It's funny now, but back then it was infuriating.

I tried to get a few comments from Bill as he was ushered to Hemenway's beige Lincoln, but he said he'd been told not to comment until the press conference the following afternoon. To this day, it's probably the only time Bill Self has ever turned down someone for an interview. Later that afternoon, I received an email from a writer in Champaign that said, "Sportswriters in KC should be throwing a party. You're about to cover the most media-friendly coach in America."

Bill Self: We flew to Lawrence on Easter Sunday and, around 9 that night, I had my first meeting with the team. I didn't get a bad vibe, but I don't know that it was great, either. I think they were looking at me like, "Let's wait and see." Wayne Simien was the hardest to read of the bunch. He wouldn't talk. He just sat back and just watched and observed the whole time.

Finally, the tension eased up and someone—I think it was Aaron (Miles) or Keith (Langford)—said, "Can we get red uniforms?" I'm thinking, "Well hell, if that will make them feel better, if that's all it's going to take, let's get a set of red uniforms."

Michael Lee: The first time we met Coach Self, he looked like he hadn't slept in three days. His shirt was untucked. His tie was loose. He was just really cool. That's what everyone was saying: "This guy is cool." By that point, reality had set in. We all felt different about the events that transpired to get him there. But collectively, we were like, "Let's see what the man has to say." Coach Self really loosened us up. He was like,

"We're going to have fun, and I'm going to have fun. We're going to run. We're going to push the ball. We're going to do what you guys do best."

Jeff Hawkins: It was all positive. We were like, "OK, he's not that bad." Before we met him, we were mad. Now my impression was, "I'm going to like this guy."

Aaron Miles: Coach Self had a little swagger to his walk, a real confident walk. We didn't know him, so we were like, "He seems cool. But is he trying to be *too* cool? What's this going to be like?"

The one thing I remember was him saying is, "We're going to have fun. It's going to be different, but there's more than one way to skin a cat." I had never heard that before. To this day, that sticks out to me. With Coach Self, it's always about life lessons. In all walks of life, there are a lot of different ways to do things. There isn't a blueprint to everything. You've got to be flexible and able to adapt and adjust.

Bill Self: I remember telling them about the style we were going to play, and that it was the best way, and that we were going to win big. And their whole deal was, "Um, Coach ... we just played in back-to-back Final Fours. We've won bigger than you have. What makes you so sure your way is better for us than the way we've been playing?" Roy had done a great job of convincing them that his way was the best way to play, which is what a coach should do. But what I wanted to do was totally different. I was probably as different from Roy as anyone they could've hired.

Keith Langford: Right before they hired Bill Self, I called Roy and said I wanted to come to North Carolina. He said, "Keith, you know I'd love to have you, but there's a lot going on right now. Just see who they bring in, and if it's that bad, we'll go from there." Then they hired Bill, and he sat me down and gave me the whole spiel about how important I was to the program and stuff. I ended up staying.

Norm Roberts: We were fortunate enough to keep all the returning players, and we attempted to add a piece in Charlie Villanueva. About a month after Bill was hired, we brought him in for a visit. He played pickup with our guys and about 500 fans showed up to watch. But during the visit a tornado touched down in Lawrence. We were getting the alerts up in our offices. We didn't want Charlie to know, but we also had to take cover. So we said, "Um, Charlie ... let's go tour the locker rooms again." We kept him in the locker room about two hours and didn't tell him why. He was like, "Coach, can we go? I'm hungry." He ended up signing with Connecticut, and I'm pretty sure they used the tornado against us when they were recruiting him. It was frustrating not to get him since he had committed to us at Illinois, but we still liked our roster.

Stephen Vinson: Throughout the summer of 2003, during pickup games, Keith was as good as anyone I've ever played with. I'm not exaggerating. One week there were 35 people in the gym every day, including some really good alumni that were back in town. Keith got stuck on a team with four walk-ons, including myself. We held the court for seven or eight games in a row. Those were some of the most competitive summer pickup games you'll ever see. And Keith scored every point but maybe one or two.

Keith was so good and so driven. We all were. We'd just lost to Syracuse in a national championship game we felt we should've won—and then our coach left us. We had a lot of built up fire and anger. If it were up to us, we would've skipped the regular season and hit fast forward to March. Nobody wanted anything to change—but then everything changed.

Michael Lee: After a few months, you could really see that Coach Self was going to change some stuff around. That's understandable. He was a new coach and wanted to do things his way. The problem was that we were still trying to do things our way. Under Coach Williams, we were programmed to do certain things a certain way at a certain time. We had our whole itinerary written out on the first day of school. It was day and night compared to when Coach Self came in.

The first real shock for me was Boot Camp. I thought, "This is crazy!" It wasn't that it was bad. It was just different. He challenged us mentally and physically in different ways.

Aaron Miles: Getting up that early was the hardest part. I was thinking, "This is dumb. Why are we doing this?" With Coach Williams there was no Boot Camp. The conditioning was on Tuesdays and Thursdays for four weeks leading up to the season. That was it. There wasn't any reason to be getting up at 6 in the morning. We were 18- to 22-year-old young men. We weren't used to getting up at 5:30 a.m. We didn't want to do it. I'd sleep in my practice uniform just to cut down on the time I had to spend each morning getting ready.

Michael Lee: Aaron would go to the locker room each night and round up all the practice gear and bring it to the guys. He'd say, "Just sleep in your practice gear." I think a couple of times he even slept in the locker room so he wouldn't be late.

We'd work out for an hour starting at 6 a.m. and then do sprints at the end. We did a lot of running for guys being late to class and guys not going to study hall. And the thing was, you wouldn't know what was going to happen until you got there. You'd show up in a good mood, thinking you were going to have a good day, and Coach Self would say, "All right, guys. Since such-and-such wanted to be a jerk and not show up to class ..." and we'd be like, "Nooooo ... he didn't do it again, did he?" And then we'd have to run. Coach Self would drive us crazy. They kept a total of every time you messed up and then added that into the number of sprints you had to run at the end of practice. I remember one day we started with jump ropes, and Jeff Graves didn't have his shorts tied up. He was trying to jump rope as he was pulling up his shorts. Now instead of doing four sprints, we had to do 15. Almost every day it was total chaos because we were dead tired, our bodies were shocked and we were up earlier than we'd ever been up. It was brutal. Plus, we still had our classes, our study halls, our homework and our social life, although it was almost impossible to have one. You really have to challenge yourself. I was so relieved when Boot Camp was over. I remember calling my parents and saying, "I made it! I survived!"

Kansas opened Self's inaugural season on a high note, defeating No. 3 Michigan State in the second game. But losses to Richmond—at home, no less—and Nevada sparked panic among the fan base and tension in the Jayhawks' locker room.

Wayne Simien: I'm not going to sugarcoat it. The coaching change was tough on all of us. We had won two straight Big 12 titles and been to back-to-back Final Fours under Roy Williams, and now we had a new guy who wanted to do things totally different. Along with being hurt, we were also confused. Looking back, it was like an arranged marriage. Marriage is hard enough in its first year, even though your spouse is basically your best friend and you've had tons of communication and life experiences with her leading up to that point. But this was an *arranged* marriage, where they brought in a coach that we didn't know, a coach that didn't recruit us. We didn't have any experience with Coach Self or any of his staff. It took some getting used to.

Aaron Miles: Coach Self came in and said all the right things about how we were going to have fun and about how we were going to run. He said all the right things to keep us around. He said we were going to play a similar style of basketball. But we didn't. Hell no, we didn't. Coach Williams wanted to score 100 points and hope the other team had 99. Coach Self wanted to score 1 point and hold you to 0. He was fine playing in the 50s.

Tim Jankovich: It was not a smooth transition. It wasn't ugly or confrontational, but it definitely wasn't smooth. You could just feel it. Body language is easy to read. It was very subtle, in my mind. It wasn't defiance in any way. It was just guys thinking, "I'm seeing how this is going, and it doesn't feel like it used to feel."

Don't get me wrong. We loved the guys on that team. They were great people and great players. We enjoyed them. But the coach that they loved was gone and now they had these new guys. I don't want to paint it as this awful thing, because it wasn't. There just wasn't 100 percent buy-in like you get when your own group is 100 percent tied together.

Christian Moody: One difference between Coach Williams and Coach Self was that, at least during Coach Self's first year, we really practiced a lot. We had some long practices. Coach Williams' practices were about two hours. We were there between 3 ½ and four hours with Coach Self. That was definitely a big switch, but I understand why Coach Self wanted to practice so much. He was totally revamping our entire system—our offense—and he wanted to pound home the way he wanted things done. There were definitely some long practices, some long days. We'd practice for three hours, and I remember Coach Self, if we couldn't get something right, he'd say, "All right. Go home." And we'd be like, "All right. Yes! Go home!" Then he'd say, "Be back at 11." And that would just drain everybody.

Michael Lee: It was really bad when we lost at home to Richmond. I still vividly remember a play where they hit a huge 3 near the end of the game. I left my man to go get a steal. But right before I swiped it, the kid picked the ball up and threw it across the court to the guy I was supposed to be guarding, and he swished a 3. Then a few minutes later a kid comes down and makes a game-winning shot. I was like, "We lost at *home*? We lost in *The Fieldhouse*? To *Richmond*?" That just doesn't happen.

At that time there was a "Free for All" section in the school paper, the *Daily Kansan*. Man, that was bad. People were calling in and leaving these anonymous messages bashing our team and bashing Coach Self, and the paper was printing them all. *"These guys need to lose their scholarships. They are immature kids. They think they have it made. Self is in over his head."* Things like that made it obvious to him really quickly how high the expectation level is at Kansas. You don't come here to win 20 games. You don't come here to make the NCAA Tournament. You come here to win championships.

Aaron Miles: Keith was more frustrated than anyone. It took him a while—a *long* while—to get on board.

Keith Langford: In December, we played at Nevada, and Kirk Snyder just killed me. He was really good. Before the season I had said a bunch of stuff in the media about how I was mad that some of the preseason magazines had Snyder ranked ahead of me on the "best slashers" list. I was being borderline arrogant and I shouldn't have done it. A few days after the game, I was dogging it in practice a little bit, and Coach Self made a comment about Kirk Snyder "sticking it up my ass." He dropped a couple of other comments on me after that, and we ended up having an exchange. It wasn't good. It wasn't healthy to do that in front of the whole team and coaching staff. That was one of the low points of the year. At that point I was ready to transfer. I had my AAU coach and my mom contact the Kansas coaches over Christmas, but they refused to give me a release. They talked to me, and I agreed to stay. That's when things kind of went downhill. It was tough after that and a lot of it was my fault.

Michael Lee: Keith was a bit stubborn, but let's be honest: Keith was gifted. He had an amazing first step and he was explosive. And Keith had had an enormous level of success doing things the old way. He was on the All-Midwest Region team as a freshman in the 2002 NCAA Tournament—and he had 19 in the national title game against Carmelo Anthony and Syracuse the next year. Now someone was asking him to do things differently.

The new system really limited him. We went from Roy's secondary break—getting up and down the court and scoring easy baskets and creating turnovers—to Self's philosophy of, "It's OK to walk the ball up the court and get into our high-low game and play from the inside out."

Coach Self is more of a basketball guy. He knows what works and he's going to stick to it. He could care less about guys getting a certain amount of shots. *"Mike Lee, I don't care if you only get one shot in the first half. I need the ball to go to Wayne because he's our most efficient guy."* Keith struggled with that approach. Keith can get a first step on anyone in the world. But even when he may have thought he could've taken his man on the baseline, he knew the system called for him to reverse it to the top of the key because Coach Self wanted to play high-low. Those kind of things bothered him.

Assistant coach Joe Dooley: Early on there was a misnomer that Bill didn't want to play fast. That wasn't true. He just wanted to make sure that if we weren't making shots, we could get some stops. The guys had obviously been well-coached under Roy. But Bill wanted them to defend a little higher on the floor. He wanted to be a little more aggressive on ball screens and guard in different ways. Bill would love to hang 100 points on someone. But he'll tell you in a second that he'd go home a lot happier winning 49-48 than he would losing 101-99. There are a lot of different ways to win games. We wanted to be able to win muddy games and pretty games, too.

Bill Self: You've got to coach within your personality. You can't coach what you don't know and you can't coach what you don't feel comfortable coaching. Under Roy, they ran motion. They ran box set. They ran secondary break. We may have dabbled with those things, but those weren't things we could do as well as the staff had done here previously.

Keith Langford: We struggled so much that year with identity and finding out who we were. It was hard to focus on actually winning something, because Coach Self was trying to win us over. It was difficult.

Michael Lee: In January, Coach Self really gave us a reality check. He told us we were going to have to grow up or it was going to get worse. That's when we had to accept that there's more than one way to skin a cat. We all had to check ourselves and realize, "Man, this is on us. The coaches aren't playing the games. The coaches aren't missing the layups. Coach Self didn't get boxed out for a rebound or turn the ball over." Obviously, the assumption was that Coach Self was doing something wrong or that we weren't responding. That wasn't it at all. We just stunk it up. We weren't coming anywhere close to playing good basketball.

I was like Keith in that my transition wasn't as graceful as some of the other guys. J-Hawk was the same way, but Aaron and Wayne were different. They were carrying the load and trying to get everyone on board. As a coach, Self couldn't have asked for a better leader than Aaron in a situation like that. Aaron was a godsend for Coach Self.

Bill Self: Keith and Mike Lee were stubborn. They were *stubborn*. But that was part of their attractiveness. I liked that about them. Wayne was great, but Aaron was the best. Aaron took on the leadership role because he knew what was best for the team and best for the organization. He bought in early and tried to get everyone else to do the same.

The thing was, it wasn't going to change. We'd just gotten hired. It's not like we were going to leave or get fired after one year. Fighting it wasn't going to help anyone.

Aaron Miles: I felt like it was more important than ever to be a leader, because I could feel the tension. Initially, everyone was hurt. I was hurt. Some guys viewed it as a father walking out on a family, and a new man coming into the locker room. They looked at Coach Self like, "You're not my dad." My mindset was, "You know what? My dad didn't want to be here. Now *you* want to be a part of my life? That's cool. It'll be different, but I appreciate you for that."

It wasn't easy. But if we had to be in the same household, we might as well be on the same page and work toward a common goal. If we didn't get on the same page, those goals weren't going to be attainable. For me, it was what it was. Coach Williams wasn't coming back and Coach Self wasn't leaving. The sooner we accepted the situation, the sooner we could move on.

Kansas finished the regular-season strong with victories in five of its final six games, including an 84-82 win at Missouri in the last game ever at the Hearnes Center. Still, at 12-4, Bill Self's first team tied Texas for second in the Big 12 standings behind Final Four-bound Oklahoma State (14-2).

Bill Self: We couldn't have won the Big 12 that year. Oklahoma State was great. They were terrific.

Wayne Simien: As proud as I am to be a member of the team that started the Big 12 title run (in 2005), I'm also a little frustrated, because the streak would have an extra three years tacked onto it if we wouldn't have stubbed our toes during Coach Self's first season. Frankly, considering everything we went through, we were probably fortunate to place second.

Keith Langford: A lot of people give us credit for starting the streak, but it's kind of our fault for the record not already being broken. It was going to be a difficult year regardless. He had to come in and change the culture, and we had to adapt to it. We had to be the guinea pigs.

Still, through all of our crazy moments, through all of our highs and lows, we somehow got to the Elite Eight. It was crazy.

And things would've been even crazier had Kansas defeated Georgia Tech and advanced to college basketball's biggest stage in Self's first season. Instead, a controversial charging call against red-hot Langford in overtime squelched KU's momentum in a 79-71 overtime loss to the Yellow Jackets. It was the fifth foul on Langford, who scored 13 of his 15 points after intermission.

Keith Langford: For Jim Burr to make that call—a charging call in transition, on the opposite end of the floor at the beginning of overtime—was unbelievable. I spun around Isma'il Muhammad, and he flopped. (Burr) was trailing the play and was literally about 50 feet away when he blew his whistle. There was another ref standing right there and he didn't call anything. I had killed Georgia Tech in the second half. There was no way I was going to let us lose.

Joe Dooley: If that was a charge, I'm a supermodel. Isma'il Muhammad flopped.

Isma'il Muhammad (laughing in postgame interview): There might have been a little Hollywood (by me) on that offensive foul. He barely touched me, but I went flying a little bit. Maybe a little bit of a flop.

Bill Self: Keith's fifth foul killed us. It was an awful call—an *awful* call. (Burr) was 30 feet behind the play. He wasn't in a position to make the call. I'm not saying we would've won the game, but we'd have had a much better chance if they don't blow that whistle. Keith was on a tear.

Aaron Miles: One of the first things I ever said to Coach Self was, "We're used to Final Fours around here." I said it in a fun way, but I was being serious. That's what we do. We had been there back-to-back years. So when we started making that run in 2004, that's what we expected. People always say, "It's so hard to get to the Final Four." No, it's not. Not in our minds. We were good at it. We were right there on the brink of it again and felt like we were supposed to be there. When we didn't get in, it was a letdown.

Michael Lee: I actually thought that was one of Coach Self's best coaching years. He inherited a brand new team—granted, we'd had some past success—and he took us within a game of the Final Four. We lost two lottery picks in Nick Collison and Kirk Hinrich. I don't think Wayne was healthy all year. Aaron was playing with two taped ankles and an air cast. Yet we almost found a way to get back.

Tim Jankovich: By the end of year, it didn't feel like change to those guys anymore. We'd had success and relationships had been formed. You could feel that it was Bill's program, and there was great buy-in taking place.

Wayne Simien: There were definitely a lot of growing pains, but we got stronger as the season progressed. Getting to the Elite Eight gave us a huge confidence boost heading into the next season. Other than Jeff Graves and David Padgett, we had all of our key pieces coming back.

BEYOND THE STREAK

In an effort to most accurately portray their thoughts and feelings, all players and coaches have been directly quoted. Asterisks have been used to conceal certain curse words.

The comments expressed by players and coaches in this book do not necessarily represent the view of the authors.

## CHAPTER 1

2004-05
EMBRACING CHANGE

With Bill Self's awkward "transition period" out of the way—supposedly, at least—the expectations for Kansas basketball entering the 2004-05 campaign were higher than they'd been in decades.

Literally.

For the first time since the days of Wilt Chamberlain, the Jayhawks opened the season ranked No. 1 in the Associated Press poll. The buzz certainly seemed warranted. Wayne Simien was an All-American candidate; Aaron Miles was a lock to become the school's all-time assists leader; and Keith Langford seemed destined to crack KU's Top 10 career scoring list.

Even though the departures of Jeff Graves (graduation) and David Padgett (transferred to Louisville) left them thin in the paint, the Jayhawks had the look of a national championship squad. And that was clearly the theme when 16,300 fans crammed into Allen Fieldhouse for "Late Night in the Phog."

Wayne Simien: There was so much excitement going into my senior year. The honeymoon stage with Coach Self was over, and all of us felt like we knew what to expect. Plus, we'd added some young talent with guys like Russell Robinson and Darnell Jackson and Sasha Kaun and Alex Galindo. We were the No. 1-ranked team in America entering the season. I just remember huddling up with Keith and Aaron and Mike in the middle of the court at the end of Late Night. We were out there in tuxedos and the fans were going crazy. There was just a feeling in that moment, when we were high-fiving and looking into each other's eyes, that we were on the cusp of something special. We really thought we could go the distance.

Michael Lee: The whole theme at Late Night was that we were marrying ourselves to the national championship trophy. We had an actual ceremony, where we wore tuxedos and they brought out the trophy from the 1988 season to center court. We made vows to the trophy and everything.

Aaron Miles: Maybe that jinxed us.

Kansas surrendered its perch atop the AP poll after just one game—a narrow, 68-61 victory over Vermont in the season-opener that dropped the Jayhawks to No. 2 in the rankings. But a 14-0 start caused hopes for an NCAA title to soar even higher—at least among KU's rabid fanbase. Internally, though, something seemed amiss.

Bill Self: There were a lot of positive things happening. Our record was great. But we weren't the second-best team in the country. Instead of blowing teams out, we were winning by two or three possessions. Something just wasn't quite right.

Looking back on it, we were probably a player short—or maybe just a healthy Keith short. He had microfracture surgery on his knee before the season, and any doctor will tell you it takes 12-18 months to get your pop back. Even when he played he didn't have the same pop. It frustrated him, because his body wouldn't do what his brain told him to do.

Russell Robinson: It was tense from the beginning of the season. It's tough for young players when the veterans are only halfway on board. Some guys were still not over the Roy situation.

I played pretty well off the bench, I thought. I started off strong. One game, against Nevada, I could've led the team in scoring but I missed a layup on purpose just to keep our balance and chemistry strong. Wayne had 14 and I had 13.

There was tension. There was a big separation. The old guys did their own thing, and the younger guys didn't know what to do. We were looking for guidance, and there wasn't very much. You factor in personalities like J.R. Giddens, and things just didn't gel very well. I took it as a learning experience. Don't get me wrong. I liked those guys. There were a lot of areas where they set a great example. They were respectful of the staff and really carried themselves well in the community. I picked up on that. I learned a lot from Aaron Miles and how he led off the court. It wasn't all negative. I just learned from their mistakes, too.

Wayne was there. His body was there and his mind was probably there. But *he* wasn't there, if that makes any sense. He came in and did his job and went home. Having been a pro … that's more of a pro mentality. But at that point we needed a little more leadership, a little more guidance. But he had his larger plan and focus (religion). And to his defense, he was battling injuries. He had a lot on his plate.

Wayne Simien: The one thing I wish I could change about that season is that we weren't good leaders for the younger guys. They didn't have a clue on the court—but we didn't have a clue leadership-wise. It's tough to lead when you're in a brand new environment, just like them. I don't have a lot of regrets in my basketball career, but I feel like I could've done a better job of leading those guys … Darnell and Russell and Sasha and C.J. Giles.

The season took what could have been an ugly turn when Simien, the team's leading scorer, injured his thumb in a home win Dec. 18 against South Carolina.

Wayne Simien: It was a routine play, and I took a hard foul. I don't remember my thumb hurting. I just remember not being able to use it. It wasn't working. We immediately went to the locker room and the trainers were looking at it. I was watching the game in the back while Cheddar (Bill Cowgill) and Dr. (Jeffrey) Randall were doing their thing. South Carolina started chipping away, so I was like, "Let's take care of this later." They taped it up and I ran back out there and we finished off the win.

I got an MRI later that night, and they told me I'd torn some ligaments. I could've played with it and waited until after the season to get surgery. But Coach Self had my best interest in mind in regard to my future as a professional. He was like, "Let's go ahead and get this taken care of." I really appreciated that. My respect and trust in Coach Self increased in a significant way that night.

During Simien's four-game absence, Self adopted a new guard-dominated, ball-screen heavy offense—called "Fist"—that he continued to use in future years.

Kansas 70, Georgia Tech 68
January 1, 2005 · Lawrence, Kan.

Kansas (9-0)

Player	MP	FG	3FG	FT	R	A	F	S	TO	B	TP
Aaron Miles*	38	4-11	4-5	2-4	5	8	4	0	4	0	14
Keith Langford*	38	8-19	2-4	0-0	6	1	1	1	3	0	18
J.R. Giddens*	40	6-14	4-10	0-0	3	1	2	0	3	0	16
Christian Moody*	32	3-4	0-0	2-2	10	0	3	0	3	1	8
C.J. Giles*	11	1-2	0-0	0-0	3	0	5	0	0	2	2
Alex Galindo	26	2-8	2-5	0-4	7	0	2	0	0	0	6
Russell Robinson	17	2-6	0-1	0-0	2	3	0	1	2	0	4
Sasha Kaun	10	1-1	0-0	0-0	2	0	1	0	0	1	2
Michael Lee	2	0-1	0-1	0-0	0	1	1	0	0	0	0
Darnell Jackson	4	0-1	0-0	0-0	0	0	0	0	0	0	0
Moulaye Niang	7	0-2	0-0	0-0	2	1	0	0	0	0	0
Team					4						
Totals	225	27-69	12-26	4-10	43	15	19	2	15	4	70

Georgia Tech (9-2)

Player	MP	FG	3FG	FT	R	A	F	S	TO	B	TP
Will Bynum*	34	2-10	1-5	2-3	2	3	3	3	4	0	7
Jarrett Jack*	42	10-12	2-3	4-4	5	3	1	2	4	0	26
B.J. Elder*	7	1-4	0-0	1-2	0	0	0	1	1	0	3
Anthony McHenry*	22	2-3	1-1	0-0	7	1	5	1	1	3	5
Luke Schenscher*	37	1-7	1-1	7-8	6	2	2	0	3	3	10
Isma'il Muhammad	33	3-10	0-0	2-6	7	2	4	1	1	1	8
RaSean Dickey	8	0-3	0-0	0-0	2	0	0	0	1	2	0
Mario West	7	0-1	0-0	0-0	3	0	0	0	0	0	0
Anthony Morrow	21	3-5	1-2	0-0	3	0	3	0	0	0	7
Theodis Tarver	10	1-2	0-0	0-0	1	0	1	0	1	1	2
Zam Fredrick II	4	0-2	0-0	0-0	0	0	0	0	0	1	0
Team					3						
Totals	225	23-59	6-12	16-23	40	11	19	8	16	11	68

	1st	2nd	OT	Total	FG%	3FG%	FT%
Kansas	27	34	9	70	39.1	46.2	40.0
Georgia Tech	34	27	7	68	39.0	50.0	69.6

Officials: Tony Greene, Michael Kitts, Donnie Gray
Technicals: None

Bill Self: We changed because of Wayne's injury. We didn't have another big guy we could throw it to and get a basket, so we said, "Let's change how we play." Initially, it wasn't good. We played Georgia Tech right after that and I think we made five of our first 19 shots and got down 31-15. I turned to my assistants and I said, "Can you believe this?" But we came back, and Keith ended up making a big shot in overtime and we won the game.

Then we go to Kentucky and win with Christian Moody, a walk-on, and four freshmen—Darnell, Sasha, C.J. and Alex—as our bigs. We were playing with a makeshift lineup and we were still undefeated. It was incredible.

Keith Langford: For me, it was cool, because with the high-low, the only one benefiting was Wayne. Don't get me wrong. He was playing amazing. But there wasn't

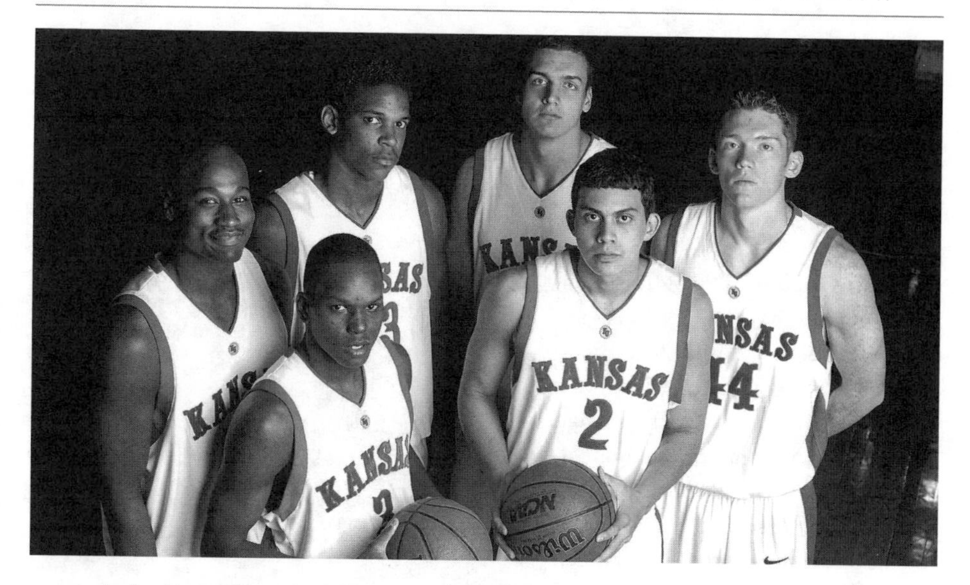

as much freedom. But when he went down and we had to change, all of us felt like, "Wow, this feels more like our first two years."

That time period, when we changed that offense, is the reason guys like Sherron Collins and Tyshawn Taylor and Frank Mason had so much success. You've seen KU guards have explosive seasons, whereas initially it was usually the bigs that had great years.

When Wayne came back, we incorporated him more. We had to because he was our best player in that system. He was a first-team All-American. You couldn't just go away from him.

Wayne Simien: I had the surgery to reattach the thumb ligaments over Christmas break and I missed two games I really wanted to play: Kentucky and Georgia Tech. But it gave other guys a chance to step up. Keith obviously hit the iconic game-winner in overtime against Georgia Tech on New Year's Day at Allen Fieldhouse. That game was huge, not only because they were ranked No. 9, but because they'd knocked us off in the Elite Elite nine months earlier. And Darnell and Sasha showed some good flashes in the win at Kentucky. That was the game when (broadcaster) Billy Packer called Moody (11 points, seven rebounds) the greatest walk-on in college basketball history.

Christian Moody: I think I got 300 text messages that night. My phone just was going crazy. I ran into Billy Packer later that year. I told him that my mom was his biggest fan in the world, because my mom just loved that he said that. I definitely let him know how appreciative I was. Michael Lee started giving me the nickname, "G.O.A.T." It's cool to get a nickname at all from anybody, even if it's a joke. That comment has kind of stayed with me. Even when I go to play at a charity game, it will come up. Coach Self always reminds the campers when he introduces me before our alumni game each summer. So that's really been cool to have something like that—even if it's not at all true—stick with you.

No love in Lubbock on Valentine's Day

The Jayhawks were 20-1 and 10-0 in Big 12 play when they traveled to Lubbock on Valentine's Day. Simien had been back for nine conference games, and the team looked untouchable since his return. He had averaged 20.1 points and 10.3 rebounds per game in Big 12 play and KU's average margin of victory was 14.4 points during that stretch.

Wayne Simien: I kept things in good perspective while I was out. We'd gotten off to such a good start—we were undefeated—and it was our last hurrah. Whether we had to tape up my thumb or amputate it, I wasn't going to let another injury sabotage my season.

I don't think there was too much of an adjustment period when I came back, because I'd been getting so many minutes before and was comfortable with what we were doing. Plus, it was an injury to an upper extremity, so I was able to run and do cardio and stay in shape. It wasn't like an ankle or a knee, where you're limited. It was a pretty seamless return.

Texas Tech 80, Kansas 79
February 14, 2005 · Lubbock, Texas

Texas Tech (16-6)

Player	MP	FG	3FG	FT	R	A	F	S	TO	B	TP
Jarrius Jackson*	49	6-16	3-7	4-5	4	4	2	1	4	1	19
Joey Hawkins*	22	0-1	0-0	0-0	1	1	3	1	1	0	0
Devonne Giles*	24	1-5	0-0	1-2	2	0	4	1	3	3	3
Martin Zeno*	50	7-16	0-0	10-14	6	2	0	0	1	0	24
Ronald Ross*	49	10-15	1-3	0-0	11	7	2	2	2	0	21
Damir Suljagic	18	1-1	0-0	0-0	0	1	4	1	1	0	2
LucQuente White	2	0-0	0-0	0-0	0	0	1	0	0	0	0
Darryl Dora	36	3-7	1-5	4-5	1	1	4	0	1	0	11
Team					8						
Totals	250	28-61	5-15	19-26	33	16	20	6	13	4	80

Kansas (20-2)

Player	MP	FG	3FG	FT	R	A	F	S	TO	B	TP
Keith Langford*	45	10-22	2-4	2-6	8	1	2	4	3	0	24
Wayne Simien*	47	8-20	0-2	4-4	13	2	3	0	2	0	20
Christian Moody*	34	3-4	0-0	1-2	8	0	5	1	2	1	7
J.R. Giddens*	45	3-13	3-9	0-0	3	2	4	0	0	0	9
Aaron Miles*	47	4-9	3-5	0-0	7	9	1	0	6	0	11
C.J. Giles	2	0-0	0-0	1-2	2	0	1	0	1	0	1
Russell Robinson	3	0-1	0-1	0-0	0	1	0	0	0	0	0
Alex Galindo	3	0-0	0-0	0-0	0	0	1	0	0	0	0
Sasha Kaun	13	1-2	0-0	2-2	3	0	3	0	0	0	4
Michael Lee	11	1-3	0-1	1-2	1	2	2	0	1	0	3
Team					3						
Totals	250	30-74	8-22	11-18	48	17	22	5	15	1	79

	1st	2nd	OT	2OT	Total	FG%	3FG%	FT%
Texas Tech	39	30	5	6	80	45.9	33.3	73.1
Kansas	33	36	5	5	79	40.5	36.4	61.1

Officials: Mark Whitehead, John Higgins, Ed Hightower
Technicals: None

Keith Langford: We were rolling through everyone. We were on our way. Then we went to Texas Tech on Valentine's Day.

Guys were acting up in the hotel before the game. We always had these wrestling matches. The night before we played it was me and Mike Lee's turn to go. Our teammates filmed the whole thing, and I kinda got the best of him. The next day before the game, Mike had this real bad crick in his neck. Coach was giving his pregame speech and Mike is sitting there with a heat pack on his neck. Coach was like, "What the hell is wrong with Mike?" Everyone was kinda snickering because we all knew, but we were trying to keep it a secret.

Bill Self: Coach (Bob) Knight had a really good team that season with Ronald Ross and Jarrius Jackson and Martin Zeno. That's the year they beat UCLA and Gonzaga to go to the Sweet 16.

Our game against them that night was one of the most exciting we'd played all year. Keith scored in the lane with 3 seconds left to force overtime. And then Christian tipped in a shot to send it to double OT.

Langford scored all five of KU's points in the second overtime to put the Jayhawks ahead 79-74 with 2:50 remaining. And it was 79-77 when Miles rebounded a missed 3-pointer by Jarrius Jackson with 7.9 seconds left on the clock.

Aaron Miles: About three guys swarmed me and started swinging their hands and arms. One of them hit me hard enough under the eye to cause a big welt that turned into a shiner after the game. Somehow, the ref called me for traveling. It was a bad call. If that call would've gone the other way, the conversation we're having now might be a little different.

Keith Langford: The whole team was swarming him and trying to foul him. He had scratches on his face and a welt under his eye. But instead, with Bobby Knight standing right there, they called traveling, which meant Texas Tech was going to get one last shot.

Even then, I remember not being worried. I thought, "We're fine. Let's just get a stop and get out of here." Instead, they inbounded the ball, and Darryl Dora banked in a 3-pointer to beat us 80-79. He wasn't even a 3-point shooter. I think he'd made about two all season.

A 6-foot-9 sophomore reserve, Dora was 9-for-27 from beyond the arc for the season before he made that shot.

Darryl Dora: That night I had taken four 3s and missed them all. The shot came out of an inbounds play, an up screen for Ron (Ross). He got it and tried to make a play. They cut him off. I screamed at him. Time was running out. I flashed up to the 3-point line. I was pretty deep. Sasha Kaun was a ways back with his hands down. I decided to let it go and, luckily, it went in.

I was actually a good 3-point shooter. That's what helped me play professionally for seven years, being a big guy that could shoot. It was a big part of my game. At Texas Tech I was just playing my role. We had very, very good guards—Jarrius Jackson, Martin Zeno, Andre Emmett—during the time I played there. In the motion offense you do your part, and my job was to screen for those guys. I handled the ball a lot and got those guys the ball. That was pretty much my role.

Dora also was the star for Texas Tech in its 2007 upset win over Kansas. He had 19 points off the bench.

Pat Knight: For years, Self would see us every summer and say, "Who the hell is Darryl Dora?" It would drive Bill nuts. He was like, "That's the best play your dad could come up with in the final seconds? A 3-pointer for Darryl Dora?"

Darryl Dora: The 2007 game was great, but my shot in 2005 is the thing I'll remember the most. Beating Kansas brings so much excitement to your campus. I walked into biology class the next day and all of the football players were like, "Well, well, well ... look who made it to class today." They said they'd never have come to class after that game.

It was a big part of my career that people still bring up all the time. I'm a coach here now, and people treat me really good in west Texas. Still, in my years here, we went to three NCAA Tournaments and a Sweet 16. Playing deep into the tournament feels much better than hitting one shot. Kansas knows that.

Wayne Simien: After Daryl Dora banked in that 3, things were never quite the same. It was shambles after that. We lost the next two games. Initially, we didn't think too much about the Texas Tech loss, other than we got hosed on a no-call in front of Bobby Knight and the Texas Tech bench. Still, by no means did we feel like the loss would be the start of a snowball effect that resulted in some big-time struggles. We lost at Oklahoma after our hotel caught on fire around 4 a.m. We had to evacuate and sit in the parking lot for a couple of hours, so no one got good sleep. They eventually let us go back in, so it must not have been too bad, but you could definitely smell the smoke in the hallways. So we thought that loss was fluky, too. But the worst was when Iowa State came and punched us in the mouth at home. We were like, "What? This just doesn't happen, especially at Allen Fieldhouse." That was the true reality check, where we knew something was really, really wrong.

Three-game losing streaks are unheard of at Kansas. I'm not sure any of us had experienced something like that ever in our entire careers dating back to little league.

Keith Langford: After Texas Tech, we stunk it up from there on out. We barely passed the finish line. Things were going great until that loss. We were 20-1 and 10-0. After we lost, Coach Self wanted to shock us into reality and get us settled again. My mentality was, "Hey, man ... relax. We just lost our second game of the season and our first game in the Big 12. Get off our ass."

That next meeting we had, he comes in and says, "Langford, all you care about is changing your shoes at halftime. You don't care about this and that." He was trying to push everyone's buttons. It was my shoes ... it was Aaron was being careless with the ball ... it was Sasha and Darnell and Alex not being tough enough. He went down the line. Obviously I shouldn't have said anything. But nobody else was, so I opened my big mouth and said, "I don't agree with anything you're saying right now," or something along those lines. It was a snarky remark and totally unnecessary, but I was being a smartass. I was just thinking, "We're 20-2 and I've been changing my shoes at halftime my whole career. Why are you bringing that up now? We're all right. We're fine." It turned into a fight. We were supposed to have the day off, but Coach Self was like, "Everyone thank your senior leader for us having to practice right now."

Sometimes I look back on that and think, "Had I just not said anything, had I just let him cuss us out, we could've gone on and done great things." I'm not saying that was the reason we struggled. But that was definitely a negative moment from that season.

Aaron Miles: Sometimes when you're winning, the flaws that you have get disguised. We wouldn't always talk about the negative things. But when we lost to Texas Tech, Coach Self pointed some things out, and Keith didn't hold his tongue. He spoke up and said something. The whole situation plummeted after that. A lot of times you can overcome things with talent, but for us things just went sideways.

That loss changed our season. We were 20-1 but we lost six of our final nine games. In some ways you could see it coming. We had been winning, but there was still tension in the air throughout the whole season. It felt different.

Russell Robinson: Everyone was acting like the sky was falling. J.R. Giddens used to keep up with the message boards and it got really bad during the three-game losing streak. (In the middle game of that streak, Giddens shot 3-of-16 in a loss to Iowa State and some KU fans booed him at The Fieldhouse.) I saw how frustrated he'd be in practice after games when he wouldn't shoot as well. He would get ripped on the message boards. He'd come into practice and say, "Yo, they're saying I'm shooting too much or they're saying y'all aren't passing to me enough." He was trying to keep up with and please people that probably didn't know anything about basketball. It was a huge mistake.

If you asked anyone that came after me, they wouldn't even know what the message board was. That's an example of something that got tweaked out of the culture. If you're playing well and they're saying good things about you, it's fun to be on there. But if you're playing bad and they're saying how they really feel, it can mess with your game. It certainly messed with J.R.'s, and that had a negative impact on our squad.

Wayne Simien: Coach Self over the years has done a great job of making sure his teams are playing their best at just the right time. But that particular season … I don't know if we peaked too early or what. He was pushing us pretty hard and wanting us to peak at the right time, and we didn't.

We were all disoriented. We were trying to figure out what was going on and how we could bounce back. I remember feeling dizzy during that time. We thought we had the Big 12 championship secured, and now Oklahoma State was right over our shoulders.

Kansas vs. Oklahoma State: The (unofficial) start of the streak

Wayne Simien: Our three-game losing streak opened the door for Oklahoma State to get back into the Big 12 title hunt. In fact, we were tied for the league lead when they came to Lawrence in late February.

It was one of the biggest games of my career—and not just because of the stakes. I took that game very personal. They'd kicked our ass (80-60) when we went down to Stillwater the previous year. It's not that our feelings were hurt, but I felt like Coach Self's nose was kind of bloodied during that game. It was his first time playing against his alma mater as Kansas' coach, and we got destroyed. That didn't sit well with me.

Now that it was his second season and we'd fully accepted him as our coach, I felt like we were playing that game for him.

Both teams were 10-3 in the league and ranked in the top 10. Even though we each had a few games left, the Big 12 championship was basically on the line. It was a Sunday afternoon game on CBS. I loved afternoon games in the Fieldhouse. Even better was that I had a chance to go against Joey Graham, who was in the conversation for Big 12 Player of the Year. I remember taking that game very personal.

Bill Self: It was a Sunday afternoon game at the Fieldhouse. I remember that specifically, because we had to adjust our pregame itinerary so Wayne could go to church. We were like, "The big fella says he wants to go to church? He can go to church."

Joey Graham: As high as the stakes were, the Kansas game meant even more to me because of the fact that my twin brother, Stephen, and I almost went there. Or rather, we *wanted* to go there.

We met (former KU coach) Ted Owens when we were 14 or 15. He was the athletic director at Saint Leo University near Tampa. We lived close by and used to sneak into the gym late at night. The lights were almost always off, but Coach Owens would sit up in the stands and watch us shoot. Then one night he turned on the lights and asked if he could show us some things. Coach Owens was the first one to work on our fundamentals, and from there our relationship grew. We worked for him at his camps. We were childhood friends with his kids, Taylor and Teddy. We were family. He was a father figure to us.

By the time we decided to transfer from Central Florida after two years, Coach Owens had moved to Tulsa. We called him for advice and we ended up going to see him. On that trip we visited Oklahoma, Oklahoma State and Kansas. At the time, Roy Williams was just leaving, but we knew about Bill Self.

We went to Allen Fieldhouse and, even though it felt old in there, I remember sensing the tradition of that program as we walked into the building. Kansas has

Kansas 81, Oklahoma State 79
February 27, 2005 · Lawrence, Kan.

Kansas (21-4)

Player	MP	FG	3FG	FT	R	A	F	S	TO	B	TP
Keith Langford*	34	6-8	1-1	1-2	3	5	2	0	2	0	14
Wayne Simien*	34	11-17	0-0	10-11	12	1	2	0	3	1	32
Christian Moody*	34	5-6	0-0	1-2	0	1	2	0	1	0	11
J.R. Giddens*	18	0-3	0-2	0-1	1	3	0	2	2	0	0
Aaron Miles*	35	5-7	2-3	1-4	1	6	1	1	1	0	13
Darnell Jackson	7	1-1	0-0	0-0	2	0	1	0	0	0	2
Jeff Hawkins	11	0-0	0-0	2-2	2	0	2	0	0	0	2
Sasha Kaun	5	0-1	0-0	0-0	0	0	1	0	1	0	0
Michael Lee	22	3-4	1-2	0-1	1	2	2	1	0	0	7
Team					1						
Totals	200	31-47	4-8	15-23	23	18	13	4	10	1	81

Oklahoma State (20-5)

Player	MP	FG	3FG	FT	R	A	F	S	TO	B	TP
John Lucas*	40	9-11	4-5	0-0	2	3	1	1	0	0	22
Ivan McFarlin*	33	1-4	0-0	6-6	5	3	3	0	2	2	8
Joey Graham*	33	9-17	1-5	0-0	4	2	4	0	2	0	19
Daniel Bobik*	27	2-4	1-3	0-0	0	2	3	0	3	0	5
JamesOn Curry*	36	6-8	2-3	1-2	5	2	2	1	1	0	15
Terrence Crawford	14	0-2	0-0	0-0	3	0	3	1	0	0	0
Stephen Graham	17	4-7	1-3	1-1	0	2	4	1	1	0	10
Team					1						
Totals	200	31-53	9-19	8-9	20	14	20	4	9	2	79

	1st	2nd	Total	FG%	3FG%	FT%
Kansas	39	42	81	66.0	50.0	65.2
Oklahoma State	39	40	79	58.5	47.4	88.9

Officials: Mark Whitehead, Ted Hillary, John Clougherty
Technicals: None

produced tons and tons of great players throughout history, and on that visit I made up my mind that I wanted to be one of them. We toured the locker room and then went through the tunnel and onto the court. When I walked out there, I saw myself being a Jayhawk, which was a good feeling coming from a small university like Central Florida. I thought, "This is what it feels like to be on a big stage at a prestigious university with tons of great basketball players." It was kind of a surreal feeling.

Coach Owens was really pushing for us to go to Kansas, because he coached there and loved it there—and he loved Bill Self. We had a chance to talk to Coach Self over the phone, but they already had a full roster and didn't have any scholarships left. Oklahoma State was actually one of our last choices at that time, probably because we hadn't visited yet. Once we went to Stillwater, we fell in love with Oklahoma State.

Michael Lee: Heading into that game, Coach Self definitely reminded us about what happened the year before in Stillwater. The day after that loss, we spent about five hours going over film. He was going through every possession. The thing about film is that players remember the points in the game where they messed up. They may not always admit it, but they're preparing for that moment in the tape where the coach is going to pause it and jump their ass.

Coach Self would pause it and say, "So, Mike, what were you thinking right here?" He let us have it, one by one by one. Joey Graham got so physical with us that game, and it showed up on tape. Coach Self said none of us are strong enough or tough enough to play in that game. He told Andrea Hudy, our strength coach: "Everybody in here needs to be bench-pressing 250 or 300 pounds!" He was upset, because we really got punked. We got bullied and pushed around and outrebounded and out-hustled. Those were grown men that made us look like boys. Coach Self even said that. He'd pause it on Joey Graham and say, "That's a man! That's a MAN right, there and you guys are a bunch of little boys."

Stephen Vinson: It wasn't hard to predict that his pregame speech that day was going to focus on the Grahams. Before the season, he had posted an article from an Oklahoma newspaper in the locker room about the Graham brothers and how they each bench-pressed 350 pounds and squatted 500. Those were Coach Self's kind of players. He had a lot of respect, in general, for that entire team simply just because of their makeup and physicality. We knew the pregame speech was going to be all about how tough and physical they were, because they were going to try to push us around.

Oklahoma State guard John Lucas III: We were always physical. That's what Coach (Eddie) Sutton preached. We didn't want to get outrebounded, because whenever we did, he made us practice in football pads. We didn't ever want to have to do that again. We even kept football pads in our lockers as a reminder, a motivator to keep us focused on winning the battle in the paint.

Keith Langford: They were strong at every position. Physically, they stand out as one of the strongest teams I've ever faced. They were grown men. A bunch of them were seniors, like 22 years old. They were built for the Big 12 and a deep college run.

Darnell Jackson: Coach Self was red in the face before the game, very nervous. Everyone wanted to win. He wanted to win. We had lost three in a row and now we were playing his alma mater.

Joey Graham: Eddie made the game a really big deal. He'd had a legendary career and some great teams, but he'd never won a game at Allen Fieldhouse. Considering how good we were that year, he knew this might be his best chance. At that point in time, Eddie's son, Sean, was the more vocal coach on our staff. He was the one that did most of the talking in the huddles. Eddie would just sit there and scowl.

Wayne Simien: I'm not an edgy guy, but I remember being very edgy going into that game. I didn't make a speech or act all rah-rah. But I pulled some guys aside and let them know what was at stake. I didn't have to do it with the other seniors. We had been in the trenches enough times to know how to act. But I remember doing it with J.R. Giddens. I remember doing it with Christian, because Coach Self had switched the matchups to where I would have to guard Ivan McFarlin so I wouldn't pick up any cheap fouls guarding Joey Graham, because Graham liked to play on the perimeter and drive. I pulled Moody to the side in the locker room and said, "Hey, you're just as capable as anyone. You guarded Nick Collison every day in practice two years ago. You've guarded me all season. This guy is nothing."

Joey Graham: I wasn't sure why they decided to put Moody on me. When I figured out that he was guarding me, I smiled, because I knew I was a lot quicker and a lot stronger than he was. My whole thing was to catch it out high and bring him out to the outside of the court and just drive around him, because my quickness and speed and strength were too much for him.

Christian Moody: I'm sure it looked like I wasn't playing defense, because, man, he had a great game. I just tried to move my feet, stay in front of him and not give him any easy stuff. I wanted to force him to take tough shots. Unfortunately, he made a lot of those tough shots. I'll give him credit for that. He scored 19 points and played an excellent game.

Stephen Vinson: Oklahoma State loved to run a reverse ball screen—a little-for-a-big ball screen. They'd run it with Joey Graham and John Lucas III, and we couldn't figure out how to guard it. Because you couldn't switch it. You couldn't switch Wayne or Christian on Lucas, and guards aren't used to hedging and getting back on a ball screen. That was a miserable set for us to figure out.

Michael Lee: JamesOn Curry (15 points) gave me all I could handle that game. I remember Coach Self just lighting me up in the huddle. "Mike Lee, you think you're a tough guy? You're not tough. He's a freshman and he's out there killing you." I was getting mad but there was nothing I could do but sit there and take it. JamesOn was good. He was *very* good.

Bill Self: It was the best offensive game played by both teams since we've been here. They were unbelievable. In the first half we only had six possessions out of the 25 where we didn't execute absolutely perfect. And they were the same way. They were unbelievable.

Graham had 19 points and Curry scored 15, but it was John Lucas III who was giving KU the most trouble. Lucas made his first nine shots and followed up a Graham 3-pointer with one of his own to put Oklahoma State ahead by seven with 5:45 left.

Keith Langford: John Lucas was playing so freaking well. I remembered him from when he played at Baylor. This wasn't the same guy. I always thought he was a good player but I had never seen him at that level.

John Lucas III: The ball was just dropping for me. One of my goals as a college player was to win a game at Allen Fieldhouse. I started my career at Baylor, and we weren't able to get it done. I knew this was going to be my last chance. I was locked in. I didn't even see the crowd. I didn't hear it. I was just so absorbed with what was going on in the game.

Joey Graham: At the 5-minute mark, we had the momentum. We had the time and the score behind us. I can remember Sean was saying, "We have to control the clock!" So when I hit that three and then John hit his, we kind of thought the worst part was behind us.

I don't know if we got complacent or a little overconfident, but anytime you go to somebody else's house, you can't ever count them out. And I can remember the fans in the stands ... it was so loud in there. It's intense—and intimidating, too. If you're not careful, it can get to you a little bit.

Kansas chipped away at the lead and eventually tied the game at 78 with 1:31 left when Simien swished two free throws, giving him a career high of 32 points.

Keith Langford: I made a play here and there, a shot here and there. A lot of us did. But that game was all about Wayne. We rode him and rode him. The whole freaking Fieldhouse was on his shoulders that day.

That was the great thing about that group. If one guy had it going, which Wayne did, none of us minded chipping in to do whatever. The will to win takes over. Whether it was a screen or grabbing someone's jersey or running a little bit faster on a break, we just did what we did to gut that game out. It was that important to us.

Michael Lee: I felt like my job was to get the ball to Wayne. That was the game where he told me, "Don't salt-shake it! When you've got the ball and you want to pass it to me, be assertive and get me the ball!" I used to jab and pump-fake. He was like, "Man, just get me the freaking ball."

BEST OF THE STREAK

CONFERENCE HOME WINS

1. Feb. 25, 2012: No. 4 Kansas defeats No. 3 Missouri 87-86 in OT: Thomas Robinson has 28 points, 12 rebounds and a key block in the final Border War.

2. Feb. 27, 2005: No. 8 Kansas defeats No. 4 Oklahoma State 81-79: Wayne Simien scores a career-high 32 points for a KU team that shoots 66 percent.

3. March 3, 2007: No. 3 Kansas tops No. 15 Texas 90-86: Jayhawks rally from a 15-point deficit to beat Kevin Durant and the Longhorns.

4. Jan. 4, 2016: No. 1 Kansas defeats No. 2 Oklahoma 109-106 in 3OT: A 46-point effort from Sooners' guard Buddy Hield isn't enough to upset the Jayhawks.

5. Jan. 9, 2013: No. 6 Kansas defeats Iowa State 97-89 in overtime: Ben McLemore banks in a three-pointer to force overtime and finishes with 33 points.

6. Feb. 13, 2017: No. 3 Kansas defeats No. 9 West Virginia 84-80 in OT: Frank Mason scores 24 points as KU rallies from a late 14-point deficit with 2:58 remaining.

7. Feb. 5, 2006: Kansas defeats Oklahoma 59-58: Brandon Rush scored 18 points and Mario Chalmers made the go-ahead bucket in the waning seconds as Kansas wiped out a 16-point second-half deficit for a 59-58 win.

8. Jan. 18, 2014: Kansas defeats Oklahoma State 80-78: Frank Mason stripped Le'Bryan Nash as the buzzer sounded as KU avenged a home loss to OSU the previous year. Naadir Tharpe scored 21 points. Joel Embiid had 13 points and 10 boards.

9. Feb. 1, 2017: No. 3 Kansas defeats No. 2 Baylor 73-68: Josh Jackson's 23 points and 10 rebounds help KU rally from a six-point halftime deficit.

10. Jan. 20, 2010: Kansas defeats Baylor 82-75: The teams were tied with less than three minutes remaining before Sherron Collins scored eight of his 28 points to stave off Baylor, which reached the Elite Eight.

Coach Self used to say that Wayne was so amazing, because even on a bad day, you could pencil in a double-double for him. Wayne had that turnaround with those great hands and soft touch. Wayne could bang with you or finesse you. One-on-one, you couldn't guard Wayne. We'd just give him the ball and space the floor and let him do his thing.

Wayne Simien: I didn't need to demand the ball. At the time, the high-low offense was our main thing. I was getting a lot of touches. If I wasn't scoring, I was getting fouled. The usual strategy is, if we're in transition and you've got a chance to make something happen, make it happen. If it was late in the shot clock, Keith had the green light to do his thing. But if it's half-court and it's early in the shot clock, it's coming to me.

Kansas pulled ahead, 80-78, with 39.4 seconds left when Miles drove around Joey Graham and made a layup. After an OSU timeout, Curry drove past reserve guard Jeff Hawkins and attempted a one-handed dunk over Moody. Curry missed but was fouled by Moody. With 25.9 seconds remaining, Curry stepped to the free throw line with a chance to tie the game.

Christian Moody: Coach Self always says a dunk changes momentum—and *nobody* dunks in Allen Fieldhouse. So when I saw Curry, a freak athlete, making a beeline to the basket, I just thought, "I've got to get in front of him and affect this shot."

Joey Graham: JamesOn was the baby, the youngest guy on the team. At that time, I was nervous for him because he hadn't played in a game like that before. He had never experienced that type of intensity. Not only was the crowd going crazy, but our coaches had put a lot of emphasis on that game, so there was a lot of pressure on him to make those free throws. I wasn't sure how he was going to handle it.

He ended up missing the first one. His morale and our whole team's morale was like, "Argghh! We needed that."

John Lucas III: I threw the ball to JamesOn and he went one on one and got fouled. He missed the first and he NEVER missed his free throws. He was crying after the game. I was like, "JamesOn, there's no need to cry. It was a hell of a game. No one is mad at you. You missed a free throw. It happens to the best of the best."

Curry made the second free throw to shave KU's lead to 80-79. The Cowboys fouled Miles, who made one of two and left the door open for Oklahoma State to either tie the game or win it in regulation with a 3. The Cowboys were out of timeouts, but they had a play ready to run.

Joey Graham: We ran one of our designed plays called "Sweep." I'd go out to the wing and one of the guards would set a screen for me. My whole job was to attack whoever was on me. If I had a lane wide open, I was supposed to go in there and dunk it. If not, I'd try to come up with something else. We ran that play quite a few times, including the year before in the Elite Eight, when we beat Saint Joseph's to advance to the Final Four.

Stephen Vinson: In end-of-game, shot-clock situations, Coach Self switches all five matchups, so he switches all screens. He'd rather get a mismatch in a last-second situation than have a team be able to run its normal offense.

The goal always on defense is to dictate to the offense what they have to run and make them adjust on the fly. In late-game situations, it's harder for them to react and execute what they need to do because it's different than the play that was called. The strategy worked against Oklahoma State.

Joey Graham: They obviously knew we were running that play. I'm sure they'd watched film on it. They pressured up on me and clogged up the paint, so John couldn't get me the ball. He had to take the last shot, which definitely wasn't a bad option. At that point he was 9-for-10 with 22 points. John had to take it.

Unable to fire a pass to Graham, Lucas hoisted a 3-pointer that clanged off the front of the rim. Simien grabbed the rebound as the buzzer sounded. Kansas shot a scorching 66 percent from the field (31-of-47) while Oklahoma State shot 58.5 percent (31-of-58).

Michael Lee: If you watch the last shot that John Lucas took, I was guarding him. I stumbled and almost fell and he got off that last shot. I wasn't able to contest it at all. If he would've made it, everything would be different. The streak might have one less year on it.

I remember Coach Self just putting his hands in the air with both of his fists balled up. It was like the Oklahoma State monkey was finally off of his back. That one felt good to him. He was relieved. We were happy for him.

Assistant coach Kurtis Townsend: I remember Wayne grabbing the rebound and running to mid-court with his arms up. Then everybody ran to half-court and celebrated. You don't see that very much from our guys. They kind of just trot over to the handshake line and shake hands. So when you see that, you can tell how much pressure there was, how big of a game it was. I've only seen it a handful of times.

Stephen Vinson: That was the most emotional I had ever seen Wayne. It was the exclamation point on an unbelievable year for him.

Wayne Simien: I wouldn't say I felt unstoppable that day, but it was one of those games where everything felt slow. And when the game slows down, it gets easier. Kansas has had several big-time games since then that certainly trump it in terms of atmosphere. But back in the day it rated as the best I'd ever played in.

It was one of those games that, while you're playing it, it's almost silent. But in between timeouts and big plays, that's when the crowd comes into effect. The way I felt that day reminded me of that phrase "clear the mechanism" in the baseball movie "For the Love of the Game" with Kevin Costner. It's a real phenomenon. (Costner) had this internal conversation with himself on the mound and things just slowed down and went into slow motion. When things get slow on the basketball court, that's when guys get really good. I didn't feel like I was unstoppable or that I needed to carry the team. We had good players who all stepped up at certain times during that year. That was just my game, my time to do it.

Christian Moody: When Coach Self talks about his greatest college players, games like that are what put Wayne at the top of the list. It was a high-pressure, win-or-go-home situation, and Wayne stepped up and performed and justified his All-American status. He cemented his place in the rafters that afternoon. It was special to be a part of it and play alongside him.

Even though Kansas needed one more victory to clinch a share of the Big 12 championship—which it secured easily 72 hours later against K-State on Senior Night—the Jayhawks' 81-79 win over Oklahoma State that afternoon is viewed as the unofficial beginning of their league title streak.

Aaron Miles: There's a great photo of Wayne after that game. He's holding his hands in the air and his fists are clinched as he's screaming. It's the perfect picture to illustrate the passion and the meaning of the streak. If we don't win that game, the record book might look a little different.

Wayne Simien: Going back to Allen Fieldhouse now and seeing highlights from that day during the pregame introduction video … it gives me chills. It brings back memories. That game meant something. We had no idea we were starting a streak that day, but that's what ended up happening.

Part of me hates that we slipped up a year earlier in 2004 and finished second, because the streak would be three years longer. But in some ways it's better that the streak started in 2005, because that way Coach Self can say it's all his. I tip my hat to him on that.

Kansas had a chance to win the Big 12 outright on the final day of the regular season, but a 72-68 loss at Missouri forced the Jayhawks to share the title with Oklahoma. Even worse, Langford suffered an ankle injury in the game's opening minutes that would alter the rest of Kansas' season.

Keith Langford: I felt really good at the beginning of the game. I had five points, including a 3-pointer, in the first three minutes. Me and Coach Self even talked about it later. He was like, "You had it going, didn't you?" And I was like, "Yeah, I could feel it."

But then I rolled my ankle and we went to the back. They gave me an injection of a pain medication called Toradol so I could play in the second half, which didn't end up happening. I didn't realize it at the time, but I was allergic to Toradol.

The next day or two, I started having these really bad back pains. I was like, "Man, I don't know what's going on, but I feel like crap." I didn't practice at all and, for some reason, I couldn't go to the bathroom. My stomach was starting to swell. On about the third night, the pain was getting really, really bad. It was really intense. I called our trainer, Bill Cowgill, around 2 in the morning. I said, "You've got to come get me. Something is wrong. My back is hurting really, really bad."

Once Cowgill saw me he took me over to the clinic on campus and they hooked me up to an IV. The next day they put me in the hospital. By then my stomach was really, really big and the pain was bad. Eventually the doctor came in and said, "Your kidney isn't functioning right but we don't know why." They finally realized it was a delayed reaction to the medicine I took at Missouri, the injections. I had an allergic reaction to them. I missed the Big 12 Tournament and was still really weak when I came back for the NCAA Tournament, when we played Bucknell.

Bucknell blues

Bill Self: Looking back on it, I wish I would've handled the situation with Keith differently. Keith wasn't supposed to play against Bucknell. We didn't have any indication that he was ready. But Keith announced to the media the day before the game at shootaround that he was going to play, despite the fact that he had told us that he was absolutely, positively out. He had told us he was done, at least for that game. He hadn't practiced in two weeks. We had prepared to play without him. But once he told the media he was playing, what were we supposed to do? He was a senior, one of the best players Kansas had had for the previous three or four years. We didn't start him, but we played him. He wasn't effective, but how could he have been? He hadn't done anything. He wasn't healthy. He hadn't practiced in two weeks.

Keith Langford: I did some warm-ups and some shooting, but when I didn't start I just figured I'd just cheer on my teammates and mentally prepare to play against Wisconsin in the second round. Then a point came in the game where Coach Self kind of looked at me. He didn't say anything, but it felt like he was telling me, "You might want to check in. This might be it." That was the feel I got from the look he had in his eyes. The whole game is a blur to me now. I don't remember my stats or what happened. I just remember being out there but not moving very well. I caught a lot of hell for not performing well in that game.

Aaron Miles: At the end of the day, Keith was our emotional leader. He was also our best scorer. Wayne may have averaged more points, but we could give the ball to Keith anywhere on the court and he'd go get a bucket.

Even when you think about Syracuse (in the 2003 national championship game), Keith was lighting them up. Then he fouled out and the game changed. The next year, Georgia Tech ... he was killing them. Then he goes out and we lose. I definitely believe things would've been different if Keith had been healthy for Bucknell.

Instead, No. 3 seed Kansas suffered an opening-round loss, 64-63, to the No. 14 seed Bison in Oklahoma City. The Jayhawks had a shot to win after Simien caught a long inbounds pass from Lee near the free-throw line. But Simien's turnaround jumper as time expired was slightly off the mark.

Michael Lee: I remember throwing that ball into Wayne all the way down the court for the last shot. He'll make that shot nine times out of 10. From my angle it looked good, but the ball bounced off the rim, and their team rushed the floor. I walked straight back to the locker room and into the shower. I started banging my head on the shower wall. I kept saying, "No! No! No!" I didn't want to believe it. After all we'd accomplished in four years, that wasn't how we should've gone out.

Wayne Simien: Everyone is always going to remember how my college career ended. I missed the game-winner against Bucknell. Not only did I miss it, but the play before that, the Bucknell guy (Chris McNaughton) banked in a running hook shot over me from about 10 feet away. That was my man. So not only did I miss a shot, but my man scored on me to win the game. I was fine after the game, though.

That's not to say I wasn't disappointed. I was mainly disappointed for Coach Self, because I knew he was going to take a lot of heat from that loss. I had agents calling me. I knew I was going to have the luxury of moving on to the next step in my career. I was going to the League. But Coach and the rest of the team was stuck with that. Still, when I looked in the mirror, I knew I'd given everything I had. I don't have any regrets about my career.

Kansas 63, Bucknell 64
March 18, 2005 · Oklahoma City, Okla.

Kansas (23-7)

Player	MP	FG	3FG	FT	R	A	F	S	TO	B	TP
Aaron Miles*	32	0-5	0-1	4-4	3	4	3	2	1	0	4
Wayne Simien*	35	9-14	0-0	6-8	10	2	2	0	2	0	24
Christian Moody*	32	2-2	0-0	1-3	8	0	1	0	1	0	5
J.R. Giddens*	22	1-7	0-5	0-0	3	3	0	0	3	3	2
Michael Lee*	31	6-9	0-1	6-6	7	2	2	2	2	0	18
C.J. Giles	7	0-1	0-0	1-2	0	0	2	1	0	0	1
Jeff Hawkins	11	1-1	1-1	0-0	0	0	3	0	1	0	3
Alex Galindo	1	0-0	0-0	0-0	0	0	0	0	0	0	0
Keith Langford	26	1-7	0-3	4-4	1	3	1	0	2	0	6
Sasha Kaun	3	0-0	0-0	0-0	1	0	1	0	1	0	0
Team					1						
Totals	200	20-46	1-11	22-27	34	14	15	5	13	3	63

Bucknell (23-9)

Player	MP	FG	3FG	FT	R	A	F	S	TO	B	TP
Chris McNaughton*	23	6-7	0-0	2-3	3	0	4	0	1	0	14
Abe Badmus*	34	0-3	0-2	2-2	3	11	5	1	0	0	2
Kevin Bettencourt*	37	5-16	5-15	4-4	2	2	1	4	2	0	19
Charles Lee*	38	5-14	2-8	3-4	8	0	2	2	3	1	15
Darren Mastropaolo*	26	1-4	0-0	0-0	6	0	4	0	0	0	2
Tarik Viaer-McClymont	3	0-0	0-0	0-0	0	0	0	0	0	0	0
Donald Brown	14	3-4	0-0	0-0	2	0	1	0	1	0	6
John Griffin	5	0-2	0-2	0-1	1	1	0	2	0	0	0
John Clark	4	0-1	0-1	0-0	0	0	2	0	0	0	0
Chris Niesz	16	2-4	1-3	1-2	2	3	2	1	2	0	6
Team					3						
Totals	200	22-55	8-31	12-16	30	17	21	10	9	1	64

	1st	2nd	Total	FG%	3FG%	FT%
Kansas	31	32	63	43.5	9.1	81.5
Bucknell	28	36	64	40.0	25.8	75.0

Officials: Ray Natili, Randy McCall, Tom Wood
Technicals: None

Bill Self: I was very nervous about the Bucknell game, because we weren't a good basketball team when we played Bucknell. We were a tired team with a bunch of holes, and they played matchup zone, and we struggled against teams that did that because our outside shooting was so inconsistent.

I wasn't ever embarrassed about the actual loss. I was just embarrassed about how the whole thing played out. We had the best kids—the nicest, sweetest kids. Yet some of them walked off the court and didn't shake hands. I remember calling Bucknell's coach and apologizing because we shouldn't have done that. On that night, we made it more about us than the moment. That disappointed me a lot. It's one thing to get your butt beat, but it's another thing to do it and look like that. Our kids were classy but we didn't handle that well at all.

When we got back to the hotel that night, I remember calling my family up to the hotel room and I said, "Hey guys, it's not going to be very much fun at school the next couple of weeks."

It was spring break. We went to Cancun so I didn't have to be around. I just wanted to get away. But still, even in Cancun, you can still watch the NCAA Tournament. It was tough on me. It was tough on everyone—especially our seniors.

Michael Lee: To go out the way we did, that hurt. All these years later, it still stings. We wanted it. We wanted it so bad.

The funny thing about that year is that I never really felt like we were in control. It could've had something to do with chemistry. We had J.R. at that point. He was a little inconsistent and tough to deal with. Keith wasn't his best self all year and then he hurt himself against Missouri.

Even when we beat Kentucky, we didn't play great. We just somehow pulled it out at the end. We beat Georgia Tech in overtime on New Year's Day. It was a great win but, again, it was at home. I don't care who it is, we shouldn't need a last-second shot to beat anyone—not even the Los Angeles Lakers—at Allen Fieldhouse.

That whole year, even though the record was good, I never totally felt confident. We weren't playing great basketball. We were just getting by. You look at how we lost in the end—to Bucknell on a last-second shot. It was almost fitting. We were hanging on by a thread all season. We were very beatable. It was a funky year.

BEST OF THE STREAK

BUCKET-GETTERS

1. Sherron Collins: Explosiveness combined with strength and power made him tough to stop

2. Keith Langford: KU's eighth all-time leading scorer had cat-quick first step

3. Frank Mason: 2017 Associated Press National Player of the Year was a great finisher

4. Wayne Simien: Turn-around jump shots were almost automatic during senior season of 2005

5. Marcus Morris: Arguably the best all-around player of the Self era

6. Josh Jackson: Incredible ball-handler for his size; played with a mean streak

7. Andrew Wiggins: One of the most skilled athletic players in KU history; disappeared at times

8. Mario Chalmers: No one was better in big moments than the 2008 Final Four MOP

9. Tyshawn Taylor: Elite speed made him scary in transition

10. Devonte' Graham: Sharpshooter sparked huge comebacks versus Oklahoma and West Virginia

A little more from ...

Christian Moody: I remember looking at Wayne, Mike, Keith and Aaron in the locker room after the Bucknell game and it was hard to hold back tears. I was really upset and sad that the senior core was done and that was my last game with them. It wasn't a fair ending for such a great group. I wanted them to have a Final Four or championship, something that honored how great of a senior class they were. I know they've got a lot of rings and hold a lot of records and even have banners in the rafters. But I definitely wanted more for their senior year.

As far as the game goes, not having Keith healthy made the difference. It had a huge impact on our team. You look at the pro player Keith became and knowing how good he was as a college player when he was healthy ... he could have carried us to the championship. I definitely don't think that game defines their legacy.

Keith Langford: Everyone talks about our senior year being the start of the Big 12 streak, but I look at it more as the start of the Self era. That season set the foundation for everything he's done, whether it's the streak or the national championship or the new facilities. We were the foundation of that.

Ever since then, the whole conference has been waiting for someone to beat Kansas. The Big 12 isn't as sexy for basketball as it used to be. Kansas will always be a sexy destination, but this region as a whole, not so much. The east and west have really started to separate themselves. Players are more interested in marketing and exposure and style of play. They're being sold on everything that Kansas is not. Kansas is about togetherness. It's about group and team and family. So many kids today want to average 25 and dribble the ball on every possession. That's not going to happen at Kansas—at least not until Coach Self leaves. He's just not going to give an inch. The level you need to be at and play at ... he's not going to give on that at all. Nor should he.

Aaron Miles: It might have taken us a while. But at the end of the day, we're all good people. When you're 18 to 22 years old, it's hard to understand some things. To this day, we're still affected by the coaching change. I would've loved to have played four years for one of the coaches, just so we could've had that consistency. At the same time, I'm blessed to have played for two Hall of Fame coaches and learn from both. For me, as a coach now, it's unbelievable. I've seen so many different styles and schemes and ways of thinking. I can call Coach Self and ask him questions. I can call and talk to Coach Williams about whatever. I can go sit in their offices and have conversations. And then there's all the assistant coaches like Coach Dooley that I can lean on.

The relationships we built were special. Wayne was great. He was *great.* As a junior he reconnected with God. It changed his whole mentality. Wayne worked hard, but he wasn't one of those guys who was the first one in the gym and the last one out. He was like, "I'm going to come in, get my work in and I'm gone." But while he was there, he went hard. And that's how it should be. You shouldn't be in the gym for four hours, where two of those hours you're bullsh****n'.

It's funny because we were only 22 years old, yet Coach Self would give us days off. As a senior you feel so old. I remember Wayne riding the stationary bike in practice while everyone else worked out. It was like he was an old, worn-down NBA veteran. It's all relative. In the college world, we *were* old. But then you go to the NBA and you're going a million miles an hour, and you're a year older. Wayne was a rookie on a team with D-Wade, Shaq and Alonzo Mourning. He couldn't walk around acting old anymore. You can't come out there shuffling your feet and wearing sweats like you're old.

One of the best parts of my career was that I got to be teammates with Mike Lee, who has been my best friend since the third grade. We lived a block away from each other growing up. His mom and my dad worked together. His dad coached my dad at a junior college in Portland. It was special going to high school and winning a state championship together. Then we had a chance to play in college together. It was unbelievable. I trust Mike. I trust in his character and what he represents.

Michael Lee: I played alongside Aaron since the second grade. He's the type of leader that will do all of your thinking for you. He's so in tune with what's going on. He's in tune with what each player needs. Aaron knew what I needed. He knew when I was mad and what he needed to say to get my mind right. He knew when Keith needed the ball. Aaron is the type of dude that people didn't talk about enough. Aaron would go to the coaches and say, "Hey, Coach, I think we need to run more in practice. We're not running enough." Or, "Hey, Coach, I know you're mad at Keith, but this is what's going on in his head." We trusted him to do that.

Aaron was a clown, too. As serious as you need to be when you're a leader, it helps to have a fun side, too. Aaron would go around campus squirting people with his Super Soaker. He'd dress up in costumes and play entrance music for our poker games up in the Towers.

I take a ton of pride in the Big 12 streak. The fact that we were a part of something special is huge, mainly because we were there—more than anyone else—to see how it started. We were there those first two years to see the ups and downs of the program before Coach Self got it to where he wanted it to be, where it really started rolling. We were the first group to go through that Boot Camp and take those lumps. In that regard, it makes it a bit more special. When we got that first one, we couldn't have envisioned it turning into something like this.

Wayne Simien: Even though our senior year ended on a sour note with the loss to Bucknell, I relished every moment of that season. I appreciate it even more when I look back, because it's so rare to see a senior class stay together all four years like Aaron, Keith, Mike and I did. I didn't know it would be an anomaly. It was a great bond that we shared and still share.

I respected Aaron because of the way he lived his life, which was very similar to the way he played. He's the school's all-time assists leader, but he was also very unselfish off the court, too—just with the way he treated his friends, always thinking of others first. On the court he always wanted others to finish the play and get the credit. Off the court, socially, he was an includer. He always wanted to involve others.

I appreciate Keith for the chip he had on his shoulder. I never saw anyone leverage a chip to the level of success that he did. Even now, he continues to do that. Someone may think that didn't start happening until later in his KU career. But even coming in as a freshman, being overlooked during the recruiting process ... he let that fuel him. I don't know if he felt like people were against him, but he certainly had something to prove, maybe more to himself than to other people. Mike Lee is stubborn, but his stubbornness comes from his loyalty. He's a very loyal guy.

Sasha Kaun: I'm not sure everyone would admit it, but deep inside, I think we knew we weren't as good as everyone thought we were. That's obviously no excuse for losing to Bucknell. We should've won that game no matter what. But there was a lot of division on that team between the seniors and the freshmen. Wayne and Aaron and Keith did their thing, and then we had a bunch of younger guys. I don't think we were ever as close of a team as we were in later years.

About halfway through my freshman year, I started to feel comfortable on the court. We lost to Villanova but I had a decent game to where I became more confident. Then I had a good game against Kentucky and, after that, I felt pretty good on the floor. We actually won that game without Wayne. I had a good start to my sophomore year and had some good games. I became a better player overall.

Matt Kleinmann: I remember distinctly feeling that 2005 was a destiny year—maybe because of how Aaron, Mike, Keith and Wayne started off Late Night with the trophy kiss. Looking back, they probably wish they hadn't been so bold about it, but they really led us as seniors. They put us on their backs and carried us.

We talk about the Big 12 championships, and I think they're great. It's an awesome honor and there's nothing that's going to take away from it. But at the end of the day, if you don't win in April, there's a sense that you let the school down and let all the fans down.

That Big 12 title meant a lot, because it was the first one. But to me, the bigger picture about that season was that it was the first building block of our national championship run in 2008.

There were guys on that team who had different opinions about how things should go. Coach Self was still getting acclimated to KU, and KU guys were getting acclimated to him. I remember 2005 as the old guard and the new guard both having a presence as Self was making the team—the program—his own. The fact that we won the Big 12 during that transition is amazing.

Russell Robinson: Having a decent freshman year yet having teammates not support me because of their own personal stuff … it taught me a lesson for when guys like Sherron (Collins) came in two years later. Instead of getting in his way and causing conflict when he started to excel, I looked at it as a positive and let him excel.

There were a few times when Sherron was a freshman when he led us in scoring every game. I thought back to when I had my little stretch as a freshman when I was doing well, and guys were going to Coach Self saying, "This is my senior year. I should be playing more." That approach didn't work out for them. I learned from that, so when Sherron came, and even Mario (Chalmers) and some of the other younger guys ... you let them shine and you let them play. You let them be them. Everybody has a skill set. Everybody that comes to Kansas is good. I let them be, whether they're freshmen or seniors. That's when that culture kind of began. Guys come in with their high school swag and we let them continue it. Coach Self is already going to be tough on you. You don't need animosity from your teammates, too.

Had Wayne hit that shot against Bucknell, maybe my line of thinking would be different. Everything might have worked out. We may have won the national title, and I'd have thought, "This is how it's supposed to be." But you look back at that whole season and how everyone was acting, and you realized, "This isn't how it's supposed to be done."

2004-05 Season Summary

Results (23-7, 12-4)

November

19	Vermont	W, 68 - 61
23	Saint Joseph's	W, 91 - 51
29	Nevada	W, 85 - 52

December

4	Pacific	W, 81 - 70
9	TCU	W, 93 - 74
11	Louisiana-Lafayette	W, 96 - 51
18	South Carolina	W, 64 - 60
22	vs. Milwaukee	W, 73 - 62

January

1	Georgia Tech	W, 70 - 68
5	Texas A&M	W, 65 - 60
9	@ Kentucky	W, 59 - 65
12	@ Iowa State	W, 66 - 71
15	@ Colorado	W, 61 - 76
19	Nebraska	W, 59 - 57
22	@ Villanova	L, 83 - 62
25	@ Baylor	W, 66 - 86
29	Texas	W, 90 - 65
31	Missouri	W, 73 - 61

February

5	@ Nebraska	W, 65 - 78
9	@ Kansas State	W, 65 - 74
12	Colorado	W, 89 - 60
14	@ Texas Tech	L, 80 - 79
19	Iowa State	L, 61 - 63
21	@ Oklahoma	L, 71 - 63
27	Oklahoma State	W, 81 - 79

March

2	Kansas State	W, 72 - 65
6	@ Missouri	L, 72 - 68
11	vs. Kansas State	W, 80 - 67
12	vs. Oklahoma State	L, 75 - 78
18	vs. Bucknell	L, 63 - 64

All-Big 12 Team

Player of the Year:
Wayne Simien, Kansas, Sr., F

Newcomer of the Year:
Taj Gray, Oklahoma, Jr., F

Freshman of the Year:
Daniel Gibson, Texas, Fr., G

Coach of the Year:
Billy Gillespie, Texas A&M

First Team
Wayne Simien, Kansas, Sr., F**
Taj Gray, Oklahoma, Jr., F
Joey Graham, Oklahoma State, Sr., F**
John Lucas, Oklahoma State, Sr., G
Ronald Ross, Texas Tech, Sr., G

Second Team
Curtis Stinson, Iowa State, So., G
Keith Langford, Kansas, Sr., G
Jeremiah Massey, Kansas State, Sr., F
Brad Buckman, Texas, Jr., F
Antoine Wright, Texas A&M, Jr., F

Third Team
Jared Homan, Iowa State, Sr., C
Aaron Miles, Kansas, Sr., G
Kevin Bookout, Oklahoma, Jr., F
Daniel Gibson, Texas, Fr., G
Jarrius Jackson, Texas Tech, So., G

Honorable Mention
Aaron Bruce, Baylor, Fr., G
Richard Roby, Colorado, Fr., G
Linas Kleiza, Missouri, So., F
Joe McCray, Nebraska, Fr., G
Terrell Everett, Oklahoma, Jr., G
Ivan McFarlin, Oklahoma State, Sr., F
Joseph Jones, Texas A&M, Fr., C
Acie Law, Texas A&M, So., G

** Unanimous selection

Kansas Awards

Wayne Simien:
Lowe's Senior CLASS Award
Concensus All-American First Team
NABC All-American First Team
AP All-American First Team
USBWA All-American First Team
Sporting News All-American First Team
Big 12 All-Tournament Team

Aaron Miles:
Big 12 All-Defensive Team

Christian Moody:
Big 12 All-Underrated Team

Season Stats

#	Player	CL	POS	HT	Hometown	G	GS	FG%	3P%	FT%	R	A	S	B	PTS
23	Wayne Simien	SR	F	6-9	Leavenworth, KS	26	26	55.2%	28.6%	81.6%	11.0	1.4	0.6	0.6	20.3
5	Keith Langford	SR	G	6-4	Fort Worth, TX	28	27	46.5%	35.2%	60.1%	4.0	2.8	0.9	0.2	14.4
15	J.R. Giddens	SO	G	6-5	Oklahoma City, OK	30	21	40.4%	33.7%	68.0%	3.8	1.4	0.8	0.7	10.1
11	Aaron Miles	SR	G	6-1	Portland, OR	30	30	45.7%	50.0%	78.8%	3.5	7.2	1.7	0.3	9.3
34	Christian Moody	JR	F	6-8	Asheville, NC	27	25	57.9%	33.3%	55.4%	4.7	0.7	0.3	0.4	5.8
25	Michael Lee	SR	G	6-3	Portland, OR	30	6	42.9%	30.4%	91.2%	2.0	1.4	0.9	0.1	4.8
2	Alex Galindo	FR	F	6-7	Mayaguez, Puerto Rico	23	1	41.9%	38.6%	72.7%	1.6	0.3	0.3	0.3	4.1
3	Russell Robinson	FR	G	6-1	New York, NY	24	0	41.2%	28.6%	70.0%	0.7	1.0	0.8	0.1	3.5
1	Jeff Hawkins	JR	G	5-11	Kansas City, KS	21	0	46.3%	48.6%	77.8%	0.4	0.7	0.2	0.0	3.0
33	C.J. Giles	FR	F	6-11	Seattle, WA	21	5	53.2%	-	60.0%	2.4	0.0	0.2	0.9	2.8
24	Sasha Kaun	FR	C	6-11	Melbourne, FL	27	2	53.6%	-	33.3%	2.3	0.1	0.1	0.6	2.6
32	Darnell Jackson	FR	F	6-9	Oklahoma City, OK	24	1	54.8%	-	58.3%	1.7	0.1	0.2	0.1	2.0
34	Nick Bahe	SO	G	6-2	Lincoln, NE	11	0	36.4%	28.6%	50.0%	0.5	0.3	0.1	0.0	1.1
55	Moulaye Niang	JR	F	6-10	El Cajon, CA	16	0	40.0%	-	33.3%	1.1	0.1	0.1	0.0	0.6
20	Stephen Vinson	JR	G	6-2	Lawrence, KS	5	0	0.0%	0.0%	-	0.6	0.6	0.0	0.0	0.0

## CHAPTER 2

2005-06

A FRESH START

Losing to Bucknell—and then bidding farewell to Wayne Simien, Keith Langford, Aaron Miles and Michael Lee—made for an emotional March for Kansas fans. And things got even worse two months later, when the Jayhawks found themselves in the headlines once again for all of the wrong reasons. Instead of getting excited about a talented crop of incoming freshmen, Bill Self spent the first part of his summer dealing with the fallout from a highly publicized fight that, ultimately, would alter the direction of his program.

The Moon Bar

Bill Self: The summer of 2005 was probably the toughest three-month stretch we've had since we've been here. Everyone was taking shots at us and making jokes about us because of the Bucknell loss. And even though we have the most supportive fans in the country, I could just sense that everyone was deflated. It was a frustrating situation—and it got 10 times worse after that fight at the Moon Bar.

Jeremy Case: Part of me feels bad about what happened with J.R. (Giddens) at the Moon Bar because, in some ways, I could see it coming. Something was going on with J.R. that day, and I'm still not sure what it was.

J.R. and I were best friends. We were roommates. That summer I had been voted team captain, and I think he felt underappreciated. He wanted to be "the guy," which isn't a surprise. He had a big ego.

We were playing pickup that afternoon, and J.R. and I were on the same team. He wanted the ball, and I was like, "Run the floor. Let's try to get going and have a good pickup game." He went off on me and started getting mad. When I threw him the ball, he kicked it into the stands and went nuts. *"Who made you the boss?"* We had a big argument and he ran out of the gym.

Michael Lee: J.R. stormed out of the gym screaming. He was so mad that he was actually crying. Something was wrong that day. He had some issues.

Jeremy Case: I got back to the Towers and J.R. was nowhere to be found. I didn't know where he was. I wanted to talk to him and tell him we didn't need to be arguing like that. I wanted to squash it.

Apparently, he'd already gone out. I'm not sure who he was with, but he ended up at the Moon Bar. He got into an argument with some guy in there, but J.R. ended up leaving. His whole group left. But then he got somebody—I think it may have been a girl—to take him back to the bar to fight the dude. None of us were around.

Michael Lee: When I got to the bar, J.R. was already there. He got into it with some dude, and they threw the guy out. After that, I left and went home. A while later, I got a call saying he'd been stabbed. I went to the hospital, and the same girls I saw J.R. with at the Moon Bar were sitting in the lobby. I was mad at them for letting it happen. I was mad at everybody. It was just a crazy situation. It was almost spooky. I don't know what he did to instigate that situation. It was almost surreal. I was like, "This dude just got his calf ripped open."

Jeremy Case: I just feel like if I was there, and that argument between us earlier hadn't happened, I would have kept him out of that situation. I just wish I would've tried harder to find him before he went out that night. Maybe I could have prevented it. Because there's no way I would have let him go back to the bar. He wouldn't have even been in that fight. Thinking about it, I feel bad, because J.R. was my guy.

Jason King: J.R. Giddens was one of the more interesting players I ever covered at Kansas. On his good days he was the most charming person in the room ... friendly, funny, full of energy and extremely likeable. He was also one of the more passionate players I've been around, which could be both good and bad.

Still, as nice as J.R. could be at times, he also possessed some ugly traits that intensified as his fame and notoriety grew on KU's campus. While investigating the Moon Bar fight for *The Kansas City Star*, my colleague, Jason Whitlock, and I interviewed multiple witnesses that said, on the record, that J.R. Giddens was the lead instigator in a brawl that left multiple people with stab wounds. The witnesses said Giddens shouted, "Do you know who I am?" before he and others used fists, bricks and bottles to beat the man with whom Giddens argued inside the bar more than an hour earlier. The man brandished a knife and began swinging it wildly, slicing the back of Giddens' leg before stabbing four others. Giddens was kicked off the team about a month later amid a sea of negative publicity.

J.R. Giddens: Any thoughts I had about leaving for the NBA ended when I got stabbed. After that I knew I wasn't going anywhere. If anything, I was trying to figure out if I was ever going to play basketball again. I think that's why they made me leave Kansas. The doctor said I would walk with a limp for the rest of my life. He said I was going to come back 50 percent and I wasn't going to be able to play basketball anymore. I'm not saying Kansas threw me out like a battery. But they get McDonald's All-Americans every day. They weren't going to let me stay around campus and be Moulaye Niang.

I wanted to stay at Kansas but I felt like they just pushed me out the door, especially after getting stabbed. As a 19-year-old who was immature and didn't understand life, I took that really hard. I left the office in tears when I knew I was leaving. I remember that day really well. I walked out of there on crutches, crying.

Darnell Jackson: Eventually, I figured everything would be cool. I thought everything would get back to normal. The last thing I ever would've guessed was that J.R. would leave. I thought it was over. Everyone told their story. Then boom ... he's leaving. I felt bad, because I know how much he wanted to be here. I was with J.R. on his first recruiting visit here, which was for Late Night in 2002. It was me and J.R. and Adam Liberty. I'll never forget it. At the time, Roy was the coach, and KU wanted J.R.—not me. I was just along for the ride. I was sitting there thinking, "Man, this is crazy. You're coming *here*?" Right before Late Night started, a ball rolled over near where we were sitting. J.R. bent over and picked it up and shot it, and it went in. The fans went wild. J.R. loved Kansas. When he left, it really hurt him. It made J.R. look like he was a bad guy, and he wasn't a bad guy.

That whole summer, things just continued to get worse. Coach Self was disappointed in us because he felt like the perception of the program had been damaged. People thought we were going out and causing problems all around Lawrence, and that wasn't the case.

Coach Self put all these restrictions on us. He wouldn't let us go anywhere. We had curfew at 9 or 9:30. They'd come and knock on our door. If we weren't there, we'd have to get up at 5 in the morning. Coach Manning would take us down to the football field and make us run hills. Coach Self ... I was scared to say anything to him after all that happened. Part of me didn't want to be here anymore. We couldn't do anything or go anywhere. I definitely didn't want to come off as that type of guy, who goes out in the middle of the night and causes trouble. But things happen.

Jeremy Case: In June, a lot of the older players came back for the alumni game we have each year at the end of Coach Self's camp. After we played, Drew Gooden said he wanted to talk to everyone in the locker room. Nick Collison and Kirk Hinrich were there, too. Obviously everybody was upset about the Bucknell loss, and the J.R. thing, too. So everybody had a lot to say. The main message was: "This isn't Kansas basketball. You guys need to fix it. We left it in a good state and we expect you guys to continue it."

Assistant coach Tim Jankovich: The Moon Bar thing was very difficult for everyone, particularly Bill. It created a depressing mood, in a lot of ways. When you're the head coach, you're responsible for the conduct of everyone on your team. Of course you can't control every single last thing. But you always feel that responsibility. You feel the scrutiny from the public. It's never fun when those things happen. Behind the scenes, it's not something you can blow off. It affects the image of your program, it affects recruiting, it affects the amount of respect people have for you. Those things are important to a coach. When stuff like that occurs, it's not fun behind the scenes. Plus, that was right after Bucknell. So you can't say everything was hunky-dory in those early years.

Assistant coach Joe Dooley: One of Coach's strengths is that, even when things might not look good, he sure makes you feel like things are all right. He tells the staff, "It's not great right now, but it's going to be all right." He thinks things through and analyzes all of the angles of a situation. Then he comes up with a solution. And if he ends up not liking the solution, he's not afraid to change course. Meanwhile, the whole time he's telling everyone that everything is going to be OK.

Bill Self: We got to a point where we really needed something good to happen. Finally, in August, our big break fell into our lap.

Rush of Excitement

Even though he was a Kansas City native, Brandon Rush had not been recruited by KU before the summer of 2005—mainly because it was presumed he wouldn't qualify academically. Also, Rush's mother (Glenda) and grandmother (Jeanette Jacobs) had some ill feelings toward Kansas following the messy courtship of Brandon's older brother, JaRon, years earlier.

Bill Self: It was late July and I was recruiting at a tournament at Okun Fieldhouse in Shawnee. I'm in the stands, and hear these guys in front of me talking about Brandon. One of them said, "I heard from a reliable source that Brandon Rush made his grades." Immediately, I started trying to find out how to reach him. I made a call and, out of the blue, Brandon called me back a few days later when I was at lunch at Set 'em Up Jacks in Lawrence. He said, "Yeah, I'll come visit." I said, "What will your mother and grandmother think? I've heard they hate Kansas." He said, "Yeah, they do." So I called them, and they were great. They bought in.

Brandon Rush: I was on a plane on the way to the airport to fly to Oklahoma for a visit. My mentor, John Walker, was on the phone with Coach Self. He was like, "Why don't you just come up here for a visit?" I talked to Coach Self for a couple of minutes and agreed to check out Lawrence. I had never talked to anyone at KU before. I heard they asked about me when I was at Mount Zion (in North Carolina), but I'm not sure. Our whole team lived in our coach's house and he basically controlled everything and didn't let us talk to anyone.

At first I was anti-KU because of the way Roy Williams had done my brother. My mom and my grandma didn't want me to come here because of that. But it was close to home, and I'd been away from home for two years. I wanted to come somewhere close so my family could come and see me play.

Russell was one of my hosts, one of my chauffeurs. He showed me a really good time. I knew Mario (Chalmers) before that because of the AAU circuit. We were best buds. I had a good time on my visit. I fell in love with it and committed.

Joe Dooley: When he visited he was quiet and on his phone quite a bit—except when he was in the backseat of Kurtis' car and Kurtis got pulled over for running a red light. That was about as amused as I've ever seen Brandon. He thought it was hilarious. He sat in the back and laughed the whole time.

Even though we felt confident he'd be eligible, it was still a process to get him cleared because he'd been to, like, five different high schools. I remember Coach and I sitting at Bigg's Barbecue dotting our i's and crossing our t's on Brandon's transcript, trying to figure out if it was going to work.

The cool thing about Brandon was that we knew he was going to be a good player, but we didn't realize what a great guy he was. He was as fun to be around as anyone we had.

Stephen Vinson: I knew Brandon's older brother, JaRon, who was a really good guy. I had met Kareem before, too, but I didn't know Brandon, even though he was from this area. He had such a bad reputation coming in. People thought he'd be cocky or entitled because of his name and that he wouldn't work very hard. And let's just be honest, we had just lost J.R. Giddens. So we were all kind of thinking, "Oh great, we traded one bad seed for another." But then this guy comes in, and he's the exact opposite of everything we'd heard. To this day, I don't think Brandon has ever said anything mean about anyone—or to anyone—in his entire life. He couldn't have been a nicer person or a better teammate. He was funny in a quiet way. He wasn't a big personality, but he was still really funny.

Rush was the cherry on top of a banner recruiting class that already included Chalmers, Downs and Wright. An awkward fit, Downs would transfer after the fall semester. The Jayhawks also returned Self recruits Russell Robinson, Darnell Jackson, Sasha Kaun and C.J. Giles—all of whom were sophomores.

Tim Jankovich: It was refreshing to have all of those guys on campus—especially after such a turbulent summer. We could finally feel some optimism in the air with all of that young talent. Whenever you have good, young talent, the future looks bright.

Stephen Vinson: There was definitely excitement, but the vibe in the locker room was completely different. You didn't have the mouthpiece, the leader, like we had with Aaron Miles. You didn't have Mike Lee's sense of humor. You didn't have proven scorers like Keith and Wayne, who you knew would combine for 35-40 points every night. We didn't have J.R. We didn't even have Omar Wilkes (Cal) or Nick Bahe (Creighton) or Alex Galindo (Florida International), all of whom had transferred.

All around it was a different atmosphere—but it also felt like it was the first KU team that was basically Coach Self's.

Jeremy Case was the lone survivor of that 2003 recruiting class. Christian and I and Jeff Hawkins and Moulaye Niang were seniors, but we weren't big enough voices to still be considered a part of the Williams regime. We had bought in and were fully on board. Still, we were support players, complementary players.

The new guys ... not only were they great players, but they were great personalities and they were fun to be around. Coach Self loved coaching them. They were young pups but they worked hard. They tried. They cared. It made for a really good environment.

Darnell Jackson: Brandon was quiet. He never talked. Initially I thought, "What's wrong with this guy?" Mario was always talking noise. He loved to pick on me. That was just the bond we had. I don't know what it was about him. We just clicked right away. Julian was one weird guy. He did his own thing. He'd walk through campus all by himself with his headphones on. My room in the Towers was by the window, and every day I could hear him coming back from class, because he'd be singing really, really loud.

All three of them brought something different to the table. There wasn't any hate or anything. I never had a problem with any of those guys. Micah stayed to himself. He'd talk to us in practice, but once we got off the court he'd go lock himself in his room and play games or something. The whole time Micah was here I didn't go out with him one time. He had a serious girlfriend back home. He was in love.

Brandon Rush: The vibe was kind of odd because we were all freshmen. We didn't know what type of team we'd have. Once the season started, we started playing better and the vibe kind of changed. Once I get comfortable with people I start opening up a bit. But when I first start meeting people I'm kind of quiet.

Jeremy Case: I'm not sure what it would have been like if J.R. was still around instead of Brandon. It definitely would have been different, because J.R. rubbed a lot of people the wrong way with his ego. Especially those older guys like Wayne and Aaron. His ego was so big that he wouldn't even respect those guys and what they'd done. It was an "all about me" type of thing. It might have been a bad influence on those younger guys. You'd like to think that he would have grown out of that, but it's hard to say.

Russell Robinson: There was an eagerness for the season to start. The tension was high because everyone was competing for a starting spot. It was wide open. The competition level in one-on-ones and summer workouts was at its highest ever. So many things were up in the air. Who was going to be our leader?

Sasha Kaun: The older guys like Christian and Hawkins and Vinson were good vocal leaders, but everyone contributed. That's what made that group so special. We didn't have a main guy, where it was like, "OK, everyone listen to him." Everybody was a voice in their own way.

Russell Robinson: Everyone blended in well. Brandon came in at the last second. He had a pro attitude, a pro mentality, and stayed to himself at first. Him and Mario's relationship was so good that it started to carry over and spread to the team. He eventually opened up.

Micah was the odd man out. He stayed to himself. It was cool while everything was good. But once things started getting bad for him he didn't have any support from his teammates. He was a loner. He really didn't want to do anything with anyone. Hanging out, playing video games, watching movies in someone's room ... he didn't want to do any of that.

Growing Pains

Kansas began the season unranked—the only time that has occurred in the Self era. The Jayhawks headed to the Maui Invitational in late November with a 1-0 record and a date with Arizona in the first round. Kansas had 27 turnovers—including seven from Mario Chalmers—and got smoked 61-49 by the ninth-ranked Wildcats.

KU lost again the next day to Arkansas by one point and left Maui with just one win—against Division II Chaminade.

Stephen Vinson: Maui was great. It couldn't have been more fun—except if we would have won some games. We played Arizona, and the game was just too fast. They weren't a great team that year, but they pressed and they had really good athletes. They got under Mario and were taking the ball from him like I'm sure no one had ever done before.

Joe Dooley: We were sitting there after two days trying to figure out how to beat Chaminade so we wouldn't get swept in Maui.

Sasha Kaun: Gosh, that was a horrible tournament for us. We had two sophomores and two freshmen in the starting lineup. Arizona and Arkansas were just taking the ball away from our freshmen like it was nothing. They were pressuring us and we choked. Man, that was ugly.

But it was definitely a good way for us to realize, "Hey, we're talented and we could be really good. But we've got a long way to go."

Mario Chalmers: It was the worst I've ever played. I was coming from a high school team where I was the star player and could do whatever I wanted to do. Coming out of high school I was a really skinny kid. I weighed about 170-175. All of a sudden I was playing against guys that were juniors and seniors in college. They were so much stronger and bigger than me and it took me a while to adjust. Against Arizona, I couldn't even get the ball past half court for the first five minutes of the game. Chris Rodgers was all over me. I barely played that game or the next one against Arkansas. After the Arkansas game is when I really started to think about transferring. I hit two 3s and—bam!—he took me out. He put me back in, and I hit another 3. Then he took me right back out again. I didn't understand at the time why he was taking me out, but I know now that it was because I wasn't playing any defense.

Still, when we got back to Kansas, I wanted to transfer. I wanted out of there. I was like, "This isn't for me." I wasn't liking playing for Coach Self, playing in that system. I didn't have the freedom to do what I wanted to do. It was the first time I'd been in that position. It was more about me than him.

When you're the star on the team, you get to make your decisions. But at Kansas we didn't have any one, single star. And we were more big-man oriented at that time. Our main objective was always to get the ball into the post and then work it out from there. That was different for me. I had never played with high-quality bigs.

Russell Robinson: I was trying to win, but I was trying to show what I could do as well. We were so young and no one had that much experience. We just tried to pull together. We could see that, "OK, we've got good players and a good team. This is eventually going to come together." We were deep, too. We were just waiting for it to click. We kept believing that everything was going to be all right.

"Shoot the ball, Brandon!"

Kansas continued to struggle after Maui and was 3-4 following losses to St. Joseph's and No. 20 Nevada, the latter of which occurred at Allen Fieldhouse. Rush had emerged as the go-to guy and leading scorer, but getting him to embrace that role was a challenge.

Brandon Rush: I'd never been challenged like Coach Self challenged me. He was always telling me to be aggressive. I took it and ran with it and did what he wanted. I tried to be aggressive and not get yelled at all the time. I made sure I played my hardest. Coach Self was always screaming, *"Shoot the f**king ball!"* Then he'd tell me to get on the treadmill until I decided to shoot it.

Coach Self even set up a treadmill each day in practice that was just for me. No one else used it. He'd make me run for not shooting the ball enough in practice, for passing up shots. If I passed up a shot I should've taken, I'd have to run. It kind of pissed me off, to tell you the truth.

Mario Chalmers: Brandon was the No. 1 guy on the team. Or at least he was supposed to be. The thing about Brandon ... he was shy. He didn't really want to be the guy to take the last-second shot. He didn't want to be the guy to get all the attention. That's just how he was. He has all the confidence in the world in his abilities, but you know how he is. He's just weird. He'd be down to take the last shot if you asked him, but he wasn't going to volunteer to take it. He didn't really put himself out there like that.

The knock on him coming out of high school was that he was selfish and didn't pass enough. Sometimes he got caught up on trying to prove everyone wrong instead of just playing his game.

Stephen Vinson: Coach Self tried everything he could to get Brandon to be more assertive and to shoot more. Apparently Brandon, when he was little, had broken his left arm while doing a backflip. To this day, he can't fully extend that arm, and we loved to give him a hard time about it. One day, Coach Self was giving one of his long talks after practice, and he was getting on Brandon about not being able to dribble with his left hand. He said, "I talked to some NBA guys, and they think we should re-break your arm so we can get it straightened out, and then you'll be able to dribble with your left hand."

Jeremy Case: A lot of us thought he was serious. We were like, "What the hell? They're really thinking about that?"

Stephen Vinson: The look on Brandon's face was priceless. He looked like he'd just seen a ghost when Coach Self said that to him. Everyone was just laughing and smiling at Brandon, but Coach is going "No, I'm serious! I'm serious!"

Brandon Rush: For a few minutes he actually had me thinking, "Damn ... maybe I *should* have it broken."

Mario's Mentorship

While Rush's transition to college was mostly smooth, Chalmers continued to struggle during his first semester and lost the starting point guard job to Jeff Hawkins. A fifth-year senior, Hawkins considered leaving the program after the 2004-05 campaign, but his performance during his final season—and his mentorship to Chalmers—proved invaluable for the Jayhawks.

Jeff Hawkins: The previous season, my junior year, I was suspended for the first semester. Coach Self told me not to even go to class, but I did anyway. I wanted to show him I wanted to be on the team. He was like, "If you choose to come back, Matt Kleinmann is going to get in the game before you." At the time, Matt Kleinmann was a freshman walk-on who was supposed to redshirt, and he was literally going to play him over me.

Still, I continued to work out with

the team, and during that fall semester I probably practiced as well as I ever had in a Jayhawk uniform. I didn't care. I knew I wasn't going to play in games, so I just went balls to the wall. I went against the top guys and they were impressed. Coach Townsend would always say, "We're going to get you in the next game," and it never happened. At that time I didn't even care. I had decided to leave after the season. I took 22 hours the first semester and 23 the second semester. I was going to get my degree and I was going to be done. My plan was to transfer to a small school that was scheduled to play in The Fieldhouse the following year—Washburn or Fort Hays State or somewhere like that. That would've been like a Senior Night for me.

Finally, Coach Self put me in for 11 seconds to guard Rajon Rondo when we were playing Kentucky at Rupp Arena. He tried me again at Iowa State to chase John Neal around off of screens. Then from there we played Villanova and got our asses kicked. Russell wasn't playing well, and I got about 16 minutes that game. Kyle Lowry punched me right in the stomach and got kicked out of the game. That got me going, and I got more playing time. Then we lost to Bucknell and, after we got back, I still hadn't made a decision. Transferring still sounded kind of good. But then Coach Jankovich called and said Coach Self wanted to meet with me.

Coach Self brought me into his office and told me he didn't want me to come back. He needed me to come back. Him telling me he *needed* me was all I needed to hear. Walking out of that meeting, I knew I'd be back for my senior year.

Bill Self: I was mad at him, but I never seriously thought about running him off. I liked him too much. Jeff Hawkins is one of my favorite all-time guys. He was ornery as hell, but I loved him. He'd fight anyone. He was competitive, but he cared about Kansas. He genuinely cared about us winning. He was crucial for us as a senior, for a lot of different reasons.

Matt Kleinmann: That first semester, Hawk was better than Rio. Nobody on the outside believed it, but he was. That's why he played more.

Joe Dooley: You knew Hawkins was always going to guard well, and he could hit some big shots for you, especially in the clutch. He was fearless. Stephen Vinson wasn't afraid, either. It's a really cool deal when you've got a guy that gives great effort every day and doesn't always get rewarded. Coach played Stephen because he was playing harder than anyone. It proved a point to the young guys that it does matter how hard you try. There were some hard lessons learned that helped us in the long run.

Stephen Vinson: I knew I was a Band-Aid and not a long-term solution. Our best team was going to have Mario on the floor. We'd have no chance of winning the Big 12 without him. Our job was to keep things stable until he was ready.

Mario Chalmers: Coach Self was a dickhead to me, only because he knew I could take it. Everyone knows I'm the type of guy you can yell at and do whatever to and I'll still bounce back strong. It's not going to faze me. So, yeah, he was hard on me. He was an absolute dickhead to me. I'd bark back at him at first, but the more I barked back, the deeper the trouble I'd be in, because it made me seem like I wasn't coachable. You either buy into the system or you're out of the system.

He's not going to play you until you do what he wants you to do, until you play how he wants you to play. Or at least that's how it was back then. Coach Self is softer now (laughing).

Jeff Hawkins: Mario was trying to get a good feel for Coach Self, because Coach Self was on him. Plus, I was heatin' him up pretty good in practice and I know he didn't like that. But I was trying to make him stronger. Looking back, Mario understands that now. But back then he didn't. He was at a breaking point.

One night I picked him up at the Towers, and we went for a drive. I talked to him about my struggles and what I'd been through. I let him know that it was going to be all right and to fight through it. It's something every KU player experiences. I needed to show him that he wasn't the only one who had fought that battle.

Mario Chalmers: I owe a lot to J-Hawk for talking to me that night. We just drove throughout the streets of Lawrence for about three hours. By the time I got back to my room it was about 3:30 a.m.

Jeff Hawkins: Before we played Yale (on Jan. 4, 2006) I went up to Coach Self and told him to start Mario. To me, a starting spot didn't mean anything because my end goal was to win a national championship. Our chances were better with Mario starting. I could've been a selfish guy and said, "Coach, I've been working my ass off for this. I want to start." But at the time I felt like Mario was ready to go. He's fearless. He doesn't care. He steps up in big moments. I was fine coming off the bench as the first guard in.

Bill Self: Hawk came to me before we played Yale and said, "Coach, it's time. Let the young fella start." I said, "Hawk, you've outplayed him." He said, "Yeah, Coach. But this will make us better in the long run. Watch." That was one of the coolest things, especially for a senior, to say, "It'll be better if he starts." Hawk deserves a lot of credit for Mario's improvement.

Rivalry Woes

A 73-46 home win against 19th-ranked Kentucky—Rush had 24 points and 12 rebounds—highlighted the Jayhawks' six-game winning streak heading into conference play. But after defeating

Colorado in the league opener, Self's squad dropped back-to-back contests against K-State (at home) and Missouri. The loss to the Wildcats ended KU's 31-game winning streak against its in-state foe.

Kansas State guard Clent Stewart: The game before, we'd played Nebraska and we lost at home 57-42. It was the worst game we'd played all season. We struggled scoring the ball. It was one of those games where, when you're done, you feel embarrassed to wear the university's jersey. We felt like we were an embarrassment to the university, the fans, the president, everyone. We just didn't play well. And then the very next game was against KU in Lawrence. *Great!*

Kansas State coach Jim Wooldridge: We only made 11 field goals in that Nebraska game. Everybody was disappointed in us. We decided to take the team out of town the night before the KU game. We spent the night in Topeka and tried to clear the air a little bit. We gave the guys a very simple game plan and told them to focus on one thing: not turning the ball over. Don't let them get in the open court. Let's play a half-court game. We had a very good rebounding team and we had some strengths on defense. But if that game got loose, I thought there was no way we could keep up with them.

Apparently my speech didn't work very well, because we went into halftime with 18 points and 13 turnovers. We did the complete opposite of what we had talked about. It was a ridiculous half of basketball. We were only down 26-18, but we were still really upset with them.

In the locker room, we kept preaching that, again, if you'll just take care of the ball and you give yourself a chance by putting it up on the rim, you'll have a shot to win. KU's locker room had one of those old-fashion chalkboards. It had a metal plate behind it, so there was no give in it. I didn't know that, so I punched it. I punched it *really* hard. I knew something was wrong, but I didn't say anything as I sent the team out. Then I turned to my assistant, Jimmy Elgas, and said, "Jimmy, I just broke my hand." It was obvious because it was bubbling up on me, and I could feel it. Something in there was crooked and the pain was intense. Jimmy said, "You need to have it looked at." But I told him we'd worry about it later. I wasn't going to miss any of the game.

Clent Stewart: We came out the second half and executed really well. Then we realized we're at the under-eight-minute timeout now and we have a chance to win. We had a couple of guys who didn't usually get a lot of minutes come up huge in that game. One of them was Schyler Thomas, a walk-on. He made a couple of shots in the second half and stayed out there. Schyler was an older guy, a senior that year. He kind of kept us together. For him, this was the last chance he had to beat KU. He was like, "Hey, let's get this done. Let's do something special."

Coach Wooldridge was really fired up. At one point he didn't like a call, so he took off his suit jacket and threw it, so of course the fans went crazy and were mocking him for that. Normally he'd stomp his foot, but for him to take off his suit jacket and toss it ... he didn't do that a lot. You could feel the energy and sense the opportunity we had in front of us to do something special.

Christian Moody: There were K-State guys making plays in that game that never made those plays in games before that season. Some of them weren't even in our scouting report. I remember thinking, "Gosh, *that* guy made another shot." Dramane Diarra made a bunch of jump shots from the elbow, and I can't remember what his average was. (Diarra averaged 5.3 PPG that season.) But that's no excuse. He made big plays.

Joe Dooley: They surprised us. We couldn't guard their flex, and they kept hitting jump shots from the elbow.

Jim Wooldridge: That offense is a pick-the-pick offense. It's a continuation from one side to the next. If you let it get rhythmatic, you're stepping into shots, you're more confident, they're not taking ball reversal away ... They didn't switch any screens. They played us straight up, and we were able to get some looks at the basket. Still, it's not like we were scoring a ton of points. We slipped into a 2-3 zone and played it throughout most of the second half. They didn't shoot the ball well, and we were a good rebounding team that year so we only gave them a one-and-out look at it.

A 3-pointer by Russell Robinson forced a 50-50 tie with 3:57 remaining, but Kansas made just one field goal the rest of the way in the 59-55 loss. Chalmers (20 points) was the lone bright spot for a KU squad that made just 32.1 percent of its field goals while being outrebounded 40-33.

Clent Stewart: Mario Chalmers missed a desperation 3 with a few seconds left. I ended up with the ball and threw it into the air as the buzzer sounded. There's a clip floating around of me popping my jersey. It was definite jubilation. Beating them in Allen Fieldhouse ... I mean, they're great everywhere, but at home they're so dominant. It's one of the toughest, if not the toughest place to play in college basketball. We knew we did something special.

We celebrated a little bit on the court, and as soon as we got to the locker room, we started checking our phones, and all these text messages were rolling in. We got back to Manhattan, Aggieville was packed and everyone was celebrating. People were chanting our names as we walked through the streets. It's something we'll remember for the rest of our lives.

Jim Wooldridge: On the bus ride home, cars that were headed back to Manhattan drove by us and were honking and people were hanging out their windows and waving. Then we got back to Bramlage (Coliseum), and there was a group of them there. It was one of those coaching moments that was truly special, partly because it was the most improbable win I've ever been a part of, based on the circumstances where Bill's team was and where our team was. All of us—the fans, the players, everybody—were so down from the previous week. Everyone wanted something bigger and better. I don't think anybody could've predicted what happened in that game. We went on from there and beat Missouri and Texas A&M. We had a really competitive team, but I don't know how competitive people thought we'd be going into Allen Fieldhouse.

That was the first time we'd beat Kansas since 1994. It was a 31-game losing streak.

It's a night I'll always cherish. They didn't put Bill Self in the Hall of Fame for no reason. He's an elite coach. Only 10 teams in 14 years have beat him at Allen Fieldhouse. We were fortunate enough to be one of them.

Mario Chalmers: I hated to lose, but I'm not going to lie. That was my first 20-point game. That's the main thing I remember.

Darnell Jackson: I don't know what happened, but it seemed like they were making every shot, and we were missing every shot. Coach Self grilled us for a week straight about that game. We shouldn't have lost.

We were trying to find ourselves. We were trying to determine who the main guys should be and who should be taking the most shots. Coach Self sat us down and said, "The only way this is going to work is if you guys become closer." Jeremy Case reached out and told everybody, "Yo, if we're going to make this work, we need to go sit down and have lunch." So we all met up and talked.

Two days later, on Jan. 16, 2006, freshmen Rush, Chalmers and Wright played their first Border War game against Missouri in Columbia. Tigers guard Thomas Gardner erupted for 40 points, including a 3-pointer that forced a 70-70 tie with six seconds remaining.

Mario Chalmers: I ended up with the ball after Gardner's 3 and, instead of taking a shot to win it, I passed it to Christian Moody, who was wide open under the basket for what should've been an easy layup. But my man (Jimmy McKinney) ran and fouled him with 0.4 seconds left.

Christian Moody: Mario made a great pass and I was fortunate to make a play and get fouled. I was ready for the free throws, but sadly they didn't go in. The game went to overtime, and things didn't go the right way for us.

I definitely felt confident going to the line, and Coach Self had confidence in me, as did my team, as they all said that during the timeout before. It all happened very quick, but those moments kind of slow down, and you wish you could do them over again. I'd do it over again and hopefully make it this time.

It was an awesome atmosphere. It didn't come close to getting as loud as The Fieldhouse gets, but the building was definitely shaking. The students were excited, and it was a packed house like it always is when KU comes to town. It was a great atmosphere and I wish we could have come out of there with a win, because it's always fun to win there.

Bill Self: I think it affected Christian quite

a bit. It genuinely bothered him for a long time. He had a hard time getting over it. He probably didn't handle it the right way. So many times, guys can use a failure as motivation. But you shouldn't do that with free throw shooting. He even hung an article up in his locker about that game. I told him, "Take that down. We know what happened. You don't need to keep reminding yourself of that. It was a freakin' free throw. Move on." If it was someone scoring 32 on you, that's one thing. But the constant reminder that he missed was not good for his confidence.

Stephen Vinson: You can either rally around a loss like that, or things can start to spiral downward. Unlike the K-State loss, there were a lot of positive things that happened against Missouri. We went into a hostile environment and competed and actually had a sizable lead. Mario (22 points, eight assists) and Russ (12 points, seven assists) had great games and showed a lot of chemistry and toughness. Brandon (14 points) played well, and it felt like we were turning the corner. All of a sudden we had the confidence we'd been missing.

Bill Self: That night in Columbia, I could see it coming together. Guys were starting to get it. I said, "Hang in there, fellas. We're getting ready to get really good." We outplayed them and let it get away at the end. But we showed a lot of poise in a tough environment. I was upset we lost, but I still told them, "We're not gonna worry about this one. We're about to take off."

From Chumps to Champs

Self's premonition was correct. The Jayhawks won their next 10 games, including nine against unranked opponents. Self settled on a starting lineup that featured the three freshmen stars along with sophomores Kaun and Robinson. Rush remained steady while Chalmers and Wright continued to make noticeable strides.

Mario Chalmers: Coming in, I was the No. 1-ranked point guard in the country. But we had other strong point guards, too. They needed me to score—and I was a better shooter than Russ, so they decided to play me at the two (shooting guard) and Russ at the point. That's what really forced me to develop my shot and work on my shot even more. A lot of that was because of Coach Dooley. He said, "We're not going to be that good unless you put yourself out there and take that next step." So he and I got in the gym. We stayed in there before practice, after practice. All we did was shoot. The K-State and Missouri games got me going, and from that point on, I averaged about 16.

The other good thing was that, even though I wasn't technically point guard, I still had the ball in my hands a ton. Coach Self opened up the system to where whoever got the ball brought it up the court. Once he opened it up, we were a whole different team. We were faster, we attacked more and everything flowed so much better.

Stephen Vinson: Mario is extremely coachable. The game was just a little fast for him early on, and it hadn't been that way his whole life up to that point. But once he got comfortable, Mario had maybe the best instincts of anyone who has ever played at KU. Between him and Russell Robinson, it felt like we stole seven or eight possessions every game just because of their instincts.

What's crazy about Mario is that he was our worst starter in November and December, but by the end of Big 12 play, he was our best player. And also the most fearless. The key to this streak is that we're the only team that goes into other buildings and consistently wins games. And Mario that year, every time the opposing crowd would get into a game, or every time our eight-point lead would get cut to two, it felt like he would hit a shot and put it back to five. And then a steal and put it back to seven. And then the crowd would sit down. That was a pretty cool year for him, especially considering where he started out.

Darnell Jackson: Russell was the heart of our team. We fed off of his energy, because his defense was amazing. Mario was more of a vocal guy. He didn't hold anything back. If he had a problem with someone, he'd say something. That really helped us. He and Russ were the tough, hard-nosed guys on the team. We followed their lead.

Stephen Vinson: We all knew how important Russell was. You take Russ on the road and put him in a hostile environment against a player that, on paper, is much more talented, much better, bigger, stronger ... it doesn't matter. When Coach Self talks about toughness, he's not talking about knocking someone down. He's talking about someone that loves to compete and doesn't take a possession off and is offended if someone scores against him. That was Russell.

Julian improving and becoming a bigger factor was huge, too. He was really fun to play with because he was such a good passer. You never knew what was going to happen. It was like having a wild stallion out there on the court who also had a ton of skill, too. The variance of how he could play was pretty incredible.

Bill Self: Julian was kind of a weird position, because at that time we played a lot of high-low, although we did move to more of a ball-screen mode team. You couldn't really play him at the 3 because we had Rush, Chalmers and Robinson. He was kind of the 4-man where he wasn't really an inside player. He's more of a slasher type.

In addition to finding a starting lineup that worked, the Jayhawks also benefitted from improved play from sophomore forward Darnell Jackson, who averaged 9.7 points off the bench in KU's first seven Big 12 games.

Darnell Jackson: What clicked for me, honestly ... it was Coach (Ronnie) Chalmers and Coach Self. And Mario and Brandon. Those guys, especially Mario, would just stay on me. Mario would say, "Yo, we're not going to win if you don't give us your all. You're a huge piece. We can't do this without you." To have people believing in me like that gave me more confidence to go out there and be free and be myself.

The Jayhawks won their first four games of the 10-game winning streak by a comfortable margin, and then they were tested when No. 19 Oklahoma came to Lawrence. KU won 59-58 and followed that up with a memorable trip to Nebraska.

Mario Chalmers: Oklahoma my freshman year ... that was my first game-winner. Michael Neal had hit a 3 for them to put OU ahead by one point (58-57), but I drove into the lane and hit a floater over Kevin Bookout with 20 seconds left. They got one more possession to try to beat us but Terrell Everett and Michael Neal both missed shots. That was huge for us because Oklahoma was the only ranked team in the Big 12 besides Texas.

Matt Kleinmann: Usually when you think of KU and Nebraska you don't think of memorable games. That year we beat them by 21 in Lincoln, but the trip was unforgettable because of what happened during pregame.

Stephen Vinson's girlfriend—now his wife—spent her first year of college at Nebraska. So we're getting ready to play them, and there's this really obnoxious Nebraska fan wearing pajamas, a wig and a suit. He looked like a character from a Dr. Seuss book, and he was standing right behind the backstop. Fans at every school always tried to get a rise out of us during pregame. Some were funny. Some made fun of my red hair. But with Stephen, they got too personal, because they started talking about his girlfriend. *"Hey Steve, we know your girl!"* Me and Hawk asked him, "Are you going to take that?" He didn't say anything.

We did three or four shootarounds before each game and, in between, we'd go back to the locker room. That day, in between one of the shootarounds, Stephen, Hawk and I drew up a plan. Hawk stood near the baseline, and Stephen and I stood at the free throw line. We were in a "V" formation, and we'd take turns firing passes to Jeff at a pretty fast pace. I had a ball and Stephen had a ball. It was just a BS passing drill.

Well, we waited for the guy with the PJs and the hat to get right behind Jeff, and as soon as Jeff kind of gave the nod, I threw a pass and then Stephen immediately rocketed a pass at Jeff, but really aiming at this annoying fan. So Jeff catches my pass and then ducks. Stephen's pass hits the guy in the face and knocks him out. He falls over, drops his water, everything. Then he hops up and runs over to the ref and tries to get us in trouble. But we were like, "Hey man, you were on the court! We're trying to get ready for a game here!" I remember driving back on the bus, me and Stephen and Jeff high-fiving each other, like, "That was awesome!"

Chalmers followed up his game-winner against Oklahoma with one of his best stretches of the season. He hit four 3s and had 20 points at Nebraska and then scored 23 in a win over Iowa State at Allen Fieldhouse. His most crucial performance, though, came under difficult conditions in a gritty win at Oklahoma State, where Chalmers tallied a team-best 13 points, seven assists and three steals.

Mario Chalmers: At Oklahoma State, Brandon and Julian were in foul trouble late, and the score was close with about six minutes left. I was on the floor with Darnell, Sasha, Stephen Vinson and Hawk. It was a lineup we'd never played before. It wasn't a good scoring lineup. Coach Self just gave me the ball and said, "We're going to run straight pick-and-rolls." That was my first time really picking a team apart in a pick-and-roll situation. We ran away with it at the end and won (64-49). From that point on, any time we needed a basket in the clutch, they'd give me the ball.

Tussles with Texas

Kansas went to Texas tied with the Longhorns for the Big 12 lead at 11-2. Unfortunately, the bigger news around the program leading up to that game was Hawkins had been cited a week earlier for leaving the scene of an accident in a McDonald's drive-thru. Self suspended Hawkins for one game and he returned for the matchup with Texas.

Bill Self: The McDonald's thing cracked me up. I mean, I hated that it happened. Only Hawk would cut in line at McDonald's. He tried to cut in line and the person behind him nudged up and they bumped fenders. We called him the Hamburglar after that.

Matt Kleinmann: I always try to get on the court early, because that's the only time I ever got to really shoot around. I remember walking out onto the court with Hawk at Texas, and nobody from either team was out there yet.

We got to half court, and the entire Texas fan base is there, all the students, and they all unravel McDonald's wrappers, each and every one of them, and in unison, right as we cross half court, they chant the McDonald's theme: *"Ba da ba ba baaahhhh ... I'm lovin' it!"*

Hawk and I just die laughing. It was one of the greatest moments ever. They loved it. We loved it. I think Hawk was mortified, but it was one of the better examples of hazing I've ever seen from a school. Whoever was in the audience at Texas that day remembers it because it was perfect.

Mario Chalmers: At K-State (the next weekend), they were holding up cheeseburgers, and they had a big picture of Jeff's face with the Hamburglar drawn all over it. We were all laughing about that.

Stephen Vinson: Back then we just played Texas once during the regular season. That year Texas had the perfect roster—literally everything you'd want if you were putting together a team. P.J. Tucker was an absolute monster in college. And I know Kareem (Abdul-Jabbar) had the skyhook, but I saw ground-level LaMarcus Aldridge shoot a right-shoulder fadeaway at the top of his head. I think his release point was 10 1/2 feet; you couldn't block it. It was just make or miss. And it just seemed like they had cloned big guys they could bring off the bench.

Daniel Gibson, their point guard, had been to Kansas on a recruiting trip, so we knew him fairly well. He was a great scorer, great shooter, great player.

A.J. Abrams, who became the all-time leading 3-point shooter in the Big 12, came off the bench for them. He was the guy you try to take advantage of—except you couldn't take advantage of him. They killed us.

Kansas lost 80-55 at Texas and then won its final two games and finished tied for first in the Big 12 after Texas had followed the KU win with a loss at Texas A&M. The two teams met again in the Big 12 Tournament championship game in Dallas.

Jeff Hawkins: I was fired up for that game for a lot of reasons. They had beat us so bad in Austin a few weeks earlier, and I was coming off the McDonald's situation where I was cited for a hit-and-run—which is something I still deny to this day. We ended up losing at Texas, and Coach Self blamed a lot of it on me because of the distraction it caused. We had really started rolling when that happened. I owned up to it. It *was* a distraction.

The next practice he was lighting into me about how A.J. Abrams had busted my butt in Austin because he had four 3-pointers against us. He'd kick me out of a drill and then let me back in, but he kept saying stuff. I got mad, so I threw an overhead pass when we were breaking the press. I threw it over everyone's heads where no one could catch it. I did it on purpose. I was being a butthead. He screamed at me and was like, "Do it again!" So I threw the exact same pass and he kicked me out. That was just me pouting and being immature.

That lit a fire inside of me, so I was excited when we got to face them again in the championship. The sound of him talking about A.J. Abrams busting my butt kept playing in the back of my mind. Obviously that was just personal for me. (Hawkins made four 3s and scored 13 points.)

The other thing was that, even though we had shared the Big 12 regular season title, they had given Texas the trophy after they won their half—but no one did anything to recognize us. That pissed us off.

So that game was to prove who was the top dog. The emotions of it had me fired up. The whole team was fired up. We thought we were better than them. They were stacked: Aldridge, Tucker, Gibson, Abrams. They had a nice little squad.

Kansas 80, Texas 68
March 12, 2006 · Dallas, Texas

Kansas (25-7)

Player	MP	FG	3FG	FT	R	A	F	S	TO	B	TP
Russell Robinson*	35	3-10	2-5	6-7	10	6	1	3	3	0	14
Mario Chalmers*	30	4-8	4-7	3-4	3	6	4	2	0	1	15
Sasha Kaun*	15	4-7	0-0	1-3	1	0	4	1	0	3	9
Brandon Rush*	37	4-14	2-7	2-2	6	1	2	0	3	0	12
Julian Wright*	32	6-11	0-0	0-0	10	4	3	3	2	2	12
Jeff Hawkins	19	4-5	4-5	1-2	3	5	1	1	0	0	13
Darnell Jackson	8	1-3	0-0	1-1	6	0	1	0	1	0	3
C.J. Giles	24	1-3	0-0	0-0	4	0	2	0	0	2	2
Team					4						
Totals	200	27-61	12-24	14-19	47	22	18	10	9	8	80

Texas (27-6)

Player	MP	FG	3FG	FT	R	A	F	S	TO	B	TP
LaMarcus Aldridge*	28	1-5	0-0	3-4	9	1	4	0	2	1	5
Kenton Paulino*	29	6-11	5-9	2-2	2	2	2	0	2	0	19
Brad Buckman*	32	5-11	0-3	2-4	11	1	4	1	1	2	12
Daniel Gibson*	33	3-12	2-8	0-0	5	4	5	2	2	2	8
P.J. Tucker*	38	5-13	0-0	6-8	11	4	3	2	6	0	16
A.J. Abrams	20	2-3	1-1	2-2	3	2	1	0	3	0	7
Connor Atchley	2	0-0	0-0	0-0	0	0	2	0	0	0	0
Mike Williams	18	0-0	0-0	1-2	10	1	1	1	0	0	1
Team					3						
Totals	200	22-55	8-21	16-22	54	15	22	6	16	5	68

	1st	2nd	Total	FG%	3FG%	FT%
Kansas	37	43	80	44.3	50.0	73.7
Texas	38	30	68	40.0	38.1	72.7

Officials: Steve Welmer, Scott Thornley, Curtis Shaw
Technicals: None

Christian Moody: I remember playing them in Austin, and it felt like we were playing an NBA team. They couldn't miss, and Aldridge had an unblockable shot. You knew you were watching greatness with him. It was like watching Wayne in that Oklahoma State game (in 2005). He was a star player. It seemed like their team was unbeatable after playing against them in Austin.

So, to come out and play against them again and have a second chance ... we knew we'd have a chance because we had a lot of confidence and so much momentum. Julian went off that game. Ball-handling, passing, making tough shots, making plays, he was doing everything. He had some crazy play where he dribbled behind his back three times and then made a pass or a shot after that—I can't remember exactly—but he was handling that ball like it was a yo-yo. You could tell Julian was having fun and playing within himself. He was very loose and relaxed. I do remember thinking, "This is Julian at his finest. He is so connected to the game and so relaxed that things are just coming to him."

Stephen Vinson: In that Big 12 championship game, we ran a triangle-and-two against them and junked the game up. They were confused offensively. What I remember more, though, was how that was the Julian Wright-Mario Chalmers-Brandon Rush show. They all played incredible that game.

That Texas team was as good of an opponent as we played in my four years at Kansas. The 2004 Oklahoma State team with Tony Allen was really good, too. There's only a few teams that I remember being on that level.

Chalmers (15 points, six assists) Robinson (14 and six) and Hawkins (13 and five) combined for 42 points and 17 assists. Still, as dominant as Kansas was in the backcourt, the x-factor was C.J. Giles' post defense on Aldridge. The No. 2 pick in the 2006 NBA draft was held to five points on 1-of-5 shooting.

Christian Moody: C.J. Giles was the only guy we had that could match Aldridge's length.

You look at C.J's raw talent and, if you're an NBA scout, you're just drooling. He's definitely a phenomenal athletic specimen with that 7-6 wingspan and those quick legs. And he had that nice, soft touch on his jump shot.

There were definitely some unbelievable moments where you'd look up and C.J. was making an NBA-caliber play, whether it was a jump hook, a jump shot, a dunk or a rebound. I wish he could've stayed with us longer. NBA scouts would've been drooling over him.

With 5:42 remaining, Wright broke open the game with a steal and a tomahawk slam that put KU ahead 67-63. Five minutes later, Wright put the exclamation point on the Jayhawks 80-68 victory with a soaring, 360-dunk in transition that surprised everyone. Even Wright.

Julian Wright: Honest to God, I didn't even think I was going to do that. I didn't know what I was going to do. I think Mario tipped it, and Russell got the rebound and threw it to me. I didn't even know where the rim was. So at the last minute, I was like, "Oh shoot," and I just did something. It's crazy. Hey, that's what basketball's about. It's just poetry in motion. I was just like, "Well, you know, this is a team that beat us pretty badly at first, so how can I just kind of add to the excitement?" That's what happened in a split-second. The game is pretty reactive, so I just did it. Coach Townsend and Coach

BEST BIG 12 OPPONENTS (TEAM)

1. Texas: 2005-06: *Coach:* Rick Barnes. *Record:* 30-7 overall, 13-3 (tied for first) in the Big 12. *Postseason:* Lost to LSU 70-60 in overtime in the Sweet 16. *Starters:* PJ Tucker (16.1 ppg), LaMarcus Aldridge (15.0), Daniel Gibson (13.4), Kenton Paulino (9.8), Brad Beckman (9.5); Sixth Man: A.J. Abrams (6.4)

2. Oklahoma: 2015-16: *Coach:* Lon Kruger. *Record:* 29-8 overall, 12-6 (third) in the Big 12. *Postseason:* Lost to Villanova 95-51 in the Final Four. *Starters:* Buddy Hield (25.0 ppg), Jordan Woodard (13.0), Isaiah Cousins (12.6), Ryan Spangler (10.2), Khadeem Lattin 5.6

3. Missouri: 2011-12: *Coach:* Frank Haith. *Record:* 30-5 overall; 14-4 (second) in the Big 12. *Postseason:* Lost to Norfolk State 86-84 in the opening round of the NCAA tournament. *Starters:* Marcus Denmon (17.7 ppg); Kim English (14.5), Ricardo Ratliffe (13.9), Phil Pressey (10.3), Matt Pressey (6.2); Sixth Man: Michael Dixon Jr. (13.5)

4. Texas A&M: 2006-07: *Coach:* Billy Gillispie. *Record:* 27-7 overall, 13-3 (second) in the Big 12. *Postseason:* Lost to Memphis 65-64 in the Sweet 16. *Starters:* Acie Law (18.1 ppg), Joseph Jones (13.4), Antanas Kavaliauskas (11.9), Josh Carter (11.8), Dominique Kirk (7.2); Sixth Man: Donald Sloan (5.2)

5. Texas: 2006-07: *Coach:* Rick Barnes. *Record:* 25-10 overall, 12-4 (third) in the Big 12. *Postseason:* Lost to USC 87-68 in the second round of the NCAA tournament. *Starters:* Kevin Durant (25.8 ppg), A.J. Abrams (15.5), D.J. Augustin (14.4), Justin Mason (7.6), Damion James (7.6)

6. Oklahoma State: 2004-05: *Coach:* Eddie Sutton. *Record:* 26-7 overall, 11-5 (third) in the Big 12. *Postseason:* Big 12 tournament champion; lost to Arizona 79-78 in the Sweet 16. *Starters:* Joey Grahm (17.7 ppg), John Lucas III (17.7), Ivan McFarlin (12.5), JamesOn Curry (9.4), Daniel Bobiik (6.7), Stephen Graham (6.5)

7. Iowa State: 2013-14: *Coach:* Fred Hoiberg. *Record:* 26-7 overall, 11-7 (third) in the Big 12. *Postseason:* Big 12 tournament champion; lost to Connecticut 81-76 in the Sweet 16. *Starters:* Melvin Ejim (17.8 ppg), DeAndre Kane (17.1), Georges Niang (16.7), Dustin Hogue (11.6); Monte Morris (6.8)

8. Baylor: 2011-12: *Coach:* Scott Drew. *Record:* 30-8 overall, 12-6 (tied for third) in the Big 12. *Postseason:* Lost to Kentucky 82-70 in the Elite Eight. *Starters:* Pierre Jackson (13.8 ppg), Perry Jones (13.5), Quincy Acy (12.0), Quincy Miller (10.6), Brady Heslip (10.2)

9. Kansas State: 2009-10: *Coach:* Frank Martin. *Record:* 29-8 overall; 11-5 (tied for second) in the Big 12. *Postseason:* Lost to Butler 63-56 in the Elite Eight. *Starters:* Jacob Pullen (19.3 ppg), Denis Clemente (16.6), Curtis Kelly (11.5), Dominique Sutton (7.2), Luis Colon (2.9) Sixth man: Jamar Samuels (11.0)

10. Oklahoma: 2008-09: *Coach:* Jeff Capel. *Record:* 30-6 overall, 13-3 (second) in the Big 12. *Postseason:* Lost to North Carolina 72-60 in the Elite Eight. *Starters:* Blake Griffin (22.7 ppg), Willie Warren (14.6), Taylor Griffin (9.6), Tony Crocker (9.6), Austin Johnson (8.6)

Self gave me a hard time. They said, "You know, I've never seen you do that one too much in practice. So we're glad you brought that one out and made it."

The Big 12 Tournament championship was Kansas' first since 1999. Chalmers was named Most Outstanding Player after averaging 16 points and 5.3 assists in three games.

Mario Chalmers: You beat guys like Aldridge and Gibson … guys that are projected lottery picks, you feel pretty good about yourselves.

Bill Self: That was such a great moment for Mario. We couldn't even play him earlier in the season and now he was the Most Outstanding Player of the Big 12 Tournament.

Another Early Exit

Unlike the previous season, Kansas entered the NCAA Tournament on a roll with wins in 15 of its previous 16 contests. The selection committee, however, did the Jayhawks no favors by pitting them against another B-school (No. 13 seed Bradley)—and this one boasted a future NBA lottery pick at center in Patrick O'Bryant.

Jeff Hawkins: With Bucknell, we were like, "Who?" and I don't think we took it seriously enough. The next year when we found out we were playing Bradley … again I thought, "Who?" But I was like, "No, we've got to take them seriously!"

Bill Self: We couldn't have been playing better going into that game. We were so loose. But our young guys weren't quite ready for that stage. I think the game before ours went long. You could see how tight our guys were getting in the locker room.

Mario Chalmers: That was the first time where it felt like the moment was too big for us. We didn't know what to do. We were all overwhelmed. We played uptight.

Kansas 73, Bradley 77
March 17, 2006 · Auburn Hills, Mich.

Kansas (25-8)

Player	MP	FG	3FG	FT	R	A	F	S	TO	B	TP
Julian Wright*	29	4-5	0-0	0-0	5	2	2	2	1	0	8
Sasha Kaun*	26	1-4	0-0	4-4	8	0	2	0	2	0	6
Russell Robinson*	36	5-13	1-2	7-11	3	7	3	5	5	0	18
Mario Chalmers*	34	6-11	2-4	1-2	3	0	5	3	5	0	15
Brandon Rush*	36	4-14	1-5	0-0	7	1	2	0	1	1	9
Jeff Hawkins	15	4-8	3-7	0-0	1	1	4	1	3	0	11
Stephen Vinson	1	0-0	0-0	0-0	0	0	1	0	0	0	0
Darnell Jackson	7	0-1	0-0	2-2	0	0	1	1	0	0	2
C.J. Giles	14	2-2	0-0	0-0	2	0	5	0	1	0	4
Jeremy Case	1	0-0	0-0	0-0	0	0	0	0	0	0	0
Christian Moody	1	0-0	0-0	0-0	0	0	0	0	0	0	0
Team					7						
Totals	200	26-58	7-18	14-19	36	11	25	12	18	1	73

Bradley (21-10)

Player	MP	FG	3FG	FT	R	A	F	S	TO	B	TP
Marcellus Sommerville*	37	7-15	5-9	2-2	7	0	0	1	5	0	21
Patrick O'Bryant*	26	3-8	0-0	2-4	10	2	4	1	1	0	8
Tony Bennett*	31	1-5	0-2	6-8	4	2	4	0	2	0	8
J.J. Tauai*	17	3-3	1-1	1-2	3	0	2	3	1	0	8
Daniel Ruffin*	26	2-4	2-3	5-6	2	7	3	1	2	0	11
Will Franklin	26	5-9	2-3	2-2	0	6	0	0	2	0	14
Zach Andrews	12	1-1	0-0	0-2	4	0	1	0	1	1	2
Lawrence Wright	21	1-7	1-3	2-6	1	0	3	0	2	0	5
Danny Adams	4	0-0	0-0	0-0	0	0	0	0	0	0	0
Team					4						
Totals	200	23-52	11-21	20-32	35	17	17	6	16	1	77

	1st	2nd	Total	FG%	3FG%	FT%
Kansas	27	46	73	44.8	38.9	73.7
Bradley	37	40	77	44.2	52.4	62.5

Officials: Steve Welmer, Scott Thornley, Curtis Shaw
Technicals: None

No one had a breakout game. I didn't even score the first half. I'd been averaging 17-plus throughout the second half of the season.

Matt Kleinmann: Bradley came out and punked us physically and mentally. They were tougher. Patrick O'Bryant and (Marcellus) Sommerville just outmuscled us.

Brandon Rush really struggled. He got rode off every screen. This was that double-edged sword with Brandon. He could be the most focused player in the world, but if he gets out of his game, he doesn't turn it back on. He's kind of a slow build, but when he gets going, you can't knock him out. That day he just didn't have it.

Rush wasn't alone. Chalmers, Robinson and Hawkins combined for 13 of KU's 18 turnovers and not a single frontcourt player scored in double figures in the 77-73 loss. For the second straight year, Kansas had lost in the first round of the NCAA Tournament.

Bill Self: Bradley was playing with house money. And the reality of it is, there wasn't a nickel's worth of difference between those two teams. There wasn't a big difference in the teams at all from a talent standpoint. They had Marcellus Somerville, a senior that was a grown man. They had a lottery pick at center. We started three freshmen. They won their next game against Pittsburgh and advanced to the Sweet 16.

The loss was bad, but it wasn't anything like the Bucknell deal, to me. The situation was completely different.

Mario Chalmers: The biggest thing about the Bradley loss is that it hurt our school and our fans more than it hurt us. The previous KU team had just lost to Bucknell, so everyone was still hearing jokes about that. And now they had to hear all about Bradley.

Matt Kleinmann: Throughout the whole game I just had this sinking feeling that it was going to happen again. My biggest memory from that night was walking to the back and seeing the seniors—Jeff and Christian and Stephen—crying in the locker room and the showers. That was it for those seniors who did so much for the program. That was the last time our group really saw that happen, because the next year we didn't have a senior class, and the following year we won the title.

When upsets like that happen, you want to turn the TV off for the rest of the summer. You don't want to read ESPN or anything. You avoid it all, because you're so embarrassed and ashamed and pissed off. You don't want to relive those moments.

I think we used what happened as fuel. We would always say that, but that year I think we really did. Granted, Bucknell was the major upset. Bradley wasn't that big of an upset. They were just older and stronger. People thought, "oh, it's the B schools." I don't ever think that got into our heads. I think what got into our heads was, "OK, it's happened two years in a row. What are we going to do to change it?"

A little more from ...

Tim Jankovich: We went to Hawaii that year and we were awful, just brutal. We got smacked.

I thought Bill did his best coaching after that with a really young team. I watched how fast he got them from there to a really, really high-level basketball team at a really young age. I thought he was tremendous, just his coaching and leadership and even how he talked to them, and not necessarily always on the floor. Films and individual meetings ... just constantly driving things into their heads to create a culture. In my four years there, I was more impressed with him during that season than any. We went from a group that got slaughtered in Maui to a Big 12 championship team.

Brandon Rush: I used to hate playing against Stephen Vinson. He would go so hard in practice. He'd play the toughest defense. He was doing everything he could to get some playing time. Whenever he was guarding me, practice was harder than the games. He made me a lot better.

Stephen Vinson: I'm biased because that was my senior year, but that year was easily, *easily* the most unexpected season of this streak, and I don't think it's close. I don't think it's in the same universe. If you look at who we tied (Texas) for the regular-season title and then beat in the Big 12 Tournament, and you compare rosters, it's laughable. I thought that was an extremely special year, but it started out with those young guys coming in and there was a process to that.

Coach Self had so much more fun coaching that year, probably because he, and everyone, knew the transition was official. It was his team. He had less pressure and felt confident in that group. I thought by the time that year was over, even though it didn't end well, the program was set up to succeed in the future under Self. You could sense it was going to work.

Trust me, with the streak still going, former players are following every game and every moment to try to keep this thing alive, because it really does kind of connect all of the classes. It was great almost winning a national championship in 2003. No doubt about that. But being a part of this streak is what I'll always look back on.

I take so much pride in the last year that I was there, because that was the group that was picked to finish fourth in the Big 12. We weren't the favorite that year, nor should we have been. Yet we were able to win it—or, technically, tie for it. And what made it even sweeter was winning the "tiebreaker" in the Big 12 tournament against the same Texas team that had whipped us so bad earlier in the year. That's one of my favorite memories.

Christian Moody: Coach and I talked before that season, and from what I had seen that summer after playing with the new freshmen and how the sophomores had gotten better over the summer, I knew that my role may change because we'd obviously added an incredible talent in Julian Wright. I told Coach Self that I just wanted what was best for the team. If that meant my role changed, then I was all for it.

There were multiple lineups throughout the year that changed. With the way the young guys were developing, Coach Self had to figure out what the best lineup for each game was.

The streak is unbelievable, what Coach Self and his staff have done, but it's not just the coaches. Guys like (trainer) Bill Cowgill deserve credit as well.

Those are the guys that are absolutely critical to the success of the team and I feel like Cowgill is as big a part of the streak as anybody, with the time he puts into keeping us healthy—before practice, after practice, before weights… his hours never stop.

Jeff Hawkins: A lot of players butted heads with Coach Self during his first two years. We weren't having the same type of success as we had under Coach Williams. We wanted to play faster.

Personally, though, that third year under Coach Self … I got to know him more and trust him more. I thought the transition was great. For myself and Coach Self, that's where our relationship turned the corner.

Coach Self always told me, "I guarantee you that we'll get along a lot better once your career is over than we will while you're playing for me." Our relationship continues to grow.

When I look back on that season now, I wish I'd have taken my role as a leader more serious and done a better job in that area. Still, I led by example and I think that had an impact, because the young guys didn't know what they were doing. I was trying to protect the program and lead in a good way. I passed on what I could, but when you're on a team that doesn't win it all, you always look back and wonder what you could've done differently from a leadership standpoint.

Mario Chalmers: That season was very gratifying because we were young. The oldest guys on the team were Jeff Hawkins and Stephen Vinson and Christian Moody, and they didn't play a ton. Once we got rolling, it made Coach Self a little happier, because his guys were finally doing something. We took off from there.

It was also great to be able to play with Hawk. He's probably one of the best defenders I've ever played against. He had long-ass arms. Still, to this day, he's the first person I call when I'm in Kansas.

Jeremy Case: That year was a grind. Practices were hard and long, and Coach was just going to get it out of us, eventually. Those guys had to grow up. Mario had to grow up. Brandon had to grow up. That year was one of the years that really got us to where we could win it in 2008.

It was pivotal as far as those young guys getting used to Coach Self and how things were going to be.

Sasha Kaun: We had everyone coming back the following year, plus we were adding Sherron and Shady (Darrell Arthur). We knew we were going to get better. Even though we lost to Bradley, it made everyone want to come back the next year and win some games in the tournament. It fueled us during the summer to work harder. We got so much better during that offseason.

2005-06 Season Summary

Results (25-8, 13-3)

November

18	@ Idaho State	W, 90 - 66
21	vs. Arizona	L, 61 - 49
22	vs. Arkansas	L, 64 - 65
23	@ Chaminade	W, 54 - 102

December

1	Nevada	L, 70 - 72
3	Western Illinois	W, 86 - 57
6	vs. Saint Joseph's	L, 67 - 70
10	vs. California	W, 69 - 56
19	Pepperdine	W, 63 - 43
22	Northern Colorado	W, 85 - 62
29	New Orleans	W, 73 - 56

January

4	Yale	W, 87 - 46
7	Kentucky	W, 73 - 46
11	@ Colorado	W, 63 - 75
14	Kansas State	L, 55 - 59
16	@ Missouri	L, 89 - 86
21	Nebraska	W, 96 - 54
25	@ Texas A&M	W, 73 - 83
28	@ Iowa State	W, 85 - 95
30	Texas Tech	W, 86 - 52

February

5	Oklahoma	W, 59 - 58
8	@ Nebraska	W, 48 - 69
11	Iowa State	W, 88 - 75
13	@ Oklahoma State	W, 49 - 64
18	Missouri	W, 79 - 46
21	Baylor	W, 76 - 61
25	@ Texas	L, 80 - 55

March

1	Colorado	W, 75 - 54
4	@ Kansas State	W, 52 - 66
10	vs. Oklahoma State	W, 63 - 62
11	vs. Nebraska	W, 79 - 65
12	vs. Texas	W, 68 - 80
17	vs. Bradley	L, 73 - 77

All-Big 12 Team

Player of the Year:
P.J.Tucker, Texas, Jr., F

Defensive Player of the Year:
LaMarcus Aldridge, Texas, So., F

Newcomer of the Year:
Michael Neal, Oklahoma, Jr., G

Freshman of the Year:
Brandon Rush, Kansas, Fr., G

Coach of the Year:
Bill Self, Kansas

First Team
Richard Roby, Colorado, So, G
Brandon Rush, Kansas, Fr., G
LaMarcus Aldridge,Texas, So., F
P.J.Tucker,Texas, Jr., F**
Jarrius Jackson,Texas Tech, Jr., G

Second Team
Curtis Stinson, Iowa State, Jr., G
Cartier Martin, Kansas State, Jr., F
Terrell Everett, Oklahoma, Sr., G
Taj Gray, Oklahoma, Sr., F
Joseph Jones,Texas A&M, So., F

Third Team
Will Blalock, Iowa State, Jr., G
Thomas Gardner, Missouri, Jr., G
Brad Buckman,Texas, Sr., F
Daniel Gibson,Texas, So., G
Acie Law,Texas A&M, Jr., G

Honorable Mention
Aaron Bruce, Baylor, So., G
Mario Chalmers, Kansas, Fr., G
JulianWright, Kansas, Fr., F
Jimmy McKinney, Missouri, Sr., G
Aleks Maric, Nebraska, So., F
WesWilkinson, Nebraska, Sr., F
Kevin Bookout, Oklahoma, Sr., F
Michael Neal, Oklahoma, Jr., G
Mario Boggan, Oklahoma State, Jr., F
JamesOn Curry, Oklahoma State, So., G
Martin Zeno,Texas Tech, So., G

All-Defensive Team
Mario Chalmers, Kansas, Fr., G
Russell Robinson, Kansas, So., G
Taj Gray, Oklahoma, Sr., F
LaMarcus Aldridge,Texas, So., F
P.J.Tucker,Texas, Jr., F

All-Rookie Team
Curtis Jerrells, Baylor, Fr., G
Mario Chalmers, Kansas, Fr., G**
Brandon Rush, Kansas, Fr., G**
JulianWright, Kansas, Fr., F
Michael Neal, Oklahoma, Jr., G

** Unanimous selection

Kansas Awards

Mario Chalmers:
Big 12 All-Tournament MOP

Julian Wright:
Big 12 All-Tournament Team

Season Stats

#	Player	CL	POS	HT	Hometown	G	GS	FG%	3P%	FT%	R	A	S	B	PTS
25	Brandon Rush	FR	G	6-6	Kansas City, MO	33	33	.474	.472	.761	5.9	2.0	0.9	0.7	13.5
15	Mario Chalmers	FR	G	6-1	Anchorage, AK	33	21	.445	.375	.788	2.2	3.8	2.7	0.2	11.5
3	Russell Robinson	SO	G	6-1	New York, NY	33	32	.371	.322	.742	3.1	4.6	2.3	0.5	9.3
30	Julian Wright	FR	F	6-8	Chicago Heights, IL	33	15	.564	.000	.548	4.6	1.8	0.9	1.3	8.5
24	Sasha Kaun	SO	C	6-11	Melbourne, FL	33	29	.562		.535	5.3	0.4	0.5	1.1	8.2
32	Darnell Jackson	SO	F	6-9	Oklahoma City, OK	23	0	.505		.769	4.9	0.3	0.6	0.1	6.3
23	C.J. Giles	SO	F	6-11	Seattle, WA	33	13	.506		.588	4.8	0.4	0.4	1.5	6.2
1	Jeff Hawkins	SR	G	5-11	Kansas City, KS	32	12	.429	.406	.692	1.9	2.4	0.9	0.0	5.4
22	Micah Downs	FR	G	6-8	Kirkland, WA	13	0	.380	.375	.545	2.2	1.0	0.1	0.2	4.3
34	Christian Moody	SR	F	6-8	Asheville, NC	31	9	.577	.333	.512	2.9	0.5	0.3	0.3	3.4
10	Jeremy Case	SO	G	6-1	McAlester, OK	24	0	.420	.333	1.000	0.6	0.4	0.3	0.0	2.5
20	Stephen Vinson	SR	G	6-2	Lawrence, KS	23	1	.321	.292	.700	0.7	1.3	0.3	0.0	1.4
54	Matt Kleinmann	FR	C	6-10	Overland Park, KS	16	0	.636		1.000	0.4	0.3	0.0	0.0	1.0
5	Rodrick Stewart	SO	G	6-4	Seattle, WA	14	0	.364	.000	.667	0.4	0.2	0.0	0.0	0.7

## CHAPTER 3

2006-07

MAKING STRIDES

Unlike the previous offseason, the summer of 2006 was filled with positive vibes. Brandon Rush, Julian Wright and C.J. Giles—all potential NBA draft picks—opted to return to school, and in May, the Jayhawks won a highly-publicized recruiting battle when McDonald's All-American forward Darrell "Slim Shady" Arthur picked Kansas over Baylor. Still, no player that summer generated as much buzz as incoming freshman Sherron Collins, a gritty point guard from Chicago who would become one of the best players in Jayhawks history.

Sherron Collins: I thought there may be some tension when Shady and I got to Kansas, but everyone took us under their wings from the very first day. I think they viewed us as the missing pieces to a national championship. There was a great vibe around the program that whole summer. No one was moping about the Bradley game. There was so much talent in the gym. Our pickup games were intense.

Mario Chalmers: I'll never forget the first day Sherron stepped on campus. The way he abused Jeremy Case in pickup that day ... he just destroyed him. Stepbacks, crossovers, blowing past him and pulling up. The only thing he wasn't doing was dunking—and we knew he could do that, too, because we'd seen him throw one down in the McDonald's game a few months earlier. Still, to watch him in person ... we were all just thinking, "Wow! We've got something special with Sherron."

Jeremy Case: I literally couldn't stop him from scoring. He'd light me up and then get the ball back a few possessions later, and I'd focus in and think, "OK I'm going to stop him this time." But I couldn't. He was definitely special. Even on a team with Brandon and Julian and Shady—all first-round draft picks—Sherron was our most-talented guy by far.

You think about his size (5-10, 205) and what he could do with the ball. His handles were tight and quick. It was like he had the ball on a string, like a yo-yo. He could get around you and pull up on a dime, and he could really guard, too. Sherron should've played in the NBA for 10 years.

Mario Chalmers: We had lost J-Hawk to graduation, so we'd been thinking, "Who is going to be the next guard to step up? Is it going to be Case? Is it going to be Rod Stewart?" But after that day in pickup, we were like, "Phew! We got one. We're going to be fine. And if we figure out a way to fit him in our system and control him, watch out!"

Sherron Collins: I remember that day against Case in pickup, but what I remember even more are the two or three days after that. Russell Robinson guarded me full court on every single possession. There were no breaks. I couldn't take a play off. Russ was in my face every single minute of every pickup game. I guess he saw what I'd done to Case and took it as a challenge to guard me.

The best thing Russell did for me was to not take it easy on me. He's half the reason I was able to get past dudes at will. He was such a good defender, I'd think, "If I can get past Russell, I can get past anybody."

Off the court, Russell was more welcoming than anyone. One time that summer, Coach Self was on me so bad. I was out of shape. I got kicked out of individuals and kicked the garbage can over. Coach Self called Hudy and she came and ran me like crazy. I did stairs and sprints and had to get on the elliptical. I was overwhelmed. I thought he was picking on me. Afterward I was in the shower and ... I'll admit it, I was crying. Russell came in and said, "Hey, I went through the same thing. Rio went through the same thing. He's just coaching you. You've got to let it roll off your back and not let it bother you." We went to eat that night and talked a little more. By the next day, I was fine. Coach said something to me and I was like, "Whatever."

Collins also found an instant connection with fellow freshman Brady Morningstar, a Lawrence native who'd signed with Kansas after spending a year at New Hampton Prep in New Hampshire. Morningstar and his parents and sisters became like a second family to Collins, whose infant son died just months after his arrival at KU.

Brady Morningstar: The first time I met Sherron, he walked into the gym at Horejsi while we were playing pickup. Coach Self was like, "Yo, come over here, Star. I want you to meet your new roommate." I went over there and met Sherron for the first time. He was wearing a thick gold chain and was cool. After pickup, I ran home and grabbed a bunch of sheets and pillows and stuff, because he hadn't brought any with him. From that day forward, I looked out for him and took care of him. But it went both ways. He looked out for me and took care of me, too. I learned a lot from him. You can imagine the stories I heard about things he'd been through. I was fortunate. I grew up in Lawrence. Life wasn't that hard for me. Listening to the s**t he'd been through, I was like, "Damn, man, this is crazy." It was stuff you'd see in movies. Him getting shot at when he was younger ... him walking out of his apartment and seeing crackheads and prostitutes in the courtyard ... him telling stories about sick family members and him having a kid that's premature and eventually passes away. He'd just had a lot of s**t happen to him, and it was ongoing.

Moving to Kansas was also an adjustment for Arthur, who committed and then decommitted from Baylor, signed with KU and moved to Lawrence—all within one week.

Darrell Arthur: My grandmother was pushing me to go to Baylor because it was close to home. After I committed, I scheduled a press conference for the next day. The Baylor coaches actually drove up for it and everything. But I never showed up. Instead we put a sign on the door that said the press conference had been re-scheduled for the following afternoon.

I knew I had to figure something else out fast. When I went to bed that night, my mom said, "Pray on it, because you have to make a decision tomorrow." That's when I went to sleep and had a dream that I was playing for Kansas. I know some people laugh about it and think I made the whole story up, but it really did happen. I dreamed that I was on the court, playing with Mario and Julian. When I woke up, I was trippin'. I was like, "Man, why the hell did I have that dream? That was crazy." The night before I had asked God to give me some sort of sign, because I didn't know what I was going to do. So when I had that dream, I was like, "I guess that was a sign that Kansas is where I need to go to school." So I got up and texted Coach Self and told him I was coming. A week later, I was in Lawrence. It all happened so fast. It was really stressful, but I felt like I made the right decision. We had a good team and, ultimately, I wanted to win more than I wanted recognition. I didn't care about being "the man."

My mom stayed with me the first week I was there. After she left, I was like, "Damn, I'm on my own now." I was a little scared because I'd never been away from home for a big amount of time. There were a lot of nervous feelings going through my mind. I was like, "Damn, what am I going to do?" I hadn't really gotten cool with all of my teammates yet.

Sherron and I had met on my official visit and got re-acquainted at the McDonald's game. We knew each other, but not very well. Then I got to meet Brady, which was really helpful because he was from there. When I first got on campus, Brady pulled up in his car, rolled down his window, introduced himself and said, "If you need anything, let me know." We used to go to his mom's house on Sundays and eat and hang out. Usually it was me and Sherron and Brady.

Being at Kansas was like being on an NBA championship team in college. All of these diehard fans want to meet you. Coach Self had a meeting with us and was like,

"Essentially, you're gods on this campus. It's like you're in your own little world. People adore you here and want to meet you. But outside of here, people won't even know who you are." I loved those fans. They're the reason I wanted to go there. I went to Late Night when Keith Langford and Nick Collison and Drew Gooden were there. I couldn't believe it was packed like that for a practice. I'd never seen something like that before. That sold me. That won me over.

Bill Self: Shady was a freak—an absolute freak. We've never had a big guy that could run like Shady. We haven't had a big guy that could slide his feet like Shady. When NBA people would come watch our practices, I'd tell Shady, "Go guard the point guard, and pick him up full court." The guard couldn't get it past halfcourt.

Darrell Arthur: My first day there, I was going against Julian and I thought, "Man, this guy is good." Then I got a chance to play against Darnell and Sasha. They were super strong and skilled. I was thinking, "Man, we've got a good team here." I didn't know those guys were that good, just from watching them on TV. I came in weighing about 215. They were 240-pound beasts. Plus, I had to get acclimated and learn all the plays and stuff. Knowing when to duck in and when not to duck in, or when to pick-and-roll and when not to. They had that knowledge over me, as well. It took me awhile to get acclimated to everything that was going on.

My high school coach used to go to Coach Self's camps to learn stuff from him. He was hard on us, too. But Coach Self took it to another level. He was trying to teach us to play together and play hard at the same time. He was teaching us that, if we win, everyone will get recognition. He was trying to get us to see his vision.

It was tough because he'd be cool and happy if you made a good play. But then if you messed up on defense, he'd be on you. It wasn't like he'd be cool and forget about it if you messed up. He was on your ass. He was trying to get the most out of you. He was trying to get you to play to your potential.

So long, C.J.

C.J. Giles was dismissed from the team Nov. 7 after being cited for misdemeanor battery of a former girlfriend the night before at his apartment. Giles had been in trouble at Kansas multiple times, forcing Self to part ways with the talented but troubled center.

Assistant coach Kurtis Townsend: C.J. had more potential than anyone. I treated him like a son. He was the victim of some unfortunate circumstances. He was a crack baby, so he had a chemical imbalance. But he had enough talent to make it. I saw it when he was a high school sophomore. He was walking around with glasses. He was 6-foot-6 and I said, if this kid grows, he's going to be all right. He grew to 6-11 and was an unbelievable athlete.

The thing that disappointed me was that he didn't have the wherewithal to listen to what you told him to do as far as what would be best for his life. He regrets it now.

We want to save kids like him and make their lives better. And a lot of the time, we do. That's one where it didn't happen. He still calls and texts me, though. He says, "Gosh Coach, I wish I'd have done what you said." I wish it'd have worked out better for him.

Darnell Jackson: C.J. was so talented. He was a special player. When Coach Self would put him in the game and he was running up and down the court and catching lobs from Aaron (Miles), I was like, "This dude is going to the NBA." I don't know what happened during his career, but the tables just turned on him and he never found a way to bounce back. He was just going through so much mentally and physically.

We all knew what C.J. was going through, but he never brought it to the court or to the locker room. He was always smiling and happy. I remember thinking, "Man, I'd be losing my mind if I was him." He was far away from home and his dad was always coming to town, putting pressure on him. No one knew specifics, but everyone knew he had it hard. We wished he would've opened up more to us.

Sasha Kaun: C.J. was one of the most talented players I've seen. He could shoot and run and jump. He was crazy-talented but, mentally, he wasn't there. He couldn't stay out of trouble. That's part of why a lot of guys don't make it at the next level. It's all about keeping the right mindset and composure to do the right things.

Texas A&M forward Joseph Jones: Kansas' whole team changed when C.J. Giles left. With him, they were on a different level athletically. I remember they ran that play where he'd get the alley-oop off the jump ball, and that would kind of set the tone for the rest of the game. I'm like, "We don't have a damn chance in hell to win if they're going to run plays like that the whole game."

He brought a different dimension to their team, a different dynamic. He would have made a big difference for them if he had been there all four years.

One week after Giles' dismissal, in its second game of the year, Kansas suffered what is easily the biggest regular-season upset of Self's KU career: a 78-71 setback against Oral Roberts at Allen Fieldhouse. With Giles missing from the paint, ORU forward Caleb Green tallied 20 points and 11 rebounds. But the biggest difference-maker was Marchello Vealy, who scored 22 points off the bench. Vealy was 7-of-8 from 3-point range after going 1-for-13 the previous season.

Darrell Arthur: We didn't want to show our faces on campus after that game. We didn't want to walk to class or anything. We were embarrassed. That was probably one of the worst experiences of my college career—and the fact that Coach Self used to coach there made it even worse.

He was like, "This team is a great team. They're capable of coming in here and beating you guys." He said that before every game, though. We were thinking, "Whatever. We're fixin' to go out there and beat the s**t out of these guys." They ended up coming in there and kicking our ass. Coach Self made us come back to the gym that same night for a practice at midnight. Then we woke up the next morning and practiced again. That was as pissed as he's ever been. For the whole next month, our practices would last three

WORST NON-CONFERENCE LOSSES

1. Nov. 15, 2006: vs. Oral Roberts, 78-71: Bench player Marchello Vealy helped Oral Roberts "shock the world" by going 7-for-8 from 3-point range and scoring 22 points in front of a stunned crowd at Allen Fieldhouse

2. Dec. 1, 2005: vs. Nevada, 72-70: Forward Nick Fazekas scored a career-high 35 points — and later got a tongue-lashing from KU assistant Joe Dooley in the handshake line — as the Jayhawks lost an unexpected game at home

3. Nov. 18, 2014: vs. Kentucky, 72-40: Bill Self joked he wished his postgame water was vodka after the shellacking in the Champions Classic, and for good reason; the Jayhawks shot 20 percent in one of their worst offensive performances ever

4. Dec. 2, 2006: at DePaul, 64-57: Exactly seven days after taking down No. 1 Florida, KU stumbled on the road at 2-4 DePaul, as the Blue Demons overcame a 14-point second-half deficit

5. Jan. 5, 2014: vs. San Diego State, 61-57: The Aztecs' big men dominated the interior with eight blocks, holding KU to 30-percent shooting as the Jayhawks' non-conference home win streak was snapped at 68 games

6. Dec. 13, 2008: vs. UMass, 61-60: The Jayhawks fell to a 2-6 team in a front of a pro-KU crowd at the Sprint Center, as Sherron Collins' potential game-winning shot was blocked in the final seconds

7. Dec. 22, 2014: at Temple, 77-52: KU shot 32.1 percent from the floor at the Wells Fargo Center in Philadelphia, suffering its worst loss (at that point) to a non-conference opponent in the Self era

8. Dec. 19, 2011: vs. Davidson, 80-74: The Wildcats led the entire second half and made 11 3-pointers, while KU made 26 percent of its 3s and 58 percent of its free throws in the Sprint Center defeat

9. Dec. 6, 2005: vs. St. Joseph's, 70-67: KU made only 6 of 19 free throws, and the setback in the Jimmy V Classic dropped the Jayhawks to 3-4 — their worst start since 1971-72

10. Jan. 10, 2010: at Tennessee, 76-68: The Volunteers, playing without four players who were either dismissed or suspended earlier in the week, took down the 14-0 Jayhawks with help from a late 3 by Skylar McBee straight hours. That's was one of the toughest times ever, losing to that team.

Matt Kleinmann: I remember the fear in all of us as we walked toward that locker room. I don't think we went out to a bar until Christmas. By that, I mean we didn't go out and have a good time until Christmas. Nobody was allowed to go out. We were all under house arrest because we lost to ORU, and for good reason. We shouldn't have lost to ORU. We shouldn't have lost at home. Mix in the fact Coach Self's pride was hurt by losing to his former team and, yeah ... I would have done the same thing.

Maddening as it was, the Oral Roberts loss served as a motivator for the Jayhawks as they traveled to Las Vegas 10 days later for a matchup with Joakim Noah, Al Horford, Corey Brewer and defending national champion Florida. The night before, however, they faced Ball State at the Orleans Arena.

Mario Chalmers: The Ball State game, we didn't cover the spread. Coach Self was hot at us. He was cussing us out after the game. The last five minutes we were up by about 20. We let them come back and cut it to eight, I think. Coach Self was livid. We watched the film and he was like, "Y'all didn't play hard for the last five minutes. What if they would've come back and beat us?" When you have a team up, that's when you have to have a killer instinct and step on their throats. We were like, "Coach, we still won the game." He was really upset, though. We were on the elevator going to our rooms and I said something like, "Dang, I can't believe Coach Self was trippin' on us like that. That's some bulls**t." Julian said something like, "Oh Rio, shut the hell up. You were out there bullsh**tin' the whole game" or whatever. So I felt like he was coming at me. We got off the elevator, and I just snapped. I tried to charge at him, but Russell and Darnell were holding me back. They put me in my room.

After I calmed down we had a team meeting later that night. We asked Coach Self, "Why are you so mad at us about the Ball State game when we're playing Florida, the No. 1 team in the nation, tomorrow night? Why are you nitpicking?" He basically told us, "It's not about nitpicking, it's about trying to make y'all better and make y'all realize that, when you have a team down, you can't let them come back. I've been in too many situations where we were up and we let a team come back. We took Bucknell lightly, and they came back and beat us." Once he said that we kind of understood where he was coming from. Me and Julian apologized to one another and made up. After that we beat Florida, and everything was cool.

Indeed, the Jayhawks toppled Billy Donovan and the No. 1-ranked Gators 82-80 in overtime. All five KU starters scored in double figures, with Wright (21 points, 10 rebounds) and Arthur (19 and nine) leading the way.

Bill Self: The Florida game was when I knew we were going to be good in 2007. Julian Wright was the best player in the United States that night. We were awful the night before against Ball State. We were just terrible. I remember going around the room and asking everybody what we did well. Somebody said, "Well, we like each other." And I said, "That's wrong. You don't like him. He doesn't like you. And you don't like this guy.

BEST NON-CONFERENCE WINS

1. Nov. 25, 2006: vs. Florida, 82-80 in OT: Just 10 days after a home loss to Oral Roberts, KU took down the top-ranked Gators in Las Vegas. All five starters scored in double figures, led by 21 points from Julian Wright. Florida would go on to win back-to-back national titles that year.

2. Nov. 15, 2016: vs. Duke, 77-75: Frank Mason hit the game-winner from the elbow with 1.8 seconds left—and held his shooting pose for a second—as KU won in front of an electric crowd at Madison Square Garden. Mason's 21-point effort was the beginning of his National Player of the Year campaign.

3. Nov. 12, 2013: vs. Duke, 94-83: Andrew Wiggins introduced himself to America with a dominating second-half effort, scoring 16 of his 22 points after halftime and outdueling Jabari Parker, the second-ranked player in the 2013 class, in the Champions Classic at United Center in Chicago.

4. Jan. 1, 2005: vs. Georgia Tech, 70-68 in OT: Keith Langford told his teammates to clear out before hitting the game-deciding jumper in the lane with 2.1 seconds left, helping KU avenge its NCAA Tournament loss from the previous year. Langford scored 16 of his 18 points in a win that came without star Wayne Simien.

5. Jan. 30, 2016: vs. Kentucky, 90-84 in OT: After losing three of five games, KU resurrected its season with help from this victory; Wayne Selden had 33 points, and the Jayhawks went on to win their next 16 games.

6. Dec. 22, 2012: at Ohio State, 74-66: Ben McLemore scored 22 points—with multiple thunder dunks—as the Jayhawks easily took down a top-10 opponent despite being a five-point Vegas underdog. This was the game when Bill Self said he knew McLemore would be a one-and-done freshman.

7. Jan. 28, 2017: at Kentucky, 79-73: Coming off a road loss at West Virginia and playing without the suspended Carlton Bragg, KU took down Kentucky in Rupp Arena with help from a 2-3 zone defense. Stars Frank Mason and Josh Jackson combined to score 41 points.

8. Dec. 5, 2014: vs. Florida, 71-65: KU overcame a 39-24 halftime deficit at Allen Fieldhouse with help from a 17-0 second-half run; Selden led the way with 21 points on 9-for-15 shooting.

9. Nov. 25, 2007: vs. Arizona, 76-72 in OT: Brandon Rush came off the bench and officially showed he was back to full strength after offseason knee surgery, scoring 17 points—including five in OT—to help the Jayhawks win despite allowing Zona star Chase Budinger to go off for 27 points.

10. Dec. 2, 2010: vs. UCLA, 77-76: Whether he was fouled or not, Mario Little took advantage of an official's whistle by making a free throw with 0.7 seconds left to give KU its 64th straight home win.

This guy doesn't like this guy."

"Well, we share the ball good."

"No, that's BS. Everybody's selfish. Everybody passes as a last resort rather than being willing passers."

We go down the whole list, and Matt Kleinmann says, "We get it out fast when the other team scores."

I said, "Hey! Isn't that great? University of Kansas, the inventor of the game was our first coach, and we're going to take pride in that we get it out fast when people score on us. Boy, we have arrived guys!"

Jank was going on and on about Florida. Jank said they could beat the Lakers. I told him, "Jank, we're in trouble, aren't we?"

He said, "Yes, we're in trouble."

Then our guys go out and they play unreal. They surprised the heck out of all of us. I think there were 13 NBA players that played in that game. It was unreal.

Kansas 82, Florida 80
November 25, 2006 · Las Vegas, Nev.

Kansas (5-1)

Player	MP	FG	3FG	FT	R	A	F	S	TO	B	TP
Darrell Arthur*	16	6-7	0-0	7-9	9	0	3	1	0	1	19
Russell Robinson*	43	4-7	1-2	3-4	7	3	1	1	2	2	12
Sherron Collins*	7	0-0	0-0	0-0	0	0	3	0	0	0	0
Rodrick Stewart*	4	0-0	0-0	0-0	1	0	1	0	0	0	0
Mario Chalmers*	38	5-11	2-6	1-2	1	5	3	0	3	0	13
Sasha Kaun	12	0-2	0-0	0-0	0	0	4	0	0	0	0
Brandon Rush	43	6-16	1-5	0-2	7	4	1	0	2	3	13
Julian Wright	42	9-12	0-0	3-4	10	3	4	3	4	1	21
Darnell Jackson	20	0-1	0-0	4-6	2	1	2	0	1	0	4
Team					1						
Totals	225	30-56	4-13	18-27	38	16	22	5	12	7	82

Florida (6-1)

Player	MP	FG	3FG	FT	R	A	F	S	TO	B	TP
Corey Brewer*	26	4-14	1-4	2-3	6	3	3	2	1	0	11
Taurean Green*	44	9-19	4-11	3-5	5	1	4	1	3	0	25
Lee Humphrey*	40	5-11	4-9	2-2	3	0	1	1	0	0	16
Joakim Noah*	33	7-9	0-0	3-5	4	1	4	0	5	0	17
Walter Hodge*	11	0-0	0-0	0-0	0	0	0	0	0	0	0
Dan Werner	4	0-1	0-1	0-0	0	0	0	0	0	0	0
Jonathan Mitchell	5	0-0	0-0	0-0	2	0	1	0	1	0	0
Chris Richard	29	1-2	0-0	0-0	5	3	3	0	1	1	2
Marreese Speights	2	0-1	0-0	0-0	2	0	1	0	0	0	0
Al Horford	31	3-8	0-1	3-7	8	1	5	1	3	3	9
Team					1						
Totals	225	29-65	9-26	13-22	36	9	22	5	14	4	80

	1st	2nd	OT	Total	FG%	3FG%	FT%
Kansas	37	33	12	82	53.6	30.8	66.7
Florida	31	39	10	80	44.6	34.6	59.1

Officials: Jeff Clark, Duke Edsall, William Bush
Technicals: None

Kansas was upset at DePaul exactly one week later, but the Jayhawks still entered Big 12 play with an impressive 13-2 record. Something, though, was threatening KU from reaching its full potential, and Self addressed the issue before it got out of hand.

"Lose 38 pounds or you're not playing."

Sherron Collins: Early in December, we played Toledo in Kansas City, and they had some really fast guards. One of them got the ball on a fast break and drove right past me. I was probably tired and being a little lazy, but I was also overweight. Coach called me into his office the next day and weighed me in. I was 238 pounds. Coach said, "You've got three weeks to lose that 38 pounds or you may not play for us this year."

I needed to lose it to help the team. We sat down and got a plan together with a nutritionist. I was getting up early to workout with Hudy. He told me, "I promise you, when you get down to 200-205, you're going to feel so much better and play so much better. Things are just going to be better."

Looking back, I can see how I'd gained so much weight. The previous spring, after the McDonald's and Jordan Brand games, I started lifting a lot of weights. And my eating habits weren't good. I was still abusing guys during pickup games in the high school gym, so I didn't realize what a problem it was becoming until I got somewhere where everyone was fast and in shape. With me, it was more muscle than fat, and it's hard to lose muscle. I got to Kansas and gained eight pounds the first week from lifting. They told me, "No more lifting for you. You're only doing cardio." I don't think I've lifted weights since.

Bill Self: He might not have been 238, but he was at least 230. I said, "Just so you know, by this date, if you're not 205, I'm not going to play you." Sherron was a guy that put on weight overnight and lost weight overnight. So a lot of it may have been water weight.

Anyway, he went home for Christmas and I told my assistants, "Just watch … if he cares, he'll come back at 220. If he doesn't care, he'll come back at 240." He came back at 217. I said, "OK, guys, he's starting to get it."

Strength and conditioning coach Andrea Hudy: Sherron is a mesomorphic guy, so he has a propensity to put on muscle mass—sometimes too much muscle mass for his performance. We could've gotten him stronger, but that could've taken away from his speed. We did a lot of cardio with Sherron.

We used to ride bikes together. We were coming up Iowa Street and some girl in a dress and flip-flops passed him on his bike. We did Dance Dance Revolution for Sherron. We tried to make things interesting for him.

It was like a love-hate relationship between us. He was like my son. It was so much energy to put into one guy. But he did what I asked him to do and he was successful. A lot of people just have the propensity to put on weight. It's genetics. But when he would eat right, it was better contained.

The biggest thing was monitoring his meals. We'd go to the grocery store and buy things that were easy for him to make or take with him. Lunch meat, sandwiches, peanut butter, yogurt. We had him on a low-carb diet—below 50 carbs a day. Usually I just threw everything into the grocery cart while he was on his phone. I was like, "Even if you don't like it, just eat it, because this is what's best for you."

Sherron Collins: I tried everything. Nutrisystem, cottage cheese, berries. I lost eight pounds the first week and nine the second week. I got down to 200 for the Boston College game on Dec. 23, but I didn't have any energy. I had hardly been eating any real food. My body was starving. I wore out so fast that game. I played like s**t and didn't even score.

The game at home against Missouri (on Jan. 15) … that's when I knew I could do this. I had 23 points that night. People thought I should be starting over Russell but I didn't agree. Russ was the head of the team. The stuff he was doing, I couldn't do yet. I didn't understand all my angles and guarding. I think it was a good decision by Coach not to start me, because I got to sit right beside him and the assistants at the beginning of the game and hear about what we weren't doing well. Then I went in and helped fix it.

Bill Self: To me, Sherron was the second-best player in the Big 12 that year behind Kevin Durant. He was *our* best player, at that time. Other players knew how good he was. Sometimes, everybody can't see it when a team is balanced. But I remember Bob Huggins, who was at K-State that year, said, "Durant is the best player, but Sherron Collins is the hardest player to guard in our league, hands down." I actually thought that, too. He wasn't as clutch as Mario, even though he was really clutch. And he wasn't as big as Brandon. But just as a pure player, I thought he could do just about anything.

Saving Darnell

Although he was averaging 7.7 points off the bench through KU's first 12 games, Darnell Jackson was struggling to focus. A car accident the previous summer in Las Vegas had claimed the life of his grandmother and left his mother with life-altering injuries. His uncle was murdered that fall and, shortly after, a friend and a cousin were killed, too. For Jackson, coping with the tragedies was becoming more and more difficult as the holiday season approached.

Mario Chalmers: Before the Boston College game a few days before Christmas, we were getting ready to go out for warm-ups. After we huddled up and said "One-two-three Jayhawks!" and broke the huddle, D-Block grabbed me and said, "Rio, I need you real quick." He just grabbed me and started crying on my shoulder and said, "I wish my grandma was here." He knew that my grandma had just died, too. He knew I'd been there before, so he was drawing strength from me just like I drew strength from him.

Darnell Jackson: Coach Self knew what buttons to push with everyone to get us to where we needed to be. Around that time, I remember thinking, "Man, this dude is constantly on me. He's always saying something." He used to always call me lazy. *"Lazy-ass. You never want to work."* It used to just piss me off. I was like, "Man, I'm trying to give this guy everything I have and show him that this is what I want to do, and he's calling me lazy." Mentally, I wasn't there. Everything I was going through, worrying about home, my mom and all of that … mentally, I just wasn't there.

One night around 1 a.m.—about a week after Christmas—I packed up some of my things and drove home to Oklahoma with my brother and my ex-girlfriend. It was a long, quiet ride. I did the driving. There wasn't really any talking, because they slept the whole way there. When I finally got home it was about 6 a.m. I walked through the door, dropped my bags on the floor and crawled into the bed with my mom.

When I didn't show up for practice the next day, Coach Self knew that something was wrong. He found out I was in Oklahoma, so he and Coach Chalmers got on a plane and came to talk to me. We were in my living room with mom and my uncle, Edred, and I asked Coach Self if I could talk to him outside. I was like, "I'm tired of seeing my mom go through this." She was in all this pain from her surgeries. She wasn't working because of that, so the bills weren't getting paid on time. It was everything. I told him I thought if I left and came back to Oklahoma City, all the bad stuff that was happening to me would stop. He grabbed me and gave me a hug. I started crying. I just broke down. I didn't know what else to do. Having him there helped me understand that he had my back. He told me anything I had ever wanted or dreamed about was about to happen for me. He was like, "Come back home." Once I got back, my attitude really changed. I'll never forget what Coach Self did for me that night. I came back to Lawrence a few days later.

Bill Self: I was scared we were going to lose him, but it had so much to do with other things that were going on. It wasn't about Kansas. He had so many things going on in his mind after the accident out in Vegas. That accident took the life of his grandmother, who helped raise him. And it changed his mother's life forever, to the point where she could never have a normal day. It was so sad. He struggled with everything. His uncle was also murdered during that period of time. He felt guilty that he was up here playing instead of at home helping his family.

Jeremy Case: Darnell was my roommate. When he got back and I first saw him, he was trying to be strong. I remember we were sitting in the living room, and he just broke down. It kind of brings tears to my eyes thinking about it. I mean, he was *hurting.* We'd sit there and talk. Other times we'd just sit there in silence.

At that point, he really started leaning on us, his teammates. He started hanging around us more than ever. Before that, Darnell was a guy that would always have other friends around, whether it was someone from back home or a random person he'd met in Lawrence and thought was cool. People I hardly even knew would come crash in his room for a couple of weeks.

But after he went home and came back that winter, everything changed. At that point, he was with us, and we were there for him.

Bill Self: Once he came back, things just clicked. He was so much better. He realized the best way to help his family was for him to do well.

Sasha Kaun: Darnell impressed me with his toughness. I was amazed that he kept such a positive attitude. He had rough years and rough stretches where he was a little bit lazy here and there. But overall, his toughness to get through all of that stuff and come out on top says a lot about what type of person he is.

Stomping on the Jayhawk

Once a perennial Big 12 doormat, Texas A&M was tied with Kansas for first in the league standings when it arrived in Lawrence for a Saturday showdown on Feb. 3, 2007. The man responsible for the Aggies' rise was Billy Gillispie, a former Self assistant at Tulsa and Illinois who was now in his third year with the Aggies. With ESPN's College GameDay crew broadcasting from Allen Fieldhouse, the battle between No. 6 KU and No. 10 Texas A&M was sure to be a classic.

Texas A&M assistant coach Jerrance Howard: We had a video crew following us that year. They were doing a documentary. I remember Coach Gillispie was like, "I don't want them anywhere near us this trip." The producers were really mad because, obviously, they wanted scenes from Allen Fieldhouse in their footage. But Billy wouldn't let them come with us. I said, "Look, we play Texas two days later on Big Monday. We'll give you anything you want. You can come to Coach Gillispie's house if you want to. But you can't come to Kansas."

Texas A&M guard Acie Law: We had played at Kansas in Coach Gillispie's first year (in 2005), and KU had a really good team with Simien and Langford and Miles. We only lost by five, 65-60. For us to do that in his first year—for us to be in a position to beat Kansas at Allen Fieldhouse—we were like, "Damn, we may be all right. We may have something going here."

Coach Gillispie could obviously sense we were thinking that way when he came into the locker room after that loss, and he blew a gasket. *"That's not acceptable. We're not about moral victories. We're not about celebrating when we play a good team close."* It was a teaching moment for us, because prior to that, Kansas was the basketball school and A&M was the school that they beat the hell out of whenever they played us.

Texas A&M forward Joseph Jones: Coach Gillispie worked under Coach Self at Illinois, so they were really good friends. Anytime we would do anything in terms of practicing or running sprints, anything we were doing—no matter what it was—we were always competing with KU. He would come in the gym and say, "Kansas did this in their game. I talked to Coach Self last night and they did this. We've got to do this." It was a battle every day. We developed a rivalry in our heads against KU.

Our practices were hard, long, intense and physical. And they were mentally taxing, too, because you'd never know how Coach Gillispie was feeling or how he'd react. He'd just attack you mentally, and once your mind starts going, your body doesn't know what to do or where to go. You just have to come in and try to be mentally tough and stay physical at the same time.

Acie Law: The year before Coach Gillispie got there, we were 0-17 in the Big 12. We were just eager to have some success. And that's the first thing Coach Gillispie addressed. He instilled a mindset within the program that we could win. And not only with the players, but the fan base, too. He brought a blue-collar, workmanlike attitude, where the theme was, "We're going to get better every single day. We're going to put our hours in, and we're going to work. That's the only way we're going to get there."

He had this thing called "Boot Camp," and I'm sure it's something he copied from Bill Self when he worked under him. It was a two-week camp where you're basically practicing four times a day, and a couple of the practices were conditioning workouts where we didn't even have a basketball. It was brutal every single day because he was so demanding. When he came in and took the job, he'd been so nice and polite. Then we got on the basketball court for individual drills, and we were like, "Man, this dude has split personalities."

He yelled at us so much. I had never experienced anything like that in my life. If it was my choice, I would've quit. I was ready to leave but my dad wouldn't let me. He said, "Him being tough on you is not a good enough reason to quit." It ended up being the best thing that ever happened to me, but at that particular juncture, it was hard to see the big picture. Once we started having success, it was easy for us to buy in and believe everything he told us.

Kansas 66, Texas A&M 69
February 3, 2007 · Lawrence, Kan.

Kansas (19-4)

Player	MP	FG	3FG	FT	R	A	F	S	TO	B	TP
Julian Wright*	29	4-10	0-0	3-4	10	2	3	1	1	2	11
Sasha Kaun*	19	1-4	0-0	0-2	5	0	2	0	2	0	2
Russell Robinson*	30	3-6	0-1	2-2	7	3	1	2	5	2	8
Mario Chalmers*	31	4-8	0-2	0-1	2	2	2	3	2	0	8
Brandon Rush*	36	3-13	1-5	3-4	6	1	2	0	1	0	10
Darrell Arthur	13	2-6	0-0	0-0	3	0	3	0	2	0	4
Sherron Collins	23	6-9	3-4	3-4	0	2	3	0	3	0	18
Darnell Jackson	19	1-1	0-0	3-4	4	0	2	0	0	3	5
Team					3						
Totals	200	24-57	4-12	14-21	40	10	18	6	16	7	66

Texas A&M (19-3)

Player	MP	FG	3FG	FT	R	A	F	S	TO	B	TP
Josh Carter*	31	3-7	3-6	2-2	3	0	2	2	2	1	11
Antanas Kavaliauskas*	34	2-5	0-1	3-5	3	0	4	1	4	2	7
Joseph Jones*	22	4-11	2-4	0-0	3	0	4	1	1	0	10
Acie Law*	39	9-18	1-4	4-5	3	7	3	2	2	0	23
Dominique Kirk*	35	4-7	2-4	0-0	4	2	2	2	1	1	10
Donald Sloan	13	1-2	0-1	2-2	1	2	0	1	0	0	4
Beau Muhlbach	1	0-0	0-0	0-0	0	0	0	0	0	0	0
Bryan Davis	12	2-3	0-0	0-0	4	1	1	0	2	0	4
Slade Weishuhn	1	0-0	0-0	0-0	0	0	0	0	0	0	0
Chinemelu Elonu	1	0-0	0-0	0-0	0	0	0	0	0	0	0
Marlon Pompey	11	0-1	0-0	0-0	3	0	4	0	0	0	0
Team					5						
Totals	200	25-54	8-20	11-14	29	12	20	9	12	4	69

	1st	2nd	Total	FG%	3FG%	FT%
Kansas	35	31	66	42.1	33.3	66.7
Texas A&M	30	39	69	46.3	40.0	78.6

Officials: Paul Janssen, Larry Rose, Hal Lusk
Technicals: None

Joseph Jones: Once we made it through Boot Camp, we felt like we could make it through anything. The games we played were cakewalks compared to our practices. That's how we approached every single day: just make it through practice and everything else will be easy.

Every time we played KU, we approached it the same way. We didn't do anything special. We knew Coach Self knew everything about us. Gillispie pretty much took the offense from him. There was nothing we could do different that he didn't already know. All we tried to do was limit some of their guys. We might try to trap a couple guys on ball screens or double some guys in the post, but we never did anything special. We just came out and played men against men. They had a bunch of big bodies—some strong, tough guys. We had a bunch of strong, tough guys, too. Everyone was just fighting one another, trying to get the win.

Darnell Jackson: I loved playing against Joseph. He and I are still close to this day. We used to battle against each other on the AAU circuit, the summer circuit. He'd say, "I can't wait to come down there. I'm going to bust your ass." We were talking noise back and forth. He was so strong, physically.

Joseph Jones: I always respected D-Block. I came on the AAU scene late and he was one of the first guys who sat down with me, joked with me and had fun with me. I didn't know too many guys, especially being from a small country town. I didn't grow up in the city like most of the guys that played AAU, so I didn't know anyone out there in the basketball world. He took me under his wing and became one of my friends. Even to this day, when I see him, it's all love.

Going up against him was always a great pleasure. He was so tough to guard. When we stepped on the floor against each other, we knew we had to bring our hard hat. We were gonna have to fight and give it everything we had.

Acie Law: When we went back to Allen Fieldhouse in 2007, my senior year, we knew they were a tough team. But we were tough, too—much tougher than we'd been when we almost beat them two years earlier. I think they respected us like we respected them. It was a bout, man. A true fight. They punched us. We punched back. They punched us. We punched back. I don't think they were surprised. They knew coming in that we were one of the best teams in the nation, just like them.

Kansas led 35-30 at intermission and was up 62-52 with 6:42 remaining. The Jayhawks then went nearly six minutes without a field goal, allowing the Aggies to claw back. Twice during that stretch Gillispie instructed Marlon Pompey to hack Sasha Kaun—a 50 percent free-throw shooter—and send him to the foul line. Each time, Kaun missed the front-end of a one-and-one.

Sasha Kaun: Nowadays it's a pretty common strategy to foul the other team's bigs and send them to the free throw line and hope they miss. But back then it was a new thing to do.

It obviously worked for them. At that time, I was struggling with my free throws, so I was pretty nervous. It sucks but it is what it is. It's part of the game.

Darnell Jackson: When Sasha got fouled and went to the free throw line, it was so quiet in the gym. He missed the first one and the whole crowd went, "Awwwww." Then he missed the second one, and (laughing) I remember a fan yelling, "S**t!"

Bill Self: People said I shouldn't have had Sasha in the game, but if I had to do it all over again, I would. Those guys were good enough players. I'm not going to take a guy out because I didn't believe in him. That could've sent the wrong message and hurt us long term.

I told Billy a few days later, "Billy, you just told your players that you didn't believe in them, that you didn't think they could guard. All you had to do was get a stop and you could still win." It was the perfect scenario for him to do it. He made the right call. But ever since I've know him, Billy's approach has been, "We're going to be tough. We're going to guard." So he went against what his character was. He went against his beliefs.

Jerrance Howard: The atmosphere was incredible. I remember Joseph Jones was at the free throw stripe late in the game. Acie Law was lined up for the rebound, and I screamed at him to match up with Brandon Rush. He looked at me and shrugged his shoulders and mouthed, "Coach, I can't hear you!"

Acie Law: At that moment, there wasn't nothing that could rattle us. We were one of the best teams in the country and we sincerely felt like we could go in there and win. There was never a doubt in our locker room. Kansas was loaded. They had five or six guys who played in the pros. But when we got down, our toughness—our mental toughness—was so rock solid, and our belief in our team was so rock solid, that we always thought we could win. It all goes back to that first year and the aura Coach Gillispie created within our program.

Kansas was up by 10, and I believe Jo made a big shot. Then Donald Sloan made a big shot and we never wavered as we got it down to the last couple seconds. Gillispie always told us, if we get down to the last play or the last couple plays, our toughness will prevail. That's what we wanted to do, just stick around and then put the pressure on them, and that's what happened.

A layup by Julian Wright gave KU a 66-64 lead with just under a minute remaining. Moments later, when the Aggies had the ball out of bounds under their basket with 28.3 seconds left, Gillispie called for one of their signature plays.

Joseph Jones: Anytime we played KU at Allen Fieldhouse, we always approached it like we were in Vegas. We went out there and rolled the dice. *Just roll the dice and see what happens.* We're not going for moral victories. We're not going for overtime. We're going to win. If they were up two, we were going for a 3. We weren't going for overtime. At KU, we were going for the win.

Acie Law: We had a play called "triangle." It was a simple play: I stand in the middle underneath the basket and both bigs stand on the box. I just pick and choose where I want to go get the ball. I get to do whatever I want to do. It's a matter of just making a play.

I knew they had length, so me taking it to the basket probably wouldn't have been the right play. Brandon Rush was guarding me. He's 6-foot-6, a long guy, and I just remember looking at him, and it was token D. He was respecting my drive, so I just jabbed. He jumped back, and I took the shot.

At that point in my career, my confidence in those moments was so high. There wasn't an ounce of self-doubt in my mind when those situations came up. All of my teammates were like that. Everybody sincerely believed that, if we got to that moment, we would make a play.

BEST BIG 12 COACHING PERFORMANCES

1. Scott Drew, Baylor: The Bears' program had narrowly escaped the death penalty when Drew took over in 2003. Since then he's turned Baylor into the league's most consistent team other than Kansas. Baylor has made two Elite Eights and two Sweet 16s since 2008 and achieved the school's first No. 1 ranking in 2017.

2. Billy Gillispie, Texas A&M: His accomplishments have been tainted by his off-the-court troubles, but let's not forget how Gillispie resurrected an Aggies program that had gone winless in the Big 12 before his arrival. Gillispie's 2006-07 squad almost ended KU's streak.

3. Rick Barnes, Texas: Kansas was forced to share two of its Big 12 titles during the streak with Texas, and Barnes is the main reason. Oftentimes his teams were the only ones in the Big 12 whose talent was even close to stacking up with KU's. Texas made the NCAA Tournament in all but one of Barnes' 17 seasons.

4. Bob Huggins, K-State/West Virginia: Even though he never got to coach the prized recruits, Huggins made K-State relevant again by luring Michael Beasley, Bill Walker and Jacob Pullen to Manhattan. Now at his alma mater, Huggins' full-court press has turned West Virginia into KU's most consistent challenger.

5. Frank Martin, K-State: A master motivator, Martin instilled a culture of toughness in Manhattan. He toook K-State to an Elite Eight in 2010 and made four NCAA Tournaments in five years before leaving for South Carolina in 2012. The Wildcats won a share of the Big 12 title the following year thanks, in part, to the players Martin recruited.

6. Lon Kruger, Oklahoma: Considered one of the best offensive minds in college basketball, Kruger is one of only two coaches (Tubby Smith being the other) to lead five programs to the NCAA Tournament. Two of Kruger's teams—Florida in 1994 and Oklahoma in 2016—have made the Final Four.

7. Fred Hoiberg, Iowa State: Considered one of the smartest coaches and best tacticians in college basketball before bolting for the NBA's Chicago Bulls, Hoiberg won two Big 12 Tournament titles and took ISU to four straight NCAA Tournaments. The Cyclones games against KU during Hoiberg's reign—particularly in 2013—were epic.

8. Bob Knight, Texas Tech: The General wasn't exactly at the height of his coaching career when he took over in Lubbock in 2001, but he made the Red Raiders relevant again by taking them to four NCAA Tournaments in six years. Knight beat KU in Lubbock in 2005 and 2007.

9. Frank Haith, Missouri: Other than the 2005-06 Texas team led by LaMarcus Aldridge, Haith's 2011-12 Missouri squad was the best Big 12 team Kansas has faced during it's Big 12 title streak. Using a four-guard lineup led by Marcus Denmon, the Tigers shot 50.4 percent from the field, a mark that ranked first among Power Five schools. Missouri finished 30-5, a huge accomplishment for a first-year coach.

10. Bruce Weber, K-State: It's no coincidence that K-State won (a share of) its first conference title since 1977 with Weber on the sideline. He's a master tactician who led Illinois to the NCAA championship game in 2005. Granted, both of those accomplishments occurred with players Weber inherited, but the feats are impressive, nonetheless.

Joseph Jones: We'd been running that play the whole year. It was a little diamond play. He comes off of two screens—a stagger on the baseline—and then I get another screen to come across the paint, and if he doesn't get a shot, he throws it inside and I get a layup. Me and AK (Antanas Kavaliauskas) always set good screens, so we knew he was going to come off and take the shot. That whole year he had been taking big shots for us.

Sasha Kaun: Brandon was guarding Acie Law. He kind of stood there with his hands out and dared him to shoot, which was a little bit of a knucklehead play, as opposed to getting all over him and forcing him to drive it.

Law's 3-pointer over Rush from the right wing swished through the net with 25 seconds remaining and put Texas A&M ahead 67-66.

Jerrance Howard: Acie hit six game-winners that year. None were as big as that.

Sherron Collins: Acie Law was one of the top players in college at the time. He was a tough cover for us. He scored points on all of us that game: Me, Mario, B-Rush. He got all of us a time or two. On that game-winning shot, he didn't even dribble. He just sized B-Rush up in the corner and hit the 3 right over him.

Acie Law: Bill Self called timeout after that shot. I remember going into our huddle and Coach Gillispie said, "We're going to switch everything." It confused them. I'm not sure they were prepared for it because they looked a little disorganized. They were stagnant for a second and then Chalmers drove to the basket on our big. He shot a floater and airballed it. I think it had a lot to do with the switch. That was coaching. We played hard and put ourselves in a position to win, but we could always count on Coach Gillispie to make those right adjustments. He decided to switch the matchups, and they weren't able to make a play. Marlon ended up rebounding Chalmers' miss, and he threw me the ball like it was a hot potato. We laughed about that after the game in the locker room.

Kansas immediately fouled Law, who made a pair of free throws to put Texas A&M ahead 69-66 with 5 seconds remaining. Kansas' attempt to tie the game was thwarted moments later when Chalmers, pestered by Law and the Aggies' defense, missed a 3-pointer at the buzzer.

Joseph Jones: It was the same hand-off play they ran to win the national championship the next year. We knew it was coming from the beginning, so Coach said to make sure we switched on the hand-off and to make sure we didn't foul the jump shooter.

Sherron Collins: The last play ... Coach Self told me to keep the ball but Rio snatched it from me and missed the 3. I was pissed and Coach was pissed, but Rio was our clutch guy, so I can live with that.

Joseph Jones: We celebrated on the court. I know this doesn't sound great, but back then our whole goal after we got a big win was to stomp on logos. So that's what we did. We went to midcourt and stomped on the Jayhawk. We were ecstatic.

Acie Law: That was Jo. (laughing) I wasn't going to admit that. But, yes, that was something that we talked about, and it came from him. *We're going to go in there, we're going to beat them and we're going to stomp on their logo.* That was us marking our territory. We were moving up and knocking off these heavy hitters, and that's just what that was.

I remember watching College GameDay and all of them picked against us. They respected me as a player, but I don't really feel like they respected our team. I got a lot of credit, but everybody picked us to lose. They thought that we were solid, but they thought a lot of our success had only to do with coaching. We looked at that game as our coming-out party. If you look at that film, after I made that shot and Chalmers missed his shot and the clock went out, the College GameDay crew—Jay Bilas and all those guys—were sitting to the left of the basket, and I ran over there, holding my jersey up. It was an opportunity to bring relevance to our name, to put our team out there and let them know we were for real.

Bill Self: I know coaches find this hard to believe, but even though I never like to lose, there have been times when I'm happy for coaches that have beaten us, even if I hated every second of it. That was a big deal for Billy in his career. I think on Monday, they turned right around and beat Texas and Durant.

Acie Law: We were dead tired after that game. Even though it was cold and snowing up there, that gym was real hot and the locker room was even hotter. Everybody had given it everything they had. We'd had a tough week of practice that week, and we didn't have anymore to give. If we had gone to overtime, it would have been tough for us to win because we tried to give it our all during regulation.

Jerrance Howard: After the game, everyone was celebrating in the locker room, jumping up and down, and Acie Law almost passed out. They had to rush the doctors in there because he was so exhausted. He was breathing really, really heavy—almost hyperventilating—and his head was down. They finally got him situated and out of the locker room and onto the bus. I said, "Acie, you couldn't hear me when I was yelling at you out there?" He said, "Coach, the floor was shaking. I couldn't hear you and the floor was shaking."

Sasha Kaun: Their work ethic and how tough they were was impressive. Gillispie taught them to be a hard-nosed team. They didn't have many big-time, NBA-caliber players, especially compared to a lot of other schools. But they just played hard. That's what made them so tough to beat. They played until the end. That game was the prime example. We don't lose in The Fieldhouse very often. When a team beats you there, they're usually really, really, really good. They played hard without backing down. It didn't matter what name was on the other jersey. They weren't scared.

Bill Self: My dad, after the game, said, "Hey Bill … I'm sorry, but I don't see how you can recover." He thought it was that big of a loss. I'm going, "Gosh, dad. It was a big loss, but jeez …"

Jerrance Howard: Coach Gillispie couldn't enjoy it. He even called Coach Self the next day and apologized. It meant so much to our program, but I know how he feels about Coach Self. That's his mentor, his family. When we came back we had thousands of fans waiting for us at the airport. It was the biggest win in our program's history. Everyone else was so excited, but he kind of just sat there and didn't enjoy it.

Midway through the Big 12 season, Texas A&M (7-1) now led Kansas (6-2) by one game in the standings.

Darnell Jackson: They busted our ass. Everyone was mad. Everyone was pissed. No one talked after that game. We truly felt like we should've won, but everything went their way. We had a chance to win and we blew it. We knew we still had a chance to win the league. We came back the next day and just went to work.

The Kevin Durant Show

Kansas won seven straight games after the A&M loss to move to 13-2 in conference play. That put the Jayhawks one game ahead of Texas and Texas A&M in the Big 12 standings when the Longhorns came to Lawrence on March 3, 2007—the final day of the regular season. The 16,300 in attendance witnessed not only one of the most memorable games in Allen Fieldhouse history, but also one of the greatest players the sport of basketball has ever seen.

Darnell Jackson: The day we played Texas for the Big 12 title, I walked into Allen Fieldhouse two hours before tipoff and there was only one person in the entire gym: Kevin Durant. He was shooting all by himself, and he was absolutely soaked in sweat. I remember thinking, "What is he doing?"

Texas forward Kevin Durant: No matter where we were playing, my routine at Texas was to get to the gym early and get up extra shots before the game. I liked being the first one on the court, especially on the road. All of the fans would sit there and watch and boo. It happened every game, and it was fun. When we went to Kansas I knew the stands would be packed long before the game started.

It was an early-morning tipoff, and I was really excited to be in Lawrence that day, because everyone had told me the history and the tradition there was on another level. I mean, they've still got the wooden seats there and everything. I was very excited about playing there and seeing what it was all about.

Texas guard A.J. Abrams: When we walked into Allen Fieldhouse, we expected everything to be made of gold, because people always talked about it like it was some holy place. We were like, "Urgh, this is it?" I guess it's more about the name and the history and not the actual facility.

The buildup and anticipation to that game was crazy. Kevin was going there for the first—and only—time. Back then, we only played Kansas once a year during the regular season, so it was our only chance with that group to go into Phog Allen and show what we've got. With K.D. on our team, we were like, "Man, we've got a chance."

We weren't nervous. The thought of losing never crossed our minds. We weren't afraid of the mystique. We just wanted to go in there and beat Kansas.

At the same time, I don't think any of us really understood the magnitude of the game. We didn't get caught up in the conference race or that kind of stuff. We started four freshmen and I was the veteran as a sophomore. We were young and naive.

We had K.D. and D.J. Augustin, who I think is the best point guard to ever come through the University of Texas. We didn't have any sort of set offense that year. We just took it and ran with it. We freelanced. It played into our hands, because that's what we were good at.

Sherron Collins: The hype for that day had been building all week. Whenever we played those high-stakes games, there was a different feel in practice. Coach Self didn't joke around as much. The environment that week was intense. He brought up K.D. over and over and kept saying, "This guy can kill us. He can beat us. He can score on all of us."

Deep down, I think Shady wanted to guard Durant. And Shady probably *could've* guarded Durant, because he moved his feet really well.

Darrell Arthur: Coach Self was on me all week. He was like, "Durant is having this great season and doing this and that. Shady, what the hell are you doing? What the hell have you done?" He kept going on and on about Durant, and finally I was like, "Man, f**k Durant!"

I definitely wanted a shot at guarding him. I'd met him at Nike Camp our freshman year of high school. That was the first time he really jumped onto the scene. Before that he was like 6-foot-2 or 6-foot-3—but then he shot up to 6-foot-9. The improvement he made from that year to his freshman year of college was amazing.

Mario Chalmers: One of our ex-players, Billy Thomas, came to practice that week and played the role of KD on the scout team. He shot it nearly every time he touched it and didn't miss, no matter who we put on him. I was like, "Wow, if K.D. is gonna be like this, it's going to be a long night."

The day before the game, Coach Self was like, "Julian, we're putting you on Durant." B-Rush and I looked at each other like, "Uh-Oh." JuJu was a great defender, but he gets lazy at times. He gets spacey. He's loosey-goosey. With K.D., you can't do that. You've got to be locked in. That's one thing about Brandon. When Brandon is locked in, it's hard to score on him.

Durant entered the Kansas game averaging 25.8 points and had posted back-to-back 30-point efforts in wins over Oklahoma and Texas A&M. He'd shot 54.8 percent (17-of-31) in those wins while connecting on nine-of-12 attempts from beyond the arc.

Kurtis Townsend: I think everyone respected him because of the numbers he was putting up, but it was tough to gauge just how good he truly was until you saw it in person.

Darnell Jackson: Durant was getting all of this hype on TV, but I kept thinking, "He's not going to do that against us." Then when the game started, I was like, "Oh, this guy is the real deal." He was unbelievable. He looked good on tape, sure. But in person it was at a different level.

Russell Robinson: In the back of my mind I was thinking, "Sure, he's been playing really well. But he's still a freshman. The pressure of The Fieldhouse is going to get to him. The fans are going to be turnt up and we've got a strong team with lottery picks, as well." We felt like we'd be fine. How much can he really do? We thought it was more about keeping guys like Abrams and Augustin from getting hot.

Durant—the Big 12-leader in points, rebounds and blocks—opened the game by making eight of his first 10 shots. He hit the 20-point plateau with a three-pointer at the 7:55 mark of the first half, as Texas surged to a 51-35 lead.

Russell Robinson (laughing): Boy, did he surprise us that first half. I remember going back to the bench for a timeout. I walked in last, just as the coaches were huddling up, and I heard Coach Self asking Coach Dooley, "What are we going to do with this guy?" Dooley was speechless for a minute, and then he just shook his head and said, "I don't know. I really don't know."

Kevin Durant: I was just lost in the game. I was so happy to be there and to be playing in that arena at that time against that great team.

They had Chalmers, Shady, Julian Wright, Brandon Rush, Darnell Jackson, Russell Robinson, Sasha Kaun … they had a *squad.* They were all pros. I'd known Julian for a long time. He started off on me and then they switched to Brandon Rush and eventually to Darnell Jackson.

My first shot went in and, from there, my confidence level kept rising and rising and I was able to knock down some shots.

It was fun, man. It was fun to look over and see Coach Self shaking his head and to hear the crowd get quiet when we built that lead. We were up by 16 at one point. To suck the air out of that historic arena, even for a half ... I'll take that.

Kurtis Townsend: Julian Wright started off on him. He's a good athlete and we thought he could give Durant some trouble with his length. But he was just killing Julian. He had 25 in the first half. We switched Julian off of him and gave Brandon a chance. Brandon was our best perimeter defender and we thought maybe Brandon playing underneath him would be good. That was eight minutes into the first half. I remember the next timeout Brandon came to the bench and said, "I can't guard that mofo. He's too big. He's too good."

Kansas 90, Texas 86
March 3, 2007 · Lawrence, Kan.

Kansas (27-4)

Player	MP	FG	3FG	FT	R	A	F	S	TO	B	TP
Sasha Kaun*	17	3-6	0-0	3-3	5	0	2	1	0	1	9
Julian Wright*	34	8-14	0-1	1-2	13	5	2	1	3	2	17
Russell Robinson*	30	5-9	3-4	4-7	4	2	3	2	2	2	17
Mario Chalmers*	35	7-9	5-5	2-4	3	5	3	2	2	0	21
Brandon Rush*	36	5-12	3-6	2-2	7	3	0	0	4	1	15
Darrell Arthur	19	3-7	0-0	1-4	2	1	3	0	0	1	7
Sherron Collins	19	0-4	0-2	0-0	5	5	0	0	2	0	0
Rodrick Stewart	2	0-0	0-0	0-0	0	0	0	0	0	0	0
Darnell Jackson	8	2-2	0-0	0-2	2	0	0	0	1	0	4
Team					1						
Totals	200	33-63	11-18	13-24	42	21	13	6	14	7	90

Texas (22-8)

Player	MP	FG	3FG	FT	R	A	F	S	TO	B	TP
Damion James*	31	4-7	0-0	4-4	7	1	3	0	0	1	12
Kevin Durant*	34	13-22	6-8	0-0	9	2	4	4	3	2	32
A.J. Abrams*	37	6-17	5-13	1-1	3	0	1	1	3	0	18
D.J. Augustin*	40	7-14	2-4	3-4	4	13	3	1	3	0	19
Justin Mason*	27	1-6	1-4	0-0	2	2	4	0	0	0	3
J.D. Lewis	1	0-0	0-0	0-0	0	0	0	0	0	0	0
Matt Hill	13	1-1	0-0	0-0	3	1	1	0	0	0	2
Craig Winder	7	0-0	0-0	0-0	2	0	1	0	0	0	0
Connor Atchley	8	0-1	0-1	0-0	1	0	2	1	2	0	0
Dexter Pittman	2	0-0	0-0	0-0	0	0	0	0	0	0	0
Team					1						
Totals	200	32-68	14-30	8-9	32	19	19	7	11	3	86

	1st	2nd	Total	FG%	3FG%	FT%
Kansas	42	48	90	52.4	61.1	54.2
Texas	54	32	86	47.1	46.7	88.9

Officials: Kelly Self, Steve Olsen, David Hall
Technicals: None

Assistant coach Tim Jankovich: We started Julian on him and Durant starts shooting it from 25 feet. Then he moves back and tries to hit a shot from every logo on the court. He was making every shot.

I look up at the 8:00 mark of the first half, maybe just under eight minutes, and they've got everyone's scoring total up on the scoreboard. He had 20 points! I leaned over to Bill and whispered, "He's going to get 80 on us! *He's going to score 80!*" I'll never forget thinking, "Oh my God, this guy is going to come into The Fieldhouse as a freshman and hang 80 on a team that has five pros on it."

Assistant coach Joe Dooley: Jank was always so positive.

Bill Self: At one point, I turned to Danny Manning, who'd had a decent game or two at Allen Fieldhouse during his career. I said, "Danny, you have any ideas?" And he said, "That's the baddest man to ever play on this court. He's a *baaadddd* man."

Director of Student-Athlete Development Danny Manning: You always appreciate guys that are able to do things you hardly ever see. You can't help but marvel at talent like that.

You'd like to think you could play better defense, but he was making some tough shots. He was catching the ball, squaring guys up, jabbing them off, rising up, shooting pull-up Js and scoring at all three different levels. He was out there balling and we didn't have anything to stop him.

Jeremy Case: I remember sitting in there thinking, "Can anybody guard this guy?" Coach Self's like, "OK, Julian, you try to guard him." He scored like five straight on Julian. *"OK, Darnell, you try."* I'm sitting there like, "We're going to have *Darnell* guard him? Come on, Coach, what are you thinking?" Then he scores on Darnell. I'm like, "Are we going to box-and-one this dude? What are we going to do?"

Brandon Rush: I didn't know he was that good and that tall. He was killing Julian. He was tearing Julian's ass up, left and right. Then it was my turn.

Then they put me on him and, right off the bat, he hit a shot over me and he goes, "Uh oh, it's about to be a long night! You're too little!" He was talking trash and I couldn't say anything back. How could I? He damn near had 30 points—in the first half!

Texas coach Rick Barnes: The first 20 minutes of that game was the best half of basketball Kevin Durant ever played collegiately. We were isolating him and giving him the ball, just daring them to double-team him. They tried to double-team him from every possible angle you could double-team him, and he always made the right read. He got wide open shots. That first half … they had no answer. No matter what they did, he had an answer for anything.

Brady Morningstar: I remember one play when he got the ball at half court, drove down the middle of the lane and dunked it. That dunk dropped the jaws of everyone in the building. It was literally the loudest silence I've ever heard, if that makes sense. You could've heard a peanut crack. There was a loud "boom" when he dunked it, but it was such a clean dunk that there was no rattle. Just ... "BOOM!!!" I looked at Case and Rodrick and was like, "God *damn*! This dude is crazy. This dude is the real deal."

Texas guard Justin Mason: Kevin was a leader by example. He thrived on sucking the life out of a building. That carried over to everyone else. We liked playing on the road, and I think it was because of Kevin. He was so good that his game traveled wherever he went. His confidence carried over to everyone.

Durant went 5-of-5 from beyond the arc in the first half and had 25 points at intermission. Trailing 54-42, Kansas' players trudged into the locker room filled with frustration.

Jeremy Case: Before Coach Self came in, we were talking and I said, "Brandon, don't let him catch the ball. Just don't let him catch it." Brandon was like, "Oh, OK! You try to stop him if you think it's that easy." (Laughs)

Then Coach Self came in and started going off. *"Y'all are going to let this guy come in here and score 50 on y'all? Seriously?"*

Brandon Rush: Coach came in and said all we have to do is stop one guy. Slow him down a little bit, don't let him have a crazy half and we can win the game.

Mario Chalmers: Coach Self was like, "OK, we took the first hit. It can't get any worse, especially at home. We're already down by 20. We're either going to come back or we're going to go down by 20 more." Then things just clicked.

We had a great defensive team that year. At times, certain people turned into space cadets on defense. When we had those moments, we looked like a bad defensive team. That happened in the first half and they picked us apart. Plus, D.J. and A.J. were hitting all sorts of crazy shots. They were hitting on all cylinders and we couldn't do anything. That changed after intermission.

Russell Robinson: We had already established our winning culture. With Coach Self and the confidence he brought, I never really felt like we were out of a game.

Indeed, Kansas looked like a completely different team early in the second half, when a 29-11 scoring run resulted in a 71-65 lead for the Jayhawks with 11:11 remaining. Moments later, Durant injured his ankle on a shot attempt near the Texas bench and was taken to the locker room for treatment.

Rick Barnes: He rolled his ankle right in front of me. When he did it, I kid you not, the outside of his ankle bone touched the ground. My initial thoughts were, "He's going to be out for two weeks."

What was impressive was that he finished the shot, almost made it and still limped to the other end to play defense. At that point, we called timeout and took him out of the game. At that point, I knew it was going to be tough for us, because he had been controlling the game, and now we'd have to depend on so many other freshmen.

Kurtis Townsend: There was a hush in the crowd when K.D. turned his ankle in the second half. But when he got up to leave the court he got a standing ovation. It just showed me, "Wow, these people get it."

Kevin Durant: That was really classy. I think they respected us and our team and our coach. And they respected me. That game was to see who won the regular-season championship. But at that moment they didn't care about any of that. It was about showing class and sportsmanship. That's a moment I'll always remember.

Bill Self: I loved how they applauded for him. Our fans realize the game was bigger than a win or a loss. They were witnessing greatness.

Rick Barnes: About 10 minutes later, Todd Wright, our strength and conditioning coach, came up and said, "K.D. is ready." He'd been back in the locker room getting treatment from our training staff. I couldn't believe it. I said, "What? Are you serious? I'm not going to play him if he's hurt!" Todd said, "He swears he's ready to go." So we put him back in the game and you'd have never known he got hurt.

Joe Dooley: Our fans gave him another standing ovation as he ran back onto the court. I was hoping he was OK, but I didn't want to see him come back in the game. I don't think any of us did. But I guess he got tired wearing Julian and Brandon out so we could actually guard him.

Kansas led 81-72 when Durant returned at the 7:19 mark of the second half. And it was 88-80 before back-to-back 3-pointers by Durant and Abrams pulled the Longhorns within two, 88-86, with 27 seconds remaining. Wright's free throw extended KU's lead to 89-86, and then Wright essentially won the game for Kansas by blocking Augustin's 3-point attempt with five seconds to go.

Kevin Durant: The momentum was gone at that point. My ankle had stiffened up. They taped it up again and I ran back on the court. I wanted to keep going but I was mad that it had stopped my momentum—and our momentum as a team. We were on a roll. It was an amazing experience in the Big 12 at that time. I'm lucky I got a chance to play in that arena.

Justin Mason: Kevin getting hurt was the game-changer. That was probably the difference between us winning and losing. It also cost everyone in Allen Fieldhouse that day a chance of witnessing something historic, because he was on his way to putting up 50. That's something no one would've ever forgotten.

Still, you have to take your hat off to Kansas. Of all the teams I played against in my career, Kansas is the one I have the most respect for. They were the ultimate competitors. We had them down by 16 and they came back and were resilient.

A.J. Abrams: I know the one thing that you never want to hear is that "Rock Chalk Jayhawk" chant near the end of the game. You *never* want to hear that. We were getting close to the end of the game and we heard it, and I was like, "S**t!"

The year before, they'd rallied to beat us in the Big 12 Tournament championship game. Now we were near the end of the game at Phog Allen and they'd come back on us again. With about two minutes to go, Russell Robinson walked up to me and kinda whispered, "Well, we did it to y'all again, didn't we?" I was like, "Bro … yes, you did! Now get out of my face!"

Kansas won 90-86 and held Durant to just seven points in the second half and he finished with 32. Augustin (19 points, 13 assists) and Abrams (18 points) also had big games for Texas. Chalmers led Kansas with 21 points and was 5-of-5 from three-point range. Robinson (17 points) and Wright (17 points, 13 rebounds) had banner performances, too.

Sherron Collins: K.D. is one guy that is always going to have the ultimate respect from me. What he did to us that day ... no one ever did that to us. Nobody ever took over a game like that. Maybe you could say Ben Woodside from North Dakota took over (in 2009), but it didn't feel the same.

That was the first time I saw our fans cheer for someone else like that. I couldn't blame them. He had our respect, too. We're lucky he sprained his ankle. We probably would've lost.

Tim Jankovich: I remember leaving that game thinking, "That's the best player I've ever been in a game with, in all of my years of playing and coaching. There's no way he won't be the MVP of the NBA one year." I'd never seen a guy his size shoot the ball that well, from that range, while under so much duress at that age. It was amazing.

Rick Barnes: You can't talk about anything except winning with Kevin. He'd give up every award he received to win a championship. Our whole thing was, "We're going to win this league." Kevin wasn't a guy you had to jack up or hype up. The bigger the moment, the better he was. We started four freshmen and had a few more coming off the bench. I promise you, they all followed Kevin's lead.

I remember calling him over to the sideline one game and saying, "You're one of the best team players I've ever been around. But we've got to forget that right now, man. You've got to take this game over." He rarely wanted to do that. He's such a team player. But the Kansas game was a prime example of him taking over a game.

Justin Mason: Kevin was a pro even before he became a pro. He handled his business like a veteran.

K.D. is a cliché. Everyone always says the politically right things about their teammates, but with him, every compliment is genuine and true. Yes, he's really that humble. Yes, he really works that hard. Yes, he was a great teammate back then. And I'm sure he is now.

Everything always seemed so easy for him. Even today, he'll have 30 and 15 and it seems like he's having a bad game. That's how it was back then, too. We'd look up and he'd have 30 and 20 and I'd be like, "Dang, I had no idea he'd scored that much."

We were so young, like little puppies out there. It started to hit us at the end of conference play just how good he was. He started rolling and putting up those massive 30 and 20 games. When he went on those rolls is when we knew he was on a whole different level.

Russell Robinson: To this day, I can say that K.D. put on the best show I've ever seen at Allen Fieldhouse.

Kevin Durant: I'll always remember the energy in the arena at tipoff, and how quiet they were in the first half. But Kansas was so good and they were so deep, they eventually just wore us down. That was their third Big 12 title in a row and now the streak is at 13. It's unbelievable. Kansas has such a great program.

Our game against them was one of my favorite experiences at Texas. You play against those guys in AAU in the summers and then you see them in college. They can relate to the journey you're on. It's pretty cool to see where we all are now and think back on that game.

Bill Self: That's the baddest man I've ever seen play in person. We had two lottery picks trying to guard him and neither one could even come close to having an effect. He was having so much fun. From a fan standpoint, it worked out perfect. Their team won, and our crowd got a chance to see something special.

I've only seen Kevin once since then to give him crap about it. It was at Cole Aldrich's wedding. I was like, "You may be leading the NBA in scoring, but you've got a goose egg against us, big fella."

Postseason

Eight days after Kansas' victory at Allen Fieldhouse, the Jayhawks and Longhorns faced off again in the championship game of the Big 12 Tournament in Oklahoma City. Much like the first meeting, KU found itself in a big hole early—it trailed 32-10—before mounting a furious second-half comeback that resulted in an 88-84 overtime win. Durant had 37 points for Texas but went just 12-of-30 from the field and was scoreless in overtime. Collins, who had zero points against the Longhorns eight days earlier, led Kansas with 20 points off the bench. Rush and Wright scored 19 apiece while Chalmers added 17.

A few hours after that victory, Kansas—which had won 11 straight—learned that it had received a No. 1 seed in the NCAA Tournament. Victories over Niagara, Kentucky and Southern Illinois set the stage for an Elite Eight showdown against No. 2-seed UCLA in the Bruin-friendly city of San Jose, California.

Kansas 88, Texas 84
March 11, 2007 · Oklahoma City, Okla.

Kansas (30-4)

Player	MP	FG	3FG	FT	R	A	F	S	TO	B	TP
Julian Wright*	33	8-13	0-0	3-4	8	2	4	0	2	2	19
Sasha Kaun*	19	0-3	0-0	0-0	3	1	3	1	0	1	0
Russell Robinson*	31	1-4	0-1	3-4	4	3	3	0	1	0	5
Mario Chalmers*	30	6-12	2-5	3-3	1	2	5	1	2	0	17
Brandon Rush*	44	6-17	4-10	3-4	7	2	2	1	1	3	19
Darrell Arthur	12	1-5	0-1	0-0	1	0	1	0	2	0	2
Sherron Collins	30	8-18	2-4	2-2	6	3	2	0	2	0	20
Darnell Jackson	26	0-3	0-0	6-6	7	0	4	1	1	2	6
Team					9						
Totals	225	30-75	8-21	20-23	46	13	24	4	11	8	88

Texas (24-9)

Player	MP	FG	3FG	FT	R	A	F	S	TO	B	TP
Damion James*	39	4-10	0-0	1-4	14	1	4	0	1	2	9
Kevin Durant*	43	12-30	3-7	10-11	10	0	3	2	4	6	37
A.J. Abrams*	42	5-16	3-10	6-7	2	0	1	1	0	0	19
D.J. Augustin*	41	2-8	0-2	4-4	6	6	3	1	5	0	8
Justin Mason*	22	1-3	0-0	0-0	1	0	0	1	2	0	2
Craig Winder	22	1-1	0-0	3-6	5	1	3	0	0	0	5
Connor Atchley	15	2-3	0-1	0-0	4	0	4	1	1	2	4
Dexter Pittman	1	0-0	0-0	0-0	0	0	0	0	0	0	0
Team					4						
Totals	225	27-71	6-20	24-32	46	8	18	6	13	10	84

	1st	2nd	OT	Total	FG%	3FG%	FT%
Kansas	34	45	9	88	40.0	38.1	87.0
Texas	39	40	5	84	38.0	30.0	75.0

Officials: John Higgins, Scott Thornley, Curtis Shaw
Technicals: None

BEST OPPOSING BIG 12 PLAYER

1. Kevin Durant, Texas: After Durant's only game at Allen Fieldhouse – a 32-point effort – Self said the freshman was "one of the best to ever play on that court."

2. Buddy Hield, Oklahoma: Hield's 46 points against KU highlighted a senior year in which he averaged 25 points while posting some of the best shooting stats of the modern era. Hield shot 50.2 percent from the field, 45.7 percent from 3-point range and 88 percent from the foul stripe en route to earning the Naismith Award in 2016.

3. Michael Beasley, Kansas State: First-team All-American averaged 26 points and 12 rebounds in his one year and also ended KU's long win streak in Manhattan.

4. LaMarcus Aldridge, Texas: Future No. 2 overall pick made 9 of 10 shots in an 80-55 home win over KU in 2006, but the Jayhawks got revenge with a win over the Longhorns in the Big 12 Tournament.

5. Blake Griffin, Oklahoma: Consensus National Player of the Year his sophomore season after posting 23 points and 14 boards per game ... though he only played five total minutes against KU in two years because of injuries.

6. Joey Graham, Oklahoma State: Tough, physical forward was Oklahoma State's best player when KU's streak started in 2005, when he was runner-up to Wayne Simien for Big 12 Player of the Year.

7. Acie Law, Texas A&M: Hit famous jab-step three over Brandon Rush to give his Aggies the lead late in a 2007 comeback win at Allen Fieldhouse.

8. Marcus Denmon, Missouri: Scored 29 points – including nine straight late – to help Missouri to a 2012 win over KU at Mizzou Arena. And he had 28 in an overtime loss to the Jayhawks in the final Border War the following month.

9. Jacob Pullen, Kansas State: Had a career-high 38 points in Wildcats' 2011 upset over KU at Bramlage. Ranked second in the Big 12 in scoring (20.2 points) that season.

10. Marcus Smart, Oklahoma State: Future lottery pick averaged 18.4 points in five games against KU ... but Jayhawk fans will remember him for the backflip he did across the Allen Fieldhouse court following the Cowboys' win in 2013.

Sasha Kaun: We got screwed that year. We were a No. 1 seed and we had to play UCLA in San Jose, which was basically its backyard. It was a home game for them. That game was just tough. It was an Elite Eight game and we'd had a tough game before against Southern Illinois—which played a totally different style—and then we had to play UCLA to go to the Final Four. For whatever reason, Kansas always struggles in those Elite Eight games.

Jeremy Case: It was like we could not get anything done against them. That's how good they were. We just knew we weren't at that level yet.

Kansas led 29-23 in the first half before UCLA went on a 12-2 scoring run that made it 35-31 at intermission. The Bruins maintained at least a four-point lead throughout the entire second half. Aaron Afflalo had 24 points for UCLA while Darren Collison added 14. Ben Howland's squad shot 53.3 percent and still won despite committing an uncharacteristic 25 turnovers. Rush (18 points) and Robinson (11) were the only KU players to reach double figures.

Sherron Collins: We felt like we were going to win the national title that year. Aaron Afflalo had different plans. He hit so many 3s late in the shot clock, after we'd played great defense. They were just daggers.

Darrell Arthur: Russell Westbrook (four points) was on that team, too. But he was just a role player that season. Afflalo and Collison were the keys. They were so patient with their offense. They played at a slow pace the whole game and really controlled the tempo and frustrated us. It didn't make it any better that we were playing in San Jose, but we can't use that as an excuse. That was one game where we can say we flat-out got beat by a better team. They whipped us. They outworked us.

Sasha Kaun: Me and Darnell went into the locker room after the game and, as we were getting dressed, they were already showing the game on replay. We were like, "Wow, we played so bad."

Kansas 55, UCLA 68
March 24, 2007 · San Jose, Calif.

Kansas (33-5)

Player	MP	FG	3FG	FT	R	A	F	S	TO	B	TP
Brandon Rush*	36	7-16	2-3	2-2	5	1	3	0	4	2	18
Julian Wright*	29	4-7	0-0	0-2	5	4	2	4	2	0	8
Sasha Kaun*	13	2-4	0-0	0-0	1	2	1	0	1	1	4
Russell Robinson*	32	4-8	2-2	1-2	2	1	4	5	1	1	11
Mario Chalmers*	33	1-8	0-2	0-0	3	7	2	6	7	0	2
Darrell Arthur	24	2-6	0-0	0-0	4	0	3	0	2	2	4
Sherron Collins	15	0-4	0-1	0-0	1	2	3	0	1	0	0
Rodrick Stewart	4	0-0	0-0	0-0	0	0	0	0	0	0	0
Darnell Jackson	14	3-3	0-0	2-5	4	0	1	2	3	0	8
Team					3						
Totals	200	23-56	4-8	5-11	28	17	19	17	21	6	55

UCLA (30-5)

Player	MP	FG	3FG	FT	R	A	F	S	TO	B	TP
Josh Shipp*	35	2-7	2-4	3-4	6	5	1	4	4	2	9
Luc Mbah a Moute*	35	3-8	0-2	2-2	6	2	1	4	5	1	8
Lorenzo Mata*	18	1-2	0-0	0-2	3	0	4	0	0	0	2
Darren Collison*	36	4-8	2-3	4-4	1	1	3	5	7	0	14
Arron Afflalo*	36	10-15	3-7	1-2	4	3	1	0	4	0	24
Russell Westbrook	5	2-2	0-0	0-0	1	1	0	1	1	0	4
Alfred Aboya	25	1-2	0-0	2-2	6	0	4	1	1	0	4
James Keefe	1	0-0	0-0	0-0	0	0	0	0	0	0	0
Michael Roll	9	1-1	1-1	0-2	1	0	0	0	2	0	3
Team					3						
Totals	200	24-45	8-17	12-18	31	12	14	15	24	3	68

	1st	2nd	Total	FG%	3FG%	FT%
Kansas	31	24	55	41.1	50.0	45.5
UCLA	35	33	68	53.3	47.1	66.7

Officials: Ted Valentine, Mark Whitehead, Paul Janssen
Technicals: None

If that loss had to happen for us to win a championship, I'll take it. We came so close to the Final Four. We were right there. It motivated us going into our senior season. Anything less than the Final Four would've been a disappointment.

A little more from ...

The Jayhawks didn't have a single senior on the roster in 2006-07, but they did lose Julian Wright, who declared for the NBA draft a few weeks after the season. Wright, who had vowed all along to spend at least three seasons at KU, was selected No. 13 overall by the New Orleans Hornets.

Julian Wright: I don't regret saying during my sophomore year that I was going to stay at KU, because at the time, that's exactly what my mindset was. I'm a person that tries not to think too far down the road, because had I had that mentality, I promise you, I think I wouldn't have even had a good season. So it wasn't that I was trying to dodge those questions. That's exactly how I felt. Honestly, when the season was over, there was more time for reflection. But during the season, I owed it to my teammates and to myself to not think about anything in the future. That's pretty much how I felt then and now.

I won't say there's regrets. With that decision, I had the support of my team. I didn't have too many people in my ear. It was more about me thinking about some stuff in terms of stock, to be honest. I just felt that with the same team we had, my stock would be pretty much the same. So I figured it would be a good year to come out. Coach Self even helped out the process in terms of contacting teams. The consensus was that I'd be taken between No. 10 and No. 16. And so, I just felt it was a good opportunity to go. Coach Self said he understood. He said that he definitely thought I could benefit from another year, honing my craft and things of that nature. But he just said, "At this point, this is probably the most important decision you've made in your life. If you've given it a lot of thought, all I can do is support that." I really appreciated that. I believe it was the right decision.

Sherron Collins: Julian was great. I feel like Kansas fans never saw the real Julian Wright. If you'd have seen Julian and Shaun Livingston going against each other in high school ... my God. In high school, Julian had the ball in his hands a lot. Here, he just had to play the three and the four, so he was always on the block. He did fine, but I'm not sure that was his strength. Julian promised three years and left after two. I wasn't surprised. The sophomore year Julian had ... it was a great year. He was a lottery pick. No one was mad at him for leaving. Ju was a leader. He was always a voice in the locker room. Ju was really big for me my freshman year. I had some up and down moments. Him being from Chicago ... he was a religious person. He prayed for me. He'd keep smiles on people's faces just because of some of the weird s**t he might say or wear. Julian would wear an all-brown shirt with white Air Force Ones with brown shoestrings. He'd play the loudest music in the Towers. Everyone knew it was him. Everyone was like, "Yep, Ju's awake."

Bill Self: Julian was fun and so unselfish and a great passer. He was a terrific all-around player, and in all honesty, I was really disappointed when he left—not in that he shouldn't have gone, but I thought another year would've helped him.

It ended up being the right decision because he was a lottery pick, but I thought he could have been a better player over time—this is just my opinion, it doesn't mean it's right. And back then, kids left early but it wasn't quite as in vogue to leave early like it is now. If we had Julian or Brandon Rush today, they would leave after their freshman year.

I thought Julian had a great two years here. Fabulous. But he probably didn't develop his perimeter shot like he needed to.

Often overlooked is the fact that Brady Morningstar was a member of the 2006, program-changing recruiting class that included Sherron Collins and Darrell Arthur. Morningstar appeared in just 16 games as a freshman before redshirting the following year. Still, his contributions to those teams was immeasurable.

Brady Morningstar: I had so much stuff going through my head that year. Along with being a freshman, I was a little scrawny white kid from Lawrence getting a scholarship to Kansas. I know what everyone probably thought—that the only reason I was going there was because my dad played there. They thought I was a waste of a scholarship, that I couldn't play at this level. What most people didn't realize, though, is that after Free State I went to prep school for a year.

Coach Self was the one that suggested I go to New Hampton. He'd seen me play at Free State. Even after I graduated, I was still growing and maturing. He was like, "Hey man ... go perform. Go do your thing and get better and develop and we'll talk here in a little bit." I played against the best competition in the country at New Hampton and averaged more than 23 points per game. Jerome Dyson, who played at Connecticut, was in our league. Brewster Academy, where Thomas Robinson and Devonte' Graham played, was in our league. It was a big-time league. I was a white kid from Lawrence putting up 24 a game. Eventually Kansas told me they were going to come to watch me practice and to see one of my games. I was like, "Don't waste your time. If you want me, I'm signing. You don't need to wine and dine me. Kansas is where I want to go." They still brought me down for an official visit the weekend of the Kentucky game in 2006. It was kind of weird taking an official visit to my hometown.

After I signed, I'd hear whispers and read stuff. People were like, "Why are we signing him?" I tried to block it out, but it actually made me more hungry. I was like, "If they don't think I'm good enough to play here, I'll make them change their mind." That's what I wanted. I wasn't mad at what they were saying, because I hadn't proven myself yet. I knew that I was good enough to play. They just didn't because they hadn't seen me play at a high level.

The Jayhawks finished one game ahead of Texas A&M that season in the Big 12, but it's one year where they needed some help. The Aggies got swept by Texas Tech, a bubble team that year. Jones and Law still lament what might have been.

Joseph Jones: The main deal of the whole season was we could have been Big 12 champions. We could have tied for the Big 12 championship if we wouldn't have lost those two games against Tech. Don't get me wrong, Tech was a pretty good team but they weren't up to our level that year. Jarrius Jackson just killed us both games and made plays the whole year against us. It killed us. It killed our spirit and it still hurts now.

We worked so hard and had a chance to do something that had never been done in a long time as far as winning a conference championship, and we just gave it away in two games.

Acie Law: I always felt like Tech was the kryptonite to how Coach G wanted to play. How Bobby Knight coached his team, their offense, the motion offense, if I was a coach that's how I would play against a Billy Gillispie team. He wanted to deny. He wanted to play aggressive, and as a team we talked about it.

The Tech week was the toughest week of practice. That was the toughest team to prepare for, because it was always going to be a bad practice because what Coach G wanted to do wasn't successful against them, and he knew it.

Our second game against them, in College Station, I had made a shot to put us up and then I think Jarrius Jackson made a game-winner at the buzzer, but their talent wasn't as good as ours. It was more so their style of play. We knew that was the reason we didn't win the Big 12 that year. The heavy hitters, we beat them. And for a team like Tech to be the reason we didn't win the title … that was unfortunate.

2006-07 Season Summary

Results (33-5, 14-2)

November

11	Northern Arizona	W, 91 - 57
15	Oral Roberts	L, 71 - 78
19	Towson	W, 87 - 61
21	Tennessee State	W, 89 - 54
24	vs. Ball State	W, 64 - 46
25	vs. Florida	W, 80 - 82
28	Dartmouth	W, 83 - 32

December

2	@ DePaul	L, 64 - 57
4	USC	W, 72 - 62
9	vs. Toledo	W, 68 - 58
19	Winston-Salem State	W, 94 - 43
23	Boston College	W, 84 - 66
28	Detroit-Mercy	W, 63 - 43
30	Rhode Island	W, 80 - 69

January

7	@ South Carolina	W, 54 - 70
10	Oklahoma State	W, 87 - 57
13	@ Iowa State	W, 64 - 68
15	Missouri	W, 80 - 77
20	@ Texas Tech	L, 69 - 64
24	@ Baylor	W, 56 - 82
27	Colorado	W, 97 - 74
29	@ Nebraska	W, 56 - 76

February

3	Texas A&M	L, 66 - 69
7	Kansas State	W, 97 - 70
10	@ Missouri	W, 74 - 92
14	@ Colorado	W, 46 - 75
17	Nebraska	W, 92 - 39
19	@ Kansas State	W, 62 - 71
24	Iowa State	W, 89 - 52
26	@ Oklahoma	W, 65 - 67

March

3	Texas	W, 90 - 86
9	vs. Oklahoma	W, 64 - 47
10	vs. Kansas State	W, 67 - 61
11	vs. Texas	W, 88 - 84
16	vs. Niagara	W, 107 - 67
18	vs. Kentucky	W, 88 - 76
22	vs. Southern Illinois	W, 61 - 58
24	vs. UCLA	L, 55 - 68

All-Big 12 Team

Player of the Year:
Kevin Durant, Texas, Fr., F/G

Defensive Player of the Year:
Mario Chalmers, Kansas, So., G
Marcus Dove, Oklahoma State, Jr., G/F

Newcomer of the Year:
Stefhon Hannah, Missouri, Jr., G

Freshman of the Year:
Kevin Durant, Texas, Fr., F/G

Sixth Man of the Year:
Cartier Martin, Kansas State, Sr., G/F

Coach of the Year:
Billy Gillispie, Texas A&M

First Team
Brandon Rush, Kansas, So., G
JulianWright, Kansas, So., F
Mario Boggan, Oklahoma State, Sr., F/C
Kevin Durant, Texas, Fr., F/G**
Acie Law, Texas A&M, Sr., G**
Jarrius Jackson, Texas Tech, Sr., G

Second Team
David Hoskins, Kansas State, Jr., G/F
Cartier Martin, Kansas State, Sr., G/F
Aleks Maric, Nebraska, Jr., C
D.J. Augustin, Texas, Fr., G
Joseph Jones, Texas A&M, Jr., F

Third Team
Mario Chalmers, Kansas, So., G
Stefhon Hannah, Missouri, Jr., G
Nate Cater, Oklahoma, Sr., F
JamesOn Curry, Oklahoma State, Jr., G
Martin Zeno, Texas Tech, Jr., G

Honorable Mention
Aaron Bruce, Baylor, Jr., G
Curtis Jerrells, Baylor, So., G
Richard Roby, Colorado, Jr., G
Mike Taylor, Iowa State, Jr. G
Darrell Arthur, Kansas, Fr., F
Sherron Collins, Kansas, Fr., G
A.J. Abrams, Texas, So., G
Josh Carter, Texas A&M, So., G/F
Antanas Kavaliauskas, Texas A&M, Sr., F

All-Defensive Team
Mario Chalmers, Kansas, So., G
Russell Robinson, Kansas, Jr., G
Marcus Dove, Oklahoma State, Jr., G/F
Kevin Durant, Texas, Fr., F/G
Dominique Kirk, Texas A&M, Jr., G

All-Rookie Team
Wesley Johnson, Iowa State, Fr., F
Darrell Arthur, Kansas, Fr., F
Sherron Collins, Kansas, Fr., G**
Stefhon Hanah, Missouri, Jr., G
Kevin Durant, Texas, Fr. , F/G**
D.J. Augustin, Texas, Fr., G**

** Unanimous selection

Kansas Awards

Julian Wright:
NABC All-American Third Team
Big 12 All-Tournament Team
Las Vegas Invitational MVP

Brandon Rush
NABC All-District (12) First Team
Big 12 All-Tournament Team

Season Stats

#	Player	CL	POS	HT	Hometown	G	GS	FG%	3P%	FT%	R	A	S	B	PTS
25	Brandon Rush	SO	G	6-6	Kansas City, MO	38	38	.443	.431	.681	5.6	2.0	0.4	0.9	13.8
15	Mario Chalmers	SO	G	6-1	Anchorage, AK	38	37	.491	.404	.770	3.0	3.3	2.6	0.4	12.2
30	Julian Wright	SO	F	6-8	Chicago Heights, IL	38	37	.549	.231	.613	7.8	2.2	1.4	1.3	12.0
0	Darrell Arthur	FR	F	6-9	Dallas, TX	38	7	.538	.000	.646	4.7	0.4	0.9	1.5	9.8
4	Sherron Collins	FR	G	5-11	Chicago, IL	38	3	.478	.405	.766	2.3	2.9	0.7	0.0	9.3
3	Russell Robinson	JR	G	6-1	New York, NY	37	36	.436	.346	.651	3.1	4.4	2.0	0.5	7.2
32	Darnell Jackson	JR	F	6-9	Oklahoma City, OK	38	3	.550		.657	5.1	0.3	0.4	0.6	5.5
24	Sasha Kaun	JR	C	6-11	Melbourne, FL	35	28	.530		.500	3.8	0.5	0.3	1.4	5.9
10	Jeremy Case	JR	G	6-1	McAlester, OK	19	0	.419	.370	1.000	0.6	0.8	0.4	0.0	1.9
12	Brady Morningstar	FR	G	6-4	Lawrence, KS	16	0	.500	.444	.800	0.8	0.5	0.3	0.1	2.1
5	Rodrick Stewart	JR	G	6-4	Seattle, WA	30	1	.357	.455	.273	0.8	0.6	0.2	0.0	0.9
54	Matt Kleinmann	SO	C	6-10	Overland Park, KS	17	0	.556		.833	0.9	0.2	0.1	0.1	0.9
10	Brennan Bechard	SO	G	6-0	Lawrence, KS	12	0	.333	.333	.000	0.3	0.1	0.0	0.0	0.3
40	Brad Witherspoon	FR	G	6-1	Humboldt, KS	10	0	.167	.000	.500	0.4	0.2	0.1	0.1	0.3

## CHAPTER 4

2007-08

THE ULTIMATE PAYOFF

The narrative of one of the most memorable seasons in Kansas' storied history actually began in an Atlanta gymnasium, five months before the Jayhawks embarked on their national championship run. It was there, during a secret workout for NBA teams in May of 2007, that Brandon Rush tore the anterior cruciate ligament in his right knee. The following morning, Rush—who had declared for the NBA draft but had yet to hire an agent—placed a phone call to Bill Self.

Bill Self: Brandon was really down, as you'd expect. He'd made up his mind that he was turning pro and he was expected to be a lottery pick, which was a goal of his long before he came to Kansas. It was right there in front of him and, just like that, he was injured and everything was up in the air.

I thought he still might want to stay in the draft, so I asked him what he wanted to do. He said, "I've gotta come back, Coach. I've gotta get healthy and get better." I said, "OK, let's get you back. Let's get you with Dr. Randall and go from there."

Brandon Rush: I still remember hearing that pop in my knee. We were doing a three-man weave drill, and I went up for a dunk and landed funny. I was hoping it was a just a sprain. Once they told me it was torn, I was scared. I couldn't understand why this was happening to me. I didn't want to tell anyone at the time but, deep down, there was a part of me that wondered if I'd ever be the same player again. I watched the NBA draft on television and wondered where I might have gone if I wouldn't have hurt myself. It definitely would've been in the first round.

JaRon Rush (Brandon's older brother): I remember my mom calling to tell me that Brandon had hurt himself. She said he was really down about it and that he was crying a little bit. I couldn't reach him because he didn't want to talk to anyone. I was pretty upset about it, too. I actually shed a few tears for him, because I had been through knee injuries before and I knew it was a long road back.

Brandon Rush: The good thing was that I didn't sit around and sulk. For a while I was going to rehab three times a day, doing all kinds of extensions and other exercises. It was pretty painful at times, but I was determined to get back.

Rush had led Kansas in scoring as both a freshman (13.5 points) and sophomore (13.8) while earning first-team All-Big 12 honors after each of those seasons.

Jeremy Case: The most impressive thing about Brandon during that time was his attitude. I'm sure he was down initially, but once he had surgery and was back in Lawrence, he didn't act like anything was wrong. He wasn't pouting. He didn't seem like he didn't want to be there. He just had this mindset of, "What do I need to do to get back to where I was before the injury?"

He was very professional about it. Our trainer will tell you … he was on time to every treatment, and he had to go twice a day. He was back on the court in five months. It was unbelievable.

All of us were thinking, "What's he going to be like when he gets back out there?" Because athleticism was such a big part of his game. But I actually think he got stronger.

Bill Self: We had no idea that Brandon would be full speed in five months. I was nervous for him. But in the end, it was good for him. It helped him mature from a discipline standpoint. He never missed rehab and he became much more responsible through all of that.

Brandon Rush: My respect for Coach Self went to a new level during my knee injury. He was calling or texting every day to check up on me and telling me to call him whenever I needed to talk. He had already treated me well, but I think our relationship got even better at that point. I know it did on my end.

Bill Self: In an indirect way, you could say the day Brandon tore his ACL was the day we won the national championship.

Darrell Arthur: You never want to see anyone get injured, but I was glad Brandon was back. I could've entered the draft that summer, too, but I didn't think I'd had a very good freshman year. Plus, I wanted to win a championship. Other than Julian, we had everyone back and we'd added Cole (Aldrich) and Tyrel (Reed). All of the pieces were in place.

While Rush spent the summer rehabbing, returnees such as Mario Chalmers, Russell Robinson, Sherron Collins, Darrell Arthur, Darnell Jackson, Sasha Kaun, Jeremy Case and Brady Morningstar led some of the most competitive offseason pickup games and conditioning sessions of the Self era. This season, they vowed, would be different. This season would be special.

Jeremy Case: We were driven, man. And I think that UCLA loss had a lot to do with it. That loss shook us. We were rattled by it, because UCLA just flat-out beat us. If you think about who they had ... damn they were good. We fought and fought and just couldn't get anything done against them. Their defense was unbelievable. So I think we were all kind of frustrated about that game, which turned out to be a good thing, because it really motivated us that summer.

Mario Chalmers: Our pickup games? Man … they were violent. There were fights, balls were getting kicked across the room, people were getting thrown down. But if five random guys had walked into the gym and wanted to play us, you'd have never known we were bumping heads a few minutes earlier.

That was my favorite thing about my last two teams at Kansas. We were a family. We were a fist. We'd fight anyone for one another. We had each other's backs.

Sherron brought that aura, that toughness, to the team. I brought it, too, and so did Russ and D-Block. The only person that didn't really bring that was Brandon, but he had it inside of him. We brought it out eventually.

Then there was Sasha (laughing). Sasha was *mean*. If Sasha wasn't on my team I would never want to cross paths with him. He's a big, strong Russian. And you know how Russians are. They don't really like anybody that's not in their circle. That's how Sasha was. He took care of us.

Tyrel Reed: I remember Sasha having the best summer ever. He was unstoppable in pickup, which is really weird because a big guy is never unstoppable in pickup because he never gets the ball. But for some reason, whenever he got the ball, he was like a bucket machine.

I remember an instance in practice where it was like, "OK, this guy is on a different level." Sasha was going in for a layup, and I literally slapped him as hard as I could across the arm, and he went up and still finished. It literally hurt *my* arm. It was supposed to be the other way around.

I thought, "This guy is a machine."

Jeremy Case: That summer it was all about getting better against each other. I think we were going so hard against each other that it caused a little tension. There were a lot of arguments, a lot of fights. The most memorable one was with Russ and Darnell.

Sherron Collins: We were playing pickup and Darnell and Russ were arguing about recruiting rankings. They were going back and forth about who was rated higher coming out of high school. It was getting heated, and then D-Block started making fun of Russ. He said he wasn't a true New Yorker, that he was from the suburbs. That pissed Russ off.

Jeremy Case: Russ found a line on the court and told Darnell, "C'mon ... cross this line right here. I dare you to cross it." So Darnell crossed the line and swung at Russ. He missed, and then Russ swung back and caught him right in the jaw. Darnell stumbled back a little and then we broke it up. I think Russ got the best of him.

Tyrel Reed: Darnell didn't go to the floor, but Russ definitely staggered him. Russ started running around (celebrating) and pickup was done.

Brady Morningstar: I can remember Sherron grabbing people a couple of times and shoving them into their locker. One time D-Block was messing around and squirted some lotion in Sherron's shoe while Sherron was in the shower. He put a ton of it in there. Sherron came out of the shower, put his foot in the shoe and felt it. He was like, "Who did this?" Everyone looked at D-Block and then Sherron rushed him and put him on the ground. D-Block would probably laugh about that now.

Mario Chalmers: Practices were competitive too. Our scout team was nice—Brady, Brad Witherspoon, Case, (Conner) Teahan and Matt Kleinmann. Kleinmann was a beast on defense in practice. He was everywhere, diving for loose balls. He was the guy that left everything out on the court. In practice, if he was on the scout team, you knew to be prepared for everything.

They made us better. They knew they weren't going to play much. They knew their role was to wear us out in practice and make sure we're ready for the game. They embraced that role.

Brady was a baby Sherron. All he did was study Sherron and follow him around and play just like he did. He got better with each and every practice. To this day I still don't think people realize and appreciate just how good of a player Brady was. In practice, he was the guy who simulated Stefhon Hannah or Curtis Stinson or LaceDarius Dunn. Whoever the best player was, that's who Brady was.

Brady Morningstar: We were just ready to get the season started and I was focused on doing everything in practice to make my teammates better. I was redshirting that year, so I knew I wasn't going to get on the court. Our red team was competitive. I'm telling you, we were *good*. It was me and Rod Stewart and Case and Kleinmann and Teahan and Tyrel and Cole. Some days the blue guys who were sitting out would come

and play with the red team. Some days we'd actually *beat* the blue team. We could all play ball. Practices were fun.

Tyrel Reed: We had group drills, and my group was Russ-Rob, Mario and Sherron. I'm sure they loved that Coach Self threw this freshman kid in with them. It was the best experience for me because I got beat up every time. If we were playing one-on-one to five, and I scored three, I'd feel pretty good about myself.

When that group of guys was firing on all cylinders, it was amazing. I think we had so much confidence because of who we were practicing against every day. We were practicing against better players than we went against in games so the practices were just as intense, if not more than the games. That's what was really cool.

We had a squad. The second team was legitimately pushing the first team. It's not like they were bums. There was some high-level basketball being played every single day.

Jeremy Case: It was frustrating to not be able to play very much, but by that point, as a senior, I kind of understood everything and had accepted it. I knew how good I was, but I also knew those other guys were really good. *Damn* good. Most of them played in the NBA. They were pros. So at that point I knew I needed to go at them as hard as I could in practice, because the players that they're going to be playing hopefully won't go as hard as I'm going to be going. I had to prepare them—and also prepare myself, so I'd be ready if I got in.

We were going at each other so hard, it brought us closer. I don't know how many times Mario and I got into it because we were competing so hard. *You fouled me! I fouled you!* I thought it made us better.

Coach Self didn't have to yell a whole lot. We knew what Coach Self wanted. We'd had guys who had been through the program. We had five seniors. It was one of those perfect storms. Everybody knew their role. And like Mario said, we were like a fist.

Mario Chalmers: I looked at Russ and learned from him. Sherron learned from me. We were like, "We're all in this together. We're not going to compete against each other. We can't do this without each other." In our rotation we only had four guards: me, Brandon, Sherron and Russ. That was our rotation.

Tyrel Reed: No one's ego got in the way. When we had Boot Camp that year, Mario showed up 30 minutes late to the last day, when we did all these sprints. This was our starting guard. Coach Self probably could have taken it easy on him and no one would have said anything. But for every minute he was late, he made him run a sprint. He was 30 minutes late, so he had to run 30 extra sprints at the end of Boot Camp with a manager watching, and he did it.

It was physically impressive, but I think that set the tone too. (Self) wasn't going to let anybody, even one of his best guys, get away with something like that.

Bill Self: That team was so bought in. That's what's great about having guys that have been there a year or two. All they cared about was winning. Sasha was a great example. Everybody should learn from Sasha. He set the tone. He had been a starter the previous two years. But in that particular season, from an energy standpoint to start the game, it was better for our team that Darnell started.

It wasn't like anybody thought that Sasha wasn't good enough to start. The reason Sasha didn't start is because he wanted to win. He sacrificed himself, because he knew it was best for the team from a chemistry standpoint—and for Darnell's psyche—if Darnell was the starter.

Look at Sasha now. He ended up making as much money as a pro as anybody by not starting. I love him.

Sasha Kaun: A lot of schools have stars that play hard half the time on offense, and that's it. They score 25 points and walk around and act cool, even though they're probably losing. Coach Self wouldn't put up with any of that crap.

A big thing for him was playing defense. Everyone that comes to Kansas is talented but, for him, it's all about playing defense and developing a good work ethic. If you took possessions off, he wouldn't accept that. It was all about playing hard on every possession.

20-0

Other than an overtime win at home against unranked Arizona and a four-point road victory over O.J. Mayo and No. 22 USC, the Jayhawks were hardly challenged by one of their worst non-conference schedules ever. They were 20-0 following an 84-49 win at Nebraska on Jan. 26—just two wins from matching the best start in KU history.

Bill Self: I remember ESPN's Hubert Davis, of all people, on College GameDay, kept saying "Kansas is the best team in the country."

The year before, when we beat Kentucky in the second round, their coaches said,

"Hey, go win it all." I'm saying, "Do you really think we can?" And they're going, "Yes, you can!" I'm not sure I believed them then—and obviously we ended up not winning the title.

But in 2008 I thought we were terrific. I really did. I thought we were great. That year we played 40 games and we probably played six or eight games where we didn't play very well, but that was about it. We were a model of consistency.

We beat Nebraska 84-49 to get to 20-0. It was a joke. We had a killer instinct. We go to Boston College (on Jan. 5), and we're killing them at halftime. They come out and go on a 10-0 run on us to cut it to 12, and we're talking some trash. Mario threw the ball at one of them. I loved it. Mario smiled and came across like a choirboy, but he was in the middle of every (skirmish). He loved moments like that, thrived on them. I told our staff right there, "You watch this. Game over." And then we go on an 8-0 run in a minute. Our guys loved it. They were cocky and had swagger. It defined our team.

Darnell Jackson: The most memorable games of that 20-0 streak were beating Oklahoma at home (85-55) and the win at Mizzou (76-70).

I was really excited to play against Blake and Taylor Griffin. At one point I thought Blake was coming to Kansas, but I understood why he went to OU. He wanted to play with his brother. I grew up around Blake in Oklahoma. We were always around each other during AAU and stuff. He was the baby out of all of us, small and skinny.

He came on his recruiting visit to Kansas and walked into the locker room, and I was like, "Dude, what have you been doing?" I hadn't seen him. He was towering over me. I was excited for him. He and Taylor are great guys. Five minutes into the game against us, me and Blake were jumping for a rebound and he sprained his knee. He spent the rest of the game on the bench with an ice pack on his knee. I was disappointed because we were really looking forward to going against him. I'm sure our fans were disappointed, too. He was a great player at OU.

Octagon of Gloom

Second-ranked Kansas and No. 22 Kansas State were both 5-0 in the Big 12 when the Jayhawks traveled west on Interstate 70 for the Sunflower State Showdown. The league race, however, was far from the main storyline leading up to tipoff. And neither was KU's 24-game winning streak in Manhattan.

The previous summer, K-State freshman Michael Beasley—who would blossom into one of the best players in school history—had irritated Kansas' players and fans with some bold remarks that found their way onto KU's bulletin board.

"We're going to beat Kansas at home," said Beasley, the No. 2 pick in the 2008 NBA draft. "We're going to beat them at their house. We're going to beat them in Africa. Wherever we play, we're going to beat them."

K-State coach Frank Martin: Heading into that season, after Bob Huggins left and I became the head coach, I instilled a policy that said freshmen can't speak to the media during their first semester. But some reporters grabbed Mike at a Catbacker function over the summer, just a month after he enrolled in school. He didn't know he wasn't supposed to talk, so he ran his mouth a little bit and said those things.

I was pissed at the media guy that did it, because he knew that I'd put the policy in place, but he disrespected me and still went up and talked to Mike.

Deep down, though, I kind of liked that Mike said those things, because we were trying to establish a mindset, and that's the kind of mindset you have to have in your locker room to beat elite teams like Kansas.

Bill Walker, Jacob Pullen, Ron Anderson, Dominique Sutton and Jamar Samuels all shared that mindset. They were like, "We don't care that it's KU. We're ready to play them wherever it's at."

K-State guard Clent Stewart: Mike's quote made it fun and it fueled some of the fire within our fans. It also showed us, before the season or practices had even started, that Michael Beasley wasn't afraid of anyone. He was going to go out there and compete, and we were going to follow suit.

Bill Self: When a guy is averaging 24 and 13, I think he has the right to talk a little bit.

K-State guard Jacob Pullen: It was a really big game, especially after Mike's comments. We were undefeated in the Big 12, so we were kind of feeling ourselves.

Me being a freshman, just like Mike ... I didn't know much about the rivalry. I didn't know that KU had won every game since they'd opened Bramlage Coliseum. I just thought KU vs. K-State was like the North Carolina-Duke rivalry, and it was going to be a big game.

Looking back on it, we didn't realize how good that Kansas team was. They had a lot of guys on that team, from Mario to Russell and Sherron, to Rush and Darnell, Darrell Arthur, Sasha Kaun, Cole Aldrich ... they had a ridiculous team.

But after Mike made that comment, we had to back it up. Luckily for us, we were in the groove, so we went out there and played without fear. We were all new to this, and we went out there and played our asses off.

Darnell Jackson: When Beasley said that, I remember thinking, "There's no way. They've got no chance." Then we got there and it was a totally different story. They just beat our ass the whole game.

The media and fans were building the game up because of the Beasley quote, but behind the scenes, Martin was considering benching Beasley and Bill Walker, another K-State star who would eventually play in the NBA.

Frank Martin: On Tuesday, the day before the game, Mike and Bill were horrendous in practice, and I threw them out of the gym. They just weren't focused. When I got to my locker room they were waiting for me. They were both like, "Coach, that was our bad. We really want to play tomorrow." I had moved on. Mentally, I was prepared not to play them.

But they came into my locker room and made me understand that they'd been waiting for this moment for a long time. I told them I'd call them later. I called them that night and said, "If this ever happens again, you're not playing." The next two days those two guys, along with Jacob Pullen, were the three best players on the court.

Pregame

Bill Self: Bramlage Coliseum, when we play there, is about as good as there is. When that place is juiced—and it always is when we play there—it's probably the toughest road game we have to play each year in the Big 12. Iowa State would be the other one. We've seen some crazy environments there, and that night was probably the craziest.

Darrell Arthur: We're out there warming up, and all of a sudden a chicken lands in the middle of the court. It was all tied up—and trust me, it wasn't a fake chicken. It was real because I could see it moving. It was insane.

Russell Robinson: It's tough to play there when they're throwing chickens at you with the heads cut off. It was literally a real chicken. That didn't sit too well with my stomach.

One thing I don't miss about college basketball is the heckling before the games. K-State fans were the worst; them and Missouri. They made it very difficult to focus and prepare before games. Fans just about anywhere are going to talk trash, but there was something different about the things you'd hear from K-State and Missouri fans. It's like their words were coming from this deep, dark, mean, disturbing place. I truly think they meant everything they said.

Clent Stewart: KU and K-State fans, when we play each other, can get nasty at times.

The interesting thing for me when I was in it ... I grew up in Oklahoma, and some of those KU guys I grew up playing with or against. I played with Darnell Jackson and Jeremy Case, and I played against Russell Robinson on the AAU circuit when he was with the New York Gauchos. Most of those guys, I either knew them fairly well or I knew their games. In the summertime, we'd even work together as counselors at Bob Chipman's camp in Wichita. We'd hang out and shoot the breeze and kick it, yet here we were, a bunch of guys who were supposed to hate each other, at least in the eyes of the fans. So it was interesting from a player's standpoint, because even though we were competitors, I think a lot of us viewed each other as friends.

The Game

Kansas—which entered the game beating opponents by a national-best 24.9 points—hardly appeared shaken by K-State's raucous crowd. Eight different Jayhawks scored in the opening half including Rush, who had 12 points on 5-of-7 shooting. The Wildcats, though, led 38-36 at intermission. And K-State caught a huge break when Arthur picked up his fourth foul less than two minutes into the second half.

Sherron Collins: Shady was giddy that day; he was amped to guard Beasley. Shady was a thoroughbred. He could run all day.

But it was hard for him to make an impact because he was on the bench so much in foul trouble. We needed him on defense. We needed him on Beasley. It was tough for Sasha to guard him. Most of the time Sasha was a great defender. We never had to double anyone with him because he could handle his guy one-on-one. But Mike Beasley was a tough matchup for him. He'd pull him out on the perimeter, and he's got moves like a guard. Beasley would just blow past him and dunk it or he'd throw a lob to Bill Walker. We tried Darnell and Cole on him, but they weren't much better. We never got over the hump defensively.

Kansas State 84, Kansas 75
January 30, 2008 · Manhattan, Kan.

Kansas State (15-4)

Player	MP	FG	3FG	FT	R	A	F	S	TO	B	TP
Bill Walker*	25	9-18	3-10	1-2	5	1	3	1	4	0	22
Michael Beasley*	38	9-18	4-4	3-4	6	2	1	1	4	1	25
Blake Young*	27	1-3	1-1	0-0	2	5	5	0	0	0	3
Clent Stewart*	36	3-5	2-3	3-4	5	1	2	0	2	0	11
Dominique Sutton*	26	1-6	0-1	0-0	6	1	4	2	2	1	2
Jacob Pullen	28	4-9	2-5	10-10	0	4	2	0	1	0	20
Chris Merriewether	1	0-0	0-0	1-2	0	0	0	0	0	0	1
Darren Kent	18	0-4	0-2	0-2	4	3	4	0	0	0	0
Luis Colon	1	0-0	0-0	0-0	0	0	0	0	0	0	0
Team					6						
Totals	200	27-63	12-26	18-24	34	17	21	4	13	2	84

Kansas (20-1)

Player	MP	FG	3FG	FT	R	A	F	S	TO	B	TP
Darrell Arthur*	17	5-12	0-0	2-2	7	1	4	0	2	3	12
Darnell Jackson*	30	2-2	0-0	3-4	4	0	2	0	2	1	7
Russell Robinson*	26	1-8	0-3	4-4	2	3	5	2	2	0	6
Mario Chalmers*	30	5-9	2-4	7-8	1	2	5	0	3	0	19
Brandon Rush*	37	6-10	3-7	0-0	7	4	3	1	2	0	15
Sherron Collins	29	5-11	1-3	1-2	0	2	3	0	1	0	12
Rodrick Stewart	6	1-1	0-0	0-0	2	0	0	0	0	0	2
Jeremy Case	1	0-0	0-0	0-0	0	0	0	0	0	0	0
Sasha Kaun	20	1-1	0-0	0-0	3	0	2	0	2	2	2
Cole Aldrich	4	0-0	0-0	0-0	0	0	1	0	2	1	0
Team					4						
Totals	200	26-54	6-17	17-20	30	12	25	3	16	7	75

	1st	2nd	Total	FG%	3FG%	FT%
Kansas State	38	46	84	42.9	46.2	75.0
Kansas	36	39	75	48.1	35.3	85.0

Officials: Ted Hillary, Brad Ferrie, Dan Chrisman
Technicals: None

Sasha Kaun: Michael Beasley was probably the top big guy I played against at Kansas. In terms of pure scoring ability, gosh, he was unbelievable. Being a lefty, he could do just about anything … shoot 3s, post up, mid-range jumpers, everything. And if you let him go to his left, forget about it. He was going to get you.

Darnell Jackson: I just couldn't believe all of the shots Beasley was making. I remember one stretch in the second half when he just went crazy. I was all over him and he pulled up for a step-back 3 from deep. *Swish!* I was thinking, "No way!"

Beasley scored 17 of his game-high 25 points in the second half. For the game he was 9-of-18 from the field and 4-of-4 from 3-point range. He also had six rebounds.

Jacob Pullen: That was one of the few games when Mike didn't have a double-double. I remember Bill Walker (22 points) playing extremely well. We started Bill at the three because we wanted Brandon Rush to have to guard him, because we could use Bill's size on the block. But then we ended up going small and playing Mike at the five and Bill at

BEST PERFORMANCES BY A BIG 12 OPPONENT

1. Kevin Durant, Texas, March 3, 2007: KU fans still refer to this as the "Kevin Durant game," as the super-freshman scored 25 in the first half with 5-for-5 three-point shooting before an ankle injury slowed him down (he finished with 32) in Kansas' 90-86 win.

2. Buddy Hield, Oklahoma, Jan. 4, 2016: The future national player of the year scored 46 points in a triple-overtime thriller, earning an ovation from KU fans at Allen Fieldhouse as he left the court after the Jayhawks emerged with a 109-106 victory.

3. Jacob Pullen, Kansas State, Feb. 14, 2011: Switching defenders and defenses were ineffective against the K-State guard this night, as he had 38 points – and 19 free throw attempts – in his team's 84-68 home win.

4. Acie Law, Texas A&M, Feb. 3, 2007: Brandon Rush said this about Law after he scored 23 points and hit late a 3-pointer to lift the Aggies to a 69-66 win at Allen Fieldhouse: "They say he's the best clutch player in the league. He proved it there."

5. Michael Beasley, Kansas State, Jan. 30, 2008: After guaranteeing victory over KU earlier in the week, Beasley delivered with 25 points, including a 4-of-4 performance from beyond the arc, in the Wildcats' 84-75 victory.

6. Craig Brackins, Iowa State, Jan. 24, 2009: The forward's 42 points in his team's 82-67 home loss were the most ever surrendered by the Jayhawks to a Big 12 opponent at the time.

7. Pierre Jackson, Baylor, March 9, 2013: The point guard repeatedly burned by KU on the dribble, scoring 28 points on 11-for-13 shooting with 10 assists in the Bears' 81-58 home win.

8. Alan Voskuil, Texas Tech, March 4, 2009: On Senior Night in Lubbock, Voskuil torched KU for a career-high 35 points on 9-for-14 three-point shooting in the Red Raiders' 84-65 upset victory.

the four, because we realized when they were playing Sasha Kaun and Darrell Arthur together, and Bill being actually a wing player, they couldn't guard him at the four.

Frank did a great job of changing his matchups during the game. It was a big moment for him. That was his first time going up against an elite coach like Bill Self, who was really good.

Clent Stewart: I had to guard Brandon Rush. He wasn't overly athletic, but he could really shoot it from the outside. The whole game plan was to make him drive. He's 6-6 or 6-7 and I'm 6-3. Anytime you have to play a guy with that much height on you, it can be a challenge. He was a quiet guy but definitely one that could score. If you left him open, it was going up and going in.

At one point, I got caught up on a screen. Of course he made a 3 in the corner, and I just wanted to close my ears, because I knew Coach Martin was going to go off on me and scream at me.

That was part of our game plan: *Make Brandon Rush drive.* You can't let him catch and shoot, so when you're playing a guy like that, you've got to make sure you know where he is at all times. All it takes is one slip-up, and he'll make the shot—and then you'll be hearing it from Coach.

Trailing 47-45, Kansas was still in the game midway through the second half. But a 10-0 scoring run by K-State made it 57-45 with 10:04 remaining. The Jayhawks—who went nearly 7 minutes without a field goal—never threatened again in an 84-75 loss, KU's first of the season.

Mario Chalmers: Looking back, I think we blew that game off. We weren't up for it like we should've been. We thought, "We're 20-0. We're about to go in there and smack them." Then Bill Walker got hot early and we were like, "Uh-oh. They really came to play." We took that game for granted. We should've won that one.

The main reason they beat us was Jacob Pullen. We knew what Beasley and Walker could do, and we weren't too worried about Clent Stewart. But when Jacob got hot, it turned the game. We weren't expecting that. It put them over the edge.

Russell Robinson: They had some terrible teams at K-State, but it was still almost always a game when we played them. Once they got those big talents in there with Beasley and Walker, we knew it was going to be different. It was one of those games that, no matter how good we played, we weren't going to win. Everything was going their way. The stars were aligned for them to win that game.

Beasley, Walker and Pullen combined for 67 of K-State's 84 points and 22 of their team's 27 field goals. Pullen was 10-of-10 from the free throw line. The victory over Kansas was the Wildcats' first in Manhattan since 1983. The 24-game streak in an opponent's gym came within one of tying the NCAA Division I record, which UCLA set against California from 1961-85.

Clent Stewart: Our fans were going crazy the entire game. I remember looking into the stands and seeing a student with a sign that said, "Nobody beats us 25 times in a row at home! Nobody!" It was funny and embarrassing at the same time.

Everyone stormed the court and celebrated. At that moment, we were at the top of the Big 12. We realized we had a chance to do something special.

Sherron Collins: Their fans rushed the court, and the security guards did a great job of keeping them off of us— except for this one guy. He was about to run Coach Townsend over and he just leveled him. Coach T just *leveled* this dude.

K-State assistant coach Brad Underwood: Twenty-four years ... that is an even more amazing record than KU's 13 straight Big 12 championships, beating your archrival at their place that many seasons in a row.

Mike had made the statement over the summer that we'd beat them in Africa or wherever they wanted to play, so there was that motivation both ways. The electricity of that game was unreal. Kevin Keitzman and the 810 radio station came from KC and broadcast in Manhattan all throughout the day. It was a different KU-KSU game. Before then it wasn't really a rivalry, because Kansas State hadn't won in forever. That win brought things back a little bit from the K-State perspective.

Frank Martin: It was as amazing of a moment as I've ever been associated with as a coach. As I walked back out to do my radio interview about 10 minutes after the buzzer, I looked into the stands and they were still full. Everybody was still there. To see people who were 75 years old with tears of joy streaming down their cheeks ... it was incredible.

Clent Stewart: That win meant a lot to me personally because it was the last time my mom got to see me play. The game was on Jan. 30 and she passed away from breast cancer on Feb. 5.

At that point I really didn't know it would be her last game. She had been sick, but up until that point, it had been manageable. But then the cancer got into her nervous system. Initially, they misdiagnosed her as having cerebral palsy, and we didn't find out it was cancer until, like, the night before she passed, when she went to the hospital because she was so sick.

My mom was at all of the games she could be at, which was amazing for her at that point in time, but the three games she always wanted us to win the most were Oklahoma and Oklahoma State—since I'm from Oklahoma—and Kansas. So for her to see that win before she passed away my senior year meant a lot to me.

After the buzzer went off, everyone was rushing the floor. Mike and Jacob were standing up on the scorer's table, puffing their chests out. Instead I went straight over to my mom and gave her a hug and shared a "We did it!" kind of moment. Somehow, just like when we won in Lawrence, I'd ended up with the ball in my hands during the final seconds. I threw it up in the air as the horn went off, but then I was like, "Why did I do that? It's been 25 years!" Luckily I ended up getting it back. The whole team signed it and gave it to me.

Everyone was so excited so, of course, we went to Aggievile that night. Had I known that my mom didn't have much time left, just five or six days, I'd have never gone out and celebrated like that. I'd have spent that time with her. But she wouldn't have wanted it any other way. She always wanted me to do well and enjoy my life and not worry about her.

A Bitter Taste

Sasha Kaun: After that game, watching on ESPN as they jumped all over the scorers table and all that other crazy stuff they did ... it definitely left a bitter taste in our mouths. The next game we really wanted to kick their ass.

Mario Chalmers: Coach Self was mad because he knew we took that game for granted. We should've taken them more seriously. Our next practice was really hard. We went *hard*. They brought out two treadmills and put them on the sideline. Every time you turned it over or got boxed out for a rebound, you had to run.

Darnell Jackson: They embarrassed us. That was a bad feeling for me. I played so soft that game. Coach Self was throwing it in my face. He was like, "You're out there playing like a girl." Except he didn't use the word "girl." He used the other word. But he was right. I got so caught up into us trying to go undefeated in the Big 12. We weren't focusing on the game, and those guys just destroyed us down low.

Sherron Collins: The bus ride home that night was the worst bus ride of our lives. Normally they'll turn on the TVs and we'll watch an NBA game or another college game. But that night we watched the replay of the game we'd just lost.

Coach Self was sitting at the front of the bus, screaming the whole time. I'd miss a block out and he'd yell, "Look at Sherron! SOOOFFFTTT!" Darnell gets beat inside. "Look at that! SOOOFFFTTT!"

He was right. We were soft the entire game. Nobody rebounded. A lot of people blame our big guys for that loss, but it was on the guards, too. We had to help them. Just like when we're playing against a high-level guard, we need the bigs to help us when the guard gets by us. As a collective group, we just played soft that night. The whole ride Coach Self was chewing us out.

It was good for us too, because we knew we were going to beat the s**t out of them when they came to Lawrence.

Indeed, Kansas cruised to an 88-74 victory in the March 1 rematch at Allen Fieldhouse. The Jayhawks led by as many as 23 points early in the second half. Beasley had 39 points in a losing effort for K-State.

Russell Robinson: It was a quiet 39 points. We showed them, "That was your one day. You had it. Enjoy it." Purple used to be one of my favorite colors, but that changed when I came to Kansas. We took that rivalry real seriously from that point on.

Sherron Collins: The day before we beat them at home, somebody snuck into the Towers and threw hundreds of pictures of Mike Beasley and Bill Walker in front of all of our doors and in the halls. They knocked and then ran away. That really pissed us off. Right then, K-State was beat. The game was over.

Mario Chalmers: I got to know Beasley when we both played for the Miami Heat. To this day, we still talk about those games. He tries to brag, but then I say, "What happened when you came to Kansas?" He'll tell me he had 39, but then I laugh and say, "Yeah, but you were down by 23 at one point."

Regrouping at Henry T's

For years now, players-only meetings have been a popular way for struggling Jayhawks teams to hit the "restart" button before the most crucial time of the season. The trend began in February of 2008 after road setbacks against K-State, Texas and Oklahoma State. All of a sudden, a team that once looked unbeatable at 20-0 was now 22-3 and clearly in a funk.

Darnell Jackson: The idea to meet up at Henry T's came from Matt Kleinmann, who lived next door to me. I texted Jeremy about it, and then he sent out the big group text.

Matt Kleinmann: If I called for the Henry T's meeting, it was probably because I was hungry and it was close to my apartment. I used to live at Sixth and Kasold. I just wanted to go somewhere where I could get home quickly. Those motivational talks we had, we never did anything. We'd just sit down and say, "Hey, try harder."

"Now what are we going to eat?"

(Laughing) OK, maybe this one was a little different.

Darnell Jackson: Once everyone was there, it was Jeremy who started the conversation. He told everyone to put everything out on the table, their likes and dislikes.

Jeremy Case: We were in a little funk. There weren't any huge issues, but I remember Coach Self saying, "We're lost. Let's get it going again." And then he left it up to us.

I wouldn't say there was tension on the team. I don't think there was any jealousy at all. We just had some guys that might have been feeling themselves a little too much, some guys who were being selfish and worrying too much about themselves. Me being one of the oldest guys and being here the longest, I felt like I needed to say something.

I don't quite remember who I was pointing out, but I remember letting them know it was about the team—and not individuals. Russell agreed with me. Darnell definitely did. Mario and Sherron and all of those younger guys, they were good with us saying it, because they respected us and realized they needed to hear it.

Sasha Kaun: We all had a voice. At every team meeting, everyone spoke up about what was going right or wrong and what needed to be changed.

Darrell Arthur: We got along really well. There was no jealousy between one another. We played video games together. We went out to eat together. We loved Pepperjax and Buffalo Wild Wings and Henry T's. Our meeting there that night ... we just got some stuff off of our chests. I don't even remember what we talked about, honestly. Even in the NBA, we do that kind of stuff. We're struggling so we'll have a players-only meeting to hash things out. I think it really works.

Darnell Jackson: Most of the stuff we talked about was just little things. *DJ, I don't like when you try to take shortcuts in practice ... Go hard on a screen! Don't half-ass a screen! ... We need that energy and physicality! ... Mario, start throwing bounce passes to Russ earlier in transition instead of holding it for so long.*

There were so many little things we could do better that would make a huge difference in helping us win.

Tyrel Reed: In a way it felt like the world was caving in. We'd started 20-0 that year and it was almost like the wheels were falling off. Everyone likes to talk about the meeting we had, but I thought Coach Self did a really good job of getting us refocused during that time. He can be really negative while he's coaching you, but he's also good at bringing in some positives. He said, "We won 20 games to start the year. It's not like we're a bad team." We needed to hear that. We needed to hear that from him. We needed to know that we weren't that far off.

The meeting definitely helped, too, because it brought us all together for a reason, and that reason was to say, "Hey, what's going on here?" I remember Russ saying, "This is my last go. We've got to fix this." And then we did. Boom! That was the turning point of the year.

Mario Chalmers: Russ was one of the few people on the team that led both by example and also with his words. With most leaders, you get one or the other. But Russell did both. Since he did both, it was like, "OK, we're going to follow you." He was the head of the snake. If it wasn't for Russ we wouldn't have done nearly as much or been nearly as good. He did all the intangibles. If we needed a guy to pick someone up full court, Russ was doing it. If we needed someone to dive on the floor for a loose ball, Russ was doing it. Russ did everything we asked of him. He was everything you'd want in your point guard.

Russell Robinson: Coach Self did a good job of managing egos and keeping everyone focused. Even in the games we lost, we were never outmatched.

Jeremy Case: I guess you could say the meeting went well, because we got back to playing how we'd been playing. But it took those guys—Mario and Sherron and those young guys—saying, "He's right."

From that point on, we stayed really humble and took things one game at a time. We weren't like, "Hey, we can actually win the title." It wasn't like that at all. It was,

"Hey, let's keep moving and doing what we're doing."

Sasha Kaun: The three games we lost ... that was the best thing that could've happened to us. After those three games we really came together and changed some things. Our attitude and our composure just weren't there. We knew we were better than everyone talentwise. We just weren't there mentally.

In terms of X's and O's, you're not going to change much midway through the season. It was all about work ethic and how we approached every game.

I don't know if we'd have won the championship if we hadn't lost those three games. It was a good thing. It turned us around in the right direction and got everyone's mind right. We realized that if we wanted to be in the Final Four, we needed to do some things different.

Bill Self: I was really disappointed when we lost at Texas (72-69). We tried to run our "Chop" play at the end, but Mario didn't run it right. He did his own thing and we lost. Looking back, maybe we learned from that, which led to us running it the right way against Memphis. Maybe it was a blessing.

At Oklahoma State, we didn't play well at all. I remember coming back in terrible weather on the bus—there was an ice storm—and I remember saying, "We are awful. How are we going to turn this around?"

The reality was we were 22-3 and we were pretty good. Then it just took two or three games and we started playing better, and we peaked at the right time. In the Big 12 Tournament, we were great.

Kansas responded to its three losses by winning the final four games of the regular season, including a 109-51 win over Texas Tech on Senior Night.

Jeremy Case: One of the coolest moments for me that season was Senior Night. I hit three 3s against Texas Tech and had nine points. It was surreal. I was like, "Damn, I kind of forgot how fun it is to be out there," because that was the most minutes (12) I'd played in a long time. To be out there and hear the crowd and actually hit some shots … it was great.

Pat Knight: At halftime, the losing coach has to speak to the sideline reporter. That day it was Holly Rowe. It was a typical game against Kansas at Allen Fieldhouse. You can hang with them for the first 10-15 minutes and, all of a sudden, you look at the scoreboard and you're down 20-something. I'm walking off the court and Holly asks what I'm going to tell my team at halftime. I'm like, "What can I tell my team? This game is over. It's *ohhhhhh-verrrr.* We've got to get ready for the Baylor game on Monday." The look on her face was classic. I just walked away.

After the game the reporters asked me what the atmosphere was like, and I said it was like putting on a meat necklace and jumping into a lion's den. I experienced it as a player and as an assistant and as a head coach. You can't win there. Guys that are still coaching wouldn't admit that, because they have to be politically correct, but to be honest with you, when you look at that game on your schedule, you just want to get it over with. When you're an assistant, you have to keep the head coach positive, but chances are you're not going to win it. So in the back of your mind, you're already getting ready for that next game so you don't lose two in a row.

I don't care what anyone says, you see that game on the schedule you know you're not going to win. The night before, you show up and those students are camped out in their sleeping bags. You have to walk over them to get to the court. That makes an impression on guys who come from a place that's not really a basketball school, where there's not that student support.

If you have a *really* good team, maybe. If you can play them tight and get them to overtime, you may have a chance of getting lucky, but probably not.

They've got a great coach with great players and fans. It has to be one of the top five places to play of all time. It reminds me of Assembly Hall when I was growing up.

Kansas then defeated Nebraska, Texas A&M (who had hired former Jayhawk Mark Turgeon to replace Billy Gillispie) and No. 7 Texas to win the Big 12 Tournament in Kansas City for the third straight year. The Jayhawks hit a tournament-record 15 three-pointers in their 84-74 title-game victory over the Longhorns. Eight of them came from Chalmers, who scored 30 points and was named the tournament's Most Outstanding Player for the second time in three years.

Darnell Jackson: When we won the Big 12 Tournament, I was like, "There's no way we can lose. There's no way." Everyone felt like that. "There's no way we can lose. We're going to win it. We're going to take the whole thing."

Title Run

The Jayhawks won their first three NCAA Tournament games—against Portland State, UNLV and Villanova—by an average of 19.3 points. But a scary opponent awaited in No. 10-seed Davidson and postseason darling Steph Curry.

The Wildcats had advanced to the Elite Eight by defeating No. 7 Gonzaga, No. 2 Georgetown and No. 3 Wisconsin. Curry averaged 34.3 points in those victories while connecting on 19-of-36 shots from beyond the arc.

Curry scored 25 points against the Jayhawks but went just 9-of-25 from the field as Kansas eked out a 59-57 win to reach the Final Four for the first time under Self.

Bill Self: They had the ball on the final possession with a chance to win, but we played great defense on Curry and forced him to give up the ball, and their guy (Jason Richards) missed the last shot.

I think I was more relieved than happy. At that time we were 0-4 in Elite Eight games as a staff. I said back then that there wasn't a monkey on our back. It was a gorilla. I thought we were loose and everything, but during that first timeout, I said, "Russell, what's wrong?" And he said, "Coach, I can't breathe."

Those guys wanted it so bad. They put so much pressure on themselves to get there. Sasha won the game for us. He was the best player in the game for us. No question. He had 13 points, six rebounds and didn't miss a shot (from the field).

Sasha Kaun: I didn't sleep the night before the game. I thought about the year before, when we had lost to UCLA in the Elite Eight. It was a bad memory. The next day I was just looking and making sure everyone was focused during warmups. I wanted to make sure everyone was on the same page. I knew it wasn't going to be easy, especially playing the underdog. I know how that happens in the tournament. If you compared us guy-by-guy, there was no way they could beat us. But they were hot. That's all that really mattered. We won, but it wasn't easy.

Matt Kleinmann: The best thing Darnell ever did, and he may not realize this, it happened in the locker room right after we beat Davidson. We were in there celebrating—you know, the water bottle champagne spray—and in the middle of all of it, Darnell yells, "Hey! Everybody shut up! We didn't come here to win four games. We came here to win six. We've got to focus in."

And that mentality shut us all up. We literally took the next week as seriously as the first week of the season. Honestly, in previous years in the NCAA Tournament, a few guys may have thought, "Man, if I play well, I might go to the NBA next year." There wasn't any of that after we beat Davidson. It was more like, "Darnell is right. We've got one more week."

For the first time in history, all four No. 1 seeds—Kansas, North Carolina, UCLA and

Memphis—advanced to the Final Four. KU's semifinal matchup pitted the Jayhawks against North Carolina and former Kansas coach Roy Williams. While that storyline dominated the pregame headlines, an unfortunate incident the Friday before the game rattled the Jayhawks locker room.

Senior guard Rodrick Stewart, a USC transfer who had been with the team since the fall of 2005, fractured his kneecap while attempting a dunk during KU's open practice.

Joe Dooley: Coach had said, "No more dunking." But it was a freak deal and he went up and did it anyway. We didn't want our guys to see his knee because it was a horrific-looking deal. Losing Rod a day before the Final Four was really jarring for our players. They felt so bad for him.

Mario Chalmers: What really changed our mindset in San Antonio was when Rodrick Stewart got hurt. We were just messing around, dunking. I was going to be the next guy to dunk after Rod. When he hurt his knee, I was like, "Oh no!" Rod was a senior. I started thinking about all of the things he'd been through. His cousin was shot, his little brother got shot. Then you throw in all the stuff that happened with D-Block's family and stuff that happened off the court with guys like me and B-Rush and Russell and Sherron's son dying. We were like, "We've all had problems. We might as well put those problems aside, win these six games and deal with these problems afterward when we're the champs."

When that happened with Rod, he was crying, and we were helping him back to the hotel with his kneecap broke. We were like, "This is a sign. Rod, we're going to win this for you." I can remember talking to him right after he got hurt. I went to his hotel room and he was lying there in bed with ice on his knee. I was like, "Rod, we're going to win this tournament for you. Mark my words. We're going to win it for you." He was crushed. He was really starting to play a lot. He was our eighth man behind Sherron and Sasha.

Rodrick Stewart: Some people ask if I have regrets about trying to dunk in practice the day before the game, but I don't. It was a freak accident. It could've happened in the North Carolina game or in the Memphis game. Throughout the whole NCAA Tournament, I had never dunked during warmups. I always just let the freshmen go. But in San Antonio—the day before we played North Carolina—I heard someone say, "All the reserves … go ahead and dunk." I thought, "Why not? It's the Final Four."

People don't understand what it's like to break your knee at the Final Four of your senior year. I had been preparing myself for that moment from the sixth grade on. Two-a-days, three-a-days, when I played football just so I could get stronger for basketball … that was all done so I could get to the Final Four someday. When you work your whole life for that moment, and then you achieve it and it gets taken away from you, it's devastating.

If I had to do it all over again—if we went back in time and I had to break my knee again for us to win it all—I'd break it again. If it would give us that extra fire, that extra energy, with players looking over at me on the bench the way that they did during the

Final Four, then I would do it again in a heartbeat. It's all about sacrifice. Maybe it did take me breaking my knee for us to really focus and say, "Whatever it takes, no matter what happens, we're going to win this for him."

The following day, Kansas played one of its best games of the season. The Jayhawks made 12 of their first 16 shots and raced out to a 40-12 lead. The Tar Heels entered the game boasting the nation's second-leading offense, but UNC shot just 35 percent against Kansas.

One of the biggest surprises was the performance of seldom-used freshman center Cole Aldrich, who had eight points, seven rebounds and four blocks while frustrating All-American Tar Heels forward Tyler Hansbrough.

Perhaps it was fitting that Aldrich played such a big role. Moments before tipoff, his father, Walt, had been the subject of a wisecrack by Self in the KU huddle.

Jeremy Case: Coach Self was just trying to relax us a little bit. Cole's dad was in the stands wearing his No. 45 jersey with no shirt on underneath. I don't know if you've ever seen Cole's dad, but he's kind of a goofy, sloppy-looking dude.

We were about to break the huddle right before the start of the game, and we were all tense, and Coach just says, "Everyone look at Cole's freakin' dad!" And then everyone looked into the stands and started laughing. It definitely lightened the mood.

Tyrel Reed: Cole was my roommate, and early on that year he was terrible. He didn't look like the McDonald's All-American they had recruited. The game was too fast for him. He was a little out of shape and overweight.

Coach Self was on Cole a lot because I think he saw the potential Cole had. Once he got things turned around, he was *really* on him—probably more—because he knew he was going to be a really good player.

What's great about Cole is that he cares, but at the same time, he's able to not care. Things just roll off his back. *"Yeah, they're yelling at me. Whatever. I'm going to go back to the room and eat and I'll come back to practice later."* He took it in, but he didn't let it eat at him. He was really good at taking criticism and moving on.

Once it got to be Christmastime, something clicked. He understood that he wasn't going to be "the guy" that year, so he just put his head down and learned and really took in what the coaches said. He just flipped a switch. Obviously he had some good games in the tournament, and that just spurred him to have a really great career.

Kansas 84, North Carolina 66
April 5, 2008 · San Antonio, Texas

Kansas (36-3)

Player	MP	FG	3FG	FT	R	A	F	S	TO	B	TP
Darrell Arthur*	32	3-9	0-0	0-0	9	2	2	0	3	4	6
Darnell Jackson*	17	5-6	0-0	2-2	4	2	3	2	0	0	12
Russell Robinson*	30	2-5	1-4	2-2	4	4	2	3	1	0	7
Mario Chalmers*	31	5-10	1-3	0-2	4	3	3	3	2	0	11
Brandon Rush*	32	11-17	2-7	1-2	7	2	2	0	3	1	25
Sherron Collins	30	4-9	1-1	2-2	4	4	4	1	7	0	11
Jeremy Case	1	0-0	0-0	0-0	0	0	1	0	0	0	0
Sasha Kaun	10	2-4	0-0	0-0	0	0	3	0	1	0	4
Cole Aldrich	17	2-4	0-0	4-4	7	0	1	1	2	4	8
Team					3						
Totals	200	34-64	5-15	11-14	42	17	21	10	19	9	84

North Carolina (36-3)

Player	MP	FG	3FG	FT	R	A	F	S	TO	B	TP
Deon Thompson*	25	2-4	0-0	3-4	4	0	2	0	1	0	7
Tyler Hansbrough*	36	6-13	0-1	5-6	9	1	3	2	3	0	17
Marcus Ginyard*	32	0-3	0-2	0-0	3	2	1	0	1	0	0
Ty Lawson*	28	2-8	1-2	4-4	3	2	1	0	2	0	9
Wayne Ellington*	33	8-21	1-9	1-1	6	0	3	3	3	1	18
Quentin Thomas	14	0-2	0-0	0-0	1	2	1	1	1	0	0
Danny Green	21	6-13	3-9	0-0	5	0	3	1	5	1	15
Alex Stepheson	7	0-1	0-0	0-0	0	0	0	0	1	1	0
Mike Copeland	1	0-0	0-0	0-0	0	0	0	0	0	0	0
Will Graves	3	0-2	0-1	0-0	1	0	0	0	1	0	0
Team					1						
Totals	200	24-67	5-24	13-15	33	7	14	7	18	3	66

	1st	2nd	Total	FG%	3FG%	FT%
Kansas	44	40	84	53.1	33.3	78.6
North Carolina	27	39	66	35.8	20.8	86.7

Officials: Tony Greene, Mike Eades, Verne Harris
Technicals: None

Darrell Arthur: When Cole first got to Kansas, it took him a while, just like it takes lots of people a while to get adjusted. Cole loved to talk trash, and the first pickup game we played with Cole, I dunked on him the first three possessions. And I mean I dunked it hard. After a while, he stopped taking that s**t. He started coming into his own. He started blocking shots. He started getting physical. His work paid off against North Carolina.

I think all of the other big guys took a little bit of pride in the way he played that night, because we felt like we helped prepare him for that. He played better than I thought he was going to play. He blocked some shots and made a couple of key baskets and got in Tyler Hansbrough's head a little bit. He was a game-changer for us, because we ended up blowing their ass out.

Cole Aldrich: I watched a bunch of extra film on Hansbrough and thought, "If I get into the game, I know what he'll struggle against. I know what's going to bother him." You've got to be physical with him. You've got to play long because he struggles to shoot over length. You've got to get him out of his comfort zone and keep him off the boards.

It didn't take long during the game to tell that he was frustrated. You could see it on his face. We rushed him with four big guys. It was only natural that he got tired.

Bill Self: I've never had a team play better for 12 minutes. That's as good as a team can play. Our guys were motivated. We didn't talk about, "We're playing Roy." We never said that. But North Carolina was the No. 1 overall seed. Our guys knew Tyler Hansbrough, Ty Lawson, Wayne Ellington, Danny Green and all those guys. In their minds, it was probably like, "We're on the big stage now. Now we get a chance to show everybody how good we are."

And then for Cole, that was his coming out party. Cole was so good.

Cole hadn't played much that season because he was our fourth big and he wasn't as good as the other three yet. We knew he'd be good, but we had no idea he'd turn out to be a lottery pick at that time. That one game gave him so much confidence.

North Carolina shaved KU's 28-point lead to five late in the second half, but Collins dished out two assists, swished a 3-pointer and made a pair of free throws in a 10-0 run that gave KU a 15-point lead and momentum it would never relinquish. Rush scored a game-high 25 points in the 84-66 win.

Forty-eight hours later, the Jayhawks took the court in San Antonio seeking their first national championship since 1988. Standing in their way were Derrick Rose and the Memphis Tigers, who were coached by John Calipari.

Rock, Chalk, Championship

Sherron Collins: The game started late on Monday night, so we had to wait all day long. We got up and ate breakfast. We couldn't read the papers because Coach Self had told the hotel people not to deliver any papers to our room. He wanted us to keep the TVs off. But of course, it's hard not to watch ESPN the day of the big game. You want to hear what everyone is saying. So everybody watched it. Later, when we were in the locker room getting ready, everyone had something to say about what we'd heard on TV. People were like, "Did you hear what they said about us losing?" A lot of analysts picked Memphis. We were pretty pissed.

Mario Chalmers: There was almost a fight before the national championship game. Memphis' players were in the tunnel, waiting to be summoned on the court, and we walked up doing our little chant. They were like, "Shut the f**k up, you gay-ass Jayhawks." Then one of the arena guys asked Memphis' players, "Are y'all ready to go on the court?" One of their bigs, Pierre Niles, was like, "Hell no! Let those bitches go first." I was the first one to say something back. Some people started shoving, but it ended pretty quickly.

Sherron Collins: When we were in the layup line warming up, people were talking s**t across the court. Big Joey Dorsey and Sasha were going back and forth. Of course, I never could understand half of what Sasha was saying, but you could sure hear him.

I don't know if it would've been smart for Dorsey or anyone to go after Sasha. He's a strong dude. I wouldn't want to go at the big fella like that.

Kansas got 10 first-half points from Arthur and led 33-28 at intermission. The most impressive performance at that point was Collins' defensive effort on Rose, who three months later would become the No. 1 pick in the NBA draft. In a matchup of fellow Chicagoans, Collins got the best of Rose by limiting him to three points and only three shot attempts in the opening half.

Sherron Collins: Coach Self had been messing with me all week. He'd say, "Memphis has that good point guard who is 6-foot-3. I don't know who to put on him. Russell might be too slow. I don't know who is going to guard him." He kept saying that in front a group of people, but he made sure I was always nearby. I finally exploded and said, "F**k that! I'm guarding him. You can stop saying all that because I'm going to guard him. He's from Chicago, and I've been guarding him all my life. I'll guard him." He looked at me with a little grin. I think he liked that. I guarded Rose pretty well until we went to that 2-3 zone in the second half. He didn't get off on us until we changed what we were doing defensively.

Referee Ed Hightower: One of the most fascinating aspects of Kansas-Memphis was the athleticism of the players from each team. A lot of the kids in that game ... they didn't just have a chance to play at the next level; they *were* going to play at the next level.

It was a game where the athletes were the stars. Not the coaches. Not the officials, but the athletes out there on the court. They were the ones that made the plays and decided the game.

As quiet as he'd been in the first half, Rose caught fire after Kansas switched to a 2-3 zone after intermission. Included in Rose's 15 second-half points was a fall-away 18-footer that officials initially ruled a 3-pointer before a video review showed that it was only a two. Still, that shot gave Memphis a 56-49 lead with 4:06 remaining. And the margin swelled to 60-51 after a pair of Robert Dozier free throws with 2:12 left in regulation.

Brandon Rush: The mood was down—or at least I know I was down. We were losing by nine with two minutes left. I thought we were going to take an L. We'd worked so hard and now we were going to come up short.

Darrell Arthur: One thing I remember was looking across the court into the stands. My little brother, Juicy, was crying. He was only six, and later my mom told me he was saying, "We're not going to win it, are we momma? We're not going to win it, are we?" That was with about two minutes left in the game, and I'm sure a lot of people were probably thinking the same thing.

Russell Robinson: When Derrick Rose hit that 18-footer off the backboard, I thought that might be the dagger. But Coach Self never allowed us to get down. I didn't always listen to what he said in the huddle, but I always paid attention to how he was saying it. That night he never panicked. He was real confident that we were going to make plays and that it was going to work out. He was calm, and that poise spread throughout the whole team.

Kansas refused to fold. An 18-foot jumper by Arthur shaved the Memphis lead to seven, 60-53. Then, after a KU timeout, Collins stole Memphis' inbounds pass and, as he was falling out of bounds, fired it to Chalmers. Chalmers tried to drive and then dumped it on the block to Robinson, who passed the ball back to Collins in the right corner. Collins swished a clutch 3-pointer that made it 60-56.

Sherron Collins: I knew the 3 was good. If you listen to the tape closely enough, you can hear me yell, "Boom!" after the ball leaves my hands. Right after I hit the shot, I ran into B-Rush's shoulder as I was running down the court. My jaw felt like it locked. I fell to the ground right as Memphis was calling a timeout. My jaw was stuck. I had to work it back into place. I was too excited to feel much pain, though. After I hit that 3, I knew we could win.

Equally important was a turnaround jumper on the baseline from Arthur that made it a one-possession game, 62-60, with 1:00 remaining.

Bill Self: Shady was the best player in the game that night. Mario was clutch, but Shady had 20 and 10. And he made two shots—the 17-footer when we were down nine, and then the baseline turnaround—that were as difficult and pressure-packed as any. He was so good that game. I don't know that people remember Shady for being as good as he was. He was terrific.

Darrell Arthur: Luckily, I had the best games of my career at just the right time.

Memphis had plenty of chances to win the game in the final minute, but the Tigers' poor free-throw shooting continued to give Kansas hope. Chris Douglas-Roberts failed to extend his team's 62-60 lead by missing two free throws with 16 seconds remaining. Memphis' Dozier snagged the offensive rebound on the second miss and passed it to Rose, who was fouled with 10 seconds left.

Rose missed the first free throw, but made the second. Trailing 63-60, Kansas' only hope was to make a 3-pointer and force overtime.

Mario Chalmers: In the huddle, Coach Self had asked everyone, "Who do you want the ball to go to?" And everyone was like, "Mario!" Maybe the guys didn't actually say my name verbally—at least not all of them—but when he asked that question, all of their heads just swiveled and turned right toward me. I said, "Wow! If y'all believe in me like that, I'm not going to let you down. I'm going to make the shot. This ain't nothin'."

Bill Self: We called "Chop," but we didn't run it the same way we had in the past—we didn't set a ball screen—because we knew they'd switch.

Sherron Collins: Once D-Rose missed that first free throw with 10 seconds left, we all lit up. We knew there was still a chance. Darnell threw me the ball inbounds, and I paused for a second so I could hear what John Calipari was yelling at Rose. He was on the sideline screaming, "Foul him! Foul him! Foul him!" At that point, I made a crossover move to get D-Rose leaning the wrong way so I could get by him.

The play was initially set up for me to come down the sideline, but instead I went to the middle and then toward the sideline. That's what made the play so hard. D-Rose was on the right side of me, just riding me and riding me and riding me. Then somehow he got behind me, and I lost the ball. I tried to put the ball in front of me so he wouldn't tap it, but I put it too far in front of me so I had to dive to toss it back.

Kansas 75, Memphis 68
April 7, 2008 · San Antonio, Texas

Kansas (37-3)

Player	MP	FG	3FG	FT	R	A	F	S	TO	B	TP
Darrell Arthur*	35	9-13	0-0	2-2	10	1	3	1	3	0	20
Darnell Jackson*	29	3-4	0-0	2-2	8	1	1	1	0	0	8
Russell Robinson*	20	1-1	0-0	0-0	4	1	3	1	3	0	2
Mario Chalmers*	40	5-13	2-6	6-6	3	3	3	4	3	0	18
Brandon Rush*	42	5-9	0-2	2-3	6	2	3	1	3	1	12
Sherron Collins	34	4-10	1-4	2-2	4	6	3	3	4	0	11
Sasha Kaun	21	2-5	0-0	0-0	2	0	2	0	1	0	4
Cole Aldrich	4	0-0	0-0	0-0	0	0	0	0	0	0	0
Team					2						
Totals	225	29-55	3-12	14-15	39	14	18	11	17	1	75

Memphis (38-2)

Player	MP	FG	3FG	FT	R	A	F	S	TO	B	TP
Robert Dozier*	39	4-11	1-2	2-3	10	3	2	1	1	1	11
Joey Dorsey*	26	3-3	0-0	0-0	2	1	5	1	1	2	6
Antonio Anderson*	42	3-9	2-7	1-3	5	1	3	4	2	0	9
Chris Douglas-Roberts*	42	7-16	2-5	6-9	1	1	4	1	2	0	22
Derrick Rose*	45	7-17	1-6	3-4	6	8	1	2	5	0	18
Shawn Taggart	24	1-5	0-1	0-0	3	0	2	1	1	0	2
Willie Kemp	4	0-0	0-0	0-0	0	0	0	1	1	0	0
Pierre Henderson	1	0-0	0-0	0-0	0	0	0	0	0	0	0
Doneal Mack	2	0-1	0-1	0-0	0	0	0	0	0	0	0
Team					1						
Totals	225	25-62	6-22	12-19	28	14	17	11	13	3	68

	1st	2nd	OT	Total	FG%	3FG%	FT%
Kansas	33	30	12	75	52.7	25.0	93.3
Memphis	28	35	5	68	40.3	27.3	63.2

Officials: Ed Corbett, Ed Hightower, Don Cahill
Technicals: None

Mario Chalmers: I just told Sherron to get it to me anyway he could. We ran that play all the time at the end of games. Sherron was supposed to be more toward the sideline, but he cut to the middle to get past D-Rose. When he stumbled, I got worried. I was just thinking, "Sherron, just get me the ball, and I'll make the shot."

Sherron Collins: I didn't know where D-Rose was at. I saw Mario's blue shirt over my right shoulder. I just flung it toward his shirt. I was so sweaty that, as soon as I hit the floor, I slid five or six feet across the court and didn't even see Mario take the shot. I just heard the crowd scream, so I knew it went in.

Mario Chalmers: Somehow he tapped the ball to me and I got it in my sweet spot. I had perfect form on the shot. It felt good from the time the pass hit me in the hands. I could've turned around and thrown the ball between my legs and it would've gone in. That's how confident I was feeling in that moment. It's a great feeling to have. So, no, I wasn't surprised when it went in. I had known the whole time that I was going to make it.

Sherron Collins: On the way to the bench, I passed by Chris Douglas-Roberts, or maybe it was Dozier ... one of them said something, and I was like, "It's over now. You'll never win."

Fueled with a newfound momentum and energy after Chalmers' shot, Kansas scored the first six points of overtime and went on to win 75-68. The game will long be remembered as one of the greatest championship bouts in NCAA Tournament history. Douglas-Roberts had a game-high 22 points and Rose added 18 for Memphis, which shot just 40.3 percent while going 12-of-19 (63.2 percent) from the foul stripe.

Ed Hightower: One thing that's unfortunate is that so many people talked about the free throws that Memphis missed. People say Memphis "lost" the game. That's unfair. It's a disservice to one of the greatest championship games ever.

Just look at the game in its totality: There was so much athleticism, so many great plays, so many great stops, so many exciting moments. There were so many opportunities for the game to be won and lost. That's how it should be when two great teams play each other. You were on pins and needles the whole time. There were so many great moments. That's how the game should be remembered instead of talking about how Memphis missed free throws.

Darrell Arthur: One of the things I'll remember the most about the NCAA title game is that my dad was in the stands, watching me play. It was the first time he had ever been to one of my college games. My dad wasn't really around when I was growing up. He got into drugs when I was about 6 or 7 and moved to Houston. I hardly saw him after that. When he showed up at the national championship game, it was the first time I had seen him in more than two years. Since then, he's been making an effort to do better. I loved playing in front of my dad that night. Around Dallas, he was a pretty big name when he was younger. I remember he had all these trophies and medals and things. When I was growing up, people would say, "Your dad used to be the man around here." His nickname was "Grasshopper" because he could jump so high. That's why I started playing basketball, to impress him. His name is Anthony Arthur. He played at South Oak Cliff, just like me. Before he moved to Houston, I used to go to his mom's house, my grandmother's house, and I'd see all his trophies. I'd be like, "Man, daddy, you won all these trophies and things?" He'd be like, "Yeah, those are mine." I remember pointing to one of them and saying, "I want to win me a big one, just like that." Well, that night in San Antonio, I won the biggest one there is to win, and he was there to see it.

Arthur's gaudy stat line earned him a spot on the All-Tournament team. Rush—largely because of his 25-point effort against UNC—was on the squad, as well, along with Chalmers, who was the easy choice for Most Outstanding Player.

Brandon Rush: Mario is definitely confident, even to this day. He has a tattoo on his arm that says, "Mr. Clutch."

Mario Chalmers: My favorite picture from that night is the one of me hugging my mom. The two of us had talked about that ever since I was little—me hitting the big shot to win the national championship. For that moment to actually come true, I was like, "Mom, all the work that we put in when I was younger, all that stuff you used to tell me, all those times you worked me out, it finally paid off." My mom used to rebound for me and motivate me when I was younger. She was a schoolteacher at Romig Middle School in Anchorage. She had to be there early in the morning, so I'd go with her and work out in the gym, take a shower and go to class. After school, while she was still there for parent-teacher meetings, I'd go back in the gym and shoot some more. When she was finished with her responsibilities, she'd come in there and help me. It'd just be me and my mom working out. She used to always tell me, "The game is on the line, 3-2-1 shoot it! 3-2-1 shoot it!" All that hard work, all the late nights and early mornings in the gym, it all paid off.

More on Mario

Texas guard A.J. Abrams: There was no moment too big for Mario Chalmers. You saw that in the national championship game. He was always level-headed. You could just see how much he loved the game from the way he played. As a competitor, that rubs off on you.

During that 2006 season when we beat them in Austin, I was at the free throw line to ice the game, and he comes up to me and says, "Hey A.J., miss these two free throws so I can come down and hit a 3." I was like, "Bro, I'm not doing that."

K-State guard Clent Stewart: There was something different about Mario. During that game my senior year when we beat them at home, there's a time when he gets the ball—the ball gets tipped out to him on the wing—and he drives toward the lane. We had big guys down there, but he rises up and dunks on everyone and screams "AAAHHHH!!!!" No one jumped with him. At that point we realized, "He's not scared. He's bringing it." No stage is too big for him, and you saw that in the national championship game.

A little more from ...

Brady Morningstar: One thing people need to remember about the title game is the role Shady and Sherron played down the stretch. Shady had a double-double, 20 and 10. And his shots were big-time shots. *Biiggg*-time shots considering how difficult they were, and even more so, the pressure surrounding them. And Sherron had those key plays at the end—the steal on the inbounds pass followed the 3 from the corner, and also the crazy pass to Mario for the historic shot. When people go back and relive that game, no one talks about those plays, which is crazy. Those guys don't care, though. We all know who came through.

Andrea Hudy: Sherron was in the best shape of his career at the Final Four. He weighed in at 199.6 before we left for San Antonio. It was a huge milestone for him.

Jeremy Case: Sherron worked really, really hard to keep his weight down that whole season. I think all of us felt for him a little bit, because we could see it was a constant struggle.

One example—and this is kind of funny, but it also shows what he was going through—happened during the first week of the NCAA Tournament when we were in Omaha. Someone always sets up a 24-hour snack table at our team hotel, and one night I got up around midnight or 1 to make a peanut butter and jelly sandwich. I figured everyone else was asleep. Instead I find Sherron leaving the snack area with a plate just *stacked* with food. Two bagels, a PB&J sandwich, chips, fruit. This was the night before a game. I was like, "Man, what are you doing?" Sherron was whispering. "Case, man ... please don't tell on me. They're starving me, man. They're starving me." I said, "Well, you definitely don't need both of these bagels, and you definitely don't need these chips." So I pulled that stuff off his plate and he went back to his room all mad.

Sherron just liked to eat. And he was probably telling the truth. They probably *were* starving him.

Russell Robinson: At Kansas you get in the habit of winning and being in control. You come to realize that, "Hey, we're representing more than ourselves out here. We're representing our university and our students and we're going to do it with class."

The stress level is there every game. It's not about the other team; it's about us. We could be 12-0 or 14-1, but when you read the papers or listen to the coaches, it's not good enough. *They beat Vermont, but it was close. They only won by seven.* Or, *they're only shooting 34 percent from 3-point range.* If you keep winning, that stuff fades away. But if you lose, it intensifies.

It's sad that it's like that. They just had an incredible year (in 2017), but that loss to Oregon is all people will talk about. If they'd have won that game and gotten to the Final Four, people would remember it as one of the best seasons in history. But one loss can change all of that. Winning that championship in 2008 completely erased anything negative that happened my previous three years there. And for the few people that remember the negative stuff, the championship still supersedes everything.

When we'd beat the K-States and the Missouris on the road, we were always in a rush to get back and party, because we knew how much it meant to the student body. We knew they'd watched the game.

To be able to come back and share that excitement with them ... everyone would be at The Hawk or Brothers. They wanted to take pictures and say thanks and offer congratulations—whether they were drunk or not. It's a positive vibe that you get, a genuine sense of school pride that helps your confidence moving forward into tougher games. It does something to you.

At the same time, when you're losing, fans can be tough. I remember going to Abe and Jake's my freshman year with Keith Langford and those guys didn't get the same kind of love that we got as seniors. They'd lost to Syracuse in the national title game two years earlier, and there was still some people who were upset, still some heckling. It's never what they're saying. It's how they're saying it. Because honestly, a lot of what they're saying might be true. Maybe Keith could've played a little better defense on Carmelo or Gerry McNamara. Those are probably facts. But the fact that people were still bringing it up was sad.

Mario Chalmers: I'm so proud of D-Block. If you look at D-Block, he's one of those people who, if he gave up, you'd understand why. If he gave up on sports and said, I don't want to do this anymore, you'd understand because of all his struggles. So to see him still fighting, to see him with the same smile, to see him out there working hard to support his family, to see him doing something positive and still playing basketball after all the stuff he went through, that's an incredible story.

D-Block is blessed. I told him the other day, "D-Block, you're blessed, man. You're an inspiration to a lot of people." Hell, he's an inspiration to me. He makes me want to keep going. I've got every reason to stop playing. I've made good money. I've got two rings. But I don't want to be done playing, and I feel like I've got a group of close friends who look up to me and live through me, so I want to keep going for them. D-Block is one of those guys.

Shady and I were roommates and we were very close. He was a freak athlete. He was the best offensive big I played with at Kansas, and he's one of the fastest, most athletic guys I've ever seen. That's something we needed at KU. We had JuJu, who was more of a play-making big. He could score, but he liked to pass and do everything else. We needed someone that could sit down in the post and give us everything we needed, and that was Shady.

To see him keep going after everything he's been through, tearing his Achilles and going through meniscus surgery … it's great to see him still out there.

Coach Self is a great coach. He always finds a diamond in the rough. He always has a backup plan. Our 2008 team … if I'd have gone down, or Brandon or Sherron had gone down, he'd have found a way to make Rodrick Stewart a star. That's the great thing about Coach Self. He knows how to get the most out of his players. There aren't many coaches like that. He showed what a good coach he was by abandoning his philosophy and letting us be more guard-dominated. That changed the program. The high-low worked with Wayne Simien. But Darnell and Sasha and C.J. weren't Wayne Simien. They were different types of players. They couldn't dominate offensively like that. But we had all of these scoring guards, these go-getters. Coach Self trusted us and we made sure he looked good for doing it.

I keep all of my rings in a box that says "Champions."

Darrell Arthur: The fans at KU are the best. I talked to (former Kentucky guard) Jamal Murray, my teammate in Denver, and he said the best place he played, by far, was Kansas. He said he and one of his teammates were supposed to switch on a pick-and-roll but they couldn't even hear each other, and Frank (Mason) ended up hitting a big 3.

Sasha Kaun: Danny Manning was the main reason I developed into the player I became. Danny was a special player. His knowledge of the game was so crazy. If you look at his body, he shouldn't have played in the league as many years as he did with everything he had going on knee-wise and injury-wise. The fact that he stuck around as many years as he did says a lot about his knowledge of the game. It tells you he knew how to play smart. That's something that definitely stood out to me.

He was very quiet and calm and very organized. Most everything he taught us, he showed us himself on the court. We'd come out and do workouts and he'd just explain stuff and show us firsthand.

One thing Coach Self is good at is getting us to play tough. It's not something most people are used to when they get to Kansas. They think they're tough, but they're not. Loose-ball drills are the worst. Coach Self would stand in the middle of the court and roll the ball across the floor. We'd have to sprint to it and dive on it. We'd do it for 10-15 minutes. There were definitely some bruises after those practices. People just hated it. After a few years it got into your head: "Hey, dive for loose balls!" If we had a bad game where we didn't dive for loose balls, we knew we're going to have a loose-ball drill at the next practice. Coach Self 's Boot Camp is harder on you mentally than physically, just because you know you have to go through it. You've got to run a lot, but you can do it.

What's tough is going to class afterward and also being expected to show up in time for tutoring and stuff. You have a lot of responsibilities for two weeks.

Assistant coach Danny Manning: In my mind, the thing that defined the championship team is how those guys relished killing the spirit of their opponent. That was the thing I was most impressed by. If something happened on the court, they tried to rally around it and take the other team's spirit. As a staff, we were all very proud of that. Our guys weren't going to be a part of anything dirty or go into any sort of retaliation mode. They were just going to create more space or distance with the score. They were going to play good basketball and let the score do the talking. That's something Coach Self stressed and continues to stress. When something goes awry on the court, you come together and your focus becomes laser sharp.

The other thing was, every game that season, it seemed like someone different stepped up to be the catalyst, the hero. It wasn't always on the offensive end. Sometimes it was, "Hey, tonight, I'm going to challenge myself the most on the defensive end and try to slow this guy down." With our guards, it might have been, "I'm going to try to make plays and get into the paint and get my teammates good shots." Everybody would chip in in some way to help the team succeed. They all had such good relationships with one another. Everyone wanted to see their teammates do well.

I loved working with Sasha and Darnell. Sasha had a businesslike mindset. A lot of that was because he was an international kid who had been in the states and away from his family for quite a while. He had to grow up fast. Darnell, like most kids in the states ... he had to develop and mature.

There are certain guys who have it a little bit tougher on their journey. Darnell was someone who definitely hit some rough, tough patches. He continued to persevere and fight. It wasn't easy for him, but he got through it. The amount of pride he should feel in what he helped the team accomplish in the midst of what he was going through, and how he developed as a young man ... it's something that was extremely impressive.

Shady's talent was undeniable. He was able to do some things out there that a lot of guys his size couldn't do, with the explosion he had and the quickness that he had. His stat line during that run was impressive. It gets lost in the shuffle. He put in a lot of work to help us win that trophy. He was the best player in the game that night.

Brandon Rush: Throughout my whole career, people were always critical of me because I didn't shoot more. They said I wasn't aggressive enough, that I was too passive. Coach Self was on me about it, the fans, the media ... it got annoying. Why should I have shot more? We were a great team. We went 37-3 and won the national championship. I didn't need to take any more shots. I always had good players around me. Everyone was happy. If I'd have started taking 20 shots a game it would've messed up our chemistry. Who knows what would've happened then.

Everyone was doing anything they could to get me to shoot more. Midway through my junior year, a dude that I've known for a long time—a family friend—started paying me for every basket I made. I'd get a little bit for a layup, a little more for a 3-pointer and a little more for a dunk. It wasn't very much money at all. I think he just wanted to give me incentive to be more aggressive so the scouts could see what I could do, because obviously I wanted to be drafted high. I don't know if I played any differently because of it, but the guy that was paying me ... he cared about me. He was just trying to help. Even today in the NBA, people say I don't shoot it enough. But I think I've done pretty well for myself.

The chemistry we had in 2008 was amazing. We had a great team. We got a little lucky with Mario hitting that shot, but we deserved to win. I think we were the best team.

Baylor coach Scott Drew: They had so many different weapons in 2008. It seemed like it didn't matter to them who stepped up and had a great game. Some teams, if the star player doesn't get his, he's not happy. With that team, there were so many people you had to stop. It seemed like no matter what holes in the dam you plugged, there were always other leaks. There were so many weapons and all of them always put the team first.

I was cheering for them throughout the entire Memphis game. I always root for conference schools to do well. Those last few minutes were tough when it looked like they were going to lose. When it's a team in your conference, you've seen them play at their best and you've seen them play at their worst. It doesn't take long to know where they're at. When they're not playing a great game and you know what they're capable of, you're like, "Dang, c'mon. Let's go!"

On that final play of regulation when Mario Chalmers hit the shot, you knew what was coming as a coach. You knew they were going to run "Chop." Still, it's one thing to know it, and it's another thing to stop it. Kansas was very hard to stop.

Clent Stewart: When we beat Kansas, we didn't know that they'd be the ones to end up winning the national championship. I joke with people all the time that they lost three games that year, so that national championship is really one-fourth K-State's. KU gets 25 percent of it and then the other three teams that beat them get 25 percent.

When we beat them at home and we were No. 1 in the Big 12, obviously we were on cloud nine and kind of felt like this could be our year. We got knocked back down the next game against Missouri. They had three of their starters suspended for something—Jason Horton and a couple other guys—and they end up beating us at their place. That was kind of that letdown after being on that high of KU.

Then we went to their place a month later and lost by 30 (actual score: 88-74). That's when we realized things were slipping away a little bit from us. That's why they're great year in and year out; they're consistent. They might have a couple bad games here and there, but through the main part of conference play, they're pretty consistent and find ways to pull out ballgames.

For us, we went on a little slide late, and anytime you go on a slide late in the season, you get a little nervous because you worry about making the NCAA Tournament. Are they going to look at these last four games? Or are they going to remember that we beat KU back when they were No. 2 and we were No. 24? We knew beating them was helpful to our resume and getting into the NCAA Tournament.

Jacob Pullen: Walking into their Fieldhouse that year, that was my first time there. I didn't know that the damn gym was that small, because on TV it looks like a huge college arena. But it's almost like a high school gym because the crowd is right next to the court, so when it gets loud in there, it *really* gets loud.

We went down 15-2, and I remember Frank calling a timeout and saying, "You guys don't understand what we're running. You guys can't run offense." And I looked over to one of the assistant coaches and said, "I can't even hear what the person guarding me is saying, so there's no way my teammates on the court can hear what I'm saying if I'm calling plays."

It was amazing. I hadn't played in a gym that loud and in that type of atmosphere in my college career yet. It was a different experience.

Frank Martin: The MVPs of that team were Bill Self and his staff. They had really good players, a bunch of NBA draft picks. But he got them to play like they were a bunch of undrafted guys. That's how hard and how together and how well they played. I think Bill was the MVP of that team. The job he did of getting those guys to play so unselfishly on offense and defense made them so hard to defend and so hard to beat.

To this day, very few people talk about the fact that we went to the NCAA Tournament with nine freshmen. As a No. 11 seed, we beat Southern Cal and were pretty close to going to the Sweet 16. Very few people talk about that when they speak about that year. They talk about Michael Beasley's great year, and they talk about beating KU. That's how powerful that moment was.

We didn't understand the hatred that Kansas State had for Kansas until we got on campus. Then everyone started saying, "Hey, you guys have to beat KU." It wasn't, "Are you guys going to win the Big 12? Are you guys gonna make the NCAA Tournament?" Instead it was, "Do you think you'll be able to beat KU?"

It's not a rivalry that's known country-wide because it's been so one-sided. But internally, within a state, it's as intense as anything I've ever been a part of.

As far as people caring, they cared as much at K-State as they cared at KU. Kansas just had better players. There's no other way to word it. When Lon Kruger had Mitch Richmond, they beat Kansas twice that year. So it's not like they'd never had success. But for a long time KU recruited at a higher level. Kansas State didn't have enough good players to match KU.

As soon as Huggs and I got there, that was our No. 1 goal. We said, "We've got to shrink this gap and address the talent deficiency." And we also had to create the mindset where we were like, "They're good. We understand that. But we're going to figure out a way to beat them." That was the whole thought process we had when we were hired.

BEST KU NCAA Tournament Wins

1. Kansas 75, Memphis 68, OT (2008, title game): The Jayhawks made one of the greatest comebacks in championship game history over a team that had just one loss coming in and featured future No. 1 overall pick Derrick Rose. Mario Chalmers became a KU legend with a 3-pointer that forced overtime.

2. Kansas 84, North Carolina 66 (2008, Final Four): The Jayhawks played near-perfect basketball in the first 13-plus minutes to jump out to a 40-12 lead and beat a group that would go on to win the national title the following year. The game marked the first time Kansas faced former coach Roy Williams, who left in 2003 after 15 seasons to return to his alma mater in Chapel Hill.

3. Kansas 64, Ohio State 62 (2012, Final Four): The Jayhawks were underdogs against the Buckeyes, a No. 1 seed with All-American Jared Sullinger. Jeff Withey's block party (7 swats) helped neutralize Sullinger (5-of-19 shooting) as KU advanced to the national title game against Kentucky in New Orleans.

4. Kansas 80, North Carolina 67 (2012, Elite Eight): The Tar Heels were loaded with seven eventual NBA draft picks. Bill Self used a triangle-and-two to flummox Roy Williams. Even though UNC was without star point guard Kendall Marshall, who injured his wrist one week earlier, this was an upset win for the Jayhawks, who had just three future NBA players.

5. Kansas 98, Purdue 66 (2017, Sweet 16): Kansas' speed killed one of the best frontlines in college basketball, headlined by All-American Caleb Swanigan. The small-ball Jayhawks outscored Purdue 51-26 in the second half in one of their best performances ever at the Sprint Center.

6. Kansas 59, Davidson 57 (2008, Sweet 16): The Wildcats were only a No. 10 seed, but the win has aged well, considering the NBA career Steph Curry has had. He was close to ending KU's historic season if not for a clutch performance by Sasha Kaun, who had a team-high 13 points off the bench.

7. Kansas 63, Purdue 60 (2012, Second round): KU trailed by 11 at one point and didn't lead until the 3:04 mark of the second half. This game helped make the Jayhawks believe there was no lead they couldn't overcome, which came in handy in the next three rounds against North Carolina State, North Carolina and Ohio State.

8. Kansas 60, North Carolina State 57 (2012, Sweet 16): Kansas trailed by 10 points in the first half but ended up winning despite making just two shots—both Elijah Johnson jumpers—outside of five feet. Jeff Withey's 10 blocks helped the Jayhawks win an ugly game.

9. Kansas 72, Villanova 57 (2008, Sweet 16): This was payback for Sherron Collins and Mario Chalmers, who had been cut the previous summer from a USA Basketball team coached by Villanova's Jay Wright. Brandon Rush scored 16 points for a KU squad that shot 53.3 percent.

10. Kansas 61, Southern Illinois 58 (2007, Sweet 16): The Jayhawks won despite only one player (Brandon Rush) scoring in double figures. The Salukis were one of the top defensive teams in the country, coached by current K-State assistant Chris Lowery.

2007-08 Season Summary

Results (37-3, 13-3)

November
9 Louisiana-Monroe W, 107 - 78
11 UMKC W, 85 - 62
15 Washburn W, 92 - 60
21 Northern Arizona W, 87 - 46
25 Arizona W, 76 - 72
28 Florida Atlantic W, 87 - 49

December
2 @ USC W, 55 - 59
5 Eastern Washington W, 85 - 47
8 DePaul W, 84 - 66
15 vs. Ohio W, 88 - 51
18 @ Georgia Tech W, 66 - 71
22 Miami (OH) W, 78 - 54
29 Yale W, 86 - 53

January
5 @ Boston College W, 60 - 85
8 Loyola (MD) W, 90 - 60
12 @ Nebraska W, 58 - 79
14 Oklahoma W, 85 - 55
19 @ Missouri W, 70 - 76
23 Iowa State W, 83 - 59
26 Nebraska W, 84 - 49
30 @ Kansas State L, 84 - 75

February
2 @ Colorado W, 59 - 72
4 Missouri W, 90 - 71
9 Baylor W, 100 - 90
11 @ Texas L, 72 - 69
16 Colorado W, 69 - 45
23 @ Oklahoma State L, 61 - 60
27 @ Iowa State W, 64 - 75

March
1 Kansas State W, 88 - 74
3 Texas Tech W, 109 - 51
8 @ Texas A&M W, 55 - 72
14 vs. Nebraska W, 64 - 54
15 vs. Texas A&M W, 77 - 71
16 vs. Texas W, 74 - 84
20 vs. Portland State W, 85 - 61
22 vs. UNLV W, 75 - 56
28 vs. Villanova W, 72 - 57
30 vs. Davidson W, 59 - 57

April
5 vs. North Carolina W, 66 - 84
7 vs. Memphis W, 68 - 75

All-Big 12 Team

Player of the Year:
Michael Beasley, Kansas State, Fr., F

Defensive Player of the Year:
Marcus Dove, Oklahoma State, Sr.,G/F

Newcomer of the Year:
DeMarre Carroll, Missouri, Jr., F

Freshman of the Year:
Michael Beasley, Kansas State, Fr., F

Sixth Man of the Year:
Sherron Collins, Kansas, So., G

Coach of the Year:
Rick Barnes, Texas

First Team
Curtis Jerrells, Baylor, Jr., G
Darrell Arthur, Kansas, So., F
Brandon Rush, Kansas, Jr., G
Michael Beasley, Kansas State, Fr., F**
Blake Griffin, Oklahoma, Fr., F
D.J. Augustin, Texas, So., G**

Second Team
Mario Chalmers, Kansas, Jr., G
Aleks Maric, Nebraska, Sr., C
A.J. Abrams, Texas, Jr., G
Damion James, Texas, So., F
Martin Zeno, Texas Tech, Sr., G

Third Team
Richard Roby, Colorado, Sr., G
Jiri Hubalek, Iowa State, Sr., C
Darnell Jackson, Kansas, Sr., F
Bill Walker, Kansas State, Fr., F
Byron Eaton, Oklahoma State, Jr., G

Honorable Mention
Henry Dugat, Baylor, Jr., G
Kevin Rogers, Baylor, Jr., F
Wesley Johnson, Iowa State, So., F
DeMarre Carroll, Missouri, Jr., F
James Anderson, Oklahoma State, Fr., G/F
Marcus Dove, Oklahoma State, Sr., G/F
Josh Carter, Texas A&M, Jr., G/F
Joseph Jones, Texas A&M, Sr., F/C

All-Defensive Team
Rahshon, Clark, Iowa State, Sr., F
Mario Chalmers, Kansas, Jr., G
Russell Robinson, Kansas, Sr., G
Marcus Dove, Oklahoma State, Sr., G/F**
Justin Mason, Texas, So., G

All-Rookie Team
Michael Beasley, Kansas State, Fr., F**
Bill Walker, Kansas State, Fr., F
Blake Griffin, Oklahoma, Fr., F
James Anderson, Oklahoma State, Fr., G/F
DeAndre Jordan, Texas A&M, Fr., F

** Unanimous selection

Kansas Awards

Brandon Rush:
NABC All-American Third Team
Big 12 Tournament MOP
NCAA Final Four All-Tournament Team

Mario Chalmers
Big 12 All-Tournament Team
NCAA Tournament MOP
NCAA Final Four All-Tournament Team

Darrell Arthur
NCAA Final Four All-Tournament Teams

Season Stats

#	Player	CL	POS	HT	Hometown	G	GS	FG%	3P%	FT%	R	A	S	B	PTS
25	Brandon Rush	JR	G	6-6	Kansas City, MO	38	30	.435	.419	.779	5.1	2.1	0.8	0.8	13.3
0	Darrell Arthur	SO	F	6-9	Dallas, TX	40	39	.543	.167	.702	6.3	0.8	0.5	1.3	12.8
15	Mario Chalmers	JR	G	6-1	Anchorage, AK	39	38	.516	.468	.746	3.1	4.3	2.5	0.6	12.8
32	Darnell Jackson	SR	F	6-9	Oklahoma City, OK	40	35	.626	.333	.691	6.7	1.1	0.8	0.5	11.2
4	Sherron Collins	SO	G	5-11	Chicago, IL	34	3	.462	.362	.776	2.2	3.1	1.1	0.1	9.3
3	Russell Robinson	SR	G	6-1	New York, NY	40	40	.424	.318	.779	2.8	4.1	2.0	0.4	7.3
24	Sasha Kaun	SR	C	6-11	Melbourne, FL	40	6	.619		.541	3.9	0.3	0.4	1.2	7.1
45	Cole Aldrich	FR	C	6-11	Bloomington, MN	40	0	.518		.684	3.0	0.1	0.3	0.9	2.8
5	Rodrick Stewart	SR	G	6-4	Seattle, WA	33	8	.493	.313	.607	2.2	1.4	0.4	0.1	2.8
2	Conner Teahan	FR	G	6-5	Leawood, KS	21	0	.593	.600	1.000	0.4	0.3	0.1	0.0	2.2
14	Tyrel Reed	FR	G	6-3	Burlington, KS	23	0	.514	.458	.000	0.4	0.9	0.3	0.0	2.0
10	Jeremy Case	SR	G	6-1	McAlester, OK	30	1	.378	.379	1.000	0.3	0.9	0.2	0.0	1.6
10	Brennan Bechard	JR	G	6-0	Lawrence, KS	12	0	.556	.400	.500	0.3	0.2	0.0	0.0	1.2
54	Matt Kleinmann	JR	C	6-10	Overland Park, KS	20	0	.429		.333	0.7	0.1	0.0	0.1	0.4
41	Chase Buford	FR	G	6-3	San Antonio, TX	13	0	.111	.000		0.4	0.1	0.1	0.1	0.2
40	Brad Witherspoon	SO	G	6-1	Humboldt, KS	12	0	.000	.000	1.000	0.3	0.3	0.0	0.0	0.2
12	Brady Morningstar	SO	G	6-4	Lawrence, KS	Redshirt									

## CHAPTER 5

2008-09

NO PRESSURE

Seven months after hoisting the national championship trophy in San Antonio, Kansas entered the 2008-09 season complaining about a lack of respect. The Jayhawks had been third in the Big 12 preseason coaches poll, behind Oklahoma and Texas and tied with Baylor. To the casual college basketball fan, the predictions didn't seem like a slight.

Brandon Rush, Darrell Arthur and Mario Chalmers had left school early for the NBA draft; and Russell Robinson, Darnell Jackson, Sasha Kaun and Rodrick Stewart all graduated.

Although Cole Aldrich had begun to emerge, Sherron Collins was the only player returning who'd averaged double-digit minutes on the NCAA title team. For KU to win a fifth-straight Big 12 title, freshmen Tyshawn Taylor, Marcus and Markieff Morris and other members of its eight-man recruiting class would have to develop. Fast.

Marcus Morris: Markieff and I originally signed with Memphis in the fall of 2006, during our senior year of high school in Philadelphia. But then we didn't qualify and had to go to prep school in New Jersey for a year. During that time, rumors started to swirl that John Calipari wouldn't be at Memphis much longer, so we got out of our letters-of-intent and opened up our options.

Dan Brinkley—our high school coach and mentor in Philly—did some research and saw that Kansas was probably going to be losing guys like Darrell Arthur and Sasha Kaun and Darnell Jackson. It seemed like a situation where we could potentially play early at a high-level school.

Bill Self: Dan Brinkley called us and said, "Hey, our two guys are not going to qualify and one of them really likes Kansas. If you recruit them, you can get them."
Sure enough, he was right.

Assistant coach Joe Dooley: Villanova was in the mix, too, but Dan and their mother, Angel, wanted them out of Philadelphia so they could focus on basketball and academics. They needed to get out of their comfort zone. They'd been brought up in a rough environment, and they'd been through the whole deal with the house fire. They just needed a fresh start.

When the Morris twins were in the 11th grade, their Philadelphia home was gutted by a fire, and Marcus and Markieff lost almost all of their possessions. They spent the next year living in the basement of their paternal grandparents. The ceiling was only six feet high, forcing the teenagers to walk around slumped over. With no central heating, Markieff and Marcus went to the gas station at 6 each morning to fetch gallons of kerosene to fill their space heaters.

Marcus Morris: When Kansas started recruiting us, I didn't know who Coach Self was. I didn't know who Danny Manning was. I didn't know anything about Kansas because they'd never shown interest in us.

Our visit was cool. It was pretty normal. We were just grateful to be taking a visit to a prestigious school like Kansas in the first place. Most people—the people that do the recruiting rankings—considered us mid-major or low-major players. Memphis and Villanova were good teams, but Kansas was the only really big program that came after us. It felt like a special place.

We took a chance on Kansas. We considered ourselves high-level competitors trying to work our way up.

The Morris twins signed with KU on Oct. 31, 2007 after also considering Villanova and St. John's.

Bill Self: After they signed, Joe Dooley and I went to watch them work out. It was an individual improvement/strength training workout where they were jumping off boxes and doing some different things. Afterward, one of them asked, "What do you think?"

Joe said, "Well, on a scale of one to 10, that was a minus-2. ... You're not going to last one day."

Joe Dooley: I was pretty frustrated, because they weren't trying very hard. I remember telling them that in pretty harsh terms. Coach gave me a hard time. He was like, "Ease up, we need to make sure we get them on campus first."

Bill Self: They were so lazy. They thought if they dunked it, it would take up too much energy and they couldn't get through practice. And if one didn't do it, the other one wouldn't do it. Everything with them had to be done exactly the same.

Joe Dooley: When they finally got to campus, it was really cool watching them develop, especially Markieff, because Marcus was a star already but Markieff kept getting better and better. Markieff was very gentle and quiet. Marcus was much edgier.

While KU's staff had been anticipating the Morris twins' arrival since the previous fall, Tyshawn Taylor was a late addition to the 2008 recruiting class. Taylor—who played for legendary coach Bob Hurley at St. Anthony's in New Jersey—originally signed with Marquette. But he was released from his letter of intent when Golden Eagles coach Tom Crean took the Indiana job that spring.

Bill Self: With Russell graduating and Rio leaving early for the NBA, we had to sign a point guard, and in our opinion Tyshawn was the best one out there that was available. We didn't really know him because we hadn't recruited him initially. But we knew *of* him. And how could you go wrong getting somebody out of Coach Hurley's program?

Tyshawn Taylor: I had signed with Marquette and got my release after Tom Crean left for Indiana. It made sense for him and his career, but it sucked for me because I didn't really know where I was going to be. I called him immediately. He told me he'd love for me to stay at Marquette because Buzz Williams is a really good coach. But at the time, that was his first head coaching job. Buzz had done a lot of my recruiting, but I was going there because of Crean's system.

Crean didn't really push me into Kansas' hands. Kansas was just an opportunity that came up a little bit later. They didn't really contact me until after my recruiting opened back up. Once that happened Coach Self was there the very next day to see me. I was working at a camp at a middle school right around the corner from St. Anthony's. Billy Donovan from Florida came, too. The two of them actually passed each other in the hallway; one was walking in as the other was walking out. At that point it was between Kansas, Florida and Georgia Tech.

Mario was still on the fence about the NBA, but they were thinking he was going to go. It made sense for me to go to KU because they were low on guards. Tyrel and Brady were coming back. Sherron was coming back. Tyrone Appleton was committed but Coach Self wasn't sure how much he'd be able to contribute. He offered me right then and there.

The main thing I was excited about was the chance to play with Sherron. I was like, "I could play with *Sherron*?"

Sherron was one of my favorite players in college basketball. I had put all my money on Kansas in the NCAA title game earlier that month—and that was as a Marquette recruit. I thought Sherron was better than Ty Lawson. He was my guy. I was like, "Hell yes I'm going to Kansas. Even if Mario stays, I'd just be competing with Tyrel and Brady."

That's what Coach said. He was like, "If you can't beat out Tyrone Appleton and Tyrel Reed and Brady Morningstar, you're the wrong guy." He didn't promise me anything, but he told me it was up for grabs. He said, "If you are who we think you are, this is going to be your spot."

I loved Billy Donovan, but they had so many guards at Florida. With Georgia Tech, I was like, "I'm not going to the ACC unless it's Duke or North Carolina."

I visited Kansas and committed right then. Sherron was my host, but he had his family and friends here. So Russell was the guy I hung with the most, even though he was leaving. He was being super real with me about Coach Self and what he was like and how hard I'd have to work. He told me about his personal ups and downs, coming in as one of the guys who is supposed to start as a sophomore, but then having Mario come in and taking minutes from him, and how hard he had to fight to get on the court.

I went out with the players and they showed me a good time. The fans were still hungover from winning the championship, so everyone was super nice and excited about having me in Lawrence. It was dope to be around that atmosphere. They brought me to the football field and played this whole video of my highlights on the JumboTron. Then they played the last minute-and-a-half of the championship game, when Mario hit the shot. They spliced my high school highlights in there. I'm not gonna lie: that made an impression.

On my visit, I questioned Coach Self about the Morris twins. I was like, "Coach, I don't really know, man. These guys are crazy."

We'd played them at a Rutgers team camp the summer before my senior year. They were coming from the South Jersey/Philly area. We were beating them by about 20 points and they were getting frustrated. Markieff scored a layup, and then he grabbed the ball out of the net and threw it in my teammate's face. The benches cleared. Their coach was arguing with Coach Hurley. It got really bad. The teams couldn't even shake hands after the game. That was the last time I'd thought of them until Coach Self came and recruited me. I was like, "I don't know if these are the types of guys I want to play with. I don't want to be having to fight all the time." But obviously Coach Self said, "These are the kind of guys you want to play with and not against. These are the type of guys you want on your team. You *need* guys like that on your team." I knew they were good. They were just short-tempered. I was, too. I was like, "Are you sure you want this, Coach? Are you sure you can handle it?" He laughed and said not to worry.

No one questioned the Morris twins' talent and potential. However, breaking Marcus and Markieff of some bad habits was often a difficult chore.

Sherron Collins: The twins were cool. They were just lazy. I really didn't blame them, though. If anything, I could relate to why they were like that. My high school coach was cool—but he was also blessed to have a ton of talent. We didn't really have plays. It was just, "Give the ball to Sherron and let him go score." When I got to Kansas, I didn't know how to guard a ball screen. I didn't know what a Gator switch was. I didn't know how to front the post or even how to close out correctly. That's s**t I should've known. Instead I was like, "Yo, I just averaged 37 points a game."

So I understood why the twins may have been a little bit lazy at first. Their coach probably allowed them to be that way because they were winning games and no one was touching them, so they thought everything was OK.

Conner Teahan: In their first individual workout, Coach Self just ripped them because they were so out of shape. They could squat 415 pounds—but they could only bench, like, 170. They were just bottom-heavy. They had no clue what hard work was. They thought they were going to skip out of everything. Anything involving cardio, they tried to skip out of it.

Director of Basketball Operations Barry Hinson: About two weeks into our workouts that fall, my wife asked me how the Morris twins were doing. I was like,

"Well, I think they're going to be pretty good. But I'm not positive because they spend the whole practice running on the sidelines." I'm serious ... every day for a month or two, it felt like they'd spent the entire practice running sprints on the sidelines or on the treadmill because they'd done something wrong. Coach was on them about everything.

Marcus Morris: Boot Camp was horrible. It was the toughest thing ever, waking up at 6 a.m. each morning. We did it, though, because we knew that if we didn't the consequences would be harsh. Still, doing all that running early in the morning, then going to workouts and to class—and then back to more workouts. Coach Self always said we didn't work hard, so he was trying to train us and show us what working hard was all about.

It was tough. I questioned whether I wanted to continue to be a hooper. I seriously wondered whether I even wanted to play anymore.

Expectations Lowered

Along with being picked to finish third in the league by Big 12 coaches, Kansas opened the season ranked No. 24 in the Associated Press poll. It was one of only three times in the last 13 years that Kansas wasn't ranked in the top 10 to start the season.

Sherron Collins: Everyone disrespected us. Even people in our own conference disrespected us. We'd just won a national championship. At least put us in the top 10.

Tyshawn Taylor: No one knew what to expect because there were so many new guys. In some ways I was surprised, because things were actually kind of easy. There wasn't a ton of pressure, because they'd just won the title, and hardly anyone besides Cole and Sherron were back. We didn't really feel like we had to defend the title. We were just there to play basketball.

The coaches didn't put too much pressure on us that year. The analysts didn't rank us very high. No one really knew what was going to happen. I don't even know if *we* knew what was going to happen. No one knew how good Cole was going to be. He'd played a really small role his first year. Everyone knew how good Sherron was, but he had never been in a position where he had to be a leader, where he had to be "the guy." No one knew what to expect from me, the twins, Travis, Mario Little, Tyrone Appleton or Quintrell Thomas. There were seven new guys.

Tyrel Reed: Some people may not have had big expectations for us, but I know we had big expectations for ourselves. Still, it was different not having that target on our backs the whole year.

K-State guard Jacob Pullen: I didn't think KU would fall back at all. The media did, but I didn't.

Knowing Sherron from Chicago and being friends with him already, I knew he was going to get the keys to a Bentley. He still had good bigs to work with. He had Cole Aldrich, and the Morris twins were coming in. They were going to have talent. I knew that when they gave Sherron a role like that, he'd be able to lead that team.

Cole Aldrich: Sherron and I were the only returning players in 2008-09 who had seen much playing time the year before. The assumption was that we were in a "rebuilding year," but neither of us wanted to settle for that. Sherron and I worked really well together. I think there was a mutual respect there that led to some really good chemistry on the court. We hung out a little bit off the court, but we had an even stronger tie on the court. In the locker room we always talked to each other and said, "Hey, this is what you need to do and this is what I need to do." There was no bulls**t between us. If he was doing something he wasn't supposed to do, I'd yell at him. I'd cuss him out. If I was doing something I wasn't supposed to do, he'd cuss me out. There was something about Sherron that made people rally around him. He was so talented and he had such a confidence about him. It's hard not to follow a guy like that.

Sherron Collins: I was planning to leave after my sophomore year but, a month after we won the title, I had to have surgery on my meniscus. I didn't have an agent or anyone advising me, so I went back to Chicago and talked to Tim Grover, who has a workout facility close to my neighborhood. He's worked with hundreds of NBA guys. Grover was like, "You can do whatever, but going back to KU wouldn't be a bad idea. It's going to be your team." I also knew that if I entered the draft I'd be a second-round pick. I thought I was better than that, so I went back.

Coach Self went to Media Day that fall and said, "Sherron is going to have to shoot about 25 shots a game for us this year." I was like, "If I have to, I will." At the same time, I didn't want the new guys to think it was going to be all about me. Coach Self always used to tell us that the pie was big enough for everyone to have a piece. That's what I told the new guys—that we'd just won a title with six or seven pros. I was like, "I *know* the pie is big enough. I just won."

Practicing Patience

As expected, Kansas fought through some growing pains during non-conference play as first-year starters such as Taylor, Morningstar and Marcus Morris adapted to their roles. The Jayhawks were 11-4 entering Big 12 play with losses to Syracuse, Massachusetts, Arizona and Michigan State. A home win against No. 24 Tennessee on Jan. 3 provided a much-needed jolt of momentum. Collins (26 points and nine assists) and Aldrich (22 points, 10 rebounds and six blocks) played like All-Americans.

Still, expectations were tempered as the Jayhawks opened league play unranked.

Tyrel Reed: Coach Self had a little bit more patience that season. The year before, when we won the title, if I messed up in a drill or wasn't getting it, he could just say, "Go over there and sit on the sideline and let one of the older guys do it." But my sophomore year, people could make mistakes and still be out there playing.

Me, Cole, Sherron and Brady were the veterans, and other than Sherron, we'd hardly been on the court at all. We'd hardly played. But we'd at least been around and understood the offense and what Coach Self was looking for.

Watching Coach Self that year ... it was pretty impressive. He went from a situation with the title team where he didn't have to say much—he just had to put the guys into the right position—to a scenario where he's teaching, coaching and managing the personalities of 18-year-old kids who are far away from home for the first time.

I don't know what his mentality was, but it was just unique to see him change and understand he had a young group of guys. He had to figure out how to get them to respond.

Sherron Collins: I was the voice for the team. If someone wasn't feeling good or something was bothering someone—maybe something that happened back home—and Coach Self was riding them and didn't know about it, I'd call timeout and sub myself out. I'd pull Coach to the side and tell him what was going on. Someone could've been sick, or maybe there was a pregnancy scare. That's why those guys looked up to me. They knew I'd do anything for them. Darnell and Russell and those guys had treated me that way when I was younger, so now I needed to step into that same role. There were times when I went to bat for guys over some stupid s**t, some wrong s**t. But I had to let them know I was by their side.

Bill Self: Sherron loved his teammates and wanted them to do great. He was proud of them. And after we won the title, when everybody was gone, he said, "This is perfect for me. It gets to be my show." He took responsibility for everything.

Sherron Collins: Coach Self coached his ass off that year. We were winning games we weren't supposed to win. We beat Tennessee.

I felt like I was playing the best ball of my career. That's when I was locked in. I was like, "If I don't play good, we're not going to win." Cole was rolling with me. We were like polar opposites. I'm city; he's country. I'm short; he's tall. I'm fast; he's slow. But we jelled.

Brady Morningstar: You had Tyrel, the little country boy, funny but quiet; Sherron was from the west side of Chicago, loud and brash and hood; Cole was the 7-foot goofy guy. To put all of those backgrounds together and have them form a bond on the court was incredible.

Tyrel Reed: It was impressive seeing Cole go from a guy who didn't have any pressure to suddenly having all the pressure and dealing with it so well. It was the Sherron and Cole show. It was just fun seeing a guy who, coming in, did not look the part, then after one year he's who everyone is talking about.

And Sherron could just be Sherron again. That's how he was in high school; he was *the* guy. He was the McDonald's All-American, the tough guy from Chicago. When he came to KU, he had to blend in a little bit and play on a team with a bunch of talented guys. Then boom, it was his show again. It was good to see him return to that role, because he flourished in it, having the ball in his hands and being a distributor and doing all those things. That year he didn't have a lot of extra weight on him and he didn't have a lot of injuries, so he could really showcase his skills.

Kansas started 8-0 in conference play, including a 73-53 road win at Iowa State when Cyclones forward Craig Brackins scored 42 points.

Former Iowa State coach Greg McDermott: Craig was incredible that game. He was in a zone, and we were coming up with a hundred different ways to get him the basketball and just let him go to work. But while he had an incredible game, it wasn't enough for our team to pull it out.

We were a team that relied on 3-pointers and usually shot it well, but that particular game our other guys were off. (Brackins went 3-of-5 from beyond the arc but the rest of his teammates combined were 3-for-21.)

I remember thinking, if he's scoring 42 against Kansas, I don't know if I'm gonna get to coach him next year because he might be off to the NBA. But he did end up coming back for one more season. Bill congratulated him after the game for an incredible performance, because he was throwing a lot of different looks at him defensively and Craig was still finding a way to score the basketball.

Tyrel Reed: I didn't even realize we started 8-0. It was just one of those things ... we figured it out. Coach Self always figures it out. Everything else changes. The teams change. The players change. But he always figures out how to get the best out of you.

Rivalry Week

With a perfect record in league play at the midway point, the Jayhawks had the daunting task of starting the second half of their conference slate with back-to-back road games at Missouri and Kansas

State. The Tigers, who would make the Elite Eight that season, rallied from a 14-point halftime deficit to beat Kansas, 62-60, on a Zaire Taylor game-winner with 1.3 seconds left.

KU responded to that loss with a win at Kansas State, 88-72. The games were entertaining, but it was often the sideshow in Columbia and Manhattan that the coaches and players remember the most.

Barry Hinson: That was my first KU-Missouri game, and Coach Self told me, "It will be different than anything you've ever seen. When we get on the bus, from the moment we leave the hotel, you're going to see more middle fingers than you've ever seen in your life." So sure enough, a mile outside of the arena, their fans were lined up, giving us the bird, booing us, all this stuff. I couldn't believe it.

We got into the arena, and they'd let the students in early. Again, it was my first year at Kansas, but I'd been the head coach at Missouri State. Now I'm back in the state of Missouri, and I kinda had my peacock feathers out. I figured I'd walk out there and everyone would know me, and that a few people may wave or clap. I was feeling a little frisky. About 10 or 20 steps onto the floor, there's a kid in the stands, a student, screaming, "Coach Hinson! Coach Hinson!" I stopped and waved at him. And then he said, "How does it feel? How does it feel to have been the head coach at Missouri State—and now you're the waterboy at Kansas?"

Their student section started going crazy and even *our* players were dying laughing. I didn't even make it to the free throw line. I turned right around and walked back through the tunnel and into our locker room. Coach Self said, "What'd you come back in here for?" I told them the story and everyone fell over laughing.

Sherron Collins: (Former Mizzou guard) Stefhon Hanna was my boy, so there was no bad blood there. But with everyone else, I was like, "F**k you, f**k your mom and everyone else that supports Missouri."

The night before the game that year, their fan group, the Antlers, ordered 30 pizzas and had them delivered to my hotel room at the Holiday Inn. I opened three or four of the boxes and they had anchovies and pineapples and mushrooms and onions all over them. The nastiest stuff in America. So it wasn't like I was going to eat them.

Coach Self always tells the security guards at every hotel not to allow anyone on our floor—especially in Columbia. So the fact that the pizza delivery dude was able to get up there told me that the hotel employees were in on it, too. So what did I do? I took all 30 pizzas and dropped them over the sixth floor-balcony. They landed right in the middle of the lobby. I didn't run away, either. I stood there, looked down and watched them land. I wanted someone to see me throw them.

Tyshawn Taylor: I didn't really respect Missouri as a team until my senior year in 2012, when they were really good. Before that, it was a hate thing. I didn't like playing them, and I felt like we were going to win every time. My freshman year, Zaire Taylor hit a shot to beat us. Even that day, it was our game—we were up by 14 at halftime—and we just blew it at the end. It was tougher to play at Kansas State. They were just better until my last year.

Sherron Collins: After we lost at Missouri, we went to Kansas State. A few days before the game, a girl had made a Facebook page pretending like she was a fan of KU. There was KU stuff all over her page. She friend-requested me, and I hit "accept." The night before the game, she was like, "Hey, I'm in Manhattan. I'm going to the game tomorrow and I want to come by and meet you." I was like, "Well, we have security at the hotel, so you can't get up onto our floor. But I'll come down to the lobby and we can chill." So I sent her my number. About two minutes later, the page was deleted. I was like, "What the hell is going on?"

The next day, we're in pregame shootaround and Brady taps me and points toward the stands. He's like, "Yo, that looks like your number." These fans are holding up a huge sign with my number on it, yelling, "Hey, Sherron! We're calling you!" I ran into the locker room and I had 100 missed calls. I called AT&T and changed my number right then and there. Literally, Coach Self was walking in there about to give his pregame speech, and I'm on the line with the phone company.

That kind of stuff used to piss me off. I'd tell fans, "Because of you, I'm going to beat the s**t out of your team tonight. I'm going to go for 30, and we're going to beat your ass, and it's all going to be your fault." And near the end of the game, when we were up really big, I'd make sure to walk by them and smile and point at the scoreboard.

Brady Morningstar: I liked the players that played at Missouri and Kansas State. Mike Dixon, Kim English, Jacob Pullen, Jordan Henriquez, Dominique Sutton ... they're all good people. But the fans are just so disrespectful sometimes. You can be disrespectful in a sporting-event kinda way. You can yell, "You can't shoot," or whatever you want to say. But the second it gets personal with family and something that's happened in your life that's bigger than the sport itself ... well, you should probably shut your damn mouth. The fans at those two schools don't really know how to do it.

Sometimes in warm-ups you'd get sick of it, so you'd find a way to smoke a fan with a ball with a hard pass or something. It was really easy at places like K-State, where fans are literally sitting on the court with those courtside seats. I'd say, "S-Dot, shoot this ball, and I'm going to rebound it and throw it at you real hard. Just move out of the way and act like you're tying your shoes or something." I'd throw the pass, Sherron would bend down and the ball would smack the dude in the face. All of a sudden, the tough man that was running his mouth is getting clocked with the ball. We'd be like, "Oops, our bad." We got a couple of people with that trick. They didn't say much after that.

Tyrel Reed: One thing I always hated about K-State is how they'd throw this stupid powder in the air and then it'd get all over the floor. It'd be the slickest court to play on. I'd ask Jacob Pullen about it, and he'd say, "Yeah man. I hate how they do that."

It was always fun to play K-State, because in the summer we would see those guys—Jacob Pullen, Denis Clemente, Rodney McGruder—and we'd get to be buddies with them in a way. We worked a lot of camps with those K-State players. They were great guys, and it made it even more fun playing against other.

Even when I got punched in the head by Denis Clemente after a free throw, and he got suspended for a game because of it, it was nothing. I knew him. I saw him that summer, and he said, "I don't know what happened there, man. It was my bad." It wasn't even a big deal. People made a big deal out of it, but it wasn't anything.

It was a free throw box-out, and I may have gone into him too far. He was the shooter, and I don't know if he made it or missed it, but with a closed fist, he hit me in the side of the head. I felt it, but it wasn't painful or anything. After the game, I got asked, "Did you see he punched you in the head?" I said I felt something but didn't think it was a punch. Afterward, I saw the video. I don't know how he ended up getting suspended for a game. It wasn't a big deal.

"No coach, I got this."

The class of the Big 12 that season was clearly Kansas and the Blake Griffin-led Oklahoma Sooners. On Feb. 23, 15th-ranked KU traveled to Norman for a game that would ultimately decide the Big 12 race, as both teams were 11-1.

The game, however, lost a bit of its luster when it was announced that Griffin wouldn't play because of a concussion—a huge letdown for fans eager to see the future No. 1 pick face off against emerging star Cole Aldrich. Highly touted guard Willie Warren did his best to step up for No.3 Oklahoma, but the Jayhawks' backcourt had an answer.

Tyshawn Taylor: Willie Warren was the freshman that everyone talked about in our conference that year. I had been playing pretty well, though. I'd won a few Freshman of the Week awards. It was a game I'd circled. I knew I was going to come out and play well.

I had 16 points in the first half. I was hitting backboard 3s and just doing s**t I don't normally do. Sherron had four points in the first half and turned it over a few times.

Coming out of the locker room, Sherron was like, "Way to play, bro. I needed you that half. But I got you this half."

I remember there were about 14 minutes left in the second half, and Coach Self called a play. But Sherron pulled up for a 3 instead and swished it. It was a long 3, too—all the way out by the OU logo. Coach Self looked at me with this "What's he doing?" face. I was like, "I got him. I got him. I'll reign him in. It's cool."

The next time down, Coach Self called another play and this time Sherron literally stuck out his arm and waved him off. And then ... *BOOM*! ... he pulls up and hits another 3. A few plays later he got an and-one. All of a sudden he went from having about four points to 13. Willie played good that game, too. He had 23. But Sherron had three or four really deep 3s in the second half when Coach Self was screaming out plays. He was just feeling it.

Bill Self: It basically just turned into a H-O-R-S-E contest between Sherron and Willie. We were just going one-four flat on offense and giving the ball to him. After he scored six straight, I called a play and he was like, "No, coach, I got this." And then he made a bomb right after that. I loved, loved, *looovvved* his competitiveness and coaching him.

Tyshawn Taylor: Nobody could do that but Sherron. It's not common to wave Coach Self off. You just don't do that. But Sherron was locked in. Truly locked in.

With Kansas clinging to a 71-68 lead, Collins swished a 3-pointer to extend the Jayhawks' cushion to six with 3:15 remaining. All but four of Collins' 26 points came in the decisive second half. Taylor also scored 26 in Kansas' 87-78 win. Warren sparked Oklahoma with 23.

Tyrel Reed: Our offense in the second half was basically, "Get Sherron the ball and everybody just get out of the way." His Chicago swag was coming out. He was saying anything and everything on the court that night. He thrived in those games where he was playing good and somebody else was playing good, too. He can go back and forth and talk and just let it hang.

He was talking but nothing personal. *"You can't stop me. Why are you even trying?"* He had so much confidence. It was impressive.

Kansas 87, Oklahoma 78
February 23, 2009 · Norman, Okla.

Kansas (23-5)

Player	MP	FG	3FG	FT	R	A	F	S	TO	B	TP
Brady Morningstar*	21	0-3	0-2	2-2	1	3	4	0	1	0	2
Tyshawn Taylor*	34	8-13	3-5	7-11	1	3	1	1	1	0	26
Sherron Collins*	38	6-14	5-8	9-12	2	3	1	2	4	0	26
Cole Aldrich*	38	5-10	0-0	5-6	20	1	3	2	0	4	15
Marcus Morris*	17	1-4	0-1	3-5	3	2	4	0	0	0	5
Travis Releford	10	0-0	0-0	1-2	2	1	3	0	1	0	1
Mario Little	7	1-1	0-0	0-1	2	0	3	0	0	0	2
Tyrel Reed	17	1-3	1-3	0-0	0	1	3	1	2	0	3
Markieff Morris	14	3-6	0-0	1-2	2	1	5	1	2	1	7
Quintrell Thomas	4	0-0	0-0	0-0	2	0	2	0	1	0	0
Team					3						
Totals	200	25-54	9-19	28-41	38	15	29	7	12	5	87

Oklahoma (25-3)

Player	MP	FG	3FG	FT	R	A	F	S	TO	B	TP
Willie Warren*	38	8-16	3-6	4-4	3	3	5	1	4	0	23
Tony Crocker*	28	2-4	1-3	4-5	1	1	3	1	3	0	9
*Taylor Griffin	26	3-5	1-2	4-5	6	2	4	2	0	0	11
Austin Johnson*	23	1-5	0-2	0-1	3	0	2	0	2	0	2
Ryan Wright*	23	0-1	0-0	0-5	7	1	4	1	1	0	0
Cade Davis	20	4-6	4-6	0-2	0	1	5	2	1	1	12
T.J. Franklin	1	0-0	0-0	0-0	0	1	0	0	0	0	0
Omar Leary	12	2-5	2-5	0-0	3	0	4	0	0	0	6
Orlando Allen	1	0-0	0-0	0-0	0	0	0	0	1	0	0
Juan Pattillo	27	4-10	0-0	7-8	6	1	4	0	3	2	15
Beau Gerber	1	0-0	0-0	0-0	0	0	0	0	0	0	0
Team					4						
Totals	200	24-52	11-24	19-30	33	10	31	7	15	3	78

	1st	2nd	Total	FG%	3FG%	FT%
Kansas	36	51	87	46.3	47.4	68.3
Oklahoma	29	49	78	46.2	45.8	63.3

Officials: Tom Eades, Curtis Shaw, David Hall
Technicals: None

Tyshawn Taylor: We wanted Blake to play. We thought we'd have won even if he were out there.

Sherron Collins: I'm going to put this on record: Blake Griffin faked that injury. Go watch a replay of the game. When Oklahoma had us down by 10 or 15 in the first half, he was on the sideline jumping up and down, which was strange for a guy that had a concussion. Supposedly they were worried about him even being out there in those bright lights, and around all of that noise. Yet that man was jumping up and down when they were winning.

But when they started losing, he was over there on the sideline holding his head like he was in pain or something. I felt like he could've played and that they held him back on purpose, because they probably knew they were going to lose that game no matter what. We were ready for Blake. He didn't get to play against us the year before, either, because he got hurt right at the start of the game. So we were excited about playing him when he was a sophomore. That whole week we studied Oklahoma because we wanted Blake.

Losers in Lubbock ... again

Kansas followed the Oklahoma win with one of its most impressive performances of the season, a 90-65 trouncing of Missouri in a revenge game at Allen Fieldhouse. The Jayhawks, though, stumbled in their next game against a mediocre Texas Tech squad that went just 3-13 in the Big 12 that season under first-year coach Pat Knight. The loss marked the third straight time Kansas had been upset by the Red Raiders at United Spirit Arena.

Tyshawn Taylor: Coach Self used to say, "If I have to get you juiced up for this game, y'all are in the wrong place." He didn't have to do much for Missouri or Kansas State. It was the Texas Techs and the Texas A&Ms that were the problem. That year we lost a game we shouldn't have at Texas Tech. They had one kid, Alan Voskuil, that had 35 on us. He just killed Brady. It was a Saturday afternoon. Hardly anyone was there. It was just tough to get up for it.

In one of the more impressive shooting displays ever by a KU opponent, Voskuil swished 9-of-14 shots from beyond the arc en route to a 35-point performance, as Texas Tech won 84-65.

Texas Tech coach Pat Knight: Voskull just went ape s**t on them on his Senior Night. The most memorable thing about that game was, the following Monday, I got a letter from a Kansas State fan just motherf**king me for running up the score. It was Senior Night and I couldn't get Voskuil out of the game. Time was running out and I told him to hold the ball. We were already up by about 15. Instead, he jacks a 3 from about half court and hits it.

I got a letter from a K-State fan—not a Kansas fan, but a *K-State* fan—telling me what a low-life asshole I was, just shredding me for running the score up on Kansas. I wish I would've kept that letter. It was the best. I got chewed out by a K-State fan for running up the score on Kansas. He was calling me bush league and everything else. I was thinking about all of the times we got our ass embarrassed at Allen Fieldhouse, even with my dad coaching, and yet I get accused of running up the score on the Jayhawks. It was hilarious.

Title-clincher on Senior Night

Kansas won the Big 12 league title outright on Senior Night with a 83-73 victory over Texas. Sparked by 20 first-half points from Damion James, the Longhorns—who fell to 0-9 at Allen Fieldhouse—led by as many as 14 points in the first half, but KU caught fire after intermission. Collins scored 21 points and Aldrich added 12 points and 10 boards for Kansas.

The Jayhawks had just two seniors: walk-ons Matt Kleinmann and Brennan Bechard. Sticking with a decades-old tradition, both players started the game.

Tyrel Reed: Dexter Pittman, who was 6-10 and weighed well over 300 pounds, played for Texas, and somehow Brennan got switched onto him early in the game and literally tried his heart out to box him out. He got pushed around pretty good, but he still almost got a rebound. I remember Coach Self talking about how that epitomized Brennan—he was going to do whatever he could. He didn't have great size or physical tools, but he was out there on Senior Night, and he's got this giant guy and he's trying his hardest to guard. That stuck out, because after the game, Coach Self was like, "Did you guys see Brennan out there? He's got Dexter Pittman out there, and he's trying. He's trying." That just epitomizes who he was as a player and a person and obviously he's successful now. (Note: Bechard is KU's Director of Basketball Operations.)

Tyshawn Taylor: That was one of the first times they showed the decibel level up on the big screen, and I remember it being super loud. I remember a big play that's on one of my highlight reels, when they were coming down the court and I get a steal. I threw it ahead to Sherron, but Dogus Balbay, the Turkish kid, was chasing him down, so he threw it back to me and I got a crazy dunk. The crowd went crazy.

Texas called timeout, but it was so loud in there that I couldn't hear the whistles. I ran back and got ready to play defense, and I looked over and my teammates were all on the bench.

Coach Self was really impressed with what we had done. Everyone was. We had all these new guys and didn't know what to expect. Plus Brady and Tyrel actually being a significant part of it. I mean, they weren't just on the team. They were reasons why we won games. Brady was our best on-ball defender at that time, and Tyrel shot the piss out of the ball.

Bill Self: Sherron had one of my favorite all-time quotes after that Texas game. We'd lost all five starters, yet we win the league and go 14-2, and somebody asked Sherron if he was surprised. His line was great. He said, "Surprised? This is what we do." He wasn't being cocky. That was truly his mindset, which is why I loved coaching him so much.

What Could Have Been ...

An opening-round loss to Baylor knocked Kansas out of the Big 12 Tournament, ending the Jayhawks streak of three straight championships. But they appeared re-energized the following weekend in the NCAA Tournament.

Kansas survived an unbelievable performance from North Dakota State guard Ben Woodside (37 points) to win its first-round game 84-74. Two days later, Aldrich posted a triple-double (13 points, 20 rebounds and 10 blocks) in a 60-43 round-of-32 victory over Dayton.

Cole Aldrich: It was the sixth official triple-double in NCAA Tournament history and the first in Kansas history, although Wilt Chamberlain probably would've had plenty if they would've kept those kinds of stats when he played. What made it so special was that the game took place in Minneapolis, just a few miles from my home in Bloomington.

I actually struggled offensively that game. I felt like I couldn't hit a shot. But they kept on driving into the lane. I'd block their shot and we'd get a little runout. I was more impressed with the 20 rebounds than the 10 blocks. I didn't think about the triple-double until I came to the sideline near the end of the game. The guys were like, "You got it! You got it! You got a triple-double!"

Next up was a trip to Indianapolis for a Sweet 16 showdown with No. 2 seed Michigan State, which had thumped KU in East Lansing back on Jan. 10. In the rematch, Kansas led by 13 at one point in the second half, but Spartans point guard Kalin Lucas led a furious comeback and scored seven of his 18 points in the final 49 seconds to help the Spartans win 67-62.

Michigan State advanced to the NCAA title game in Detroit, where it fell to eventual champion North Carolina.

Bill Self: We outplayed them. We had a 13-point lead in the first half and then it kind of fizzled away.

Kansas 62, Michigan State 67
March 27, 2009 · Indianapolis, Ind.

Kansas (27-8)

Player	MP	FG	3FG	FT	R	A	F	S	TO	B	TP
Tyshawn Taylor*	28	2-4	0-1	4-4	1	2	3	1	3	0	8
Brady Morningstar*	34	3-8	0-2	0-0	3	2	0	2	2	0	6
Marcus Morris*	14	1-4	0-0	2-2	2	0	3	1	2	0	4
Cole Aldrich*	34	6-13	0-0	5-6	14	4	1	2	4	4	17
Sherron Collins*	38	9-13	2-5	0-1	2	3	2	0	6	0	20
Markieff Morris	24	1-7	0-2	0-0	7	0	1	0	0	0	2
Tyrel Reed	21	1-2	1-2	0-0	1	0	5	0	2	0	3
Mario Little	7	1-2	0-0	0-0	1	0	2	1	0	0	2
Team					6						
Totals	200	24-53	3-12	11-13	37	11	17	7	19	4	62

Michigan State (29-6)

Player	MP	FG	3FG	FT	R	A	F	S	TO	B	TP
Goran Suton*	33	8-16	1-3	3-3	9	0	3	5	3	1	20
Raymar Morgan*	13	1-6	0-1	2-2	1	0	2	0	2	0	4
Delvon Roe*	10	0-0	0-0	0-0	1	2	0	0	0	0	0
Travis Walton*	29	1-5	0-0	0-0	5	5	3	1	1	0	2
Kalin Lucas*	35	5-15	1-4	7-7	2	7	0	4	2	0	18
Chris Allen	20	2-7	1-4	2-2	3	3	1	0	0	0	7
Korie Lucious	4	0-0	0-0	0-0	0	0	1	0	2	0	0
Durrell Summers	26	3-4	2-3	1-2	5	0	3	1	0	0	9
Idong Ibok	7	0-0	0-0	0-0	0	0	2	0	1	1	0
Marquise Gray	2	0-0	0-0	0-0	0	0	0	0	1	0	0
Draymond Green	21	3-6	0-0	1-1	1	0	1	2	1	0	7
Team					4						
Totals	200	23-59	5-15	16-17	31	17	16	13	13	2	67

	1st	2nd	Total	FG%	3FG%	FT%
Kansas	36	26	62	45.3	25.0	84.6
Michigan State	29	38	67	39.0	33.3	94.1

Officials: Michael Stephens, Jamie Luckie, Doug Simmons
Technicals: None

Sherron Collins: Everyone kind of excused that Michigan State loss because we were supposedly rebuilding and expectations weren't as high for us that year. But, hell, we wanted to win and we should've won. *We'd have beat Louisville* in that Elite Eight game and gone to the Final Four. Coach Self even said it. We'd have beat Louisville. I still blame myself, because I gave that 3-point play away to Kalin Lucas right at the end of the Michigan State game. I should've fouled the hell out of him, and he'd have only gotten two points. Then we just would've needed two points to tie it at the end instead of three. He got me in the air, and I pulled my hands back instead of fouling the hell out of him. It ended up being a 3-point play that made it 63-60 with about 40 seconds left. We couldn't come back.

Tyrel Reed: That loss hurt just as much as Northern Iowa and those types of losses, because I felt like we were really good and we were clicking. We were young, but we had a bunch of talent.

BEST BIG 12 3-POINT SHOOTERS

1. Brady Heslip, Baylor: The Jayhawks respected his jumper so much they face-guarded him. Hit 6-of-9 threes at Allen Fieldhouse his senior year in a 78-68 loss; finished career as a 44 percent 3-point shooter.

2. Buddy Hield, Oklahoma: A tireless worker, Hield made himself into one of the best shooters in the country. KU fans won't soon forget his 46-point performance at Allen Fieldhouse where he made 8-of-15 outside shots and received a standing ovation afterward.

3. Phil Forte, Oklahoma State: The Jayhawks saw early on how accurate he was, as he made 7 of 10 threes in an 80-78 loss at Allen Fieldhouse his sophomore year. Forte holds the OSU record with 329 threes.

4. Keiton Page, Oklahoma State: Scored 29 points with seven 3-pointers in his final home game against KU, a 70-58 loss; Self quipped afterward that he was glad Page was a senior.

5. LaceDarius Dunn, Baylor: The Big 12's all-time leading scorer and second for most made 3s (388). Most memorable game against the Jayhawks came in the 2009 Big 12 Tournament, as he scored 24 points and made 6-of-11 threes in a 71-64 upset.

6. Naz Mitrou-Long, Iowa State: Finished with the second-most 3s (260) in Iowa State history. He was on fire at the perfect time for the Cyclones, making 6-of-11 from deep in a 92-89 overtime upset at Allen Fieldhouse in 2017.

7. Marcus Denmon, Missouri: In the final year of the Border War, he buried 12-of-19 threes and scored 57 points in two games against Kansas. Denmon could heat up quickly, never more evident than when he scored nine straight points in a game-ending 11-0 run to beat KU, 74-71, at Mizzou in 2012.

8. A.J. Abrams, Texas: The 5-foot-11 guard is the Big 12's all-time leader in 3-pointers made (389). He also ranks 11th in the conference's all-time scoring list. Had one of the quickest releases in college basketball.

9. Alan Voskuil, Texas Tech: The game of his life came against KU, as he scored 35 points and made 9-of-14 threes on his Senior Night in an 84-65 victory. In his final two seasons in Lubbock, he shot 46 percent from deep.

10. Tyrus McGee, Iowa State: Had 22 points on 6-for-10 three-point shooting in the now-famous Elijah Johnson game when the Cyclones fell, 108-96, in overtime. His 46.4 percent shooting from deep led the NCAA in 2012-13.

I remember going up to East Lansing in January and basically getting pummeled. Coach Self came in at halftime that day and said, "Let's just not make this a blowout. Let's see if we can play. Don't worry about anything else. Let's just see if we can play with these guys." It wasn't a big screaming and yelling match. He was just like, "We're down 19 at half. Can we make this a game?"

The tournament game was totally different. I was so disappointed we lost, and I think all the guys were, too. We were up five with a few minutes to go. That just made us hungry for those next couple years. There's no way we should have lost. We would have played Louisville and we would have beat Louisville and made the Final Four. That's just the way it is, I guess.

Sherron Collins: Me and Cole have a special relationship to this day because of that season. That junior year, what we did, winning the Big 12 ... no one thought that would happen.

Following the season, Bill Self was named National Coach of the Year by the Associated Press.

A little more from ...

Cole Aldrich: My sophomore year was the season I got one of my front teeth knocked out. It happened early in our home game against Kansas State. I don't even know exactly how it happened or who did it, but I must've been hit pretty damn hard, because I had my mouth-guard in and my tooth still got knocked loose. We were shooting free throws, and my girlfriend was sitting in the family section behind the opponent's bench. I smiled at her and my mouthguard was filled with blood. She had this worried look on her face and mouthed to me, "What happened?" I could feel that my tooth was crooked in there. The doctor came over and said, "We'll probably have to take it out in the morning." I was like, "OK, can I keep playing tonight, though?" He said he didn't see why not.

Tyshawn Taylor: My freshman year didn't feel that hard. Remember, I had played for Coach Hurley at St. Anthony, which is the hardest person I ever thought I'd play for. And I came here with no pressure. No one expected much from me that first year. Coach Self just wanted me to play hard.

My freshman year was my easiest year to get through. Not knowing what to expect, I was super attentive and ready to listen and do everything right. I handled the situation pretty well. Sherron was in a position that he'd never been in before as far as having to be a leader. I think the first year he played really well, but he put a lot of pressure on himself as far as wanting to be good and go to the NBA. The rest of us didn't feel pressure to defend the national title, since we weren't really a part of it. But Sherron may have felt that pressure. When I first got here, he was cool with me. But it was competitive. It felt like we were competing against each other a lot of the time, and I don't think we should've been.

I get it. I was starting as a freshman. I had some games where I played really well. It just seemed more competitive than it should've been. I felt it during games. Sometimes, when you win, it's easy to mask stuff and cover it up. But when you lose you get exposed. We lost eight games that year, and they were all winnable games. There were two or three plays … not blaming Sherron for the losses, but as "the guy," there were plays he didn't make. It was his show. He wanted us to know that, but we already knew it.

Conner Teahan: I remember Tyshawn's freshman year, him and Sherron would get into it pretty good. Tyshawn's star was rising a little bit and Sherron's was Sherron's, so it was always up there pretty high.

During halftime of one game, Sherron and Tyshawn were yelling at each other. Sherron took both of his hands and put them around Tyshawn's neck and threw him into a locker.

They were just bitching at each other. *"You're missing me when I'm open."* When you get to that level, people know that just a quarter-second delay on a pass can mess up a shot. And if I don't want to get you a shot, maybe I look over here instead, and that can cause some resentment. I think there was maybe a little bit of that going on, but who knows how much of that was just an assumption. Tyshawn was always quick to bounce back, though. Even when things were going wrong in his life, he was able to ignore all of it and get down to business.

Sherron Collins: Ty was hard-headed, but he was hard-headed and stubborn in a good way, just like I was. Coach Self really got on Ty his freshman year; he handled it pretty well. Ty was just nonchalant a lot of the time. I felt like I had to be there for Ty like Russell was there for me. I used to always tell Ty, "Don't worry when he's getting on you. That means he likes you. The time to worry is when he *stops* getting on you."

That's my little brother, man. We vibed really well. He spent a lot of time with me. He was young and didn't know what not to do. I mean, we were athletes, but we were also still kids.

Brady Morningstar: Tyshawn respected Sherron. Even if you didn't like Sherron, you had to respect his game, because he busted everyone's ass. That's just what it was. You can't talk s**t on someone that can dog everyone on the roster.

Bill Self: Sherron would get in some guys' faces a little bit. But I know there were times where he pointed the finger at himself, too. He wasn't one of those guys that put anybody else down. He wanted everybody to be good. I really thought he helped Tyshawn tremendously. I don't think Tyshawn would have been near the player he was early in his career if he didn't have Sherron back there with him.

No one would have guessed we were going to be so good that year—not starting two freshmen (Taylor and Marcus Morris) and an unproven Brady Morningstar.

But how many teams would like to return two All-Americans? Because Sherron made third team that year and Cole was good enough to make it. We didn't know they were going to be that good, but God almighty, they were so good. And then Tyshawn, nobody knew he was any good. And the twins, nobody knew they were any good. Then Brady and Tyrel … we really exceeded expectations.

Kurtis Townsend: Everyone thought that was the year they were going to get us.

Matt Kleinmann: I'm fortunate enough to have been a part of the team that won the whole thing. All I can say is that being a part of five Big 12 championships is great, but you could ask any of those teams, "would they trade a Big 12 championship for a Final Four run? Not a championship, but a Final Four run?" They would probably all say yes, because there's something about the Final Four that defines a team's legacy.

You talk to the guys who came before us—guys like Aaron and Wayne and Keith—and they talk about being in multiple Final Fours (in 2002 and 2003). That's their legacy. We were fortunate to get even luckier and win the whole thing, but had we not gone to the Final Four in 2008, I don't think any of those Big 12 championships would resonate quite as much.

One story I remember from my senior year is when the twins did something stupid and we all got punished for it. We had this long stretch of AstroTurf in the weight room, and Hudy made us do log rolls on it. You'd lay down on your side and you'd start rolling with your arms and legs out. We had to do ten 20-yard log rolls, down and back. After a while, you'd throw up because your head would get dizzy from rolling so much. It was physical punishment, and the message was, "Don't mess up anymore. You're a team. If one of you makes a mistake on the court, you all lose. It's the same way when someone messes up off the court."

Anyway, Brennan Bechard was struggling a little bit—everybody was struggling—and I remember Marcus and Markieff said, "Nah, screw this. We're leaving." So they get up and start walking away, and Brennan, probably because he was dizzy and pissed, hops up and gets in their face and starts chewing them out. *"No, you're the reason we're here. You're the reason we're doing this. You're not leaving!"* It was an interesting experience. Brennan Bechard, senior walk-on, putting Marcus and Markieff in their place. We had to hold him back.

My favorite experience, I said this in my senior speech, was hands down being friends with all these guys while I was there and seeing them mature. As a big, goofy white kid from Overland Park, I'd never experienced anything in my life outside of playing ball. I had never been around guys with the type of life experiences some of the guys had.

To this day, whenever I hang out with them, it's nothing but hugs and old stories and fun. What I loved about KU was, whether it was Coach Self's intention or not, guys that would make it all the way through would mature. And guys that wouldn't make it all the way through ... it was typically because they didn't want to change, whether it was conscious or subconscious. The Morris twins, they matured into really good guys, and I'd say the same thing about everybody else who was there the whole time. Because to get through playing for Coach Self for four years, that's its own little marathon. You've got to really grow up and take responsibility for your actions.

2008-09
Season Summary

Results (27-8, 14-2)

November

16	UMKC	W, 71 - 56
18	Florida Gulf Coast	W, 85 - 45
24	vs. Washington	W, 54 - 73
25	vs. Syracuse	L, 89 - 81
28	Coppin State	W, 85 - 53

December

1	Kent State	W, 87 - 60
3	New Mexico State	W, 100 - 79
6	Jackson State	W, 86 - 62
13	vs. Massachusetts	L, 60 - 61
20	Temple	W, 71 - 59
23	@ Arizona	L, 84 - 67
30	Albany	W, 79 - 43

January

3	Tennessee	W, 92 - 85
6	Siena	W, 91 - 84
10	@ Michigan State	L, 75 - 62
13	Kansas State	W, 87 - 71
17	@ Colorado	W, 56 - 73
19	Texas A&M	W, 73 - 53
24	@ Iowa State	W, 67 - 82
28	@ Nebraska	W, 62 - 68
31	Colorado	W, 66 - 61

February

2	@ Baylor	W, 65 - 75
7	Oklahoma State	W, 78 - 67
9	@ Missouri	L, 62 - 60
14	@ Kansas State	W, 74 - 85
18	Iowa State	W, 72 - 55
21	Nebraska	W, 70 - 53
23	@ Oklahoma	W, 78 - 87

March

1	Missouri	W, 90 - 65
4	@ Texas Tech	L, 84 - 65
7	Texas	W, 83 - 73
12	vs. Baylor	L, 64 - 71
20	vs. North Dakota State	W, 84 - 74
22	vs. Dayton	W, 60 - 43
27	vs. Michigan State	L, 67 - 62

All-Big 12 Team

Player of the Year:
Blake Griffin, Oklahoma, So., F

Defensive Player of the Year:
Cole Aldrich, Kansas, So., C
J.T.Tiller, Missouri, Jr., G

Newcomer of the Year:
Denis Clemente, Kansas State, Jr., G

Freshman of the Year:
Willie Warren, Oklahoma, Fr., G

Sixth Man of the Year:
LaceDarius Dunn, Baylor, So., G
Matt Lawrence, Missouri, Sr., G

Coach of the Year:
Bill Self, Kansas

First Team
Craig Brackins, Iowa State, So., F
Cole Aldrich, Kansas, So., C
Sherron Collins, Kansas, Jr., G**
DeMarre Carroll, Missouri, Sr., F
Blake Griffin, Oklahoma, So., F**

Second Team
Denis Clemente, Kansas State, Jr., G
Willie Warren, Oklahoma, Fr., G
James Anderson, Oklahoma State, So., G/F
A.J. Abrams, Texas, Sr., G
Damion James, Texas, Jr., G/F

Third Team
Curtis Jerrells, Baylor, Sr., G
Cory Higgins, Colorado, So., G
Leo Lyons, Missouri, Sr., F
Ade Dagunduro, Nebraska, Sr., G
Byron Eaton, Oklahoma State, Sr., G
Josh Carter, Texas A&M, Sr., G/F

Honorable Mention
LaceDarius Dunn, Baylor, So., G
Kevin Rogers, Baylor, Sr., F
Jacob Pullen, Kansas State, So., G
J.T. Tiller, Missouri, Jr., G
Austin Johnson, Oklahoma, Sr., G
Terrel Harris, Oklahoma State, Sr., G
John Roberson, Texas Tech, So., G
Alan Voskuil, Texas Tech, Sr., G

All-Defensive Team
Cole Aldrich, Kansas, So., C
J.T. Tiller, Missouri, Jr., G**
Ade Dagunduro, Nebraska, Sr., G
Terrel Harris, Oklahoma State, Sr., G
Justin Mason, Texas, Jr., G
Derrick Roland, Texas A&M, Jr., G

All-Rookie Team
Marcus Morris, Kansas, Fr., F
Tyshawn Taylor, Kansas, Fr., G**
Denis Clemente, Kansas State, Jr., G**
Zaire Taylor, Missouri, Jr., G
Willie Warren, Oklahoma, Fr., G**

** Unanimous selection

Kansas Awards

Sherron Collins
Consensus All-American Second Team
NABC All-American Second Team
NABC All-District (8) First Team
AP All-American Third Team
USBWA All-American Second Team
Sporting News All-American Third Team
CBE Classic Sprint Subregional Team

Cole Aldrich
NABC All-District (8) First Team

Season Stats

#	Player	CL	POS	HT	Hometown	G	GS	FG%	3P%	FT%	R	A	S	B	PTS
4	Sherron Collins	JR	G	5-11	Chicago, IL	35	35	.434	.376	.795	2.9	5.0	1.1	0.0	18.9
45	Cole Aldrich	SO	C	6-11	Bloomington, MN	35	35	.598		.792	11.1	1.0	0.6	2.7	14.9
10	Tyshawn Taylor	FR	G	6-3	Hoboken, NJ	35	33	.506	.364	.724	2.2	3.0	1.1	0.2	9.7
22	Marcus Morris	FR	F	6-9	Philadelphia, PA	35	22	.495	.400	.604	4.7	1.1	1.0	0.3	7.4
12	Brady Morningstar	SO	G	6-4	Lawrence, KS	35	34	.419	.420	.793	3.0	2.6	1.2	0.1	6.5
14	Tyrel Reed	SO	G	6-3	Burlington, KS	35	2	.407	.389	.825	1.9	1.1	0.7	0.0	6.5
23	Mario Little	JR	G	6-6	Chicago, IL	23	3	.512	.375	.625	3.2	0.9	0.5	0.2	4.7
21	Markieff Morris	FR	C	6-10	Philadelphia, PA	35	7	.448	.188	.650	4.4	1.0	0.4	0.7	4.6
24	Travis Releford	FR	G	6-6	Kansas City, MO	32	0	.569	.375	.531	1.4	0.2	0.3	0.0	2.7
1	Quintrell Thomas	FR	F	6-8	Newark, NJ	26	1	.440		.680	2.0	0.1	0.0	0.2	1.5
32	Tyrone Appleton	JR	G	6-2	Gary, IN	21	0	.538		.500	0.3	0.3	0.0	0.0	0.8
2	Conner Teahan	SO	G	6-5	Leawood, KS	21	0	.182	.118	1.000	0.9	0.1	0.1	0.0	0.7
54	Matt Kleinmann	SR	C	6-10	Overland Park, KS	17	2	.600		.333	0.6	0.0	0.0	0.1	0.4
41	Chase Buford	SO	G	6-3	San Antonio, TX	11	0	.500	.000		0.5	0.0	0.0	0.0	0.4
10	Brennan Bechard	SR	G	6-0	Lawrence, KS	11	1	.000	.000	.500	0.1	0.2	0.0	0.0	0.1
25	Jordan Juenemann	FR	G	6-3	Hays, KS	5	0	.000			0.0	0.0	0.0	0.0	0.0

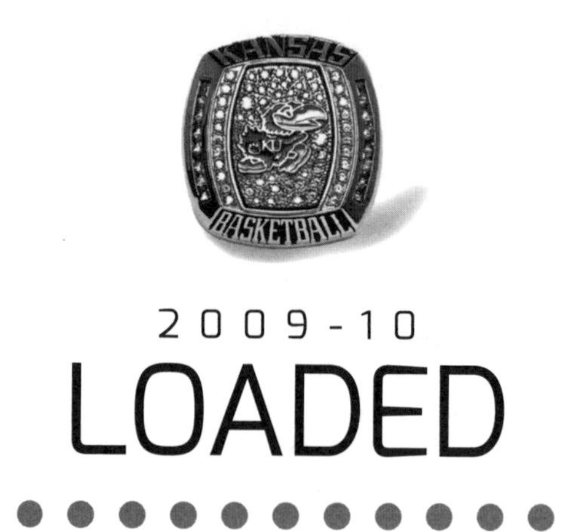

2009-10

LOADED

The sting of Kansas' Sweet 16 loss to Michigan State subsided quickly. It was easy, after all, for KU fans to get excited about all that lay ahead. The Morris twins would be back along with Cole Aldrich, Tyshawn Taylor, Brady Morningstar and Tyrel Reed. And promising freshmen Xavier Henry, Elijah Johnson and Thomas Robinson were joining the roster along with transfer Jeff Withey (Arizona).

No one player, though, generated as much hype as Sherron Collins, who shocked Bill Self by announcing he'd return for his senior season.

Sherron Collins: Even though we lost, I still went to the Final Four in Detroit that year because I was a finalist for the State Farm Player of the Year award that Blake Griffin won. I was at the banquet and Coach Self was there, too. After it was done, Coach Self was like, "Have you decided what you're going to do yet? I'm not trying to pressure you to do anything. But do you know what's going on?" I told him I was coming back. He stopped in his tracks and said, "What? Wait, wait, wait. Are you serious? Can I tell people?" He didn't believe me. He called me about three times that night just to make sure. I was like, "Yeah, I'm coming back." It was that simple.

Bill Self: I really didn't know what Sherron was going to do after his junior year in regard to the NBA draft. I didn't think he'd be a first-round pick. He had had some knee issues and stuff, so his logic for coming back was good. And it was obviously huge for our team. It definitely set the tone for our team from the get-go.

Sherron Collins: The main reason I came back for my senior year was because of my mom. She had been getting sick and wanted me to finish my degree. She had breast cancer throughout most of my college career. Luckily, they caught it so it never got too serious until my junior year. She had to have surgery and get some lumps removed a few days before the NCAA Tournament. Our first two games were in Minnesota that year and then we played Michigan State in Indianapolis. She drove both places. I wasn't going to let her fly. After we lost to Michigan State, I went and talked to my mom in her hotel room and she told me she wanted me to go back to school. I thought about it for a week and then I said, "OK, I'm going back." I was the first male in my family to get a degree.

Elijah Johnson: From day one that season, it was S-Dot's show. He let everyone know it. And to his defense ... you're damn right it was his show. He had the most experience of anyone on the team and he had a ring on his finger. There weren't many people in the country who could say that. He was on the cover of *Sports Illustrated* and all of these other magazines and he had the respect of pretty much every coach and analyst in the nation. He had earned all of that because he'd put the work in. And, don't forget, he'd chosen to come back to be with *us* when he could've left. So you're damn right we were going to give him his respect. If Sherron didn't come back for his senior year, we wouldn't have been the No. 1 team in the country.

Brady Morningstar: It was hard to not give that dude respect, on the court or off of it. His presence was felt everywhere he went. In Chicago, everyone knew him. In Lawrence, everyone knew him. He was just so damn good. His game was so pretty. He wasn't trying to be flashy, but he was. He couldn't help it. That was just his game.

Bill Self: Even to this day, I'd say that Sherron is the best basketball player we've recruited here. Joel Embiid would be the other one. But when you talk about a guy that could pass, dribble and shoot, a guy that was explosive but could also think ... we haven't had anyone here that was better than Sherron. His ceiling wasn't as high because he wasn't very tall. But, my God, he was a good basketball player.

Stacked

With Collins returning, Kansas' 2009-10 squad ended up being the most talented of the Bill Self era. The roster included eight future NBA players—two of whom (Robinson and Withey) barely saw the court—and five future lottery picks. Five others would go on to play professionally at some level.

Aldrich had established himself as an All-American-caliber player the previous season, and the Morris twins had returned determined to elevate their game as sophomores.

Strength and conditioning coach Andrea Hudy: After we lost to Michigan State in Indianapolis, Marcus texted me on the bus on the way back to the hotel. He said, "Hey, Hudy. I'm ready to tighten up. I'm ready to change my body." I was like, "I'm here. It's your choice."

Marcus Morris: As a freshman I didn't feel like I made the impact I wanted to make. Strength was the biggest reason. So after that season, we told Hudy that we wanted to be great. We said, "We want to build our bodies to be able to play at a high-major level." That entire summer, we trained with her twice a day. We were running hills and across

BEST KU TEAMS

1. 2007-08: Using statistics guru Ken Pomeroy's adjusted efficiency margins, the 2008 national champs are the second-best team of the last 16 years in all of college basketball—behind 2015 Kentucky. It was the perfect blend of talent and experience... and a little luck (Brandon Rush returning to school because of a torn ACL). The champs finished 37-3 and won the title in the only year there's ever been four No. 1 seeds at the Final Four.

2. 2009-10: This was arguably Bill Self's most talented roster ever with five future lottery picks and three others—including All-American Sherron Collins—who would play in the NBA. The 2010 Hawks went 33-3, lost just one game in the Big 12 and were the No. 1 overall seed in the NCAA Tournament.

3. 2010-11: The 2011 team wasn't as loaded as the year before but the chemistry was better. Everything revolved around the Morris twins, who were efficient monsters. Junior year Marcus Morris is arguably the best college player Self ever coached, and seniors Tyrel Reed and Brady Morningstar were two of his best leaders.

4. 2006-07: This group had a four-game stretch in the middle of Big 12 play when they outscored opponents by 31.8 points. Made up of the championship core plus Julian Wright, they were dominant defensively. They had three signature wins—knocking off eventual champion Florida and beating Kevin Durant-led Texas twice.

5. 2015-16: This was another team that seemed to have the perfect chemistry and right mix of experience and talent. It featured Perry Ellis at his peak and a stacked backcourt with Frank Mason, Devonte' Graham and Wayne Selden. The Big 12 was as strong as ever and KU won it by two games, earning the No. 1 overall seed in the NCAA Tournament.

6. 2011-12: One of Self's best coaching jobs, he took a team that returned just one starter to the national title game. The pieces fit together well, built around the inside-outside duo of All-American Thomas Robinson and senior guard Tyshawn Taylor. This was one of KU's best defensive teams, thanks to Jeff Withey's rim protection.

7. 2016-17: The Jayhawks had the best player in the country, Frank Mason, and arguably the nation's top one-and-done freshman in Josh Jackson. It was another strong year in the Big 12 and they won the league by four games. Self embraced a small-ball lineup that gave defenses fits trying to contain Mason and Jackson in space.

8. 2012-13: Jeff Withey was the best defender in the country and his experience playing volleyball—and ability to control where his blocks went—led to a lot of easy transition buckets. Withey also became a solid offensive threat and was complemented well by Ben McLemore. The 2013 team earned a No. 1 seed and was a Trey Burke miracle 3 away from making the Elite Eight.

9. 2004-05: The end of the season was spoiled by injuries, but when healthy, this veteran group was tough to beat. Led by All-American Wayne Simien, the 2005 team was preseason No. 1 and got out to 20-1 start. Simien, Aaron Miles and Keith Langford were a talented (and accomplished) senior trio who went to two Final Fours and an Elite Eight.

10. 2013-14: This is another "what could have been" team that never reached its potential because of an injury to Joel Embiid. From a pure talent standpoint, Self has never had two players better than Andrew Wiggins and Embiid. They were 9-1 in Big 12 play and starting to show their potential before the injury bug bit Embiid and kept him out of the NCAA Tournament, where KU was upset in the round-of-32 by Stanford.

football fields. We were lifting damn near every day. I think I gained like 20 pounds of muscle that summer. Just straight muscle. We took off after that.

Bill Self: We've never had a frontline as good as the one we had that year with Cole, Marcus, Markieff, Thomas Robinson and Jeff Withey. That was about as good as it gets. In the backcourt we probably had one too many players, because we had Tyshawn, Elijah, Brady, Tyrel, Xavier and Sherron. It was hard to find minutes for all of them. We had to redshirt Travis (Releford) because it was just so crowded back there.

Sherron Collins: My scoring decreased from my junior year (18.9 points) to my senior year (15.5). A lot of people thought it was because I didn't play as well, but I didn't feel like that was the case. We were just better that year. We had more weapons. Tyshawn and the Morris twins had gotten better, and we added Xavier. All of those guys could score. Brady and Tyrel were factors all of a sudden, so I didn't have to score as much. My junior year, I was always counted on to score. I had to score. I'd look to the sideline for the play, and Coach Self was like, "Four down for you."

We were so good my senior year that Coach Self would have to invent ways to convince us that other teams could hang with us. Sometimes you could tell when Coach Self was "gassing" a player, as in "gassing him up" by making us believe he was better than he actually was. Then we'd come out and the dude would score about 10 points and we win by 30. We'd go in the locker room and say, "Coach, that dude was a bum." That happened when we played Memphis in St. Louis that year, and he was telling us about how good Joe Jackson was going to be. He was only a freshman, I think. He turned out to be OK, but at that point he wasn't anything. He couldn't do anything against us.

Tyrel Reed: In some ways our team that summer reminded me of the 2008 team. We had so many guys that had been there and had an understanding of what it meant to be a Jayhawk. Most everyone was on board with how we did things.

Having so many veterans on the roster proved beneficial for newcomers such as Thomas Robinson and Elijah Johnson.

Thomas Robinson: Going against Cole every day in practice really helped me when I was a freshman. He tried to kill me every day. He didn't have the mindset of, "I'm an All-American and you're a freshman. I'm going to take it easy on you." He tried to bust my ass every day. The twins did the same thing, to the point where I was thinking about leaving. But then I realized that those were All-Americans and lottery picks I was going against. If I was holding my own against them, then I'd do pretty well against everyone else.

Elijah Johnson: When I got to Kansas, everything felt so big to me. I was overwhelmed at first. Coming into a program that had been so successful for so long … it was like an unwritten book that people had all read before.

There was never a schedule given to us. You're just expected to catch on. It was like being thrown into the wind. Even when you had a slow moment when you wanted to do something else, there wasn't any leeway. There was nothing you could do about it. It was like, "This is Kansas. These coaches don't want to hear it."

When I first got here, I didn't even play basketball. I had just had surgery. I just sat there and took everything in. A lot of former players came back that summer and said, "Dang, they're building y'all a practice gym? Dang, they're building y'all murals and doing all this stuff to your locker room? We helped create this for y'all. Appreciate this. Embrace it." They weren't being cocky or rude. They just wanted us to remember the people that came before them, the ones that made it all possible.

Those first few months were a great experience. I could never go back and describe how that made me feel. I stayed up late and then woke up at the crack of dawn to see what my teammates were doing. When we got done working out, it wasn't like we took showers and went to our rooms to be by ourselves. Everyone would shower and then go hang out in Mook and Kieff's room. It was a true program, a true family.

While not much was expected of Johnson and Robinson as freshmen—they combined to average just 4.9 points—the situation was different with Xavier Henry, a five-star recruit who was headed to Memphis before John Calipari bolted for Kentucky. Henry, whose father, Carl, played at Kansas, was a projected lottery pick who was thrust into a starting role immediately.

Also joining the roster that fall was Xavier's older brother, C.J., a former first-round pick in the Major League Baseball draft whose career on the diamond never panned out.

Tyrel Reed: The Henrys came in late that summer. Initially, I think they may have felt like outcasts a little bit. They didn't feel like they were a part of the team. I remember coming in late at night to get a workout in, and those two would be working out together without any of the other guys around.

Sherron Collins: Right after they signed that spring, their father (Carl) came out with these quotes in the paper about how his sons—both of them—were better than me. He put his sons in a bad spot, because we were going to take what he said out on them. I stood up and said that in the locker room, and everyone was like, "We're with you. Who are these dudes?" At the same time, we had to remember that Xavier and C.J. weren't the ones that said that stuff. It was their dad. Still, they weren't there all summer while we were there working. We heard they were back in Oklahoma City working out, but that didn't mean anything. They weren't there working with us. So they were already coming in on a bad note.

They finally got to school, and it was time for pickup games. I told Coach Self, "I'm gonna be on C.J. for 94 feet, since he's supposed to be better than me. I'm gonna guard them all 94 feet (of the court)." The second he touched the ball, I was on him tight. Our whole team was going hard at them at first. After the first couple of days—after we got a feel for Xavier's personality—we were like, "He wasn't behind all that stuff his father said. He doesn't think those things." Xavier was a cool guy. C.J. was a little cocky. He had played pro baseball a little bit. It was different with him. It was like, "All right, man, we're going to bust your ass and let you know how things are. We know Kansas recruited you way back in 2005 or whenever, but things are different now." He was pretty rusty. I scored on him at will and got a little rough with him. After a week or two, things were normal and everything was cool.

Xavier Henry: A few months before I got to Kansas, an article came out that portrayed me and my family really badly. It caused some tension between us and the guy that we let come into our house and do the interview. He turned around and made us look like prima donnas. Once we got to Kansas, people got to know us, and they realized that wasn't the case. We thought the article was shady. There was just a lot of stuff in there that wasn't true. We couldn't do anything about it, though. We just forgot about it and moved on with our lives.

There were probably some people that didn't understand why my brother (C.J.) and I didn't work out in Lawrence the summer before our freshman year. There were just a few people—fans or whatever—that were like, "Why wasn't he here this summer?" or "What was he doing?" or "I can't believe he didn't come down here and work out with the guys." But that summer, I had my braces taken off. I had, like, four root canals and I had my wisdom teeth removed. My face was hurting, my head was hurting, my body was tired. It was a tough summer. When I finally got to Lawrence, it was great. Everyone acted like they were excited to see me. It was so fun, because everyone knew who I was. Everyone was coming up to me and talking and taking pictures with me. You could fall in love with the attention quick. The best part about it was that I was always with my teammates. We were experiencing it all together.

Football Fight

On Sept. 22, an altercation between members of the KU basketball team and football team broke out in the Burge Union parking lot. A day later there was nearly a second fight between the two groups outside of a classroom. Much like the J.R. Giddens incident four years earlier, the program faced a lot of bad press.

Sherron Collins: We got in the brawl with the football team, and we got in trouble for it like it was our fault, but they lied. The football team lied. I wish there would've been a tape that we could've watched. Me and Ty Appleton were shooting pool. Cesar Rodriguez was in there drunk off his ass and poked TA in the face and said, "I don't like you." There were two other linemen in there that weighed about 260, so I got on the phone and called the Morris twins and said, "Get up here now." We saw them pull up so we walked toward the door. Cesar blocked the door and said, "You're not leaving." He lied and said we started the whole thing. Coach Self was like, "You guys went up there looking for a fight." No we didn't. We were just up there shooting pool and these two big, drunk linemen started messing with us and got in our face. We got out the door and Cesar rushed us and one of the twins laid him out. He hit him in his face. They kept getting up. They were so drunk. They kept getting up and rushing me and Ty, the Morris twins and Rio (Little) ... I didn't get touched.

I was looking for anyone on the football team and I was going to knock them out.

Conner Teahan: I remember that night that it all happened, I was trying to get money out of the ATM and I didn't realize what was going on and the next thing you know there's this huge mob right at the Burge Union yelling back and forth.

Tyrel Reed: I had just left training table and was up in my room. My room faced the Burge Union, so you could see The Fieldhouse and the Union parking lot, and I remember looking out there and could see cop cars. I'm thinking, "OK, that's not good."

Shortly after, I got a text that said everybody needed to come to the locker room. We were specifically told that nothing else could happen—and then the next day something else happened on campus...

Sherron Collins: We went to class the next day. There were 1,500 people in the class, including about six football players in there. There was already bad blood from the fight at the Burge the day before. Apparently one of them called some of their teammates and told them we were there, because we got out of class and there was a whole group of them waiting for us. It felt like their whole team was there. There were dudes down in three-point stances like, "Yeah, c'mon."

It was me and Mario Little and the Morris twins. I didn't want Brady or Teahan or Tyrel to get involved. They didn't need to be in a situation like that. The rest of us came from neighborhoods where you might have to fight every now and then to survive. We didn't want them feeling like they had to help us. I called Coach Dooley and they all hurried over there and saw it.

Tyrel Reed: I was going to class and I saw Coach Dooley jogging up the hill. I'm like, "What's going on?" He says, "Turn around and follow me." I jog up with him to break up the fight. People were snapping pictures of us while they loaded us all into vans to get us out of there. We felt like a bunch of criminals. It wasn't the finest moment in Kansas basketball history.

Conner Teahan: I was walking to class and (director of basketball operations) Brett

Ballard and (graduate student manager) Brennan Bechard ran past me, and I said, "What's going on?"

They said, "Come with us! There's another fight going on. We've got to break it up."

I started sprinting with them. I had to send an email to the teachers of my next two classes to tell them I wasn't going to be there, because they called emergency meetings for the football and the basketball teams. Then we went to Coach Self's that night, and he was talking to us and telling us how pissed he was. And then he says, "You know what I've decided? We're starting Boot Camp a week early."

He didn't start the actual Boot Camp, but we were basically subjected to anything Andrea Hudy wanted to do. We woke up at 5:30 the next morning and started lifting weights. It was basically weightlifting hell for the next five or six days.

Some people were upset about it. But outside of some minimal yelling at each other—*"Hey, you're the reason we're doing this"*—there was not a lot of divisiveness, because there were so many guys involved in it.

You get it ingrained pretty quickly that, "Hey, we're in this as a team. There's nothing we can do that's going to change it. We're going to handle this together."

Sherron Collins: There were more of them than us. We were trying to stick together. We could've gotten hurt. In the first fight, Thomas got a concussion and Tyshawn broke his thumb. I felt bad because as a freshman I didn't have to go through that. Thomas Robinson's mom was calling all worried, wondering if she should pull him out of school. As a senior I felt like that was my responsibility. I was pissed.

More Mistakes

As if the skirmishes with the football team weren't enough, Kansas dealt with more negative publicity after Taylor took to social media—particularly Twitter—to express frustrations and fire back at critics.

Tyshawn Taylor: I was already in the doghouse for not handling things well when I came back. No one expected anything from my freshman year, and I had a good season. The whole summer before my sophomore year, everyone was patting me on the back and telling me about all the good things I was going to do, all the points I was going to average and all the awards I was going to win. That s**t started going to my head. I went to this USA Basketball event and played well. I was playing with Gordon Hayward and Shelvin Mack and Klay Thompson and all these future pros. There were lots of reasons for optimism. My plan was to come back and have a great sophomore year and then leave (for the NBA).

Coach Self saw things completely different, and that's when things got bad. Coach was on me about everything I did. Anything I tweeted, anything I said, turnovers, if I looked mad, if I looked too happy, if I missed a class, if I was late to a class ... he wasn't letting anything go. He wasn't sweeping anything under the rug.

I guarantee my sophomore year might have been the least amount of minutes I

played during my career, because he'd pull me after every mistake. A turnover, a missed shot ... I'd get pulled. It was hard to play like that, especially since, in my mind, I was supposed to be a pro after the season. I thought I was supposed to be averaging x amount of points and x amounts of minutes. I just didn't handle it very well.

I felt like I got in the most trouble for the Twitter stuff. He was already on me, so that just made it worse. I remember doing an interview around that time, right before a practice, and someone asked me, "Do the guys not know their role?" And I said something like, "I don't know if it's super clear to everybody." Coach Self walked out of the locker room a few minutes later and one of the reporters told him about what I'd said. I'm telling you ... bro, this man walked onto the court screaming! *"Oh, so no one knows their roles, huh Taylor? I'll show you what your role is."* This was right around Christmas, which is the worst time to be in trouble. Every time I turned it over that day, I was running stairs or suicides. Anything I did, there was punishment for it.

All that being said, we were a really good team. I played pretty well. I feel like I should've been better, but I played good. I played with Sherron that year and Elijah was my backup, so we had more of a point guard presence if I had to sit. Coach Self was able to mess with my minutes a little bit, because we had a deeper roster.

Sherron Collins: Tyshawn was young and didn't know what *not* to do. We were athletes—but we were still kids. It's tough when you're 18 and some dude tweets that your mom is a prostitute or you're trash or whatever. You naturally talk back to them and Ty got in trouble for that. Coach had to shut down all of our Twitter accounts for a while. The biggest thing for Ty was that he shouldn't have cursed so much in his tweets. He should've just said, "Shut up, dweeb" or something like that. It wouldn't have been as big of a deal. Ty was going through stuff, so he was emotional. He was lashing out.

I did some dumb s**t that year, too. I was overweight. Coach Self told me to come back from Christmas break at 207 and I was 210. So he made the whole team run while I watched. That pissed me off. But the whole thing about it ... they were like, "It's cool, Dot. We got you." Some of them were probably mad. I'd have been mad, too. But it meant a lot to me. I loved those guys.

Taylor wasn't the only Kansas player having issues with Self. Early in the 2009-10 season, Marcus and Markieff Morris were frustrated about rarely being on the court at the same time. Marcus was getting quality minutes as a starter but Markieff was a reserve.

Elijah Johnson: We were in the weight room and the Morris twins got mad. One of them said, "I'm not messing with this anymore. I'm out. C'mon, dog. We're out. Let's go up to his office right now and tell him. We're *done*." They were pumping their fists and getting all animated, saying, "We're going to say what we need to say to Coach."

Marcus Morris: I really was done. It was immaturity. I wanted to play with my brother and I didn't want to wait. We wanted to be on the court at the same time. Instead we were competing against each other for minutes, and we really weren't feeling it.

Elijah Johnson: At that time, there was a window in Coach Self's office that overlooked the weight room, so we could see up in there. Those guys walked in there and sat with their hands in their laps. They told Coach what they wanted to say—and he started laughing.

He got up, opened the door, smacked them on the back and let them leave. I don't think he even said anything to them. Maybe something like, "Y'all are just frustrated. Get back in the weight room."

Bill Self: Yeah, they came in my office and quit. It was before the season started. And they said, "Hey, we're going to quit."

I said, "OK, why?"

This was their way of saying they didn't like me.

"It's just not exactly going the way we'd hoped, so we're going to transfer at Christmas."

I said, "OK, that's fine. Do you know where you want to go?"

"No. We'll just play the rest of the first semester and then we'll decide when we get finished playing."

I said, "So you're going to quit, but you're going to play the first semester?"

And they said, "Yeah."

I said, "Nah. Let's just do it this way. Why don't you just quit now? Turn in your stuff. You're done. You're done! Now you can do whatever you want to do."

They said, "But Coach, what about... I mean, we've gotta play."

I'm like (laughing), "Well, the only way you're going to play is if you don't quit."

They left the office and everything went back to normal. It was funny. They just wanted to talk.

Elijah Johnson: Now those dudes are making seven figures a year if not more. We laugh about that all the time.

Brady Morningstar: They knew they were at the place they should be, and they were going to buy in regardless. They were going to get their words in, too. But hell yeah they bought in.

Marcus Morris: Our first two years there, we were hardly ever together on the court. Looking back, I actually think it made us better, giving us that time apart on the court. It forced us to grow up and to learn how to function when the other one of us isn't there.

Bullying Baylor

The Jayhawks' rivalry with Missouri began more than a century ago. The hiring of Frank Martin at Kansas State and Fred Hoiberg at Iowa State heightened the anticipation for the annual showdowns with the Wildcats and Cyclones. In recent years, however, one of Kansas' biggest rivals has been Baylor.

The Bears' improvement under Scott Drew (two Elite Eights and two Sweet 16s since 2008) is one reason for increased interest in the Jayhawks game vs. the Bears. But the underlying reason for KU's animosity toward Baylor traces back to their meeting on Jan. 20, 2010 at Allen Fieldhouse, when Drew moved his team off the floor and into the tunnel as KU's pregame video played on the JumboTron.

Sherron Collins: They started calling our lineup and they left the court. We were all pissed about that. We were going crazy in the huddle. *"Did you see that s**t?"* That's what created our little rivalry with them. That really got to us.

Tyshawn Taylor: All of Coach Self's feelings about Scott Drew came out in that moment. He was like, "You're going to let them disrespect you like that? Go kick their asses."

Baylor forward Quincy Acy: Kansas thought it was disrespectful of us to leave while their introductions were going on, but seriously … who cares? It was because we couldn't hear a word Coach Drew was saying. It was like he was screaming, but there was no sound coming out. We had to actually go into the tunnel to hear the game plan for the first play of the game. It was nothing more than that. Coach Drew is not a controversial guy. He's not confrontational. He doesn't have a bad bone in his body. Kansas didn't like it, though. They came out and hopped on us pretty good. I guess Coach Self used that for some added fuel.

Bill Self: I don't know that I used it to try to motivate them too much. I maybe said, "Can you believe this?" But Scott and I have gotten close since then. They've done an unbelievable job down there. At that time, I probably didn't take it the way it was intended. That happens all the time.

Collins scored 28 points and Marcus Morris added 22 as third-ranked Kansas beat the No. 25 Bears 81-75. LaceDarius Dunn scored 27 for Baylor, which lost to eventual national champion Duke in the Elite Eight.

Baylor coach Scott Drew: In no way would I ever try to disrespect Kansas. The noise level there right before tipoff, with the introductions, gets so high that it's nearly impossible to communicate with your guys. We simply thought, "Hey, let's take them into the tunnel so we can talk to them and give them last-minute instructions and go over our game plan." Afterward, I understood the Kansas perspective. I just hadn't analyzed it or thought about it beforehand. It was a split-second, knee-jerk decision that I made before I thought through it. Again, I just wanted to go over our game plan one last time. At every other arena in the country, you're able to do that in that moment. But on that particular night, when no one could hear me, I tried something different and it was taken the wrong way.

Being in the Big 12 now for 14 seasons, I have a huge amount of respect for what Kansas has done. It's unprecedented. Their fans are educated and passionate. You love that as a coach.

"Give me the ball and get out of my way."

Second-ranked Kansas, off to a 5-0 start in Big 12 play, traveled to No. 11 Kansas State for the most anticipated matchup between the two schools since the 2008 game featuring Michael Beasley. This game was billed as a showdown between Sherron Collins and K-State's Jacob Pullen. The star guards did not disappoint.

Kansas 81, Kansas State 79
January 30, 2010 · Manhattan, Kan.

Kansas (27-8)

Player	MP	FG	3FG	FT	R	A	F	S	TO	B	TP
Cole Aldrich*	37	5-13	0-0	8-12	11	0	4	0	0	3	18
Marcus Morris*	31	5-11	1-1	2-3	10	1	5	0	3	0	13
Brady Morningstar*	39	4-5	2-3	4-4	1	2	4	3	1	0	14
Xavier Henry*	16	3-5	0-0	0-0	4	1	1	1	4	0	6
Sherron Collins*	41	7-14	2-6	0-1	1	4	2	0	3	0	16
Tyshawn Taylor	30	2-4	0-0	8-9	0	2	4	1	3	0	12
Markieff Morris	20	0-1	0-0	0-4	6	2	3	0	0	1	0
Thomas Robinson	1	0-0	0-0	0-0	0	0	0	0	0	0	0
Jeff Withey	1	0-0	0-0	0-0	0	0	0	0	1	0	0
Tyrel Reed	9	1-1	0-0	0-0	0	1	1	0	0	0	2
Team					4						
Totals	225	27-54	5-10	22-33	37	13	24	5	15	4	81

Kansas State (17-4)

Player	MP	FG	3FG	FT	R	A	F	S	TO	B	TP
Denis Clemente*	43	4-15	1-5	4-5	2	2	3	0	2	0	13
Luis Colon*	6	0-1	0-0	0-0	1	0	2	0	1	0	0
Curtis Kelly*	36	5-11	0-0	0-2	6	2	3	1	5	2	10
Jacob Pullen*	41	8-18	4-11	2-3	1	5	3	2	1	0	22
Dominique Sutton*	28	4-10	0-0	1-1	7	2	3	1	1	0	9
Jamar Samuels	20	4-4	1-1	2-4	3	0	5	0	2	1	11
Chris Merriewether	1	0-0	0-0	0-0	0	0	0	0	0	0	0
Martavious Irving	4	0-1	0-1	0-0	1	1	0	0	0	0	0
Wally Judge	24	3-6	0-0	4-4	9	1	5	0	1	1	10
Nick Russell	1	0-0	0-0	0-0	0	0	0	0	0	0	0
Rodney McGruder	19	1-1	0-0	2-3	6	1	1	1	0	0	4
Jordan Henriquez	2	0-0	0-0	0-0	0	0	0	0	0	0	0
Team					2						
Totals	225	29-67	6-18	15-22	38	14	25	5	13	4	79

	1st	2nd	OT	Total	FG%	3FG%	FT%
Kansas	31	38	12	81	50.0	50.0	66.7
Michigan State	30	39	10	79	43.3	33.3	68.2

Officials: Scott Thornley, Paul Janssen, Duke Edsall
Technicals: None

Jacob Pullen: In the second half at about the eight-minute mark, right before the media timeout, Jamar Samuels was at the free throw line. Sherron told one of his teammates, "I'm about to take the game over. I got this. We about to win." I think they were down like four points.

I remembering hearing Sherron say that, and I walked up to that same teammate of his and told him, "If you think that's about to happen, we're about to have a shootout, because I'm not about to lose."

Director of External Relations Barry Hinson: The score was close and we were in a timeout. KT comes up to me and says, "Watch what happens." I asked him if something was wrong and he said, "No, but just watch what Sherron does." Sherron walked out of that huddle and just took the game over. I was thinking, "Holy moly."

Jacob Pullen: Sherron scored eight points really quick after that and I answered one of his 3s with a 3, and then we scored again to go back up. They called a timeout and Sherron walked past me. I told him, "It's not going to be that easy."

The game went to overtime. Collins had tweaked his ankle late in regulation and was dealing with cramps. Collins left the game at the 2:44 mark with his team ahead by one. When he returned with one minute left, KU was still ahead by one, 77-76. That was the score when Self called timeout with 16 seconds remaining.

Sherron Collins: Coach was like, "What do you want to do?" I told him, "Give me the ball and get out of my way." At that point, I was taking all of those shots unless someone doubled me. I hit the and-one over Wally Judge to win it.

Indeed, Collins' layup and ensuing free throw proved to be the difference in KU's 81-79 victory. Collins finished with 16 points while Cole Aldrich had 18 points and 10 rebounds. Pullen scored 22 for K-State.

Bill Self: Sherron got the and-one, and I think he was kind of like, "Hey, this is what we do. This is what I do." I love that about Sherron.

Sherron Collins: We ran that play for most of the rest of the year. "Flat" was my thing. It was how I liked it. The shot clock is at 10. I get the ball and everyone just moves out of the way and I can do what I want.

I'd run "flat" on purpose sometimes, just to make people look bad. If we were up big enough and some dude had been talking s**t and I wanted to f**k him up, I'd milk the clock and call out, "Flat! Flat!" My handle was pretty good and guys like Brady used to love to watch me cross people over.

Brady Morningstar: Late in the game, if we were up a little bit and still had a couple of possessions before it was over, I'd say, "Get 'em, Dot! Mess 'em, Dot! Play with 'em, Dot!" He loved those moments, when he could just freelance and do his thing.

Barry Hinson: As far as a true competitor, there wasn't anyone in my time there that could match Sherron Collins. He had something different inside of him, something special.

All of our players, at some point, had a moment when they were really feeling it, when they were like, "Put the ball in my hands." But I watched Sherron do it game after game after game. His teammates loved him. Even more than that, they respected him. He had a bubbly personality. He was funny. He had the biggest, cheesiest smile you could see on a kid.

Jacob Pullen: Sherron and I talked s**t all the time, because we were friends. We were competitive enough that we could talk s**t and talk to each other during the game where it wasn't like we were about to fight or anything like that.

The funny part was, my whole four years of playing against Kansas, there was never any animosity or a feeling that a fight could start. I think it was because Lawrence to Manhattan is so close, and in the summertime we would meet them at camps. We all worked the same local camps, and if we were going to the LeBron camp or something, we would all hang out with each other. So we got to know each other pretty well. That's why there was never any tension. We had more animosity toward somebody like Missouri. We wanted to fight the kids at Missouri. But with Kansas, it was just a good competitive rivalry. We wanted to win. They wanted to win. But there was never anything dirty like that.

Tyshawn Taylor: I loved when they had Denis Clemente and Pullen and Curtis Kelly and Jamar Samuels. They talked so much trash. S**t, what *didn't* they say? We heard everything from those guys. None of it was good. They were fun games, though. A lot of those guys were from the East Coast, so I knew them. Pullen was from Chicago so he had a relationship with Sherron and knew Mario (Little) a little bit. It was all love. It was always competitive. It was like, "We hate y'all's school, but we respect you guys, because you always give us a game here."

Jacob Pullen: I had a lot of respect for Bill Self, too. The way he took us out of the game was amazing to me, because he utilized our own team against us. He played a triangle-and-two, sometimes a box-and-one, and he just continued to make other people on our team be more effective than they should've been at the time, yet not allow our stars to beat him.

Granted, we were good players, so we figured out a way to get going throughout the game, and I think I still finished with 22, but he just always did a great job of making me work. To this day I still tell people, Bill Self is by far the best coach I played against in my college career other than playing against Coach K (Duke coach Mike Krzyzewski) my senior year. Coach K was really good also. But those two guys from an offensive and defensive standpoint … wow. They change small things to affect both teams—their team and the other team.

Walk the Ball or D Up

KU's lone loss in Big 12 play occurred in an 85-77 setback at Oklahoma State on Feb. 27. The Cowboys shot 60.7 percent, and Keaton Page and James Anderson combined to go 8-of-10 from 3-point range. The following day at practice, Self addressed his team's porous defense with a threat.

Sherron Collins: There was a little bit of jealousy going around. Everyone wanted to be the dude to win a game or take the big shot. The thing we took the most pride in—playing defense—had become secondary. Coach did a smart thing. He knew we loved to run, and we weren't guarding as well as we needed to be. So he said, "If they score on us, we're going to walk the ball up the court." The only way you can run is if they miss. So that made us guard. It made us get back to that feisty defense we were known for and trusting each other. For the most part, I think everyone was just a little tired. Maybe we got our second wind after that, I don't know. But something clicked. After we lost to

Oklahoma State … Coach was pissed. It turned after that.

Bill Self: I'd tell them that all the time. "I want to run, too, but if you're not going to guard them, we're not going to run."

Tyrel Reed: I don't think there was much jealousy. I never felt that in my entire career there, because Coach gave everybody a fair chance. If you were giving 100 percent in practice, you'd get a chance in the game. If you weren't, you didn't get a chance. I don't know if I'd call it jealousy, but it was tough when you had so many guys who deserved to have the ball in their hands and couldn't.

Senior Night

Four days after stumbling in Stillwater, the Jayhawks returned to the court to face No. 5 Kansas State on Senior Night at Allen Fieldhouse. The evening should've been renamed "Sherron Collins Night" as KU paid homage to one of the best players in school history.

Sherron Collins: I was emotional as hell. One minute, I was happy. My KU career was ending and I was going to the NBA. The next minute, I got to thinking, "Damn, I don't want to leave. If I could stay an extra year, I would. I couldn't sleep that day. I was up at 7 a.m. Laughing, crying, remembering stuff, looking back at old YouTube videos and pictures from the national championship. When I walked out on the court that night with my mom and uncle, I couldn't hold back the tears.

Collins struggled that night, going just 5-of-15 from the field for 17 points in KU's 82-65 win. However, Chicago native Jacob Pullen—Collins' off-court friend and on-court nemesis—made sure his final game at Allen Fieldhouse ended on a high note.

With 33 seconds remaining and Collins' sub waiting at the scorer's table, Pullen relaxed his defensive stance and hardly challenged Collins as he drove to the basket for a layup that sent the crowd into a frenzy. Moments later, during a stoppage in play, Collins walked off the court to a standing ovation.

Sherron Collins: Jacob not contesting that layup … I think it was a respect thing. I went up and hugged him and he said, "Man, you set the tone tonight."

Jacob Pullen: When you have a respect for somebody and a respect for their career and what they've done …

Sherron wasn't playing good that night. I remember because I guarded him the whole damn game. He wasn't playing good. So at the end, I told him, "Go get you a bucket. It's your Senior Night. It's your last home game."

Those two points weren't going to change the game. We had already lost. I remember we had cut the lead down to four with 11 minutes left, and they made another run to push the lead back to double digits and it was never close again.

I'm not the type of guy to be petty, especially with somebody who I'd considered a friend throughout college. I had all the respect for him and his career and what he had done. He'd won a national championship, he was first-team All-Big 12 multiple years, he had multiple runs in the NCAA Tournament. When I was growing up watching college basketball on CBS on Saturday mornings ... that's the career I wanted.

I watched guys like Mike Bibby and Miles Simon and Gilbert Arenas and Baron Davis show respect when they played other good players. In Chicago I saw Will Bynum, Luther Head, Deron Williams and Dee Brown do the same thing. You've got to show respect to people sometimes, and I felt like that was a moment where, out of respect, you give up the bucket.

Sherron Collins: I remember shaking Frank Martin's hand after the game, and he was like, "I'm so glad I don't have to f**king deal with you anymore." Jeff Capel at Oklahoma basically said the same thing: *"I'm glad it's over."* I've got a lot respect for Frank Martin. He said some really nice things. He said I was the best competitor he's ever seen. He said he wished he could've coached me.

Frank Martin: For four years, we tried to rattle him defensively, and we could never get him rattled. Every game that came down to the last possession, he'd make the big play on offense or defense and not let us win. That's why I said what I did that day. I meant it. I was so happy I didn't have to coach against him anymore. I was a big, big fan of his.

Sherron Collins: That day went by so fast, and then it was over. It was bittersweet.

What stuck with me was when Coach Self introduced me. I was tearing up. He was telling people how stubborn I used to be. He was talking about life events—from me losing my kid, to all of the other issues I'd had with family and friends. He said, "Everything is going to be OK now. Everything you do now is for them."

Barry Hinson: Sherron did a lot for Kansas basketball, and on Senior Night I think it was obvious that Kansas basketball had meant a lot to Sherron, too. You see it with almost all of the guys on Senior Night, when that bottom lip starts quivering. That's when you realize how much it means to those kids. You look up in the stands on Senior Night and you see people crying. It's an emotional night, because you've got kids reflecting on the past four years, and they're remembering what Bill Self told them about Kansas basketball back when they were being recruited: "If you give it a chance, it'll change your life." Almost every time, if the kids do their part, that promise comes true.

Bill Self: I had a lump in my throat that night. I don't for everybody. Not because I don't care about everybody, but usually the ones I have the biggest lump for are the ones where I just know how much crap they've gone through to see the finish line.

For instance, my son Tyler... it was so great for me. But I wasn't emotional with him, I was proud. Or Landen (Lucas). I was proud. So proud. Frank (Mason) ... that was a little bit different, because of all the heartache he'd been through and to see where he's come from and see how this place has changed him. It was tough not to get emotional. Brady, Tyrel, Wayne... that's such a proud moment. With Jamari (Traylor), looking

back and thinking how six years ago this kid was homeless; those are the ones that get you. Darnell Jackson, thinking everything he went through, those are the ones that get me. And, of course, Sherron. That may have been the toughest of all.

Jacob Pullen: Sherron and I went to dinner after the game that night. I stayed down there because it was near the end of the regular season and we had the next day off. He was just like, "It flies by, man." Me being a junior and going into my senior year that next year, I realized it really does fly by. You're having fun and you're always doing something; it's not like you're sitting still for long periods at a time. So time's really just flying by.

We really didn't even talk about basketball that much. We just talked about life and how we're just enjoying life. In college, you're an adult but you're not really an adult. You don't have bills. You don't have responsibilities like that, but you're on your own so you have to be responsible. It just was a good time.

Sherron Collins: Me and Pullen, there was a mutual respect there. We're both from the same city. He came to Lawrence to hang out—but I was never going to go to Manhattan.

That's why we have the best fans in America. I can't go to Missouri and go out in Columbia. I'd probably have to fight. Someone is going to say something to you. Ron Anderson was boys with Brady and Pullen was my boy. They came up and we went to Quinton's and The Hawk and everywhere. Everyone was coming up to Pullen and telling him how good he was. They treated him great.

While Senior Night was all about Collins, the presence of another "celebrity"—adult film star Samantha Ryan—generated quite a buzz the morning after the game.

Assistant coach Kurtis Townsend: Her real name is Jamie Mance. I'd met her on a Southwest flight from Los Angeles to Kansas City on the way home from a recruiting trip earlier that summer. She recognized me as a KU coach and sat next to me. She was like, "I love Kansas basketball. I went there and I used to camp out for tickets when Jacque Vaughn played there. I've never had great seats. Can me and my brother come to a game sometime?" I asked her what she did in LA and she just said she was a model and an actress. I gave her my card, and she called before the K-State game and I left her and her brother good seats.

The whole thing blew up the next morning, because, using her porn account, she'd tweeted out a picture from the stands during the game, thanking me for the tickets. People were saying, "You left tickets for a porn star named Samantha Ryan?" I was like, "No, I left tickets for Jamie Mance. She never told me what she did."

So that whole thing blows up and, of course, three days later we have to play at Missouri. They had guys dressed like women with balloons under their shirts. They had signs that said "Coach T, I need tickets!" and "Free Mustache Rides" and "Wanna Make A Movie?" Every time I walked by, they bowed. Sherron and all of the guys were cracking up and giving me such a hard time. It was funny, although my wife didn't think so.

So Much Pressure

The Jayhawks handled the Tigers, 77-56, and finished Big 12 play with a 15-1 record. They won their three Big 12 Tournament games by an average of 11 points and were 32-2 entering their first-round NCAA Tournament game against Lehigh and star guard C.J. McCollum in Oklahoma City—the home state of Self and star freshman Henry. And also the site of KU's 2005 loss to Bucknell.

Sherron Collins: I felt so much pressure going into the tournament because President Obama picked us to win—and he even said my name on television. "My Chicago boy, Sherron Collins ... I'm going with the Jayhawks."

Right then, I felt pressure. I didn't want to make Obama look bad, and even though we'd been winning, there was still so much I had to worry about as the leader of the team. The main issue was Xavier. I had to get him under control because he was still so worried about how many shots he took and how many points he scored. Most of that was coming from his dad.

Bill Self: Xavier played well for us. He was our second leading scorer (13.4 points). But it was a hard year for him.

Sherron Collins: Xavier showed flashes sometimes. But he worried too much. He was worried about the wrong things. It may have messed up our chemistry a bit, but not too much. Any freshman that comes in and starts is going to mess up chemistry. The only thing he messed up was a chance for everyone else who had been waiting. Guys like Mario Little and Travis Releford ... the guys that were ready to step in and play, he messed it up for them. But that's recruiting, that's college basketball. At times Xavier really helped us. There were also a lot of games when he just shot so much. I was like, "Daaaammmnnn! Come on, dog! Seriously?"

We never knew the kind of pressure Xavier was under until he told us one day. He said when he had a bad game, his family let him know about it. We used to get mad at him because he was always pouting on the court and crying and this and that. We played UCLA on the road, and his father was standing behind the rim at Pauley Pavilion, telling Xavier not to pass the ball, just shoot it every time. I told Coach Self, and Coach made him move into the stands and leave Xavier alone. That's what he went through all year, but he didn't tell us about it until we were going into the Big 12 Tournament. We had one game where we were up by about 30, and he was still pouting. I went off. I was like, "What's your problem? We're up by 30. It doesn't matter if you're having a bad game. We're winning." I snapped. Coach took him out. When we got to the locker room he told me what the deal was, and I went and told Coach Self, "Man, his father is f**king with him." I felt bad because I was on his ass all year, but I never knew what he was going through.

Bill Self: If you go back and look at the NCAA Tournament, we played Lehigh in the first game, and when Xavier finally made a basket, you could just tell the pressure was off of him. It was in Oklahoma City, worst place in the world for us to play because of all the pressure on him. He was such a sweet kid. We all loved him. He had a great year, but I don't think he was quite as good down the stretch as what he could have done.

Brady Morningstar: When we played Lehigh, CJ McCollum busted my ass. I took him for granted. I didn't know much about him because I hadn't seen him on TV, and he just busted my ass. I couldn't guard him. He was killing me. Shifty, shaky, getting to the basket and scoring. Now look at him. He's one of the best players in the NBA.

McCollum scored 26 points—but so did Kansas' Marcus Morris. And his tally came on 12-of-15 shooting in what turned out to be a relatively easy 90-74 victory for the Jayhawks.

Awaiting KU in the next round was a well-coached Northern Iowa squad that had advanced by beating UNLV 69-66. The key player in that win was guard Ali Farokhmanesh, whose 3-pointer with 4.9 seconds remaining propelled the Panthers to their first NCAA Tournament win in 20 years.

Ali Farokhmanesh: When I was a freshman, I used to sit in my dorm at Kirkwood (Iowa) Community College and watch Sherron Collins play for Kansas. I loved watching him play. You talk about someone who had the perfect combination of strength and quickness ... wow. There weren't many guards like him, even in the NBA. He was like an Isaiah Thomas-type. We're the same age, but back then, I never would've imagined I'd have a chance to play against Sherron.

That's what I kept telling my roommate, Adam Koch, the night before we faced Kansas in the NCAA Tournament. We were sitting in our hotel room in Oklahoma City, and I was like, "This is crazy. I used to watch this guy in my dorm room at a D-II junior college. I looked up to him, and now we're about to be on the same floor."

In our film session that night at the hotel, we watched highlights of Kansas. Obviously—and as a coach now (at Drake) I realize this even more—whenever the coaches are making the highlight reels of the personnel and clips of their offense and defense, it's a great highlight film. But nobody's highlight film looked quite like theirs. They had length. They had size. They could shoot the ball. There weren't any flaws, really. Cole Aldrich was an All-American and Xavier Henry had a 6-10 wingspan. They had talent everywhere, even on the bench with a future lottery pick in Thomas

Robinson. We were pretty nervous, but we were excited, too. I just remember watching it and being like, "They're really good."

Northern Iowa coach Ben Jacobson: We obviously had a lot of things to be concerned with as we prepared for Kansas, but one thing I wasn't worried about was our mentality. I wasn't worried about our toughness. We were older, and whether it would have been Kansas or anybody else—and this is not a shot at Kansas—our guys were not scared.

As good as they were, and as tough as Collins was, and as hard as they played, and as impressive as their will was and all of that, I wasn't concerned about the toughness part, because we had some tough guys. I knew we were going to play our tails off, because we always did. I knew we would get to some loose balls. I knew we would get some offensive rebounds, because that's what our guys did.

Bill Self: I really felt like we had a team that could win it all, but the Northern Iowa game ... things didn't feel right before the game. There was something that was wrong.

Ali Farokhmanesh: During our pregame interactions with them, they were talking the whole time. In the NCAA Tournament, you can't touch the ball until 60 minutes before tipoff. It's kind of ridiculous. You're all just standing out there doing nothing before you can actually grab a basketball, and I remember them just talking to us the whole time. That was the biggest interactions I remember...

Collins talked a little bit, but he wasn't really trash talking. It was mainly the Morris twins who were really getting after it. They were saying everything in the book. It was like, "You f**king white boys don't know what's coming." It was everything imaginable you'd predict the No. 1 team in the country would say to a bunch of kids from nowhere in Iowa. It was mainly stuff like that. "You guys don't have a chance. It's not happening. You guys might as well pack up your bags right now." It went on for probably 10 minutes straight, and we're just sitting on the other end stretching.

It made me laugh, because there's 70 minutes before the game. Whatever you're saying to me now, I'm not even going to remember by the time the jump ball happens. At least save it for when I'm on the court with you. If you're busting out all the good lines now, what are you going to say once the game gets going? I more laughed it off. One of our guys, Lucas (O'Rear), the guy with the muttonchops, he was talking back to them a little bit because he likes that stuff and he doesn't care. But really, we're on a basketball court. What are you going to do to me? If we were going to fight, yeah, you can probably beat me up. I can't even reach your head. I've never understood that. There's some guys who will let you get into their heads. But we were a bunch of seniors who had won 60 games already. We weren't questioning ourselves at that point.

Northern Iowa set the tone early when Jordan Eglseder—a 7-foot, 280-pounder—hit a 3-pointer from the right wing. One possession later he swished a mid-range, turnaround jumper over Aldrich that gave the Panthers a 5-2 lead and, more importantly, a huge jolt of momentum.

Cole Aldrich: Eglseder had gone 1-for-9 from 3-point range all year. One of the first shots he took was a 3. I wasn't going to guard him because I knew he wasn't going to make it. He missed it, but then he made his next two. In my head I was thinking, "What the hell? This isn't what they've done all year."

Sherron Collins: There was something different about Cole that game. He let their big fella (Eglseder) set the tone for them. He came out and scored seven points in the first few minutes. He hit two 3s that game and had that left hook. We were like, "Damn, Cole, we told you to be ready to get out there and guard him." That was always our problem with Cole, getting him to guard on the perimeter. Anytime he faced a big 7-footer or somebody that was supposedly decent or good, he got timid.

Ali Farokhmanesh: I think we shocked them a little bit. They weren't expecting us to come out like that. One key to pulling a big upset is to jump ahead early, and that's what happened. That started the whole thing and we played with momentum the rest of that first half.

Sherron Collins: Everything felt different. Everything went wrong. First of all, we weren't used to being down by 10 points. We were down by nine or 10 points most of the game. We weren't used to playing from behind. Being down by a few points is OK—but not double digits.

Northern Iowa's biggest lead of the first half came at the 3:31 mark, when Farokhmanesh swished a 17-foot jumper that put the Panthers ahead 33-24. Farokhmanesh was a perfect 4-of-4 in the opening stanza and made all three of his shots from behind the arc.

Ali Farokhmanesh: At one point, Sherron Collins and I were checking in at the same time, and he said, "Damn white boy, you can shoot."

The Panthers led 36-28 at intermission.

Sherron Collins: When we got into the locker room at halftime, everyone was arguing, including myself. Tyshawn said something to me about a loose ball that I didn't get. I was like, "Shut the f**k up. Why don't you start guarding Farokhmanesh so he'll stop scoring all over your ass?" Coach Self came in and flipped a table over and screamed at us. All the 3s we were hitting two days before against Lehigh weren't falling. We couldn't hit anything.

Bill Self: At halftime, we go in and we're getting beat by eight and it wasn't the feeling of, "All right guys, we're better than this. Let's pull together." It was more of, "Hey men, y'all need to get your ass in gear." It didn't have the same feel. Something was off.

Ben Jacobson: Going into it, we felt like we had to find a way to keep Collins somewhat under control if we could, and our point guard Kwadzo Ahelegbe did a terrific job. That was the best defensive game of his career.

And then, outside of the X's and O's, we felt like we could play Cole Aldrich one-on-one when Jordan Eglseder was in. We felt like we were going to have to double some of the other guys on the block. Our guys executed a lot of those things almost to perfection.

So I felt like some of that would happen. The part that was outside of our control was that they were going to have to miss a couple 3s—and we were going to have to make a couple, and that played out. That's why we had a big lead for a lot of the middle part of the game. We made some 3s and they missed some 3s.

Kansas made just 6-of-23 threes for the game and just 2-of-12 in the second half, when Northern Iowa refused to let KU gain momentum. The Jayhawks trailed 52-41 with 10:21 remaining and, twice over the next seven minutes, they pulled within three points, but each time the Panthers responded with a basket to thwart Kansas' run.

Ali Farokhmanesh: We just kept playing our game. Coach Jacobson kept us focused. We weren't really thinking about winning the game, necessarily. It was more of, "make the next play, make the next play, make the next play," and I think that's how you have to approach it. You start thinking "we're about to beat Kansas" ... that's how you *lose* to Kansas. That's the biggest thing. We stayed with the process of making the next play. We didn't really think about winning the basketball game at that point.

They definitely gave us a run at the end, though. I've watched replays of the game before and I thought we were going to lose in the last two minutes. They were definitely making plays and seemed pretty confident to me.

Using a suffocating full-court press, the Jayhawks started getting easy baskets off Northern Iowa turnovers—the biggest of which occurred when Ahelegbe, who was being pressured by Marcus Morris, stepped on the line after catching an inbounds pass under the KU basket.

Kansas capitalized seconds later with a layup from Collins that pulled KU within a point, 63-62, with 44 seconds remaining.

Ali Farokhmanesh: We hadn't really worked on a press break because they didn't press anybody all year. We weren't expecting it and we made a lot of bad decisions. That happens when teams make runs. It wasn't like some guy was going off on us. We made a lot of bad choices and they made us pay for it.

Still, there was no sense of panic. Of course now, if I was watching the game all these years later, I'd be thinking, "Oh, they're about to lose." But that night it was crazy. There was absolutely no sense of panic, and you've got to give a lot of credit to Coach Jake. He kind of built that demeanor into our team, where you never saw us too high or too low. That was key in that moment, although I'm sure everyone in the stands thought we were going to crumble. There's a picture of my mom at that point in the game and she looks like we'd already lost.

Kansas called a timeout after Collins' basket to set up its defense and, sure enough, the Jayhawks applied their full-court press as soon as Northern Iowa inbounded the ball. This time, though, the Panthers didn't flounder under pressure.

When Tyshawn Taylor gambled and went for a steal on a pass from the baseline to midcourt, Farokhmanesh was left all alone. Ahelegbe fired a chest pass to the senior, and Farokhmanesh caught it on the right wing, just beyond the 3-point line, and eyed the basket. Tyrel Reed was the nearest defender.

Tyrel Reed: I was the last guy back. We were pressuring them full court, and I was the last guy back. I did a jab and retreat on him. I was trying to stop him, or at least rattle him. But I had to make sure I protected the hole as well. The court was wide open.

Plus, who thinks you're going to shoot a 3 at that moment, right?

Sherron Collins: No one knew it was coming. I never thought for a second that he'd shoot that 3. They were up by one point with 40 seconds left. Who is going to take that shot in that situation? You're supposed to pull back, run some clock and let the other team foul you.

Northern Iowa 69, Kansas 67
March 20, 2010 · Oklahoma City, Okla.

Northern Iowa (30-4)

Player	MP	FG	3FG	FT	R	A	F	S	TO	B	TP
Johnny Moran*	23	2-3	2-3	2-2	2	2	0	0	4	0	8
Jordan Eglseder*	18	6-11	2-3	0-0	5	0	2	0	1	0	14
Ali Farokhmanesh*	31	5-12	4-10	2-2	1	1	0	1	1	0	16
Adam Koch*	24	4-5	0-1	0-0	5	2	4	0	0	0	8
Kwadzo Ahelegbe*	30	1-11	0-3	3-4	1	5	2	1	2	0	5
Marc Sonnen	15	1-2	0-1	0-0	3	0	2	3	0	0	2
Kerwin Dunham	20	1-2	0-0	1-1	3	1	1	2	0	1	3
Anthony James	2	0-0	0-0	0-0	0	0	0	0	0	0	0
Jake Koch	20	1-7	1-5	7-8	2	0	3	0	1	0	10
Lucas O'Rear	17	1-2	0-0	1-2	5	0	2	2	0	0	3
Team					3						
Totals	200	22-55	9-26	16-19	30	11	16	9	9	1	69

Kansas (33-3)

Player	MP	FG	3FG	FT	R	A	F	S	TO	B	TP
Cole Aldrich*	27	6-8	0-0	1-2	10	1	1	1	2	2	13
Marcus Morris*	28	5-8	2-3	4-6	4	0	4	1	3	0	16
Tyshawn Taylor*	220	0-6	0-5	2-2	2	3	1	0	0	0	2
Sherron Collins*	38	4-15	0-6	2-2	3	4	3	0	5	0	10
Xavier Henry*	32	3-6	2-4	0-1	8	0	2	2	1	0	8
Brady Morningstar	8	0-1	0-1	0-0	0	1	2	0	0	0	0
Tyrel Reed	26	3-6	2-4	0-0	2	0	4	1	2	0	8
Markieff Morris	19	3-4	0-0	4-5	3	0	2	0	2	1	10
Team					6						
Totals	200	24-54	6-23	13-18	38	9	19	5	15	3	67

	1st	2nd	Total	FG%	3FG%	FT%
Northern Iowa	36	33	69	40.0	34.6	84.2
Kansas	28	39	67	44.4	26.1	72.2

Officials: Bob Donato, Mike Nance, Joe Lindsay
Technicals: None

Ali Farokhmanesh: It was the first time I saw the basket in probably three minutes. I didn't realize it at the time, but I had missed my last seven shots in a row. I was 4-for-4 to start and then I was 4-of-11 going into that big shot. But that's the whole mentality Coach Jake instilled. He had the utmost confidence in me since the day I got there. And think about it. It was a great situation. Wide open shot on the wing, up by one with a nine-second difference on the shot clock. I knew if I made it, we'd win.

Ben Jacobson: Ali always took those shots. We had a game at Iowa State where we were down by one with 25 seconds left, and we threw it up to him on the sideline and he caught it and threw it in, so we were up two. Nobody shoots that shot. You're down one with 25 seconds left on the road at Iowa State. You make sure you get it inside. You don't shoot a transition 3. He did. He made it. Two nights earlier in Oklahoma City, against UNLV, the game was tied and he hit a 3 with five seconds left.

So contrary to popular belief, it wasn't a "no-no-no … yeah!" kinda deal. When the ball got thrown to him, Tyrel Reed started moving out to him, but then he had another guy to worry about—it was kind of a two-on-one—so he backed up ... I knew Ali was going to shoot it. All of our guys did. We knew he'd take that shot.

That's probably the best part of it. It wasn't, "S**t, what should I do?" As soon as Reed moved back, he knew he was going to shoot it.

Farokhmanesh's heroic shot gave Northern Iowa a 66-62 lead with 35 seconds remaining. Kansas turned the ball over on a charge by Reed on its next possession, and the Panthers took advantage when Ahelegbe split a pair of free throws to make it 67-62 with 18 seconds left. The game was essentially over after Collins and Taylor each missed 3s moments later.

A pair of free throws by Farokhmanesh (who tallied 16 points) and a 3 at the buzzer by Marcus Morris rounded out the scoring in Northern Iowa's 69-67 win.

Ali Farokhmanesh: It was a feeling of euphoria, a once-in-a-lifetime moment. You work so hard for something your whole life, and then you get on that stage and to do it with a group of guys you've been battling with and running lines with and going through tough practices with ... there's nothing like it.

The best part was accomplishing something not a lot of people thought we could do, something we'd set our eyes on for a long time.

Tyrel Reed: You've got to give him credit. He took the shot and it went in, and he's a hero because of it. If he misses and we win, it's never talked about again.

While Farokhmanesh's shot made him a national name, the bigger story around Lawrence was that KU's loss to Northern Iowa marked the end of Collins' time as a Jayhawk. Collins had one of the worst shooting nights of his career against Northern Iowa, making just 4-of-15 shots—and going 0-of-6 from deep—while committing five turnovers in 38 minutes. Considering all he'd accomplished in his career, going out in that fashion didn't seem fitting.

Sherron Collins: I feel like I completely flopped. Cole did, too. The guys that were supposed to produce didn't produce. I can live with that. It was our fault. I'll live with that. We should've won the title that year. We were the best team.

Tyshawn Taylor: We were the best team in the country. We easily should've won the championship. We were the No. 1 overall seed in the tournament. We lost because, again, Sherron had to be the man, and we all knew it. He was throwing his weight around too much. Xavier did the same thing.

We didn't lose just because of Sherron, though. I didn't play great either. Cole and Marcus played good. Brady and Tyrel were solid. But Sherron wanted to be the man and go out with a bang.

Strength and conditioning coach Andrea Hudy: If you don't win a national championship, your season is a disappointment. To enjoy the wins and stuff is fine. But remembering the faces of guys looking for comfort after a loss that ends their season and their career … it's pretty sad. Sherron and Cole, I really felt for them after we lost to Northern Iowa. Cole was a hard worker. Sherron was great. We weren't supposed to lose to Northern Iowa. Just walking into that locker room, I couldn't hold back my tears.

Sherron Collins: The loss didn't hit me at first. I didn't cry in the locker room. Everyone else was crying. I just remember looking at everyone crying and shaking my head. I went around to all the young guys and said, "Don't let this happen again. Y'all still have some time, but this is it for me. It ain't a good feeling." I got back to Lawrence the next day, and my whole place was quiet. My brothers were there. They hadn't made it to Oklahoma City for the game because they figured we'd win easily and then they would just go to St. Louis for the Sweet 16. That's when it all hit me. I flew home to Chicago the next day.

Bill Self: At that moment, when it's a one-and-done situation and the pressure's mounting and you're the favorite and things aren't going well ... sometimes that's a harder situation than being behind and playing with house money.

When you look at that game, guys that had had great years—unbelievable years—just didn't play well. Sherron wanted it so bad that he put pressure on himself. But he shouldn't blame himself. Nah. He won so many games for us. Those two (Sherron and Cole) … you could never say that. You could never say it was their fault. We just weren't very good that weekend.

After the season, Aldrich and Henry left school early and entered the NBA draft, where they were both lottery picks. Collins went undrafted but signed with the Charlotte Bobcats, who were coached by Larry Brown. The Morris twins, Reed, Morningstar and others returned the following season, but the pain of the Northern Iowa loss has never completely subsided.

Tyrel Reed: All these years later, I've let it go now. I try not to dwell on things. I have patients come in, and I won't even talk about basketball. I'm pretty good at letting things go. Still, it's frustrating to think about, because we had such a great team that year. For it to end like that ...

Bill Self: We've had some disappointing losses, obviously, but I still think the toughest would be Bucknell, VCU and Northern Iowa. Even though Oregon was tough (in 2017) and Villanova was tough (in 2016), those were great teams. If we played them 10 times, we'd go 5-5. It wasn't like we were a lot better or anything like that. But those other three teams, I thought we were better than them.

Tribute to Sherron

During interviews for this book, opposing players and coaches were often asked to name the Jayhawk that impressed them the most. The answers were usually the same: Sherron Collins. Bill Self—a man that has coached 11 NBA lottery picks at Kansas—believes he's the best player he's ever had at KU. These next few pages are a tribute to Collins from those who played with him and against him.

Brady Morningstar: With Sherron's background, Coach Self knew it'd be helpful if Sherron had people in town—people outside of the basketball program—to kind of take him in and look after him. My family and I seemed like the perfect fit since we lived in Lawrence. We could show him around and take him places and take care of him. Coach Self came to me and said, "Hey, I'm going to put you in a room with Sherron," and I was like, "No problem."

Sherron had so many friends and family members back in Chicago who looked up to him. And here's the thing: They were all looking at him to get them out of where they were. He was the prodigy out of Chicago. He was the best player in the city. He had a chance to do something with his future. Basketball was taking him to Kansas and maybe to the NBA. Basketball was supposed to take him everywhere. *"C'mon Sherron, you can do this. You've got to do this!"* You know how much pressure that put on him? Yet he still performed every night. And they're all thinking he's going to the NBA, which he did. As much pressure as people put on him, he performed about as well as anyone could perform at the college level.

A week into me and him staying in the Towers together, my parents went out of town, so I brought my boxer, Mackie, to our apartment at the Towers. Sherron wasn't there when I showed up, and then I had to leave for about 10 minutes, so I left Mackie by herself in the living room. Sherron shows up while I'm gone and Mackie ran up and jumped on him, because she was so excited to see someone and wanted to play. Sherron ran outside and sprinted down the hall and called me and said, "Yo, there's a f**king dog in our room." I told him it was mine and he was like, "Get that thing out of here." For the next year, when he'd come to our house, he wouldn't come in until Mackie was barricaded or upstairs. It took her about a year, but finally my mom convinced Sherron that Mackie was harmless. Sherron ended up loving her and giving her treats all the time.

Elijah Johnson: Sherron was a different kind of leader. With Sherron, where you were from and your history determined how your relationship with him was going to be. Sherron was from Chicago and he never forgot that. A lot of people forget where they're from, but Sherron was from Chicago and he never for one second forgot that. He was proud of it.

If you can't adapt to how a Chicago person can be toward you—up, down, feeling good one day, feeling bad the next—if you can't respond to that, you're not going to get along with Sherron. Xavier had a tough time with it. Sherron was a good leader for me. He let me bump my head. He called me stupid when I was being stupid. I'm from the Chicago area. I responded well. Same with Tyshawn. Same with the twins and Mario Little. It worked well for us. People like Cole and Xavier ... it wasn't that they didn't like Sherron, but they might look at it differently than I do.

In practice if you weren't going hard or getting your work in, Sherron wasn't going to mess with you. It's not like he was always cussing at people or being a butthole. It was just his demeanor and how he came off. He'd come in there some days and wouldn't say a word to anyone. He'd just walk out onto the court and be on another level than anyone

in the gym, where he might not miss more than one or two shots the entire workout. He'd be in his own zone and then sub himself out. People saw that and were motivated by it. He was as real as he could've been.

I don't think there was another senior captain in the country that could've gotten to me better or impacted me more. He set a great example. He put his work in. Regardless of his weight—whether he was heavy or in perfect shape—he was getting up at 5:30 in the morning to do extra stuff, and he did it for years and years and years. People wanted to criticize him for his weight, but I think he had a weight disorder that he couldn't always control. Sherron never showed me that he didn't want to work. He never gave me the chance to say, "He doesn't want to work today. He's lazy." He was the last of a dying breed. You can't get that out of too many people anymore. Everyone now tries to be too nice. Sherron wasn't worried about being nice. He was like, "You're either helping us put another banner on the wall, or you can put your shoes on and get out of here."

When Sherron got to the NBA, he was used to being on top of the world at KU. He got knocked down a little bit and had to climb back to the top of the world again. Sherron had the world in his hands in Lawrence. He didn't have anything left to prove to us at the collegiate level. Every college coach was scared to play against him. Everyone respected him. He made his mark. His picture was plastered everywhere. He was a big shot.

Jeremy Case: Every time I see him, I'm like "That mofo should be playing in the league right now." He was way better than Ty Lawson. Way better. He just couldn't keep his weight down. I don't think that's a secret. He had issues.

Conner Teahan: They didn't allow Sherron or Rodrick Stewart to lift weights because they just were too big and I guess they put on muscle weight too quick.

At the end of my freshman year, I'd been been working out all summer long. We were doing our maxes and I think I was doing 260 on the bench press. It was a struggle for me, but I was feeling great about it.

Sherron had just come down from doing 35-40 minutes on the elliptical. He asks, "How much you got on there?" I tell him 260. He lays down on the bench, with no practice reps or warmups, and presses it five times. He racks the weight, gets up and says, "I could've done more," and walks away.

Bill Self: I never let him lift. Every time the team lifted, all he did was cardio. He was already so strong. There was an elliptical up there that, of all the athletes that have used that thing at KU, Sherron probably accounts for half of it. He lived on that thing. But he never complained.

Jacob Pullen: Sherron was a dog. Sherron was arguably the best guard in Chicago in his class and the best guard in the city period from his sophomore to senior year. Sherron was somebody when you walked into the gym, you heard people saying, "Oh, Sherron Collins is here. He's about to play." And then everyone grabs a seat to watch. Or you'd hear other guards say, "Oh s**t, I've got to play against Sherron." I've seen Sherron have battles with the best guards to come out of Chicago, from Will Bynum to Derrick Rose to Luther Head... Sherron, in his prime in high school and college, was by far one of the best guards I ever played.

With him and Derrick Rose, it was a fight. There was never a game when they played each other that one of them just destroyed the other. D-Rose in high school was a freak athlete, so that kind of put him in a different category because his athletic ability was beyond anything people had seen in high school at that point, but as far as a basketball player, Sherron Collins could dribble the ball better than anybody, could shoot the ball as good as anybody and he was athletic in high school. Sherron was dunking on people. People forget that in the McDonald's All-American game, Sherron was dunking on people. He had bounce at that point in his life. He hadn't put on that college weight. He was an NBA player in high school, some would say. He was that legit.

Iowa State coach Greg McDermott: Most of the KU players I wished I could have coached because they were so talented, but I really loved Sherron's game. There was a toughness to what he did. You had to figure out a way to stop him and it was very difficult to do it one-on-one because he was so powerful. As soon as you brought help and started plugging up the lane, he was able to spray it and make plays for his teammates. During that era, you had some pros that came through there, but he was one that stuck out to me, and those teams took on his mentality of toughness and followed his lead in that regard.

Ben Jacobson: Sherron Collins, with his mentality ... you didn't have to watch film very long to figure out he was in charge. He was the one that made everything go. He just had that toughness to him that "my team is not going to get beat." And then they had so many weapons, so many things you were going to have to defend. I think the mentality that Collins had, that was the thing that really struck me, the thing that set the tone.

Northern Colorado coach Tad Boyle: Sherron Collins was tough as nails. He knew what it took to win. He had so much talent but he was also a junkyard dog. Bill likes those kinds of players. He was special.

Kansas State assistant coach Brad Underwood: Sherron Collins ... he was dominant. He's one of the best college players I've ever coached against. He was an incredible winner. He got up for big games. We always saw his best. He elevated everybody else.

A little more from ...

Ali Farokhmanesh: I wouldn't say I felt bad for Kansas for having to play us. If anything, I felt bad for us. We were 28-4. We did have some bad losses, so I get it, but we were 28-4 and rolled through a pretty good Missouri Valley Conference that year. I don't think we should have been a 9 seed, but it goes back to the whole idea of a mid-major bias. I get that, and Coach Self has said that before that we weren't a 9 seed. But as much as it sucked for them, it sucked for us, too. We didn't want to play the No. 1 team in the second round.

I guess you could say that hitting that shot and winning that game changed my life—at least some aspects of it. I'm a coach in Iowa now, at Drake, and I go around and people still recognize me. We've gone to, like, five different restaurants just in Des Moines, and there's a picture of me making that shot up on the walls. Even when I text recruits now, or text or call their parents, usually it gets brought up at some point, especially with kids in the Midwest. *"Oh wait, you're that guy ... "* It's fun to get to relive that moment.

In 2015, when KU opened the NCAA Tournament in Omaha, a TV station had me go around and interview KU fans about the Northern Iowa game. It was funny seeing if anyone would recognize me. The first person we interviewed had no idea. He swore he was the biggest Jayhawk fan ever and been to every single game in history—but he had no idea what I was talking about. I'm like, "Wow, I don't know if this is going to work that well." We almost packed it up after the first two because it didn't go so well. Then the next one went really well. The guy was like, "No f**king s**t?" It was fun. Fans are awesome. It was really cool. They embraced it more than anything else. They had fun with it. Nobody was really mad that I was doing it. They treated me great.

Quincy Acy: Cole and I ended up being teammates on the Knicks. I was impressed with his work ethic. I'm a guy that likes to get to the gym early and leave late. Every time I'd get there early, Cole would be there already. He's a worker, a hard-nosed, blue-collar kind of guy that doesn't complain much. He's the kind of guy our coach wouldn't play for five games straight, but then they'd put him in and he'd get a double-double. He's a high-spirited, high-energy type of guy. He was a great teammate. Whenever we'd talk about Kansas and Baylor, he'd have the bragging rights. Those conversations were usually pretty short.

Sherron Collins: When we won the Big 12, the celebrations weren't too big. We'd jump around in the locker room for a few minutes and take a picture with the trophy. But then it was like, "We've got a tournament coming up" and we'd start thinking about that. But we knew we were getting rings, and that was a big deal. I buried one of them with my uncle, Walt, who walked out on the court with me on Senior Night. I put one in his jacket pocket.

I loved the Morris twins. I just wish I could've played with them another year or two. That's when they really got good. They are fun to be around. They're jokesters. They could be dead serious and then say something, "Yo, Dot, man. I almost died, man."

I used to love when someone pissed them off in a game with a dirty play or something. There were times when someone did something to me and I'd be like, "Yo, when that dude comes down the court, lay him out." The next play I'd look up and the dude was keeled over on the court or hobbling back to the bench. I'd looked over at Kieff or Mook and they'd just nod their head and smile a little bit. They took care of me. That's how we all felt about each other: Right or wrong, we had each other's backs.

Thomas Robinson: I handled my first year at Kansas pretty well, because the year before I was in prep school. So I was used to being away from home and having more responsibility. It was still a tough transition, though, because basketball-wise, it was a different level for me, a new intensity. From the coaching to the playing to the practicing, it was a whole new level. I started to question, "Is this for me, or is this *not* for me?" I thought about leaving. I was going to transfer or go back home, probably to a smaller school.

Remember, a year before, Kansas and big schools like that weren't even on my radar. It had been such a slow recruiting process for me and then … boom! It all just took off. In a little over a week I went from being unranked to all of these schools wanting me. So in my eyes, going back home to a smaller school wasn't as crazy as it might sound now, because that's the level a lot of people had pegged me for anyway. And at that point, after barely playing as a freshman, I wasn't chasing NBA dreams. The twins talked me into staying. I worked my butt off that next summer before my sophomore year so I could get on the floor somehow. I played about 15 minutes a game.

As a freshman, you have no clout. You have no pull. You haven't done anything. You haven't won anything for the school yet, and they treat you like that. I was like, "I need to hurry up and win something around here to put some clout on my name so they won't be on my ass every day." I was chasing that more than anything. I wanted to show Coach Self that, while the challenge he had given me may have been hard as hell, I could handle it.

The challenge was more mental than physical. Coach Self breaks you down to where you have no self-esteem, no confidence. It won't last very long, but he breaks you down. Then he instills all the right things in you and lets you find yourself and figure it out. One day he's telling you you're the worst player in the country, and the next he's saying, "No one can f**k with you. No one can touch you. You're going to dominate." It makes you feel good when you reach that point, because you try so hard to please him. This is the same guy who used to make you feel like you can't dribble a ball, and a year later he's making you feel like you're invincible.

Tyshawn Taylor: The Xavier Henry experience was unique that season. His family seemed to have a lot of say on what went down with him. I almost forgot about C.J. having that much influence on us the first semester. For a while he practiced with us and had a chance to be in certain drills when we didn't think he should, talentwise. Finally Coach Self got tired of it and was like, "He's not good." Cool dude, but he wouldn't be at Kansas if his brother wasn't there.

This is my feeling about Xav. He came in with a lot of hype—a really good high school player. But college is a different game. You're on a team with better players. Even if you're the BEST player, the second and third options are usually really good, too. Plus, at Kansas, there's a system. It's not about one player. It's a system. The players have to fit within the system.

Xav did a great job of fitting in a system when he was making shots. But when he wasn't shooting well, the system didn't work for him, which made it harder for him to play. But he had to play, because he had to be one-and-done. Coach Self needed that. If Xavier had come here and not turned into a one-and-done, Coach Self may have never got an Andrew Wiggins or a Joel Embiid or a Kelly Oubre. Xavier had to leave, no matter how good or bad he played. It kinda sucked for him. I felt like, at the end of the year, he didn't know if he wanted to leave. He was on the fence about it, even though we were all like, "Yo, we knew you were leaving the minute you got here." I don't know if he felt like he played great. He had some good moments, but they all came early.

If you don't buy in, Coach Self doesn't give a f**k if you're supposedly a lottery pick. Brannen Greene came in here and was supposed to be a key guy and couldn't buy in. Even Kelly Oubre went through that stage where he struggled to get on the same page, and had to sit on the bench until he decided to get with the program.

Coach Self is the best at hiding people's weaknesses until they're supposed to be exposed. Xavier was a great example. Xavier was a great shooter but wasn't the best at putting the ball down and getting his own shot. He was a catch-and-shoot guy. The best games he had are when his shots came within the offense, where he didn't have to put the ball on the court.

Cole Aldrich: Xavier and I got along really well. He definitely helped our team, because we added another guy that was offensively polished. The year before, Sherron and I took most of the shots. If we didn't get those shots up and we didn't score, we probably weren't going to win. So having Xavier really helped. He could've been a Brandon Rush-type of a player if he stayed at Kansas longer. He was really athletic and he could defend and score. If he stayed two or three years he could've really been special. I don't think Xavier did anything to hurt our team chemistry. He's one of the nicest guys I know. He was always smiling. It got to the point where I had to tell him to stop smiling. We spent a ton of time going to dinner and doing this and that. I know he enjoyed his time here.

I lived with Tyrel Reed throughout my time at Kansas. It was really fun watching him improve so much my junior year. He definitely came a long way. His freshman year, he was so nervous. He couldn't do a thing without being nervous. He'd call out a play in practice, and then he'd dribble that ball 50 frickin' times before he passed it. Then he'd get it back and dribble it 50 more times. Coach Self would jump on him and he didn't know how to react. I still give him crap about it. I used to have some fun with Tyrel once I lost my tooth. I had a fake tooth made that was attached to a retainer. Each night, I'd take it out and place it right next to his toothbrush, so it'd be waiting for him when he woke up each morning. I'm pretty sure it grossed him out.

Tyrel Reed: For Xavier, coming right out of high school and trying to connect with a group of guys was tough. He had a great personality. I loved Xav. I saw him last year in San Antonio—I was down interviewing for a physical therapy job with the Spurs and he was in as a free agent doing a workout—I went into his room and we talked for 30-40 minutes about life and how he was doing. It was a unique thing. That was the start of the one-and-dones. It was a new thing and we were all trying to figure out how it was going to work.

Xavier Henry: I definitely didn't expect my one season at Kansas to end like it did against Northern Iowa. Personally, I think we walked the ball up the court too much. When we used to blow teams out, we'd play really fast and score a bunch of fast-break points. That game, for whatever reason, we walked the ball up the court a lot and took our time with everything. If we would've just run at them they wouldn't have been able to do anything to stop us. We had too many good players on our team. Still, even after all of that, I still can't believe Farokhmanesh made that last 3-pointer. I've been in some tough locker rooms before, but never after a game that was played on that big of a stage. We knew we shouldn't have lost that game. We just had to live with it. We sat there and didn't say too much, but it was hard. Most of the time, we were quiet. But there were guys in the locker room that would stand up and yell, "We shouldn't have lost." Then a couple of other guys would stand up and scream, "We've got to come back strong from this. We've got to do better next year," and blah, blah, blah. Not everyone had next year. Sherron didn't have next year. We were hurting for Sherron. We knew Sherron wanted that one bad. He deserved it. We all put the work in. We all tried.

Marcus Morris: During that season, there was one particular time when me and Danny Manning had a heart-to-heart conversation. He told me I wasn't playing hard enough, and that I should be benefitting more from the talented guys that I was around. Guys like Sherron and Cole. He told me to start focusing on the small things: getting offensive rebounds, diving for loose balls, making quicker moves, seeing where I could fit in and do my things. We sat there and watched countless hours of film, like I was in the pros or something. Danny Manning really changed it for me.

Growing up, I never really had a father figure. I had a couple of male mentors I really respected. But my father was never in my life. When I went to Kansas, in just three years, Danny Manning became the closest thing to a father I ever had. He took us in. He showed us the ropes. I really felt that he cared about us. It meant a lot to us. It was about more than just basketball. He really embraced us. He invited us to his house all the time. People would tell us that, before we got there, Danny would never take anyone to his house. But he would call and check on us. It was really genuine. It made us feel comfortable, because there were times when I wanted to transfer, times I wanted to leave. It was tough, but sitting and talking to Danny always made it easier for us.

Coach Self was a great basketball mind, but Danny Manning was the biggest reason for my development. Danny is like me. I feel like when I get older, that's how I'm going to be. Calm, cool, always saying the right stuff, always making people feel good. I've never really had a bad day.

He spent countless hours with us in the gym, countless hours watching film. Just giving us so much advice on how to make the game easier and more efficient. There were times when I wasn't going to class. He was killing me. He'd talk to me about what next level I want to get to and not having to go back to Philly. I love my neighborhood, but I wanted to make it out. He gave us the drive and the push to make it out. He showed us the right steps to take.

Danny Manning: The twins and I had a special bond. We talked a lot of basketball, but a lot of the times it was about other things. It was about life. "How are you handling your academics? How are you handling your responsibilities away from the court?" A lot of those guys come in and don't understand the importance of that. They don't understand that all those things go hand-in-hand. Everyone goes through it at some point. You get away from the home life you had, the freedom. You get a chance to taste college life and you try to enjoy that moment. Then you realize you need to lock in on your responsibilities in order to get better as a person, and also at your craft as basketball player.

2009-10 Season Summary

Results (33-3, 15-1)

November

13	Hofstra	W, 101 - 65
18	vs. Memphis	W, 57 - 55
19	Central Arkansas	W, 94 - 44
25	Oakland	W, 89 - 59
27	Tennessee Tech	W, 112 - 75

December

2	Alcorn State	W, 98 - 31
6	@ UCLA	W, 61 - 73
9	Radford	W, 99 - 64
12	vs. La Salle	W, 90 - 65
19	Michigan	W, 75 - 64
22	California	W, 84 - 69
29	Belmont	W, 81 - 51

January

2	@ Temple	W, 52 - 84
6	Cornell	W, 71 - 66
10	@ Tennessee	L, 76 - 68
13	@ Nebraska	W, 72 - 84
16	Texas Tech	W, 89 - 63
20	Baylor	W, 81 - 75
23	@ Iowa State	W, 61 - 84
25	Missouri	W, 84 - 65
30	@ Kansas State	W, 79 - 81

February

3	@ Colorado	W, 66 - 72
6	Nebraska	W, 75 - 64
8	@ Texas	W, 68 - 80
13	Iowa State	W, 73 - 59
15	@ Texas A&M	W, 54 - 59
20	Colorado	W, 94 - 74
22	Oklahoma	W, 81 - 68
27	@ Oklahoma State	L, 85 - 77

March

3	Kansas State	W, 82 - 65
6	@ Missouri	W, 56 - 77
11	vs. Texas Tech	W, 80 - 68
12	vs. Texas A&M	W, 79 - 66
13	vs. Kansas State	W, 72 - 64
18	vs. Lehigh	W, 90 - 74
20	vs. Northern Iowa	L, 67 - 69

All-Big 12 Team

Player of the Year:
James Anderson, Oklahoma State, Jr., G

Defensive Player of the Year:
Cole Aldrich, Kansas, Jr., C

Newcomer of the Year:
Ekpe Udoh, Baylor, Jr., F

Freshman of the Year:
Alec Burks, Colorado, Fr., G

Sixth Man of the Year:
Jamar Samuels, Kansas State, So., F

Coach of the Year:
Frank Martin, Kansas State

First Team
Cole Aldrich, Kansas, Jr., C
Sherron Collins, Kansas, Sr., G
Jacob Pullen, Kansas State, Jr., G
James Anderson, Oklahoma State, Jr., G**
Damion James, Texas, Sr., G/F**
Donald Sloan, Texas A&M, Sr., G

Second Team
LaceDarius Dunn, Baylor, Jr., G
Ekpe Udoh, Baylor, Jr., F
Craig Brackins, Iowa State, Jr., F
Marcus Morris, Kansas, So., F
Denis Clemente, Kansas State, Sr., G

Third Team
Tweety Carter, Baylor, Sr., G
Cory Higgins, Colorado, Jr., G
Kim English, Missouri, So., G
Tommy Mason-Griffin, Oklahoma, Fr., G
Bryan Davis, Texas A&M, Sr., F

Honorable Mention
Alec Burks, Colorado, Fr., G
Marquis Gilstrap, Iowa State, Sr., F
Xavier Henry, Kansas, Fr., G
Zaire Taylor, Missouri, Sr., G
WillieWarren, Oklahoma, So., G
Obi Muonelo, Oklahoma State, Sr., G
Avery Bradley, Texas, Fr., G
John Roberson, Texas Tech, Jr., G
Mike Singletary, Texas Tech, Jr., F

All-Defensive Team
Ekpe Udoh, Baylor, Jr., F
Cole Aldrich, Kansas, Jr., C
Jacob Pullen, Kansas State, Jr., G
J.T. Tiller, Missouri, Sr., G
Dogus Balbay, Texas, Jr., G
Bryan Davis, Texas A&M, Sr., F

All-Rookie Team
Ekpe Udoh, Baylor, Jr., F
Alec Burks, Colorado, Fr., G
Xavier Henry, Kansas, Fr., G
Tommy Mason-Griffin, Oklahoma, Fr., G
Avery Bradley, Texas, Fr., G

** Unanimous selection

Kansas Awards

Sherron Collins
Lute Olson Award
Frances Pomeroy Naismith Award
Consensus All-American First Team
NABC All-American First Team
NABC All-District (8) First Team
AP All-American Second Team
USBWA All-American First Team
Sporting News All-American Second Team
Big 12 Tournament MOP

Cole Aldrich
Academic All-American First Team
Consensus All-American Second Team
NABC All-American Second Team
NABC All-District (8) First Team
AP All-American Third Team
USBWA All-American Second Team
Big 12 Championship All-Tournament Team

Marcus Morris
NABC All-District (8) Second Team

Season Stats

#	Player	CL	POS	HT	Hometown	G	GS	FG%	3P%	FT%	R	A	S	B	PTS
4	Sherron Collins	SR	G	5-11	Chicago, IL	36	36	.426	.370	.855	2.1	4.5	1.1	0.1	15.5
1	Xavier Henry	FR	G	6-6	Oklahoma City, OK	36	36	.458	.418	.783	4.4	1.5	1.5	0.5	13.4
22	Marcus Morris	SO	F	6-9	Philadelphia, PA	36	33	.570	.375	.660	6.1	1.0	0.9	0.3	12.8
45	Cole Aldrich	JR	C	6-11	Bloomington, MN	36	36	.562		.679	9.8	0.9	0.8	3.5	11.3
10	Tyshawn Taylor	SO	G	6-3	Hoboken, NJ	36	25	.438	.339	.716	2.4	3.4	1.3	0.2	7.2
21	Markieff Morris	SO	C	6-10	Philadelphia, PA	36	2	.566	.526	.622	5.3	1.1	0.4	1.0	6.8
14	Tyrel Reed	JR	G	6-3	Burlington, KS	36	0	.496	.473	.833	1.4	1.1	0.8	0.1	5.1
12	Brady Morningstar	JR	G	6-4	Lawrence, KS	27	9	.402	.396	.636	2.3	2.9	1.1	0.1	4.1
13	C.J. Henry	FR	G	6-4	Oklahoma City, OK	13	0	.583	.524	.500	0.7	0.3	0.4	0.1	3.1
0	Thomas Robinson	FR	F	6-9	Washington, DC	33	1	.485		.395	2.7	0.3	0.2	0.5	2.5
15	Elijah Johnson	FR	G	6-4	Las Vegas, NV	23	2	.553	.286	.667	1.0	1.3	0.3	0.0	2.4
5	Jeff Withey	FR	C	7-0	San Diego, CA	15	0	.538		.556	1.4	0.0	0.1	0.4	1.3
2	Conner Teahan	JR	G	6-5	Leawood, KS	19	0	.318	.333	.600	1.0	0.3	0.2	0.1	1.1
25	Jordan Juenemann	SO	G	6-3	Hays, KS	9	0	.500	.500	.500	0.2	0.0	0.0	0.0	0.9
41	Chase Buford	JR	G	6-3	San Antonio, TX	11	0	.333		.571	0.5	0.1	0.2	0.0	0.5

## CHAPTER 7

2010-11

FAMILY OVER EVERYTHING (FOE)

With Sherron Collins, Cole Aldrich and Xavier Henry moving on to the NBA, the 2010-11 Jayhawks took on a new look. Not necessarily in scheme, but in style.

Marcus and Markieff Morris became the figureheads of KU's program, and the tone they set on the court was unlike anything Kansas basketball fans had ever seen.

Bill Self's first seven KU teams had prided themselves on grit, fire and —Self's favorite word— "toughness," both physical and mental. The Morris twins, though, took things a step further. They were intimidators. They were trash-talkers. They were bullies and, at times, their teammates followed suit. "They got in opponents' heads," Brady Morningstar said of the twins. "People were scared of them." Maddening as it often was for Self and his staff, the approach served the Jayhawks well throughout the 2010-11 season.

Or rather, most of it.

Marcus Morris: Most times, Kieff and I could tell during warm-ups whether we were in for a battle—or if we were going to rip out a team's heart. Before every game our junior season, usually while we were stretching, we'd look across the halfcourt line and stare down our opponents. We'd glare right into their eyes. If they looked away, we knew we'd already taken their heart. If they stared back at us and looked us up and down, we were gonna have to have to fight to win. That only happened six or seven times that whole season.

Assistant coach Joe Dooley: The twins liked that persona. Starting with the pregame stretch and all the way through warm-ups, they wanted to make sure that people felt their presence. We didn't always like it as coaches, but we liked that they weren't afraid. We liked that they weren't going to back down, that they were going to compete.

Baylor forward Quincy Acy: The Morris twins didn't give a damn. I remember playing them in Waco. I dunked on one of them—I'm not sure which one—and I was talking a little trash as I was back-pedaling down the court. All of a sudden, the other one sneaks up behind me and stiff-arms me in my back. Stopped me dead in my tracks.

Those two looked out for each other. When you messed with one, you messed with the other. Looking back, I respected that. They really brought a different dynamic to that team. They set a new tone for the program. Everyone that stepped on that floor with the twins would match their energy and toughness. Thomas Robinson really fed off of that and kept it going after they left.

Travis Releford: The twins were really good their first two years, but they were on a different level as juniors, when they were the main guys on the team. All offseason, they were really getting after it. I don't know what people were telling them, or who they had in their corner advising them, but they were in the gym often—late nights, early mornings, between classes. You could see it paying off every day when we played pickup against those guys. They were getting better and better. They worked their butts off. All they did was stay in the gym. And it helped that there were two of them. They could play against each other and rebound for each other and all that extra stuff. They were driven and focused and it rubbed off on everyone.

Brady Morningstar: The twins were our identity that year. They brought a new mentality, an air of toughness that was different than the ones we'd had before. They're wild. They're *crazy* wild.

They're from the streets. They had some s**t going on when they were growing up, with their house burning down and all kinds of other stuff. They've been through some hard times. All of those dudes—T-Rob, Sherron and those guys from the big cities—have gone through some stuff that made them stronger. They were ready to roll at any time.

Bill Self: The biggest difference with the twins going into that year was they knew they were both going to be starters, instead of just Marcus starting. They'd been waiting for two years to get on the court together, and that was their big chance.

They took on more of a leadership role, a vocal role, with Sherron and Cole not being there. They're two of the best leaders we've ever had here. The problem is that with leaders, you can be a good leader, or a not-so-good leader. They were lazy when they first got here, but as they matured, they set a better example of how to practice and how to compete. Their work habits had improved.

Elijah Johnson: Those dudes talked in their own language or something. It was like they had their own little way to communicate, their own codes. They were on the same page all the time.

They were all about working and learning and exploring and figuring stuff out.

They were winners—and the best captains I had during my time here. Actually, I don't even think they were the official captains. But whether they had the title or not, they were the captains.

Marcus Morris: It's hard to follow one guy, but it's easy to follow two that are on the same page. We were two tough, strong dudes coming from the streets of Philly, but we were lovable guys, too. That's why we had so many friends. People liked being around us. It was like that when we were younger and then it carried over at Kansas.

It wasn't something that we planned or did intentionally. The love and the bond that Kieff and I have with each other just opened up to the entire team. We weren't the captains but we felt like people looked up to us because, even when we weren't saying much, we were working our asses off. People respected that.

Tyrel Reed: The twins were freshmen on the 2009 team that lost to Michigan State. People gave us a hall pass for that one because we weren't that great. The next year, though, we didn't have a hall pass. We were the No. 1 overall seed in the tournament and we lost to Northern Iowa. They felt some genuine disappointment about that. They felt guilty, like they'd let everyone down. It gave them a little extra edge, and things changed for them. They were like, "Let's prove ourselves next year."

Brady Morningstar: They made the game so easy. All I had to do was throw it into them, and they'd go score. They'd make it seem like I threw some great pass, but I really didn't. They'd just catch whatever got thrown in there and put it in the basket.

They're two big guys with guard skills. When you have one guy like that, it's special. But when you have two that can play together and have been doing it for a while, and can read each other and play off each other, that's even cooler. Very few teams have that. I'm not sure what other teams thought of the twins, but I know this: no one wanted to play them. They got in opponents' heads. People were scared of them.

Marcus Morris: I've always been team-oriented because I've always been with Kieff. One time when we were growing up, I hit the 30-point mark in a game, and I stopped scoring on purpose until Kieff was at 30, too. That's how we always did it. Even in college, if I had 20 and Kieff had nine, I'd slow down so he could get to 15.

The team that year was like a family. It was the best team I ever played on. Everybody loved each other. Everybody fed each other the ball in their sweet spots to make it easier for them to score. It's like you see with Golden State now … they all move the ball, they all pass well, they all shoot 50 percent. That's how we were. You could talk to guys like Tyshawn or Brady or Tyrel and say, "I want it here" or "I want it there" and they'd hit you right in rhythm. The game was so easy. And we had a great coach that made it even easier.

The other leaders that year were Morningstar and Reed, both seniors who were well-respected by their teammates. Their willingness to embrace their roles as complementary players enhanced Kansas' team chemistry and on-court cohesion. The Jayhawks shared the ball, they took good shots and their spacing was incredible. When it was clicking—and it almost always was—KU's offense was precise and surgical. The Jayhawks led the nation in field goal percentage (51.4 percent) during the regular season.

Tyrel Reed: When you've got a lot of guns, sometimes you don't know which one to use. It's tough. You have so much talent, and getting everybody to buy in and on the same page isn't always easy. That year, though, everything just fit. Everyone knew their role and was OK with it. We knew the twins were going to be studs. We knew Tyshawn was going to be the primary ball-handler. Brady and I were going to defend and shoot 3s if we were open. Everything just came together a little more.

Marcus Morris: Tyrel was always a hard worker, and Brady had that white-boy swag. His confidence helped him become a huge contributor. He talked a lot of trash but he always backed it up. We needed that.

Elijah Johnson: I respected "Squeeze" (Reed) because he could do anything any of those other guards could do. My freshman and sophomore years, we had six or seven guards that were all about the same height: me, Tyshawn, Brady, Tyrel, Josh Selby, Royce Wooldridge. We'd have competitions in the weight room. Lifting, vertical jump, squats, pull-ups … all kinds of stuff. Tyrel would win a lot of those categories. He was a great athlete—and he was studious. He kept his thinking cap on all the time, on and off the court.

Brady is the craziest dude KU has ever had (laughing). Not on the court, but in general. The main thing about Brady is that he rides for his team. He'll do anything in the world for a teammate, and for the University of Kansas. He played with pride. He had the whole state of Kansas watching him. He wanted to make Kansans proud.

Thomas Robinson: Brady and Tyrel and Conner Teahan helped our team so much. They were tough. They weren't pushovers at all. Brady is one of the toughest white boys I know. They knew their role. They didn't take bad shots and they played defense. You'd have to understand basketball to understand why Coach Self loved them so much. I totally get why he loved them. We all did.

Tyrel Reed: Early on my freshman and sophomore year, Brady and I were competing against each other for playing time, so maybe we didn't have the best off-court, buddy-buddy relationship like he and Sherron did, or me and Cole. But as we got to be juniors and seniors, we were bros.

Brady was one of the few guys who actually loved playing defense. He was such a good defender and so smart. He would love just getting into people, whether it was Sherron or Xavier when he was there. It got him pumped up. He might not talk a ton. He'd just "yay, yay ... you can't score on me."

He was just this 6-3 white guy who could defend. There was something about him. He knew where to be, and he had active hands and quick feet. Lots of guys talk trash on offense, but he was a guy who would talk trash defensively. And he'd piss you off, because he was always there, always around you, always getting deflections and touching you. He frustrated a lot of people in practice, because he doesn't look like anything. He's not a physical specimen, but he'd stop you.

Brady Morningstar: Sometimes, at the start of a game, I could tell when someone would look at me and get a little happy that I was guarding them, probably because I'm

MOST UNDERRATED JAYHAWKS

1. Brady Morningstar (2006-11): Bill Self said the Lawrence native is one of the best defensive guards he's ever coached. Scored 18 points in a Sweet 16 win over Richmond as a senior.

2. Tyrel Reed (2007-11): Career 40-percent 3-point shooter whose best performances always seemed to come against Missouri. Weight-room warrior was a favorite of strength coach Andrea Hudy.

3. Kevin Young (2011-13): Late recruiting find opened his career at Loyola Marymount and was set to play at San Diego State before changing his mind and picking KU. Key piece in the Jayhawks' 2012 run to national title game.

4. Travis Releford (2008-13): A versatile player who could defend big men in the post and also small guards in ball-screen situations. Bishop Miege grad averaged 11.9 points and shot 57.4 percent as a senior.

5. Michael Lee (2001-05): Signed by Roy Williams as a package deal with Aaron Miles, the guard proved he belonged by developing into a part-time starter as a senior. Ended his career as a 38-percent 3-point shooter.

6. Jeff Hawkins (2001-06): Weathered tough times during the coaching transition and started 12 games his senior year, when he shot 41-percent from beyond the arc and made four 3s in the Big 12 Tournament title win against Texas.

7. Landen Lucas (2013-17): It was always believed the 6-foot-10 forward would be a rotation player, but he turned into a three-year starter thanks to his solid defense, intelligence and hustle. Averaged 8.0 points and 8.3 rebounds as a senior.

8. Conner Teahan (2008-12): Rockhurst High School grad became an all-important sixth man for the 2012 Final Four team after originally dabbling in both football and basketball at KU. Went 6-for-6 from 3-point range against Missouri that season.

9. Jamari Traylor (2011-16): The Chicago forward, who went through a brief stretch of homelessness in high school, was always a favorite of Bill Self because of his attitude and work ethic. Averaged 15 minutes per game throughout his career.

10. Mario Little (2008-11): The Chicago native and Team FOE member was the type of physical junkyard dog that Bill Self loves; got caught up in a numbers game at KU and was under-utilized but has excelled in the NBDL and overseas.

white or whatever. They'd think they might have a chance to go off. That lit a fire in me.

I was always guarding the other team's leading scorer on the wing. I didn't give a damn about scoring. I didn't need the spotlight. But I wanted to make sure we had the best chance to win. The guard that scored the most ... I didn't want him to score s**t. That was my mindset.

Ask (Baylor's) LaceDarius Dunn—the leading scorer in Big 12 history—who the hardest person he had to play against and score on was, and he'll say it was me. He told me that plenty of times.

My first two years at Kansas, basically all I did was play defense, because I was on the red team. Look at who I was guarding; Brandon, Mario, Rodrick, Sherron ... all guys that made money playing basketball. Doing that for two straight years, and learning how to play off the ball against shooters and penetrators and guys with handles ... when I finally started playing a lot my redshirt sophomore year, it seemed easy. The players I was guarding weren't nearly as good as the guys I was going up against in practice. I'd been guarding McDonald's All-Americans, lottery picks, pros. In games I just had to guard guys that aren't as skilled. That's how I learned to play defense, and how to play off the ball. I knew I was good at that. I realized that's how I could really help the team. I was a glue guy, a ball-mover ... everything but a scorer and rebounder.

Bill Self: Neither one got nearly the credit they deserved for being how good they were. Tyrel, go back and look at his stats. It may not seem like much, but the dude averaged like 8 points for his career. That's pretty good, considering he was on some stacked teams.

Nobody gave Brady the credit he deserved, because he was our best passer, a high-percentage shooter and our best defender. He did a lot of things well, and they were both ridiculously smart and fun to coach. And they loved Kansas so much.

Struggles with Selby

One player who never became a fixture in the Jayhawks rotation was prized recruit Josh Selby, a scoring guard who Rivals.com ranked as the No. 1 prospect in the Class of 2010. The NCAA suspended Selby for KU's first nine games for receiving impermissible benefits while he was in high school.

Selby scored 21 points and hit the game-winning 3-pointer in his college debut against USC on Dec. 18. He started 11 of his first 13 contests and averaged 12 points. But a foot injury suffered in early February caused him to miss three games, and he was never the same once he returned.

Tyshawn Taylor: Josh played really, really well in that first game against USC and everyone got really excited. He was actually solid his whole first month. I think his mindset was, "This is what I do. This is what I'm here to do. I'm going to continue to shoot the ball and score a lot." That's just not realistic when you go through a whole season. You're going to have some bad games—especially as a freshman. It just happens. He realized that when we played Michigan and he went 1-for-10.

Coach wasn't the easiest person to deal with at the time. He was a little bit tougher on Josh than he was on Xavier the year before. Josh was definitely not like Xavier as far as how he handled it. He struggled dealing with Coach Self and with Coach Self's methods of getting through to players. It was tough on him. Like I said, if you don't buy in, you're going to have a hard time. That goes for anyone. It doesn't matter how good you are.

Conner Teahan: Initially, we thought he was a good fit, because he wasn't a selfish player—but he knew when to be selfish, if that makes sense. He'd come up with some big plays. That guy was so good when he got into the paint. I remember Brady, Tyrel and I, looking at each like, "How is he making these shots?" He'd penetrate and crash into somebody in the paint and then start falling down, and somehow he'd flick the ball up—while he's almost on the ground—and it'd go in. We were like, "Holy s**t!"

Then his foot got hurt, and I guess he put on some weight, and he just had a bad attitude from that point on. At the beginning of the season, we thought he was going to be great for the team, but Coach Self can pull the trigger on you pretty quickly sometimes. If you don't get an opportunity to get out there and feel really comfortable, then you aren't as effective, and I think that's what happened to Selby. That's what happened to

Mario Little too, because that guy was one of the best one-on-one players I've ever seen.

Bill Self: The NCAA suspended him for nine games, but then he started every game once he was allowed to play until he broke his foot. I remember calling Josh into my office and giving him an option. I said, "Hey, Josh … this is going to take a month to heal—or you can have surgery. You can play and tolerate it, or you can shut it down." I remember telling him that. He said, "I want to play." I said, "OK, but you're not going to be yourself, and you're not going to play as much." But that's what he wanted to do.

Tyrel Reed: Josh had a stress fracture in his foot at the same time I was dealing with an ankle injury. We both flew out to North Carolina with our trainer to see a specialist. I remember thinking, "I wonder how this trip is going to be." The whole season, everyone knew Josh was going to be a one-and-done. He was the No. 1 player in the class coming in, and I'd been playing in front of him. I thought he'd have a lot of hostility toward me, but he didn't. He was cool. We got along. He was just dealt a bad hand with that injury. I always respected him for how he acted toward me on that trip. Me and him were the only people on the plane and the only people in the hotel room. But it wasn't awkward. He wasn't like, "You shouldn't be playing in front of me. You're not as good as I am."

I saw on Twitter the other day somebody said J.R. Smith is the best pickup player they've ever seen. That's kind of what you get with Josh. When he could just let it all go and freelance and not think about sets or specific plays, he was phenomenal. He was a guy who could go get a bucket at any time. He could shoot it. He was tough. But coming into a system and trying to learn everything and fit in was challenging for him.

Bill Self: People assumed something was wrong. What was wrong was that he wasn't healthy. He started getting some of his swagger back toward the end of the season, but there was about a six-week stretch where he could hardly move. The injury—along with a combination of holding him out of practice and games—really set him back. I thought he was a terrific talent, but one of the things that made him so good was his athletic ability. When he lost that, he wasn't nearly as effective. It wasn't his fault. It was just unfortunate.

The Marcus Morris Show

Kansas opened the Big 12 season with a 84-79 win at Iowa State, and Marcus Morris established himself that night as the best player in the Big 12. Morris erupted for a career-high 33 points on 11-of-15 shooting. Markieff chipped in 17 points, 11 rebounds and three blocks.

Marcus Morris: It was a huge game for us on ESPN, so I knew all of my friends and family would be watching back home. I was just feeling it that night. Coach Self's system is not meant for 30-point scorers. It's built for three or four guys to get between 13 and 17. That's why me scoring so much that night made it kind of special.

Iowa State forward Melvin Ejim: Marcus was tough to guard because he had such good size and such good touch. He could shoot the ball and finish around the rim. It also made it harder that he and his brother were identical. You never knew which one you were guarding unless you looked at their jersey numbers, but he obviously is a great player and he was tough to guard because of his versatility and his skill around the basket.

Bill Self: Up until that point in our time here, when you talk about pure talent, I don't know that we had anybody that was better than Marcus Morris. Wayne obviously had a better year overall as a senior (in 2004-05). But I don't know that we'd had anyone as talented as Marcus up until that point. You could make a case for Julian and Sherron. But to me, Marcus Morris was as talented as we had. He could post. He could shoot. He could handle and pass and he had vision. He was 6-8. There wasn't anything about his game that I didn't like.

After beating Nebraska at Allen Fieldhouse, the Jayhawks hit the road again for a Jan. 17 showdown with Baylor at the Ferrell Center. Once again, the Morris twins dominated, combining to score 44 points on 19-of-24 shooting in an 85-65 win on ESPN's Big Monday.

Marcus Morris: I loved playing Texas and Baylor—even though we dominated Baylor every time we played them, I still loved going against those guys. They always had a lot of pro prospects. We always knew we were going to win. That year they had Perry Jones, who was projected as a top-five pick in the draft. I had a great game (25 points on 10-of-14 shooting) against him in Waco. Once I had that game I shot up the draft boards. He was one of those dudes whose heart we took from the beginning.

Dan Brinkley (mentor/agent to Morris twins): There was a moment in that game when it hit me—a moment when I knew that was going to be the twins' last season at Kansas.

At the time, Perry Jones was projected as the No. 1 overall pick on most everyone's draft boards, so they were extra motivated to have a good game. Kansas was absolutely

Kansas 84, Iowa State 79
January 12, 2011 · Ames, Iowa

Kansas (16-0)

Player	MP	FG	3FG	FT	R	A	F	S	TO	B	TP
Josh Selby*	31	5-12	2-5	2-4	2	1	0	1	3	1	14
Tyshawn Taylor*	25	1-6	0-3	0-0	4	4	2	0	3	1	2
Tyrel Reed*	28	1-5	1-3	0-0	1	3	1	2	1	1	3
Marcus Morris*	27	11-15	0-0	11-14	13	2	2	0	2	0	33
Markieff Morris*	27	6-12	0-3	5-11	11	1	3	1	3	3	17
Thomas Robinson	6	1-1	0-0	0-0	3	0	3	1	3	0	2
Mario Little	19	3-8	1-2	1-2	4	0	2	1	0	0	8
Elijah Johnson	8	0-0	0-0	0-0	0	0	1	0	0	0	0
Brady Morningstar	29	2-5	1-3	0-0	5	4	0	1	1	0	5
Team					4						
Totals	200	30-64	5-19	19-31	47	15	14	7	16	6	84

Iowa State (13-4)

Player	MP	FG	3FG	FT	R	A	F	S	TO	B	TP
Jake Anderson*	37	6-15	1-5	3-3	6	4	4	0	1	1	16
Scott Christopherson*	40	4-13	1-5	0-0	3	3	3	0	0	0	9
Diante Garrett*	40	11-25	3-10	2-2	2	5	0	1	4	0	27
Melvin Ejim*	29	2-4	0-1	2-2	10	3	4	2	1	1	6
Jamie Vanderbeken*	39	6-12	4-10	3-3	8	1	2	0	2	0	19
Calvin Godfrey	9	0-0	0-0	0-0	1	0	5	1	2	1	0
Bubu Palo	3	0-1	0-1	0-0	1	0	0	0	2	0	0
Jordan Railey	3	1-1	0-0	0-0	0	0	4	1	0	0	2
Team					3						
Totals	200	30-71	9-32	10-10	34	16	22	5	12	3	79

	1st	2nd	Total	FG%	3FG%	FT%
Kansas	40	44	84	46.9	26.3	61.3
Iowa State	34	45	79	42.3	28.1	100.0

Officials: Mike Stuart, Doug Simmons, Kipp Kissinger
Technicals: None

annihilating Baylor throughout the first half. I remember right before intermission, Baylor called a timeout—and then they came back out and had to call another one about two minutes later because Kansas was whipping them so bad.

Anyway, as Kieff was walking back to the bench, the camera caught him looking over his shoulder at the Baylor bench. He had this mean, menacing, intense look on his face. It was like he was saying, "Being up by 22 points isn't enough. This isn't over. I still want to drive you into the ground." When I saw that look, I said to myself, "This is their last season at Kansas. They're ready. They're entering the draft." Marcus wasn't even very high on the draft boards at that point, and Kieff wasn't listed at all. But it didn't matter. I knew they were ready.

Together in Tragedy

Kansas was 18-0 and ranked No. 2 in the country after winning at Baylor on Big Monday. But that Friday around 11 p.m., on the eve of a top-10 matchup with 10th-ranked Texas, tragedy struck the Jayhawks program when Thomas Robinson's mother Lisa Robinson, just 37-years-old, died of a sudden heart attack.

Making Lisa's death even more heart-breaking was that Thomas had lost his grandfather six days earlier—and his grandmother had passed in December. After Lisa's death, the only immediate family member Thomas had left was his 7-year-old sister, Jayla.

Travis Releford: We had just left curfew check, where we all meet downstairs at the Towers and the managers bring us a late-night snack. Everyone was laughing and having fun, just like we always were when we were together. We were excited about playing Texas.

Elijah Johnson: Almost everyone had family in town, because our games against Texas were always big and everyone wanted to be there.

Thomas Robinson: I got back upstairs and my cell phone rang. I answered it, and I heard my little sister crying. I asked her what was wrong, and she told me Mom had passed.

Elijah Johnson: I was Thomas' roommate and, at that moment, I was by myself in my bedroom. Everyone else was down the hall. I remember my brother coming in and saying, "Hey man, you need to go check on T-Rob. Something happened."

I went out in the hallway, and T-Rob was punching the brick wall inside the Towers. Then he just fell on the floor and started crying. The twins came out of their room and they were crying, too. No one knew what to do. Everyone was acting like they were scared to approach T-Rob. Most everyone stayed in their room. You'd hear doors open and heads would peep out, but hardly anyone went out there at first. No one knew how to handle it.

Tyshawn Taylor: When I went to Thomas' room, the whole team was there. The coaches and everyone. It was mad emotional. Everyone broke down. He was super out of it and sad. Everyone was rubbing his back and letting him know they'd be there for him.

Tyrel Reed: The coaches came and we're literally just sitting there, stone-faced. We'd just heard about it, and nobody was talking. We were just sitting in there, just trying to let him know that we were there for him.

Bill Self: Going over to the Towers, I remember asking Thomas, "Is there anybody we can call? Is there anything that we can do for you?" He said, "Coach, you don't understand. Other than my little sister, I don't have anybody anymore." He'd lost his grandparents and his mom all right there together in a two- or three-week span.

Thomas Robinson: The twins pulled me into the bathroom at the Towers that night. This was late January and, by that point, it was obvious that Marcus was going to be an All-American and enter the NBA draft. He told me, "You're my brother from now on. I'm going to look at you like I look at Markieff." We were both in full-blown tears.

Marcus Morris: That was one of the toughest days I've ever been a part of in my life. I felt like it was *my* mom. He was just a big, college kid, only 19-years-old. All of a sudden it was just him and his little sister. It was tough for me to watch. From that point on, I felt like we became tighter than ever. He became my brother that day. From then on, anytime we get a chance to hang out and see each other, we do. I don't even call him Thomas anymore. I call him my little brother.

Thomas Robinson: Josh Selby's mom was living in town, and she let me go to her house that night, just so I could get away from everyone and out of the dorm. I stayed in a spare bedroom the rest of the night and all throughout the next morning. I walked in and closed the door and I didn't come out for 12-14 hours. I was in there by myself until it was time to go to Allen Fieldhouse the next day for the Texas game. I wasn't going to go at first, and then something just hit me, where I was like, "Get up and go to shootaround. You're playing in this game."

Bill Self: I told Thomas before the game, "Thomas, is it OK if we have a moment of silence to honor your mom?" He said, "No, I don't want to." I think he was afraid he'd be uncomfortable with all of the attention. But I said, "Thomas, she never got to come to a game here. At least let the people honor her." He said, "OK, Coach." When the PA announcer acknowledged her, there wasn't a dry eye in the house. That was a unique time, very sad.

Thomas Robinson: Coach Self told me I didn't need to play, but I definitely wanted to be there with my team. I think they were surprised when I showed up. That was the moment when I felt like I earned my respect from Bill Self. I think he realized that I knew my back was against the wall, and instead of cowering and crumbling, I was going to step up to the plate. I wasn't going to let the tragedy defeat me. That kind of thing is big with him. He likes kids that respond to challenges.

Tyrel Reed: T-Rob could have sat out. No one would have said anything. But he felt it was his duty and his mom would have wanted him to be out there playing. I remember coming out guns a blazing. We were up 15 or something early in the game. That was all energy and all adrenaline, knowing we're doing this for T-Rob.

Travis Releford: When we were in the locker room, getting ready for the game, our energy just wasn't there. But once the jump ball went up, we turned it on. The fatigue disappeared. The only time I think we really thought about what had happened was when we weren't on the court playing. I'm sure T-Rob had it on his mind every second of the game, but once we got going and started competing, a lot of that stuff vanished for that moment.

Tyshawn Taylor: We were playing on pure adrenaline, pure emotion.

Thomas Robinson: I got tangled up with Tristan Thompson going for a loose ball. No one could grab it. Mentally, I wasn't even there. I ended up fouling Tristan and kinda holding onto him for a minute. I was out of it. After the whistle, he kinda hugged me real quick and gave me that look, like he kind of knew I was struggling. He just said, "It's OK, man. It's OK." That's a moment I'll never forget. Coach Self took me out right then and I didn't play the rest of the game.

Texas coach Rick Barnes: Kansas jumped on us really quick and it was 12-2 during the first media timeout, but I wasn't discouraged. We were getting really good shots—I'm talking point-blank looks—and just missing them. I knew that wouldn't continue. During that timeout I told our players, "Look, these guys have had a week off, and we're getting every shot we want. If we just keep playing as hard as we're playing, I guarantee we're going to win this game." I could just sense it. Even when they went up 18-3, I felt confident. And sure enough, I was right. We were down 12 at intermission and came out and played the best half we played all season.

Indeed, as strong as they looked in building a 35-23 lead, the emotions of the day—not to mention a lack of sleep—caught up with the Jayhawks in the second half against a Texas squad that featured three first-round NBA draft picks in Tristan Thompson, Jordan Hamilton and Cory Joseph. The best player for the Longhorns that day, though, was J'Covan Brown, who scored 23 points off the bench in the Longhorns' 74-63 victory.

The loss snapped Kansas' national-best 69-game home winning streak.

Tyshawn Taylor: J'Covan Brown, the Kansas killer. He's so good. I worked out with him a couple of times after our senior year. We had to do one-on-one workouts together. He's just a good-ass shooter. He's slow and he's not athletic at all. He can't jump. He went to Boston for a workout and they make you run this line drill. He could hardly get through it. But when it came time to shoot 3s, he made 20 or 30 in a row.

Travis Releford: We were up at halftime and we felt like we could win it. We're like "let's do it for T-Rob's mom." We just burned out late second half and Texas ended up pulling it out. Everybody in the locker room was crying. There really wasn't much Coach could say after the game. He wasn't disappointed in us. It was just a situation none of us had ever been in.

Bill Self: We had no chance. We got out to an 18-3 lead, but then the emotion ran out and we had no chance. We had no energy, no enthusiasm. We had guys that hadn't slept. They hadn't been to bed. That's one reason we played so well against Texas in the Big 12 Tournament a few months later. We were like, "Texas has a good team and all. But we didn't have a chance to show them our best stuff because of the circumstances."

Tyrel Reed: Usually, if we'd have lost a game that we'd led by 18, we'd get lit up ... a clipboard smashed, markers broken. But that day it didn't feel like a loss. Coach Self didn't come in the locker room yelling and screaming. It was bigger than basketball that time.

It was the weirdest feeling to me. We were all sad we didn't play well at the end. We ran out of gas. It was just a way bigger moment in somebody else's life who had just lost a loved one.

Kansas played without Robinson in an 82-78 victory at Colorado the following Tuesday. After the game, the Jayhawks flew to Washington, D.C., to attend Lisa Robinson's funeral. Thomas and Director of Basketball Operations Barry Hinson had arrived earlier in the week to plan the service.

Barry Hinson: The most difficult experience I had at Kansas—and probably the most difficult time of my entire career—came after Thomas Robinson's mother passed away. I tried to be a dad. I tried to put myself in his shoes. I thought, "Here's a kid who is 19-years-old and I'm watching him plan out his mother's funeral." I'm thinking, "Could I have done that at 19?" I don't think I could have. Picking the outfit out she was going to wear in the casket, making decisions about the music at the service and how things were going to go ... I was amazed by Thomas' maturity. We met with the funeral director in the lobby of the hotel where we were staying, right there by the Georgetown Bridge. It was terrible weather, all sorts of snow and ice. He was quiet for most of the trip. I tried to talk to him a little bit, but for the most part I left him alone. I just said, "Buddy, I'm here if you need me."

When the team showed in D.C. a few days later and got off the bus, it was perfect timing. He needed that. Heck, I needed that. We needed to see someone from home.

Brady Morningstar: It was a beast getting there. We took a big charter plane but we landed at one of their main airports, and most of the airport had closed. It was the biggest snowstorm they'd had in D.C. in a long time. I'd never seen something like that. I remember looking out the window and thinking, "How are we going to land this plane?" We flew in at night. I don't know how the pilots could see anything. After we touched down, they said we probably shouldn't have landed. But someone said, "We're not missing this funeral. Land it!"

Once we landed, we had to wait for an hour-and-a-half because the bus that was taking us to the hotel couldn't reach us. Then, once it arrived, it took us three hours to get to the hotel, which was about 10-15 miles away. We were just stopped on the highway because everything was backed up. We tried to stay in good spirits, but it was tough because it was a frustrating situation weather-wise, and plus, we were thinking, "We shouldn't even be out here for this. Thomas' mom should still be alive." There were a lot of different emotions we were experiencing. It was like, "Why is this happening to such a good dude? Why is this happening to anyone?" You just have to make sure that the person going through it is getting as much support as he can. It meant a lot to him that we were there.

Bill Self: It was so icy that, for a time, they weren't even sure if they were going to be able to have the funeral, because the streets weren't cleared. But it was a very nice service and very well-attended.

Thomas Robinson: Everyone went out of their way to show support. In the middle of an ice storm, Coach Self put the whole team on an airplane to Washington D.C. because he wanted to make sure they were at my mom's funeral. They had to take some crazy way there, but they made sure they got there.

Travis Releford: To see someone like that, a guy that worked so hard and was all about his family ... to see him lose his mom and all of a sudden have to take care of his little sister, that was a tough couple weeks for us as a team for sure. He slowly got better. Over time, he started laughing and smiling and being himself again, and we got back to winning games. I'm sure it's still hard for him, though. All these years later, I'm sure it's still tough.

Thomas Robinson: At that moment in my life, my team became my family. I was only close with my immediate family my entire life. All of my cousins and uncles had been distant since I was younger, so it was literally just me and my immediate family, with my mom and my grandparents and my little sister. When I experienced that tragedy, everyone around me became a support system. I felt like I should return the favor by calling them my family.

Elijah Johnson: Honestly—and I feel bad about this to this day—but I don't think I was there for T-Rob like I should've been when he was going through that stuff. T-Rob was very hard for me to read. Stuff that you'd think would bother him didn't bother him. Other times, when you were worried you said something that could have upset him, he'd start laughing and smiling. He was laughing and smiling at his mom's funeral. It wasn't because he was happy. He was just a different type of dude. I felt like I never knew what to say to him after that. I'm not going to say I'm a coward, but I didn't know how to console my friend and brother at that time. And I'm from a place where people die and get killed all the time. So it's normal to me, but that situation was just so different.

I think he felt like I distanced myself from him. He actually said that to Tyshawn one time. He didn't say we weren't close or anything. But he noticed that I stepped back. I hate that he felt that way, because that wasn't my intent.

Eight days after his mother's death, Robinson returned to the court for a Jan. 29 home game against Kansas State. Robinson—who had yet to score in double figures in Big 12 play—finished with 17 points and nine rebounds in a 90-66 victory.

Also, by that point, the NCAA had signed off on Self's request to launch a fundraiser for Robinson's sister, Jayla.

Thomas Robinson: When I walked onto the court, it was like time stopped. The refs, both teams, the fans, everyone ... it was like they were all looking at me. It was crazy. The officials and K-State players were telling me they were glad to see me. I felt like the crowd was with me every moment. When I shot the ball it felt like someone was directing it through the rim. It was 16,300 against five.

Barry Hinson: When we checked him into the game ... I still get emotional about it (voice cracking). I've never heard The Fieldhouse get that loud. But it didn't surprise me, because Kansas has great fans—and those fans support those players unconditionally.

Danny Manning: That outpouring of love and support that was displayed for Thomas and his family at that moment ... it was beyond impressive. It was powerful. It was moving. It's something that brought many, many tears to a lot of faces.

Bill Self: It was a special deal for all of our fans to acknowledge him like that. And he felt good because the NCAA allowed us to do that fundraising thing for his sister. I don't know how much money it generated, but it was a couple hundred thousand dollars, at least. It will pay for her education all the way through school. Everything from piano lessons to college tuition. He was so appreciative of all the KU faithful.

Thomas Robinson: Coach Self is the one who did all the leg work to start the fund for my little sister. He got all the players' moms involved and also the coaches' wives. I know it wasn't easy because of all the NCAA loopholes, so for him to devote so much time to doing that during the season says everything you need to know about Coach Self.

Those guys ... I'm getting emotional just talking about them and what they meant to me during that time. I still talk to all of them, even the guys that didn't play. Conner Teahan is about to become my financial advisor. Jeff Withey, Christian Garrett and Jordan Juenemann, our walk-ons ... I don't go more than two months without talking to any of them. We became brothers.

Bill Self: For the rest of that season, Thomas was terrific. He was playing with an extra chip, an extra motivation. He realized he was playing for more than himself.

At 24-1 overall, the Kansas Jayhawks waltzed into Bramlage Coliseum with an extra strut in their step on Valentine's Day in 2011. That morning they'd catapulted to the top of the Associated Press poll for the first time all season after curb-stomping their previous five opponents by an average of 21.2 points. The Morris twins were bullying anyone in their path, Morningstar was becoming more of a scorer and Mario Little was providing a spark off the bench.

Kansas State, meanwhile, was a desperate team. After opening the season with a No. 3 national ranking, Frank Martin's squad had tumbled out of the polls and was just 4-6 in the Big 12. The Wildcats and senior leader Jacob Pullen knew a win over KU was imperative if they had any hopes of salvaging their season and making the NCAA Tournament.

Jacob Pullen: We were at a critical point in our season. We had just lost to Colorado by two points (58-56) in Boulder. Late in that game, it was tied with 30 seconds left, and Alec Burks picked my pocket at the top of the key, went and dunked the ball and we were down three. On our next possession, I pulled up for a 3, but Frank called timeout just as I released the ball. The shot went in but it didn't count. I went berzerk in the huddle. I was mad that I got picked—and even more mad that Frank called that timeout when I was about to score.

We ended up losing, and the next day, my oldest brother and my middle brother called me on three-way and were laughing at me, like "Ahhh. You too Hollywood! You ain't the same Jake no more. You soft. I ain't never seen you get picked since you've been in college. You just too Hollywood. You should have just went to the NBA. You don't want to play college basketball no more. You're not a dog anymore. You soft!" I remember hanging up on my brothers and I was just so enraged, and I remember telling myself, "I'm going to kill everybody I play for the rest of the season."

We were playing KU the next day on Valentine's Day. I went to practice that afternoon and I told everybody on my team, "If y'all don't want to play basketball, just get off the court and I'll do whatever I've got to do to win by myself. If you don't want to fight, if you don't want to take charges, you don't want to rebound, if you don't want to do your job, just don't come on the court. Don't come to practice." Then the next morning, at shootaround, somebody was out there acting up when Frank was trying to instruct, and I was like, "Man, just get out. Get out of the gym. Go to the locker room. Frank, don't play him tonight. I'm not losing with him. If I'm going to lose, I'm gonna lose with people who want to play."

Bill Self: I loved competing against Jacob. He was a good player in high school, but he got so much better at K-State. He turned out to be a damn good college player. Him and that other guard that used to drive us crazy, Denis Clemente. I loved competing against him, too. God, they were good together.

Tyrel Reed: We'd had success against K-State in the past when we went box-and-one or triangle-and-two against Jacob and Denis. It really got them out of sorts, because their other three guys couldn't pass and Denis wasn't a very good shooter. They really struggled to run their offense. But in that game, Jacob went off and no matter what we did—going over screens, going under screens—he was tough to stop.

In one of the best performances ever by a Kansas opponent, Pullen scored a career-high 38 points—he averaged 20.2 for the season—as the Wildcats upset the No. 1-ranked Jayhawks, 84-68. The victory marked just the third time in 45 meetings that K-State had defeated its in-state rival. The Morris twins, who got in foul trouble early, combined for just 16 points and four rebounds.

Tyrel Reed: When I went on my recruiting visit to K-State, Jacob was there and we got along great. I always had so much respect for him. Obviously, I didn't want to be the guy who ended up on his highlight reels getting scored on, but he was a stud.

Jacob Pullen: I really respected Tyrel Reed and Brady Morningstar. They guarded me all the time and still found ways to make big plays on offense. No matter how many points I had against KU, they always did a good job on defense and still went out and did what they were supposed to do on offense.

Almost every time I lost to KU, Tyrel and Brady were the reason. Sherron made the big play my junior year in overtime, which everybody remembers, and Cole Aldrich had a big offensive rebound. But from my sophomore to my senior year, Tyrel Reed and Brady Morningstar are the two guys who consistently made the biggest plays to beat us. They always did their job. They never got out of body. They always lined up and did what was asked of them, whether it was guarding me for 40 minutes or deferring to their teammates on offense, even if they had an opening to score that other, more selfish players would've taken.

Those are the type of guys that help you win Big 12 championships. Those are the type of guys you need on your team when you want to win. Those are the kind of guys you want to play with. They do anything it takes to win and don't complain about minutes, about touches. I remember one game Brady was 3-for-3, and he didn't complain one time about not getting to shoot more when he was open. Instead, he guarded the hell out of me and Clemente the whole game. That's the type of stuff you don't get from a lot of people anymore, because when somebody hits a couple shots, they want the ball back. They feel like they should be able to score at will. Then, when they don't get the ball back, they get mad and pout and don't play defense. It's little stuff like that a lot of people don't see on TV. If you're watching the game on TV, you're not going to notice that Brady Morningstar wasn't complaining because he didn't get any more shots after making his first three. You see Sherron Collins make a big basket, and you're like, "Oh, Kansas won," and all you talk about is Sherron. But I'm sure Bill Self noticed the little stuff. The little stuff is the reason they win.

Tyrel Reed: Jacob probably just has a lot of nice things to say about me because he went off against me.

Bill Self: I was so mad at our guys after that game. But the biggest thing I remember

BEST KU PLAYERS

1. Marcus Morris (2009-11): One of the most versatile players of the Bill Self era, there simply wasn't much Morris couldn't do. Lottery pick was named second-team AP All-American and Big 12 MVP as a junior in 2011.

2. Sherron Collins (2006-10): The fifth all-time leading scorer in school history (1,888 points) helped KU average 30 wins per season during his four-year career. Ranks third all-time in 3-pointers (232) and ninth in assists (552).

3. Frank Mason (2013-17): Became the only player in school history to be named National Player of the Year by the Associated Press. Averaged 20.9 points in 2017, the most by a Jayhawk since Danny Manning (24.8) in 1988.

4. Wayne Simien (2001-05): Leavenworth native earned first-team AP All-American and was named Big 12 MVP after averaging 20.3 points as a senior in 2005.

5. Thomas Robinson (2009-12): Spent two years as a reserve before earning first-team AP All-American honors as a senior in 2012, when he averaged 17.7 points and 11.9 rebounds.

6. Brandon Rush (2005-08): One of two players in history to be named first-team All-Big 12 three times. Led Jayhawks in scoring all three seasons. Shot 43.5 percent from distance for his career.

7. Mario Chalmers (2005-08): Named Most Outstanding Player at the 2008 Final Four after his heroic 3-pointer forced overtime in a title game victory over Memphis. Ranks second all-time in steals.

8. Cole Aldrich (2007-10): KU's third all-time leading shot-blocker keyed a 2008 Final Four win over North Carolina and earned third-team All-American honors as a junior in 2010. Averaged 11.1 rebounds as a sophomore and recorded KU's first official triple-double against Dayton.

9. Perry Ellis (2012-16): Ranks ninth on KU's career scoring list with 1,798 career points. Crafty forward with a soft touch led the Jayhawks in scoring as a junior (13.8 points) and senior (16.9). Second-team AP All-American as a senior.

10. Tyshawn Taylor (2008-12): One of the most underrated players of the Bill Self era was among the best point guards in the country as a senior, when he led the Jayhawks to the Final Four. Ranks seventh all-time in assists. Third-team AP All-American as a senior.

was talking to our players in the locker room and saying, "You know what the definition of class is? Jacob Pullen. He had 38 points against Kansas—the No. 1-ranked team in America—and had a chance to take another shot at the end, and he chose not to. He could've made another basket and bragged for years about hanging 40 on your asses, but instead he pulled the ball back and ran out the clock. That's the definition of class.

"Destroy Them"

Kansas had already secured a share of the Big 12 championship when it traveled to Missouri for the final game of the regular season. As if playing their rival for a chance to win the title outright wasn't enough, the Jayhawks found even more motivation when they looked into the Mizzou Arena stands during pregame warm-ups.

Marcus Morris: One year at Missouri, I was walking through the tunnel and people were spitting down at us, and some of it caught me in the face. That was pretty disrespectful. But what they did right after Thomas' mother passed away … that's something I'll never, ever forget.

Elijah Johnson: It was really tough to play at Missouri after the situation with Thomas' family. They held up signs. I don't even want to say what the signs said, but it was terrible. I remember everyone saying, "Damn, that's f**ked up."

Thomas Robinson: I had gotten into some minor trouble before the game, and Coach Self had told me I might not play. But during pregame warmups, a Missouri fan held up a sign that said "No Mom Tom," so Coach Self came to me and said, "You're going to play, and you better f**king destroy them!"

They kicked the fan out of the game, but I was still really pissed. If the guy—I'm guessing it was a student— hadn't have been so far up in the stands I may have run up there and taken care of it myself. What he did was way overboard. I know it's conference play and the fans get into it, but I just felt like that was too much.

Ever since then, I've hated Missouri. *Hated* them. That was the thing that flipped it for me and made me say, "OK, I'm a part of this rivalry now." Before, people would try to explain the rivalry to me, and how the schools have hated each other for 100 years. But it's not attached to you. I was always, "I just got here. I don't know about any of that stuff. I don't hate those guys." But when that happened … that's when my hate started to build for them.

Tyrel Reed: I thought it was pretty impressive how Thomas was able to continue to play and not go into the stands to bash somebody's head in.

Instead, Robinson got his revenge on the court with a stat line that was almost unfathomable: 15 points and 13 rebounds—in only 17 minutes off the bench, as the Jayhawks defeated the 22nd-ranked Tigers 70-66.

At 14-2, Kansas finished a full game ahead of Texas (13-3) to win the Big 12 title for the seventh straight year.

Heading into the Big 12 Tournament, it was clear that the 2011-12 season would be the last at Kansas for the Morris twins. Marcus was named Big 12 Player of the Year, and Markieff led the league in rebounds (8.3) and field goal percentage (58.9 percent). Behind the scenes, though, coaches feared the individual success may be going to the twins' heads.

Getting Refocused

Tyrel Reed: Brady and I got in a fight with the twins. We were in the practice gym and they were just kind of "not all there" for consecutive days. I think the coaches put a bug in our ear, like, "Somebody's got to say something to these guys. Who's going to be the one to say something?" With the twins, if you mess with one, you mess with both. So Brady and I stepped up and got into it with them, and we were at half court just screaming in each other's faces. There was some pushing and shoving.

Eventually we went outside, where there's a loading dock for vehicles and all of our gear. Once we all calmed down, we said, "Listen, you're our guys. If you guys don't play hard in practice, nobody else is going to play hard in practice. How *you* play is how *we* play." We were just trying to make sure everybody was on the same page. Maybe it took things getting a little bit uncomfortable. I'm not a confrontational guy who wants to get in a bunch of fights, but at the time, I thought it was the thing that needed to be done and Brady did, too.

I think they understood that Brady and I just cared about them. I love those guys to death and I always wanted them to be locked in, but maybe that's what made them great, too—that they were a little bit loose and it didn't always look like they cared. When it came down to it, they did care. Hopefully they knew that we cared about them and we weren't doing it to be d**ks.

I think they changed after that. I know practices got a lot better and anytime we had good practices, that translated into our games. Coach Self was a big believer in that how we practiced was how we were going to play.

It was their last year at KU. They knew they were going to the NBA, but me and Brady—knowing it was our last go-round—wanted to make sure they were locked in too. *"This is it, fellas. If we suck now, we're done and my career is over with."*

Tourney Time

Kansas marched through the Big 12 Tournament and got a revenge win against Texas, 85-73, in the title game. All five starters plus Robinson scored in double figures. At 32-2 overall, the Jayhawks were rolling.

KU was awarded a No. 1 seed in the NCAA Tournament and advanced past the first weekend in Tulsa with ease following double-digit wins over Boston University and a Bruce Weber-coached Illinois squad. Up next was a trip to San Antonio for a Sweet 16 tilt with No. 12 seed Richmond.

Thomas Robinson: We were actually worried about Richmond, because they had beat someone really good to get to that point. (Note: The Spiders advanced to the Sweet 16 by defeating No. 5 seed Vanderbilt and No. 13 seed Morehead State, which had upset fourth-seeded Louisville.)

We got into it with them in the tunnel before the game started, because one of their guys pushed either Brady or Tyrel. Marcus walked up to the guy and said, "Don't do that." Looking back, I'm pretty sure Brady started it. (Laughing).

Brady Morningstar: We came out of our locker room, and we were doing our little get-together before we ran onto the court. I guess we were blocking the tunnel a little bit and Richmond was like, "Screw it, we're going to push through them" I was the first one to say, "Chill, chill, chill." But the twins saw it and stepped in. They were like, "Hell no, y'all are going to wait for us." There was some pushing and shoving. That got us going. That got us fired up. We didn't have much trouble with them thanks to that.

Tyrel Reed: The twins just liked to test people. They'd test us, their teammates. They'd test the coaches every day to see if they could get away with maybe not touching the line on a sprint. They just liked to test people. That kind of epitomizes their toughness, and when we played Richmond and were pushing each other in the tunnel ... that was just fun to them.

Bill Self: They always liked playing with a chip on their shoulder, but as far as them trying to bully and intimidate people ... I didn't start noticing that until after the regular season. I didn't like it, and we talked about it. If there's a little bit of trash talk under your breath that no one notices, that's fine. But we had the situation against Richmond, and I still don't know what caused it. I don't know if our guys were at fault anymore than Richmond's guys being at fault, because in all honesty, you should never have two teams entering the court from the same tunnel at the same time.

Still, with the twins and the intimidation factor ... sometimes that type of mindset can be taken too far.

An 18-point performance from Brady Morningstar propelled Kansas to a 77-57 win over Richmond. Now 35-2, the only thing blocking KU's path to the Final Four was 11th-seeded Virginia Commonwealth University—which almost didn't make the bracket.

Shaka Smart's squad was the beneficiary of a new format that was implemented in 2011, when the NCAA expanded the tournament field from 64 to 68 teams. As one of the "last four in," VCU was pitted against USC in a "play-in" game in Dayton, Ohio, with the winner advancing to the field of 64.

VCU guard Joey Rodriguez: After we got beat by Old Dominion in the title game of the CAA Tournament, no one thought we'd get picked for March Madness. We'd lost five of our last eight games, so most people figured we were headed to the NIT.

Still, the more I kept watching the games and looking on the internet, the more it seemed like things were falling into place to where we might have an outside chance, a slight chance, of making the field. Coach Smart never talked about it, though. We never talked about it once.

Assuming they wouldn't be chosen, the Rams opted not to have a watch party on Selection Sunday. In fact, only a handful of players watched the telecast of the brackets being revealed. Leading scorer Jamie Skeen was across town at a sandwich shop. Others were napping. But not Rodriguez.

Joey Rodriguez: I was one of, like, three or four guys who watched it. I'm a junkie. That's all I do is watch hoops. When they called our name and said we'd made it, I completely lost it. We all lived together in the same complex, so I was banging on doors and screaming really loud. It was pretty cool, because once everyone got wind of it, the players and students that lived there went out into the courtyard, and everyone started cheering. A few minutes later, we got a bunch of phone calls to come back to the Siegel Center for meetings. We started getting pumped up—and the more we watched ESPN, the more motivated we became.

Jay Bilas and Dick Vitale were ripping the selection committee for picking us. Hubert Davis was, too. One of them said, "The selection committee doesn't know the ball is round if they have VCU in the tournament." As a collective group, that got us pretty worked up.

Using Smart's full-court, Havoc defense—which is similar to Nolan Richardson's Forty Minutes of Hell—the Rams beat each of their first three opponents (USC, Georgetown and Purdue) by double figures before heading to San Antonio to face Florida State in the Sweet 16.

Joey Rodriguez: That year, every time we played a big-name school, we played pretty well. We had a lot of under-recruited guys with chips on their shoulders, so if it was a big-time school, we were ready to go. When we saw a school like Georgetown, we were licking our chops.

Our confidence soared higher and higher with each win. We kept proving to ourselves, in our own minds, that we belonged there. Coach Smart toughened us up and made us believe we were supposed to be there and that this was supposed to be happening.

During pregame or at the hotel, he'd talk to us individually. He'd say, "Hey Joe, I need you to go up to Jamie Skeen and tell him he's a bad dude. Tell him he needs to go manhandle some of these guys." He was pressing all of the right buttons.

A Bradford Burgess layup off an inbounds pass with 7.1 seconds remaining in overtime gave VCU a 72-71 victory over Florida State—and catapulted the Rams into an Elite Eight showdown with Kansas.

Joey Rodriguez: I'd been watching Kansas since the days of Nick Collison and Wayne Simien. I was ready to run through walls. I was super excited. We all were. It was an awesome opportunity. You've got Bill Self and Danny Manning sitting on the sideline. For any hoops junkie, that's your dream to play in that scenario, to play them in the Elite Eight in the AlamoDome in San Antonio.

As much as we respected Kansas, we weren't scared or awestruck. The game before, we saw them run through Richmond's huddle on the way to the court. Richmond just let it happen. We watched that and said, "There's no way they're doing something like that to us." We went into the game knowing they may try to intimidate us.

Marcus Morris: They had been on a great run in the tournament, but I went up to them during warmups and told one of the dudes it was about to end. I just said, "Hey, the Cinderella story stops today. We're not going down to no Cinderella." But that was one team whose heart we couldn't take. That was one team that didn't back down.

Thomas Robinson: Yeah, the twins were trash-talking the VCU players before the game. By then, everyone knew that's how they got going. Brady, too. He'd start stuff. Teahan, Tyshawn, Mario Little … we had a lot of players who played off of emotion.

Joey Rodriguez: Before the game, the Morris twins were like, "Y'all had a good run. It's about to come to an end." And I'm using nice-guy words. But during the game, they were cool and competitive. They were talking a little trash, but it was nothing off the wall. We did that to one another every day in practice. We were used to it.

VCU 71, Kansas 61
March 27, 2011 · San Antonio, Texas

VCU (13-4)

Player	MP	FG	3FG	FT	R	A	F	S	TO	B	TP
Bradford Burgess*	35	3-5	2-3	1-2	5	4	3	1	3	1	9
D.J. Haley*	5	1-2	0-0	0-0	1	0	0	0	0	0	2
Ed Nixon*	27	1-6	0-1	1-2	1	1	4	0	1	0	3
Joey Rodriguez*	34	2-8	2-6	3-4	5	5	3	2	4	0	9
Jamie Skeen*	38	6-17	4-7	10-12	10	0	0	2	2	0	26
Rob Brandenberg	4	0-1	0-1	0-0	0	0	0	0	0	0	0
Juvonte Reddic	6	1-1	0-0	0-0	0	1	2	0	0	0	2
Brandon Rozzell	27	4-8	4-7	0-0	4	1	1	1	1	0	12
Darius Theus	8	1-1	0-0	0-0	1	2	2	0	1	0	2
Toby Veal	16	2-4	0-0	2-2	5	0	3	1	0	0	6
Team					3						
Totals	200	21-53	12-25	17-22	35	14	18	7	12	1	71

Kansas (35-3)

Player	MP	FG	3FG	FT	R	A	F	S	TO	B	TP
Brady Morningstar*	32	1-7	0-3	0-0	3	3	4	3	1	1	2
Marcus Morris*	37	8-19	0-3	4-8	16	1	4	2	1	1	20
Markieff Morris*	32	5-12	1-2	2-4	12	0	3	2	8	2	13
Tyrel Reed*	34	1-9	1-7	6-8	5	0	0	1	1	0	9
Tyshawn Taylor*	33	6-9	0-2	2-5	2	3	2	0	2	1	14
Elijah Johnson	6	0-0	0-0	1-2	0	1	1	0	0	0	1
Mario Little	5	0-1	0-1	0-0	2	1	2	0	1	0	0
Thomas Robinson	6	0-0	0-0	0-1	1	1	3	0	0	1	0
Josh Selby	15	1-5	0-3	0-0	1	0	1	0	0	0	2
Team					3						
Totals	200	22-62	2-21	15-28	45	10	20	8	14	6	61

	1st	2nd	Total	FG%	3FG%	FT%
VCU	41	30	71	39.6	48.0	77.3
Kansas	27	34	61	35.5	9.5	53.6

Officials: Tony Greene, Mike Eades, Ted Valentine
Technicals: VCU (1 Coach), Kansas (0)

We knew the only way to win was to stop those two guys—or at least slow them down. They had been tearing up teams all season.

Shaka Smart: About three minutes into the game, Brandon Rozell hit a 3, and he turned and looked at our bench. He gave that look, like, "This is our day." The rest of the guys just followed suit.

Joey Rodriguez: We had respect for their guards, especially Tyshawn Taylor, who was very quick with the ball. But our guards had played at that level. We felt like we could really go at them and attack them.

I think the x-factor was Jamie Skeen. Coach Smart did a good job with him. He told him, "No one thinks you can hang with these guys." He came out firing. He was cooking. It was 3s, it was inside … he was all over the place.

Shaka Smart: I had to build Jamie up big time. But he did it. He showed up.

VCU swished 9 of its 12 three-point attempts in the first half alone and led 41-27 at intermission. Skeen had 15 of his game-high 26 points before the break and forced Markieff Morris into six first-half turnovers.

Kansas whittled the lead to 46-44 with 13:11 remaining, but a 10-2 run by VCU squelched the Jayhawks' spirits.

Joey Rodriguez: We knew they were going to go on a run. We were up by 18 at one point, but in the second half there was about a six-minute stretch where they kept scoring and chopping away at the lead.

Shaka got a tech, which never happens. We came back to the huddle and were all looking at him like, "Are you crazy? Why are you doing that?" But I think it kind of helped us, because we really got fired up and started talking and trying to motivate each other. *"Stick together, it's just a run, it's going to be fine."* Somehow we held it together and made some big plays down the stretch to where the game wasn't even that close.

The Jayhawks' backcourt was particularly brutal as KU missed 19 of its 21 3-point attempts. Morningstar, Reed and Selby went a combined 3-for-21 from the field.

Joey Rodriguez: We really tried to run them off the line. Our wings did a good job of doing that. Most of their shots were contested. I think they might have had two or three that weren't challenged. They might have been tired from having to chase our guards around. (Brandon) Rozzell was really cooking at that point. We had some other freshmen that came in that were really athletic.

Remember, Kansas didn't go that deep into their bench with their guards. The only guards they brought in were Selby, who wasn't 100 percent, and the kid from Vegas (Elijah Johnson).

Bill Self: We let them think they could beat us. Obviously, they got confidence early and then they played lights out. We had been on such a roll for so long. We didn't play with the same reckless, aggressiveness that we had in other games. Maybe we were playing not to lose, I don't know. But we played awful, absolutely awful.

The Morris twins each posted a double-double—although Markieff had eight turnovers—and Tyshawn Taylor scored 14. But it wasn't enough for the Jayhawks, whose season ended with a 71-61 loss to VCU and Smart, the Rams' 33-year-old head coach.

Making the setback even tougher to stomach was that KU's opponent in the Final Four would've been Butler, a No. 8 seed. And on the other side of bracket, both No. 1 seeds had been eliminated. Everything was set up for Self's squad to win the title, and the Jayhawks couldn't capitalize.

Brady Morningstar: They busted our ass. Talk about bad games … I had a terrible game. You can't harp on it your whole life. But the biggest letdown I had as a player at Kansas was that game. I wanted to play in a Final Four. I wanted to be able to say I helped take a team to the Final Four. And I didn't and it sucks. I wanted the students that were there that year to experience the joy of advancing to a Final Four, partying on Mass Street and all of that. We were right there. We were the best team in the country that year and we laid an egg. I hate it. I've never gotten over it. That was six years ago and I still think about it every day. It's on me. It's on us. We let everyone down. We let our fans down.

Tyrel Reed: It was another Northern Iowa. They played better than we did that day. If we had a three-game series, we'd have won the other two. If we had a five-game series, I think we'd have won four of them.

I know I shot terrible—one of nine. One of the twins had a ton of turnovers in the game. Everything that could have gone wrong went wrong, and I don't know why. Everything is magnified in the NCAA Tournament. I almost have a tough time watching the NCAA Tournament sometimes. I wish it was double elimination, because in that scenario I would have taken our teams every year to have a really good chance of winning it.

It was frustrating because I wanted to get back to the Final Four so bad. My freshman year we got to the Final Four and won the national championship. It would have been a dream of mine to have that same chance my senior year. I played two minutes against North Carolina in 2008. In 2011, I was a starter but I couldn't get it done. It's unfortunate. I'm not happy about that.

It almost made it worse that I had to go to the Final Four in Houston for the Lowe's Senior Class award I was up for because of community service. I didn't want to be there for something like that when I wasn't playing.

I'm sure Coach Self has driven himself crazy, thinking, "Did I do something wrong to prepare them?" I don't think it's that at all. I just think it's pressure. Guys are a little bit tighter. I won't lie about that. Everyone says they're going to try to be as loose as they can. Sure, you're going to try, but you realize if you lose, you're done. That's the nature of it. A lot of the really good teams get beat because it is a one-game tournament. I can't put my finger on anything. I just think it's about trying to really be as loose as you can. I don't know how you do a better job of that. Do we need to have a DJ come in and play some crazy music and get everybody hyped? I don't know.

Bill Self: Bucknell was a hard loss and so was Northern Iowa, although we got the shaft on that one from a seeding standpoint. They were 28-4. They weren't a freaking No. 9 seed. They could've beat anybody, and we were the perfect team for them to play. Their big guy made two 3s to start the game and he'd only made one all year long. They got into a good rhythm and they were so well-drilled. Even though that was an upset, and we had a chance after we pulled within one, they deserved to win that game.

As for VCU, Shaka's team controlled the game from start to finish. Both losses hurt bad, but to me, the VCU game hurt more. Maybe it was because we had been upset the year before. But that was a big loss. VCU controlled the game. We got our butts handed to us.

Joey Rodriguez: It was a special moment then, and it's even better to look back on now. That Final Four run jump-started everything for VCU. I coach here now and this campus is totally different. We've got a $25 million practice facility. I don't think we'd have that if we didn't beat Kansas that day.

We've got more support than ever. Alumni are coming back, boosters are helping us out more. It all started with that run. After that run, it all kind of took off. Shaka had a few top-10 teams. We've been to seven straight NCAA Tournaments. It kept going and we took it to another level.

Marcus Morris: Like I said earlier, most games we could just stare at someone during warmups and take their heart. VCU was one team that didn't back down.

More on the twins ...

Bill Self: I loved coaching those guys. Now, they were pains from time to time, just like all good ones can be, but they were competitive and they showed up on game days. The twins were some of the smarter guys we've had here. They had better feel, basketball-wise, than anybody. They were so smart.

Andrea Hudy: I'm an east-coaster. I'm from Pennsylvania and they're from Philly. I spent nine-and-a-half years at Connecticut. I was used to the people there. I'd had athletes like them before. They wanted to slow the operation down, slow the process down. With them it was always push-push-push.

Conner Teahan: The twins are so misunderstood. They were always a lot more mature than people gave them credit for. Some of their actions, like shooting the BB gun out of their window ... yeah, that may signal immaturity. But they will never lose sight of where they came from. That's both positive and negative. They are two of the hardest working people I've ever been around in my entire life.

They made huge strides from their freshman to sophomore year, because they knew what they wanted in life and they kept themselves accountable. I don't know if they changed a ton at KU, other than they took more of a leadership role as they got older. But they were always confident. They always worked hard. And they were always a lot more mature and a lot more intelligent than people give them credit for.

They're actually some of the smarter guys I've ever played with. They get it, and they get what it means to actually take care of business when it's time to take care of business. They were some of the best advocates for the program we had, because they always talked about getting better and learning every single day and having respect for people like D-Manning. They took care of everyone around them and never changed and never compromised anything. That's who they are. They will never change, because they see no reason to.

I had a lot of fun with those guys. We'd always slap box, and I'd run up on one of them jokingly just to see where the other one was and what he was doing. You'd get within a foot or two of one, and the other one would just appear. They know! I swear they know.

They might be my favorite Jayhawks of all time. To think about everywhere they've been in their lives, and to think about how hard they worked, they definitely deserve everything they've gotten.

Thomas Robinson: It's actually sad, because I get a lot of backlash for being friends with the twins. People judge them. They don't look the friendliest. But they are like teddy bears. Of course, any male has some sort of pride and ego and anger inside of them. They had a couple of dumb and immature mistakes they made, and an image of them got locked into people's heads that wasn't accurate. That's not right.

NBA GMs and front office people have told me that they don't think it's a good idea for me to hang with them and be friends with them. But they don't realize ... it's not a friend thing to me. I don't have any immediate family. I don't. I'm not close with my distant cousins. It's hard to rekindle relationships with people I haven't seen since I was nine years old, especially considering I have a little money now, which makes me extra cautious. I've been through a lot. I don't trust a lot of people. But I trust those guys. They're my family. They're doing much better now cleaning their image up. They keep my confidence up. They keep me going.

A little more from ...

Barry Hinson: I enjoyed working with Brady Morningstar maybe more than any kid I've ever coached. I loved him. He was one of the goofiest suckers I'd ever been around. He was an elite defender. Only twice did we ever have to move Brady off of someone. There was the kid at Oklahoma, Willie Warren, and Brady just couldn't guard him in Norman. And when we lost to Michigan State in Minneapolis in the Sweet 16, Brady had a tough time with Kalin Lucas. But other than that, he won damn near every battle he fought.

Think about that ... over his entire career, we only had to switch him off a guy twice. This is a kid that wasn't all that athletic, but he was Bill's kind of player. He was a hard-nosed kid. Bill would ride him like a rented mule and Brady would just fight him back. It didn't matter what you said or did, he'd just fight you. He had the best attitude. I'd text him after every game, just messing with him and having fun with him. But I loved him. Brady is one of those people that walks into a room and it just brightens up.

Brady Morningstar: I knew I could play at Kansas. I knew how good I was and I knew I could help out other good players around me. I wasn't a guy who was going to go out and get you 30. I knew that. I was a scrawny white boy. I was a good athlete, but when I got to Kansas, my athleticism dropped down because I was playing against a bunch of real athletes—quick-twitch NBA dudes. I didn't have that, so I had to find another way to make an impact and actually get on the court.

For me, that was playing defense and making the right passes and making the ball move and knocking down open shots. I didn't need the ball in my hands. Give it to Sherron and let him go. Throw it into the twins or Cole. I just wanted to be impactful at Kansas and I worked my ass off to do that.

Barry Hinson: My favorite story from that season is when Nebraska came to Allen Fieldhouse. It was the final year Nebraska was in the Big 12. At that time Nebraska was coached by Doc Sadler, who actually ended up replacing me on KU's staff when I went to Southern Illinois. Anyway, right before the game, our manager comes into the locker room and says, "Nebraska's manager just contacted me and said Doc forgot his tie. Does anyone have a red tie? If it's not red, then something close to their school colors?" Danny was the only one with a red tie, and he's damn near 7-foot tall. Still, he handed over his tie for the manager to give to Doc. Now, this was before Doc had lost all his weight, so it fit him perfectly. It draped right over his big belly. It was almost the perfect tie. Nebraska played great that night, too. (KU won 63-60.) They almost beat us with Doc wearing Danny's tie.

Marcus Morris: Elijah was one of the most athletic dudes I've ever seen, going through his legs for 360 dunks. He became one of my brothers on the team.

He's like my blood brother. He knew who we were when no one else really knew. Now me and Ty talk everyday. He's one of my closest friends. He's an NBA point guard. He should be in the league right now.

Conner Teahan: I was always surprised that Josh Selby didn't make it in the NBA. There were always a couple guys who you'd observe ... for instance, I would have told you in 2007, after his freshman year, that Darrell Arthur would have been the best KU basketball player I'd ever see in the pros. I'd never seen anybody like him before. He was 6-9, freakishly athletic. He would win the sprints, he could dunk it like it was nobody's business, and he had a good jump shot. ... I'm surprised he hasn't done more in the NBA.

With Selby, I always thought he was going to be so much better than he was in the NBA. But after that one year at Kansas, you knew there was going to be some problems.

Andrea Hudy: Tyrel Reed is great. He has a PHD in physical therapy. He had a passion for this and a passion for basketball. He was a better athlete than people realize. Same with Brady Morningstar and same with Mitch Lightfoot. Those guys are very good athletes.

Tyrel Reed: Some of my favorite memories are from wrestling in the locker room. One time the twins wrapped my neck in a towel and drug me around the room. I was about to pass out. I got this huge rug burn on my arm, and I had to have Cheddar keep looking at it because I thought I got staph because it was on our locker room floor. They're like "just give up. Just give up!" and I said, "No, I'm not going to." I probably should have, looking back. I loved to mess with the guys and pick on them or do something that would just annoy them. I'd sing a country song or push them or touch them or grab their stuff and throw it across the room. Anything to kind of mess with them. *"Man, you always playing."*

Once, T-Rob and I started wrestling and somehow we got to the floor. I wrestled when I was in seventh grade, so I felt like I had an advantage when we got to the floor even though he was way stronger and tougher than I was. But somehow I got on top of him and I was pushing his neck into the bottom of a rolling chair right into the roller, and he gave up. Everyone went crazy. He's like, "All right. All right. Stop!" I felt pretty good about myself. T-Rob would remember but he'll say he doesn't remember. That's my one shining moment on T-Rob.

Jacob Pullen: After my freshman year, I always tried to explain to my teammates what it was like to play at Allen Fieldhouse, because the next three years we were still good, and I wanted us to be ready.

My junior year (in 2010) we were No. 5 going in there, and I really thought we had a chance to win. I felt like with the experience that we had and how we were rolling in the Big 12 that we could go in there and win. We had our chances in that game. We ended up losing by 17, but there was a point in both halves where we would pull close and then somebody made a big play. And when you make a big play in Allen Fieldhouse, the crowd gets behind you, and that leads to another big play or turnover or something, and you look up and a one-point deficit turns into a nine-point deficit—or a two-point lead can turn into a 10-point deficit in a matter of four or five possessions. It was never easy to explain that to my teammates that hadn't played. My junior year we had a lot of freshmen—Wally Judge, Rodney McGruder, Martavious Irving—and I would continue to try to explain to them that this was going to be a different atmosphere. This was going to be a different type of game. We had to be in sync because we wouldn't be able to hear each other. And the same thing happened. We started that game down 18-6. That's the toughest place I played in the Big 12.

I respected those guys at Kansas. Honestly, against Kansas, I didn't talk trash that much unless it was with Sherron. Anybody else in the Big 12, if you ask them about Kansas State, they'll say we talked s**t all game and we never shut up. Between me, Curtis Kelly and Jamar Samuels, we just talked s**t all game. We felt like we were tougher than everybody. Especially Missouri. We used to talk s**t to Missouri before the game started. If we saw them in the hallway, we'd tell them, "We'll fight you." All of that stuff. We just really didn't like them.

My freshman year was the only year that we stayed in Lawrence, and the fans found out what hotel we were in and people would call the rooms all night so we never did that again. So I was never in Lawrence again except for the few times I went up to party, and at night it wasn't like people cared about basketball. We were partying. We were having a good time. Nobody was bothering us. *"Ahh, you all go to K-State."* It wasn't like that. We went up here to party and have fun. We left the next day. They actually came up to Manhattan for a party too. There was never a situation where the teams didn't like each other or wanted to fight. It was always competitive.

2010-11 Season Summary

Results (35-3, 14-2)

November

12	Longwood	W, 113 - 75
15	Valparaiso	W, 79 - 44
19	North Texas	W, 93 - 60
23	Texas A&M-CC	W, 82 - 41
25	vs. Ohio	W, 98 - 41
27	vs. Arizona	W, 79 - 87

December

2	UCLA	W, 77 - 76
7	vs. Memphis	W, 81 - 68
11	vs. Colorado State	W, 76 - 55
18	USC	W, 70 - 68
22	@ California	W, 63 - 78
29	Texas-Arlington	W, 82 - 57

January

2	Miami (OH)	W, 83 - 56
5	UMKC	W, 99 - 52
9	@ Michigan	W, 60 - 67
12	@ Iowa State	W, 79 - 84
15	Nebraska	W, 63 - 60
17	@ Baylor	W, 65 - 85
22	Texas	L, 63 - 74
25	@ Colorado	W, 78 - 82
29	Kansas State	W, 90 - 66

February

1	@ Texas Tech	W, 66 - 88
5	@ Nebraska	W, 66 - 86
7	Missouri	W, 103 - 86
12	Iowa State	W, 89 - 66
14	@ Kansas State	L, 84 - 68
19	Colorado	W, 89 - 63
21	Oklahoma State	W, 92 - 65
26	@ Oklahoma	W, 70 - 82

March

2	Texas A&M	W, 64 - 51
5	@ Missouri	W, 66 - 70
10	vs. Oklahoma State	W, 63 - 62
11	vs. Colorado	W, 90 - 83
12	vs. Texas	W, 85 - 73
18	vs. Boston University	W, 72 - 53
20	vs. Illinois	W, 73 - 59
25	vs. Richmond	W, 77 - 57
27	vs. VCU	L, 61 - 71

All-Big 12 Team

Player of the Year:
Marcus Morris, Kansas, Jr., F

Defensive Player of the Year:
Dogus Balbay, Texas, Sr., G

Newcomer of the Year:
Ricardo Ratliffe, Missouri, Jr., F

Freshman of the Year:
Tristan Thompson, Texas, Fr., F

Sixth Man of the Year:
Quincy Acy, Baylor, Jr., F
Levi Knutson, Colorado, Sr., G

Coach of the Year:
Bill Self, Kansas

First Team
LaceDarius Dunn, Baylor, Sr., G
Alec Burks, Colorado, So., G**
Marcus Morris, Kansas, Jr., F
Jacob Pullen, Kansas State, Sr., G**
Marcus Denmon, Missouri, Jr., G
Jordan Hamilton, Texas, So., G/F

Second Team
Perry Jones III, Baylor, Fr., F/C
Diante Garrett, Iowa State, Sr., G
Markieff Morris, Kansas, Jr., F
Tristan Thompson, Texas, Fr., F
Khris Middleton, Texas A&M, So., F

Third Team
Cory Higgins, Colorado, Sr., G
Rodney McGruder, Kansas State, So., G
Lance Jeter, Nebraska, Sr., G
Marshall Moses, Oklahoma State, Sr., F
Gary Johnson, Texas, Sr., F
David Loubeau, Texas A&M, Jr., F

Honorable Mention
Quincy Acy, Baylor, Jr., F
Scott Christopherson, Iowa State, Jr., G
Brady Morningstar, Kansas, Sr., G
Tyrel Reed, Kansas, Sr., G
Laurence Bowers, Missouri, Jr., F
Ricardo Ratliffe, Missouri, Jr., F
Cade Davis, Oklahoma, Sr., G
Andrew Fitzgerald, Oklahoma, So., F
Cory Joseph, Texas, Fr., G
B.J. Holmes, Texas A&M, Sr., G
John Roberson, Texas Tech, Sr., G

All-Defensive Team
Brady Morningstar, Kansas, Sr., G
Jacob Pullen, Kansas State, Sr., G
Laurence Bowers, Missouri, Jr., F
Dogus Balbay, Texas, Sr., G
Tristan Thompson, Texas, Fr., F

All-Rookie Team
Perry Jones III, Baylor, Fr., F/C**
Ricardo Ratliffe, Missouri, Jr., F
Jéan-Paul Olukemi, Oklahoma State, So., F
Cory Joseph, Texas, Fr., G
Tristan Thompson, Texas, Fr., F**

** Unanimous selection

Kansas Awards

Marcus Morris
Consensus All-American Second Team
NABC All-American Second Team
AP All-American Second Team
USBWA All-American Second Team
Sporting News All-American Second Team
Big 12 Tournament MOP
Las Vegas Invitational MVP

Markieff Morris
NABC All-District (8) Second Team
Big 12 Championship All-Tournament
Las Vegas Invitational All-Tournament

Tyrel Reed
Academic All-American First Team

Travis Releford
Las Vegas Invitational All-Tournament

Season Stats

#	Player	CL	POS	HT	Hometown	G	GS	FG%	3P%	FT%	R	A	S	B	PTS
22	Marcus Morris	JR	F	6-9	Philadelphia, PA	38	35	.570	.342	.688	7.6	1.6	0.8	0.6	17.2
21	Markieff Morris	JR	C	6-10	Philadelphia, PA	38	34	.589	.424	.673	8.3	1.4	0.8	1.1	13.6
14	Tyrel Reed	SR	G	6-3	Burlington, KS	38	37	.408	.379	.798	3.1	1.7	1.5	0.2	9.7
10	Tyshawn Taylor	JR	G	6-3	Hoboken, NJ	36	30	.479	.380	.719	1.9	4.6	1.0	0.3	9.3
32	Josh Selby	FR	G	6-2	Baltimore, MD	26	11	.373	.362	.757	2.2	2.2	0.8	0.0	7.9
0	Thomas Robinson	SO	F	6-9	Washington, DC	33	2	.601		.510	6.4	0.6	0.4	0.7	7.6
12	Brady Morningstar	SR	G	6-4	Lawrence, KS	38	24	.488	.410	.743	2.2	3.3	1.4	0.2	7.1
23	Mario Little	SR	G	6-6	Chicago, IL	32	1	.481	.367	.694	2.9	0.8	0.4	0.3	5.1
24	Travis Releford	SO	G	6-6	Kansas City, MO	29	3	.500	.378	.640	1.4	0.7	0.4	0.1	3.7
15	Elijah Johnson	SO	G	6-4	Las Vegas, NV	36	6	.500	.400	.667	1.3	1.8	0.5	0.1	3.4
5	Jeff Withey	SO	C	7-0	San Diego, CA	26	1	.647		.515	1.8	0.2	0.2	0.7	2.3
25	Jordan Juenemann	JR	G	6-3	Hays, KS	15	0	.556	.800		0.6	0.1	0.0	0.0	0.9
22	Royce Woolridge	FR	G	6-3	Phoenix, AZ	16	0	.250	.200	.500	0.5	0.6	0.0	0.1	0.6
20	Niko Roberts	FR	G	5-11	Huntington, NY	12	0	.167	.000		0.4	0.1	0.2	0.0	0.2

ROCK CHALK CHAMPIONS
MARIO, ill be your PRINCESS PEACH
RockChalk
KANSAS 23

E WARNER CABLE THE UNIVERSITY OF KANSAS HOSPITAL
UMB
PHILLIPS 66 BIG 12 2011 CHAMPIONS
PHILLIPS 66 BIG 12 2011 CHAMPIONS
PHILLIPS 66 BIG 12 2011 CHAMPIONS

2016 BIG
UMB

Jayhawks
22
Jayhawks
21
PAY ALL WHO
HEED ENTER
adidas
SPALDING

KANSAS
25

11

KANSAS

PHILLIPS
66
BIG 12
2011 CHAMPIONS
KANSAS
10

NCAA
2008
DIVISION I

CHAMPIONS
KANSAS
XII
CHAMPIONSHIP
2016 BIG 12
MEN'S BASKETBALL
CHAMPIONS
KU

SIMIEN
23

KANSAS
31

Wilson

KANSAS
32

BIG 12 CONFERENCE
XII
2008
CHAMPS!
CHAMPIONS
KANSAS
BACK TO BACK TO BACK!

Wilson
KANSAS
15
STATE

KANSAS
0

GRAHAM
4
MASON III
0

KANSAS
22

KANSAS
1

KANSAS
45

KANSAS
12
Wilson

KANSAS
14

KANSAS
15
KANSAS
24

KANSAS
24

KANSAS
23

LR
adidas
KANSAS
22

25
Wilson

KANSAS
5

KANSAS
40
Wilson
NCAA

KANSAS
33

KANSAS
KANSAS
30

5
KANSAS

KANSAS
23
MICHIGAN
2

KANSAS
21
Colorado State

KANSAS
22

11

KANSAS
34

KANSAS
1

KANSAS
2

H&R BLOCK
GREAT TASTE.
KANSAS
1
KU
LOBOS
1
LOBOS
3

Wilson

Jayhawks
25

BACK
to
BACK
BACK
BACK
BACK
TO
BACK
TO
BACK
BIG 12
BACK
TO

KANSAS
NCAA
adidas

Wilson
INDOOR GAME BALL
3
6
5

## CHAPTER 8

2011-12

LEAVING A LEGACY

In some ways, the summer of 2011 felt like 2008 all over again, as the Jayhawks appeared to be entering a rebuilding phase. Brady Morningstar, Tyrel Reed and Mario Little graduated, and Markieff and Marcus Morris left school early to enter the NBA draft, where they were selected with the Nos. 13 and 14 overall picks, respectively. Another early defection, Josh Selby, was picked at No. 49.

Still, deep down, Bill Self was far from panicked. While Kansas fans lamented the departures of some of their favorite players, the Jayhawks coach knew another star was about to emerge—a star that, if he reached his ceiling, could produce one of the greatest seasons in KU history.

Thomas Robinson: Things really changed for me when I came back from my mom's funeral. My first game was against K-State and I had 17 points and nine rebounds off the bench. Throughout the rest of the conference season I damn near averaged a double-double—even though I was only playing about 15 minutes a game.

At that point, reality had set in. Basketball was all I had. I had no other option. Literally. I had *no other option*. I was 19-years-old, and I wasn't thinking, "Oh, if basketball doesn't work out I can go home and get a job." I knew what was back home, and it wasn't a job. I didn't want to go back to Washington D.C. I'd have been broke and resorted to doing something stupid. From that point on, I was racing the clock to get to the NBA.

After my sophomore year I was going to leave for the draft. Tyshawn was thinking about it, too, and for four or five days, we didn't answer our phones. I was like, "Man, I want to go. I want to leave. I need this money. I can't have my sister go through another year without having anybody. I've got to go." Then I saw Markieff. He had come back in town from his NBA workouts, and he sat me down and told me I should come back to school for one more year. Houston, which picked No. 13, had already guaranteed me that they'd take me that year. But Markieff was like, "Yo, you haven't done enough at Kansas. You haven't had the feeling of being the main person here, the feeling of being 'the man.' You need to experience that. If you leave now, you won't be leaving a legacy."

Bill Self: Thomas could've gone that year and been a late first-round pick. But he still hadn't done what he set out to do. I also think the way people treated him at Kansas after his mother passed ... that really touched him. He wasn't ready to walk away. He probably thought, "Unless there's a 100 percent chance I'm going to be drafted in the top 10, I should probably go back and see what I can do."

Tyshawn Taylor: Thomas' attitude was that he wanted to be the best. In his mind he was already better than what we thought he was, skill-wise. We knew he was a freak. Expectations for him never had been that high. *Just come play hard and be a beast.* No one really respected his skill as a basketball player. He got his ass beat every day the summer going into his sophomore year. Marcus was killing everyone in pickup, and it hurt T-Rob's confidence. He'd been thinking about how good he was going to be that year, and then Marcus went out and killed him and didn't give him a chance to do anything. He took those ass-whippings and kept working hard and getting better. When his number was called, he was super ready. He was the next guy up.

Thomas Robinson: Once I realized I was coming back, I went to talk to Coach Self. He sat me down and said, "Everything is right there. I'm going to play you a ton next year. If you do everything we ask, I guarantee you'll get drafted in the first round." When I went back to school my goal was to be the No. 1 pick. I locked my mind on that and convinced myself it was going to happen.

I didn't even go in the gym that summer and work on moves. The main thing I did was get in shape. That was supposed to be a horrible year for us. The early predictions—the ones that come out right after the season, in the spring—said we might even go to the NIT that year. I think we were picked to finish fourth in the Big 12. But then, that summer, I started going to camps. I ended up going to the LeBron Camp and the Adidas Nation camp. The college kids had to get called to the next camp.

My whole plan was to get invited to the LeBron Camp. Everyone knows that, if you're there, you're somebody. The invite list was very limited. I think there were about 30 of us—all guys who were supposed to be draft picks. At that point, though, I hadn't played that much, so I was still kind of under the radar with some people. Guys like Brandon Knight, Kenny Boynton, Anthony Davis, Quincy Acy, Quincy Miller, Perry Jones ... they were all there at the camps, and they were literally asking me if we were going to be any good the next year. Then they were like, "Did your coach pull some strings to get you here?" and I was like, "No, I got an invite." Once we got out onto the court, they figured out why. They realized, "Oh, OK. Kansas *does* have a star for next year."

Elijah Johnson: I think T-Rob was greedy enough to take his—or maybe the better phrase is "hungry enough." T-Rob was a dog, man. He was a dog that was hungry enough to take his food once he got the chance to eat. His junior year, that was his mindset.

Bill Self: He was a pretty focused guy. He's so stubborn. He'll fight anybody. You tell him he can't do something and he'll try to prove you wrong. He was a fun guy to coach in that regard.

Kevin Young: Everyone knew that T-Rob was our best player and that he was going to have to lead us. We were going to need him to put us on his shoulders a couple of times. I remember one game he was getting close to the 30-point, 20-rebound mark, and we were all on the bench going, "Come on, T-Rob!" We were cheering him on. We all knew he could do it because that's the type of stuff he was doing in practice every day. Grabbing rebounds, dunking over people …

The best thing about T-Rob as it related to the team that year was that everyone liked him. Everyone respected him. Tyshawn, too. I transferred in that summer and, immediately, I was impressed with how well those two guys had taken to their leadership roles. I've yet to see leaders like that on another team.

The first week I was there, before an open-gym workout, those two pulled all the newcomers to the side and explained Coach Self's "two-game" offense to us. None of the coaches were there. It was only players, and a lot of us had never run two-game before. They were like, "This is a play we're going to be running all season, so let's go ahead and start running it now in pickup." So they showed us the play before Coach Self showed us the play. It said a lot about their leadership and how much everyone respected them. No one thought, "Oh, we're not going to do this until Coach Self tells us to do it." We all listened to every word they said and moved right into the positions they told us to be in.

The Trials of Tyshawn

Tyshawn Taylor is one of the most polarizing players in recent KU history, and his play was a topic of conversation early in the 2011-12 season.

Tyshawn Taylor: We had a really good non-conference schedule that year. We went to Hawaii and lost to Duke in the championship game of the Maui Classic, and I had 11 turnovers. I know people were thinking, "This is the point guard for our team this year? Jesus Christ." (laughing)

If that had happened the year before, or my sophomore year, Coach Self may have pulled me out at halftime and not looked my way for a couple of games. But after that game he was fine with me. I had three charges, which were turnovers. I threw a few lobs to Jeff (Withey) that were a little high, but super-catchable. Still, they were my turnovers. I had a bad traveling violation at the end that hurt us. I felt terrible, but Coach was like, "Don't feel terrible. You just tried to do way more than you had to do.

We're not the best yet, but you've got to trust your teammates. You don't have certain guys here anymore, but you've got to trust Elijah. You've got to trust Travis (Releford) and (Conner) Teahan. He's a huge part of our team now."

Conner Teahan: Tyshawn had a really tough time after that Duke game. He was devastated, and he was taking a lot of heat. A *lot* of heat. He was at the back of the bus crying. He was literally in tears after that game as he was looking at his Twitter. I think that was right around the time when he said he should delete his Twitter. Stuff like that kind of makes you disappointed in the fan base at times. It makes you think, "Are these people behind us through thick and thin?" You never really know who is real and who is fake. I'll just never forget the sight of Tyshawn at the back of that bus, crying.

I have a bunch of friends in this area, and after that game, they were like, "Gosh, Tyshawn … he did this, this and *this*." And I said, "Well, guess what. He also did this, this, this and this, and he's the whole reason we were even in the game in the first place.

Kansas 78, Ohio State 67
December 10, 2011 · Lawrence, Kan.

Kansas (7-2)

Player	MP	FG	3FG	FT	R	A	F	S	TO	B	TP
Elijah Johnson*	37	5-8	5-7	0-0	2	1	0	0	2	0	15
Travis Releford*	32	3-5	1-2	3-4	5	2	2	2	1	0	10
Thomas Robinson*	30	7-9	0-0	7-8	7	1	4	1	5	0	21
Tyshawn Taylor*	35	3-9	0-0	3-6	3	13	3	1	7	0	9
Jeff Withey*	21	1-2	0-0	0-0	7	0	2	1	0	2	2
Conner Teahan	18	2-6	1-5	0-0	1	0	1	1	2	0	5
Justin Wesley	2	1-1	0-0	0-0	1	0	2	0	0	0	2
Kevin Young	24:00	6-8	2-3	0-2	4	1	2	0	1	0	14
Naadir Tharpe	1:00	0-0	0-0	0-0	0	0	0	0	0	0	0
Team					1						
Totals	200	28-48	9-17	13-20	31	18	16	6	18	2	78

Ohio State (8-1)

Player	MP	FG	3FG	FT	R	A	F	S	TO	B	TP
William Buford*	40	8-23	1-6	4-4	5	3	2	1	2	0	21
Aaron Craft*	38	4-11	1-3	2-2	5	6	5	2	3	0	11
Evan Ravenel*	25	2-7	0-0	5-6	5	0	5	0	4	0	9
Lenzelle Smith, Jr.*	25	1-2	0-0	1-2	4	1	2	3	2	0	3
Deshaun Thomas*	40	7-14	3-7	2-2	5	1	2	1	1	0	19
Shannon Scott	1	0-1	0-0	0-0	0	0	2	0	0	0	0
Jordan Sibert	15	1-2	0-1	0-0	0	1	1	1	2	0	2
Amir Williams	15	1-2	0-0	0-2	3	0	3	0	1	0	2
Sam Thompson	1	0-0	0-0	0-0	0	0	0	0	0	0	0
Team					3						
Totals	200	24-62	5-17	14-18	30	12	22	8	15	0	67

	1st	2nd	Total	FG%	3FG%	FT%
Kansas	35	43	78	58.3	52.9	65.0
Ohio State	29	38	67	38.7	29.4	77.8

Officials: Mark Whitehead, Tom O'Neill, Terry Oglesby
Technicals: None

Turnover issues weren't the only thing limiting Taylor. In a practice leading up to a Dec. 6 game against Long Beach State, Taylor tore the meniscus in his right knee. He still played against the 49ers and again four days later in a huge contest with No. 2 Ohio State. Amazingly, with a bum knee, Taylor had nine points and 13 assists in a 78-67 win.

Taylor had surgery the following morning and never missed a game, as he returned for KU's Dec. 19 matchup against Davidson at the Sprint Center. The Jayhawks were upset, 80-74, but Taylor had 15 points, seven assists, five turnovers and three steals. His toughness left an impression on his coaches and teammates.

Naadir Tharpe: I remember him telling me, "I think I've got to have this surgery, and I don't want to get it." Then he had the surgery and he was like, "Yo, I think I'm going to be back before you know it." And he *was* back. It was crazy. He almost had a double-double against Davidson. It just showed how much he cared about winning and cared about the school.

Bill Self: Tyshawn will always be one of my favorite players, because he's tough as nails. He may not come across as tough because he's frail in stature. But he's a poor man's version of a bigger Allen Iverson. He'd give his body up.

When he played against Aaron Craft here, and we knew he was having surgery right after the game, and then he came back and played the next game, when we lost to Davidson, I was just amazed. I thought, "This dude is a warrior." I loved coaching Ty. We had to deal with some stuff with him early, some maturity stuff, but we were glad we had him. He was competitive and he knew how to play. When he wanted to defend, he'd lock in. He was so long and so fast. I just loved his toughness.

Missing Pieces

Kansas entered Big 12 play with a 10-3 record. Pleased as he was with the Jayhawks' progress, Self couldn't help but wonder how things would've been different if Ben McLemore had been a part of the rotation. McLemore and Jamari Traylor had both been ruled academically ineligible by the NCAA prior to the season. As "partial qualifiers," they weren't allowed to practice with Kansas until the end of the first semester.

Ben McLemore: Jamari and I were so geeked about the season. We'd been on campus and everyone was asking about us and talking about Late Night and what kind of team we were going to have. I'd been playing pickup the whole summer and was feeling good. The day before Late Night, Coach Townsend called Jamari and I into the office and said, "They're not going to let you guys participate in Late Night. You're not going to be able to practice the first semester, and then you've gotta redshirt. You won't get to play in games until next year." I thought he was f**king with us. That's something he liked to do a lot. I thought it was all a big lie. I was like, "C'mon, Coach. Are you f**king with us?" He had a real serious look on his face and just shook his head: *No, I'm not.* I literally broke down. I got really emotional. I kept thinking, "It's not fair, it's not fair. I did all of this hard work to get here and now I can't play."

Conner Teahan: Everyone thought Ben was going to be able to play. So when we heard the news right before Late Night, one of the first things in our minds—or at least in my mind—was the Big 12 streak, which at that point was at seven years. You don't want to be the team that kills the streak. You don't want to be the team that isn't as successful as all the other teams.

When you looked at Jamari and Ben not being able to play ... we had Jeff Withey and T-Rob, and that was great. But we also had Kevin Young, who we didn't know much about; and we had myself, and even though I'd been fine in practice, I was unproven in game situations. Travis and Elijah were the same way. They were unproven. And so you get that feeling in your stomach, where you're like, "Oh s**t, this is us now. This is what we've been given. These are the cards we've been dealt. Let's see how we handle it." That collar got tighter, no doubt.

The Jayhawks had a core rotation of seven players, and the lack of depth was a factor not only in games, but in practice. The situation improved dramatically once McLemore, a smooth shooting, athletic wing, and Traylor, an active, bouncy, quick-twitch forward were cleared to begin working out with the squad Dec. 18.

Ben McLemore: Once I was able to practice and stuff… awww man. I can remember it to this day. Larry Brown was there!

We had T-Rob and Tyshawn and Jeff Withey on the court—all guys that ended up getting drafted and playing in the NBA. Yet Coach Self asked Larry Brown who the best player in the gym was, and Coach Brown said, "Ben McLemore." That gave me goosebumps and made me realize what type of potential I had.

Coach Brown was at a lot of our practices that year. I'd talk to him almost every day. He'd say, "You're going to be great. Keep doing what you're doing and working hard. You're going to be a great player for this school and also in the NBA."

Jamari Traylor: Our first official practice was at the Sprint Center. I wanted to go out there and give it my all. We wanted to prove to everyone that we had some skill and that we belonged. Thomas was just a man in the paint. Later in my career, when I had a chance to go against some big-name guys, I didn't even worry about them, because I had gone against Thomas so many times. He would bring it every day. He didn't take any days off. Coach Self always pushed me to go hard against him and to try to get under his skin. Coach Self was really good about that. Whenever I would make a good play, he used that to motivate Thomas. If I did one good thing, he'd let Thomas know, and usually things wouldn't end up too good for me, because Thomas would "turn it on" even more. Coach Self was good at turning Thomas and I against each other to motivate him.

That first practice, me and Ben took it to everyone pretty good. I remember everyone talking about how much better practice was that day because Ben and I were there, making it more competitive. At the time, I thought they were just filling my head up. But everyone was saying it. It made me want to go even harder.

Bill Self: Jamari was so good for Thomas because he pissed Thomas off so bad, because he tried so hard. Thomas saw that as, "You're trying to make me look bad."

Kevin Young: They came in there with so much energy. They made us so much better. I don't know if they realize it. They gave us a whole new look on the practice court. At that point we were kind of tired of practicing against each other. We were getting frustrated with each other. We were arguing over fouls and we were starting to get more physical with one another, throwing elbows and stuff. They came in and changed everything for us.

Tyshawn Taylor: I practiced against Ben every day my senior year. His job was to guard me and make me mad and f**k me up and foul me. Coach told him to shoot every time he touched it—and not to let me catch the ball or touch it. He'd foul the hell out of me and they'd never call anything. He had the ultimate green light. He looked like a pro, and he was only four months into being a freshman.

Naadir Tharpe: When we found out those guys couldn't play and couldn't travel with us, it was tough. Those are the guys I'd come in with. They were my friends. When Ben finally got a chance to practice with us, I'll never forget how much he helped us. In practice, we were competing every day, and he was guarding Tyshawn Taylor, and I remember one day Ben was playing so good that Coach Self was getting on Tyshawn. He said, "This guy is a freshman and he's killing you. You can't do anything."

Tyshawn got the ball at the top of the key and looked at Coach Self and said, "Oh, he's killing me, huh?" Tyshawn did a move and just took off. He blew right past Ben, dunked the ball and walked away.

The Jayhawks finished the non-conference portion of their schedule strong, winning three straight—including a road victory at USC—and Taylor started to take better care of the ball, finishing with 19 assists and just six turnovers over that three-game span.

Tyshawn Taylor: As the season kept going, it got easier. My turnovers went down and my shooting percentage went way up. I just played really well. I'd played with great players for three years, and now it was *my* chance. Coach Self couldn't move anyone ahead of me and he couldn't sub me out. We were going to win or lose with Thomas as our big and me as our point guard. Knowing that allowed me to play with a lot of freedom.

My confidence also went up because we started conference play. I knew the Big 12, and it also seemed like I was playing against a lot of sophomores and freshmen. I might go against a few upperclassmen like Pierre Jackson or Phil Pressey, but for the most part I had the experience factor over everyone. I knew what to expect. I was shooting the ball well and playing carefree, and I wasn't getting subbed out after every turnover. I wasn't being told not to shoot. Not that he ever told me that, but there wasn't anything happening to hurt my confidence.

Plus, with T-Rob playing as well as he did, I was the second option, which made things even easier for me. I averaged about 17 points my senior year, but in conference it was like 18 or 19. And I shot about 47 percent from 3, which was uncharacteristic for me.

"Forget Perry Jones"

Kansas opened Big 12 play with a 67-49 win over No. 23 Kansas State and looked dominant through the first two weeks of Big 12 play. But it was No. 3 Baylor, not Kansas, that appeared to be the class of the league. The Bears were 17-0 overall and 4-0 in the Big 12 when they came to KU for a Big Monday contest on Jan. 16.

Tyshawn Taylor: Baylor came in there full of confidence. They had a bunch of guys that were going to the NBA, guys like Perry Jones and Quincy Miller and Quincy Acy. They ended up going to the Elite Eight that year.

Baylor point guard Pierre Jackson: That was my first game at Allen Fieldhouse. It was a marquee matchup and we were feeling pretty good about ourselves. I had no idea what I was walking into. I didn't know Kansas and Baylor had a little bit of a rivalry, and I had no idea what I was about to encounter at Allen Fieldhouse. It was still early in the season and I wasn't starting yet. That was probably a good thing that particular game, because I could take in the atmosphere from the bench to start the game. It was ridiculous in there. I literally felt the floor vibrating. As the introductions were playing, I started getting nervous—more nervous than I'd been before any game in my entire life.

Thomas Robinson: Coach Self pissed us off the whole week. All he did was talk about how good Perry Jones was and where Baylor was ranked. They started off 17-0 and were looking like *the* team. We'd had a good tournament in Maui and I'd already had a 30 and 20 game. I was like, "Forget Perry Jones. He's not going to do anything." As soon as that ball was thrown up, it was on.

Neither team did much in the early going and the score was tied 2-2 after three minutes. Then, the game changed in a split second when Taylor caught the ball along the right sideline on a fast break and lobbed a pass to Robinson…

Tyshawn Taylor: It was a terrible pass. I thought I threw it a little bit late. He had to hang in the air for it, but he caught it behind his shoulder—right over Perry Jones—and just threw it down.

Thomas Robinson: Somehow I jumped up and caught it with one hand and dunked it. I think that erased any energy or heart Baylor may have had coming into that game. It wasn't even close after that.

Quincy Acy: The best alley-oop dunks always come off the worst passes. That dunk was the momentum-shifter. It was the turning point of the game—and it happened really early, which meant we were in for a long night. We never recovered from that.

Pierre Jackson: T-Rob was one of the biggest, strongest, most muscular players in the Big 12 that year, and when he caught that ball behind his head on the baseline and threw it down, the place went absolutely crazy. We couldn't hear each other talking on the bench after it happened. That's when I got subbed in. Coach Drew was hoping I could help get us some momentum, but after that dunk, I don't think we ever recovered. We were young and our guys got rattled. We were done less than 10 minutes into the game.

Kansas 92, Baylor 74
January 16, 2012 · Lawrence, Kan.

Kansas (15-3)

Player	MP	FG	3FG	FT	R	A	F	S	TO	B	TP
Elijah Johnson*	29	4-7	1-1	2-2	5	3	2	1	1	0	11
Travis Releford*	36	5-7	0-1	1-2	3	4	2	2	2	0	11
Thomas Robinson*	35	11-18	0-0	5-6	14	2	1	0	1	1	27
Tyshawn Taylor*	33	10-14	4-6	4-7	2	6	1	1	5	0	28
Jeff Withey*	30	3-10	0-0	4-4	10	2	4	3	3	3	10
Jordan Juenemann	1	0-1	0-1	0-0	1	0	0	0	0	0	0
Merv Lindsay	1	0-0	0-0	0-0	0	0	0	0	0	0	0
Conner Teahan	20	1-2	1-2	0-0	0	3	0	1	2	0	3
Naadir Tharpe	2	1-1	0-0	0-0	0	0	0	0	1	0	2
Justin Wesley	9	0-0	0-0	0-0	0	0	1	0	0	0	0
Kevin Young	4	0-1	0-0	0-0	1	1	1	0	0	0	0
Team					3						
Totals	200	35-61	6-11	16-21	39	21	12	8	15	4	92

Baylor (17-1)

Player	MP	FG	3FG	FT	R	A	F	S	TO	B	TP
Quincy Acy*	27	7-10	0-1	0-0	5	1	4	2	1	3	14
Brady Heslip*	26	1-3	1-3	0-0	0	2	1	0	0	0	3
Perry Jones*	31	8-17	1-4	1-2	5	1	2	2	3	2	18
Quincy Miller*	30	5-12	2-5	5-5	2	1	2	2	2	0	17
A.J. Walton*	24	3-6	0-2	0-0	1	2	5	2	0	0	6
Deuce Bello	8	0-1	0-0	0-0	3	0	1	0	1	0	0
Gary Franklin, Jr.	13	1-2	1-2	0-0	0	2	0	1	0	0	3
Pierre Jackson	33	3-9	2-5	3-4	2	11	3	3	3	0	11
Cory Jefferson	4	1-2	0-0	0-0	2	0	1	0	1	0	2
Anthony Jones	4	0-1	0-1	0-0	1	0	0	0	0	0	0
Team					3						
Totals	200	29-63	7-23	9-11	24	20	19	12	11	5	74

	1st	2nd	Total	FG%	3FG%	FT%
Kansas	39	53	92	57.4	54.5	76.2
Baylor	29	45	74	46.0	30.4	81.8

Officials: Mark Whitehead, Tom O'Neill, Terry Oglesby
Technicals: None

Baylor coach Scott Drew: Several media people told me that was the loudest they'd heard Allen Fieldhouse in a while. At the end of the half we were in decent shape (down 39-29), but Perry had tweaked his ankle. He'd been playing super. If you look at his first-half stats (10 points on 5-of-12 shooting), he was playing great. In the second half, he wasn't the same. That affected the game some. In the second half we didn't match their level of intensity. When you're at Allen Fieldhouse, everything has to click.

Quincy Acy: I really wish we would've not run our zone that game. They always killed our zone. Out of all the teams we played, Kansas really destroyed our zone. Personally, I wanted to match up with Thomas Robinson. Instead, he and Tyshawn Taylor tore our zone up that game.

Their penetration was so tough to stop. Tyshawn and Elijah, and Sherron Collins before them. Then they'd finish with some good plays drawn up by Coach Self or whatever. Overall the penetration from their guards that whole game really killed us.

Tyshawn Taylor: As many athletes as they had on that team, I felt like they should've been able to stop people without playing zone. We knew how to tear that zone up. Coach Self is a madman when it comes to X's and O's and breaking down plays. We've got a million plays just for that 1-3-1. If they're in the 1-3-1, we're going to put two high and one in the middle and two low. They can't guard that. How do you guard two low if you've only got one guy there?

Thomas Robinson: I loved going against Baylor. We'd beat them bad every year, but when you look at the rosters you wouldn't think that would happen. But every year we beat them bad.

Kansas won 92-74 and shot 57.4 percent with all five starters scoring in double figures. The Jayhawks were led by their two stars. Robinson had 27 points and 14 rebounds while Taylor posted a career-high 28 points.

Pierre Jackson: I had so much respect for Tyshawn Taylor. He was one of the hardest guys to guard in the Big 12. He had great size and athleticism and could really finish at the rim. And he's fast, so when he gets downhill, he's pretty much already at the rim. It's tough to keep up with him.

Border War: Round 1

By the time they took the court at Mizzou Arena for the first installment of the Border War on Feb. 4, it was clear that Kansas and Missouri were the class of the Big 12. The Jayhawks were in first place at 8-1. The Tigers (7-2) were tied with Baylor for second place, but they had already defeated the Bears, and their four-guard offense under new coach Frank Haith was clicking at ridiculously efficient levels.

Missouri forward Kim English: (Mike Anderson leaving) was a blessing. Frank came in and stabilized the program. It was in disarray. I was going to transfer to Maryland. Michael Dixon was thinking about leaving. Phil Pressey wasn't happy. Frank changed everything. He gave us an offensive system that, statistically, was one of the most efficient in the last 10 years in college basketball. We knew we were talented and that we were better than most of the teams we'd gone up against. Now we had an identity.

It's nothing against the former coach. But when you play a motion, freedom offense, you can't have eight 1,000-point scorers. There are no rules. There is no continuity. It's all so random. That can hurt you. Phil Pressey needs the ball in his hands. He needs ball screens. Ricardo Ratliffe needs post touches. Marcus Denmon and myself need screens to be set for us. Structure is needed. That really helped.

Missouri guard Michael Dixon: Coach Haith nipped everything that was negative in the bud right when he got there. The only thing we cared about was winning games. We didn't care about who was scoring or who was doing what. We really thought we were the best team in the country. That's the mentality we took into each game every single night. We didn't think anyone was better than us. That's why we won a lot of games. We had spent so much time with each other. We played every day and competed every day.

Missouri guard Marcus Denmon: We were actually a really close-knit bunch. We had a lot of guys who had been there. We were excited about going out and proving ourselves. We felt like we had a good team my junior year but we had a lot of injuries that hurt us.

My senior year, we were excited to go out and show that we meant business. We wanted to go out and prove that the coaching change wasn't going to hurt us at all.

Missouri coach Frank Haith: That group was hungry because they didn't like how they ended the year before, with a first-round loss to Cincinnati in the NCAA Tournament. Then we lost Laurence Bowers to an ACL injury before the season even started.

Michael Dixon: What made the injury to Laurence even more frustrating was that it happened during a pickup game in early October. It was so terrible because right when it happened we all knew it was really bad. It was almost like a gunshot, where you knew someone had been hit and that it was bad. He was screaming and holding his knee.

It hurt all of us, but it also brought all of us together. I hate to say it, but it might have been a blessing in disguise, because if that didn't happen, Kim plays at small forward, Marcus plays the two … it would've been a totally different look.

Frank Haith: I don't know that I thought we'd be any good. I thought we'd be solid, because we had talent. But we only had seven scholarship players and we didn't have a lot of size.

Until we played in Kansas City in the CBE Classic, I had no idea how good we could be. We beat Notre Dame (87-58) and Cal (92-53) pretty handily. Cal was ranked No. 20 and both teams ended up having good seasons. At that point, I said, "We can be pretty good." We figured out the way we needed to play, which was unique, because Kim (English), who is 6-foot-6, played the four-spot for us as a guard. That made us hard to defend.

As we went along, the team started to get more and more confidence in what we were doing. We had a swagger about us when we went into games. I'd look out there before the jump ball and say, "Oh my God … look at how small we are." Marcus Denmon was our small forward at 6-2 and Kim English was our four-man at 6-6 and Ricardo Ratliffe was our center at 6-7. But we found a way.

With Missouri ranked No. 4 and Kansas at No. 8, the Jayhawks-Tigers showdown was college basketball's marquee matchup of the weekend, especially with College GameDay broadcasting from Columbia.

Kim English: It was tough because College GameDay was there and all of our friends and family members were in town. People were wanting to take me to lunch. Plus, I wanted to watch GameDay with Digger Phelps and Jay Bilas and all of that hoopla.

Marcus Denmon: That morning I didn't want to go to College GameDay. I stayed to myself and let some of the other guys do the College GameDay stuff. The fans were into it. The campus was buzzing. I knew it'd be a fun atmosphere, a fun game.

Missouri led 39-34 at intermission, but Kansas battled back and used a 7-0 run to surge ahead 71-63 with 3:25 remaining. KU sixth-man Conner Teahan made the second of his two 3s during that stretch.

Conner Teahan: In the first half, I remember making a bad pass and Denmon got in front of it and went in for a layup, and Coach Self got on me pretty good. The second half started, and Coach Self told me he needed a big one out of me. He said, "I need you to hit a big one."

Denmon and I were pretty good friends and had played on the same AAU team along with Michael Dixon, Steve Moore and Travis Releford, but that game Denmon was getting in my ear. Whenever I'd get the ball, he'd yell, "Heat him up! Heat him up!" because Missouri wanted me to dribble. I wasn't as good dribbling. They didn't want me to shoot the ball. They wanted me to pass or dribble as much as possible.

It was kind of annoying to me, because I'm not saying I was as good as Denmon or Dixon or Moore, but when we were in Kansas City, I was the Gatorade Player of the Year back-to-back years. *I was the player in Kansas City, and you're going to come talking all this trash?*

Fast forward to the last four or five minutes, and Coach Self was saying we needed a big play. I was able to knock down a 3 in the corner, and then a few minutes later, one of the Pressey boys made a really dumb pass and I was just sitting in the passing lane like you're supposed to—right foot up, right hand out—and he threw it right at my hand. Boom. I stole it and passed it up to Tyshawn and we ran a very similar play, where I fade out to the corner, and I hit another 3, at which point I say to Denmon, "Heat this up!"

After KU's 7-0 run, Denmon cut the lead to five with an and-one layup, and then the game turned on a controversial call.

Thomas Robinson: I drove and got the and-one, but it didn't count because they said I charged. Steve Moore flopped on me, though. He was, like, 300 pounds. I can't believe they called that foul.

ESPN color man Dick Vitale couldn't either. "That's a bad, bad call," Vitale said on the broadcast. Instead of going back up seven—or eight, had Robinson made the free throw—the Jayhawks' lead was still just five points, and at that point, Denmon, who had already scored 23, took over.

Frank Haith: The game before our first game against Kansas, we had played at Texas. Marcus was passing up shots because he was in a slump. He was 3-for-12 that game with six points. I jumped him and said, "You shoot it every time you're open! I don't care if you miss every shot. I'm tired of you turning down shots."

Conner Teahan: Late in the game, I don't know that I could have played defense on Denmon much better. I got through the screens pretty well. I got my hand up in his face and everything. But the last one ... Coach Self broke it down in a film session pretty good later on. What I'd had success with earlier in the game was, if the guy I was guarding gave up the ball in a dribble hand off, I would stay back in the middle of the lane, because I was taller—taller than Dixon and Matt Pressey. If they dribbled into the lane, I could put my hands up and make it a tough pass for them.

But this time, I didn't do what I'd done when I stole the ball from Pressey. I didn't keep a hand and foot in the passing lane. I held back into the middle of the lane because Dixon had gotten the ball, and I was thinking, "This guy is going to drive, and I'm going to kind of double team him." I was going to try to be a hero—the exact opposite thing that Coach Self would tell you to do or what any defensive coach would tell you to do. I hesitated for that one second, and Dixon saw he had an open line to Denmon and made a great pass and I was too late. My hand wasn't there. So I come up on Denmon late, jump up and next thing you know ... boom, swish.

To this day, I'll come into work, and someone will have printed off a picture of

Denmon making that 3 over my head, and they'll leave it on my desk as a joke. It was stupid of me to try to take that much responsibility and try to make that play. It's discouraging to think about what could have been. There were a lot of different things we could have done in those final minutes, but I was really hard on myself and Coach Self was really hard on me about that one, too.

Denmon's 3-pointer—and his personal 9-0 run—put Missouri ahead by one with 55 seconds left, but the Jayhawks still had their chances. Taylor would get fouled and miss both free throws. He'd get another chance to put Kansas ahead when Self designed a play for him out of a timeout with 17.4 seconds left, but Taylor drove into the lane and was called for charging.

Thomas Robinson: We let up so bad that game. That was our fault.

Travis Releford: Denmon went off. He had a great game. You had to give him credit for that. He played great, but I felt like we had that game under control until he made those shots. We were in the locker room just frustrated with ourselves, because we gave them the game.

We knew it was going to be a tough game. It's always a tough game going to Mizzou. Very few times we went up there and it was a cakewalk.

Kim English: That day was that fine line of wanting to play the game and wanting to enjoy the moment. It's amazing that we won that game, because we really did enjoy the moment, too. I went to the arena that morning to be with the fans. I watched GameDay from the locker room. I went to Shakespeare's for pizza with my girlfriend's family. I did everything like a fan that day and then still played the game. I'm happy we won, because in hindsight I probably didn't handle it the way an athlete should as far as being super locked in. But we were really good. When the ball was thrown up, we could really dig in and focus on what mattered.

Michael Dixon: Kimmie hugged me so tight in the locker room after that game. He'd get mad at me if I said he was crying, but there were definitely tears in his eyes. He was emotional. We all were. Coach Haith was kind of in shock. He didn't understand how big the rivalry was until that day.

Roughing Up the Big 12

Losing to Missouri hardly sent the Jayhawks into a tailspin. In fact, Kansas appeared to use the setback as fuel, winning its next five games with ease as anticipation swelled for a Feb. 25 rematch against the Tigers.

It was during that time that a new star began to emerge for Kansas, a defensive force that gave Jayhawks fans reasons to dream of a trophy much bigger than the one awarded each year by the Big 12. His name: Jeff Withey.

A 7-foot sand volleyball star from San Diego, Withey had signed with Arizona out of high school but quit the team when Hall-of-Famer Lute Olson retired a few months after his arrival on campus in the fall of 2008. Withey transferred to Kansas that winter and toiled on the scout team for two-and-a-half years, taking elbows from Cole Aldrich and getting pushed around by the Morris twins while anxiously awaiting his chance. At one point, Self expressed fear that he may be "too soft" to ever play a major role for the Jayhawks.

Danny Manning: Bill says that about everyone (laughing).

Strength and conditioning coach Andrea Hudy: I don't know if Withey was passionate about basketball when he came here. I thought that might have been why he left Arizona, possibly because it was too tough. But then he came here and he was probably like, "Whoa, this is really tough, too." You have to be passionate about basketball here, because it's a full-time job. It's all the time. Eventually, Jeff became passionate with working out and passionate about the game. He got to where he enjoyed it. I don't know if he always did.

Bill Self: I think he fell in love with basketball. I think he'd always liked it, but he played because he was tall. I think he absolutely fell in love with the game when he started seeing himself get better.

Jeff Withey: I always loved basketball. That was never an issue. But when I transferred, I definitely went through a lot of hardship. There was a time when basketball wasn't my sanctuary anymore. It brought me a lot of anger and pain. When I decided to leave Arizona, they wouldn't give me my release, so I literally had to quit the team and pay for school to be able to transfer and not lose a year. That fall I was still going to school there, because I had to keep my grades up to be able to transfer. I'd walk through campus and people were looking at me all dirty, like, "What are you doing?" That sucked.

When I signed with Arizona, I thought I was going to be a starter. That's what Coach Olson was telling me, that I'd start as a freshman. So to go from having those kind of expectations about your college career to having to sit out a year-and-a-half was really tough. You always want to play whenever you're in any program, but at Kansas I was behind a couple of guys like Cole and the twins. In the long run, it really benefited me. Those guys made me better. But when I was going through it, it wasn't easy. I learned a lot about myself and I learned a lot about the game, and I definitely got tougher.

That was one of Coach Self's biggest things with me my first two years: toughness. In that area, I was definitely out of my comfort zone at Kansas, at least initially. I'm a laid back guy. That's something I've always had to work on. That's something I'm still dealing with right now in the NBA.

It helped me a lot to play with T-Rob. He's a tough guy and he obviously brought the best out in me. I saw him elbowing guys and being tough, and I was right there next to him. We were in the trenches together. It made me play with an attitude.

T-Rob and I had a great relationship. We wouldn't go out and go to The Hawk and party together or anything. But when we were together on the court, I definitely feel like we vibed off of each other and had good chemistry. We both knew our roles. Thomas was the focal point on offense and he was going to take that brunt. And he knew that I was always going to take the defensive brunt. I was going to guard the better post and try to block shots. And I knew I could go after blocks because Thomas was going to get every rebound.

After going scoreless in KU's loss to Missouri in Columbia, Withey put together a three-game stretch so impressive that it's still talked about in Lawrence all these years later. In victories over Baylor, Oklahoma State and Kansas State, Withey averaged 20.3 points, 12 rebounds and 6.3 blocks. He went 20-of-31 from the field during that span. A Jayhawks team that was an afterthought during the preseason was suddenly the talk of college basketball.

Not that everything was perfect.

Robinson had drawn criticism in back-to-back wins for some after-the-whistle antics that infuriated Bill Self. The first came when he hovered over K-State's Thomas Gipson, taunting him after Gipson had taken a charge. One game later, Robinson was assessed a technical foul for shoving Texas A&M's Ray Turner. Robinson had been frustrated by his own poor play, not to mention his benching against the Aggies for not running back on defense.

K-State forward Thomas Gipson: Thomas Robinson was a good player but I couldn't respect how he tried to belittle me. You can see on the video … I took a charge and I fell. There was a split second where he looked at me all crazy. He was standing over me and he just looked at me crazy. I'm tough. I don't tolerate that. It seemed like some sort of power, ego-type s**t. It was weird. If you watch the video, everybody saw it. I got up and pushed him. I'm tough. You can't do that to me. People thought since I was a freshman I wouldn't react. But I was like, "Naw, that's not happening. I don't care what your name is." I wasn't about that.

Thomas Robinson: I never liked playing at K-State. I could never have a good game there. I remember one time I stood over Thomas Gipson and taunted him a little bit. People back then either liked me or hated me. To this day, I see guys I played against in college and they won't even look my way. That's just how I play. Off the court I'm nothing like that at all.

Elijah Johnson: They called us the Goon Squad. That was just the demeanor of some of our players. When Tyshawn made a 3, he had to let you know, so he put a 3 over his eye. Coach told him to stop doing it, but he didn't. He told T-Rob to stop yelling at people, but he kept yelling. That's just how they were. It worked for them.

Thomas Robinson: We tried to be very intimidating. We trash-talked. You have to sometimes. At the end of the day, it's a competition. You have to use every tactic you can to take out your opponent. Some players were better than me and I knew it. But they weren't as tough as me. If I got in their head mentally, it knocked them down a little bit and gave me an advantage. Plus, when I'm hyped and fired up about the game, I'm a better player. So a lot of my energy was fake. I wouldn't even have a problem with the guy. But I know if

I shove him one time, he's going to push me back and lose his head a little bit.

Danny always used to tell us, "Damn, y'all are going overboard." But deep down I think he loved it. He just couldn't say it. He'd always give us little tips about things we could do to make our opponents lose their cool. Elbows to the ribs, kicking people's feet on the free throw line, fake swim moves where your forearm ends up popping someone in the face on a rebound, and it looks accidental. He gave us a lot of little tricks. The cool thing about him is that he doesn't give you everything at once. He wants you to keep begging for knowledge.

Elijah Johnson: I don't feel like T-Rob is a basketball player. He's just this "thing." As long as you feed the "thing" it'll work for you and do whatever you need it to do. He was an animal. He'd catch the ball on the block, give a head fake that didn't work, then step toward the defender, elbow or pork chop him in the ribs, and then go up and dunk the ball—and then mug for the camera. I'm like, "T-Rob, that's not basketball, dude. You're out here playing prison ball or something." It was crazy seeing it firsthand like that.

One Final (Border) War

The Jayhawks' winning streak had earned them a No. 4 national ranking—and a one-game lead over third-ranked Missouri in the Big 12 standings. With three games remaining in conference play, the stakes in the Border War had never been higher.

The same could be said about the pressure.

With Missouri headed to the SEC the following season, the Feb. 25 showdown in Lawrence would mark the final regular-season meeting between the Jayhawks and Tigers. Missouri had expressed interest in continuing the series by playing KU in a non-conference game each season. Self—who was agitated that Mizzou was leaving the league after initially promising to stay—had said he wanted no part of it.

Tyshawn Taylor: Coach Self tried not to make any one game bigger than the others, but he had a different look in his eyes in the days leading up to that last Border War. He wasn't happy about Missouri leaving the Big 12 and he let us know it. He explained all of that to us. He knew this was the last time we were playing them, and he wanted to beat them worse than ever. It felt personal. I'm sure the Missouri players felt the same way.

Marcus Denmon: I don't think anyone liked going to Lawrence and playing, because most of the time you were going to lose. Not too many people win in Lawrence. I'm not one of those KU haters. I tried to kill them every time I got the chance. But I respected the fact that they won and were well-coached.

The fans were different. They were always loud and obnoxious. The last time we played there … I've got an image of one guy's face in my brain that will never go away until I'm 100 years old. He was an older guy wearing a farmer's hat, with a red flannel shirt on under his overalls. I could see the hate in his eyes. It wasn't about basketball. He really hated people from Missouri and Mizzou. He was standing in the tunnel, on the

other side of the ropes, just a few feet from our team as we huddled up before running onto the court. We broke out of our circle and our eyes locked. He stared right into my eyes and his face crinkled up. He said, "We're going to burn you just like you burned our town down." It was a deep, genuine look of hatred that I'll never forget.

Frank Haith: I was in my first year at Missouri and, to be honest, I had no idea how much hatred the fans of each school had for one another. It brought out the worst in people.

I didn't really notice it during the actual games that year. It was mainly just stuff I'd hear from fans and media and people in the community. I had our equipment guy get me the DVD of "Outlaw Josey Wales" with Clint Eastwood. It kinda gives the story of how the Kansas-Missouri rivalry started. I needed some background on the hatred. I needed to know more about it.

Thomas Robinson: Those Missouri players were all tough, inner-city kids. They talked so much trash. It was an ego thing. It was never a cakewalk against them. You knew you were about to get pushed. You knew you were about to get elbowed. You knew someone was going to call you a punk and get up in your face. I loved that. I wanted that.

Marcus Denmon: At the hotel on the morning of the game, we watched film. But we didn't watch much of Kansas. We watched film of ourselves. We watched ourselves and some of the things we had done well that year. We thought we had a great game plan to beat them.

Shortly after the starting lineups were announced, and just seconds before the jump ball, the decibel level in Allen Fieldhouse measured at 121, which is comparable to the sound of a jet taking off less than 100 yards away. Ushers and elderly fans wore neon earplugs and children covered their ears. Videos poking fun at the Tigers played before the game. In the stands, former KU greats such as Raef LaFrentz, Nick Collison and Marcus and Markieff Morris had prime seats for one of the most hyped games the building had ever seen. Missouri, though, was hardly rattled.

Kim English: It's hard to win at Kansas unless you have older guys. Your first time playing there as a freshman, you're in awe. The second time, you're less in awe, but the atmosphere—the crowd and the officiating—is still a factor. Your third time playing there, you may not be in awe anymore, you may not be affected by the crowd anymore, but it's still a road game. But when you're a senior, it's finally a non-issue. You're not impressed. You've been there. You don't care about the banners anymore. You don't care about the cool intro anymore. You're ready to play the game.

We had a great game plan. We had a ball screen offense that we knew they would struggle with. It worked to perfection for about 29 minutes. Going out there, what we said was, "We're not going to look at the score early in the game. We're just going to lock in and focus on getting great shots. And then we're going to lock into getting a stop. And then to getting a great shot ..." That's literally what we said we were going to do—and also to not look at the score. We knew they were going to throw their biggest punch to start the game. The crowd was going to be as loud as it was going to be. All we needed was for the score to be 9-9 at the first media timeout. If it was there, or close to there, it would turn into a normal basketball game. Sure enough, at the first media timeout, the score was 9-9.

Frank Haith: I told our guys, "They're going to come out so intense and playing so hard. We've just got to stand our ground early, and at that first media timeout, if we're toe-to-toe and even with those guys, it's 'game on.'" But let's absorb that blow, because we know it's going to be fierce. They're going to come

Kansas 87, Missouri 86
February 25, 2012 · Lawrence, Kan.

Kansas (24-5)

Player	MP	FG	3FG	FT	R	A	F	S	TO	B	TP
Elijah Johnson*	29	3-6	2-5	0-0	2	8	4	0	0	0	8
Travis Releford*	34	1-7	0-3	5-8	3	2	0	2	1	0	7
Thomas Robinson*	38	10-21	0-0	8-9	12	0	3	1	2	1	28
Tyshawn Taylor*	44	7-13	3-7	7-8	4	5	3	0	1	1	24
Jeff Withey*	9	1-1	0-0	0-0	1	0	2	0	0	0	2
Conner Teahan	37	4-4	4-4	0-0	1	1	1	1	3	0	12
Justin Wesley	6	0-0	0-0	1-4	1	0	0	0	0	0	1
Kevin Young	28	2-6	0-0	1-4	8	0	3	0	2	4	5
Team					2						
Totals	225	28-58	9-19	22-33	34	16	16	4	9	6	87

Missouri (25-4)

Player	MP	FG	3FG	FT	R	A	F	S	TO	B	TP
Marcus Denmon*	44	10-15	6-10	2-2	5	2	1	2	1	0	28
Kim English*	44	4-12	2-6	1-2	6	1	2	1	2	0	11
Matt Pressey*	15	0-2	0-1	0-0	2	1	5	1	2	0	0
Phil Pressey*	33	2-8	1-3	3-4	3	12	5	2	2	0	8
Ricardo Ratliffe*	27	8-13	0-0	6-6	12	0	4	0	1	1	22
Mike Dixon	42	6-15	2-9	3-4	1	6	3	1	0	0	17
Steve Moore	20	0-0	0-0	0-0	7	0	2	0	1	0	0
Team					1				1		
Totals	225	30-65	11-29	15-18	37	22	22	7	10	1	86

	1st	2nd	OT	Total	FG%	3FG%	FT%
Kansas	32	43	12	87	48.3	47.4	66.7
Missouri	44	31	11	86	46.2	37.9	83.3

Officials: Mark Whitehead, Gerry Pollard, Brent Meaux
Technicals: None

so hard at us at the beginning. Let's just stand our ground.

We were up by 12 at halftime. We were playing well and we were confident and we were shooting the ball well. We were playing a matchup zone that we hadn't played that much before. I think that stymied them a little bit. It made them work.

We didn't try to run any plays. We ran our "Flow" game. We knew it was going to be so loud in there, it would be hard to call out plays.

Michael Dixon: We had already played them and beat them, so it was like, "Hey, let's just go in there and weather the storm and see what happens." When we came out and we were scoring so easily—we were doing that to everyone that year—it was just another day.

Travis Releford: They came into our house with the confidence—*oh, we've already beat KU once*—and they were hot. They couldn't miss a shot, especially Denmon (13 first-half points).

I'm like, "Yo, what's gotten into this guy? Where was this Denmon during our AAU days?" That's what I was thinking. I'm not saying he wasn't good in high school, but he wasn't doing that for our AAU team. We would have never lost.

He played great against us both times that year. He was coming off screens and making tough, contested shots where I was in his face. There was nothing I could do, other than say, "Hey, good shot!" And then move on and try to keep him from getting the ball next time.

Marcus Denmon: Our goal was to capitalize on mismatches, especially every time they put Jeff Withey on the court. We wanted to exploit it when Kim English was guarded by Withey or Robinson. We wanted to punish them for that. And we wanted to find our spots for our guards, mainly me and Phil.

Tyshawn Taylor: Withey hurt his ankle on an early possession and had to come out. I was really mad, because when I looked at the video, and when I talked to Cheddar, our trainer, on the bench, I thought, "He just doesn't want to have to guard Kim."

Jeff Withey: I twisted my ankle really bad. I went back and got taped up and tried to play on it, but I could tell immediately that I wasn't going to be quick enough to guard those guys. I remember telling Coach Self, "My ankle is slowing me down. I think we should go with a smaller lineup." We did that and it turned out to be an epic game.

Travis Releford: We had to go small, because Jeff couldn't really guard anybody. At one point, Missouri's tallest guy on the court was my height (6-4). They were a tough guard because they had all shooters on the court. Anybody could knock down a 3.

Michael Dixon: As a team, we finished second in the nation in field goal percentage that year (50.4 percent). And remember, we weren't a big team. We weren't scoring all of our points on easy baskets in the paint. We were ahead of our time. Now, everyone plays small ball. Just look at the Golden State Warriors. Hell, even Kansas did it last year. It's just not as big of a deal anymore.

Conner Teahan: I was forced to play the four, because they had Kim English at the four and Ratliffe at the five, and Ratliffe was a problem for Jeff.

Jeff kind of became a non-factor in both of those games, and that's why I played a lot more, because they needed someone to guard Kim English, or I would guard one of the Pressey boys.

That's why they were so successful all year. They were one of the first teams to really play that small-ball style. Teams just weren't used to preparing for it or defending it. It was unorthodox back then.

Withey played only three minutes in the first half and picked up two fouls during that time. In two games against Missouri that season he scored just one basket.

Tyshawn Taylor: It was a tough matchup for Jeff, but it'd have also been tough for Missouri to guard him inside, too. Ratliff couldn't get any fouls because they had no depth in the paint. If he got any fouls, they were done. But Jeff just didn't make them pay.

So Jeff came out, T-Rob was in foul trouble and the lineup at one point was me, Elijah, Teahan, Kevin Young and Justin Wesley. That's a non-scoring lineup. Nobody could get a bucket. It just seemed like we couldn't do anything. And they were hitting big shot after big shot.

A basket by Thomas Robinson forced a 31-31 tie with 5:33 left before intermission. Kansas, though, went 0-for-5 from the field and 1-for-5 from the free throw line the rest of the way as Missouri closed the half on a 13-1 scoring run. Marcus Denmon scored eight points during the march, all in the final three minutes. Kansas entered the locker room trailing 44-32.

Thomas Robinson: They jumped out on us. They were so hot. I was out of it. I wasn't playing well at all. Tyshawn wasn't playing well. Nobody was hitting shots. They were beastin' us. Marcus Denmon … oh my God! He was on fire from the tip. At halftime Coach Self was cussing us out and telling us that we were embarrassing everybody.

Bill Self: There was too much pressure. It was probably the most pressurized game I've ever felt in the regular season. There was so much juice about it because it was going to be the last time we ever played Missouri. We had to win that game, and our guys knew it. They played so tight in the first half. They were trying too hard. I kept saying, "Someone will make a shot and the lid will come off the basket and everything will be OK." But they were trying too hard.

Travis Releford: Coach Self told us at halftime, "There's no way these guys are going to continue to shoot like this. After this next 20 minutes, we're going to be in this locker room celebrating. I need everybody to believe that!"

BEST KU WALK-ONS

1. Christian Moody (2002-06): Dubbed "the best walk-on in history" by CBS analyst Billy Packer; started 25 games as a junior and nine as a senior.

2. Conner Teahan (2007-12): Rockhurst High School product averaged 21 minutes and 5.5 points per game as a senior in 2011-12; had four 3s in historic overtime win against Missouri in Lawrence.

3. Nick Bahe (2003-05): Played sparingly in two years at KU before transferring to Creighton—where he became a starter—after the 2004-05 season.

4. Stephen Vinson (2002-06): Lawrence native played significant minutes in fall of 2005 while Mario Chalmers adapted; had big game (six points, six assists) in win over Cal.

5. Matt Kleinmann (2004-09): Blue Valley West power forward was widely regarded as one of the top practice players on KU's squad from 2004-08.

6. Evan Manning (2012-16): Son of Jayhawks legend Danny Manning could've started at many smaller Division I schools.

7. Justin Wesley (2011-14): Half-brother of Keith Langford transferred from Lamar and played in every game as a sophomore in 2011-12 before role decreased in final two seasons.

8. Brad Witherspoon (2006-08): Former rec league star played two seasons at Kansas and was one of the key practice players on 2008 NCAA championship team.

9. Jordan Juenemann (2008-12): Fan favorite scored seven points against Texas Tech in 2012; has a Final Four ring for all of his hard work.

10. Niko Roberts (2010-14): Son of KU assistant Norm Roberts improved as much as any walk-on during his four years in Lawrence.

Conner Teahan: The thing I remember most clearly was the music that was playing when we were coming out for the second half. It was some Lil' John song, and we got out there, and there was something that felt totally different. We felt like we weren't going to lose.

Kansas may have opened the second half with swagger—but the Tigers did, too. Missouri made its first six shots after intermission during an 11-4 scoring run that resulted in a 58-39 lead. With their team trailing by 19 points, Kansas fans didn't know how to react.

Michael Dixon: It was scary quiet in there. It felt like we were in the rec or something.

Kim English: I remember walking toward the huddle for a timeout. I said to Mike Dixon, "Man, it's quiet in here. I've never heard it this quiet in here." The next timeout, I looked up at the scoreboard and I said to Marcus Denmon, "We've got to keep this up. We're up by nine." I'm obviously not good at math, because he said, "Bro, we're up 19!" I couldn't believe it. We were just clicking. We were executing. We played a flawless game for a long time.

Marcus Denmon: I'd played in Lawrence four times at Missouri and other times for AAU games. When The Fieldhouse is amped, it's so loud that you can't understand what your coaches and teammates are saying in the huddle.

That game my senior year was the quietest I'd ever heard Allen Fieldhouse. It was quiet enough that, if someone cracked a peanut in the stands, you could hear it. I could hear everything Coach Haith and my teammates were saying.

Tyshawn Taylor: One thing I remember is Coach Self being so cool. He didn't lose his cool at all. I remember looking at him in the huddle and coming out and feeling like we had a chance every time. I remember being so poised in that game. Every possession is important. We literally chipped away.

Travis Releford: Everybody believed. There were a few times we came into the huddle during the second half, and I'm pretty sure I said something to remind us, "Hey, let's keep smiling. We're about to make a comeback and win this game." We slowly came back.

Conner Teahan: The one thing we were really, really good at that year was taking things possession by possession—just chipping away. You're not going to get 19 points back in two or three possessions. We had to really hunker down defensively, run the right sets on offense and remember that we were in Allen Fieldhouse. If we got that energy behind us we'd have a good probability of winning.

Missouri still maintained a sizable lead, 67-51, with 10:51 remaining. At that point, though, the momentum began to shift. A dunk by reserve forward Kevin Young started a 15-2 Kansas scoring run that cut the Tigers' lead to three, 69-66, with less than four minutes left.

Kevin Young: I played 28 minutes in that game, which was the most for me all season. I had a chip on my shoulder, because I'd committed to Missouri when I was 16 years old. My senior year of high school, they came to a couple of my practices and a few of my games. Right before I was going to graduate, they called my travel-team coach and told him they were dropping my scholarship offer. They said it was because of grades, but that didn't make sense because I graduated with a 3.8 GPA. It was really tough for me. I had visited a couple of times and was excited to go there. I felt like I was a good fit for Coach Anderson's system … 40 minutes of hell, full-court press, on the ball the whole time. And it was a bigger school compared to all of the other schools I had offers from at the time.

Even worse was that it happened in June, at the end of the recruiting season. It was almost summer. A lot of college coaches contacted me and suggested I go to prep school, but that's not something I wanted to do. I ended up signing with Loyola Marymount in August.

So for me, that was a big game. The first time we played them at their place, I didn't get to play very much and they beat us. I didn't want that to happen again.

The atmosphere that day was like nothing I'd ever seen. Tyshawn would be two-or-three feet away from me in the huddle and I couldn't hear him talk. I remember in the team huddle, Coach just started laughing. He just said, "Go out there and play," because we couldn't hear him. At the time, it was measured as the loudest indoor crowd in history.

I remember setting a screen for Tyshawn and just rolling. He threw me the lob for that dunk and the crowd just went crazy. We took control of the game after that.

Walk-on Conner Teahan, who played a career-high 37 minutes, followed Young's dunk with his fourth 3-pointer of the day. Teahan did not miss a shot against the Tigers.

Conner Teahan: We knew we were playing for the Big 12 championship. I guarantee we were all thinking, "Let's not be the team to end this streak. Let's leave nothing to chance, because we control our own destiny."

The guys were trying to get me the ball as much as they could. They knew I had a hot hand, and they wanted to give me the opportunity to shoot. That just describes our team. We knew if somebody was feeling it, it didn't matter who, get them the ball and get out of the way and just be unselfish. We never gave up and we were unselfish.

Bill Self: Teahan against Missouri that year, in two games, was 6-of-6 from 3.

Thomas Robinson: I told everyone in the huddle, "We are *not* losing this game. We are *not* losing to these guys twice in a season." That first game, I was really hurt by that. It hurt our ranking, too. I was pissed.

As hot as Kansas got offensively, the Jayhawks were equally impressive on defense. Missouri went seven minutes without a field goal during KU's momentum-changing scoring run and missed nine of its final 11 shots in regulation.

Kim English: We had three straight possessions with no passes, just quick shots.

That's the antithesis to ball movement. Three straight no-pass shots. And I think the result by KU on the other end was a 3, another 3 and then a basket in the paint. That cut our lead from 19 to 11. All of a sudden, it went from the crowd not being a factor, to the crowd being a bigger factor than any crowd in America.

Frank Haith: Phog Allen was at its best, and it affected the game this way: it motivated and encouraged them to play unbelievable. And it affected some of the other stuff that happened in the game. You can't tell me the atmosphere doesn't affect someone trying to officiate that game. It had an impact on it. It had an impact on us. We were a veteran team, but it was so loud in there, it obviously got to us a few times. We took some quick shots a few times in the second half. We really rushed some things instead of continuing with our ball movement, particularly after Phil Pressey, our point guard, got his fourth foul. I had to sit him. That really hurt us. He was the guy that was in charge and really held us together. When we didn't have him in the game during that stretch, they made up some huge ground. We took some really quick shots, and they capitalized on those mistakes and got some easy buckets on the other end.

With 25.9 seconds left, Kansas trailed by three and called timeout. Bill Self called for the Jayhawks to run their famous Chop play—the one that resulted in Mario Chalmers' heroic basket against Memphis in the NCAA title game four years earlier—but this version had a twist.

Conner Teahan: With Chop, for every option, there's a counter option, too. There were 10 options, and there's actually 20, because if they try to deny you on the hand off, you can back cut. I think we ran that play legitimately five or six times in a row at the end of the game. On that one, T-Rob set the down screen and cut, and he slipped the screen.

Kim English: We were up by three and we were saying in the timeout, "Whatever you do, don't foul!"

Thomas Robinson: I caught the pass and went up for the shot, and Michael Dixon went under me, just a little bit. I could barely feel it. Actually … did he touch me? I'm not sure (laughing). I sold it pretty well. He made enough contact where I could make it look like it affected the shot. I must've done a good job because I got the whistle.

Michael Dixon: Coach Haith was so mad at me after that. If a guy goes up thinking there's going to be contact, I like to move out of the way and not touch him at all. That throws them off a little bit—thinking they're going to get hit, but then not getting touched at all—and sometimes they'll shoot a bad shot. Once Thomas caught the ball on the backdoor pass, I knew I wasn't going to block his shot, and I didn't want to foul him, so I moved out of the way. Still, somehow, when he went up for the shot, one of his feet grazed against me, and he fell as he made the basket.

Let's say he wears a size 16 shoe. If he'd have been wearing a 15, he probably wouldn't have ever touched me. I barely even felt it. I was just trying to get out of the way. I'm mad at myself to this day, because I saw the ball in the air on the pass. I should've knocked it out of bounds, but instead, I let him catch it. I was like, "URGH!" I faked like I was going to foul him and then moved out of the way. He ended up getting the call and the and-one.

Kim English: Mike tried to pull his hands back to get out of the way. He might have clipped him a little bit. (Official) Jerry Pollard said he wouldn't have called it if Thomas didn't fall. Thomas sold it.

Thomas Robinson: Then I had to go to the free throw line. That was big. That was the biggest moment I'd had in a game at that point in my career. The fans were going crazy. The Morris twins were at the game. I remember that's who I was staring at when I was sitting under the basket after the foul. I was sitting on the floor, just staring at them. They were sitting behind our bench.

Kim English: Thomas was on the free throw line after that play, and I was praying for him to miss it. When someone has tragedy in their life, I feel like the sports gods are going to give them the win. I was on the right block, ready to box out whoever to get the rebound. I looked at Thomas and, in my mind, I'm saying, "Miss this free throw. Miss this free throw. C'mon, God. Make him miss this free throw."

Then Thomas did something I'll always remember. He rubbed a tattoo of his mom that was on his left shoulder, and he mumbled something, presumably about his mom. When he did that, I thought, "I can't root for this kid to miss this shot. He's been through enough. Give him this free throw, God." And of course he made it. That's something small that I'll always remember from that game. Me hoping he missed that free throw but, at the same time, being happy for him that he made it.

Thomas Robinson: We wore a patch honoring my mom on the left shoulder of our jerseys. It had her initials on it. And I have her name tattooed on my wrist. I'd say "Lisa" and then I'd just rub her tattoo.

The game now knotted at 75-75, Missouri called timeout and then inbounded the ball to Pressey at mid-court. The point guard blew past his defender, Johnson, on the left wing and penetrated into the paint, where he attempted a layup over Robinson.

Thomas Robinson: We knew that refs usually swallowed their whistles on the last play of the game. Our coaches really preached that to us in practice when we were working on end-of-clock situations. If someone got to the rim on us and we didn't foul them, we'd get in trouble.

I watched Pressey match up against Elijah, and I kind of knew he was going to beat him—not because Elijah is a bad defender, but because Pressey was smaller and so quick and explosive. I just sat over there in the short corner and waited. I knew he wasn't going to try to hit a pull-up on Elijah, because Elijah is 6-4 and Pressey is 5-something.

He was going to come all the way to the rim. Initially I was thinking, "Why doesn't Marcus Denmon have the ball?" But Marcus was two passes away in the corner, so I knew Pressey was going to shoot it.

Robinson swatted Pressey's game-winning attempt cleanly and with force as the buzzer sounded. He appeared to make contact with Pressey after the shot, but no foul was called.

Thomas Robinson: I told Phil a year or so later that he should've floated it. I don't know why he'd come all the way to the rim against me like that. He knew he wasn't going to get that call at that point in the game. A floater would've been the best shot for him. They swallowed their whistle. There was too much going on. It was bananas in there. I give myself credit for being aware of the situation. It was a good play by me. I got a clean block. There was definitely contact after the shot, but it didn't affect the shot. It was a great call. Or I guess I should say it was a great no-call.

Tyshawn Taylor: The referee is never going to call that. Pressey threw the ball up and jumped into T-Rob. The shot was already blocked and then he threw his body into T-Rob. Plus, we were like, "Do y'all really want to win a game like that? On a questionable call with no time left? Throw that bitch up and let's play five more minutes."

Frank Haith: They could've called a foul. But there were a few other questionable calls before that, including an and-one where Michael Dixon had minimal contact with Thomas on a shot he made under the basket.

Marcus Denmon: I understand them not wanting to end the game on a foul, but that was the play at hand. It was a clear foul, I believe. It was a missed call, but hey, there were probably some missed calls that went the other way in Columbia.

Travis Releford: They ran an iso with Phil Pressey, and I don't even think he looked at the rim. He saw T-Rob and just threw it up. T-Rob blocked his shot, and there was contact coming down after the shot, but Mizzou fans and players will say there was contact before the shot, which obviously isn't true.

After the block, you saw how crazy it was. That's the loudest Allen Fieldhouse has been, hands down. You couldn't even hear your own thoughts in there. Missouri knew they had nothing left because they gave it all the first half and tried their hardest to keep us down. With the energy in there at that point … there was no way we were going to let the fans down. They deserved that win just as much as we did.

Kansas opened overtime with a 3-pointer from Tyshawn Taylor that gave the Jayhawks their first lead of the game. The Jayhawks controlled the early parts of the extra period—leading 80-76 at one point—but the Tigers stayed close and eventually took back the lead, 84-83, with 38.6 seconds left when Marcus Denmon made his second 3 of overtime. Denmon's guarded shot came from five feet beyond the 3-point line on the left wing.

Tyshawn Taylor: It wasn't a shot. It was a hoist. He had two people on him. Me and Travis were right there.

Elijah Johnson: They were irritating to play because they were relentless. They didn't stop. They reminded you every second that they were a top-three team, too. As soon as you'd go up by four, they'd make a 3 and be down one point. They were hard to put away.

The years before that, I felt like Missouri kind of bowed down to us. They'd try to fight, but once we punched them two or three times, they'd fold. But that year they actually fought the whole time.

Tyshawn Taylor: In overtime, it felt like it was our game. But yet it was still a one- or two-possession game the entire time.

Conner Teahan: I remember them not going away. Denmon and Dixon and all of those guys that were on the perimeter, every time they got an opportunity, you thought it was going in. They had such a green light that they were playing so loose.

We still had supreme confidence, especially being at Allen Fieldhouse. When Denmon made that shot, in most situations, teams would be like, "OK, maybe this wasn't meant to be."

But those kind of thoughts don't go through your mind as much when you're at home. Maybe at Mizzou Arena you'd have that. But at Allen Fieldhouse, after we'd forced overtime, our mindset was that nothing was going to stop us.

In the last minute of the game when we had a timeout, T-Rob was yelling "we're not going to lose this game. It can't happen. It won't happen." All these events kept occurring that made it feel like we were invincible in Allen Fieldhouse and destined to win.

Kansas called timeout with 34.6 seconds left with Mizzou ahead by one point, 84-83, and once again, Self called for his team to run Chop. Only this time, things were different.

Elijah Johnson: People all over the country were starting to run Coach Self's Chop play, and Missouri was waiting for us to run it in that moment. But they didn't realize the play has a million options. We'd mostly been running the same one for three or four years. So I was like, "Let's run a different option."

To backtrack, in practice the scout team is allowed to foul you whenever it wants, so it's hard to get the ball in handoff situations. Earlier that year, we'd improvised and came up with an adjustment. I was like, "Ty, just backdoor your man when he's about to foul you." He did it, I passed it to him as he was cutting and it was smooth. Coach Self lit up and was like, "I love it." We never used it in a game until we played Mizzou. We couldn't think of anything else to do. At the last second, I was like, "Backdoor it." And it worked.

Sure enough, Taylor started to trot from the right corner toward the top of the circle to take the hand off from Johnson. But when Phil Pressey cheated up, Taylor cut back door and raced toward the basket. Johnson hit him in stride with a perfect bounce pass, and Taylor threw down the go-ahead dunk.

Denmon, of course, had the answer again, this time driving around Releford for a baseline floater that put Mizzou ahead 86-85 with 12.6 ticks left.

Kim English: Marcus is a stoic guy, but he always wanted the ball at the end of games. We all wanted the ball at the end. Me, Mike Dixon ... we all hit big shots at the end of games. But that day there was something about Marcus' conviction that told you he wanted it a little bit more, so we had to concede.

After Denmon's bucket, Releford immediately passed the ball into Taylor. One of the fastest, most athletic guards in the country that season, Taylor used his elite speed to try to get down the court and make a play before the Tigers could set their defense.

Bill Self: The play of the game that no one talks about is the one that Tyshawn made right after Denmon's basket. They went up by one point and we didn't call timeout. Back then, the rule was that coaches could call timeouts. We'd told our players, "You get the ball in as quick as you can. If we take the timeout, we take it." Travis threw the ball in to Tyshawn underneath the free throw line, extended. In just two dribbles, Tyshawn got all the way down to the other end of the court to shoot a layup. Again, two dribbles, and he's shooting a layup. Athletically, to me, that was one of the most impressive plays I've ever seen.

Tyshawn Taylor: We used that play a lot. It was something we did when we didn't have any timeouts, or when we didn't want to take a timeout. It was something we practiced. We'd talked about it in the previous timeout. *If they score, we've got to get it in fast.* That's what I was thinking: "Get it in fast and push it. Just try to make a play." It wasn't the shot I wanted to take, but I got fouled.

Missouri players thought the foul on Pressey—his fifth—was another questionable call.

Kim English: I'm friends with (officials) Jerry Pollard and Mark Whitehead. But the calls they made at the end of the game were bad. Those guys ... they're human. They feel the environment. No offense to them, but they do. I'm not upset about them not calling the Thomas Robinson foul on Phil at the end of regulation. Let the game be won with the ball going through the net. I'm OK with that. But they fouled out Phil with a softer play on Tyshawn Taylor driving right, which was ridiculous. That fouled out our point guard and it really hurt us. I'm all about consistency in officiating. Just be consistent. That's all I ask.

Marcus Denmon: I thought it was a little bit of home cooking.

Whatever the case, Taylor went to the free throw line with 8.3 seconds remaining and his team trailing by one. The foul stripe was a spot that had haunted Taylor since KU's 74-71 loss to Missouri in Columbia on Feb. 4. In that game, Taylor clanked two free throws with 41 seconds left. This time—down 86-85, with the Big 12 title streak on the line, not to mention pride—Taylor could not afford to miss.

Conner Teahan: You sit there and you think, "These free throws *have* to go in." And in that type of situation, it's not uncommon to see someone miss a free throw, right? You'd probably expect for them to miss the free throw, because pressure breaks the pipes.

But just sitting there, watching Tyshawn, you knew that he'd been through so much, not just that season, but throughout his entire career. He'd gotten beat up so much that that type of thing—getting to that line and being in that situation—was exactly what Tyshawn wanted. He wanted to be the guy that was going to take on all the responsibility. *It might as well be me.* And I think he approached it that way. I remember having full confidence in his ability to knock them down, even as nervous as he might have been.

Tyshawn Taylor: I'm going to be completely honest. When I stepped to the line, I was nervous as hell. I felt as much pressure in that moment as I ever had in my KU career.

I thought back to that night in Columbia where I missed those two free throws in the final minute. That stuck with me for a while. One of my friends, a guy from Chicago named Pete, a guy that Sherron had introduced me to ... he said, "Bro, you're going to get that opportunity again." That statement is what I thought about when I stepped to the line. I thought, "This is the opportunity he told me I would have again."

The first one, I kind of prayed it in. That took the pressure off. The second one felt regular, it felt normal. I definitely breathed a sigh of relief when it went through the net.

Naadir Tharpe: Everybody was saying, "You're not a good free throw shooter." Blah. Blah. Blah. In crunch time, Ty made them. He always responded. That was something he did throughout his career at Kansas. He responded to negativity. He let that fuel him.

Thomas Robinson: I loved how stubborn he was. He never turned down a moment that called for him to be brave. He embraced it. I pulled a lot of weight that game, but in those last few minutes of overtime, I was running out of gas. Tyshawn stepped up and sealed it for us. He put us on his back and just did it. He's very emotional. I love that about him. I love playing with people who care.

With Pressey on the bench, the Tigers inbounded the ball to backup point guard Michael Dixon, assuming he would push the ball up the court quickly to set up—or take—the final shot. At that point Denmon was 10-of-16 from the field for 29 points and had made six of his nine 3-point attempts.

Kim English: We didn't get the ball up to the frontcourt fast enough. We kind of jogged it up.

Marcus Denmon: We ran a play but we just didn't execute it like we were supposed to. Mike Dixon was cramping up a little bit and he brought the ball up a little slower than he normally would.

Michael Dixon: I was trying to make sure we got the last shot with no time on the clock, because if we would've made it with some time remaining, who knows what could've happened? They'd have come down and scored or got fouled. I didn't think I took that long, but apparently I did.

Marcus was hot that game, but I played well, too. I'm not saying I wanted to take the shot, but man ... it was so loud in there. It just all happened so fast. The plan was to get it to Marcus. We wanted to have him come off of a handoff and shoot it. Elijah Johnson was guarding me and played good defense. I got by him a little bit but then Thomas Robinson came over to help and clogged up the lane. I passed it out to Marcus on the wing, but he couldn't get the shot off in time. I guess I just took too long. The horn sounded about one second before he released it. Marcus made the shot, too. That's what made it even worse.

Marcus Denmon: Usually, I could get a shot off out of that set. That time I released it a second too late. It wasn't because of anything Kansas did. It wasn't because they pressured us. We just didn't execute quickly enough.

Michael Dixon: I was just devastated. I cried like a little baby in the locker room. Everyone was trying to make me feel better, but I felt like it was my fault because of that last play. I wasn't as mad at myself about the foul on T-Rob in regulation, because I didn't feel like I fouled him. It was a bad call. I wasn't going to beat myself up over that, because I didn't foul him. But the play at the end, where Marcus' shot was a second too late ... I beat myself up over that one for a long time.

I wanted to win that game and celebrate on that court afterward. I needed that for myself and I never got it. It tore me up for a while.

Tyshawn Taylor: Dixon was a great player but he had a bad game. He had some crucial turnovers at the end and took a couple of bad shots that helped us. Travis and I are good friends with Dixon. We always tease him and say, "You were the best player on our team those last couple of minutes."

Frank Haith: At our place, when we won, I held my hands up at the buzzer and pumped my fists. Bill kind of gave it back to me a little bit when they beat us at Phog. He gave me the old two-handed, "Yeah, Frank, right-back-at-you" fist pump. There was nothing I could say to him because he was so amped up. Bill's never like that. He won a national championship and he wasn't like that. It shows you just how emotional that game was. And that's OK. I understood. It was a great game. I love Bill. We are great. I have a tremendous amount of respect for what he's doing there.

Bill Self: I was happy. I acted like an idiot. There was a lot of emotion in that game.

Kansas' 19-point, second-half comeback for a win marked the biggest in school history.

Assistant coach Kurtis Townsend: Coach was really pumped. He knew how much winning that game meant to the people around here. It's great to watch guys playing that hard. That will go down as one of the greatest games I've ever been a part of as a coach.

Tyshawn Taylor: I was so tired after that game that I couldn't even go out to celebrate. I wanted to, but I didn't have any energy left. I was exhausted. Plus, we had to go play a really good Oklahoma State team on the road 48 hours later.

Elijah Johnson: I just remember being so tired after that game. I've never in my life played a game that left me that tired. Other than a couple of big plays, I don't remember anything about the game except being tired. My chest had me feeling like I was about to die. The Fieldhouse was so turnt up for that game. People don't realize it—and trust me, I'm not saying it's a bad thing—but hearing all of that noise takes a toll on you. It drains you. Imagine trying to communicate over noise like that for 40 minutes. I felt like I was yelling for three hours straight. I never could catch my breath. I remember my chest feeling crazy. I don't want to ever feel like I felt that day again. People mention that Missouri game and they think sparks are going to go off in my eyes. But the first thing I do is think of my chest.

Thomas Robinson: I woke up the next morning and people were saying it was the greatest game in Kansas history. I was like, "S**t, this is crazy." I started thinking back to my freshman year, when Hudy was purposefully trying to make me throw up, and I was thinking, "Man, I want some respect here." At that moment, I realized, "I've got it now."

I was like, "This is why players like Mario Chalmers and Darnell Jackson and Darrell Arthur and all the guys from the 2008 team get worshipped every time they come back here." These fans love us, but they worship those guys. I've seen it firsthand. Time stops when Mario Chalmers walks through Lawrence, Kansas. I wanted that for myself. Hopefully that game gave fans something to remember me for.

Kevin Young: Six weeks later, while we were in our hotel waiting to play in the Final Four, we turned on the television and that game was already on ESPN Classic.

Michael Dixon: We were up 19. I'm still trying to figure out how we lost. There was so much time left on the clock. Conner hit some big shots. We didn't get some calls down the stretch, but they didn't get some calls down the stretch in Columbia, either. If you're up 19 in the second half and you lose, it's your fault. You can't blame the officials or anyone else.

Marcus Denmon: We rushed some possessions and there were some questionable calls, but that's how it goes. That's part of college basketball. The credit goes to them. They still had to make some tough shots, some tough plays. The momentum started to go their way. Add that to a couple of swallowed whistles, and we had really good, close games.

Bill Self: We were upset and pissed and everything else after losing that first game in

Columbia. It was a game we for sure should've won. The game at Allen Fieldhouse is a game Missouri should've won. They outplayed us the whole game until the very end.

Frank Haith: I think Phog Allen won that game. I heard Bill Self say it was the loudest he'd ever heard that building. We were playing so well, but then Teahan got going and made some unbelievable 3s. Then all of a sudden, when Phil fouled out, it was tough for us.

We never talked about it being the last game against them, at least not with our players. We were going into the SEC the following year, so our fan base was talking about it and so was the media. But in that locker room, it was just a game to give us an opportunity to win the conference championship. That was it. That was the focus. We knew that the Big 12 championship goes through Kansas. That was all that we talked about.

I knew they had a bad taste in their mouth with how we won the game at our place and how it ended. Plus, the magnitude surrounding this game and what was on the line ... if they won, they won the championship. So there was a certain amount of pressure on them, too.

I did call (Big 12 Coordinator of Officials) Curtis Shaw from the Allen Fieldhouse parking lot right after the game. That's the worst time to call, because you're heated. You're upset. You need time to cool off. You need time to go back and look at it. I actually felt comforted after talking to Curtis. He had watched the game on TV and he said, "Look, there were definitely some tough plays, some tough calls." Obviously, I felt the same way. The plays that I was complaining about—the "and-one" and the last two foul calls on Phil—weren't even the plays he was referencing. He mentioned some other ones that I hadn't seen.

But look ... I don't blame the officials. It was such a hard game for them to work, with the environment and the crowd and everything that was at stake.

There isn't a tougher place to play in America. I've been in the ACC and coached at Duke and Maryland. I've been in the SEC and coached at Rupp Arena in Kentucky. There is no place I've been that compares to Allen Fieldhouse. I couldn't hear my assistant coaches and we were sitting side by side. I had to look at their mouths when they were talking so I could read their lips. Their fans were great. There was no bashing Frank Haith or personal attacks on our players. It was just a great atmosphere. Absolutely off the charts. I've always told myself that, if I was officiating in that environment, there's no way it wouldn't affect me. It's human nature. As good of an official as you may be, there are going to be some things that happen that are going to rattle you. Those fans are relentless. There's no let-up. It starts two hours before the game.

Still, Bill will tell you that, in his last game at Mizzou Arena, our fans were the best. There were times when he heard some God-awful stuff. But I remember him commenting on how great our fans were in Columbia during that final game, and I certainly had the same experience at Phog Allen.

Two days after beating Missouri, the Jayhawks claimed the Big 12 title outright by winning at Oklahoma State. Then came a 73-63 victory over Texas on Senior Night. It was a proper send-off for

Taylor, who scored 22 points, and Robinson, who had 25 points and 14 rebounds.

Thomas Robinson: Coach Self had made it known that I was leaving for the draft, even though everyone pretty much knew. Still, Coach Self usually doesn't do that. I'd watched lottery picks like Cole and the Morris twins and top picks like Xavier go through similar situations leaving early, and Coach Self never did that. He never acknowledged underclassmen on Senior Night like he did with me the night we played Texas.

At the end of his speech, he looked toward me and said, "This will be this guy's last game here, too." I looked into the stands, and people were crying. It was hard for me to keep it in. I thought that man hated me at one point. But by the end of my career he was going out of his way to show me he loved me.

Big 12 Tourney Letdown

Kansas and Missouri fans were crossing their fingers the Jayhawks and Tigers would meet for a third time in the Big 12 Tournament in Kansas City the following month. Those hopes were dashed, however, when KU fell in the semifinals to Baylor, 81-72. Missouri went on to capture the tournament championship in a win over the Bears the following night.

Tyshawn Taylor: Baylor came out of the zone and went man and we couldn't score. We weren't the most talented team that year. If me and T-Rob weren't playing well, Elijah had to play well. And if Elijah didn't step up, we were in trouble.

Quincy Acy: We finally calmed down and played a solid game. In the past, they'd capitalized on turnovers and mishaps and technicals, and we didn't give them anything easy that time. I think we were pretty focused, too. We were locked in because, once again, it was basically a home game for them in Kansas City. Luckily we were able to get them. We actually played three "road games" that year in the Big 12 tournament. We beat K-State and KU and lost to Missouri. I'm not sure any team has ever been forced to play three straight games under circumstances like that in a conference tournament. We never complained, though. We locked in and got to the title game and could've won it.

Michael Dixon: I don't know how they lost to Baylor. They had killed them twice that year. I honestly think they didn't care about playing us again. I know Coach Self didn't care about Missouri. Who knows what would've happened? But it would have been fun. It would've been a storybook ending to the rivalry.

Comeback Kids

As the No. 2 seed in the Midwest Region, Kansas entered the NCAA Tournament upbeat and loose. The Jayhawks also knew they had little margin for error, as their five starters accounted for 84 percent of their offense. Foul trouble for a key players such as Robinson, Taylor or Withey could spell doom for Self's squad.

The Jayhawks opened with a 15-point win over Detroit in Omaha but then lived dangerously for the next three rounds.

They fought back from a 10-point second-half deficit against No. 10 seed Purdue, winning 63-60 thanks to a go-ahead bucket by Johnson with 23.3 seconds remaining.

In the Sweet 16 in St. Louis, they escaped with a 60-57 victory over No. 11 NC State despite making just two shots from beyond five feet and going just 1-of-14 from beyond the arc. Withey blocked 10 shots against the Wolfpack.

Jeff Withey: They just kept trying to come at me. They obviously wanted to challenge me early on and things were kind of going my way. They just kept shooting layups and doing the same thing all over again. It was easy to get block after block after block.

Travis Releford: During every tournament game, we'd be down, and at some point we'd look at each other and say, "What do we have to lose? We have nothing to lose. We've got 20 more minutes to play. Let's go all out." Clearly T-Rob was going to leave early, and Tyshawn was a senior. So the mood was like, "This might be our last 20 minutes to play together. What do we have to lose? We're not even supposed to be here."

It was the least amount of pressure we ever felt in the tournament, and I think that played a role in us doing so well. Most of the time, everyone expects us to make it to the Final Four. Even with the teams they had in 2016 and 2017, everyone expected them to make the Final Four, and they felt that. That's pressure they were putting on themselves without even trying. We didn't have that pressure. We were ranked No. 13 in the preseason poll. It was, "We're not even supposed to be here. Let's go out here and show the world what we can do." And that's what we did.

It also helped that everyone knew their role. That was key. You had six or seven guys going into every game knowing exactly what they needed to do. There wasn't anyone trying to step out and do anything extra. I wasn't going to go out there and shoot 10 threes.

Needing one more win to advance to the Final Four, Kansas found itself pitted against Roy Williams and No. 1 seed North Carolina (32-5) in the Elite Eight. The high-scoring Tar Heels, along with Kentucky, had been considered the top team in America for most of the season, but UNC had taken a major hit when star point guard Kendall Marshall fractured his wrist in a round-of-32 win against Creighton.

Bill Self: We were tied 47-47 at halftime, and everyone in the locker room was talking about what a great first half we'd had. I said, "Yeah, we're getting ready to get our ass beat." We weren't playing defense. Our guys were like, "You're right. This isn't how we play." Then we went out there and got tough and defended and won the game. It was a tie game when we went triangle-and-two, and we ended up outscoring them by about 16 down the stretch. They didn't have a field goal for the last six minutes of the game. UNC had a good team. Obviously, we caught a break because Kendall Marshall didn't play.

Jeff Withey: Everyone had us losing to them. Coach Self got us hyped up before the game and we went out there and just kicked their ass. The game was about over, and I remember the feeling being unreal as the final seconds ticked away.

Still, we knew we were going to win from the get-go. The score was tied at halftime and we hadn't defended at all. We felt like, "Hey, we can score with these guys, no problem. But we're a way better defensive team than them. We can easily beat these guys if we just step it up on that end of the court." We ended up doing that.

Withey's Wall

Kansas arrived at the 2012 Final Four in New Orleans feeling like an underdog. Along with having zero depth, the Jayhawks had looked far from dominant in their previous three wins, and now they'd be facing a revenge-minded Ohio State squad that was without All-American forward Jared Sullinger when KU topped the Buckeyes 78-67 back on Dec. 10 at Allen Fieldhouse. Much like Ohio State, though, Kansas had taken on a new look since that game, too, as Withey had improved at warp speed and blossomed into one of the top shot swatters in America. Withey—the Big 12's Defensive Player of the Year—entered the matchup with the Buckeyes averaging 5.5 blocks in his first four NCAA Tournament games.

Thomas Robinson: Everybody knew Jeff was good, but for a while he wouldn't do it in games. That was everyone's problem with Jeff. We knew he was a good player, but we were like, "Jeff, you've got to bring it *every time*." When I left, he got better. He got meaner. He can thank me for that. When I had him by myself in 2012, there were a few times when I got up in his face and said, "You better stop acting like a bitch out here." Toward the end of that season he started getting five blocks one game, seven blocks the next. We started climbing the rankings and taking off and making a run at the championship. Jeff protects the rim. That's his gift. He threw stuff all over the gym.

Danny Manning: Jeff and Thomas Robinson came in at the same time and, every day, they were going up against Cole and the Morris twins in practice. Going against those guys, you've got to find it within yourself to compete. If you don't, you're going to get embarrassed.

Jeff was a different type of athlete than those other guys because of his body makeup. As he continued to get stronger and develop more confidence, he continued to blossom. He always had a good skill set, and he had good feel. I thought his volleyball background was instrumental in him being the defender that he was, especially as a shot-blocker and rim-protector. There were a lot of times he was able to contest shots at a very high point going straight up in the paint. Most guys don't have the finesse that Jeff had, to be able to block and alter shots while still being in control of your body.

Withey came up huge for the Jayhawks against Ohio State by blocking seven shots and limiting Sullinger to 13 points on 5-of-19 shooting.

Much like it did in its first three wins, Kansas had to claw back from behind against the Buckeyes. After scoring the game's first bucket, KU didn't lead again until Releford made two free throws with

2:48 remaining. A pair of clutch foul shots by Taylor put KU ahead 64-61 with 8 ticks left. The Jayhawks intentionally fouled Aaron Craft with 2 seconds remaining. Craft made the first free throw and then clanked the second one off the rim on purpose. He was called for a lane violation. Kansas dribbled out the clock and celebrated the 64-62 win.

Jeff Withey: Sullinger wasn't the most athletic guy, but he was strong and big. He had a lot of hype behind his name. I knew I needed to disrupt his rhythm and try to make him more of a shooter. Everything that he did, I tried to make it tough for him. I tried to make him catch the ball out a little bit further and not let him back me down. I forced him to take jump shots. He was definitely their best offensive player. I knew if I stopped

BEST OF THE STREAK

BEST KU DEFENDERS

1. Jeff Withey: Two-time Big 12 Defensive Player of the Year who set a single-season record for blocks in an NCAA Tournament (31) in 2012.

2. Cole Aldrich: Ranks third all-time at KU in blocks (253) despite only playing three seasons.

3. Brandon Rush: Self routinely puts Rush at the top of the list when asked about the best defenders he's had at KU.

4. Mario Chalmers: 2006-07 co-Big 12 Defensive Player of the Year had a knack for anticipating passes for steals.

5. Tyshawn Taylor: Underrated on that end, Self has previously called him "one of the best defenders we've ever had here without question."

6. Aaron Miles: Self has cited him as one of the most unselfish (and best) defenders he's had during his KU tenure. Ranks third all-time in steals (264).

7. Russell Robinson: Pesky player on defensive end who ranks fifth all-time in steals (247).

8. Travis Releford: Selfless defender who slid feet well and was excellent at challenging shots with his length.

9. Brady Morningstar: It was hard to get a good look against the Lawrence native, who pestered many of the Big 12's top perimeter scorers.

10. Landen Lucas: Improved as much defensively as any player during the streak. KU never had to use double teams when Lucas was on the court.

him, our guys would take care of the rest. I was just super-pumped to play. There was no bigger stage than that.

Tyshawn Taylor: Jeff was unbelievable that year. He was soft when he first got to Kansas. California kids have a reputation of being soft, or at least that's what we say on the east coast. When he came he was a big softie. Then we had another big in Cole that was the opposite of that. He embraced the fact that he got his tooth knocked out. And we had Thomas and the twins. Those are guys you can't be soft around. Basically, Jeff got beat up for three years and then his time came. He was ready. He took all of those ass-whippings and he didn't tuck his tail. He didn't have to do that much. We didn't need him to score a lot, although he had some really good scoring games. But he didn't have to do that to be effective. We just needed him to play big and block shots and play hard. Sometimes you need to pop him in the chest to wake him up because he's so calm and cool and laid back.

"The Standard for College Basketball"

Kansas' victory over Ohio State propelled them into the NCAA title game against an opponent many considered to be one of the best college basketball teams in decades: Anthony Davis-led Kentucky.

The Jayhawks and Wildcats had met in the Champions Classic back on Nov. 15 at Madison Square Garden. Even though the game was tied at halftime and the final score (75-65) was relatively close, Kansas had looked inept at times against John Calipari's squad, shooting just 33 percent overall and trailing by as many as 17 points after intermission.

Five months later, when the two teams met for a rematch on college basketball's biggest stage, the Jayhawks were determined to show the world—and Kentucky, for that matter—that they were a different team.

Thomas Robinson: I remember laying in my room in New Orleans, thinking about everything we'd accomplished. I thought about going to all those camps the previous summer and listening to people tell

Kansas 59, Kentucky 67
April 2, 2012 · New Orleans, La.

Kansas (32-7)

Player	MP	FG	3FG	FT	R	A	F	S	TO	B	TP
Elijah Johnson*	36	5-13	3-7	0-0	2	2	1	1	2	0	13
Travis Releford*	30	1-6	1-2	1-2	1	0	5	1	0	0	4
Thomas Robinson*	36	6-17	0-0	6-7	17	1	2	0	1	0	18
Tyshawn Taylor*	36	8-17	1-1	2-3	4	3	1	1	5	0	19
Jeff Withey*	32	2-8	0-0	1-1	7	1	2	2	1	4	5
Conner Teahan	17	0-1	0-1	0-0	0	1	1	1	0	0	0
Justin Wesley	2	0-0	0-0	0-0	0	0	0	0	0	0	0
Kevin Young	11	0-0	0-0	0-2	3	0	4	0	0	1	0
Team					5						
Totals	200	22-62	5-11	10-15	39	8	16	6	9	5	59

Kentucky (38-2)

Player	MP	FG	3FG	FT	R	A	F	S	TO	B	TP
Anthony Davis*	36	1-10	0-0	4-6	16	5	2	3	3	6	6
M. Kidd-Gilchrist*	35	4-7	0-1	3-4	6	1	2	0	1	1	11
Terrence Jones*	30	4-7	0-1	1-2	7	0	4	1	2	2	9
Doron Lamb*	35	7-12	3-6	5-6	2	3	2	0	1	0	22
Marquis Teague*	34	5-14	2-3	2-3	2	3	2	0	2	0	14
Darius Miller	25	2-5	1-2	0-0	6	0	2	0	2	2	5
Eloy Vargas	3	0-0	0-0	0-0	0	0	1	0	0	0	0
Kyle Wiltjer	2	0-1	0-1	0-0	0	0	0	0	0	0	0
Team					3						
Totals	200	23-56	6-14	15-21	42	12	15	4	11	11	67

	1st	2nd	Total	FG%	3FG%	FT%
Kansas	27	32	59	35.5	45.5	66.7
Kentucky	41	26	67	41.1	42.9	71.4

Officials: Mike Stuart, Mark Whitehead, Verne Harris
Technicals: None

me that we weren't going to be any good. Then we got beat pretty bad by Kentucky to start the season, and even more people doubted us. Now here we were, playing them again in the last game. It was almost storybook. I was so proud of what we'd accomplished.

Jeff Withey: I remember being in the hotel room the night before. All of the commentators on ESPN were saying we had no shot. I was thinking, "Man we're going to go out there and shock everybody." I felt like we came out pretty strong. Right at the beginning, Michael Kidd-Gilchrist went up for a layup and Thomas and I both went up to block it. He flew to the ground. We were like, "This is our game. We're more physical and we're going to be able to get these guys."

Tyshawn Taylor: Losing to Kentucky pretty bad earlier in the year was actually good for us, because it gave us a measuring point and something to shoot for. Kentucky was the standard for college basketball that season. They were who we wanted to be.

Looking back, I don't know how the hell we got to that championship game. We kind of roughed it throughout the whole tournament. Every game was so close. After each win we were like, "Pheeww!" We were breathing a sigh of relief. We didn't even have time to enjoy it because it was on to the next one. Purdue, North Carolina, NC State, Ohio State ... all of those wins were under six points, or something like that. We barely won.

By the time we got back to playing Kentucky again in the finals, we were like, "We've already done what we were supposed to do. We've actually done *way* more than we were supposed to do." We were definitely happy to be there. But we wanted to show them that we could beat them. At the very least, we wanted to show them that we were a better team than the one they'd played back in November. We felt slept on a little bit.

Jeff Withey: I was excited to go against Anthony Davis. He's gotten a lot better since then but, at that time, he couldn't really shoot the ball. He was more of a rebounder/shot-blocker—kind of like me. I didn't think he had much of an offensive game at that point of his career. Now he's an all-star. I tried to make it difficult for him and turn him into a jump-shooter just like Sullinger. I knew I couldn't give him easy baskets on offensive rebounds and putbacks.

The 2011-12 Kentucky squad was one of most talented teams in college basketball history. The Wildcats' top six players were each selected in the 2012 NBA draft. Davis and Kidd-Gilchrist were the top two picks, respectively. Terrence Jones (No. 18) and Marquis Teague also went in the first round, while Doron Lamb and reserve Darius Miller were snapped up in the second.

The Wildcats' talent—and Davis' overwhelming length and athleticism—were huge factors early, as Kentucky led by as many as 18 points in the first half. It was 41-27 at intermission.

Tyshawn Taylor: I remember going into halftime thinking, "Damn, that happened fast." But I also remember the first 10 minutes of the second half, thinking, "If we can just chop their lead to single digits—if we can just get it to where we're only down by eight or nine points at the 10-minute mark—then we'll have a chance."

Kansas nearly accomplished the feat by pulling within 10 points, 48-38, midway through the second half. But back-to-back 3-pointers by Lamb (who finished with 22 point) increased Kentucky's cushion to 16 points with 10:05 remaining.

Tyshawn Taylor: Those shots were the killer. Coach Self called a timeout after the second one, and I remember we all looked at each other like, "Damn." We definitely dropped our heads a little bit.

But the Jayhawks didn't fold. Kansas fought back with a 19-8 scoring run that, at least for a few moments, put the game in question. With about four minutes remaining, Johnson looked toward the Kentucky bench and made eye contact with coach John Calipari.

Elijah Johnson: He looked nice and comfortable. I kind of smiled at him and he smiled back at me, because I knew that was our time to make him as uncomfortable as he'd been the whole game. I wanted to see how uncomfortable we could make him.

No one could tell us that we were going to lose except for the scoreboard. We said, "If they're going to beat us, they're going to remember us. They're going to feel the last of us."

Kansas had a chance to pull within three points when Johnson rose up for a 3-pointer from the left corner with 24 seconds remaining.

But just as Johnson was about to release the ball, Davis came soaring through the air, his right arm extended for a block. Instead of letting Davis swat the shot, Johnson landed, took one dribble to his left and then fired the 3. The shot swished through the net, but it didn't matter, as Johnson was called for traveling. Instead of pulling within three points, the Jayhawks still trailed 65-59 and had no choice but to foul. Lamb made two free throws to round out the scoring.

Bill Self: Elijah definitely traveled. He took the sidestep. I think Verne Harris made the call. I'd have liked to have been able to argue it, but I think it was the right call. We got behind a lot of folks that year and came back. You can't get behind 18 to them. They were too good.

Elijah Johnson: Every time I see someone from that team, they always blame that loss on me. I put it down on the ground. Anthony Davis was going to block that s**t. No one else agrees with me, though. Everyone's like, "You should've shot it. You should've shot it." They blame it on me and say I should've shot it regular the first time. That would've brought us within three and it would've been our time. We were the comeback kids that year. We were coming back on Kentucky.

Jeff Withey: They wore us down a little bit. They were just a little too much for us, I guess.

Kevin Young: Coach said at the end of the game that we just ran out of time. We were right there. We were pushing for a comeback. If Elijah doesn't travel or if he hits that 3, things could've been different.

I think we were all very proud of that season. Three years before that, I was a freshman on the worst team in America. I played for Loyola Marymount and we only won three games the whole season. To go from that to playing in the national championship team was almost surreal for me.

Travis Releford: Before the year, people said that was one of the worst teams KU had had in years. They talked about how T-Rob and Tyshawn had played more minutes in their careers than the rest of the team combined. We heard everything, and it played a big role in our success, because all season that's what we would hear. *This is one of Bill Self's least-talented teams.*

We all knew how good we were. Most of us just hadn't had a chance yet. That's what the writers and people who were saying those things didn't understand. We'd been there the last three or four years playing against all these guys who had been the top players in the country. Why would anyone think we wouldn't be able to compete? We just ran with that all season. *We're not even supposed to be here.* That's what we kept telling each other. *We're not even supposed to be here.* Everybody counted us out before the season and we rode on that the whole year. That brought us close and I think that's what the key was.

A little more from ...

The 2011-12 run to the NCAA title game wouldn't have occurred without Robinson. Along with being chosen as a first-team All-American, Robinson was named Big 12 Player of the Year, and he was the runner-up to Anthony Davis for AP National Player of the Year. The 2011-12 season—and his overall journey—made Robinson a KU legend.

Joe Dooley: A friend of ours told us about Thomas before he'd really taken off. Coach Self went and saw him at one of the All-American camps and he exploded. We got in on him early and just kind of hung around. He ended up visiting KU the same weekend as John Wall. He wanted to commit but his mom wanted him to take one other visit. We were sweating it out and going back and forth to New Hampshire to see him at Brewster Academy. He thought he was under-recruited. He hardly played as a freshman and sophomore, but he toughed it out and decided not to transfer. The next thing you know, he's the No. 5 pick in the NBA draft and runner-up for national player of the year. He kept working and didn't worry about anything. A lot of guys, if they don't get immediate satisfaction, they leave. He didn't. He kept working.

Thomas Robinson: One thing that stuck out initially about Coach Self was that he wasn't scared to come into my neighborhood to recruit me. He showed up to my house early and no one was home. The door was locked, so he and Coach Dooley were sitting out on my porch for a while. I lived in a really tough neighborhood. There were about

20 random dudes lurking down on the corner, doing who knows what. But he didn't care. After the years passed, I realized nothing fazed him. He's as tough as they come.

I loved how he talked to me and gave it to me up front. He wanted me to earn everything. He wasn't going to give me anything. I was Top 50 in high school but I wasn't Top 10 or anything. I wasn't even the top player in my class. We had Xavier (Henry) and Elijah above me. I just liked how he was straightforward with me. It gave me security, because when people tell you something that's not too fairy tale-ish, most of the time it's true.

Kansas is crazy. I got the full, 100 percent college basketball experience during my time there. The publicity we received from being at Kansas was great. It was perfect. It was surreal, too. I come from a neighborhood where we'd have to run down the street to get home. At Kansas, everyone wanted to be outside so they could see us and talk to us. They wanted us to be at their parties and in their classes and at the same restaurants. They made you feel so wanted, so welcome. It was something I'd never felt before. It was tough not to let it go to your head. Coach Self used to always say, "This is a fake world you're living in. It's not the real world. People aren't going to kiss your ass your whole life." He preached that to us repeatedly.

The Player of the Year race my junior year ... I honestly didn't pay attention to it. Even when the draft rolled around, I made some comments about how I should've been National Player of the Year, but I was literally told to say that stuff and make it into a tug-of-war thing. That was just for publicity. Me and Anthony Davis were actually hanging out throughout the whole week of the draft. We were really cool.

I'm glad I came back for my junior year. If I'd have left, I'd have only been remembered as a player who had one decent year at KU. I think the next year made them respect me more as a player. All of the respect I receive now is based off of that last year, especially since they knew what I was up against.

I'm glad I made the decision I did. Jeff got more attention that year, and Tyshawn—who had been on a bit of a downfall since his freshman year—was able to get his name back. We were winning and he was one of the main reasons. So a lot of people benefitted from it.

Conner Teahan: The story of T-Rob is not a fairytale. It's the opposite. How does a guy lose his grandparents and his mom in a matter of like 45-60 days? And the way that he acted... I still think about T-Rob and the fact that he was able to get through that. He was crying. His mom was all he had—his mom and his sister. For him to be able to power through it, especially at a time when things weren't going all that well for T-Rob on the court ... I mean, he had shown a lot of promise, but it wasn't until his junior year when he busted out. He was having a lot of problems, because we had the twins and Jeff Withey, and then it was T-Rob. You throw in losing people that are really close to you with all of that responsibility in the middle of the season, I'm still impressed with how mature and how focused he was throughout the whole thing.

He did not want to be babied, but how do you not baby someone that just went through all of that? *I don't know how you feel. I wish I could give you some advice, but I have no advice, because I haven't been through it.*

I hadn't lost a grandparent at that time. I hadn't lost a mom. I hadn't lost anybody that was significant as the people he lost. What do you really say outside of, "We're here for you. You need anything, you let me know." I think that's what made us stronger that year. There was this sense of, "This is all we have. We've just got to depend on each other."

I wouldn't have even been around that season if I hadn't redshirted. The first time my redshirt came up was my junior year (in 2009-10). Mario Little redshirted that year instead. Coach Self had talked about me having an opportunity down the road. He could see where there might be a year where we lost some of our more tenured guys. He thought having someone around that was a little bit older would be good.

Then, my senior year (in 2010-11), about a day or two before the first exhibition game, he asked me what I wanted to do. We had to decide before the exhibition games, because when you're not a freshman, you can't play those exhibition games and then redshirt. We were at shootaround when he asked, and I said, "If you're comfortable with it, I think redshirting is probably best for myself and the program." I had Tyrel and Brady in front of me, and Coach Self wanted to have somebody that was more experienced for that next year. It was basically like a conversation the day of the exhibition game.

My last year at Kansas (in 2011-12), Ben was a great player, but he redshirted. I get people all the time, to be completely candid, who say "you guys would have won a national championship if Ben would have been in your spot." And there was a part of me that maybe used to believe that, but now I don't know. That would have been a badass team, but you've still got to have a TEAM. Hey, you would have thought that Joel Embiid, Andrew Wiggins and Wayne Selden would have put together a hell of a run. They couldn't make it past Stanford.

We knew what our bread and butter was, and it was Tyshawn and T-Rob, and as much as I would have loved to have made more 3s, there were a lot of things I did in and out of the locker room that helped make the team better. Although Ben was far more athletic, far more skilled than me, I do think that my redshirting a year earlier so I could be a part of that team was critical in us getting to where we needed to be.

Ben McLemore: Everyone was helpful to me that year. They knew I was going to be a big part of that team. That second semester, once Jamari and I were able to practice ... we were a big part of that team getting to the Final Four. I think I helped those guys a lot by going hard each and every day in practice and making them better. Everyone saw, the second round, after the Big 12, they kicked it up a notch.

Jamari Traylor: My redshirt freshman year, I was definitely a little frustrated at first. I thought I'd come in and be able to play. But the good thing is that I was able to sit back and learn and get a visual of how everything was going to be. In practice, I went against guys like Thomas Robinson and Tyshawn Taylor and Elijah Johnson—guys that became pros. Even at the games, there was a point where Larry Brown was always there. I don't know how, but I always ended up sitting next to him. He'd talk and explain things to me throughout the whole game, and I'd just sit there and take it all in. He'd coach me non-stop. He'd talk about schemes and breakdowns and what we should've done in certain situations. He'd see things before they would even happen, or as they were happening. He'd just point stuff out. At the time, my mind wasn't geared to think like that, so that helped me a lot to be around people like him and Danny Manning.

Conner Teahan: What helped our team the most that year—the main reason we got to the title game—was that we had the perfect duo for Coach Self's system. Outside of Joel Embiid, all of KU's one-and-dones have been wings. It's the least important position in his entire offense.

Every year, he needs an experienced guard and an experienced big man. His offense is about the high pick and rolls and getting the ball from side to side so you can get the big guy isolated. If you look at his best teams, most of them have a great point guard and a big man who is a huge presence. Those wings can get lost, because they don't really know how to function. They don't get a lot of dribble opportunities because it's supposed to be one or two passes. You don't get a lot of isos. It all comes down to the point guard and big man.

Naadir Tharpe: We used to have a little thing between the older guys and the younger guys on the team. The Morris twins and Travis and Tyshawn were all part of team FOE and guys like me and Ben and Jamari were part of KU Cash Money Brothers (KUCMB).

We always tried to jump each other, especially when we'd find someone alone. One day we captured Travis while he was playing Call of Duty Zombies. We were setting him up, because I was actually playing the game with him while Jamari, Ben and Niko Roberts were coming up with a plan. We ended up wrestling Travis onto the floor, and someone said, "Let's tape him to the chair."

So we tape Travis up to a chair, and then we made this little ransom video, and we sent it to T-Rob. We were like, "Yeah, we've got your boy, Travis. It's KUCMB!" Thomas comes down to the room and bursts through the door. He's a huge guy, and he's like, "Give us back Travis!" I don't know who did it, but someone grabbed a fire extinguisher and started spraying down the whole room. I ran into the bathroom and tried to hide, but I hit my knee on the door. My knee started bleeding and then it got swollen. I was like, "S**t, we've got practice the next morning, and my knee is messed up." I couldn't tell Coach Self how I hurt it, but I needed to get treatment, because it was really hurting. Tyshawn was like, "This is what we're going to do. You're going to play defense on me and we're going to fall down and you're going to hold your knee." So I had to fake an injury in practice the next day in front of Coach Self that way I could get a knee brace. It wasn't something where I couldn't play, but I needed to get it wrapped up and needed to see the trainer.

Kevin Young: One reason we had such great chemistry that year is because we didn't have as many players. There were only 11 or 12 of us that year and the coaching staff did a great job of making sure we were all together. We had team meals. We walked to class together—and when we missed class we were running together at 6 a.m. We just did little things to bring us together, like barbecues at Coach Self's house and that kind of stuff.

I met Tyshawn the year before I got to Kansas. I played against him in the 19-and-under world championships in New Zealand. I was playing for Puerto Rico and he was with the U.S. On my team I had Mike Rosario and Jio Fontan, both of whom played high school ball with Tyshawn at St. Anthony's. They were like brothers. They're really close.

The first thing that stood out to me about Tyshawn was his speed and his quickness and his IQ. He could dribble up the court between four or five players without losing the ball—and he could see the wide open man. He had total confidence in all of his teammates.

From the beginning of the season, after every huddle, we said, "Big 12 Champs!" The psychology of it—keeping us in that mindset, that we were champs and we're going to win— molded our attitudes and shaped our goals.

Quincy Acy: When we played Kansas, it was different. It was special. At least it was for me, because I wanted to beat them so bad. They were the Big 12 champs throughout my college career. We wanted to shut them up and be the team that knocked them off of their high horse. But hats off to them. We couldn't do it. No one could.

They had great talent every year, obviously. But Coach Self did a great job of getting them to play hard for him. They all really enjoyed each other. People throw the word brotherhood around loosely, but it was obvious by watching them that they really embraced that every year. They had a great group of guys and it was obvious they had a close relationship with each other. The twins and Thomas Robinson are still very close to this day.

Playing at Allen Fieldhouse is surreal. That Rock Chalk chant when you're losing at the end is something that haunts you. It's a different feeling than anywhere, a completely different realm.

Iowa State forward Melvin Ejim: Thomas Robinson and I were roommates in high school. I had a little extra juice and was a little bit more motivated when we played each other in college. He had been having a great year (in 2012) and it's always fun when you play against guys you know.

In high school, he was a lot like he was at Kansas. He was really talented and really ahead of his time in some ways. Really mature at times. He was a fun guy. He showed flashes of what he could do at our school. He led us in a lot of categories and really dominated on a really good team. We all knew he was league bound. He had so much raw skill and athleticism. We all knew he had the potential, and he led our high school team to a pretty good season. When he signed at Kansas, we were all super happy for him.

I really respected Thomas—just from our relationship that we built and then watching his journey at KU. There was a respect factor there. He didn't break out until his last year at Kansas, and yet he stayed and was a role guy who worked his way up, and when his opportunity came, he made the most of it, and I think that's admirable. A lot of guys, for whatever reason, would try to opt out and go different places in that scenario, but he was able to grit it out and ended up having a really successful career there.

It's hard for Kansas fans to look back at the 2011-12 season and not think about Missouri. Although they were rivals on the court, many of the players from both teams remain close off of it.

Travis Releford: I played with Marcus on the same AAU team. Mike Dixon played on the younger squad. Steve Moore was on the team. We were tight before college. We didn't really talk much while we were in school because of the rivalry. But we talk about it now, because we're training at the same gyms and playing pickup at the same gyms during the summer. We bring up how crazy it was and how we should have won at their place and they should have won at our place that year.

Michael Dixon: When me and Bill Self see each other, we hug each other. Bill Self is my guy. I talk to Bill Self just like I'd talk to anybody. My dad coached his son, Tyler, in AAU. Bill told my dad that he really made a mistake not recruiting me.

After I left Missouri, I wanted to come to Kansas so bad, but I know Coach Self would've taken a lot of heat. I didn't talk to him at all during that time. I was trying to go through my AAU coach, LJ Goolsby, to get it done. They might have talked about it. I'm not sure. If I'd have gone there I probably wouldn't even be playing in Europe. I'd probably be in the NBA.

I tell everyone this: I don't care if you're talking about a college arena or an arena in the NBA or in Europe: There is no place in the world that's louder than Allen Fieldhouse. No place in the *world.*

The first time I played in there, when I was a freshman … it was nuts. I was going against Sherron. In high school I had watched Sherron. For that game, I can't remember if Zaire Taylor was hurt or what, but Matt Zimmerman, one of our assistants, wrote the starting five on the dry erase board. I wasn't thinking about starting at all. I looked up and he was writing my name on the board to start. I was like, "I'm starting against Kansas, as a freshman, in Allen Fieldhouse?" I couldn't believe it. I went into straight focus mode. I was overly excited to play. I remember shooting my first shot hard off the glass. It didn't even touch the rim. I wasn't scared. I was just geeked up to play.

To this day, I don't think that Bill Self gets enough credit. I don't know anything about his coaching tactics, but from the outside looking in, the stuff that he runs … he always adapts to the players that he has. That's what coaches are supposed to do. Tyshawn was great that year. He has the perfect basketball body. He's 6-foot-3 with long arms. He used to dunk effortlessly. His senior year he was as good as any point guard that has ever played at Kansas. He was so fast and big and athletic, and then once he started hitting shots, it was like, "How do you guard this guy?"

Kim English: Our team that season definitely had a special feeling. It's something I've been searching for ever since from a basketball standpoint. I didn't get it in the NBA. I didn't get it in Europe. I haven't experienced it in coaching yet. When I find it again, I'll hold onto it. When everyone is happy and playing the right way, it's special.

Kansas was so well-coached. Coach Self is one of the best in the country at getting his guys to buy in to what he wants them to do. Whether it's running a high-low offense, or crashing the offensive glass, or defensively ducking in, or running the dribble-weave late in the game, or executing any of the wrinkles to their "Chop" play at the end of the game, they always do a tremendous job. Talent plus coachability is a special combination.

That year I got caught up in the moment with the whole Big 12/SEC thing. I love Big 12 basketball. I've never been a huge fan of SEC basketball, especially for Missouri. I understand why they were looking for a new league when it appeared the Big 12 was about to fold after Colorado and Nebraska and Texas A&M left. But when I put on that SEC shirt at the Sprint Center after we won the Big 12 Tournament championship ... I wish I wouldn't have done that. Because I love Big 12 basketball. I'm a Big 12 guy. That was just me being spiteful and feeling like we got cheated out of an outright title by them taking the game from us in Lawrence. That was my slash back at the league office or the officiating crew or whatever. I was only 21. I was immature. I probably shouldn't have done that.

Kansas and Missouri should play. I think a lot of the administrators that were there during that time are gone now, so hopefully they can reconcile and find a way to play that game again. But honestly, thank God they didn't play that game the last three years (2015-17). It would've been a bloodbath.

I had a lot of respect for Tyshawn. He had a lot of mental toughness. The ball was in his hands for three years. He grew as a player all throughout his career. I respected him. I grew up playing against the Morris twins. Thomas was from D.C. and I knew Tyshawn. Josh Selby was like my little brother. I have a relationship with all those guys. I don't hate them. I hate their fans.

It's gotten better since I graduated, but I just don't like their fans. I don't think their true alumni, the people that actually graduated from there, are that bad. It's their sidewalk fans that annoy me, people that I know didn't graduate from the University of Kansas and instead got some cheap tickets to a second-round NCAA Tournament game in Tulsa. It's not the alumni or even the students. It's the people that don't have any affiliation to KU but pretend like they do. They get under my skin.

Jeff Withey: I went to Arizona because of Lute Olson, but right after I got there, Lute retired. The way it all happened, he was with the team first couple of weeks of the year, and then he just disappeared out of the blue. We all found out he was leaving because it was on ESPN. It left a really bad taste in my mouth. I knew that the interim head coach (Russ Pennell) wasn't going to stick around. I didn't know who was going to take over there. Maybe I wouldn't fit into their system. I wanted to be in control of my future. Not them.

I had been to Late Night in 2006. I really enjoyed it, but the reason I didn't want to go to Kansas initially was because it was too far from home. Arizona was only an hour flight from California. But after being at Arizona, I realized that being further away from home might benefit me more in the long run. That's the reason I transferred to Kansas.

I had also been paying attention to what Danny Manning was doing with all of the bigs. What he did with Sasha Kaun, in particular, left an impression on me. He'd gotten so much better during his time there.

Danny spent so much extra time with me practice. He'd give me little details about the game that really helped out. Whenever you're playing in games and can go to the bench and talk to a guy that is one of the best college players to ever play, he really gives you insight. When you're frustrated, he's been there. He can talk you through it. Obviously his knowledge of the game and his basketball IQ is really high. I learned a lot about footwork from him. Not to mention his knowledge about the game, where the defense is going to be, all that stuff. I owe a lot of where I am today to Coach Manning.

2011-12
Season Summary

Results (32-7, 16-2)

November

11	Towson	W, 100 - 54
15	vs. Kentucky	L, 65 - 75
21	vs. Georgetown	W, 67 - 63
22	vs. UCLA	W, 56 - 72
23	vs. Duke	L, 68 - 61
30	Florida Atlantic	W, 77 - 54

December

3	South Florida	W, 70 - 42
6	Long Beach State	W, 88 - 80
10	Ohio State	W, 78 - 67
19	vs. Davidson	L, 74 - 80
22	@ USC	W, 47 - 63
29	Howard	W, 89 - 34
31	North Dakota	W, 84 - 58

January

4	Kansas State	W, 67 - 49
7	@ Oklahoma	W, 61 - 72
11	@ Texas Tech	W, 46 - 81
14	Iowa State	W, 82 - 73
16	Baylor	W, 92 - 74
21	@ Texas	W, 66 - 69
23	Texas A&M	W, 64 - 54
28	@ Iowa State	L, 72 - 64

February

1	Oklahoma	W, 84 - 62
4	@ Missouri	L, 74 - 71
8	@ Baylor	W, 54 - 68
11	Oklahoma State	W, 81 - 66
13	@ Kansas State	W, 53 - 59
18	Texas Tech	W, 83 - 50
22	@ Texas A&M	W, 58 - 66
25	Missouri	W, 87 - 86
27	@ Oklahoma State	W, 58 - 70

March

3	Texas	W, 73 - 63
8	Texas A&M	W, 83 - 66
9	vs. Baylor	L, 72 - 81
16	vs. Detroit-Mercy	W, 65 - 50
18	vs. Purdue	W, 63 - 60
23	vs. NC State	W, 60 - 57
25	vs. North Carolina	W, 67 - 80
31	vs. Ohio State	W, 64 - 62

April

2	vs. Kentucky	L, 67 - 59

All-Big 12 Team

Player of the Year:
Thomas Robinson, Kansas, Jr., F

Defensive Player of the Year:
Jeff Withey, Kansas, Jr., C

Newcomer of the Year:
Royce White, Iowa State, So., F

Freshman of the Year:
Quincy Miller, Baylor, Fr., F
Le'Bryan Nash, Oklahoma State, Fr., G/F

Sixth Man of the Year:
Michael Dixon, Missouri, Jr., G

Coach of the Year:
Fred Hoiberg, Iowa State
Bill Self, Kansas

First Team
Royce White, Iowa State, So., F**
Thomas Robinson, Kansas, Jr., F**
Tyshawn Taylor, Kansas, Sr., G**
Marcus Denmon, Missouri, Sr., G
J'Covan Brown, Texas, Jr., G

Second Team
Quincy Acy, Baylor, Sr., F
Pierre Jackson, Baylor, Jr., G
Rodney McGruder, Kansas State, Jr., G
Ricardo Ratliffe, Missouri, Sr., F
Keiton Page, Oklahoma State, Sr., G

Third Team
Perry Jones III, Baylor, So., F
Scott Christopherson, Iowa State, Sr., G
Jeff Withey, Kansas, Jr., C
Kim English, Missouri, Sr., G
Phil Pressey, Missouri, So., G

Honorable Mention
Quincy Miller, Baylor, Fr., F
Chris Allen, Iowa State, Sr., G
Melvin Ejim, Iowa State, So., F
Jamar Samuels, Kansas State, Sr., F
Romero Osby, Oklahoma, Jr., F
Steven Pledger, Oklahoma, Jr., G
Le'Bryan Nash, Oklahoma State, Fr., G/F
Myck Kabongo, Texas, Fr., G
David Loubeau, Texas A&M, Sr., F
Elston Turner, Texas A&M, Jr., G

All-Defensive Team
Quincy Acy, Baylor, Sr., F**
Jeff Withey, Kansas, Jr., C**
Jordan Henriquez, Kansas State, Jr., F
Rodney McGruder, Kansas State, Jr., G
Michael Dixon, Missouri, Jr., G

All-Rookie Team
Pierre Jackson, Baylor, Jr., G**
Quincy Miller, Baylor, Fr., F
Royce White, Iowa State, So., F**
Le'Bryan Nash, Oklahoma State, Fr., G/F
Myck Kabongo, Texas, Fr., G

** Unanimous selection

Kansas Awards

Thomas Robinson
Consensus All-American First Team
NABC All-American First Team
AP All-American First Team
USBWA All-American First Team
Sporting News All-American Third Team
NCAA Final Four All-Tournament Team
Maui Invitational All-Tournament Team

Tyshawn Taylor
NABC All-District (8) First Team
AP All-American Third Team
NCAA Final Four All-Tournament Team

Season Stats

#	Player	CL	POS	HT	Hometown	G	GS	FG%	3P%	FT%	R	A	S	B	PTS
22	Marcus Morris	JR	F	6-9	Philadelphia, PA	38	35	.570	.342	.688	7.6	1.6	0.8	0.6	17.2
21	Markieff Morris	JR	C	6-10	Philadelphia, PA	38	34	.589	.424	.673	8.3	1.4	0.8	1.1	13.6
14	Tyrel Reed	SR	G	6-3	Burlington, KS	38	37	.408	.379	.798	3.1	1.7	1.5	0.2	9.7
10	Tyshawn Taylor	JR	G	6-3	Hoboken, NJ	36	30	.479	.380	.719	1.9	4.6	1.0	0.3	9.3
32	Josh Selby	FR	G	6-2	Baltimore, MD	26	11	.373	.362	.757	2.2	2.2	0.8	0.0	7.9
0	Thomas Robinson	SO	F	6-9	Washington, DC	33	2	.601		.510	6.4	0.6	0.4	0.7	7.6
12	Brady Morningstar	SR	G	6-4	Lawrence, KS	38	24	.488	.410	.743	2.2	3.3	1.4	0.2	7.1
23	Mario Little	SR	G	6-6	Chicago, IL	32	1	.481	.367	.694	2.9	0.8	0.4	0.3	5.1
24	Travis Releford	SO	G	6-6	Kansas City, MO	29	3	.500	.378	.640	1.4	0.7	0.4	0.1	3.7
15	Elijah Johnson	SO	G	6-4	Las Vegas, NV	36	6	.500	.400	.667	1.3	1.8	0.5	0.1	3.4
5	Jeff Withey	SO	C	7-0	San Diego, CA	26	1	.647		.515	1.8	0.2	0.2	0.7	2.3
25	Jordan Juenemann	JR	G	6-3	Hays, KS	15	0	.556	.800		0.6	0.1	0.0	0.0	0.9
22	Royce Woolridge	FR	G	6-3	Phoenix, AZ	16	0	.250	.200	.500	0.5	0.6	0.0	0.1	0.6
20	Niko Roberts	FR	G	5-11	Huntington, NY	12	0	.167	.000		0.4	0.1	0.2	0.0	0.2

## CHAPTER 9

2012-13
THE LEFTOVERS

He may not have realized it at the time, but being forced to redshirt the 2011-12 season was the best thing that could've happened to Ben McLemore.

And to the Kansas Jayhawks.

By sitting out his inaugural year in Lawrence, McLemore had a chance to hone his game—both mentally and physically—during practices and film sessions and conditioning drills. By the time he was eligible to take the court a year later, McLemore had developed into a polished, NBA-caliber wing who elevated the ceiling for a 2012-13 Jayhawks team otherwise lacking in starpower following the loss of Thomas Robinson, the fourth overall pick in the NBA draft, and Tyshawn Taylor, a second-round selection at No. 41.

Elijah Johnson: If Ben would've played that first year and not redshirted, he probably would've gone to the NBA. And if he'd have gone to the NBA, I'm not sure we'd even be talking right now. The streak probably would've ended, but Ben saved it.

That's not to say the rest of the 2012-13 Jayhawks didn't have talent. Jeff Withey was the Big 12's reigning Defensive MVP and just months removed from setting an NCAA Tournament record for blocks. Johnson had turned in some clutch performances while averaging 10.2 points as a junior, and Travis Releford was a battled-tested senior. With those players alone, the Jayhawks would've been good. McLemore, though, had the potential to make them special. Bill Self had known it all along.

Ben McLemore: When Kansas made the Final Four with T-Rob and Tyshawn, Jamari and I weren't even allowed to travel with the team. We were redshirting that year, and the NCAA wouldn't allow it. Still, we'd been practicing with those guys that whole second semester. We felt like we should be a part of it, so we got in the car and drove 15 hours to New Orleans. It wasn't all that bad. Jamari and I split it up.

It was tough sitting there and watching them. I wanted to be out on the court so bad. It really helped motivate me. I wanted to experience that and Jamari did, too. I remember saying, "We're going to be all right. We're going to come back even stronger next year.'

That whole offseason, I was excited about getting on the court that next fall. I had always been a Kansas fan. I loved watching them growing up, especially Paul Pierce. I wanted to be a part of that tradition.

Coach Self first saw me when I was playing AAU ball with the St. Louis Eagles and Bradley Beal. I wasn't the top-rated guy at the time, but obviously I was ranked in St. Louis. I was performing well on that team, and everyone was like, "Who is this guy?"

I remember Coach Townsend showing up at all of my games and watching me play. That really made an impression. It motivated me to go out and perform at a high level every day.

Convincing my mom that KU was the right place for me was tough. It was between Missouri and Kansas. I wanted to sign in November but my mom wouldn't agree to it. And since I was only 17 at the time, my signature meant nothing without hers next to it. She didn't want me to sign with Kansas. She was a big Missouri fan. I actually had my uncle, her brother, talk to her. He was a Kansas fan, too. He loved Danny Manning. He was one of the best players at his high school growing up. His name was Daniel Reid, but people actually called him Danny Manning because that's who he reminded them of on the court.

He talked to her and she took a visit with me to Late Night. I told her, "Just come to Late Night. It's going to overwhelm you and you'll change your mind. You'll see why I want to go there." She went and there were 16,300 crazy people there. Her opinion started to change. I could see her thinking, "Wow! My son has a chance to play for a school like this every night?" I think that's what convinced her. Eventually, she was like, "At the end of the day, it's your decision. I'm still going to support you. You're my son." The next signing period, I wrote my name on the dotted line.

I was bummed when I had to redshirt my freshman year, but I think it ended up being really great for me. I turned it into a complete positive. I hear a lot of young guys today saying, "Man, I don't want to redshirt." But I tell them the redshirt year is the best thing for them, because they're going to improve their game and it will help them mentally and physically. And it helps you get acclimated to school.

Bill Self: I knew from the get-go in recruiting that Ben was going to be great. I didn't know he'd be a lottery pick, but it was obvious that the ceiling for him was high. He was quiet, but he was a great teammate. He got more and more competitive as the year went on. He wanted to be coached so bad. The other players liked him a lot.

Director of basketball operations Doc Sadler: Ben was very quiet and tried to take in everything Coach Self said. If there was a definition of a pleaser, it'd be Ben McLemore. He wanted to make everyone happy. I don't know of anyone who didn't like Ben.

Starting alongside McLemore on the wing was Releford, a fifth-year senior who had also benefitted from a redshirt year in 2009-10.

Travis Releford: I didn't play much my freshman year (in 2008-09) and at the time I was thinking about leaving KU. I talked to my mom about it and also my AAU coach. We never got into other potential schools. I just told him about my experience at KU to that point, and then we talked about what I wanted for my future. He told me he'd help me out if I decided to leave and would support any decision I made.

It was a tough decision. Coach Self called me into his office and said, "I see you being a three-year starter here and a 1,000-point scorer. We're going to be really loaded next year and I don't want you to waste another year—but I want you to stay here." Then he told me I should redshirt that next upcoming season.

I waited a few nights, thought about it and decided to stay and prove that I could play. He wasn't lying about us being loaded that year. Xavier and Elijah came in. Brady and Tyrel were becoming factors. We had Tyshawn and, of course, Sherron. With all those guys, it was going to be tough to get minutes on the perimeter. I decided to stay at Kansas and prove that I could play, and that's what I did.

For me, hands down, that was my best year of college—both on the basketball court and as a student. I got a chance to live like a regular student. I still went to practice each day and traveled with the team if I wanted. But I also had the choice to stay in Lawrence when the team was on the road, so I was able to go to restaurants and watch the games and see how excited and into the games fans would get. It was a great experience, and it made me better on and off the court. I went to Kansas thinking I'd be *the* guy. A lot of guys do, coming from where they come from, being the best player in their city and

state. It didn't happen for me right away. It humbled me. I saw things I needed to work on and I did that. I picked up a lot of confidence playing against guys that were one-and-done like Xavier—everybody knew he was only going to be there for one year—and Sherron, a potential draft pick, and all the other guys that were actually playing. I was able to compete with them and give those guys trouble in practice. It built a lot of confidence being able to do that.

Releford set the tone on the perimeter for one of the best defensive teams of the Bill Self era, as the 2012-13 Jayhawks led the country in field goal percentage defense (.361). The main reason for that low number was Withey, who entered his senior campaign with a new swagger following his success in the second half of the 2011-12 season, when he was named Big 12 Defensive of the Year before setting the record for blocks (31) in a single NCAA Tournament.

Jeff Withey: Elijah and I were really close. After the Final Four, we actually thought about turning pro. We considered putting our name in the NBA draft, because we thought there was a chance we'd get picked. Finally, Elijah was like, "I'll come back if you come back." I was like, "Let's do it."

Kevin Young: Jeff made me a better defender. He made it easy for me to funnel guys straight to him. I could just send them right to Jeff, because I knew he'd be there. They hardly ever called fouls on him, which made it even better.

He's a California kid. He's a really mellow guy. There were times in practice when I'd make Jeff mad. I'd catch him with an elbow every now and then and he'd come after me, but it only made us better. He got pretty intense a couple of times. One time we were playing K-State and Jamari drove baseline and threw a bounce pass to him. He dunked on one of their centers and he started flexing and everything. He got really excited.

Ben McLemore: Withey saved my ass a lot, especially because I liked to gamble a little bit on defense. Even if my guy got by me, I knew he'd be there to block his shot.

Travis Releford: Withey didn't change how I played because Coach Self always told me "don't look for help. Play as if no one is going to help you." That's how I played on the defensive end, but overall as a team, it was a cushion to know that we had Jeff under the rim blocking everything or at least changing somebody's shot. It took away some of the pressure, because if there was a mistake being made, Jeff was going to come and fix it.

The only issue I had is that Jeff didn't guard the best players every game. We joked about that. *You didn't guard anybody. All you did was block shots.* He won Big 12 Defensive Player of the Year, and I think it should have been a tie, because I had to guard all the best players. He set the record for blocked shots, so you've got to give the big guy credit for that. He blocked shots that led to fast breaks and easy buckets.

Self had two potential plans for his frontcourt that season. Self had long prepared for the arrival of McDonald's All-American Perry Ellis, a Wichita native who'd been attending Jayhawks games for years. Another possibility was Kaleb Tarczewski, a 7-footer from New Hampshire who likely would've started next to Withey inside. KU landed Ellis—but Tarczewski, a five-star recruit, surprised everyone by signing with Arizona.

Conner Teahan: I still think that was such a dumb mistake for him to go to Arizona. So stupid. Kansas wanted him bad. Dooley wanted him bad. Coach Self wanted him really bad. I was his host on his recruiting trip and we really hit it off. I had convinced him KU was the place to go. I was like, "Dude, look at the offense. It revolves around the big man. We need you." We got along so well that he told me to get a job in Kansas City once I graduated so we could hang out. I remember telling Coach Dooley that I'd bet my life savings, everything I had in the bank—which was only about $500—that (Tarczewski) comes to Kansas. But then his AAU coach or someone like that got offered a job at Arizona, and that's where he ended up.

Ellis knew all along that Kansas was the best place for him, but he needed time to get acclimated to the college game.

Perry Ellis: Some guys reach the spring of the their senior year of high school—or even the summer after it—and still don't know where they want to go to college. I was lucky. I pretty much knew I was going to be a Jayhawk in the eighth grade. I talked to some other schools during the recruiting process but, honestly, none of them really had a chance.

The decision to come to Kansas was easy for me. I couldn't see myself playing anywhere else. I'd been a regular at Allen Fieldhouse since middle school. I knew all of the coaches and had gotten close with some of the players, and even some of the fans. Before I ever committed and enrolled, I felt like that was my home.

On the court, things were pretty awkward during my first three or fourth months in Lawrence. Coach Self wants his players to play with a free mind, but it was hard for me to do that as a freshman. I was trying so hard to fit in. I was always worried about what Coach Self was thinking about me. I wanted to please him so bad. Basically, I was trying TOO hard, and it was affecting me on the court, because I was playing very timid. I didn't have the confidence I needed at that time. I wanted to do everything right, and that just doesn't happen in basketball. You're going to mess up. I didn't really figure that out until later in the season.

Luckily, Kansas didn't have to force Ellis onto the court for extended minutes before he was ready thanks to the presence of Kevin Young. A role player as a junior one year earlier—and a huge factor in the overtime victory over Missouri in the final Border War—Young emerged as the Jayhawks "glue guy" in 2012-13. Young began his career at Loyola Marymount and then sat out a year before pledging to San Diego State, which is where he was headed before KU swooped in during the summer of 2011.

Kevin Young: I ended up at KU because a guy they thought they were going to get (DeAndre Daniels), who surprised everyone and signed with Connecticut in early June, at the last minute. They were looking for another player. One of the KU assistants called my phone and asked if I wanted to come on a visit. I told them I didn't want to say "yes" right away until I talked to Coach Self. So Coach Self called me and he said the only way I'd be able to come on a visit was if I talked to Coach (Steve) Fisher to let him know my plans. At that point, I had signed a financial aid agreement with San Diego State, but it was non-binding. Coach Fisher wasn't happy when I told him I wanted to look at Kansas, but I went ahead and took my visit and never left. I mean, I literally moved in during my official visit. I loved it so much that I enrolled in summer school right then and started getting myself situated.

I had been in Puerto Rico that summer, training, so I'd already had a ton of clothes with me. I brought all of them with me on the visit, and that was enough to last me through the end of summer school, when I could go back to California to get the rest of my stuff.

Obviously, everyone at San Diego State was mad at me, but the way I looked at it was, if Kansas had called any of those coaches who were mad at me and offered them jobs, they wouldn't have said "No" either.

Coach Self told me he wanted a player with high-energy, and I fit that description. In one of the first conversations I ever had with him, he told me I wouldn't play very much my first few months. He told me I might not play a single minute until around February (of 2012). Looking back at it now, I played some before then, but I got most of my minutes toward the end of the season. I started gelling with the team and learning the offense around that time. I got to play a lot in that huge game against Missouri and then in the Final Four. Those are experiences I'll never forget.

The next season, my senior year in 2012-13, I knew I was going to play a lot because we had lost Thomas Robinson and we were pretty thin down low. I tried to be selfless. I never tried to do too much with the ball in my hands. I rarely looked to score. If it was there for me, I'd take it. But I understood from the beginning that I wasn't going to be the star of the team. As the season went on, I began to understand the type of player Coach needed and wanted—a guy that hustled and brought energy, even if it meant diving on the floor and getting a couple of bruises or going up and trying to get a rebound over five guys, which wasn't an impossible task for me.

Early on that year, we were feeling really good. The only game we lost was against Michigan State in the Champions Classic. I only played two minutes in that game. I'd broken my hand going up for a rebound in practice a few weeks before the season started. I had surgery and sat out for two weeks. That was my first game. I think I gave up six points in two minutes.

I eventually got my starting spot back. I felt like we were gelling really well.

Kansas finished its non-conference slate with a 12-1 record, highlighted by a 90-54 home win against Colorado and a 74-66 road victory against No. 7 Ohio State in Columbus. McLemore scored 24 and 22 points, respectively, in those two contests.

Colorado coach Tad Boyle: They trounced us in Lawrence. It's not a good memory for me. We had two pretty good guards in Askia Booker and Spencer Dinwiddie, who is in the NBA right now. Kansas pressured the heck out of them and got into their heads. They drilled us. *They drilled us.* They could've beat us by 50 if they wanted.

Bill Self: Ben had his coming out party at Ohio State. After that I'm going, "This dude is gone!" And he should've been. He had a great year for us.

The one key player who didn't fit seamlessly into his role was Johnson, a veteran guard who had played off the ball most of his career and had to move to point guard after Taylor graduated.

Elijah Johnson: I wish I could've played the one and Tyshawn could've played the two the whole time. I think it'd have been better for me and him. I didn't have my explosiveness. I was hurting the whole year. The years before that, I wasn't great. But I still had some of my edge. I just envision me getting the ball off the glass and kicking it to Tyshawn on the wing. We would've been dangerous because of how fast he is. Plus, I'd have gotten more reps, so my senior year would've been different.

My senior year at point guard ... people didn't even see half of my ability. I remember wishing I had my health. I just didn't feel good. It's pretty obvious when you look back at the film. You can see it. Even in the NCAA Tournament my junior year, I wasn't myself. That's why I had surgery as soon as the season was over. I was having a lot of swelling. I had to get the micro fracture surgery. That kept me down for four months before my senior year. We went to Europe and we prepped for that a little bit before we went out there. My confidence wasn't down. I just didn't feel good. I just wish I had a little more time in the offseason to get my health right. I wish I'd have communicated better and told them how I was feeling instead of putting so much pressure on myself to get back as fast as possible. I think that would've changed a lot of stuff.

Naadir Tharpe: Elijah had to adjust to playing point guard, but he was up for the challenge. He tried to mirror his game after Sherron's because he really admired how Sherron played both on and off the ball. As long as you knew what Coach Self wanted in terms of the plays, it was smooth sailing, because with some of our guys ... all they needed was to get the ball in the right spot, and they'd score it.

While Johnson's play on the floor was up and down—like Taylor before him, he struggled with turnovers—he still made an impact as a leader.

Perry Ellis: I don't think Elijah got nearly enough credit for "taking one for the team" during his senior year, when he had to play point guard—even though he wasn't a point guard.

I really liked playing with Elijah. He was a smart dude. He knew how to relate to anyone. My first year, more than any teammate, I felt like I could go and talk to him and feel comfortable. He helped me out with basketball and just life in general. He had a lot of knowledge about life. He's a cerebral guy. He opens up to people. He's really cool.

He was really able to read me as a player. He'd say, "Man, I see what you do in practice. When you're playing with that mentality, where you're trying to score, you can take over. You've got to take that into games.'"

McLemore's Miracle

Every Big 12 coach—except for Self, who couldn't vote for his own team—had picked KU to win the league in the preseason poll, and those opinions certainly hadn't changed in early January when the Jayhawks took the court Jan. 9 for their conference opener against Iowa State in Lawrence.

McLemore scored 13 first-half points to give KU a 42-38 lead at intermission. But the redshirt freshman didn't attempt a shot in the first 12 minutes after the break as the Cyclones surged ahead by four.

Ben McLemore: There were nights when I could feel it. I was like, "This is going to be the night." I'd get easy buckets early and then I'd start making tougher shots. That's the best way to get into a rhythm. I could definitely feel it. I could sense when it was about to happen.

That night against Iowa State, we were down in the second half, and I was like, "We're not losing this f**king game." I took over the game and obviously Coach Self believed in me and let me take the shots I needed to take to bring my team back.

McLemore scored 12 points in a seven-minute span to keep his team close, but the Cyclones were able to maintain their lead.

Iowa State forward Georges Niang: When you go to another Big 12 school, all you hear about is how hard it is to win at Kansas, and their record and this, that, and the other. Me being a competitor, I was kind of like, "Screw that. How hard could it be? I'm going to go out there and win." That night, I thought we'd done it. I fouled out with 21 seconds left in regulation, and we were up four. Elijah Johnson missed a free throw, so as I walked back to the bench, I winked at the fans, thinking we had it.

Trailing by three moments later after a pair of free throws by Iowa State's Korie Lucious, Kansas inbounded the ball with 8.4 seconds left and ran the "Chop" play for which they'd become famous.

Iowa State forward Melvin Ejim: We knew what play they were going to run. They always run the same play—they're just really good at running it. We had a miscommunication, because our guards were supposed to switch, and I think one guy might have got hung up a little bit and missed the flair. Ben came off clean and he got a good look at it.

Iowa State coach Fred Hoiberg: We went through it at shoot around, the exact scenario, and one of our guys messed up on the switch.

Kansas 97, Iowa State 89
January 9, 2013 · Lawrence, Kan.

Kansas (13-1)

Player	MP	FG	3FG	FT	R	A	F	S	TO	B	TP
Elijah Johnson*	38	4-10	2-6	2-4	6	10	3	3	6	0	12
Ben McLemore*	40	10-12	6-6	7-7	3	1	2	1	2	2	33
Travis Releford*	39	3-6	0-2	6-8	4	2	3	0	1	0	12
Jeff Withey*	38	6-10	0-0	3-7	12	1	1	1	1	3	15
Kevin Young*	31	5-10	0-0	0-2	12	1	1	1	2	0	10
Perry Ellis	7	0-2	0-0	2-2	2	1	2	0	0	0	2
Naadir Tharpe	23	2-11	0-5	4-4	2	0	2	1	1	0	8
Jamari Traylor	9	1-1	0-0	3-4	2	0	3	0	1	0	5
Team					2						
Totals	225	31-62	8-19	27-38	45	16	17	7	14	5	97

Iowa State (10-4)

Player	MP	FG	3FG	FT	R	A	F	S	TO	B	TP
Chris Babb*	41	3-11	3-10	2-3	4	4	4	1	0	0	11
Will Clyburn*	36	6-12	1-4	3-6	7	2	3	1	2	0	16
Melvin Ejim*	36	7-14	2-5	3-3	11	5	4	1	1	0	19
Korie Lucious*	42	4-10	3-8	4-5	1	2	2	2	3	0	15
Georges Niang*	27	5-11	2-5	1-1	7	2	5	0	1	0	13
Anthony Booker	3	0-1	0-0	0-0	1	1	3	0	2	0	0
Percy Gibson	12	2-7	0-0	0-0	2	0	3	1	1	0	4
Naz Long	1	0-0	0-0	0-0	0	0	0	0	0	0	0
Tyrus McGee	27	3-7	3-6	2-2	2	1	5	1	1	1	11
Team					3						
Totals	225	30-73	14-38	15-20	38	17	29	7	11	1	89

	1st	2nd	OT	Total	FG%	3FG%	FT%
Kansas	42	37	18	97	50.0	42.1	71.1
Iowa State	38	41	10	89	41.1	36.8	75.0

Officials: Mark Whitehead, Paul Janssen, Keith Kimble
Technicals: Iowa State (1(Bench), Kansas (0)

Ben McLemore: I remember that same play happened earlier in the season, and I'd messed up on it. We'd lost to Michigan State in the Champions Classic 67-64 in Atlanta. I didn't read my defender well and couldn't get open to take the game-tying shot. Travis Releford had to shoot it instead, which is not what we wanted, and we took a tough L. I told myself the next time that situation came up, I was going to make a better decision.

We raced up the court and Chris Babb, their best defender, was guarding me. I respected Babb. He was a big guard that really made you work. Travis came out to set a screen and I thought, "If (Babb) goes under the screen, it's a wrap." I popped back and Elijah threw me a perfect pass. As soon as it left my hand, I knew it was either going to be off the glass, or it was going to be a swish, because Tyrus McGee was rushing at me and I had to shoot it really high.

Fred Hoiberg: When McLemore shot it, it looked so far to the left that I took a couple steps toward their sideline to go shake Bill's hand.

Melvin Ejim: It just looked long. He had really rushed the shot and it looked long so I didn't think it was going to go in.

Georges Niang: I'm thinking, "That's far left..."

Fred Hoiberg: Then the thing banked off the top of the left side of the backboard.

Ben McLemore: I didn't call "bank," but who cares? It counted.

Georges Niang: I have never heard a place get so loud in my life. It was ear piercing. And then the energy continued all the way to the start of freaking overtime, where they're blaring their music before they come out for the jump ball. We were sort of in trouble then.

Bill Self: Hoiberg still talks about that. We were dead. We didn't have anything going. We pulled one out of our hat there at the end of regulation. Then we got them good in overtime.

Fred Hoiberg: I've never been in a louder arena. They came out and hit a couple 3s right away and it was over.

McLemore opened overtime with another 3-pointer and that started an 11-0 KU run. The Jayhawks went on to win 97-89. McLemore scored a career-high 33 points on 10-of-12 shooting—and he was a perfect 6-of-6 from beyond the arc.

Kevin Young: If you'd had asked any of us when we were down with four minutes left if we were going to lose, we all would've said, "No."

Iowa State guard Naz Mitrou-Long: I can't explain to you how quiet it was the possession before they ran their Chop play—and then how *loud* it was after McLemore hit that bank shot. One extreme to the next. That place just erupted.

It hurt us when Georges fouled out. Georges was balling, too. Me and him, as close as we are, he came back to the bench and it was weird, because the "Pay Heed" sign that they have, it just looked a little extra brighter. It was weird, man. We started looking around and just seeing how electric it was in there.

We had no choice but to give them our respect for their home-court advantage, but man, we were so close to winning that game. That was one of the most heartbreaking losses we had in our career.

Fred Hoiberg: The one thing I always regretted was not fouling when we were up three. But again, we knew what they were going to run. You go through it countless times and we didn't execute the switches the way we'd talked about. But you can look at it a different way, too. We had two guys who had fouled out, and we're small, so we took our chances with our guys, knowing the play they were going to run.

Melvin Ejim: We knew what they were going to run. One stop and we win the game. It was tough to swallow when you go into Phog Allen and you play so well, but you still can't get that win. A lot of teams probably have that same feeling.

McLemore's heroics against Iowa State set the tone for KU in January, as the Jayhawks went 7-0 for the month. Most to Self's delight, Kansas was playing particularly well defensively, holding six straight opponents to under 60 points. That included No. 11 Kansas State, which was now coached by Bruce Weber. Self's squad defeated the Wildcats 59-55 in the final game at Bramlage Coliseum for KU seniors, Releford, Young, Johnson and Withey.

Assistant coach Norm Roberts: It was fun watching Elijah and those guys that night. They were hyped. Before the game, they were like, "We are winning here!" Then Elijah and Travis said, 'We're going to blow kisses to their crowd." And they did. They popped their jerseys and blew kisses to everyone.

Flippin' Out

At 19-1 and 7-0, Kansas had risen to No. 2 in the Associated Press poll when Oklahoma State arrived in Lawrence on Feb. 2. The Cowboys weren't ranked, but after a 2-3 start in league play they were feeling good about themselves following back-to-back home wins against Iowa State and West Virginia. And with players such as guards Marcus Smart and Le'Bryan Nash—both McDonald's All-Americans—and Markel Brown, OSU touted arguably the best talent in the conference. Also on the roster was sixth man Phil Forte, Smart's best friend. The Cowboys had edged out Kansas and a host of others on the recruiting trail for the Smart-Forte package deal.

Bill Self: I liked Marcus Smart. Of all the guys that we recruited here that got away, he was one of the biggest ones. If we could have signed him, we would've had a great chance at a few more national championships, because his mindset and his toughness and energy was fabulous.

Phil Forte: Both of my parents went to Kansas, so I was a huge, diehard KU fan. It was always my dream to play there. I grew up watching Kirk Hinrich and Nick Collison. I was in San Antonio when Mario Chalmers hit the shot against Memphis to force overtime. I was at the national championship game in New Orleans when they lost to Syracuse and Carmelo Anthony and Gerry McNamara. I cried after that game. That's how big of a fan I was. My room was painted blue and red. There were KU posters everywhere, and the big Jayhawk was painted on the wall. Hinrich, Nick Collison … and I was a big Keith Langford fan since he was from the Dallas-Forth Worth area. Anytime they played the Big 12 Tournament in Dallas, I'd skip school to go watch.

I don't know if I could've been a bigger KU fan growing up. Looking back, you just laugh at it, because in college I tried to do everything I could to beat them.

I didn't talk to Bill Self very much during the recruiting process. I talked to Danny Manning a little bit. Me and Marcus were obviously very close. We'd been best friends since the third grade. I just wanted to go somewhere where I could play right away.

As good as Kansas is every year, I knew it would've been hard for me to do that there. They're getting players that go to the NBA every single year. There's a reason they've won 13 straight.

They offered me a scholarship, but part of me wondered if it was just because of Marcus. I was having other schools offer me as part of a package deal to get Marcus and I wondered if Kansas was doing the same. I wondered if they really believed I could play there. I had to go to the school that was best for me individually. The fact that I'd always wanted to play for them was an added motivation the first time I took the court there.

Travis Ford: Anytime you're going into Allen Fieldhouse, you're just trying to give yourself a chance. I don't know if you tell your team, "We're going to go down there and win!" I never did that. But you go down there with confidence. You just have to understand that it's a different beast, a different ordeal. And when you take players that have never been there before, it's *really* a different deal. You try to prepare for it in practice. We turned the sound up. We had our older players trash talk to the younger guys. You don't try to psyche them out, but you've got to get them somewhat prepared rather than just throwing them out there. We tried to talk to them about what it's like playing in Allen Fieldhouse. You don't want them to be caught by surprise.

Phil Forte: When you play at Allen Fieldhouse, there's really no pressure. You're never going to be the favorite going into that game, so it's a really relaxed mentality. You just go in and leave it all out there like you've got nothing to lose. They're the ones who are ranked higher. They're the ones who have the streak. They're the favorites. The pressure is on them. Coach Ford had a way of getting us to believe we could beat them no matter where we played them. Going in, I remember having a weird feeling. I was like, "I think we're going to win this game."

Ben McLemore: We started off sluggish, and Markel Brown got 22 on us before halftime. It was ridiculous on my part. I should've been better. Me and Travis, being the defensive stoppers on our team, we let our team down. We definitely heard about it going to the locker room.

Naadir Tharpe: Markel Brown was hitting 3s on us like he was J.J. Redick and Ray Allen rolled into one. He was knocking s**t down. He could not miss.

Oklahoma State led by 14 points at one point in the first half, but KU pulled ahead 64-60 on a 3-pointer by Tharpe midway through the second. The Cowboys, though, kept things close and then surged ahead late with a 13-2 run that started with Forte's 3 with 4:15 left.

A pair of free throws by Forte gave OSU an 83-80 cushion with 7.9 seconds remaining. The game ended moments later when Smart stole the ball at midcourt and passed to Forte for a layup at the buzzer.

Brown (28 points) and Smart (25) had huge games for the Cowboys while Forte added 11 off the bench.

Travis Ford: My philosophy was to try to stay in the game as long as you could and hopefully have a chance at the end. That's kind of what happened in that game. We got way up and they came back. Right at the beginning of the second half, they went on a big, big run and took the lead. That's the hardest thing when you're playing there. Once you give up a lead, it's nearly impossible to get it back.

Phil Forte: We were up big early. They came back and, in the last couple of minutes, things started going their way. In the back of my mind, I was thinking, "Here we go. We're going to be like all the other teams that come so close in here and then fall short." But we made a couple of plays down the stretch and Marcus made a big steal to seal it.

I had to hit about four free throws to win it. I was thinking, "How ironic. I grew up wanting to be a Jayhawk, and now I'm shooting free throws at the end of a game to beat the Jayhawks." I was almost speechless, like, "This isn't happening."

Travis Ford: I told our team in the locker room after the game, the biggest thing I'm proud of is that we gave up a lead, got it back and won it in regulation. It took some incredible performances. Obviously Marcus was really good. Markel Brown was off the chart in the first half. Phil Forte made big shots. But you're not ever going to take a team in there and have one or two guys beat Kansas. It's going to take a collective effort from everyone.

Phil Forte: I remember walking off that court and seeing the look on all the fans faces. They were stunned. They had no idea what hit them. We weren't ranked at that point. Some of them were crying. They had no idea what hit them. Usually you walk off a court and fans are yelling at you or cussing. Their fans were *crying.* It's something I'll never forget.

The loss ended Kansas' 33-game winning streak at Allen Fieldhouse, and it marked OSU's first road win against a top-five team since beating KU in Lawrence in 1958. Much to the chagrin of Jayhawks fans, players and coaches, Smart celebrated by doing backflips across the hardwood moments after the final horn.

Ben McLemore: I didn't see him flip until we watched the tape a few days later. I'm cool with Marcus now. But I didn't like him for a while because of that. I didn't like him—or (Michigan's) Tim Hardaway or Trey Burke, either. They're my guys now, but for my first two or three years in the league, every time I played against them, I wanted to go out there and bust their ass because they beat us.

Travis Releford: He was hyped. Not too many teams come in and win at KU. I'm surprised the whole team wasn't doing backflips. Of course it was disrespectful, but you've got to understand not a lot of teams come in and have moments like that.

Perry Ellis: Even though I didn't like what he did that day, I couldn't help but be impressed with Marcus Smart. He was a hard-nosed competitor who played with a lot of fire.

To this day, Coach Self won't let his players forget about that moment. We had footage of him doing that on all of our Oklahoma State (scouting) tapes. Even after he was gone, they'd play that tape back to remind us of what he did on our court. The coaches would always bring that up and say, "You let him come into our home and do backflips on our court?" They'd replay it over and over again, on a loop.

Bill Self: Doing the backflip on the floor, that didn't bother me at all. But I was almost glad he did it because it was great to show the guys that we allowed that to happen. But no, I didn't have a problem with him personally at all. I thought it was beautiful—like a 9.6.

Phil Forte: The backflip was a spur of the moment thing. If he'd planned it, he didn't tell me about it. I remember afterward, we were on the bus back to Stillwater, and he called me over. He said, "Do you think that backflip was too much?" I was like, "Dude, what we just did ... that doesn't happen. So, no, I don't think it was too much."

Travis Ford: We bussed there. On the way home, about halfway through the bus ride, you could hear everyone in the back giggling and laughing. Somehow it got back to me. Everyone was like, "Oh man, it's on YouTube." Someone brought it up to the front and showed it to me. That was the first I'd heard about it. We talked about it a little bit. It was a split-second, knee-jerk reaction. A lot of people thought it was disrespectful. I guarantee he didn't mean it that way at all. It was just a celebration, and he probably didn't choose the best way to celebrate. It wasn't anything disrespectful.

Phil Forte: People still talk about that backflip. Kansas fans and Oklahoma State fans are going to be talking about that forever. It's part of his legacy. Those fans are always going to remember that game because he did the backflip on the beak of the Jayhawk. That bus ride was probably the best bus ride I've ever had as a player. We were getting on ESPN.com and reading about how we'd broken the longest winning streak in the country.

TCU vs. Topeka YMCA

The Jayhawks had what appeared to be the perfect game to get back on track after the Oklahoma State loss: a road tilt with TCU. The Horned Frogs were 0-8 in Big 12 play.

Bill Self: There was an official who monitored our shootaround who, years later, told me, "Bill, just so you know, I did your shootaround (for the 2013 TCU game), and I've never seen a team look better before a game. Your guys had so much energy. They didn't miss a shot. It was unbelievable."

Norm Roberts: That game was like the Bermuda Triangle. It was the weirdest game atmosphere I'd ever been in. Leading up to the game, our shootaround was one of the best we've ever had. Coach was like, "Man, our guys are juiced up." We missed a couple of shots early, and from that point it was almost like a fog was over us.

Kevin Young: Coach changed the lineup that game. It messed us up a little bit. Perry started ahead of me. We couldn't score hardly at all.

Bill Self: Perry got off to a bad start and we couldn't throw it in the ocean. We were awful—*awful*. Then we got tight and everything snowballed.

Jamari Traylor: I was the first person to score in that game, which tells you all you need to know about how bad we played (laughing). We had six points in the first 16 minutes of the game and only 13 in the first half. Nothing went well for us. It was a terrible feeling.

Ben McLemore: We were 0-for-everything.

Kevin Young: We went into the locker room really confused. The ball wasn't going in. I think we all were confused. We missed a lot of open shots but they did their part as well.

In the second half we started to force stuff. Everyone was trying to get the ball in the net and it wasn't going in.

Norm Roberts: We made jokes about it. It was almost like we became the Monstars (from *Space Jam*). Coach was like, "You guys are like the Monstars? Who took your powers?" We couldn't do anything. We missed dunks off of lobs. We missed wide-open shots, layups, bunnies, free throws. We couldn't make anything.

Travis Releford: Coach was just trying to keep us calm. It was clear we had more talent than that TCU team did. They came out and they wanted it more. With them wanting it more and us thinking they're just going to give us the game, it didn't work out. Every time we'd come in the huddle, he wasn't yelling at us. He was just like, "you guys need to calm down. I know you're better than what you're playing right now."

Elijah Johnson: I was trippin' that game. I didn't shoot the ball well. But I didn't have the confidence to shoot the ball then. I wasn't moving

Kansas 55, TCU 62
February 6, 2013 · Fort Worth, Texas

Kansas (19-3)

Player	MP	FG	3FG	FT	R	A	F	S	TO	B	TP
Perry Ellis*	10	0-1	0-0	0-0	1	0	0	0	0	0	0
Elijah Johnson*	31	3-12	2-8	0-2	3	1	5	0	3	1	8
Ben McLemore*	36	6-16	0-6	3-4	9	3	4	0	3	1	15
Travis Releford*	36	0-1	0-0	1-2	6	4	5	0	1	0	1
Jeff Withey*	33	4-6	0-0	4-5	8	0	3	0	2	3	12
Rio Adams	3	0-0	0-0	0-0	0	0	0	0	0	0	0
Niko Roberts	1	0-0	0-0	0-0	0	0	2	0	0	0	0
Naadir Tharpe	25	2-15	1-6	6-6	6	2	3	0	2	0	11
Jamari Traylor	7	1-1	0-0	0-0	1	0	2	0	0	0	2
Justin Wesley	3	0-0	0-0	0-0	1	0	1	0	1	0	0
Kevin Young	14	2-7	0-0	2-4	9	0	1	1	0	0	6
Andrew White	1	0-2	0-2	0-0	0	0	3	0	1	0	0
Team											
Totals	200	18-61	3-22	16-23	44	10	29	1	13	5	55

TCU (10-12)

Player	MP	FG	3FG	FT	R	A	F	S	TO	B	TP
Kyan Anderson*	21	2-6	1-3	3-4	1	1	4	0	1	0	8
Nate Butler-Lind*	27	3-6	1-1	3-8	2	2	3	2	1	1	10
Connell Crossland*	32	3-6	0-0	2-6	15	1	2	0	0	0	8
Garlon Green*	36	7-13	2-4	4-5	2	1	2	1	1	0	20
Adrick McKinney*	25	1-5	0-0	5-8	8	1	3	0	2	0	7
Devonta Abron	21	1-1	0-0	4-4	4	2	4	0	2	1	6
Charles Hill, Jr.	20	1-7	0-4	1-3	2	1	2	0	2	0	3
Clyde Smith III	17	0-2	0-1	0-0	0	2	0	0	0	0	0
Chris Zurcher	1	0-0	0-0	0-0	0	0	1	0	0	0	0
Team					5				2		
Totals	200	18-46	4-13	22-38	39	11	21	3	11	2	62

	1st	2nd	Total	FG%	3FG%	FT%
Kansas	13	42	55	29.5	13.6	69.6
Iowa State	22	40	62	39.1	30.8	57.9

Officials: John Higgins, Darron George, Doug Sirmons
Technicals: None

BEST OF THE STREAK

MOST MADDENING BIG 12 LOSSES

1. Feb. 6, 2013 at TCU (62-55): Bill Self famously said afterwards it was the "worst team Kansas has ever put on the floor since Dr. Naismith was here."

2. Jan. 30, 2008 at Kansas State (84-75): This game snapped the other "Streak" – a string of 24 straight wins for KU at Bramlage Coliseum.

3. Feb. 3, 2007 vs. Texas A&M (69-66): The Aggies overcame a 10-point deficit in the final 6 ½ minutes, posting the first win ever for a Big 12 south team at Allen Fieldhouse.

4. Feb. 14, 2005 at Texas Tech (80-79): Following no-call after Aaron Miles was blatantly (and intentionally fouled), Darryl Dora hit a game-winning 3-pointer with 3.6 seconds left that gave the Red Raiders a double-overtime win.

5. Feb. 2, 2013 vs. Oklahoma State (85-80): Markel Brown scored 28 as Oklahoma State ended KU's 33-game home-court winning streak, and Marcus Smart celebrated with postgame backflips that drew the ire of Jayhawks players, coaches and fans.

6. Jan. 14, 2006 vs. Kansas State (59-55): K-State overcame a 12-point second-half deficit, broke a 31-game losing streak to KU ... and still couldn't save coach Jim Wooldridge's job, as he was fired after the season.

7. Jan. 16, 2006 at Missouri (89-86): Thomas Gardner scored 40 points, as the Tigers made up seven points in the final 30 seconds of regulation on their way to the overtime win. Christian Moody missed two free throws with 0.1 ticks left in regulation.

8. Feb. 23, 2015 at Kansas State (70-63): A sub-.500 K-State team sent Bramlage into a frenzy – starting a postgame celebration in which fans made contact with Jamari Traylor and Bill Self.

9. Jan. 22, 2011 vs. Texas (74-63): An emotionally spent KU team had a 69-game home-court winning streak snapped the afternoon after Thomas Robinson's mother died unexpectedly.

10. March 9, 2013 at Baylor (81-58): Instead of claiming the Big 12 title outright, the Jayhawks had to share it with K-State following a blowout loss to the Bears—who didn't even make the NCAA Tournament—on the final day of the regular season.

like my normal self. I started thinking too much. I didn't take over the game like I should've. If I'd had taken five more shots—whether I made them or not—we'd have won that game. My team was waiting on me and I didn't respond. I didn't freeze up. No one made me nervous or anything. But it was a situation where everyone was just playing around, and all of a sudden it was like, "Uh-oh, they have a chance to beat us." We just weren't there.

Norm Roberts: TCU was almost as awful as we were, but they kicked in a couple of shots and got some confidence. It was the weirdest day. It wasn't that we weren't prepared or that we were having chemistry issues. It wasn't really any of that. We were just out of sync and we couldn't get it right.

Kansas made just 18-of-61 shots from the field and lost 62-55. It was one of only two conference wins for TCU that season.

Travis Releford: That one hurt. We were like, "Urgh, we've got to fly to Texas and play the worst team in the league. Let's get this win and move on." I'm sure that's what everybody was thinking, and if they weren't, I'm sure it crossed their mind. They shocked us. We were sitting in the locker room, like, "There's no way we lost this game to that team."

Coach was upset. During the game, Coach Self had tried to keep us calm. But after the game he was not happy. No one that was a Kansas fan was happy that night.

Ben McLemore: Coach Self was furious. Who wouldn't be? No matter how bad things are going in a season, the last thing you ever expect is to get the floor rushed on you by TCU.

Norm Roberts: Coach was pissed at the guys. He thought even though we played bad, we should've found a way to win.

Perry Ellis: It was one of the worst tirades I ever saw from Coach Self. He was irate.

Self's quotes from his postgame press conference that night still live in infamy, especially this one: "It was the worst team that Kansas ever put on the floor since Dr. Naismith was there. I think he had some bad teams when he lost to Topeka YMCA."

Bill Self: There's a ball in my office that was there when I took the job. It was used in Kansas' first-ever win, and it was against the Topeka YMCA. That's why I said that. Win No. 1 … Topeka YMCA.

Kevin Young: After that loss, we were in the film room and Coach Self started to tell us how we were all selfish. He was like, "Nobody in here would take a bullet for anyone else." Pretty much the whole team spoke up right then and said, "Kevin would." For my teammates to say something like that about me was an honor. It definitely came during a bad moment, but it still made me feel really good.

Jamari Traylor: When we got back to Lawrence, I didn't want to go to class. I didn't want to be seen on campus. Coach handled it pretty well. He was definitely disappointed in us. But he was like, "Hey guys, did the sun come up today?" He let us know that we were going to be fine.

But the Jayhawks weren't—at least not immediately. Three days after the TCU debacle, Kansas suffered a 72-66 setback against Oklahoma in Norman. For the first time since 2005, the Jayhawks were on a three-game losing streak. Even worse, all of the defeats were against unranked opponents.

With a Big Monday game against rival Kansas State just 48 hours later, the Jayhawks were looking for something, anything, to get them back on track.

Harlem Shake-Up

Travis Releford: Coach Self was trying to figure out what was going on. We were 19-1 and all of a sudden we lose three straight games? *What's going on? Are you guys on drugs or something?*

We had a quick Saturday-Monday turnaround with K-State, and Coach was like, "You all need to figure it out." We were sitting in the locker room, just trying to think of a way to relax and have fun and laugh and smile again. Justin Wesley came to the locker room and he was talking to all us seniors, and he said we should make one of those Harlem Shake videos. He showed us a video of another group of people making it, and I was first to jump on board. A few guys were like, "Man, I don't know. I don't know." I'm like, "Let's do it! I'll go ask Coach Self right now." We got Coach to be in the video. He said, "Whatever gets you guys going and playing good again, I'm all for it. Let's do it. Let's have some fun again."

Kevin Young: We recorded it the Sunday before we played K-State at Allen Fieldhouse. I remember it well, because I was the one that went to the Goodwill store to buy all the props and costumes for the video. I got vests and cowboy hats and couple of masks and two little guitars. I only spent about $20. It was just a bunch of random things.

It was pretty fun, and Coach Self being a part of it helped us out a lot, just for our confidence and our self-esteem. Before that, no one wanted to go see him in his office for about two weeks. We were too scared (laughing). It helped us off the court and on the court, just knowing that, even in tough times, we can still laugh and have fun and enjoy each other's company.

Ben McLemore: The dance you see me doing at the beginning of the video, I actually started doing that after we beat Ohio State on CBS in December. After we won, I came in the locker room after my interview and started dancing.

A few months later, we were on that losing streak, and everyone was down and upset. I was like, "Everyone is down. Everyone is moping. Coach Self is pissed. We've got to get past this. Let's do something fun to get everyone's minds off of basketball, something to lighten the mood so we can finish conference play on top."

Travis Releford: That video helped. That was the only moment we took away from basketball. At that moment, it was just us. We had the music and we were able to be ourselves again and loosen up. I wouldn't say that changed our season, but that played a role. And having Coach Self involved really put the icing on the cake. We were like, "Wow, he's going to be in the video?" He said he wasn't going to dance but he would be in it. Once he did that, we said, "OK, now we've really got to go out and play." After making that video, we knew there was no way we could go out and blow another game.

With Kansas—which fell from No. 5 to No. 14 in the rankings—on its three-game losing streak, a new team was atop the Big 12 standings: Kansas State.

The 10th-ranked Wildcats arrived in Lawrence with an 8-2 conference record while Self's squad was 7-3. None of it mattered, though, as KU raced out to an 18-point halftime lead in what turned out to be an 83-62 curbstomping. McLemore hit six 3s and scored 30 points on 9-of-13 shooting.

Ben McLemore: The Harlem Shake really seemed to work. Twenty-four hours later, we looked like a different team. When it was time for us to pick it up, we picked it up.

K-State coach Bruce Weber: McLemore went crazy, no doubt about that. They got on one of their runs, like they always seem to do at home, where they play with a great deal of confidence. I told our guys I wasn't sure they believed they could win. When you go to Lawrence, you get that feeling that the Jayhawks *know* they're going to win each time and they play with those runs. Those earlier teams that I went against in my first few years at K-State were so good defensively, and they used it and went on runs with their defense leading to fast-break dunks, and then the crowd gets involved.

We were ahead by one game in the league. There was no doubt that the fans and their players came with a different level of hype and energy in the building that was probably the best of the five times I've been there. They came out and played at such a high level. It wasn't like our guys were awful or anything. They just kicked our butts. It was impressive.

Travis Releford: The video was a hit. That was the end of that dry spell.

Payback

Kansas followed up the K-State win with a victory over Texas and then headed to Oklahoma State. At 9-3, the Cowboys were in a three-way tie with the Jayhawks and K-State for first place in the Big 12—and it had only been 18 days since their victory (and Smart's backflips) at Allen Fieldhouse.

Travis Ford: We thought we could win the league. We had already beat them and we knew that game was basically for the conference championship. They came to our place and they were on edge and they were pretty good.

Travis Releford: Every time we played a team for a second time, we had to watch film of the first time we played them, whether we won or lost. So of course, they had those backflips playing on repeat. We're like, "Come on! This is getting out of hand."

Naadir Tharpe: That was the year the streak almost ended. That was the game, "Are we going to end the streak? Are we going to mess it up for everybody?" That thought was definitely lingering. I couldn't make any shots that game. They were going in and out. It was weird. They'd look like they were going in and they were just missing.

With Johnson in foul trouble, Tharpe played extended minutes off the bench in Stillwater, but for most of the game he couldn't have thrown the ball through a hula-hoop. Tharpe was just 1-of-10 from the field and 0-of-6 from 3-point range as the final seconds ticked away in the second overtime.

Naadir Tharpe: When Elijah Johnson fouled out, I had to finish the game. We were basically playing for the championship in double overtime, and I had the ball in my hands. I drove past Phil Forte and got into the lane and hit a floater to win the game. I'll never forget that.

Travis Releford: Coach was saying, "If we win this game, I don't want you guys doing anything crazy on the court." We knew it was going to be a tough game, because they had the confidence from beating us at home and figured they could do it at their house, too. But we ended up pulling it out in double overtime.

Kansas improved to 10-3 with the victory, placing them in a first-place tie for the league lead with K-State.

Another payback victory—74-48 over TCU—upped KU's record to 11-3 and, two days later, the Jayhawks traveled to Iowa State for a rematch of what had been a classic round one at Allen Fieldhouse.

Elijah's Masterpiece

With just two weeks remaining in conference play, McLemore's banked-in 3-pointer to force overtime against Iowa State had been the biggest moment of KU's 2012-13 campaign. When all was said and done, however, that OT win back in January didn't prove to be the most memorable game of the season. It wasn't even the most memorable game against Iowa State. That matchup occurred Feb. 25 in Ames, and one particular Jayhawk was motivated more than others.

Elijah Johnson: Leading into that game, I'd had some crazy experiences at Iowa State, stuff you couldn't see on TV. Some of their fans lost their cool more than a couple of times. Our team knew about it and the coaches knew about it, but that was about it.

The year before, in 2012, when they beat us up there, they stormed the floor and hurt a referee. He was bleeding from his head. That same game, one of their fans spit in my face as I was running up the tunnel before the game. There was a guy in the stands that was trying so hard to get my attention. He didn't get it, but he got the attention of the person next to me. I believe it was Merv Lindsay. Merv looked up and said something smart to him, and he started grabbing the rail and lunging at us—and then another guy spit toward us. I happened to look up just as that spit was coming down and it hit me. I turned around and lunged in his direction, but then I thought about what was happening, and I regained my composure.

Assistant coach Joe Dooley: The spit hit him right in the face. I was right behind him when it happened, and I was amazed that he kept his poise. He was definitely pissed off, and I was scared he was going to run into the crowd. I remember thinking, "How could someone do something like that?"

Elijah Johnson: I got to the locker room and lost my cool. I was the last one in the locker room and Tyshawn was already giving a speech. I walked right past him and Ty said something, but Merv was like, "Someone just spit in his face. Leave him alone. He's mad right now. He's *real* mad." Then we went out there and they beat us. They rushed the court and wouldn't let us off, and then they hurt that referee. The KU people helped take him to the locker room. My blood boiled about that night for a whole year. I couldn't wait to go back up there.

Georges Niang: No offense to Elijah Johnson, but we felt like he was having a down year as a senior. As good of a career as he'd had, he hadn't been as dominant that year as we thought he was going to be.

That description rang true throughout the first half of Johnson's final game in Ames, when he had nine points on 3-of-8 shooting as KU went into halftime with a 41-40 lead. Self lashed out at Johnson several times during the opening 20 minutes, and the senior snapped back.

Elijah Johnson: Coach Self was irritating me. He was getting on my nerves. He knows how to do that kind of stuff at the right time. Stuff just wasn't going well—and he was there to remind me every second how bad stuff was going. He was in my head and bothering me so much. I was like, "Dude, leave me alone!" He tried to sub me out for Naadir and I barked back at him. I was like, "I'm not coming out!" and I stayed in the huddle. He called Naadir's name again, and I was like, *"I'm not coming out!"*

Johnson was a non-factor for the first 10 minutes of the second half, too, before hitting his first shot—a 3-pointer—to give KU a 66-64 lead with 9:42 remaining. Johnson would connect on a handful of other clutch baskets to keep the game close, but it wasn't until the final minute—or, more specifically, the final 29 seconds of regulation—that his performance reached legendary status.

The drama started when a 3-pointer by Johnson shaved Iowa State's five-point lead to two, 87-85. With the shot clock off, KU fouled Iowa State point guard Korie Lucious with 23.1 seconds left. The foul was clearly on Withey, which would have been his fifth, but the officials gave the foul to Young, who had also been reaching but did not make contact with Lucious.

Fred Hoiberg: Jeff Withey basically tackled our guy and they called a foul on Kevin

BEST OF THE STREAK

INDIVIDUAL PERFORMANCES BY A JAYHAWK

1. Wayne Simien vs. Oklahoma State, Feb. 27, 2005: Scored a career-high 32 points on 11-for-17 shooting before ending the game with a celebration for the highlight reels, screaming with both fists in the air while getting mobbed by teammates after an 81-79 win.

2. Elijah Johnson at Iowa State, Feb. 25, 2013: Johnson scored 39 points – and 30 after halftime – to will KU to a 108-96 victory in overtime. Bill Self said afterwards it would go down as one of the best performances ever by a KU guard.

3. Julian Wright vs. Florida,, Nov. 25, 2006: Joakim Noah, Al Horford, Corey Brewer and the defending national champion hardly intimidated Wright, who scored 21 points on 9-of-12 shooting and also snared 10 rebounds in an 82-80 overtime win in Las Vegas.

4. Joel Embiid at Iowa State, Jan. 13, 2014: The big man took over late, using a flurry of post moves to score 12 of his 16 points after halftime in a 77-70 win. Iowa State coach Fred Hoiberg said afterwards that Embiid was the best player in the country.

5. Mario Chalmers vs. Texas, March 17, 2008: Notched a career-high 30 points (his previous best was 23) and was 8-of-12 from 3-point range as Kansas won 84-74 and claimed its third straight Big 12 title. Each of the three championship-game victories came against the Longhorns.

6. Marcus Morris at Iowa State, Jan. 12, 2011: Saying he was inspired by the hostile Hilton Coliseum crowd, Morris posted career highs with 33 points and 13 rebounds while making 11 of 15 shots in an 84-79 win.

7. Thomas Robinson vs. Missouri, Feb. 25, 2012: Tallied 28 points and 12 rebounds in the final Border War—which KU won 87-86—but he'll be remembered most for his game-saving block of Phil Pressey's floater with 2 seconds left in regulation.

8. Sherron Collins at Oklahoma, Feb. 23, 2009: After KU fell behind by 14 early, Collins hit three consecutive 3s in crunch time on his way to 26 points as the Jayhawks knocked off Blake Griffin-less Oklahoma, 87-78, in Norman.

9. Andrew Wiggins at West Virginia, March 8, 2014: The Canadian phenom posted a KU freshman record with 41 points on 12-for-18 shooting, but it wasn't enough as KU fell on the road, 92-86.

10. Cole Aldrich vs. Dayton, March 23, 2009: Posted the first "official" triple-double in KU history, going for 13 points, 20 rebounds and 10 blocks as Kansas advanced to the Sweet 16 with a 60-43 Round of 32 victory over the Flyers.

10. (tie) Devonte' Graham at Oklahoma, Feb. 14, 2016: Scored a career-high 27 points on 8-of-13 shooting, but equally important was his defensive effort on national POY Buddy Hield, who had 24 points but went just 5-of-15 from the field.

Young. It was just one thing after another at the end of that game.

Lucious made both free throws to put the Cyclones back ahead by four, 89-85. Kansas—surprise!—ran the same Chop play that had freed up McLemore for his big shot back in January. This time, though, Iowa State defended it perfectly, so it was Johnson who was forced to hoist a 25-footer over Lucious to keep his team's hopes alive. He made it, and KU now trailed 89-88 with 12.1 seconds left.

Fred Hoiberg: That's their late-game play. You know that's what they're going to run and they still find a way. They won a national championship on that play.

Georges Niang: Everybody knows the Chop play. They've been running it since (Mario) Chalmers hit that 3 against Memphis. So everybody knows what's coming late in a game. I don't know how it happened, but it happened.

Kansas 108, Iowa State 96
February 25, 2013 · Ames, Iowa

Kansas (24-4)

Player	MP	FG	3FG	FT	R	A	F	S	TO	B	TP
Elijah Johnson*	37	13-22	6-10	7-7	5	7	4	0	3	0	39
Ben McLemore*	38	2-6	0-1	3-3	3	4	2	0	1	0	7
Travis Releford*	42	6-12	5-9	2-4	4	3	2	2	3	0	19
Jeff Withey*	36	5-7	0-0	3-5	10	2	5	1	4	0	13
Kevin Young*	23	6-8	0-0	1-2	9	1	5	0	1	0	13
Perry Ellis	15	2-5	0-0	4-4	6	0	0	0	0	0	8
Naadir Tharpe	26	3-7	2-5	1-2	3	4	3	1	3	0	9
Jamari Traylor	8	0-1	0-0	0-0	1	0	1	1	0	1	0
Team					6		1		2		
Totals	225	37-68	13-25	21-27	47	21	23	5	17	1	108

Iowa State (19-9)

Player	MP	FG	3FG	FT	R	A	F	S	TO	B	TP
Chris Babb*	39	2-7	2-7	5-6	1	3	1	1	0	0	11
Will Clyburn*	38	4-9	2-3	6-8	7	0	0	2	2	0	16
Melvin Ejim*	22	2-5	0-2	0-0	7	0	5	1	0	1	4
Korie Lucious*	39	5-13	3-7	10-12	4	5	4	0	3	0	23
Georges Niang*	31	3-17	3-9	6-6	2	7	5	0	0	0	15
Anthony Booker	13	1-4	1-3	2-2	5	0	2	0	1	0	5
Percy Gibson	3	0-0	0-0	0-0	0	0	0	0	0	0	0
Tyrus McGee	33	8-15	6-10	0-0	5	0	1	0	0	0	22
Bubu Palo	7	0-0	0-0	0-0	0	1	1	0	1	0	0
Team					2				1		
Totals	225	25-70	17-41	29-34	33	16	19	4	8	1	96

	1st	2nd	OT	Total	FG%	3FG%	FT%
Kansas	41	49	18	108	54.5	52.0	77.8
Iowa State	40	50	6	96	35.7	41.5	85.3

Officials: Mark Whitehead, Tom O'Neill, Bert Smith
Technicals: Kansas (1 Bench), Iowa State (0)

Iowa State inbounded to Lucious and he headed back to the line after being fouled with 11.6 seconds left. The Cyclones had made 22 straight free throws, but Lucious missed the first. He made the second to put ISU ahead by two, 90-88. Kansas inbounded the ball to Johnson, who drove the length of the court for a game-tying layup. As he went up for the shot, which he missed, Johnson crashed into Niang on what appeared to be a charge. The officials thought otherwise and didn't whistle Johnson for a violation.

Bill Self: We did get a good no-call late.

Georges Niang: When Korie missed that free throw, I was like, "Dang! But we still got it. One stop. What's one stop?"

I was waiting to see what Elijah was going to do, and then I saw him lock into picking up his dribble. His eyes looked toward the rim. So I stood in there, and I probably should have had my hands around my crotch to make the charge look more realistic, but he ran me over, and there was a no-call.

Fred Hoiberg: Georges Niang did a great job, I thought, of establishing position and took a charge. They didn't call it.

Elijah Johnson: Those fans wanted my head for that (laughing). They probably should've called something, either a block or a charge. I never looked at where Niang's feet were, but it was something. The reason I say that is because the ball never hit the rim, so the shot wasn't the focus of that possession. The contact was the only focus of that possession. Everybody saw that contact. It was the only thing that happened on that possession.

The ball actually did graze the rim after hitting the backboard and when Withey tried to rebound the miss, he inadvertently tipped the ball to Johnson, who was still on the ground. Johnson caught the ball sitting up, and Niang, who was laying on the floor next to him, reached in and tried to grab it.

Georges Niang: Then I got called (for a foul) trying to grab a loose ball. It happens. I'm not going to go back and say we got screwed. I'm sure there were some calls that we got when I was in college that other teams were not too ecstatic about. It's the game of basketball.

Fred Hoiberg: It was a bogus foul on Georges—at home, with 4 seconds left—and it gave Elijah two free throws, which he made to tie the game (90-90).

In 29 seconds, Johnson had scored eight points and single-handedly forced an extra period in Ames. Boos rained down at Hilton Coliseum, and the jeers only got worse when Johnson scored KU's first four points in overtime. Moments later, Releford and Johnson made back-to-back 3s to put the Jayhawks ahead 100-92 with 2:06 left.

Georges Niang: It was the same thing that happened in Lawrence. They were in a groove going into overtime, and in college when you have a momentum shift like that, it's the team that gained the momentum that usually takes the game.

Still, the Cyclones weren't finished.They went on a 4-0 run to pull back within four after Will Clyburn made 1-of-2 free throws with 1:32 left. On the ensuing possession, the Jayhawks tried to milk the clock.

Naadir Tharpe: The shot clock was going down and Elijah drove to the basket and shot a layup. It didn't hit the rim, but I thought it did. Elijah got his own rebound and passed it to me. I didn't realize the shot clock was still going. I thought it had reset, but I hear everybody on the bench screaming, "Hurry up! Shoot the ball!" Elijah looked right at me and said, "Throw me the ball." I threw it to him, and he shot it falling away, right by the sideline. *Launches* it ... money! Three!

Elijah Johnson: He threw it to me and I let that thing go. I can't even say how that feels because that's how I'm used to playing. I'm not a guy that shoots a ton each game. I score in bunches. In high school I'd have two points entering the fourth quarter and then end up with 20. That's how I've always played. I just didn't play like that a lot at Kansas.

Bill Self: He had one of the best halves I've ever seen. That was Kevin Durant-ish.

Joe Dooley: Elijah went crazy. You talk about getting on a roll. He was banking shots in. We were in harm's way and Elijah bailed us out. He was very underrated because he had a quiet, laid-back personality. That was different than our previous point guards like Tyshawn and Sherron, who were demonstrative.

Kevin Young: He just turned it on. It was fun to watch. We just gave him the ball and got out of the way. Especially in overtime. He couldn't miss.

Georges Niang: We didn't think he was capable of that. That was a surprise when all of that happened.

Up 106-96, the Jayhawks were in control after Johnson's buzzer-beating 3, but he wasn't finished yet. As the final seconds ticked away, Perry Ellis snared a long rebound off of a missed Iowa State 3-pointer and fired a pass in transition to Johnson, who put the cherry on top of his revenge game by throwing down a one-handed jam at the buzzer. Johnson finished with 39 points, including 30 after intermission and 20 after the 29-second mark of the second half.

Elijah Johnson: When I dunked at the end of the game, I didn't feel any remorse. It was a heated situation. Anyone that got mad at me, I reminded them of what happened to me the year before. Iowa State was my punching bag that day, and that dunk was the last punch of the workout.

Most basketball players don't really have an on or an off button. I'm one of those people. I've had that same thing happen to me in Europe, where the game is pretty much over, but I continue to play defense or shoot the ball, and people end up getting mad. Sorry, but I've never been taught to stop playing before the buzzer goes off. I hate when you're watching an NBA game and the players are shaking hands while there's still four or five seconds left. I've always hated that. I've always been a play-to-the-end-of-the-buzzer type of player. I understand sportsmanship, but I really had tunnel vision on that play. I didn't know if there was three minutes or three seconds left—and I didn't care. Anytime I have that ball and can do something with it, I try. Maybe I was too focused in, but if I wasn't focused in, maybe we wouldn't have won that game.

The people booing didn't know about all of that stuff from the year before, when I got spit on. The last thing I cared about was a boo. If anything, it made me want to dunk even more when I may not have had the energy to do it otherwise. *"I'm tired right now but I'm going to go down here and dunk this ball because I know that's what you don't want to see."* Coach said he understood. I had to apologize in the press conference, but that was it.

Bill Self: I didn't think anything bad about it. The kid was just excited. People can say whatever. We were up by what … 10? Then he goes in and dunks it? Big deal. If the clock is running out it's one thing. Or if you're playing five-on-five and you act like you're going to stall it, and then you dribble in and score, that's B.S. But this was in transition. He could've dribbled it out. But trust me, the fans would've still been pissed, because they got a couple of bad calls that game. They would've been pissed regardless.

Georges Niang: I was livid about it, and our fans were, too. It was like a circus, with stuff flying everywhere at the end. I think Kansas had to get escorted out.

Fred Hoiberg: Sure, stuff like that always rubs you the wrong way, but these are kids. The more memorable part was our fan on the court going after Bill.

That fan was Iowa State booster Melvin Weatherwax, who confronted Self after his postgame interview with Holly Rowe.

Bill Self: He just kind of came at me. I don't know what he said. "Thugs," or whatever. Everyone made a big deal out of it but it wasn't a big deal to me. The next couple of years, I walked by where everyone told me he usually sat. I was going to say, "Hey" to him but he was never there.

Joe Dooley: We always joked that Coach was lucky that security was there because that guy would've kicked his ass. We were back there making odds on who would've won that fight. The odds were heavily in Coach's favor that he would've kicked the guy's ass, but we never got to see that one.

Bill Self: Everyone got a kick out of it. Doc (Sadler) got to know him the next year when he joined Fred's staff, and said he's a good dude. I told him, "Go ask that dude what he's got against me. What did I do to him?"

Kurtis Townsend: What I remember the most is the hate after the game by their fans. I was walking out with Elijah. He dunked at the end of the game and those people were pissed. They were yelling the n-word and things like that. Some of the worst stuff you can imagine. Then he had death threats on his phone. People were texting him, "I'm going to come out to the bus and blow your head off, ni**er." You tell them to have blinders on and not to listen. But when it gets that vile it's hard not to hear that stuff.

Jamari Traylor: That was one of my favorite games to be a part of. I didn't even play that much. When you watch the tape, you can see me on the bench getting excited about everything that was happening. When we go to Ames, it's a different level of hate from their fans. That night they were spitting at us and throwing those cones—those plastic megaphones—at us. I picked up one off the court, took it into the locker room and had Elijah autograph it for me a few minutes after he smoked their ass. I kept it in my locker for the rest of my career. I still have it.

Known for his calm demeanor on the sideline, Hoiberg was heated after the game and had words with the officials as soon as the buzzer sounded before heading to the handshake line. Hoiberg later became upset when he learned that, multiple times during KU's comeback—when it became obvious the Jayhawks would win—the ESPN broadcast repeatedly showed his 10-year-old twin boys, Sam and Charlie, crying in the stands. The network received heavy criticism for showing the images over and over and over again—not just during the game, but on all of the recap shows that followed.

Fred Hoiberg: I hate when they do stuff like that. People sent me comments about that. Here's a little kid obviously wearing his emotion on his sleeve. There's no need to embarrass a kid like that.

Years later, the loss still stings Hoiberg—especially when he's asked to talk about the game.

Fred Hoiberg: You mean the game when we got f**ked? And yes, you can quote me on that. It was a heartbreaking loss. I thought we did everything to deserve that game and win that game. Elijah Johnson was unbelievable. It was the best game of his career.

You feel good in your home gym being up five with 45 seconds left, but the series of things that happened in that last minute were very bizarre. I got an email that next morning from one of the refs from that game. He said he'd never sent an email like that before, and he felt awful about the way that last minute went down. It obviously didn't help. It didn't reverse things.

We had them beat twice that year. I think in the two games combined we hit 32 threes—15 at Allen Fieldhouse and 17 at home—and lost both times. That shouldn't happen. They were two great games, and two games we should have won.

Georges Niang: I still see that ref around and I've never got an explanation. I was livid, but like I said, mistakes happen. I don't need an explanation now. It'd probably hurt worse now hearing that explanation. I guess I was holding someone when I was going for a loose ball.

Melvin Ejim: I thought the NCAA changed the rule based on that play and a couple others, but a lot on that one because it was such a big game and a big call that won it for them and lost it for us. I think the fact the NCAA changed the block-charge call the following season speaks volumes to the difficulty of that call. It could have gone either way and probably should have went our way.

Elijah Johnson: That game wasn't reffed the best, but it was a dogfight kind of game. I don't think anyone should be mad with how it was officiated or how it turned out. They got hot and we got hot. At the end of regulation, the score went back to 0-0. We had five more minutes to play—and we won by 12 points. We didn't leave any question.

Kurtis Townsend: It was great and well-deserved for Elijah. He was such a strong presence in our locker room. I had guys tell me that multiple times that, when things were going poorly, our staff would leave the locker room and Elijah would stand up and say, "Would you guys just listen to the coaches. They know what they're doing."

BEST OF THE STREAK

TOUGHEST BIG 12 ARENAS

1. Hilton Coliseum, Iowa State: No fans boo louder, or more frequently, than the ones at Iowa State. The rowdy crowd in Ames has helped the Cyclones to four home wins over the Jayhawks in the Self era. "Hilton Magic" is definitely a thing.

2. Bramlage Coliseum, Kansas State: The Octagon of Doom is one of the toughest places to play in America—when the Jayhawks are in town. Other times ... eh, not so much. The proximity of the court to the student section makes it tough for KU players to block out the insults, which never stop.

3. Gallagher-Iba Arena, Oklahoma State: Although it's not nearly as intimidating as it was during the Roy Williams era, Gallagher-Iba still gives the Jayhawks fits. Bill Self lost six of his first 10 games in Stillwater after taking the KU job before the 2003-04 season.

4. WVU Coliseum, West Virginia: Kansas has kept its Big 12 title alive despite four straight losses (from 2014-17) in Morgantown, which boasts the most underrated home-court advantage in the Big 12.

5. Mizzou Arena, Missouri: The Jayhawks claim the most vulgar, tasteless remarks they heard on any road trip came from the fans in Columbia, where Kansas and Missouri split eight meetings before the Tigers left for the SEC in 2012.

6. United Spirit Arena, Texas Tech: Bill Self lost his first three games in Lubbock (in 2005, 2007 and 2009) before winning his next seven. Typically a dead atmosphere—but, like most places, fans come out in droves when KU is in town.

7. Frank Erwin Center, Texas: Bill Self suffered his worst Big 12 loss in here in 2006 when LaMarcus Aldridge, Daniel Gibson and P.J. Tucker led the way in an 80-55 drubbing of KU.

8. Lloyd Noble Center, Oklahoma: Though Oklahoma fans typically don't pack the arena, the Sooners have been able to topple the Jayhawks three times at home since the Big 12 streak began.

9. Coors Events Center, Colorado: Long dubbed "Allen Fieldhouse West" because of the large contingent of KU fans that showed up for games, the arena became more challenging when Tad Boyle began to change the culture after taking over in 2010.

10. Ed and Rae Schollmaier Arena, TCU: Previously known as Daniel-Meyer Coliseum, the newly-renovated venue could become a hornet's nest now that Jamie Dixon is making the Horned Frogs competitive again.

Norm Roberts: That game was going back and forth and back and forth. Elijah got really hot. But it wasn't like, "Wow! Elijah!" It just happened in the flow of the game. When it was over and they said he had 39, I was like, "Wow! Really?" It was just two teams making play after play. Going up there, no matter who they have on their team, for whatever reason, they play unbelievably there. It seems like they make every big shot. Even if you know it's coming, it's going to happen.

Those games are the most fun. You know your guys aren't scared. They're trying to make plays to win the game. They're playing the right way. But Iowa State is, too. It can fall on a call—or a no-call. As coaches, we all get hyped and enjoy those games, win or lose. Even when we lose, we leave there thinking, "We played our tails off. They just made some shots." If we get beat in a game like that, Coach will come in and he won't go nuts. After the game he won't get too crazy, because he realizes it was a hell of a game against a hell of a team.

Travis Releford: It was hard for me to sit back and watch and appreciate what Elijah was doing, because I was a part of it. A lot of the shots he was taking, I was throwing him the ball. So it was hard for me to be a fan and enjoy it. But going back and seeing the highlights a few days later, I was like, "Man, you were really out there killing it. That was a hell of a game and your numbers show it." The things he was doing out there ... he was unbelievable.

Elijah Johnson: I've never watched that game. I'll get to that one day. Right now I'm still trying to make a living.

Welcome to the Big 12

The 2012-13 season was West Virginia's first year in the Big 12. It's the only season that the Jayhawks have swept the Mountaineers. West Virginia's introduction to Allen Fieldhouse on March 2 was a cruel one. Ben McLemore dropped 36 points and Kansas won 91-65.

West Virginia guard Gary Browne: As soon as we got off the bus, it was freezing outside. I had, like, three jackets on, and I get off the bus and I see a loooong, loooong, long line to get in the game. I'm like, "This is serious out here, because if the weather is like *this* and there's people outside waiting, I can't imagine what it's like inside. As soon as they get in, they're going to go crazy."

That's why we got blown out, because of the crowd. McLemore had a good game, but the crowd was one of the best crowds I ever played in front of.

Tied

Kansas and K-State entered the final day of the regular season tied atop the conference at 14-3. K-State played first that afternoon against Oklahoma State in Stillwater. The Cowboys won 76-70, leaving the door open for the Jayhawks to win the Big 12 title outright.

Bruce Weber: It was so disappointing, because we coulda won, shoulda won. Obviously a couple plays, calls, whatever down the stretch, changed the momentum of the game. It was just disappointing because you left an opportunity there. We got home and I didn't even think Kansas would lose. I didn't have it in my mind.

Few people did as the Jayhawks took the court against Baylor in Waco with a chance to win the Big 12 title outright. Ranked as high as No. 16 at one point, the Bears had struggled down the stretch with losses in five of their previous six games.

The Jayhawks—who had defeated Baylor 61-44 back in January—had never lost at the Ferrell Center under Self. But that changed on Baylor's Senior Night, when Pierre Jackson turned in one of the best performances ever by a Big 12 opponent, scoring 28 points on 11-of-13 shooting and dishing out 10 assists. Big man Cory Jefferson made only three 3-pointers that season, and they were all in that game. He finished with 25 points to help lead the Bears to an upset 81-58 win. For the first time since 2008, KU—which got 25 points from McLemore—would have to share the Big 12 title. Baylor missed the NCAA Tournament but won the NIT title.

Travis Releford: We were all so focused on what other teams were doing that day that we weren't really worrying about our own game. I think that's what it came down to. All the players we were all watching other games and more focused on that than the Baylor game. They came out with nothing to lose.

Ben McLemore: We let Pierre go off on us, and then it was contagious. Hell, Cory Jefferson made three 3-pointers on us. I'm not sure he'd made that many in his whole career.

Scott Drew: Pierre Jackson was a monster. Cory Jefferson had a super game. Senior Night, as a coach, you always want your guys to have a great feeling when they leave the arena. If you're going to play a great game, every coach would say, "this is the game you want it to be."

Pierre Jackson: It was my last home game so all of my family and friends were there. My grandmother had flown in from Vegas. It was her first time ever on an airplane. They had guys like Ben McLemore who were going to go high in the draft. I took it personal and my teammates backed me up and had great games, too. It was a great way to cap off the year. They could've won the title outright that day but, because we beat them, they had to share the title with Kansas State. I'm sure they didn't like that.

Bruce Weber: I didn't watch the game. In fact, I still remember my wife and I were walking the dog. At that time we lived near the baseball stadium, and all of a sudden this loud noise erupted and people are going crazy. I'm like, "Gaahh, they must have had a grand slam or something." But then all of a sudden my phone just lit up. I had literally a hundred texts in seconds. It just kept going boom, boom, boom. And then my wife said, "What happened?" Then our AD, John Currie, called me and said, "Hey, congratulations." We went from being very low that afternoon to very high that night.

It was great for our kids.

Even though they lost to Kansas in both regular-season meetings, the Wildcats claimed a share of the conference title for the first time since 1977.

Thomas Gipson: We were pretty pissed off that day. Later that night I was at the house, and we weren't really watching the KU game, but we were tracking the updates. At one point Baylor was up by like 20. Once we found out they won, you could just hear it outside. People were going nuts in our neighborhood and at the bars. People were going crazy. We got the title through Baylor, but you can't take it away from us.

Bruce Weber: Someone from the Big 12 had been in Stillwater that day with the trophy. They were going to present it to us had we won, but obviously that didn't happen. Some of our boosters who had come down for the game had stayed in Stillwater, and they were having dinner. So when Kansas ended up losing, some people called back to those guys from Manhattan and said, "Hey, is there any way you could go get the trophy from Oklahoma State and drive it back?" So those guys drove the trophy back and we had a nice presentation the next day at our place. They were so nervous driving the trophy back.

Ben McLemore: I forgot we had to share the title with K-State, even though we kicked their ass twice—three times, if you count the Big 12 Tournament. I don't think they felt like they really earned it. It was rightfully ours. We still owned the Big 12.

The Real Champs

Kansas entered the Big 12 Tournament as an angry team. The Jayhawks stomped Texas Tech in the quarterfinals and then beat Iowa State for the third time that year, 83-73. It was a breakout game for freshman Ellis, who scored 23 points against the Cyclones.

Perry Ellis: I played well and the crowd was cheering my name. "PER-ry ELL-is! PER-ry ELL-is!" I just remember getting bucket after bucket. They kept going in. I remember being lined up next to Georges Niang while someone was shooting free throws, and he laughed and said, "Man, I was waiting for this day to come. I knew it was going to happen for you." From that point on, I knew I could do it. I had been up and down my freshman year. But at that point, I was like, "Man, the hard work paid off."

Much to the delight of restaurant and bar owners in Kansas City's Power & Light District, the top two seeds—No. 1 Kansas and No. 2 K-State—advanced to the title game to essentially break the tie from the regular-season standings.

Kevin Young: I always tell K-State fans that K-State was my favorite team in the Big 12—mainly because I got five wins against them. I never lost to K-State in my two years.

That game was special for me, too. We beat them at their place that year (59-55), but I was only 1-for-6 and had a horrible game. I got a big offensive rebound near the end of the game to get Ben a wide-open 3. One of their forwards, Shane Southwell, told the media after the game that I should've never gotten that rebound. He said, "I mean, c'mon … it's Kevin Young."

My cousin immediately sent me the clip of him saying that, and then he sent it to me again the day of the rematch. I had a little extra motivation. The refs were about to T me up, because after every basket I scored, I just glared at him.

Young filled the stat sheet with nine points, nine rebounds and three assists to help the Jayhawks cruise past the Wildcats, 70-54. Withey was named the Big 12 Tournament's Most Outstanding Player after putting up 17 points and nine rebounds in the championship. Johnson added nine points and had one of the most memorable plays of the game.

Norm Roberts: I used to get mad at Elijah. He was so athletic and could do so many things, but sometimes he'd drive you crazy. When the game was on, though, he was engaged. Especially in big moments. He had a non-fearing way about him.

In the Big 12 championship, it's a six-point game late, and he goes off and throws the ball between Will Spradling's legs, catches it on the other side and scores. The game was on the line and he throws it between Spradling's legs and gets it on the other side. And I'm like, "Are you kidding me?" He shrugged his shoulders and said, "That was the move. I had it." Part of the reason that happened was Coach Self. Coach gets our guys to believe they can accomplish anything. *Believe in yourself.* He gives them the freedom to do those things.

That story reminds me of Kevin Young. We played Texas Tech in Lubbock that season, and we weren't playing very well, although we ended up beating them (60-46). Kevin caught a pass in transition and he went in and tried to dunk it really hard, and it bounced off the back of the rim. Coach was like, "What are you doing? Don't do things you're not capable of. Just go in there and lay it in and make the simple play."

You'd think he'd listen, but instead Kevin gets the ball on a breakaway—and it's still a six-point point game—and he windmills it and goes under the rim and dunks it backward. In his mind he's like, "OK, you said I couldn't do it. I'll show you—and I'll do it even bigger, because I've got that kind of confidence in myself." Deep down, Coach likes that. He wants guys to be aggressive. Make the right basketball play, but also play with a free mind. You have to play with a free mind.

Bruce Weber: Bill's group was tougher. They just didn't give in with their toughness and defense. When all was said and done, I'm not sure our guys totally believed they could win. You have to give credit to them. They beat us three times that year—a fairly close game in Bramlage and then pretty soundly in Lawrence. And then it was kind of a typical championship game in the Big 12 Tournament. Just a battle. It was an impressive thing. That team was experienced, older, tough, defensive-minded and just knew how to play.

They didn't have bonafide NBA, first-round, lottery-pick guys. But they had a lot of veterans. It was kind of like, "This guy left, that guy left, these are the guys who are still here, let's find a way to be great again." And they were. They played with a vengeance.

That KU team impressed me as much as any of them.

Tourney Time

A day after beating Kansas State for the third time, the Jayhawks were awarded a No. 1 seed by the NCAA Tournament selection committee. Even better, KU was given the chance to play its first two games in front of a hometown crowd at the Sprint Center in Kansas City.

Kansas was sloppy in its first-round game against Western Kentucky but still managed a 64-57 victory. Up next—for the third time in six years—the Jayhawks faced North Carolina. The Jayhawks trailed by nine at intermission before outscoring UNC by 21 in the second half en route to a 70-58 win. Releford (22 points) and Withey (16 points, 16 rebounds and five blocks) led the way for KU.

Bill Self: The thing I was happiest about the most was that Travis was the best player in that game. I was so happy for him. Doing it in Kansas City, his hometown, against North Carolina was great for that kid. We were behind by 11 that game, and we went on a 51-23 run, and he keyed it all. It was unbelievable.

Travis Releford: Coach Self and I had another talk late that season, and that's what he wanted me to do. He said, "I need you to step up more." We had Ben and he was a young guy. We knew that he was going to be great, but we knew that he was going to have times where he didn't play well. That happens with every freshman. It's very rare for a freshman to score 20 points all 30-something games. Coach told me he wanted me to score more. My role changed. My shot got better and my confidence was clearly sky high after playing in the national championship the year before. I was ready.

Cheap Shot

The victory over the Tar Heels propelled Kansas into a Sweet 16 showdown with No. 4 seed Michigan at AT&T Stadium in Dallas. Led by National Player of the Year Trey Burke, the Wolverines were playing their best basketball of the season thanks to a late-season decision by coach John Beilein to insert freshman big man Mitch McGary into the starting lineup.

McGary was coming off a career-high 21 points on 10-of-11 shooting in a round-of-32 win over VCU. Less than two minutes into the Sweet 16 game, as Michigan was trying to inbound the ball, Johnson tried to get around a McGary screen and smacked him below the belt.

Elijah Johnson: That was an accident. I'm not that type of player. I don't try to get in your mind by poking you in the back or blowing in your ear.

Bill Self: I didn't know what happened until after the game. The official walked over to our bench, and I said, "Hey, do I need to be worried about this?" And he said, "He's going to get a Flagrant 1, and Bill, it's not something you can argue." I said, "OK."

It was a bad play, but we had made such a big deal on scouting about what a great screener McGary was. And he was. He was a great screener, with that big ol' wide base and big body. And it was hard to guard Burke coming off ball screens with McGary setting them. In Elijah's mind, he may have thought, "Maybe if I hit him once, he won't set such good ball screens." I don't know if he meant to hit him like he did. Obviously it didn't affect him. It didn't hurt the guy. Even with all that being said, we were up 14 with 8 minutes left.

Indeed, other than the Johnson's flagrant foul, everything else went right for the Jayhawks over the first 32 minutes. Much of that was because of McLemore, who was a combined 2-of-14 overall and 0-of-8 from 3-point range in the first two rounds of the NCAA Tournament. McLemore bounced back against the Wolverines, scoring 20 points and burying 4-of-8 shots from long range.

Ben McLemore: I had never had a shooting drought, ever. I just kept shooting the ball. That's what I learned. When you're cold, keep shooting until you snap out of it. I tried to find ways to get rolling by getting easy buckets. I told myself not to put my head down. Even great shooters miss. After playing Western Kentucky and North Carolina, and going into the Sweet 16 against Michigan, I even told reporters I was in a drought, but it didn't mean I was going to be in a drought forever. I just needed to find a way.

I started off really slow against Michigan, but I started getting easy buckets and layups and going to the free throw line. That's when my jumpers started falling. We had a veteran team. We were more skilled than them. We were one of the most veteran teams in the NCAA at the time with four seniors (Withey, Johnson, Releford, Young) and a freshman.

We were up by 14 with less than seven minutes left. Even with that lead, a veteran team should've known not to let up. Anything can happen in college, especially in the tournament. It's all about runs. We thought we had it in the books but we really didn't. They started making runs and Trey hit some big shots and, all of a sudden, it was a close game.

Burke was scoreless in the first half but heated up after intermission. His 3-pointer with 1:15 left cut KU's lead to five. That was still the margin with about 35 seconds left when Michigan's Tim Hardaway Jr. shot a 3 in transition and missed.

Bill Self: The biggest play of that game … there was a loose ball under their basket (after Hardaway's missed 3) that Ben had a chance to dive on. We were up by five and we had the possession arrow. Even if Ben just dives and holds onto it, we'd have it. Instead he bent down to dribble it or pick it up, and somebody dove on it and took it from him, and they got a layup to cut it to three.

Johnson put Kansas back up five, 76-71, with two free throws with 21 seconds remaining, and then Burke cut it back to three after he quickly drove past the KU defense and scored a layup. Forced to foul, Michigan sent Johnson back to the line with 12.6 ticks left. The senior missed the front end of a one-and-one, and Hardaway grabbed the rebound and passed to Burke. Trailing 76-73, the Wolverines would have one more chance.

Kevin Young: I just remember looking down for a split second when their big man (McGary) fell down after Elijah ran into his screen. The next thing you know I'm looking back up and Burke has the ball a few feet away from me on the left wing—but way behind the line. He went up to shoot and I'm like, "Oh, he's shooting it from way out here? He's six feet past the 3-point line. He's way too far. All I have to do is put a hand up and we'll get the rebound and win." That ball hung up there forever and then, somehow, it ripped through the net. I was shocked when it went in.

Travis Releford: I couldn't believe Burke made that 3. Once it went in, that took all the momentum that we had and gave it all to them. I can't even remember how the overtime went. It all went by so fast after that shot. It was all a blur.

The lead changed hands five times in the extra period, and Kansas had a chance to tie or win when it got a stop with 9 seconds remaining. Trailing 87-85 on the

Kansas 87, Michigan 85
March 29, 2013 · Arlington, Texas

Kansas (31-6)

Player	MP	FG	3FG	FT	R	A	F	S	TO	B	TP
Elijah Johnson*	24	4-8	2-4	3-4	5	0	3	1	5	0	13
Ben McLemore*	39	8-15	4-8	0-0	2	1	4	0	1	1	20
Travis Releford*	42	6-10	0-0	4-4	5	6	1	1	1	0	16
Jeff Withey*	39	6-11	0-0	0-0	8	2	3	1	1	5	12
Kevin Young*	29	6-6	0-0	0-1	7	1	3	0	1	0	12
Perry Ellis	15	4-7	0-0	0-1	5	3	0	1	2	0	8
Naadir Tharpe	32	1-8	0-4	0-0	2	7	3	1	2	0	2
Jamari Traylor	5	1-1	0-0	0-0	0	1	0	0	0	2	2
Team					1						
Totals	225	36-66	6-16	7-10	35	21	17	5	13	8	85

Michigan (29-7)

Player	MP	FG	3FG	FT	R	A	F	S	TO	B	TP
Trey Burke*	44	9-21	4-11	1-1	2	10	3	1	4	0	23
Tim Hardaway Jr.*	39	4-11	1-3	1-2	5	3	3	0	0	0	10
Mitch McGary*	35	12-17	0-0	1-3	14	1	2	3	1	1	25
Glenn Robinson*	42	5-11	1-4	2-3	8	1	0	3	2	0	13
Nik Stauskas*	39	4-7	1-4	2-4	2	3	1	0	1	0	11
Spike Albrecht	11	1-1	1-1	0-0	1	0	2	0	1	0	3
Jon Horford	7	0-1	0-0	0-0	0	0	0	0	0	0	0
Caris LeVert	3	0-1	0-0	0-0	0	0	1	0	0	0	0
Jordan Morgan	5	0-1	0-0	2-4	3	0	0	0	0	0	2
Team					3				1		
Totals	225	35-71	8-23	9-17	38	18	12	7	10	1	87

	1st	2nd	OT	Total	FG%	3FG%	FT%
Kansas	40	36	9	85	54.5	37.5	70.0
Michigan	34	42	11	87	49.3	34.8	52.9

Officials: Karl Hess, Gary Maxwell, Lamar Simpson
Technicals: None

final possession, Johnson drove into the right side of the lane but penetrated too deep—he almost stepped on the baseline—to get a shot. So the senior fired a wild pass to Tharp on the left side of the perimeter, and his hurried, off-balance 3-pointer at the buzzer was well off the mark. The bumbled play capped a frustrating night for Johnson, who had three turnovers (including a 10-second violation in the backcourt) in the last four minutes of regulation and another in OT. Johnson had 13 points in his final game as a collegian along with five turnovers and no assists.

Ben McLemore: At the beginning, once Elijah did what he did to McGary, that right there should've told Coach Self that something was off with him. Something happened to him. He should've sat him down and figured out what was going on with him and let him get his mind right. When he started the game off like that, everyone was thinking, "What are you doing, Elijah?"

Travis Releford: It was a tough one for Elijah. He probably doesn't like talking about it. He hit McGary and they almost kicked him out of the game. I didn't even see it. I had my back turned and the next thing you know the guy is on the ground. I think that play kind of took Elijah out of the game mentally. It messed him up. I don't think he was the Elijah that everybody was used to seeing.

Elijah Johnson: I've never read blogs and stuff like that. But it killed me to hear that people thought I was trying to throw the Michigan game on purpose. I thought that was the craziest thing. Looking back at the situation, I was more aggressive that game than I'd been in a while. I was getting and-ones and talking all kinds of stuff. Being on that stage took me back and reminded me of playing in the Final Four the year before.

Ben McLemore: I've never talked to him about why he did that (to McGary). It's probably just something that happened in the spur of the moment. I doubt he planned it or anything. Sometimes people just do dumb things before really thinking it through. It's happened to me, too. It was a big stage. The stakes were high. There was a lot of pressure and Elijah just made a mistake. I've never brought it up to him. He wouldn't like talking about it, and I don't blame him. I don't like talking about it, either. There's no reason for one bad moment to overshadow all the good he did for KU over four years.

Jeff Withey: People give Elijah way too much grief for that game. That thing with Mitch McGary ... Mitch was a dirty player. Elijah wasn't going to take it from him. We were watching film of them before the game, and I remember Elijah telling me, "Hey man, I'm going to try to get him with an elbow, just so it gets him off of me and he doesn't try to knock my teeth out with a screen." I think he was just trying to set a tone and he accidentally went a little too low. He definitely made a mistake with the low blow. It happens. I do think It messed with his mind for the rest of the game—but we still had a shot at the end. That one thing didn't change the course of the game. I've heard a lot of people give him a hard time about that loss. But you know what? He gave it his all, both during that game and throughout his entire career. Elijah was a great teammate.

Bill Self: I thought Elijah had a great year. He just made the one bad play in the Sweet 16.

Ben McLemore: One of the leaders, including myself, should've stepped up. Instead we all made mistakes. It's easy to beat yourself up and look back and say, "We should've done this or that." But the bottom line is that we were up by 14 points with seven minutes left. We should've won that game.

Michigan beat Florida in the Elite Eight and Syracuse in the Final Four before falling to Louisville in the NCAA championship game in Atlanta.

Travis Releford: The way the brackets were set up for us that year, it should have been us and Louisville in the championship. Going into that game, I felt great about the team and the team we were playing against. They had some really great shooters and the big guy (McGary) was a really good screener and we knew that, and we knew what we needed to do to stay ahead. I think we did a pretty good job throughout the game, because I don't ever remember being down until they went up late. We had control up until Trey Burke made the shot to send it to overtime.

Kevin Young: That shot by Burke was the dagger. He was already so far out, and when he came off the screen he went backward. I stood my ground. I looked over because I was shocked there was no call on the screen. They were calling the game really tight. He shot it and I contested it and he made it. People don't let me forget that I was guarding him on that play. Every March someone will send me the clip on SnapChat or Instagram.

Bill Self: That team was good enough to get to the Final Four, but it wasn't one of our best teams. Withey had an unbelievable senior year. Kevin did what he could do. He was great. Elijah and Ben and Travis ... they all had really good years. But that wasn't one of our more talented teams.

Naadir Tharpe: It was tough being in that locker room, because we had so many guys that would never get that chance again. Elijah, Travis, Kevin Young, Withey ... they were seniors. That was it for them. And everyone knew Ben was gone. We had that game won and then everything just changed so fast. That's not how it should've ended.

A little more from ...

Ben McLemore: After the Ohio State game that season, the NBA buzz started. At that time, I was like, "I'm not even going to think about that stuff. I'm coming back next year, regardless." I was telling Naadir and Jamari and all my guys that I'd be coming back.

I was even saying that after we lost to Michigan. I was like, "I'm coming back. I want to win a championship." I probably just got caught up in the heat of the moment, but I really wanted to go out on a good note, and that loss was tough to take.

It all happened so fast. I was like, "What am I going to do?" There were guys in my corner—family and friends and AAU coaches—helping me through it. With the financial situation I was in with my family, I was like, "I've got to go. I've got to help my family out the best I can."

During the season, there was no pressure at all. I was focused on winning.

I hated to leave. I hate "what-ifs" and reminiscing about what could've been. But to this day, when I think about my time at Kansas, my mind just goes "what-if, what-if, what-if?"

What if I could've played that next year with Wayne and Wiggs and JoJo? What would things have been like? Would we have won a championship? I'll never know.

Johnson had a productive career at Kansas, but injuries limited his athleticism, which meant most fans never really saw what he was truly capable of on the floor.

Conner Teahan: I remember Elijah Johnson on his recruiting visit. He was standing at the free throw line. I think his shoes were untied. He took one dribble and did his between-the-legs 360 dunk. He was a freak.

Elijah Johnson: I don't look at the dudes I played with as my friends. I look at them as my brothers. If I was just out and about and had never played basketball, me and Kevin Young probably wouldn't be close friends. We're so different. But he's my brother. Same with Travis. He's very different than the rest of us. But he's my brother. I accept everyone for how they come.

I don't know any of these new guys in the program. I'd be lying if I said I was overseas studying which high school players are the best in the country or what college players are the best. Yeah, I check and see stuff every now and then. But I don't have it down to a tee. I wait until they sign and get on campus, because I don't care what Kentucky or UCLA or North Carolina or Duke did. I wait to see who comes to Kansas. I meet them and check them out. They have the same look on their face that I had on mine when I first arrived. They're getting thrown into the wind. They're confused, but they feel on top of the world.

Coach Self tells you from the get-go what it's like and how it's going to be. You either get on the boat or you watch it sail away. Coach Self is 96.3 percent the reasons this is happening. He picks the lotto numbers. He decides who he wants here. He tells them what to do. He puts the game plan together. He doesn't always get the guys he wants, and the ones he gets don't always do what he wants them to do. But he still figures it out every year.

Jeff Withey: We had a really good team, but we weren't as good as the year before, as evidenced by us losing to a team like TCU. There was something we were missing. Elijah was a great point guard, but his knees were a little shaky at the end of the year. That hurt us a little bit, even though he still had a really good year, especially since he was playing out of position. Travis definitely stepped up big that year and Kevin played great.

We were built to go pretty far in the tournament because we had seniors who had been through it. It was just unfortunate that Michigan hit those big shots to end it for us. Trey Burke just went off. It hurt going out that way, but when you look back on our time at KU, it was amazing.

Kevin Young: You've got to give most of the credit to Coach Self when it comes to the streak. He finds a way to win every year. It's not just about recruiting talent. It's about getting those talented players to play well with each other. Think about it: in one class, he had Joel Embiid, Andrew Wiggins, Wayne Selden and Frank Mason. Earlier in his career he had the twins at the same time as Sherron and Elijah and Tyshawn. To have all of those guys and keep their egos in check and continue to win ... it's amazing.

Jamari Traylor: I don't know how the Iowa State fans knew it, but that season right before we played there, I had a dog named "Sosa" that died. I looked into the crowd and someone had a sign making fun of it. They had a picture of me on the posterboard with my dog's name and something mean written next to it. I can't remember exactly what it said, but I was like, "Man, how did they know that?" He had just died a week earlier. After stuff like that I didn't even look in the stands anymore.

One guy I learned a lot from that most people probably wouldn't guess is Kevin Young. He did some things that I tried to copy as far as my energy plays and everything. There would be points in games where he'd come up and trap the ball. I saw that and I started doing it, and then Coach Self started putting me in just to do that. A lot of my energy plays and hustle were based on things I picked up from watching Kevin Young. I think our careers mirrored each other's in a lot of ways. He was a guy that didn't get nearly enough credit.

Elijah Johnson was a guy that showed me the ropes on and off the court as far as things I should do and how I should carry myself. Even now as a pro, I still come to Elijah for advice. He's a professional overseas and he knows a lot more than me because he's been doing it for a while now. Tyshawn always tries to help me out. When I trained in LA, I was with Thomas, as well. He tells me about everything. These guys are like my big brothers.

I'd played with Ben before college, because we were in an all-star game in Chicago.

We were out there dunking and everything. I was like, "You're going to Kansas, too?" We got pretty cool with each other. When I got to school he ended up being my roommate. He would do some amazing things in practice. He could glide and shoot. I didn't see many guys that could do the things he was doing. He did some amazing things.

Ben is also one of the most clumsy people I know. A lot of people wouldn't guess that, but it's true. He was always breaking stuff and falling, just being real goofy all the time. He'd drop stuff and trip as he was going up the stairs. As smooth and athletic as he is on the court, he's the exact opposite off of it. He was always tripping and stumbling. One time we were leaving Jefferson's and he had a big order of wings in a bag, and he tripped and dropped his food and ruined everything. We couldn't even eat it.

Barry Hinson: It wasn't uncommon for famous people to end up in our locker room after games. I remember one night when Jason Sudeikis and Rob Riggle, the actors and comedians, showed up after a big win. I'm sitting here and thinking, "Here are two guys that we've watched on Saturday Night Live or Hangover or whatever movie, and now they're in our locker room, and they're absolutely giddy." They seriously looked like kids in a candy store as they went around and talked to our players. They were starstruck. It blew my mind to see how excited those guys were. You'd have thought they were backstage at the Oscar's.

Another time (Hall of Fame Major League Baseball manager) Tommy LaSorda came into our locker room after a game. I can't remember who we'd played, but they weren't great. Anyway, LaSorda walks out of the restroom. He'd been at the urinal and didn't realize he'd dripped all over his gray pants. There were splashes of urine all down his leg. We're all just dying laughing.

So we're sitting there and LaSorda goes, "Hey Bill, great game, great atmosphere ... wow, what a game!" We hadn't played very well, and Bill said, "Yeah, it was OK but we didn't play very well." LaSorda put his hand out and stopped him. He said, "Bill, all wins are good. There are no bad wins." And Bill said, "You're right, you're right." I'm sitting there as a coach and I'm thinking, "I'm going to have my chance to be a head coach again one day, and I'm going to remember this. I'm going to enjoy every win." I'd never met Tommy LaSorda in my life, but that stuck with me. Now, after every win, regardless of how we play, I'm like, "Great win! Great win!" I appreciate them more.

2012-13 Season Summary

Results (31-6, 14-4)

November

9	Southeast Missouri State	W, 74 - 55
13	vs. Michigan State	L, 64 - 67
15	Chattanooga	W, 69 - 55
19	vs. Washington State	W, 78 - 41
20	vs. Saint Louis	W, 73 - 59
26	San Jose State	W, 70 - 57
30	vs. Oregon State	W, 84 - 78

December

8	Colorado	W, 90 - 54
15	Belmont	W, 89 - 60
18	Richmond	W, 87 - 59
22	@ Ohio State	W, 66 - 74
29	American University	W, 89 - 57

January

6	Temple	W, 69 - 62
9	Iowa State	W, 97 - 89
12	@ Texas Tech	W, 46 - 60
14	Baylor	W, 61 - 44
19	@ Texas	W, 59 - 64
22	@ Kansas State	W, 55 - 59
26	Oklahoma	W, 67 - 54
28	@ West Virginia	W, 56 - 61

February

2	Oklahoma State	L, 80 - 85
6	@ Texas Christian	L, 62 - 55
9	@ Oklahoma	L, 72 - 66
11	Kansas State	W, 83 - 62
16	Texas	W, 73 - 47
20	@ Oklahoma State	W, 67 - 68
23	TCU	W, 74 - 48
25	@ Iowa State	W, 96 - 108

March

2	West Virginia	W, 91 - 65
4	Texas Tech	W, 79 - 42
9	@ Baylor	L, 81 - 58
14	vs. Texas Tech	W, 91 - 63
15	vs. Iowa State	W, 88 - 73
16	vs. Kansas State	W, 70 - 54
22	vs. Western Kentucky	W, 64 - 57
24	vs. North Carolina	W, 70 - 58
29	vs. Michigan	L, 85 - 87

All-Big 12 Team

Player of the Year:
Marcus Smart, Oklahoma State, Fr., G

Defensive Player of the Year:
Jeff Withey, Kansas, Sr., C

Newcomer of the Year:
Will Clyburn, Iowa State, Sr., G

Freshman of the Year:
Marcus Smart, Oklahoma State, Fr., G

Sixth Man of the Year:
Tyrus McGee, Iowa State, Sr., G

Coach of the Year:
Bruce Weber, Kansas State

First Team
Ben McLemore, Kansas, Fr., G
Jeff Withey, Kansas, Sr., C
Rodney McGruder, Kansas State, Sr., G
Romero Osby, Oklahoma, Sr., F
Marcus Smart, Oklahoma State, Fr., G

Second Team
Pierre Jackson, Baylor, Sr., G
Will Clyburn, Iowa State, Sr., G
Travis Releford, Kansas, Sr., G
Angel Rodriguez, Kansas State, So., G
Markel Brown, Oklahoma State, Jr., G

Third Team
Isaiah Austin, Baylor, Fr., C
Melvin Ejim, Iowa State, Jr., F
Amath M'Baye, Oklahoma, Jr., F
Steven Pledger, Oklahoma, Sr., G
Le'Bryan Nash, Oklahoma State, So., G/F

Honorable Mention
Cory Jefferson, Baylor, Jr., F
Korie Lucious, Iowa State, Sr., G
Tyrus McGee, Iowa State, Sr., G
Elijah Johnson, Kansas, Sr., G
Shane Southwell, Kansas State, Jr., G
Michael Cobbins, Oklahoma State, So., C
Jaye Crockett, Texas Tech, Jr., F
Eron Harris, West Virginia, Fr., G
Deniz Kilici, West Virginia, Sr., F

All-Defensive Team
Chris Babb, Iowa State, Sr., G
Travis Releford, Kansas, Sr., G
Jeff Withey, Kansas, Sr., C**
Angel Rodriguez, Kansas State, So., G
Michael Cobbins, Oklahoma State, Fr., G
Marcus Smart, Oklahoma State, Fr., G**

All-Rookie Team
Isaiah Austin, Baylor, Fr., C
Will Clyburn, Iowa State, Sr., G
Georges Niang, Iowa State, Fr., F
Ben McLemore, Kansas, Fr., G**
Amath M'Baye, Oklahoma, Jr., F
Marcus Smart, Oklahoma State, Fr., G**

** Unanimous selection

Kansas Awards

Ben McLemore
Consensus All-American Second Team
NABC All-American Second Team
AP All-American Second Team
USBWA All-American Second Team
Sporting News All-American Third Team
CBE Classic All-Tournament

Jeff Withey
Consensus All-American Second Team
NABC All-American Third Team
NABC Defensive Player of the Year
AP All-American Third Team
USBWA All-American Second Team
Sporting News All-American Second Team
Big 12 Tournament MOP
CBE Classic All-Tournament

Perry Ellis
Big 12 Championship All-Tournament

Travis Releford
CBE Classic MVP

Season Stats

#	Player	CL	POS	HT	Hometown	G	GS	FG%	3P%	FT%	R	A	S	B	PTS
23	Ben McLemore	FR	G	6-5	St. Louis, MO	37	36	.495	.420	.870	5.2	2.0	1.0	0.7	15.9
5	Jeff Withey	SR	C	7-0	San Diego, CA	37	36	.582	1.000	.714	8.5	0.9	0.8	3.9	13.7
24	Travis Releford	SR	G	6-6	Kansas City, MO	37	36	.574	.415	.789	3.8	2.6	1.3	0.2	11.9
15	Elijah Johnson	SR	G	6-4	Las Vegas, NV	37	36	.382	.331	.763	3.1	4.6	0.9	0.2	9.9
40	Kevin Young	SR	F	6-8	Perris, CA	36	32	.562	.000	.596	6.8	1.2	1.1	0.6	7.8
34	Perry Ellis	FR	F	6-8	Wichita, KS	37	3	.475	.667	.738	3.9	0.6	0.4	0.3	5.8
1	Naadir Tharpe	SO	G	5-11	Worcester, MA	37	0	.343	.330	.886	1.5	3.1	0.6	0.0	5.5
3	Andrew White III	JR	G	6-7	Richmond, VA	25	0	.333	.278	.625	1.2	0.0	0.2	0.1	2.2
31	Jamari Traylor	FR	F	6-8	Chicago, IL	37	1	.429		.579	2.1	0.3	0.5	0.8	2.1
2	Rio Adams	FR	G	6-3	Seattle, WA	24	0	.400	.400	.385	0.3	0.3	0.3	0.0	1.1
10	Evan Manning	FR	G	6-3	Lawrence, KS	12	0	.429	.333		0.4	0.1	0.2	0.0	0.7
4	Justin Wesley	JR	F	6-9	Fort Worth, TX	19	0	.500		.600	1.1	0.2	0.1	0.0	0.4
11	Tyler Self	FR	G	6-2	Lawrence, KS	11	0	.333	.000	.000	0.2	0.2	0.0	0.0	0.4
20	Niko Roberts	JR	G	5-11	Huntington, NY	15	0	.143	.000	.500	0.3	0.2	0.2	0.0	0.3
21	Christian Garrett	SO	G	6-3	Los Angeles, CA	14	0	.000			0.3	0.1	0.0	0.0	0.0

CHAPTER 10

2013-14

One-and-Done

One good thing about Kansas fans is that they get over NCAA Tournament losses rather quickly—usually because there are so many reasons to be excited about the next season. No time period backs up that theory more than the spring and summer of 2013.

The only difference was that the majority of the offseason hype back then centered not on the team, but on a single player.

Tabbed as "the next LeBron" by Sports Illustrated before he ever graduated high school, Andrew Wiggins sent Jayhawks fans into a frenzy when he committed on May 14, choosing KU over Florida State, Kentucky and North Carolina. Later that month, autograph seekers tracked his flight from his native Canada to Kansas City and were waiting for Wiggins at the airport when his plane touched down. Some even followed his vehicle to Lawrence, where about 10,000 fans showed up in June to watch the nation's No. 1-ranked recruit compete in an open scrimmage.

"I've never seen anything like it," KU coach Bill Self said. "It was insane."

Wiggins may have been the main reason for the chatter, but he wasn't the only one. Seven-foot center Joel Embiid had recently shot up to No. 6 in the ESPN.com rankings and was hailed as the nation's best center. Wayne Selden, a wing, was a McDonald's All-American ranked No. 14 in his class and shooting guard Conner Frankamp, a Wichita native, was the all-time leading scorer in his city's history. Rounded out by gritty guard Frank Mason and sharpshooter Brannen Greene, KU (along with Kentucky) boasted one of the nation's top two recruiting hauls.

And everyone in Lawrence knew it.

Wayne Selden: It was like we were all rock stars when we first got there. I'd been asked for my autograph before, but never in restaurants or when I was just walking down the street. Everyday, students would come up to me and recognize me and ask to take pictures. I'd actually gotten a taste of it the previous fall at Late Night. I was a high school kid from New Hampshire, but everyone in Lawrence knew who I was. It was the type of feeling every kid wants to feel. It was new for me, and I loved it.

Late Night in the Phog was my first official visit, but I committed that weekend. I didn't want to be anywhere else. I wasn't used to that. We had me, Joel, Frank, Andrew... there was so much hype around our class. Everyone had such high expectations for us, and people were just so happy.

Landen Lucas: Even though it was my second year there, it was fun to be a part of it all. We realized how big of a deal everything was right before Late Night. We were inside Allen Fieldhouse eating, and we looked outside and there were thousands of people lined up, and then some of them got turned away. Then Coach Self called for an open practice a few weeks later and Allen Fieldhouse was packed. That kind of showed us how big that year was going to be, and how much hype our team was going to have.

And make no mistake. As excited as fans were to see all of Kansas' new players, Wiggins was the headliner, the guy who generated the most interest not just locally, but nationally, too.

Bill Self: The hoopla wasn't fueled by Andrew's family and it wasn't fueled by him. They were perfect. They were down to earth, humble people. Wiggs is as sweet of a young man as there is. He tried to shy away from the attention, but he couldn't hide from it. He was on the cover of everything. It was too much at times and it wasn't fair to him, but it was something he'd grown used to. By the time he got to Kansas, he already knew what it was like to be in the spotlight.

Assistant coach Kurtis Townsend: We got lucky to get in on Wiggs when we did. I was on my way to his high school, Huntington Prep in West Virginia, to recruit Xavier Rathan-Mayes, who ended up signing with Florida State. It was September of 2012 and, if you remember, Wiggs was initially supposed to be in the Class of 2014, so we hadn't started recruiting him yet. My plane landed, and their coach, Rob Fulford, called and said, "KT, are you on your way?" I told him I'd be there in 40 minutes and asked if everything was OK. He said, "I don't know if you read *USA Today*, but Wiggs just announced he's reclassifying to 2013." I was like, "Oh really?"

I got there and asked Wiggs if he'd be interested in Kansas. He was like, "I don't know much about it. Call my mom and dad." He gave me the number for his father, Mitchell, and I started recruiting him hard that month. I had seen him a few years earlier, as a freshman, in a tournament in Orlando. I thought he was Kobe Bryant, as quick and explosive as he was.

I followed him through high school and had always intended to recruit him hard. He was a Nike kid, though, and every school who was recruiting him was sponsored by Nike, except for us. He started asking me questions in the spring that gave me a clue we had a chance. He was like, "Coach, would I have to wear Adidas?" I told him that he had to wear Adidas during the games, but as far as walking around campus or around Lawrence, he could wear Nikes. He said that was fine. But I told him, "When it's time to sign with a shoe company after college, you need to go with whoever pays you the most money." He ended up going with Adidas because it gave him more money than Nike did.

Anyway, back to his recruitment ... Wiggs wasn't real big on talking on the phone. We mainly just texted. He saw me at all of his games. He knew how bad we wanted him. Sometimes he'd call me after he scored 25 and say, "Coach, I didn't play that good." I was thinking, "Yeah, right."

Eventually, he started asking me more questions, like whether he had to come to summer school. I started getting the feeling we were going to get him.

But I didn't know for sure where he was going until the day of his announcement, when he called and told us he was coming to Kansas. I'd been talking to his mom and his dad all along, and Grandma was big, too. Coach Self and I went up to Canada and visited with all of them, but not until after he committed.

Bill Self: It was easy to recruit a guy like Wiggs. I'm not saying it was easy to *get* him, because everyone wanted him. What I mean is, Wiggs didn't need to be shown a bunch of love. We didn't need to call him every day or send a certain amount of letters every week. He didn't care about that stuff. He knew everyone wanted him and he knew what each school had to offer. We gave him some space to make his decision. I think he appreciated that.

Assistant coach Jerrance Howard: I was at Illinois in 2005 when we made the Final Four. Dee Brown and Deron Williams and Luther Head ... the players on that Final Four team were like rock stars. They had to go through kitchens to get into restaurants and secret elevators to get to their hotel rooms because it was so crazy. It was like that with Wiggins. Fans wanted to see him and touch him. I've never seen anything like it. He was a celebrity. Wiggins justified the decision to build McCarthy Hall, where there was a little more privacy. It was already in the works, but that just solidified it.

I think the attention made him uncomfortable. He was turning down almost every media request. We had to force him to do a *GQ* photo shoot and force him to talk to *Sports Illustrated.* Most kids like that kind of thing, but all he wanted to do was play basketball.

Another addition to the Jayhawks that summer was Tarik Black, a former top-50 recruit who started for three years at Memphis before transferring to KU for his senior season.

Tarik Black: For his stature, Wiggins is the most humble person you'll ever meet. His humility is unbelievable. I think he had times when he was like, "Man, this is getting to be too much." But Wiggs had also grown used to it before he ever got there. He was the next best thing since sliced bread even in high school. His dad was an NBA player, his mom was an Olympic gold medalist (in track) and Andrew had been "the man" since eighth grade. People had been watching his YouTube highlights for years and he'd been projected as the No. 1 draft pick since his 11th grade year. He was raised in the spotlight.

Perry Ellis: He was a quiet, happy, goofy dude. Coach always messed with him.

Being from Canada, Wiggs used say, "Pardon me" a lot. So when Wiggs was guarding someone in practice, Coach would tell the player to say, "Pardon me" and just blow right past him. He was very polite and quiet. But he was a good kid and a great athlete.

Naadir Tharpe: What made it so cool was how he handled everything. If you knew Andrew Wiggins, you wouldn't even know that this guy was the No. 1 this or No. 1 that. His demeanor and how he moved through life was so smooth and humble. He didn't think he was better than anybody. He showed his team love. He understood, "We're all in this together." And we already knew he was special. We knew it was real big time when *Sports Illustrated* did the cover story and compared him to Wilt Chamberlain. That's when we figured out this guy was on a different level.

Kurtis Townsend: When we recruited Wiggs, we told him, "You could go to Kentucky and share (the spotlight) with everyone else, but is that what you want? And, yes, we know your parents went to Florida State, but there's no guarantee that they'll be in the NCAA Tournament every year. They're not even the best team in the ACC. You deserve to be at a school that's the best of the best, and where you'll be the best player on the team." Little did we know that Joel was going to come on and be just as good, especially that fast.

A native of Yaounde, Cameroon, Embiid didn't begin playing competitive basketball until he was 16, when he attended a camp in his native country hosted by NBA player Luc Richard Mbah a Moute.

After the final session, Mbah a Moute tabbed Embiid—who was 6-9 at the time—as one of the top five performers at the camp, with the reward being an invitation to attend a larger, more prestigious event, Basketball Without Borders, in Johannesburg, South Africa, the following month. Despite his inexperience, Embiid held his own against the elite competition, making it obvious that basketball was his future.

After finally getting the blessing of his father—who had wanted his son to pursue a volleyball career in Europe—Embiid left Cameroon for Lake County, Fla., and Montverde Academy, which is also Mbah a Moute's alma mater.

Montverde coach Kevin Boyle: A few of our kids were laughing at him during our first practice because he was really clumsy, dribbling the ball off his feet and stumbling around a little bit. I told Joel to go get a drink of water and then I called our players to center court. I said, "Laugh all you want, but in five years, you're going to be asking him for a loan, because he's going to be worth about $50 million." I told them, "You have no idea how good this kid is going to be."

Then an assistant at Florida, Norm Roberts had been recruiting Embiid for the Gators. But when he joined KU's staff for his second stint in the summer of 2012, he immediately told Self about the up-and-coming prospect.

Norm Roberts: We watched one of his AAU games and I asked Coach, "Well, what do you think?" He didn't say anything for a few seconds, and I was like, "Listen, I know he's raw. I know he's a project and all, but ..."

Then Bill interrupted me and was like, "Are you frickin' kidding me? This dude could be the No. 1 pick in the draft. He can run. He's got good feet. He's got touch. He's unbelievable. He'll be the best big man we've ever coached if we can get him."

Bill Self: I fell in love with him. I thought he could be the best kid I ever recruited.

Joel Embiid: I took my visit during Late Night, and it was crazy. Wayne was there, too. We walked in there and everyone started clapping and yelling. I didn't know what was going on. I was scared. I was like, "Are they clapping for us?" I just looked down at the ground. I couldn't believe it.

In November of 2012, Embiid—who had transferred to The Rock, a prep school in Gainesville, Fla.—announced he'd chosen Kansas from a list of favorites that also included Florida and Texas. He arrived in Lawrence the following summer having played just one year of varsity high school basketball.

Joel Embiid: I was pretty nervous, but I also knew that I was young. I'd only been playing basketball for a few years, so I really didn't expect to do very much my first year.

The first time we played pickup basketball, I got dunked on by Tarik. It was in front of a bunch of people, like the women's basketball team. I was so embarrassed. I felt like I was the worst player out there. I went up to Coach Self after practice and told him I wanted to redshirt.

Bill Self: After the very first practice, he came to me and said, "Coach, I'm not good enough. I'm going to need to redshirt." I said, "Nahhhh, I think you'll be OK, big fella."

Joel Embiid: I didn't think I was ready, but he told me not to worry about it. He said, "If you work hard enough, you'll be the No. 1 pick in the draft after your sophomore year."

I remembered hearing during the recruiting process that college coaches lie a lot. At that time I didn't know Coach Self very well, so I figured he was just making all that stuff up. I was just like, "OK, whatever." But he kept telling me, "Just keep working hard. You'll see."

Embiid drew Self's ire during an intrasquad scrimmage at Late Night in the Phog. Self had told players to have fun and to "show their personality" at the annual event, and Embiid responded by hoisting ill-advised shots, attempting fancy passes and dribbling behind his back a few too many times.

Bill Self: I told them to have fun, and he thought that meant jumping around and acting stupid while the game was going on.

Norm Roberts: Coach got on him pretty good. He was like, "You looked like a jackass out there. I don't know about you, Jo. Your attitude stinks. You're soft. I don't know if I can coach you, Jo. Maybe you should just take your ass back to Cameroon."

I called him the next night and his voice was all soft. He said he was at the gym, shooting by himself. I went up there and he was like, "Coach is not pleased. He's not happy with me at all." I told him, "That's because he knows you can be great. He's not going to treat you with kid gloves when your attitude isn't right. He's trying to bring out the best in you." He nodded and said he understood. He really took off after that.

One thing about Joel … he was good with the guys. He was funny. When Joel was with us, we had Tarik and those guys, so he was kinda looked at as 'Little Joel,' the little baby. He was immature and goofy, but he engaged with his teammates. But then he'd get on the court and become a different person. He'd act like a 17- or 18-year off the court. But then he'd step onto it and he'd carry himself like he was 25 or 26.

When we first got Joel, I was worried about whether he'd understand the offense and what we were trying to do. But Coach would show him plays, and and he never had to go over it twice with Joel. After a while, we'd throw it to him in the post, and he'd start telling the guards what to do. *"Cut! Cut! Set a screen!"* We couldn't believe it.

Perry Ellis: JoJo was one of the smartest athletes I've ever been around. He picked up things so quickly. If you told it to him, he'd understand immediately.

Jason King: In October, a few days after the start of official workouts, I requested a pass to practice because I wanted to get a good glimpse of Wiggins to see what the hype was about. After about 10 minutes, though, I couldn't take my eyes off of Embiid. The way he moved, the touch on his shot, his coordination, his ball skills for a 7-footer … I was flabbergasted. Then he started draining 3s. And he was talking noise, too, which I loved. At that point in my career I'd been covering college basketball for 13 years, so a decent amount of time. And I had never seen anything like Embiid at the college level. I seriously felt like I was in the presence of a once-in-a-lifetime type of talent.

Jerrance Howard came up to me after the workout and asked me what I thought. I said, "You've got the No. 1 pick on your team, all right, but it's not Wiggins. It's him." I pointed at Embiid and Jerrance started laughing. I was like, "What? Am I missing something? Am I a bad judge of talent? Or are you laughing because I'm right?" He just put his finger up to his lips and went, "Shhhhh!"

Jerrance Howard: We knew at an early stage—basically from the day he touched down in Kansas—that Jo was going to be special. He'd go through the entire practice without shooting a 3-pointer, because he knew that wasn't going to be a part of the game plan. But once the workout was over, and all of the NBA scouts had left, he'd stand at the top of the key and say "Coach Self, watch this." And then he'd make 20 or 22 three-pointers and then just walk off the court. He's showing off, kinda like, "Yeah, I can do this, too." He was just messing with us.

Everything was so natural, from his left to his right jump hook. He was so smart. He knew all five positions. He knew where everyone was supposed to be. He had a high IQ. When you have a high IQ and you're skilled and athletic and have good footwork, that's a scary combination.

BEST OF THE STREAK

MOST CANDID KU PLAYERS

1. Keith Langford: A journalism major, Langford was not only honest with the media, he shared his opinions with the coaching staff—at times, to a fault.

2. Tyshawn Taylor: Ask KU beat writers their favorite KU player to cover, and Taylor is a popular answer. He gave colorful answers and treated everyone with respect.

3. Tarik Black: He arrived at Kansas older than his teammates as a graduate transfer, and he was even wiser beyond his years.

4. Elijah Johnson: A deep thinker, no one put more thought into his answers than Johnson.

5. J.R. Giddens: He was confident in his abilities, and he let everyone know it. In fact, some might say Giddens was downright cocky.

6. Russell Robinson: Off the court, he was as nice a guy as you'll ever meet. But he wasn't afraid to voice his feelings if you crossed him.

7. Sherron Collins: One of the all-time great Jayhawks is a reporter's dream, not afraid to say anything and an awesome storyteller.

8. Marcus Morris: Teammates said he was hilarious. He could also be mean, usually to opponents. Marcus could fill a notebook with his feats on the floor and words off it.

9. Landen Lucas: He spent five years in Lawrence, so he was the elder statesman and he acted like it. Similar to Tarik Black, Lucas was an old soul who saw the bigger picture.

10. Joel Embiid: JoJo has become the most entertaining character—especially on social media—in the NBA. That wasn't always on display at KU, but he was still hilarious—at one point convincing reporters he killed a lion as a child.

Tarik Black: I showed up on campus in August of 2013, right after I graduated from Memphis. Most of the newcomers—Andrew, Frank, Wayne and Joel—had been there earlier that summer, but they'd gone back home to relax for a few weeks before the start of the fall semester.

Before Joel got back on campus, Coach Self called me into his office to have a talk about him. He was like, "Tarik, Joel is going to be really good. I'm not sure how good he'll be *this* year or how long it's going to take. But I want you to work with him. He's a freshman and you're a senior. This is *your* time. Once you leave here, I want him to be ready." I told him I'd help as much as I could. That's the type of guy I am. I don't care if someone plays my position. If I can take him under my wing, I'll do it. Nobody can stop what's meant for me and my future. I believe that wholeheartedly. God's got me. I'm OK.

When JoJo got on campus, we played pickup ball and I saw how talented he was, although right at first he didn't play too well. He wasn't just out there killing everyone. What stood out to me more, and what made me think he was a one-and-done, was watching him in his workouts. He was a 7-foot guy with a 7-foot-to-infinity wingspan, shooting right- and left-handed hooks, and he had good footwork. I'd been around the college game for a while and seen the No. 1 draft picks. I had seen and played against talent. I could just recognize that he had all the tools. I was like, "This guy is going to be a problem for people."

Whenever we had free time, I'd go to his room and say, "C'mon, we're going to work out." I'd take him to the gym and teach him little things and, man, he just started taking off. I remember during those summer workouts one day, me and him were in the locker room. We got in the hot tub. It was just me and him. By that time I realized how talented he was. Being a senior, I knew how fast the college season goes by and how overwhelming it can be for kids that age. I also know how quickly guys can progress during their freshman year because I'd done it myself. Sitting in that hot tub, JoJo was like, "I don't know how good I'm going to be. I don't know how long it's going to take." I told him, "JoJo, I'm willing to bet you're going to be one-and-done." He laughed and was like, "No, no. I'm not ready for it. I'm not mature enough. I'm not talented enough. That won't happen." I was like, "OK, let's see how things pan out and let's have this conversation again midway through the season."

Jerrance Howard: It was a big brother, little brother relationship. Everyone really embraced Tarik for the way he embraced Jo because, when you think about it, Jo took his spot. Tarik wasn't happy at first. But Jo was so good that Tarik had to accept it. He had to honor it. He did it in a way where it made him better, Jo better and our team better. Jo was super-talented but he could be a little immature when things weren't going his way. Tarik would say, "Get your head up, stop pouting and go a little bit harder. Coach is pushing us because he wants to win." He stayed with him after practice and challenged him and went right at him. Jo wouldn't have been as good as he was if it wasn't for Tarik.

Joel Embiid: Tarik is a great guy. He went out of his way to be nice to me. I was actually kind of surprised by it, because I was the main reason he lost his starting position, but he was still helping me. He was like my big brother.

Bill Self: Tarik Black is, without question, one of the best teammates we've had here. He was a graduate transfer. It was his last year to play. He came here with dreams of winning a national championship. He was staring over Joel. But Tarik, if you remember, had more fouls than points five games into the season. We put Joel into the starting lineup to replace him, and I think Tarik realized, from a talent standpoint, that this dude was different. He was special. He became his mentor, and then Tarik ended up having a great year for us. Tarik had all of the intangibles, all of the good ones. Signing him was one of the best decisions we made.

Tarik Black: When I signed with Memphis, we had the No. 1-ranked recruiting class in the country. We had a really talented team, but we didn't live up to the glory—and that includes me, in particular. I had a lot of accolades to live up to. You know how every player has their time? My time was supposed to be my sophomore year. I was in all of the preseason mock drafts, including some that had me in the lottery. I was featured in *Sports Illustrated*. I had all of these things lined up and they all fell through, and then the whole situation at Memphis fell through. After my junior year I knew I needed a change of scenery. I'd grown up in Memphis and then gone to college there. I'd been there my whole life. I needed to get out of Memphis and try something different. I decided to transfer.

I didn't know what was going to happen. I didn't know that Kansas and Duke and all these schools were going to call me. It didn't matter. I just wanted to get out of Memphis. With the graduation rule and me getting my diploma, I knew I could play immediately. So I threw my name out there and, lo and behold, I was getting calls from everywhere. In the spring of 2014, I was probably the No. 1 recruit in the country behind Andrew Wiggins.

Me and Coach Self talked when he came to my house to recruit me. He was like, "Well Tarik, I'm at your house. I like you. I like how talented you are and what you can do. But if you come to Kansas, I want you to be a leader for us. I've seen you play. You can play pretty well. But at the same time, I see you as an older statesman on a team full of young guys. I need someone to help me in leading some of these young dudes." I knew when I signed that that would be a major part of my role there.

I visited Kansas, Georgetown, Oregon and Duke and I also looked at Ohio State.

But I was particularly interested when Coach Self called me, because I already had so much respect for Kansas because it was Big Man U. All of the big men that go to Kansas end up playing professionally, if not in the NBA then overseas. I'd played against the Morris twins and Thomas Robinson my freshman year at Madison Square Garden. I always thought we were similar. We all have similar builds. We're all athletic, 6-foot-9 guys. Their success made me put Kansas high on my list.

But what sold me, too, was when Coach Self showed up at my house for my home visit. He came all by himself. No other school did that. Most schools assign an assistant to make most of the calls and do most of the recruiting, and then the head coach shows up at the end to close the deal. But Coach Self recruited me all by himself. I don't think I talked to anyone else from KU during that time. Every text and every call was from him. He'd say, "Tarik, I just want you to know that I want you." Then I went on the visit. I just felt good with the guys. I was like, "Kansas is the place for me."

One of the last players KU's staff discovered during the 2013 recruiting cycle was Mason, a Virginia native who had originally committed to Towson. Townsend first watched Mason in a back gym at a Las Vegas tournament near the end of the summer of 2012.

Kurtis Townsend: I actually went to watch Jordan McLaughlin, who went to USC. But Frank kicked his ass and was glaring at him the whole time. I called his AAU coach and said, "Does he play like that every game?" The coach said, "He does. He'll play like that every game." Frank asked his coach, "Do you think Kansas recognized me?" I told him to tell Frank I'd be back to watch his game the next day. They got back from that tournament and he said, "Do you think Kansas will call me?" I did and he said, "Coach, Kansas is the only place I want to go."

Naadir Tharpe: Coach Self told me we had a recruit coming in and he wanted me to show him around. I took Frank to Jefferson's, and I asked him what other schools he was considering. He named the other schools, and they were all low mid-majors. I'm like, "You don't need to go to any of those schools. You need to come here." He said, "Yeah, I don't know. I think so." By the end of the trip he told me, "I'm coming to Kansas. I'm going to commit. I'm coming here."

Kurtis Townsend: We were recruiting Cat Barber, who went to North Carolina State, Demetrius Jackson (Notre Dame) and Chris Jones (Louisville). Those were all ahead of him. I told Coach, "If we don't sign any of them, Frank will come and stay all four years, and he'll be second-team all-league by his junior year." Coach said, "What? You're saying he'll be one of the best players in the league by his junior year?" He actually ended up being second-team all-league as a sophomore.

Fifth-ranked Kansas opened the 2013-14 season with five straight wins, the highlight being a 94-83 victory over No. 4 Duke at the United Center in Chicago. Wiggins scored 16 of his 22 points in the second half against the Blue Devils and Jabari Parker, the nation's No. 2-ranked recruit. Still, as good of a moment as it was for Wiggins, there were some maddening ones in store, too.

The Jayhawks started 5-0 but then lost three of four games during a frustrating stretch for the country's most talked-about player. Wiggins scored just 10 points in a loss to Villanova in the semifinals of the Battle 4 Atlantis in the Bahamas and only six in the third place game against Texas-El Paso the next day. Wiggins only made 28.8 percent from 3-point range (14-of-45) in non-conference play and, at times, seemed disengaged and passive.

Andrew Wiggins: Everything was moving so fast for me at first. Coach would get on me for not being aggressive or not running the floor hard every possession. He was hard on me. He was hard on everyone. He doesn't care who you are.

Kurtis Townsend: He was facing all sorts of double-teams and junk defenses. I remember him stopping by my office and saying, "Is it always going to be like this? All of these defenses are geared to stop me. I'm not getting any run-outs. I can't get a good look. I can't get a good shot." I think he thought he'd just come here and score 20 points a game and have a blast.

There's a ton of stuff he wasn't ready for.

Even though he'd attracted attention in high school, Wiggins was overwhelmed with how the spotlight intensified in college—especially at a tradition-rich school such as Kansas. By the end of September, Wiggins had conducted individual, one-on-one interviews with reporters from USA Today, Sports Illustrated, Sporting News, CBSSports.com, ESPN Insider, ESPN The Magazine and ESPN television. When a reporter from 60 Minutes called in October and requested an interview, Wiggins told Self he'd had enough.

Bill Self: He was like, "Coach, do I have to?" It was just wearing him down. He's not a kid that embraces that kind of stuff. In college, you should have a favorable experience and enjoy it. Instead all the extra stuff was making him miserable. We had to shut it down.

Norm Roberts: I never felt he was totally engaged. Wiggs was a nice, private type of kid. He'd come to practice, finish, laugh and joke on the court for a few minutes, and then he was gone. We'd have a get-together at Coach's house, and he'd show up for a half-hour, and then he was gone. Wiggs liked being around his teammates, but he was worried about himself a little more. He was just a little bit different.

Of course, he was from Canada, so that played a part in it. He'd be like, "You guys cuss so much. Y'all think that because I don't cuss and because I say "Pardon me" that Canadians aren't tough." We'd tease him and say, "What war has Canada ever won?" He was fun to be around, but I don't think he was totally engaged. Wiggs would have opportunities where we could do some circus-like dunks, and he'd just lay it in lightly. Coach was like, "Wiggs, show off your athletic ability. Show it off!" And he'd be like, "OK, Coach, maybe next time."

But he was the nicest kid, the best kid ever. We all loved him. We never had any troubles with him. One time he was walking down the hall wearing some KU sweatpants we had given him that were way too short. They were supposed to go down past his ankle but they damn near stopped right below his kneecap. I was like, "Wiggs, you're the No. 1 player in America. You're going to be the No. 1 draft pick. Get some sweats that fit." He was like, "It doesn't matter to me, Coach. I'll wear whatever you give me."

While Wiggins was struggling with consistency issues, Embiid was beginning to flourish thanks, in part, to the opportunities he was getting when Black would go to the bench with foul trouble. Black committed at least three fouls in all but one of KU's first three games and averaged just 11.1 minutes and 3.5 points during that span.

Embiid replaced Black in the starting lineup in the ninth game of the season, a 67-61 loss at No. 19 Florida on Dec. 10. Four days later, however, in a meeting with New Mexico at the Sprint Center, Embiid became a national name with an 18-point, four-block effort in KU's 80-63 win. But it wasn't Embiid's stat line that generated the most buzz.

Landen Lucas: I remember I went into his room a week before the New Mexico game, and he was watching videos of Hakeem Olajuwon. He told me about how he liked watching him, and then he showed me a YouTube clip of one of Hakeem's moves that he liked. I forgot about it until a couple of days later, when Joel did it at practice. It was the exact same move we had been watching in his room on YouTube, and he did it to perfection. I was like, "Oh, he's a quick learner."

Still, it's one thing to do it in practice. To do it in a game is completely different. But a few days later he did it against New Mexico. He called it "The Dream Shake." I haven't seen too many post moves make SportsCenter Top 10, but his did. It was crazy. In just a few days he'd found a video on YouTube of a guy doing something 99.9 percent of the country probably couldn't do, taught it to himself and used it in a game in front of thousands of people. That's when I knew he was on a different breed. I've never seen anybody progress like he did. There were times when he would do something and everybody would look at each other in awe, and that was just in practice.

Wayne Selden: He got so good so fast. Joel would be in his room calling me in. "Hey Wayne. Look at this. Look at this. Look at this." It'd be Hakeem Olajuwon on YouTube doing moves. He's like, "I'm going to do this move tomorrow, and they're not going to be able to stop me."

He goes out and just does the move and it's so effortless how he picked up on things and became that much better so fast.

Joel Embiid: The New Mexico game is when the hype started picking up. That's what opened everybody's eyes. I was actually surprised myself with "The Dream Shake." That was a pretty good move. For the two years I was in high school and my first year at Kansas, I had a tape of Hakeem that was 45 minutes long. I'd watch it nearly every day and then come in and try to repeat the same move by myself. I'd do it over and over until I got it.

Coach Self pushed me a lot. He talked to me and encouraged me. At the same time, he was on me all the time. He was trying to make me better. That's what I loved about him. I started to realize that, every time he was hard on me, it was part of his plan. In practice, he would put me on the second team. I'd be the only one who could shoot the ball. He'd literally say, "Play through Joel. Joel is the only person who's allowed to shoot." Offensively, that really made me better than most people realized. Obviously on the court I didn't feel as comfortable showing my skill set as I am in the NBA. But he helped me by pushing me a lot. He was talking a lot of trash, too. I loved that. If someone tells me I can't do something or if someone pushes me, that makes me want to do better.

The Story Behind the Goggles

Kansas opened Big 12 play with a 90-83 win at Oklahoma. Embiid wore goggles to protect his left eye and had one of his worst games in Big 12 play with six points, six rebounds, one blocked shot, three turnovers and four fouls. It was reported that he "caught a blow" from center Hunter Mickelson in practice. There was a little more to the story than that.

Wayne Selden: That was during a time when we were trying to be tougher. Coach Self thought we were technically a "soft" team. So after a practice leading into that OU game, he had us do a rebounding drill where you just throw it up and go get the ball. No rules. Just go get it. They threw the ball up and Hunter elbowed JoJo in the eye. That's why JoJo was wearing the goggles. He fell down and then got up, not looking, and winds up and swings as hard as he can. Just swung wild. *"I'm going to f**k you up! I'm going to f**k you up!"* Hunter ducked it and then JoJo took another swing and fell back, and then we separated them. They took him to the trainer. His eye was messed up.

JoJo definitely had an edge to him. One day during pickup, he saved Brannen Greene. Brannen was talking trash to Frank, and Frank's not about the talking. Frank's not going to talk with you. Frank told Brannen, "Hey, keep that talking up and see what happens." Then JoJo set a screen on Frank, who was already mad. Frank said, "You set a screen like that again and I'm gonna..." You can fill in the blank. So JoJo came right back down the court and set another screen the exact same way, and they just went right straight to squaring up. I think they swung a couple times and hit each other once or twice before we broke it up.

Too Much Noise

Kansas' conference-opening victory over Oklahoma was followed by the Sunflower State showdown against No. 25 K-State at Allen Fieldhouse. Now in his second season with the Wildcats, Bruce Weber was willing to try anything he could to avoid a blowout like the 83-62 thumping his squad had endured one year earlier in Lawrence.

K-State forward Thomas Gipson: Frank (Martin) already knew what it was like to play at Allen Fieldhouse when he took over, because he had been there the year before as an assistant with Bob Huggins. He was always prepared for it. My freshman year (in 2011-12), I didn't know what to expect, and he told me, "It's a crazy place, a crazy environment." It was something I had to see for myself, and I did.

On the flip side, that next year, when we won the Big 12, Coach Weber didn't realize what it was going to be like. The players knew it was crazy. The players knew about the sound. But Coach Weber and his staff didn't. They'd heard about it but never experienced it, and we got beat really bad. One of the assistant coaches was like, "Yo, this is the loudest gym I've ever been in by far, hands down." A lot of the staff was surprised.

So the next year, my junior year (in 2013-14), Coach Weber came up with a new way to prepare. He used a crowd simulator on our speakers while we were practicing. The whole week leading up to that game, we were having to practice with that noise. We had to talk over it and listen to Coach over it. It was like we were in Allen Fieldhouse.

K-State coach Bruce Weber: Through the years whether it's Indiana, Purdue, Michigan State ... places like that in rivalry games—or even the Illinois-Missouri game in St. Louis—it continually stays loud. But Allen Fieldhouse was impressive. The energy in the building and the hype from the crowd was incomparable. You definitely could tell that it helps their players perform at a high level.

The big thing we found out the first time was how hard it was to call out plays or switch defenses or whatever. It's just really tough to communicate over that noise. You go to football practice, and Coach (Bill) Snyder always uses the noise simulator at the stadium and puts the speakers on. So we tried it in our gym. We played some four-minute segments where you couldn't look at the bench; you just had to play the game and keep attacking. So we tried to simulate it a little bit, but obviously it didn't help too much.

Thomas Gipson: The scary thing is that you can't simulate Allen Fieldhouse. Bruce did the best he could, but I lost all four years in Allen Fieldhouse.

Bruce Weber: They played at a high level. The big guy (Embiid) just played so well and then Wiggins. They were still trying to find themselves. It was early in the conference season, and they were still trying to figure it out a little bit. They were good, don't get me wrong, but I don't think they had that chemistry going yet.

Still, once they got going and got running, whew, it was an avalanche we couldn't stop. They beat us pretty soundly.

K-State's Marcus Foster had been one of the best players in the Big 12 up to that point. He'd been named National Freshman of the Week a few days before the KU game, but he was outplayed by the Jayhawks' young stars in KU's 86-60 win. Foster scored just seven points on 3-of-12 shooting. Wiggins (22 points), Selden (20 points) and Embiid (12 points) all reached double figures for Kansas.

Thomas Gipson: I knew Embiid would be good. Me and Shane Southwell said all the time that someone must've sat him down and said, "Watch Hakeem Olajuwon play, because you're going to be just like him." His skill set is nice. He's 7-foot and people think he's skinny. No, he's not skinny. He's strong as hell. He's 250 now. Maybe 260. He was a big boy and he had moves, too. It was a big challenge for me being 6-7 going against him. I've always been used to going against bigger guys, but skill-wise, he's the most-skilled player I ever went up against. He was the best big I went up against. I probably respected him more than any KU player I ever faced. He didn't talk much on the court. He just did his job.

America, Meet Joel Embiid

The hype surrounding Embiid was building when No. 15 Kansas traveled to Ames to face No. 8 Iowa State on Jan. 13. By the time the night was over, there weren't many basketball fans in America who didn't know his name.

Joel Embiid: I remember having a bad first half (four points and two rebounds), and Coach Self got on me really bad in the locker room. He got on Wiggs, too. He was on all of us for playing bad, even though we were tied.

I came out in the second half and I was unstoppable on offense. Defensively I was all over the place. I was playing out of the double teams and no one could stop me. That's all because Coach was in my head, talking s**t and letting me know that I needed to play better, and I did.

Tarik Black: JoJo had been playing really well, but that game is when he really turned it on. That's when people were like, "OK, this kid is going to be the No. 1 draft pick this year." He almost single-handedly won that game.

Kansas opened the second half on a 16-5 run, turning a 36-36 tie at intermission into a 52-41 lead. Tharpe scored a season-high 23 points and Wiggins had 17 points and 19 rebounds. Still, even though his stat line wasn't as gaudy, it was Embiid who generated the most buzz. He scored 12 of his 16 points after intermission, blocked five shots and frustrated Iowa State forward Georges Niang into a 4-for-20 performance from the field.

Wayne Selden: Georges is so crafty. We were high school teammates, and no one could ever guard him. Nerlens (Noel) was on that team, too, and when he and Nerlens first got in the gym, Nerlens would mess with him and wouldn't let him score. But they were in the gym so much that Georges eventually figured him out. I had never seen anybody be able to guard him until we played Steven Adams, and it was when Steven Adams had a bare face. He looked like he was 17, and Steven Adams was putting that s**t on the glass—each side, each side.

When Georges got to college, he really took his game to the next level and slimmed down, but that was the funniest moment seeing him get a little frustrated. Georges is one of the best offensive players I ever played with, but he couldn't do anything against JoJo. Every other year, he killed us and he talked a lot of stuff. A few years later he was like, "I always killed y'all—except when you had Embiid down there."

Joel Embiid: Niang was good. Offensively he was so sneaky. He's not athletic, but he's crafty and he knows how to score the basketball. Being 7-feet gave me an advantage. And me being a big man and being able to move the way I do really gave him some challenges.

Georges Niang: I remember watching him on film before the game and thinking, "Man, he has better post moves than me and he's 7-foot—and he can shoot! His whole game translated to the NBA. It was tough to do anything against him.

Iowa State guard Naz Mitrou-Long: The way he dominated that game was insane. They dominated us. I hated that feeling.

Iowa State coach Fred Hoiberg: Embiid's performance against us at Hilton was one of the best I'd ever witnessed.

Joel Embiid: At the end of that game, at his press conference, Coach Hoiberg called me the best player in college basketball. I see him now in the NBA, when we play Chicago. We still joke about that. But that was definitely the game. After that night, people started saying, "This guy could be the No. 1 pick."

Kansas 77, Iowa State 70
January 13, 2014 · Ames, Iowa

Kansas (12-4)

Player	MP	FG	3FG	FT	R	A	F	S	TO	B	TP
Perry Ellis*	27	4-13	0-0	0-3	6	1	4	0	2	0	8
Joel Embiid*	28	7-8	0-0	2-3	9	2	5	2	7	5	16
Wayne Selden*	33	2-7	1-5	2-2	3	6	2	0	1	0	7
Naadir Tharpe*	36	7-9	3-4	6-7	6	4	1	1	4	0	23
Andrew Wiggins*	38	7-16	1-5	2-4	19	3	3	1	6	1	17
Tarik Black	5	1-2	0-0	0-0	1	0	5	0	0	0	2
Conner Frankamp	1	0-1	0-1	0-0	0	0	0	0	1	0	0
Brannen Greene	4	0-1	0-0	0-0	1	0	1	0	0	0	0
Frank Mason	9	1-2	0-1	0-0	0	0	2	0	0	0	2
Jamari Traylor	19	1-2	0-0	0-0	5	0	3	0	3	0	2
Justin Wesley	0+	0-0	0-0	0-0	0	0	0	0	0	0	0
Team					3						
Totals	200	30-61	5-16	12-19	53	16	26	4	24	6	77

Iowa State (14-2)

Player	MP	FG	3FG	FT	R	A	F	S	TO	B	TP
Melvin Ejim*	37	5-15	2-5	3-3	5	0	5	3	3	0	15
Dustin Hogue*	35	3-10	0-1	7-8	9	0	3	0	0	0	13
DeAndre Kane*	37	6-13	1-3	8-16	8	3	1	4	2	0	21
Naz Long*	16	0-2	0-2	0-0	3	1	1	0	0	0	0
Georges Niang*	31	4-20	0-9	3-4	6	3	3	0	2	0	11
Monte Morris	28	3-5	0-1	1-2	1	4	3	4	0	0	7
Matt Thomas	16	1-5	1-4	0-1	2	1	1	1	0	3	3
Team					2				1		
Totals	200	22-70	4-25	22-34	36	12	17	12	8	3	70

	1st	2nd	Total	FG%	3FG%	FT%
Kansas	36	41	77	49.2	31.3	63.2
Iowa State	36	34	70	31.4	16.0	64.7

Officials: Gary Maxwell, Tom Eades, Joe DeRosa
Technicals: None

Naadir Tharpe: The better JoJo got, the better everyone else got. He made the game so much easier for everybody. Who are you going to guard? Are you going to double JoJo? Cool, we'll just go to Wiggs. You going to double Wiggs? Fine, we'll throw it to Wayne. You going to try to double team Wayne? Go ahead, we've got knockdown shooters. With JoJo on the floor, it opened up everything and took some pressure off of guys, especially on the defensive end. Because now anybody who was going to try to get layups or dunk on us, we had another Jeff Withey back in the building. It was JoJo. He was blocking everything and that got us fast breaks. That just got us excited.

Tarik Black: Right around that time, not long after that Iowa State game, we were back sitting in the same hot tub at KU, just me and him again, like we had been back in the summer. I said, "Do you remember the conversation we had before the season?" He just started laughing and flicking water at me. He didn't want to answer me. By that time I thought he could be the No. 1 draft pick. A few months ago, Andrew was the clear-cut No. 1 draft pick, but now everyone realized it was up in the air. So I said again, "You don't remember that conversation?" He just started shaking his head. That's what he does when he knows you're right but doesn't want to admit it. I said, "Jo, you're super-talented. You're starting to develop. Big things are about to happen for you." He just turned and faced the wall and shook his head.

I poured as much energy as I could into him. I saw a kid who was super-talented and needed some direction. That's just how my heart is. I didn't care that he played my position or that he could take minutes away from me. That didn't bother me. I knew that's what was meant for me to do. I wanted to help him mature. The talent was there. I wanted to help him mentally and be there for him. His family wasn't there. They were in Africa. I took it personal. I was like, "Man, he needs someone around that cares about him, especially considering the level he's ascending to … he needs someone to be genuine." I didn't want anything from him. I just wanted to make sure he was OK, because I cared about him in that manner.

Smartin' Off

Other than the arrival of Wiggins, the biggest Big 12 storyline during the preseason was Marcus Smart's decision to return to Oklahoma State instead of entering the NBA draft, where he was projected to be a lottery pick. Smart was irked that Wiggins had been voted Big 12 Preseason Player of the Year by league coaches. "They are saying he is the best college player there is and he hasn't even played a game yet," Smart told USA Today in October. "It's all talk. It's all potential. I'm not saying he can't do it. But he hasn't done it yet."

Obviously, Smart had plenty of reasons for motivation when his ninth-ranked Cowboys took the court in Lawrence for a Jan. 18 showdown with KU. The Jayhawks, though, were anxious to face Oklahoma State, too, following Smart's infamous backflips on their logo at midcourt the previous season.

Oklahoma State guard Phil Forte: Marcus had won Player of the Year the season before as a freshman, but then Andrew Wiggins came and he was supposed to be the next

LeBron James. We were seeing all this stuff about him. It was just natural competitiveness. In Marcus' eyes, if someone is supposedly better than him, he doesn't like that. That's what makes him so good to this day. I think that definitely drove him. It drove all of us.

Norm Roberts: With certain guys we've had here, guys like Wayne Selden and Josh Jackson, someone talking trash like (Smart) did would fire them up. We could say, "Wayne, this guy thinks he's better than you." And Wayne would say, "OK, I'll kick his ass." Or someone like Josh would go, "Oh, OK. I'm about to dunk on this dude's head!"

But when Smart said that stuff, Wiggs was like, "I don't care what he says. It doesn't matter." With Wiggs, the feeling was always, "Give us more." It was just really hard to fire him up.

That was obvious against Oklahoma State, when Wiggins scored a season-low three points in his highly-anticipated showdown with Smart. Kansas still managed to squeak out an 80-78 win thanks to 21 points from Tharpe and 13 points and eight blocks from Embiid. Still, most of the postgame buzz centered on the lack of effort by Wiggins, who attempted just five shots.

Smart (20 points) struggled offensively and went just 3-of-14 from the floor. But he still got to the foul line often and made all 10 of his free throws. He also had 10 rebounds and nine assists. His effort, unlike that of his counterpart, was phenomenal.

Oklahoma State coach Travis Ford: Marcus held Wiggins to three points, but Kansas won. We had the final shot to win the game. They missed a free throw that would've put them up by three. Le'Bryan Nash got the rebound and dribbled up the court. He went up for a 3-pointer at the buzzer to win it, but Frank Mason stripped it. We had been down 17 and came all the way back. We came so close to winning there two years in a row but we fell just short.

Phil Forte: Marcus didn't get too caught up in the individual battle. Even though Wiggins didn't do much, at the end of the day, we lost.

Kansas 80, Oklahoma State 78
January 18, 2014 · Lawrence, Kan.

Kansas (13-4)

Player	MP	FG	3FG	FT	R	A	F	S	TO	B	TP
Perry Ellis*	18	3-8	0-0	0-2	4	0	0	0	0	0	6
Joel Embiid*	32	5-6	0-0	3-7	11	1	2	0	4	8	13
Wayne Selden*	34	2-9	1-6	4-4	3	4	2	2	5	0	9
Naadir Tharpe*	39	7-8	3-4	4-4	2	6	0	3	6	0	21
Andrew Wiggins*	23	1-5	1-2	0-0	2	1	3	0	2	1	3
Tarik Black	9	4-5	0-1	0-0	2	0	1	0	0	1	8
Conner Frankamp	1	0-1	0-1	0-0	0	0	0	0	0	0	0
Brannen Greene	7	2-3	1-2	0-0	1	0	1	0	0	0	5
Frank Mason	18	2-4	1-2	1-3	4	0	2	1	1	0	6
Jamari Traylor	19	3-3	0-0	3-3	3	1	3	0	1	1	9
Team					5						
Totals	200	29-52	7-18	15-23	37	13	14	6	19	11	80

Oklahoma State (15-3)

Player	MP	FG	3FG	FT	R	A	F	S	TO	B	TP
Markel Brown*	28	5-13	5-9	0-0	3	1	5	0	1	0	15
Kamari Murphy*	38	5-10	0-0	2-2	1	1	4	1	1	2	12
Le'Bryan Nash*	22	5-11	0-0	0-2	5	2	4	0	3	0	10
Marcus Smart*	39	3-14	0-6	10-10	10	9	2	4	3	0	16
Brian Williams*	21	1-5	0-1	0-0	3	0	2	1	0	0	2
Stevie Clark	14	0-1	0-1	0-0	0	2	3	0	1	0	0
Phil Forte	30	7-11	7-10	2-2	5	2	1	2	0	0	23
Marek Soucek	8	0-1	0-1	0-0	1	0	1	0	0	1	0
Team					5				2		
Totals	200	26-66	12-28	14-16	33	17	22	8	11	3	78

	1st	2nd	Total	FG%	3FG%	FT%
Kansas	47	33	80	55.8	38.9	65.2
Oklahoma State	30	48	78	39.4	42.9	87.5

Officials: John Higgins, Doug Sirmons, Keith Kimble
Technicals: None

BEST BIG 12 DEFENDERS

1. Marcus Smart, Oklahoma State (2012-14): Two-time All-Big 12 defensive team selection caught a lot of grief for flopping. Averaged 4.5 steals in his team's two wins versus the Jayhawks

2. Dogus Balbay, Texas (2008-11): Named one of the top two defensive guards in all of college basketball in 2011 by ESPN's Jay Bilas. And Sherron Collins said: "Balbay was the toughest defender I played against in college."

3. DeMarre Carroll, Missouri (2007-09): Nicknamed the "Junkyard Dog," Carroll was a menace at the top of Mike Anderson's full-court press. His ability to guard multiple positions has made him a lot of money in the NBA.

4. Marcus Dove, Oklahoma State (2004-08): Two-time Big 12 Defensive Player of the Year who also hit late 3 to help Oklahoma State to upset win over KU in 2008

5. Jevon Carter, West Virginia (2014-18): Led the Big 12 in steals as a junior with 92 and was named the Big 12 Defensive Player of the Year. A repeat performance in 2017-18 would place him second all time on the Big 12's career steals list.

6. Ekpe Udoh, Baylor (2009-10): Posted the most blocks (133) in a Big 12 single-season by anyone not named Jeff Withey. Udoh's length in the middle of Scott Drew's zone helped the Bears advance to the Elite Eight in 2010.

7. J.T. Tiller, Missouri (2006-10): The 2009 Big 12 Defensive Player of the Year, he was the stopper on the best two defensive teams (2009 and 2010) that Mike Anderson ever coached. Snagged four steals and held Sherron Collins to nine points in Mizzou's 62-60 home win over KU in 2009.

8. Jacob Pullen, Kansas State (2007-2011): A two-time All-Big 12 defensive team member, ranks 10th on the Big 12's all-time career steals list. He brought a toughness to Frank Martin's defensive-minded teams.

9. Tristan Thompson, Texas (2010-11): The anchor on one of the best defensive teams KU has faced during the streak. Had five blocks and helped hold the Morris twins to 8-of-24 shooting in UT's 74-63 win at Allen Fieldhouse in 2011.

10. LaMarcus Aldridge, Texas (2004-06): Ranked second in the Big 12 in rebounding (9.2) and blocks (1.9) as a sophomore. Swatted four shots in Texas' 80-55 victory over KU in 2006 — the Jayhawks' worst margin for a Big 12 loss in the Self era.

That's the only thing Marcus cared about. He wasn't thinking, "What did Wiggins do?"

Kansas went on to win five of its next six games—losing only at Texas, when Wiggins scored seven points on 2-of-12 shooting—and was 9-1 in league play heading into its second game of the season against Kansas State. The Jayhawks rallied from a nine-point deficit late in the second half to force overtime. But this time they fell just short in an 85-82 setback. The victory over KU was the first for Weber in five tries.

Bruce Weber: We had the Saturday-Monday quick-turn, with the game against Texas first on Saturday. We just annihilated them (74-57). Marcus (Foster) went crazy and had 34 points and it was never a game. We were up 25-9 at one point.

With the Kansas game two nights later, we had the game won and Wes (Iwundu) had a transition opportunity where he should have just dribbled it out, but instead he tried to flip it behind his head to somebody, trying to get the crowd excited, and then they stole it and made a couple plays, and it went to overtime.

Sitting there waiting for the overtime, looking at our guys, I thought we were done. It felt like a disaster you couldn't recover from. But the first minute or so went back and forth, and then Will Spradling hit one of the biggest shots of his career, if not the biggest one, the corner 3, and got us the lead again. Then we went on a run and ended up winning, and it was bedlam in Bramlage. Storming the court and all that stuff.

Obviously it was huge. You've beat the best team, a team that's been the perennial power in the Big 12, along with your state rival. And you do it in a year when they have two iconic players like Wiggins and Embiid. It meant a lot to our fans, there's no doubt. I remember I fought the crowd and got back to our locker room. It was just me and (assistant coach) Chris Lowery in there. We were just sitting there laughing, because the players didn't come for a while. No one came for a while. It was a great night for the kids and for the program.

Best Dunk Ever at Allen Fieldhouse?

Kansas bounced back from the K-State loss with four straight wins, including a payback win over Texas. The Longhorns had given the Jayhawks their first Big 12 defeat back on Feb. 1 in Austin. But the rematch turned into a laugher, with the most-lasting moment being a ridiculous one-handed dunk by Black over Texas big man Cameron Ridley.

Tarik Black: I still watch the video of that dunk to this day, mainly because I like watching the part where Wayne Selden jumps over his chair on the bench and runs into Niko's (Roberts) arms. Jamari pushes me after I did it. Coach Self, in the postgame interview, says, "I'll be honest, that might be the best dunk I've ever seen in The Fieldhouse." That type of stuff makes me feel really good. It makes me appreciate my time there.

In No Mood to Celebrate

By the time they took the court at Oklahoma State on March 1, the Jayhawks knew they had won the outright Big 12 title. Iowa State and Texas had suffered losses earlier in the day, making it mathematically impossible for them to catch KU in the standings. Self had planned a celebration in Stillwater after the game—but it never happened thanks to Marcus Smart.

With Oklahoma City Thunder stars Kevin Durant and Russell Westbrook watching from courtside, Smart scored 20 of his 21 points after intermission to lead the Cowboys to a 72-65 victory. Wiggins had another disappointing game. He scored 15 points but went just 5-of-16 from the field and had six of his team's 23 turnovers.

Tarik Black: Coach Self had the managers bring these huge boxes of Big 12 championship shirts to Stillwater so we could celebrate winning the title after we beat Oklahoma State. But we just didn't show up that night. We got on the bus and Coach Self was pissed. He was hot. He was so mad. He was like, "I brought these shirts for us to be able to celebrate. Now I ought to burn them."

We didn't know he'd brought the shirts to celebrate us clinching the title. We all felt so bad on the bus. It was quiet. No one was looking at each other. No one said anything to each other. We felt like crap.

At the same time, at least we knew we had the title wrapped up. We didn't want to be the first team to lose it. That would've been embarrassing. If the streak had only been at two or three years—or even six or seven—it wouldn't have been as bad. But we were going for number 10. Imagine being the team that loses it now. That team will go down in history. We've made history, now that team will go down in history, too. We didn't want it to be us.

Bill Self: To me, we missed our opportunity to celebrate.

Disappointing as the loss at OSU may have been, it was far from the only thing on Self's mind as Kansas departed Stillwater. Self said Embiid "tweaked" his back during a fall near the end of the second half. At the time, the extent of the injury was unknown.

Naadir Tharpe: When he went down, we were like, "Wow! Everything was looking so good for us and now this happens." We knew things were about to be different. We had to figure out a way to work through it.

Kansas bounced back from the loss in Stillwater with an 82-57 win over Texas Tech on Senior Night at Allen Fieldhouse. Black, the lone senior in KU's rotation, was honored along with reserves Niko Roberts (Norm's son) and Justin Wesley.

Tarik Black: I had 19 points and went nine-for-nine from the field, which tied the Kansas record for field goal percentage in a single game. It was an amazing game and an amazing way for me to finish my time at Allen Fieldhouse.

That year in the Big 12 was nuts. At one point we had four teams in the Top 10. We had us at the top of the list. You had Oklahoma State and Baylor and Iowa State and Texas. K-State was good that year. Every time you stepped into the gym you were

BEST KU DUNKERS

1. Andrew Wiggins: A 44-inch vertical leap helped secure his spot as one of KU's best all-time dunkers.

2. Julian Wright: Long arms and crazy hops helped him attempt and make dunks that others wouldn't be able to attempt.

3. Ben McLemore: His best one was against Texas in Allen Fieldhouse, as on a breakaway, he spun for a 360 that even had Jay Bilas in awe.

4. Thomas Robinson: No Jayhawk has been better at power dunks in the Self era.

5. Wayne Selden: There were times when injuries sapped his athleticism, but when healthy, his jams were as good as anyone's.

6. Josh Jackson: He finished second in the nation in missed dunks during his one year, but when he connected, the freshman finished his jams with force.

7. Keith Langford: Perfected the "two-handed, pull-your-knees-up-to-your- chest-while-swinging-on-the- rim" slam at KU.

8. Rodrick Stewart: His top highlight came against Arizona, as he took it the length of the floor and threw a right-handed dunk directly over the top of future pro Jerryd Bayless.

9. Tarik Black: His throwdown over Texas' Cameron Ridley will remain on highlight videos for years to come.

10. Elijah Johnson: KU's best dunker as a point guard, one of his top highlights came against Kansas State when he finished a set-play alley-oop off a feed from teammate Tyrel Reed.

facing one of the top teams in the country. That was an unreal season.

Naadir Tharpe: *"We cannot be that team to end the streak."* I tried to instill that thought into my teammates heads, because that's what the older guys instilled in me. I said, "We can't be the ones to end it, because that's going to be *the* story, and that's all people are going to talk about—that we were the team that messed up the Big 12 legacy."

There wasn't a doubt in my mind that we weren't going to win it. To be the team to win the 10th title, I felt like that was pretty cool.

After the game, Kansas players donned the Big 12 championship hats and t-shirts Self had initially hoped to give them a few days earlier in Stillwater. All 10 of the Jayhawks' Big 12 championship trophies were lined up at center court as Black delivered his Senior Night speech. Self also made sure the crowd applauded Wiggins, who was playing his final home game. And he made mention of Embiid, who did not suit up for the game. "Didn't you guys think Joel looked great in a suit tonight?" Self asked the crowd. "But Jo, listen, everybody thinks you look much better in a uniform."

Alpha Wiggs

With Embiid sidelined indefinitely, additional pressure was now on Wiggins to perform at a superstar level. That finally occurred in the season finale against West Virginia. Kansas trailed by 25 early in the second half and would go on to lose 92-86. Still, college basketball fans got a glimpse of how good Wiggins can be when he's aggressive, as he rallied his team almost single-handedly by scoring 41 points and making it close.

Tarik Black: That's when Wiggs quieted all the critics that questioned whether he had any fire, whether he was assertive enough. He had 41 that game and then went out the next game (in the Big 12 Tournament) and had 30 against Oklahoma State. He put up 71 points in two games. It was crickets after that. We didn't see those articles anymore. He just single-handedly took over those games. At one point, Coach Self said, "Andrew, go win us this game." In a way it was a slap in the face to everyone else on the team, but he was just being honest. That's what we needed him to do.

Bill Self: That's how he was. He would be kinda, "La-di-da" and then somebody would challenge him, and he'd step up.

He should've been the Big 12 Player of the Year, but people voted before that game. Not that Melvin Ejim didn't deserve it, but I was really disappointed in that, because I thought Wiggs earned it.

Naadir Tharpe: A couple practices before, Coach Self was getting on Wiggs, telling him, "You need to score the ball more. You need to be more aggressive. You need to be a little selfish."

I remember watching his highlights before he got to Kansas, and before he did any of his dunks he always did a hop step. And I remember going to his room before we

BEST OF THE STREAK

MOST TALENTED JAYHAWKS

1. Joel Embiid (2013-14): A back injury forced a premature end to his only collegiate season, yet even in just 28 games, it was easy to see that Embiid's physical gifts and skill set could make him one of the top centers in NBA history. If, of course, he remains healthy.

2. Andrew Wiggins (2013-14): The most-hyped recruit in Kansas history averaged 17.1 points in his one KU season, but he often no-showed in big games and was rarely in attack mode. Likely would've benefitted from better point guard play.

3. Marcus Morris (2008-11): Scoring, passing, shooting, banging, rebounding, defending, leading. During his junior season at KU, Morris did just about everything at an elite level. The 2011 Big 12 Player of the Year had the most well-rounded skill set of any player in the Bill Self era.

4. Josh Jackson (2016-17): Assistant coach Norm Roberts says Jackson was "the best one-and-done we've ever had here." A 6-8 wing, Jackson relished playing defense and despised losing—two qualities not often found in one-year players.

5. Ben McLemore (2012-13): Sitting out the 2011-12 campaign as a partial qualifier did wonders for the 6-5 shooting guard, who averaged 15.9 points and shot 42 percent from 3-point range the following season. One of the smoothest, most athletic players Self has coached.

6. Darrell Arthur (2006-08): Heroic as Mario Chalmers' 3-pointer may have been, KU wouldn't have won the 2008 NCAA title without Arthur. Along with 20 points and 10 rebounds, Arthur connected on two difficult, heavily-contested shots in the final two minutes to spearhead KU's comeback.

7. Julian Wright (2005-07): With the ball skills of a point guard and the wingspan of a pterodactyl, the 6-8 Wright was one of the more unique players of the Self era. His court vision and flair for the dramatic led to countless highlight reel passes and dunks. The 2007 NBA lottery pick averaged 12 points as a sophomore.

8. Brandon Rush (2005-08): During his three-year KU career, the Kansas City native made 43.5 percent of his shots from beyond the arc, a mark that ranks third in school history. Rush's ability to shoot—and, also, his defensive skills—enabled the 6-6 wing to make millions in the NBA.

9. Sherron Collins (2006-10): So tight were Collins' handles that his teammates joked that he "had the ball on a string, like a yo-yo." Collins' combination of power and quickness and burst made it impossible to stop his penetration. He ranks fifth on KU's all-time scoring list.

10. Wayne Simien (2001-05): Not many things were as automatic as Simien's soft turnaround jumper during his senior season. Self has said multiple times that the 2005 All-American was the best college player he's coached. Simien is one of just two KU players in the last 20 years to average 20-plus points in a single season.

Honorable mention:
Thomas Robinson, Keith Langford, Cole Aldrich, Markieff Morris, Josh Selby

took off for that trip, and I'm like, "Yo Wiggs, how come you don't do your hop step anymore?" He kind of looked me, like "I don't know." I said, "Yo, you need to get back to your hop step when you go in the lane and start dunking how you were."

We got to West Virginia, and West Virginia is one of the craziest places we play. You walk in there and you think, "This place is so small," and then you come out before game time and people are doing stuff on the court and the atmosphere is crazy. I remember looking at him and he had a different kind of focus. He had four or five dunks that game that were just crazy. He stole it and went coast to coast. That game showed, "This is Wiggs. He's feeling free."

Jerrance Howard: Wiggs didn't get enough credit. He was such a great teammate in that he accepted all of the responsibility with the media attention, whether we lost or won. It allowed the other guys just to be them. The attention wasn't on the other guys. The other guys didn't catch blame like Wiggins did when things didn't go well. He took all of that and accepted it. He was very mature for his age. He was a different breed of person, and a different breed of athlete.

Coach would tell him what other people would say about him, and about how he had to prove them wrong. Wiggs was even-keel at first. But as he got more comfortable, the better he was.

Wiggs liked the fact that Coach would challenge him just like anyone else. He didn't care who you were. He was going to get after him just like he got after Wayne Selden. He chewed everyone out the same and coached everyone hard. Guys like him and Billy Preston—guys who have supreme talent, but when their motor doesn't go, they're just another player—people knew that this would be a good place for them, because they need to be pushed.

He was low-key and mild-mannered and humble. But he also had some dog in him, a little killer streak. If you pissed him off, that's where he'd let you know he wasn't always so sweet. If you challenged him or said he was overrated, that would piss him off. That would get underneath his skin. The West Virginia game in Morgantown, people saw that.

Tarik Black: Wiggs could've done whatever he wanted on the court at Kansas, but he chose to pay homage to those of us who were older than him and especially those who were there before him. Wiggs' dynamic was to respect Naadir as our starting point guard. Even though he knew he was supposed to be the first option, he wanted to take care of Naadir and a native Kansan like Perry Ellis that everyone loved. He wanted him to have a breakout year, and he wanted to JoJo to do well because he'd become one of his best friends.

It's not like he wanted to take a backseat, but he wanted to pay homage and respect to everyone else. It wasn't like he was reluctant or scared, because now we see him in the NBA and he's putting up 20 shots a game and scoring 40 on people. That fire is there, but it's different when you come in as the No. 1 draft pick and an organization is leaning on you to be its top player for the next decade. You need to go ahead and start shooting. But in college, other guys were trying to make it, too, and he respected them. He looked up to them. Still, you saw him go out there and dominate games at times. He had a great freshman year.

Five days after his onslaught on West Virginia, Wiggins took the court against Oklahoma State in the Big 12 Tournament in Kansas City. Unlike the previous two Cowboys-Jayhawks meetings that season, Wiggins came to play and finished with 30 points in KU's 77-70 overtime victory. Smart had 14 points but was just 4-of-14 from the field. In three games that season, Smart made 14 of his 42 shot attempts (28.5 percent) against Kansas.

No Embiid, No Big 12 Title

The victory over Oklahoma State catapulted KU into the Big 12 Tournament semifinals against Iowa State. Along with the win in Ames, Kansas had defeated the Cyclones 92-81 in Lawrence. This time, without Embiid, the Jayhawks weren't as fortunate.

Georges Niang: The game at their place was close, and Andrew Wiggins was about to hit a free throw to put them up five. So it's the first free throw, and I'm bent over. Wiggins hits the free throw, and Joel leans over to me and in his African accent, he says, "Well, that's it."

I was so pissed off, like, "F you man." Now that I look back on it, I think it was pretty funny, but I really wanted to beat them in the Big 12 Tournament.

Niang's wish was about to come true. He dominated the Jayhawks with 25 points and seven assists, and his team led by eight when he took a charge with 1:23 left on the clock.

Georges Niang: Brannen Greene was driving and I stepped in front of him. This time they called it and it probably wasn't a charge, but they owed me one from the year earlier with Elijah. His elbow came down on top of my eyebrow and sliced it open.

I remember a bunch of blood came out and I was walking and the doctor said, "I can get you back out there in five minutes." I said, "All right, let's go."

So I started sprinting back to the locker room and I'm getting lightheaded. I don't know what I was thinking. Then I did a quick concussion protocol and tried to get back out there, but by the time I got my stitches in, it was already too late.

I was trying to get back out before the end and then he said Kansas wasn't fouling. They were just letting the clock run down so they could take the loss and move on. So I couldn't make it back out there. I was mad, because I wanted to see what their faces were like after we beat them. That's just how it was beating Kansas back then. You took pride in doing that. I just remember asking my teammates after, "What did Bill Self's face look like after we won? Was he pissed?"

Naz Mitrou-Long: When we got back to the locker room, Georges kept asking that. I told him, "Yeah, Coach Self was definitely salty about that L."

It was amazing. There was no other way we wanted it. We all said that. After losing to them at home and then losing in Lawrence, we didn't want them to be on the other side of the bracket. We wanted to see them right away. We knew the place, Hilton South, was going to be split red and blue. We kind of wished Joel Embiid played.

Georges Niang: In college when you have a rim protector and a guy that can score at that level, it makes a world of a difference. I was going to the rim not even having to worry about getting my shot blocked because I was shooting over smaller guys. I hated going up against Embiid.

After we won, I remember we were leaving the hotel and I ran into Bill Self at the elevator and I had stitches and my Band-Aid over my eye. He said, "Man, I'd really like to punch you in that other eye."

Naz Mitrou-Long: I'm not going to lie and let pride get in the way. They were a different team without Embiid. I think Wiggins definitely stepped up and showed the world why he was a superstar, but Embiid ... he's just dominant. The dude is a 7-footer who can catch and shoot at the mid-range area. He'd get double-teamed in the post, spin baseline and finish, hit guys cutting, hit guys for 3s, block shots. His presence was felt when he was on the court. Nobody can deny that. You can't take that away from him. He's a great player.

Would it have been a different game? Maybe. But coming into that game we were hungrier than ever, and it felt amazing. It really put an exclamation mark on the rivalry and what Iowa State was about. It really spearheaded the winning tradition that we got going there at Iowa State.

What if ...

Kansas entered the NCAA Tournament as a No. 2 seed after losing three of its previous five games. While KU fans crossed their fingers that Embiid would return for March Madness, the Jayhawks prepared as if they wouldn't have him.

Bill Self: Every doctor he went to said he'd fractured a small bone in his back, which a lot of people do. A lot of offensive lineman have that issue. It's one of those deals where you can't hurt yourself any worse. It's just a matter about how much discomfort you're having and how much you can tolerate. You can't blame him. You can't blame anybody. The money is so big. All it takes is one person to say there's a one-in-one-hundred chance that playing could hurt him further or cause risk, and he's going to sit out.

Jerrance Howard: I remember walking into Coach's office the day we found out Jo was out for the first weekend. He was like, "This may have cost us the national championship." That really hit me in the gut, because he meant so much to our team. Going into the tournament without one of your best players was a major blow.

Jo wanted to play but the people around him, the people in his inner circle, wouldn't let him. Plus, as coaches, we had to be smart and do what was best for his future.

Kansas survived an opening-round scare—it was tied at halftime—and beat No. 15 seed Eastern Kentucky 80-69. Up next was Stanford, the No. 10 seed that was fresh off an upset of No. 7 New Mexico. Tipoff was at 11:15 a.m. in St. Louis.

Tarik Black: The NCAA cheated us. Well, not literally. But the start time of that game was terrible. I had played in a handful of NCAA games at Memphis. We'd been to the tournament every year and we'd won our conference tournament every year. I had already experienced what it felt like. But we had a team full of freshmen who had never been in that situation before. I'd played in morning games, but most of those freshmen hadn't. They were used to playing games at night.

In the NCAA Tournament, you have to wake up in the morning and be ready to play by 11 a.m. Those guys were used to going to class, taking a nap, eating a good meal and then going to shootaround and playing at 7 p.m. It's a totally different dynamic.

I tried to warn them before the Stanford game, and I probably should've been more forceful. I told them, "It's not the same. Don't stay up all night. Go to bed. Wake up early. Do something to get yourself going. Eat a good breakfast." But we didn't do that. At the hotel that morning, I saw guys yawning and acting sluggish as they were leaving the pregame meal. Their eyelids were heavy and their faces were drooping a little. I was like, "Wake up, guys! We've got a game! Wayne, why do you have a hoodie on, barely looking awake? We've got to get on this bus and go play!" I recognized it then. Everyone was still asleep. A lot of guys just weren't prepared. Then Stanford ran a zone the whole game and threw us off. If we'd have played that game at 5 or 7 p.m. and we weren't sleepwalking, we would've beat Stanford and won the championship.

Naadir Tharpe: Our whole demeanor was off—from the time we were eating before the game to the moment we rolled into the locker room. It was definitely a different type of vibe than we usually had on

Kansas 57, Stanford 60
March 23, 2014 · St. Louis, Mo.

Kansas (25-10)

Player	MP	FG	3FG	FT	R	A	F	S	TO	B	TP
Tarik Black*	26	6-8	0-0	6-8	6	0	5	0	0	0	18
Perry Ellis*	26	3-10	0-0	3-4	8	0	2	0	3	0	9
Wayne Selden*	18	1-5	0-1	0-0	1	2	4	3	1	0	2
Naadir Tharpe*	26	2-8	1-3	0-0	2	2	5	1	2	0	5
Andrew Wiggins*	34	1-6	0-2	2-2	4	1	3	1	4	2	4
Conner Frankamp	18	4-8	4-7	0-0	2	0	0	1	0	0	12
Brannen Greene	3	0-0	0-0	0-0	0	0	0	0	0	0	0
Landen Lucas	2	1-1	0-0	0-0	0	0	0	0	0	0	2
Frank Mason	22	0-4	0-3	2-2	2	2	0	1	1	0	2
Jamari Traylor	25	1-8	0-0	1-2	5	0	3	2	3	0	3
Team					5						
Totals	200	19-58	5-16	14-18	35	7	22	9	14	2	57

Stanford (23-12)

Player	MP	FG	3FG	FT	R	A	F	S	TO	B	TP
Anthony Brown*	33	2-5	0-1	6-9	5	1	3	1	2	0	10
Josh Huestis*	39	2-8	0-1	2-4	8	2	0	1	1	2	6
Stefan Nastic*	31	4-5	0-0	2-3	4	0	4	0	1	1	10
Dwight Powell*	30	5-10	0-1	5-6	7	1	4	1	5	1	15
Chasson Randle*	40	6-12	0-2	1-2	4	1	1	6	7	0	13
Marcus Allen	4	0-0	0-0	0-0	1	0	0	1	0	0	0
John Gage	17	1-6	0-4	2-2	3	1	2	0	0	0	4
Robbie Lemons	5	0-0	0-0	0-0	1	0	0	0	0	0	0
Grant Verhoeven	1	1-1	0-0	0-0	0	0	1	0	0	0	2
Team					4						
Totals	200	21-47	0-9	18-26	37	6	15	10	16	4	60

	1st	2nd	Total	FG%	3FG%	FT%
Kansas	24	33	57	32.8	31.3	77.8
Stanford	22	38	60	44.7	0.0	69.2

Officials: Bryan Kersey, Lamont Simpson, Michael Greenstein
Technicals: None

game day. We just couldn't find any type of groove that game. There was no type of rhythm. That starts with me being the point guard and being a leader that year. I felt like I didn't uplift my guys enough going into that game. I don't know if it was because we were so keen on getting JoJo back for that game, and then finding out he wasn't going to play when it came time … or maybe our minds were just somewhere else. I don't know.

Kansas' 60-57 loss to Stanford was one of the more disappointing postseason efforts of the Self era. Only two players—Black (18 points) and Frankamp (12 points, all on 3s)—reached double figures for a Jayhawks squad that shot just 32 percent from the field.

Wiggins, once again, failed to show up in the big moment. He scored four points and attempted just six shots in 34 minutes. He only got to the free throw line one time and had four turnovers in what proved to be his final game.

Bill Self: Wiggs was a little too laid back, in our eyes. I never thought he was quite the assassin that he could've been. Not because he didn't try hard. I just thought he should've dominated more.

Norm Roberts: Wiggs wasn't the type of guy who looked down toward the other end of the court and said, "Yeaaahhh, buddy! I'm coming! Try to stop me!" He knew it didn't matter. Wiggs was so gifted and so athletic and such a good kid. He already knew he was the golden boy.

What made the Stanford loss so difficult to stomach was that Embiid and his people had indicated he would return the following weekend.

Bill Self: I was under the understanding that, if we'd have won that game against Stanford, he was going to play in the Sweet 16. But obviously we played bad that game and it didn't happen. That was a bad distraction for our team. I would've been better off saying, "OK, Jo is done for the year." But we let it linger, because the doctors said it could happen, and Jo was telling us all along that he wanted to do it. He did the exercises and everything. But the reality was that it was the right thing for him not to play. And it may have been the right thing for him not to play the next weekend. Who knows? But the thing about it is, there was always that thought, "If we could get Jo back …" whereas we probably would've been better off just saying, "We're going to shut it down."

Norm Roberts: We thought he could probably play. I think he wanted to play, but there were other factors that were there. It hurt him because he wanted to be on the court with his team. But we didn't want him to hurt himself anymore. Had we gotten past Stanford, he would've played the next week. I also think we would've gotten past Stanford had we had him. Stanford had all that length and it was bad for us. They neutralized Wiggs and he didn't do much. Joel was so big. He'd have been able to protect the rim for us better than Tarik and he'd have been a problem down low.

Perry Ellis: It was a tough time for him. He knew how much he could help and we knew how much he could help. We were so much better with him.

Jamari Traylor: I'm sure it killed him not to play in the end. It killed us, too.

Joel Embiid: It was hard not to play. I hated it, because I would've played in that next game. That was the plan. Us losing to Stanford actually played a role in my decision of whether to stay or leave for the NBA. I actually decided to stay, but then I was forced to leave. I really wanted to stay because I felt like I didn't accomplish anything. People were talking about me being the No. 1 pick, but to me, I only averaged 11 points and eight rebounds. I was thinking, "If I come back I can average 20 and 10 and go to the Final Four and win the whole thing." I wanted to stay but I didn't get the chance to do that.

Norm Roberts: Joel didn't want to enter the draft. He sat in my office in tears. He kept saying, "I don't want to go. I don't want to go. Call my mom and dad and tell them I want to stay." Then it was like, "Joel, you're going to be a top three pick. You could be the No. 1 pick."

Luc, his mentor, said, "Norm, how could this kid not go in the draft when he's going to be a top-three pick? How am I going to go back to his country and tell them that I told him to wait? What if something happens with his back or his foot? How can Joel do that and let his country down?" He said that, and Joel was sitting right there. We all got up and started walking out of my office, and Joel turned around and looked at me and said, "Coach, can I call Coach Self? I'm going to have to go. I've gotta go, Coach. I've gotta go." I said, "OK, big fella. OK."

Bill Self: He had to leave. It was the right decision. With him, it was sad about his back injury, because that kept us from having a chance at the title. We would've had a chance with him and Wiggs.

Joel Embiid: I remember telling them that I was going to stay. Then I talked to a few guys in the league and my mentor. My stock was already so high and I was supposed to be the No. 1 pick. There was really no reason to stay. I told them I was staying, but after talking to a few people, I was like, "I don't want to, but I kinda have to."

Did I feel like I was ready for the NBA? No, I didn't feel like I was ready. Mentally and physically, I didn't think I was ready.

Coach was never opposed to me leaving. He just warned me, "That's a different life. You've got to live by yourself. You've got to be a professional." I looked at myself, as young as I was, and not being from this country, my parents not being here and not having any family, I felt like I wasn't going to make it. Luckily I had good people around me who have been helping me through the whole thing.

Norm Roberts: He knew from a maturity standpoint he wasn't ready. He sat in my office and said, "I'm not mature enough. I'm not ready."

(Luc) said, "Norm, he may not be mature enough. I don't think he is, either. But Africans adapt. We have to when we come over to this country. We have to adapt. He will adapt." I couldn't argue with that. Luc is a good man. He looked out for Joel.

One More Exit

Wiggins and Embiid shocked no one with their decisions to leave school early for the NBA draft, where they were selected No. 1 and No. 3, respectively. (Note: A foot injury to Embiid a few weeks before the draft likely kept him from being the top overall pick). What wasn't expected was the departure of Tharpe, who still had one season of eligibility remaining.

Naadir Tharpe: That was definitely hard for me. My mind was going crazy. There were a lot of things pulling me in different directions. Should I try to go back to school? Should I try to do this? I just remember being so frustrated. I didn't trust anybody and I wanted to be on my own. I decided to leave and play in the D-League.

I couldn't see myself playing at another college. That's not how I should have been thinking, but that's how I felt. That's all I really knew. I played at Kansas for three years. There was no other school that was going to be able to bring that much excitement. That's how I felt about Kansas. I didn't want to go anywhere else.

A little more from ...

Bill Self: That (2013 class) was the best recruiting class we ever had, hands down. We knew Wiggs was great but we didn't know Jo would be that good and we certainly didn't know Frank would be National Player of the Year. That was a darn good class.

Jerrance Howard: I didn't know (Mason) could score the ball so well. Some of his finishes with either hand—and with contact—was impressive considering it was a 5'9" guy doing that. I didn't know how crafty he was around the basket. But I knew he had some dog in him. He's one of the toughest kids I've ever been around. He didn't say a lot as a freshman, but he competed. When Coach challenged him, he went harder. That's when you know ... a lot of kids, as freshmen, they have bad body language and feel sorry for themselves. Frank would just turn it up another notch.

We had a drill called block out and break. It was basically the red team vs. the white team. The starters against the subs and the walk-ons. You'd put 10 minutes on the clock and, basically, you just go up and down. Frank was turning it over. Coach was like, "You're not playing hard! You don't say anything!" From that point on, Frank just dominated for the last five minutes. He had something to do with every basket, either by scoring or with an assist or a steal. He didn't say anything to Coach, but his body language was basically saying, "Take that, Coach." All of us looked at each other like, "OK, this is a bad boy." He was the best player on the court that day.

Jamari Traylor: There was so much hype when Wiggins committed. I just remember thinking, "I want to see what all of this is about." We were having open gyms and he was doing some crazy things. It was impressive. With JoJo it was completely different. Coach Self told me, "Everyone is saying all this stuff about Wiggs, but watch out for Jo. He's going to be special." Coach Self was always his biggest fan. I give him credit for that. At first I didn't see it, but he ended up doing some eye-popping things when he got out there. He might end up being one of the best guys they've ever had at Kansas. He could end up being one of the best players in the entire NBA if he stays healthy.

Joel Embiid: I loved (the attention) at Kansas. It prepared me for the environment I'm in with Philadelphia, because 76ers fans are crazy, too. The difference is, at Kansas, they're always nice no matter what. No one talks trash if you don't play well or if you lose. No matter what, they're going to be camping out days before games to get tickets. People respected me and gave me my space. But when it was basketball time, it was crazy.

I thank Wiggs, because I benefitted from him a lot. We all did. He had so much hype coming out of high school; it brought attention to Kansas. All of the scouts were coming to watch him play, and at that point I was "the other guy." But the more people watched me play, the more the hype started picking up. I thank him a lot for that. He's a great guy to be around. He's an athletic freak in the league. He's one of the best scorers in the NBA. He's a quiet dude, but he's fun to be around.

Coach called (Mason) the Bulldog because he's tough. It was a fun group. We had a lot of hype. Unfortunately we didn't make it very far, mainly due to my back injury. I wish we could go back and see what would've happened if we were healthy, because I think we'd have had a good chance of winning it all.

Wayne Selden: Our whole team changed when Joel went down. We had to really adjust. We obviously weren't as good, but we had Tarik, so we still had a solid five. We just had to figure out what our new roles were going to be. That group never really came into its own. We never developed an identity. We just didn't have the right leadership I guess. There are so many "ifs." Naadir did a good job, but if Frank would've been our point guard—not even senior-year Frank, but maybe sophomore-year Frank—that team would've been scary.

It was tough playing without a true point guard. It was, "Go get your own basket." With Wiggs and his athletic ability and how good he was, he was able to go do that. Everybody else wasn't.

The outgoing personality Embiid displays in the NBA was actually molded at Kansas, where Embiid says he became "a man of the people."

Bill Self: He was funny and really, really smart. He'd act like he didn't understand English if he didn't feel like talking to you. You'd get onto him and he'd said, "Oh, Coach. I don't understand ..." He understood everything we were saying.

He convinced people that, for his tribal initiation, he had to fight a lion. And people actually believed him. He was fun, but I had no idea he had this much personality, in terms of how he's acted since he left Lawrence.

Tarik Black: JoJo embellishes his accent when he wants to play dumb. When he was doing an interview and he wanted it to be over, or if he was shy or anxious, he'd turn up his accent so that you couldn't understand him. When he did something wrong and Coach Self was on him, his accent got super heavy and he'd pretend like he didn't understand. He's doing the same thing in the NBA, but he's not fooling me.

Naadir Tharpe: The way that he acts now, he was the same way at KU. Now he's just got a little bit bigger platform for it, so he can show everybody. He was the same exact way in Lawrence. We'd go to the bar and he'd be in there dancing in front of a crowd. It was hilarious. It was just JoJo being himself.

Wayne Selden: He's always the life of the party. When he first got to Kansas, he was a little quiet and a little shy but he really came into his own with confidence. It just took him a little while to find himself. We're all young coming into college and I felt like him coming into his own was a big step.

We were roommates. When we first got there, we went through a tough stretch where we weren't seeing eye to eye. Not on the court, but as roommates. This guy ... he left the chicken potpie on the counter for, like, two months. You know how Boston Market has the little boxes for their pot pies? I thought he had already ate it. Every day, I'd walk inside and think, "what's that smell?" I'm cleaning out the fridge and taking everything out of the freezer. *What's that smell?* I finally look in this box on the counter and it's a bunch of meal worms and bugs in this chicken pot pie box. It had to have been there for two or three months, and I didn't think there was anything in the box. I thought he ate the pie and just left the box there. I show him the box and say, "Jo, what are you doing?" He's like, "Oh .... " And he ends up bringing it out and throwing it away, but he dropped a little bit of it in the stairwell, and the stairwell smelled for a year, probably.

Tarik Black: One time we had a party, a gathering, at one of our teammates' parents house. Before dinner was even ready, JoJo ate an entire plate of brownies. Seriously, they were meant for the entire team, but Jo walked away with the plate and ate all of them by himself. All of a sudden I couldn't find him, so I walked into another room and he was sprawled out on the couch, holding his stomach. He was like, "I'm gonna be sick. I'm gonna throw up." We had a game the next day and the coaches were like, "Is he going to be able to play?"

I sat down next to him and said, "JoJo, what are you doing? You didn't even eat dinner. You've got to take care of your body. Now you're sick and you might not be able to play tomorrow. That's not a cool thing to do to your teammates. That's an immature thing to do." He just looked at me and shook his head. He knew he was wrong. I was like, "C'mon, Jo. I understand that you're young and you're going to make some mistakes. But you're on the fast track right now. You're the one who said you wanted to be great. If that's what you want to do, you need to grow up fast. You're not going to have the luxury of having four years to do it like I did."

Bill Self: If you gave him some Nutella, he'd be happy. The dude had terrible eating habits.

Perry Ellis: He was funny off the court. He loved Shirley Temples and brownies. We had a lady that would bring us brownies after games, even on the road. Sometimes she'd show up at the airport or the arenas. We'd look for them but he'd already eaten them all. Also, he loved Shirley Temples. At restaurants, that's all he'd drink.

Tarik Black: Every time (Embiid and I) play each other in the NBA, we have a talk either before or afterward. We played in L.A. and went to In-N-Out afterward. When we played in Philly I went by his apartment. We communicate. Even when we're not playing against each other I check in on him every month or so. Everyone always asks him about basketball and stuff, but I don't go there with him. My thing with him is, "Jo, how are you really doing? *How are you?* That's what I care about."

I definitely think (Wiggins) enjoyed his time at KU. How could he not? We had such a great team and everyone got along. That's not to say he didn't like his privacy. He'd lock himself in his room all the time. He'd talk to his brother and his parents on the phone a lot and sleep a lot. Honestly, he's kind of introverted. I talked to him in Minnesota last year about potentially coming to speak to some kids in my hometown, and he was like, "I can't do that. I can't talk in front of people like that." But if he knows you, he'll talk to you. If you're by yourself and hanging out, he can have a conversation and talk. But in public, he's a very shy guy. Wiggs hasn't changed since KU, either. He still talks, acts, walks the exact same. He's more confident and deservedly so, because he's become a star. But he's the humblest guy, though.

Hudy is at the top of the class. She sets the standard and the bar. Her style of lifting … I hadn't done that until I got to Kansas. I had knee surgery coming out of high school. My whole time at Memphis, my body-fat percentage was up. I was still an elite athlete, but I wasn't at the level I should've been. Hudy started off slow with me. We built it up where, near the end of the year, I was doing these lifts and my body felt great. I was power-cleaning numbers that I had never done before. I was doing the same weight as guys like Jamari, who had already been there two or three years. She worked with me and helped me with my body so much.

When I was at Memphis, Coach (Josh) Pastner was hard on us, but it wasn't like Kansas. He had that thing about not cursing. Most of the time, when guys don't curse, they get labeled as soft. But he was definitely hard on us. Coach Pastner has done some amazing things. He went down to Georgia Tech and won ACC Coach of the Year. That's off the charts and I respect it. But that stuff comes with experience. Now he's more of an experienced coach because of the trials and tribulations he went through at Memphis. Those Georgia Tech kids are getting a more experienced coach. I was a part of his first crop, his first recruiting class. It's a different situation.

Coach Self was experienced when I walked through the door. He had already won

national titles and understood how to deal with guys that grew up in my environment, guys who were chasing their passion. He understands that this means the world to us. He cared as much about us doing well as we cared about doing well ourselves.

Norm Roberts: I was one of the guys from the very start—and some guys differed with me—that said, "Tarik Black is going to play in the NBA. He can guard ball screens. He's athletic. He rebounds and he's got some toughness, and he has a pretty good basketball IQ." He got better and better at the skill stuff. He improved as much in one year as anyone we've had here. He wasn't even on anyone's draft board, and look at him now. Making millions in the NBA.

BEST OF THE STREAK

RANKING KU'S ONE-AND-DONES

1. Josh Jackson: Self calls him "the most prepared freshman we've ever had." Assistant coach Kurtis Townsend called him a queen on a chessboard you could move anywhere. He delivered no matter where he played, earning All-Big 12 and third-team All-American honors.

2. Joel Embiid: Arguably the greatest talent Self has ever coached, he might be No. 1 on this list if not for injuries. He averaged 11.2 points, 8.1 rebounds and 2.6 blocks per game, and his impact was even greater than numbers reflect.

3. Andrew Wiggins: Sometimes left fans and coaches wanting more because of his freak athleticism, but it's hard to fault his production: 17.1 points, 5.9 rebounds and second-team All-American honors.

4. Ben McLemore: He made the game look easy, gliding all over the court and effortlessly draining picture-perfect 3s. McLemore averaged 15.9 points and shot 42 percent from distance.

5. Xavier Henry: He faced a lot of outside pressures—mainly, from his father—but when he'd just play carefree, he was one of the best wings Self has coached. Henry averaged 13.4 points and shot 41.8 percent from distance on a 33-3 squad.

6. Kelly Oubre: It took some time for him to figure out his role, but once he did, Oubre was a menace defensively and an opportunistic scorer. He averaged 9.3 points, 5.0 rebounds and 1.1 steals per game.

7. Josh Selby: Teammates said he was awesome in pickup games. Selby wasn't as good in a structured setting, but he was also slowed by a foot injury at KU. Before his injury, he started 11 of 13 games and averaged 12 points.

8. Cliff Alexander: He struggled to grasp the KU offense, but when he was on the floor, he'd make an impact because of his raw strength. He was an efficient scorer, averaging 7.1 points on 56.6 percent shooting.

9. Cheick Diallo: A five-game suspension because of an NCAA investigation put him behind his teammates, and he never really caught up. He did have a motor that Self loved, and in limited minutes, he was KU's best defensive rebounder and shot-blocker.

2013-14
Season Summary

Results (25-10, 13-5)

November

8	Louisiana-Monroe	W, 80 - 63
12	@ Duke	W, 83 - 94
19	Iona	W, 86 - 66
22	Towson	W, 88 - 58
28	vs. Wake Forest	W, 87 - 78
29	vs. Villanova	L, 59 - 63
30	vs. UTEP	W, 67 - 63

December

7	@ Colorado	L, 75 - 72
10	@ Florida	L, 67 - 61
14	vs. New Mexico	W, 80 - 63
21	Georgetown	W, 86 - 64
30	Toledo	W, 93 - 83

January

5	San Diego State	L, 57 - 61
8	@ Oklahoma	W, 83 - 90
11	Kansas State	W, 86 - 60
13	@ Iowa State	W, 70 - 77
18	Oklahoma State	W, 80 - 78
20	Baylor	W, 78 - 68
25	@ TCU	W, 69 - 91
29	Iowa State	W, 92 - 81

February

1	@ Texas	L, 81 - 69
4	@ Baylor	W, 52 - 69
8	West Virginia	W, 83 - 69
10	@ Kansas State	L, 85 - 82
15	TCU	W, 95 - 65
18	@ Texas Tech	W, 63 - 64
22	Texas	W, 85 - 54
24	Oklahoma	W, 83 - 75

March

1	@ Oklahoma State	L, 72 - 65
5	Texas Tech	W, 82 - 57
8	@ West Virginia	L, 92 - 86
13	vs. Oklahoma State	W, 77 - 70
14	vs. Iowa State	L, 83 - 94
21	vs. Eastern Kentucky	W, 80 - 69
23	vs. Stanford	L, 57 - 60

All-Big 12 Team

Player of the Year:
Melvin Ejim, Iowa State, Sr., F

Defensive Player of the Year:
Joel Embiid, Kansas, Fr., C

Newcomer of the Year:
DeAndre Kane, Iowa State, Sr., G

Freshman of the Year:
Andrew Wiggins, Kansas, Fr., G

Sixth Man of the Year:
Tyler Neal, Oklahoma, Sr., F
Phil Forte, Oklahoma State, So., G

Coach of the Year:
Rick Barnes, Texas

First Team
Melvin Ejim, Iowa State, Sr., F**
DeAndre Kane, Iowa State, Sr., G
Andrew Wiggins, Kansas, Fr., G**
Marcus Smart, Oklahoma State, So., G
Juwan Staten, West Virginia, Jr., G

Second Team
Joel Embiid, Kansas, Fr., C
Marcus Foster, Kansas State, Fr., G
Buddy Hield, Oklahoma, So., G
Markel Brown, Oklahoma State, Sr., G
Johnathan Holmes, Texas, Jr., F

Third Team
Cory Jefferson, Baylor, Sr., F
Georges Niang, Iowa State, So., F
Perry Ellis, Kansas, So., F
Cameron Clark, Oklahoma, Sr., F
Jaye Crockett, Texas Tech, Sr., F

Honorable Mention
Isaiah Austin, Baylor, So., C
Wayne Selden Jr., Kansas, Fr., G
Naadir Tharpe, Kansas, Jr., G
Thomas Gipson, Kansas State, Jr., F
Will Spradling, Kansas State, Sr., G
Ryan Spangler, Oklahoma, Jr., F
Le'Bryan Nash, Oklahoma State, Jr., F
Kyan Anderson, TCU, Jr., G
Javan Felix, Texas, So., G
Cameron Ridley, Texas, So., F
Isaiah Taylor, Texas, Fr., G
Eron Harris, West Virginia, So., G

All-Defensive Team
Isaiah Austin, Baylor, So., C
Joel Embiid, Kansas, Fr., C**
Marcus Smart, Oklahoma State, So., G**
Demarcus Holland, Texas, So., G
Cameron Ridley, Texas, So., C
Juwan Staten, West Virginia, Jr., G

All-Rookie Team
DeAndre Kane, Iowa State, Sr., G
Joel Embiid, Kansas, Fr., C**
Andrew Wiggins, Kansas, Fr., F**
Marcus Foster, Kansas State, Fr., G
Isaiah Taylor, Texas, Fr., G

** Unanimous selection

Kansas Awards

Andrew Wiggins
Consensus All-American Second Team
NABC All-American Second Team
AP All-American Second Team
USBWA All-American Second Team
Sporting News All-American Second Team
Big 12 Championship All-Tournament

Joel Embiid
NABC All-District (8) First Team

Perry Ellis
NABC All-District (8) Second Team
Battle 4 Atlantis All-Tournament

Season Stats

#	Player	CL	POS	HT	Hometown	G	GS	FG%	3P%	FT%	R	A	S	B	PTS
22	Andrew Wiggins	FR	G	6-8	Vaughan, Ontario	35	35	.448	.341	.775	5.9	1.5	1.2	1.0	17.1
34	Perry Ellis	SO	F	6-8	Wichita, KS	35	34	.549	.471	.763	6.7	1.0	0.8	0.6	13.5
21	Joel Embiid	FR	C	7-0	Yaounde, Cameroon	28	20	.626	.200	.685	8.1	1.4	0.9	2.6	11.2
1	Wayne Selden	FR	G	6-5	Roxbury, MA	35	35	.437	.328	.629	2.6	2.5	0.7	0.3	9.7
10	Naadir Tharpe	JR	G	5-11	Worcester, MA	34	31	.436	.377	.821	2.1	5.0	0.7	0.0	8.5
0	Frank Mason	FR	G	5-11	Petersburg, VA	35	3	.417	.327	.662	1.3	2.1	0.5	0.0	5.5
25	Tarik Black	SR	F	6-9	Memphis, TN	33	15	.692	.000	.600	3.9	0.3	0.3	0.5	5.5
31	Jamari Traylor	SO	F	6-8	Chicago, IL	34	0	.674		.667	4.1	0.8	0.4	0.8	4.8
23	Conner Frankamp	FR	G	6-0	Wichita, KS	27	0	.344	.313	.800	0.6	0.6	0.1	0.1	2.5
14	Brannen Greene	FR	G	6-7	Juliette, GA	28	0	.385	.333	.842	1.0	0.4	0.2	0.0	2.4
3	Andrew White III	SO	G	6-7	Richmond, VA	18	0	.441	.320	.500	1.2	0.2	0.3	0.2	2.4
33	Landen Lucas	FR	F	6-10	Portland, OR	22	0	.571		.500	1.4	0.0	0.1	0.3	1.5
5	Evan Manning	SO	G	6-3	Lawrence, KS	6	0	.250	.333	.500	0.0	0.2	0.2	0.0	0.7
20	Niko Roberts	SR	G	5-11	Huntington, NY	6	1	.000	.000	.500	0.5	0.0	0.0	0.0	0.3
4	Justin Wesley	SR	F	6-9	Fort Worth, TX	14	1	.000	.000	.500	0.6	0.0	0.0	0.1	0.1
15	Christian Garrett	JR	G	6-3	Los Angeles, CA	7	0	.000		.000	0.1	0.1	0.0	0.0	0.0

## CHAPTER 11

2014-15
TRANSITION

Losing a pair of one-and-dones in a single year would cripple most programs. The Kansas Jayhawks? They simply responded by signing two more. Granted, Kelly Oubre and Cliff Alexander didn't fare nearly as well in their lone college season as Andrew Wiggins and Joel Embiid. Luckily the Jayhawks of 2014-15 boasted a better supporting cast that kept the squad in the hunt for an 11th straight conference crown.

Forward Perry Ellis, the second-leading scorer from the previous season, returned for his junior campaign along with Wayne Selden, a sophomore wing who had initially only planned to be at Kansas for a year. The biggest improvement, though, was at point guard, where Naadir Tharpe's decision to leave the program created an opportunity for an undersized—and under-valued—bulldog who would eventually become one of the best players in the program's rich history.

Frank Mason: Naadir and I had a good relationship when I was a freshman. He was a good leader for our team. He was an older guy who had experienced a lot and knew the system. We competed for the job, but going in, Coach Self felt like he should be the one that started. He told us everyone should get an equal opportunity and a chance to start. All along, I felt like it was my job and I was going to be the one who started, but he won.

Naadir Tharpe: Frank went hard every day. Coming into my junior year, I had a couple injuries—a few knickknack things going on—and I just remember him pushing me. For real. One practice he was just destroying me. This was in front of the coaches, and I think CBS was there and a couple other media people. It was good for me. After practice, I told Frank, "I need you to do that all the time." That's how he was. He always played hard. He's just a dog.

It was just about him picking up the system and learning the spots where he needed to be. That's how it is for anyone at Kansas. If you understand the system, you figure out the spots where you can score and, just as important, where you can create for others. That's when the game really opens up for you.

Jamari Traylor: Frank is a workaholic. He's always in the gym. He's a guy that, whenever he fails, he's going to come back 10 times harder. His freshman year he felt like he should've started over Naadir and it didn't happen for him. He didn't like that at all. His sophomore year he wanted to come back even harder and improve.

Landen Lucas: I was very close with Naadir and I was supportive of him through the whole thing. We had a tough finish to our season. That was hard on everybody. A couple weeks after the loss, everybody was kind of in that state where we weren't very happy and we didn't want to even think about basketball—and then some of the crazy things happening off the court didn't help. Naadir made a decision with Coach Self, and it was tough, because we lost somebody who had a lot of experience, but we also knew what the potential was for Frank.

While it was hard losing a good friend from the team, from a basketball perspective, I think everybody quickly realized it was just going to bring Frank along more quickly the following year.

It pushed him to the forefront where he had to be ready to go. He was definitely prepared to answer that challenge and it sped up the process. It was good for his development. It made him into the player he is now, to have to take over at a young age and develop some of the qualities we saw his junior and senior year.

Frank Mason: I love competing, and it doesn't really matter how it works out. When Naadir left, there was just more opportunity for me and I took advantage of it. I felt like our issues my freshman year, when Wiggins and Embiid were there, started with the point guards. We didn't do a great job of leading the team and of getting guys easy shots. We also didn't score enough. Growing up, I always had the ball in my hands, but I really wasn't like a point guard. I was a scoring guard. All I knew was where I needed to go... but I didn't know where everyone else needed to be.

After so much went wrong that first year, it pushed me to work hard over the summer after Naadir left. I knew I was the guy next up. I knew a lot of pressure would fall on me and I got ready for the summer and worked out a lot. I watched a lot of tape. I changed my shot.

That season I also learned how to get into the lane and pass first, without just thinking the shot should be for me. I learned to get into the lane and make the defense collapse and get guys easier shots. Before, I'd get into the lane and look to shoot first. It shouldn't be that way. Coach Self told me I can get in the paint any time I want, and I felt that way, too. He was always on me about getting into the paint and making plays for others.

I just learned to be a point guard. I knew my teammates' strengths, where they were good at finishing, what they could do in transition—like where each guy shouldn't catch the ball and where he's comfortable catching it. As point guard, everyone should know that. I always had confidence. I could have done some of the same things my freshman year that I did as a sophomore, but that wasn't my role.

Wayne Selden: I knew Frank had it in him from the first week we started playing together as freshmen. He plays with a chip on his shoulder. He loves when the odds are against him. His freshman year, he always had the game, he just didn't know how to apply it right. But come sophomore year, besides Perry, he was really the best player on our team.

Bill Self: By the end of Frank's sophomore year, when we ran bad offense, we just said, "Frank, go get a shot." You knew that he was going to be a special guy, but nothing like a National Player of the Year or anything. I thought he became a great shooter, which was never his reputation. He was just so competitive and getting smarter and understanding the game more.

Vital as Mason was to the Jayhawks' chemistry, Ellis and Selden were equally important pieces of a squad that would depend heavily on inexperienced underclassmen. Ellis averaged 13.5 points as a sophomore but was overshadowed by the hoopla surrounding Wiggins and Embiid. A McDonald's All-American once pegged as a potential first-round draft pick, Selden had fallen short of expectations in his inaugural season. Although he started every game and averaged a respectable 9.7 points, Selden shot only 43.6 percent from the field and 32.8 percent from 3-point range. And he often struggled in big moments, as evidenced by his two-point performance in KU's NCAA Tournament loss to Stanford.

Wayne Selden: Initially, when I first came in, I thought I was going to do my time, my one year, and get out. But that definitely wasn't the case. And then, my sophomore year, I felt like everything would magically happen for me, that it'd be easy. I worked hard that summer, but I still think I was just expecting good things to naturally happen.

Perry Ellis: I was a quiet kid, but that didn't stop Coach Self from getting after me. He loved to yell at me and challenge me. I didn't have a problem with it at all. It didn't phase me one bit. He did it every season, from my freshman to my senior year, although it wasn't as bad the last few years.

My first two seasons, he kept trying to convince me to talk and be more vocal. But by the time I was a junior, he adjusted—or, at the very least, tweaked—his approach, because he realized I was never going to be a real vocal guy. That just wasn't me. It wasn't my personality. So he got away from that and just made sure I was playing as hard as I could every single play. He let me lead by example.

My freshman and sophomore years, everything was a straight-line to the basket. I'd just get the ball, make one move or head fake and go straight to the bucket. But by my junior year I was doing different things. I'd stop and start again. Or I'd bring the ball behind my back or do a spin move. I relied a lot on my quickness. I had a good first step that helped me get by a lot of people.

Creamed

The Jayhawks were still adapting to their roles—or in some cases, trying to determine them—when they traveled to Indianapolis to face No. 1 Kentucky in the Champions Classic on Nov. 18. The Wildcats returned the Harrison twins in the backcourt and also had landed the best recruiting class in the country, led by eventual No. 1 overall pick Karl-Anthony Towns, who teamed with Willie Cauley-Stein to form a huge frontline.

Wayne Selden: Kelly Oubre started for us that game because we needed athletes—and we *still* didn't have enough athletes. Our game plan was to take it at them and drive it. It just didn't work. Game plans don't always work. They were just too big. I couldn't see anything except tall guys out there. I feel like that was one of the best college basketball teams ever assembled. It has to be when you look at where those guys are at now after just a few short years in the NBA, guys like Towns and Devin Booker and Tyler Ulis.

Bill Self: I thought we were awful. Of course, I knew they were really good. They also had an advantage because they were able to take a trip to the Bahamas in August, so they got to practice 10 times and then they played against great competition. They were just way ahead of us, and we weren't ready to compete. I mean we tried hard, but it was men against boys. It was just a different level that we weren't ready for at that point in the season.

The Wildcats smoked the Jayhawks, 72-40, in a game that was never close. KU made just 11 baskets and shot 19.6 percent from the field, and its point total remains the lowest of the Self era. As he took his seat for the postgame press conference, Self picked up a glass of water on the table before him and said, "I was hoping that was vodka."

Wayne Selden: After we lost to Kentucky, we came into the gym and started practicing passing the ball around, and we messed up a little bit. Coach Self said, "All right, I'm going to give you guys one more chance." We used up that chance pretty quickly, and next thing I know we're on the line, running 46 suicides. One suicide was half court and back, the free throw line and back, and then all the way down and back. We had to do 46 of them! But that wasn't it. We were doing (defensive) slides, then running, then slides, then running ... We did all that for over an hour, and then he said, "Are you guys ready to start practice now?" We tried to start practice but nobody could do it because we'd been running so much.

Where's Kelly Oubre

One thing that puzzled Kansas fans early in the season was the lack of playing time for Oubre, a McDonald's All-American and surefire one-and-done who was expected to be one of the Jayhawks top players in 2014-15. Oubre played 13 minutes against Kentucky and 15 minutes in a win over Rider six days later. But then came a four-game stretch in which Oubre played single-digit minutes. He scored a combined four points in those contests.

Assistant coach Norm Roberts: When you have guys that come in with that "one-and-done" tag, some people probably assume there's pressure on the staff to play them no matter what. Coach doesn't look at it that way. If you're a one-and-done type of guy here, you have to understand that faces may change, but expectations don't. The bottom line is, even if you're a one-and-done guy, you're going to have to come in and work. There's an expectation level that you're going to have to reach.

Bill Self: When a guy is 6-foot-8 and has never really been a guard, and all of a sudden he goes to college and he's a guard, there's going to be an adjustment period. The things that Kelly had to do for us to be good was defend, rebound and steal possessions. Stuff like that. It took a while for him to understand the attention to detail and effort he needed to give to those areas, and that's fine. It's that way for a lot of guys.

Still, think about it ... how many freshmen have started for us? Just about every one of those (high-profile) kids we've signed have come and started for us as a freshman at some point. It just took him some time to work into it.

Oubre returned to the starting lineup on Dec. 20 and tallied a season-high 23 points and 10 rebounds in a win against Lafayette. He'd start all but one game the rest of the season.

Bill Self: People can say what they want to, but Kelly averaged like 27 minutes a game after we made him a starter. He just didn't start early because I didn't think he was playing good enough.

Another Fast Start in the Big 12

Other than the clunker against Kentucky and a bizarre, 25-point setback at Temple, the Jayhawks felt good about their performance in non-conference play. Highlights included a 61-56 victory over No. 20 Michigan State in the championship game of the Orlando Classic and a 63-60 win against 13th-ranked Utah at the Sprint Center.

Kansas was 12-2 after opening Big 12 play with a one-point win against Baylor in Waco, and by the end of January the record had swelled to 18-3 overall and 7-1 in the league. The lone conference loss came against Iowa State on Jan. 17 in Ames. The two teams took the Allen Fieldhouse court for a Feb. 2 rematch with KU holding a one-game lead over the Cyclones in the standings.

Iowa State forward Georges Niang: My junior year I had just lost a ton of weight, and I was coming out to shoot during pregame. Usually I'd wear baggy shirts to shoot, but that day I was wearing a Dri-Fit shirt—a tight one. I was feeling myself. You know how all the KU fans are there early? I walked out and some kid was like, "Hey Niang, you still need this." And he had a pink sports bra he was swinging around his finger. Ruthless.

The slimmed-down Niang came out firing and hit two early 3s to help his team build a 18-11 lead. Selden, Niang's close friend and high school teammate, struggled early on in that game. He was 0-of-3 with two turnovers early in the second half when Self decided he'd seen enough.

Fred Hoiberg: I remember Self was so pissed at Wayne Selden. He was about to yank him. He had a sub at the scorer's table, but there was never a stoppage. While his sub was sitting at the scorer's table, Selden went off and hit five 3s, and he stayed in the rest of the game. Those are the kinds of things that happen at Allen Fieldhouse.

Naz Mitrou-Long: I was matched up with Wayne Selden, and I'd had a good game when we played them at home (Mitrou-Long scored 20 points) and won that matchup. But when we played them in Lawrence he hit five 3s. They were clutch ones, too, and he was letting me hear it.

Niang scored 24 points, but Selden's second-half surge helped KU to a 89-76 win. Selden scored 19 of his team-high 20 points after intermission.

The Jayhawks slipped up in their next game—losing for the third straight year at Oklahoma

State—but they rebounded with a road win at Texas Tech. Then a hungry Baylor squad arrived in Lawrence looking for payback.

Baylor forward Rico Gathers: We jumped out to a 13-point lead and were up by six (33-27) at halftime. But we ended up shooting ourselves out of the game. Instead of forcing outside shots, I felt like we should've stuck with what was working in the first half, which was pounding it inside and getting to the free throw line. When you're taking too many outside shots (Baylor attempted 23 threes), that can really be a drain.

I liked playing there. I always had decent games there. We should've won that game. Hell, we should've beat them twice, because we lost to them by one point (56-55) at home. We just made the same mistakes we always make down the stretch that would derail us.

Struggling Down the Stretch

Kansas headed to Morgantown on Feb. 16 with a two-game lead in the conference standings over Iowa State. This was their first meeting of the season with West Virginia, which had undergone a bit of a facelift. Frustrated after missing back-to-back NCAA Tournaments, Mountaineers coach Bob Huggins decided to employ a full-court press. This was KU's first look at "Press Virginia."

West Virginia guard Gary Browne: Man, it changed our entire team, our entire program. It gave us an identity. From that point on, every game, all we thought about was, "Are they going to be able to handle Press Virginia?" Maybe they could do it for five minutes or 10 minutes, but for a whole game? It was going to be hard because we did it every day, all day at practice. We did it to ourselves, and we were teammates, so when we did it to other teams, we were going to make their lives horrible. We were going to make it 10 times worse when we play somebody else, because we were already pissed off that we had to do it every day in practice.

That game against Kansas was exciting. We were playing at home and we'd beat them at home the year before when they had Andrew Wiggins. That was my first court rush. Now we had the advantage again, because we had the great home court—and we had Press Virginia, which they had never seen before. We didn't think they'd be able to handle it.

Jamari Traylor: The worst part about playing West Virginia was the practices before we played them. Coach Self would try to do things to mimic their press. There would be times where it'd be five offensive guys vs. five defensive guys—plus the managers. So it was five vs. 10. He'd do all of that and West Virginia would still give us problems. For the most part I think we handled it pretty well.

Kansas trailed 33-30 at halftime but started the second half on fire, going on a 10-0 run to take the lead.

Gary Browne: They handled it well, but we kind of let off the gas. They came back, but I don't think it was because of them. It was us.

Kansas led a majority of the second half and was up 61-60 with 8.3 seconds left when West Virginia rebounded a missed layup by Mason and called timeout.

The Mountaineers had to inbound the ball under KU's basket, and Juwan Staten went the length of the floor to make a layup with 3.9 seconds left to give his team the lead.

Jamari Traylor made a heads up play to grab the ball immediately and throw a football pass from the baseline to Ellis, who caught the ball on the run in the lane and attempted a finger-roll layup for the win.

Bill Self: Perry had the layup to win it and short-armed it.

West Virginia guard Jevon Carter: That would have been bad because I was supposed to be back on defense, but I was just standing there. I saw Perry Ellis run right by me, but I was just stuck. I just couldn't move.

Gary Browne: Juwan made a tremendous layup and then he made a tremendous play trying to run back and stop Perry from making the layup. He missed it and we won.

Wayne Selden: I didn't even consider that a miss. I thought the game was over before that shot, honestly. Nobody on the team said anything to Perry about missing that shot because the game, in our head, was kind of over. I didn't consider it really a good look. Maybe if you slow it down, he might have been able to lay it in, but we never thought it was his fault for missing that.

Gary Browne: It's all about the home-court advantage. I look at the game West Virginia had at Kansas last year. It would have been the first time we beat Kansas at Kansas, and KU was down like 10 with a minute-and-a-half left, and KU came back to win in overtime. That game shows you the power of home-court advantage. Perry missed the layup that day, but it was meant to happen.

Afterward, our fans rushed the floor. The first time, the year before, it was so fun. The second time, I was like, "Look, get me outta here before I suffocate. This ain't no fun." People don't understand how suffocated you get. *I'm trying to have fun, but get me out of here.* But it's always fun. For all college athletes, it's great to have fans out there on the floor, because in professional basketball, unless you win a championship, you'll never experience that again.

The Jayhawks rebounded with a home win against TCU, but then they went back on the road to another hostile environment at Kansas State. After a 5-2 start in the Big 12, the Wildcats' season had gone south. Bruce Weber's squad had lost seven of its previous eight games entering the showdown with KU.

K-State coach Bruce Weber: Our guys rose up. We had a lot of people play well. Justin Edwards and Wes Iwundu and Nigel Johnson. They played at a high level. Down the stretch, we made the plays. It's usually KU making those plays. Even last year (2017), the game was tied and Josh Jackson made a great kick-out and they hit the 3. They always seem to make the big plays. This game, if you go back and watch it, it seems like we made the big plays and the big shots when it mattered. Our guys started believing that they could win.

Thomas Gipson: We probably wouldn't have won if it wasn't for Nigel. He had a great game.

Nigel Johnson had 20 points off the bench after going scoreless in K-State's previous two contests. The Wildcats won 70-63 and students responded by rushing the floor at Bramlage Coliseum. During the court storm, a K-State student intentionally bumped into Traylor from behind.

Jamari Traylor: I was so bummed that we lost. I just wanted to get to the bench, go through the handshake line and get out of there. When it happened, it was so quick. It just felt like someone bumped me. I didn't pay much attention to it. I figured it was just an accident, but when I turned and looked, the guy was running toward the crowd and he disappeared. So then I figured it might have been intentional. Then we got on the bus, and we saw the replay of it on TV, and I was like, "Man, that guy really made a beeline to me."

At the time, people were giving me so much praise for not reacting. But if I'd have realized what actually happened, and that he did that intentionally, I might have reacted differently. I was just so bummed about the loss that it didn't affect me. From then on, every time we played K-State, we'd talk about how they bumped me, and it'd make us want to go out there and crush them.

Bill Self: I wasn't nervous about getting hurt or anything. I just was nervous that it could be a bad situation, because nine out of 10 times if somebody did that to Jamari, he isn't going to let the little dude just walk off. Instead, he just let it go. I was really proud of him for that.

As students danced beneath them on the court below, K-State's players stood atop the scorer's table and celebrated the win. ESPN sideline reporter Holly Rowe used a chair to climb onto the table to interview Thomas Gipson.

Thomas Gipson: It felt good to win my senior year, and then helping Holly Rowe onto the table ... I guess that was a big moment for everybody. That was an act of kindness for me. She needed help.

The Jayhawks were in a funk. They had lost three of six and were now tied for the Big 12 lead with Iowa State at 11-4. Oklahoma was just one game back at 10-5. No KU player was struggling more than Selden, who had just seven points against K-State along with four turnovers.

Wayne Selden: I didn't necessarily suck. I just didn't do what I wanted to do. It was a down year for me, and even for the team as a whole. We weren't the best team overall, and I think we let a lot of distractions get to us.

We were winning games but we never really became anything. We never really found our identity. We really struggled with leadership. Our two best players were Perry and Frank, and neither one of them were big talkers. And then there's me, who is a good leader but I wasn't playing well, so I didn't have the confidence to tell anybody else what to do.

Then you had the freshmen in Kelly, Cliff, Svi (Mykhailiuk) and Devonte' (Graham), so there was really nobody to turn to, so we struggled with leadership.

The NCAA Calls

Another issue for the Jayhawks was that Alexander's transition to the college game hadn't gone nearly as smoothly as Self had hoped. Especially when compared to that of Joel Embiid one year earlier. Alexander, though, had finally begun showing positive flashes in February and had started five straight games. But after the loss at Kansas State, Self was notified that Alexander was under investigation for receiving impermissible benefits.

Bill Self: We had too many distractions. I remember getting the call and being told, "Hey, Cliff can't play or practice." *What?* We were down on the practice floor and our compliance office is calling my cell phone. *"Bill, you have to pull him out."* There were too many things like that.

Jerrance Howard: It was unfair to Cliff. He was really starting to take off in practice. He was starting to figure it out. He was playing his best basketball at the time he was suspended.

Wayne Selden: It was a tough time for Cliff with everything going on. And it was tough for everybody else, not knowing our role and the bigs not knowing their role and not knowing whether Cliff was going to come back and play. And if he comes back, people were like, "Is he going to start over me?" There was a lot of uncertainty, a lot of distractions.

Perry to the rescue, and then ...

One bright spot amid the drama was Ellis. The junior forward helped Kansas get a much-needed, 69-64 win over Texas following the Alexander news. Ellis scored 28 points and had 13 rebounds. Including the victory over the Longhorns, Ellis was averaging 18.7 points in his previous six games. Iowa State, meanwhile, lost its second straight game that day and was now 10-6 in the league—one game behind Oklahoma (11-5) and two behind KU (12-4).

Bill Self: Oh, Perry was doing great. I thought he was going to be Player of the Year in the league. I don't know who ended up winning it that year, but I thought Perry was so good.

West Virginia's Juwan Staten was named Big 12 Player of the Year, a honor he claimed despite missing a key game when the Mountaineers played Kansas at Allen Fieldhouse on March 3. Staten, who had eclipsed the 20-point barrier in his previous three games against KU, was out with an undisclosed injury, and so was Gary Browne. Still, even without those two, West Virginia led by 18 points late in the opening half and by eight points with 3:41 remaining. Kansas, though, battled back and won 79-69 in overtime thanks to big games from Mason (19 points) and Traylor (14). Ellis left the game with a knee sprain late in the first half and did not return in a victory that clinched an 11th straight Big 12 title for the Jayhawks.

Four days later, with Ellis watching from the bench, Kansas lost its regular season finale to Oklahoma in Norman, 75-73.

Oklahoma assistant coach Chris Crutchfield: We scored to go up by three points with eight seconds left. KU threw a home-run pass on their inbounds play. Mason ended up with the ball, and we fouled him while he was shooting a 3 from the right wing. Of course, he made all three free throws to tie it.

We ended up drawing up a shot for Jordan Woodard at the end, and Jordan got to the basket and missed the layup—by the way, he was fouled on the drive (laughing) and it didn't get called—and Buddy (Hield) gets the tip-in at the buzzer.

We beat them 75-73. I remember it was one of those games where it went back and forth and we ended up getting lucky at the buzzer with a lucky tip-in.

Oklahoma forward Ryan Spangler: We knew we weren't going to win the Big 12 with that game, but all season, you're gearing up for a big run in March, and we thought that win would get us going. Or at least we hoped it would.

On the bright side for the Jayhawks, their frontline without Ellis had fared well in Norman. Traylor scored 12 points on 5-of-6 shooting and Lucas had a double-double with 13 points and 12 rebounds.

Landen Lucas: I was just going through the ups and downs of the season. I had gotten a couple opportunities, but nothing consistent. Now here we were, in the last Big 12 game against Oklahoma, and I had my first 30-minute game and was able to get out there and get comfortable. Until then, I hadn't had a chance to do that in my whole career. That was a good feeling. After that, the rest of the year went well as far as getting out there and doing what I do best.

Ellis Returns

The Jayhawks headed to Kansas City for the Big 12 Tournament, and Self decided to hold out Ellis for the opening game against TCU. KU survived, 64-59, thanks to a 25-point effort by Oubre. Ellis returned for the semifinals against Baylor, but it was Selden who emerged as the hero with 25 points in a 62-52 win that propelled the Jayhawks into the title game against Iowa State, a team they'd split with during the regular season.

Selden was brilliant again, scoring 20 points, but Ellis made just 2-of-10 shots and KU didn't have enough. The Cyclones came back from 17 points down to win their second straight Big 12 Tournament with a 70-66 victory.

Fred Hoiberg: We won two Big 12 tournament championships in Kansas City. Those are always very memorable games, especially the last one (in 2015). We were down 17 in the second half and found a way to come back and win it. To find a way to win in the Sprint Center when it was 60 percent blue on their side and 40 percent red on our side, those are experiences you never forget. The intensity is so high. Being able to cut down the nets there twice, beating Kansas in the semis (in 2014) the first time and then in the title game the next year ... those were really fun games.

Naz Mitrou-Long: That place was completely red and blue. It was insane. I remember looking around and seeing the place go crazy. Abdel Nader (13 points) came off the bench and gave us the spark that we needed to get that win.

One thing that I'll never ever forget that made me feel good about myself and the program was when I heard Bill Self say to the media that the Iowa State-Kansas rivalry is bigger than any other game they play in conference. There's a rivalry with K-State, because they're in the same state, but he said the rivalry with Iowa State is their most-anticipated game in the conference. When he said that, I knew that we were on the map and I have nothing but respect for that program. Without those battles, my college career wouldn't have been as fun. I wish we would have broken the streak, but those were definitely some special times.

Bill Self: After Perry got hurt, we didn't have much. He tried to play in the Big 12 Tournament and he wasn't himself.

Shell-Shocked

While the Jayhawks have always been the state's flagship program, a second team from Kansas had become a mainstay in the national spotlight in recent years. Led by fiery head coach Gregg Marshall, Wichita State advanced to the Final Four in 2013 and finished 35-1 the following year, when it earned a No. 1 seed in the NCAA Tournament before falling to Kentucky by two points in the round-of-32.

Naturally, the Shockers' rise to national prominence created a yearning among some fans for an annual KU-Wichita State showdown, either at a neutral site like the Sprint Center or Intrust Bank Arena, or a rotating series at each school's home facility.

Marshall supported the idea but Self said the Jayhawks—who hadn't played Wichita State since 1993—wouldn't have any interest because there was nothing for KU to gain.

In the 2015 NCAA Tournament, though, Kansas didn't have any choice. After beating New Mexico State in the opening round, the Jayhawks squared off against Fred VanVleet, Ron Baker and the Shockers (who'd defeated Indiana) at the CenturyLink Center in Omaha with a Sweet 16 berth on the line.

Wichita State coach Gregg Marshall: Our players had high character, but they also had a lot of pride. To always be looked down upon from the fans or whoever, to always be viewed as second-rate in your own state ... *You've got a nice little program down there, but you're not at our level* ... that sticks in your craw.

Wichita State point guard Fred VanVleet: The whole Kansas-Wichita State thing had been an issue ever since I arrived on campus, and probably long before that. The fans in Wichita thought we could compete with KU. They had been trying to get that game on the schedule for a long, long time, but Kansas didn't want to do it.

I always wanted to play the game. My thing was always, "If you're better than us, just beat us and get it over with." That was my stance. I did see both sides of the argument, though. I understood when Bill Self said they had nothing to gain by playing us. That made sense. But as a competitor, you want to play the game and see what happens. I thought it would've been good for the entire state. I don't think us beating Kansas would've taken away from their recruiting or that type of thing. I don't know if that was their worry or what.

Bill Self: When the bracket came out, it wasn't a deal where we cringed and said, "Oh my God, in the second round we might play Wichita State!" It had more to do with all of the attention it got from fans. It was a bigger deal to them than it was for us.

Fred VanVleet: Coach Marshall lives for situations like that. That's just him. That's his personality. They'd been going back and forth for years and years, trying to get that game done. As much s**t as he talked, now we were in a situation where we had to put our money where our mouths were.

He's still a coach at the end of the day. He had to prepare us to play Indiana first. But I know that, in the back of his mind, he was itching for KU. We all were. We wanted them.

Gregg Marshall: When you finally get an opportunity to confront the situation, after all the buildup … I mean, how many shots are you going to get? I told our guys, "This may be your only chance at Kansas. You better take advantage of it."

Mainly because of the loss of NBA draft pick Cleanthony Early, the 2014-15 Shockers weren't quite as intimidating as the unit that won its first 35 games a year earlier before falling to a grossly-underseeded Kentucky squad in the NCAA Tournament's round-of-32.

Still, while they may have lost Early, the Shockers were still fueled by a "Play Angry" mindset that had resulted in a 28-4 record entering the Big Dance. After rallying for an 81-76 victory over Tom Crean's 10th-seeded Indiana squad, Wichita State turned its attention to the No. 2 seed Jayhawks, who'd defeated New Mexico State.

Kansas 65, Wichita State 78
March 22, 2015 · Omaha, Neb.

Kansas (27-9)

Player	MP	FG	3FG	FT	R	A	F	S	TO	B	TP
Perry Ellis*	34	4-9	0-1	9-10	8	0	3	1	2	0	17
Landen Lucas*	22	1-2	0-0	0-0	10	1	2	0	0	1	2
Frank Mason*	29	5-11	3-5	3-5	6	1	5	0	5	0	16
Kelly Oubre, Jr.*	23	3-9	0-3	3-4	5	1	5	1	2	0	9
Wayne Selden*	23	0-5	0-1	0-0	1	0	1	1	2	0	0
Devonte' Graham	29	5-13	3-8	4-4	1	3	1	5	1	0	17
Brannen Greene	20	0-2	0-2	0-0	0	1	3	0	1	0	0
Svi Mykhailiuk	3	0-1	0-1	0-0	0	0	1	0	0	0	0
Jamari Traylor	17	2-5	0-0	0-0	5	1	2	0	1	0	4
Team					2						
Totals	200	20-57	6-21	19-23	38	8	23	8	14	1	65

Wichita State (30-4)

Player	MP	FG	3FG	FT	R	A	F	S	TO	B	TP
Ron Baker*	37	5-10	2-5	0-0	3	2	1	0	0	0	12
Darius Carter*	16	3-5	0-0	4-5	4	1	3	1	2	0	10
Tekele Cotton*	37	7-12	1-3	4-6	2	3	0	2	2	1	19
Fred VanVleet*	37	4-12	2-4	7-9	6	6	2	4	5	1	17
Evan Wessel*	30	4-6	4-6	0-0	9	0	1	0	0	0	12
Zach Brown	13	2-4	1-2	2-2	1	1	3	1	0	1	7
Rashard Kelly	6	0-0	0-0	0-0	1	0	3	1	1	0	0
Shaquille Morris	10	0-2	0-0	0-0	1	0	4	1	1	0	0
Tom Wamukota	14	0-0	0-0	1-2	2	0	3	0	1	0	1
Team					3						
Totals	200	25-51	10-20	18-24	32	13	20	10	12	3	78

	1st	2nd	Total	FG%	3FG%	FT%
Kansas	26	39	65	35.1	28.6	82.6
Wichita State	29	49	78	49.0	50.0	75.0

Officials: John Higgins, Kipp Kissinger, Gregory Nixon
Technicals: None

Fred VanVleet: When they announced the bracket that year, we felt really disrespected to get a No. 7 seed. We were 28-4 and had beat some really good teams—not to mention we'd made the Final Four in 2013 and gone 35-1 the next year. They still weren't taking us seriously.

After you go 35-1, the next thing is the Final Four or a national championship. That was a realistic goal for us, or at least that's what we thought. We had our sights set really high. Looking back, though, with the group that we had, we probably did a lot more than we should have or could have considering the actual talent we had on the team.

Bill Self: I actually thought Wichita State was extremely talented. And even more than that, their guys were hard-nosed and tough. They had two future pros in the backcourt in Baker and VanVleet, both of whom were veterans. Compare those two with who we were starting at that point in their careers … it was a coin flip game.

Oubre didn't do Kansas any favors during the mandatory media session the day before the game. When a reporter asked Oubre if Wichita State had impressed him during its first-round victory over Indiana, Oubre said he didn't watch the game because he was taking a nap.

Fred VanVleet: I don't know if it was just inexperience on his part or what. But you're in the tournament. You're not going to watch the team you're going to be playing at all? Really? Even if you don't watch it, just lie and say you're about to play a tough team. Just play the part, instead of saying, "I didn't watch them because I was asleep." I couldn't imagine saying something like that in any situation.

On the surface, what he said wasn't all that terrible. But as an athlete, I feel like it's so easy to go out of your way to not be disrespectful in any way. What he said, to me, was careless. So I said, "All right, let's use that as a bulletin board thing." We were always looking for extra ways to get motivated. Then he didn't play well, so it made it even better.

Gregg Marshall: Fred VanVleet ... man, don't cross him.

Fred VanVleet: I vividly remember our forward, Darius Carter, playing Hit 'Em Up by Tupac on his Beats Pill while we were getting ready to go onto the court. He played it about five times in a row. There was just this feeling in the locker room, where we knew we were going to win before the game even started.

Kansas jumped out to a 24-16 lead, but the Jayhawks went more than 6 minutes without a field goal and went into intermission trailing 29-26. KU shot just 32.1 percent in the first half against the Shockers' menacing defense.

Bill Self: They controlled the game and, frankly, we weren't very good. The whole game just had a bad feel to it. You know how we talk about teams peaking at the right time? That team wasn't peaking. Plus, Perry wasn't healthy because of the knee sprain. He wasn't close to being himself.

Wichita State forward Evan Wessel: Our game plan never changed no matter who we were playing. We wanted to come out and force them to play our speed. We wanted to defend and pressure them, like we did with a lot of other teams. And then execute. We thought we had some good matchups with Fred and Ron against their guards. As long as we could contain their athletes and runs, we knew we'd be right there with them.

Wessel averaged just 4.2 points as a junior that season. But against the Jayhawks he scored 12 points—all on 3-pointers. Wessel was teammates with KU's Ellis at Wichita Heights High School.

Gregg Marshall: Evan was guarding his high school teammate of three years, a guy that everybody in the country recruited. I remember being in the gym when I was recruiting Evan and Perry, and everybody was there—Duke, Kentucky, Kansas, K-State and maybe North Carolina and Stanford. They would all line up to go talk to Perry, and I would be the only one to go talk to Evan. He had to deal with that for two or three years, and it was probably pretty personal for him to play well against Perry in that situation.

I didn't have to challenge him. He's self-motivated. He was going to compete like no other. He was stepping out and hitting 3s on one end and guarding Perry Ellis on the other. He knew everything that Perry did. He'd watched him. He's a student of the game. He could have written the scouting report on that matchup.

Evan Wessel: Anytime you got to play against a school that didn't offer you or didn't even give you a look, sure, it adds fire and gives you a little motivation. Perry is obviously a tremendous player. With him being a good friend, I'd watched a lot of his games because I wanted to see him do well. I'd seen a lot of the KU games and then played with him and played against him. And vice versa, too. It was a little weird in warmups, and then shaking hands during introductions—we came out together—but after that, once that ball goes up, I'm not your friend anymore. You want to do everything you can to win and you want to stop him at all costs.

A 3-pointer by Wessel at the 16:51 mark of the second half gave Wichita State a 37-30 lead, and the Jayhawks would never get closer than that. Each time KU appeared to be gaining momentum, a shot by Wessel, Tekele Cotton (19 points), VanVleet (17) or Baker (12) would squelch their enthusiasm.

Gregg Marshall: I think we popped them in the nose and let them know it was going to be a ballgame. I don't know if we had broken their spirit at all.

They had to call their fourth timeout very early in the second half, and I'm thinking, "Wow, they've got one left and there's 16 minutes left in the game. There's a lot of time left to comeback and only have one timeout." I don't know why they had used so many timeouts that early, but they had, and at that point I started to feel really good.

Bill Self: They were so much better than their seed. You watched them and thought, "Damn these guys are good."

No player was as effective as Cotton. Along with his game-high point total, Cotton completely shut down KU's Selden. One year after his two-point performance in an NCAA Tournament loss to Stanford, Selden went scoreless against the Shockers. He missed all five of his shots.

Gregg Marshall: No offense to Wayne Selden, but Tekele did that to a lot of people. He was a dynamic defender, tough and strong. I don't think Selden even came close to scoring. I'm not sure he even got a good look. And that was big, because he was obviously very talented and one of their key cogs on the perimeter. Not only did he shut down Selden, but he was our leading scorer.

Wayne Selden: That s**t hurt. It just summed up how my whole season went. It was up and down all year, and that was the biggest down of them all. Going through that Wichita State game and losing to Stanford the year before, from then on I had a different mindset. But for a while after my sophomore year, I was messed up in the head a little bit.

MOST MADDENING NCAA TOURNAMENT LOSSES

1. No. 11 VCU 71, No. 1 Kansas 61 (2011, Elite Eight): With all three other No. 1 seeds losing, the path to the NCAA title was set up perfectly for the Jayhawks—as long as they got by VCU. Instead, Kansas trailed by 14 at halftime and never recovered against the fourth-worst team to ever make the NCAA tournament, according to KenPom.com. KU went just 2-of-21 from 3-point range.

2. No. 9 Northern Iowa 69, No. 1 Kansas 67 (2010, Round of 32): With Sherron Collins, Cole Aldrich, Tyshawn Taylor and the Morris twins, this was arguably Bill Self's most-talented team. Ali Farokhmanesh's gutsy 3-pointer in transition put Northern Iowa up by four with 35 seconds remaining, and KU could never recover. KU's starting guards went 7-of-27 from the field and 2-of-15 from distance

3. No. 14 Bucknell 64, No. 3 Kansas 63 (2005, first round): Wayne Simien's 12-foot turnaround jumper at the buzzer was off the mark, as Roy Williams holdovers Simien, Aaron Miles, Keith Langford and Michael Lee experienced bitter ends to what were otherwise brilliant careers. Langford, who hadn't played a full game in 16 days for health reasons, shot 1-of-7.

4. No. 3 Oregon 74, No. 1 Kansas 60 (2017, Elite Eight): Fueled by a hometown crowd at the Sprint Center, Frank Mason and KU seemed destined for the Final Four after beating their first three opponents by an average of 32 points. But early foul trouble for Josh Jackson and a dismal shooting night by Devonte' Graham doomed Kansas, as Bill Self fell to 2-7 in Elite Eight games.

5. No. 10 Stanford 60, No. 2 Kansas 57 (2014 Round of 32): Playing without injured center Joel Embiid (back), the Jayhawks needed a big game from Andrew Wiggins to advance to the Sweet 16. They didn't get it. Wiggins made just one basket and attempted only four field goals for a team that shot 32.8 percent. Even more frustrating: Embiid was set to return the following week.

6. No. 2 Villanova 64, No. 1 Kansas 59 (2016, Elite Eight): Even though the Wildcats went on to win the NCAA title—annihilating Big 12 foe Oklahoma in the process—this one was still difficult to stomach. Kansas committed 16 turnovers, including two costly ones in the final minute, and leading scorer Perry Ellis was held to four points on 1-of-5 shooting.

7. No. 4 Michigan 87, No. 1 Kansas 85 OT (2013, Sweet 16): Leading by 14 with less than 7 minutes remaining, the Jayhawks thought they had this one wrapped up. But Wolverines guard Trey Burke led a furious late charge and forced overtime with a 30-foot 3-pointer with four seconds remaining. Ben McLemore had 20 points for a KU team that over-achieved all season.

8. No. 13 Bradley 77, No. 4 Kansas 73 (2006, First round): Five days after beating a loaded Texas squad in the title game of the Big 12 Tournament, the youthful Jayhawks—Mario Chalmers, Brandon Rush and Julian Wright were freshmen—seemed overwhelmed by the hype and hoopla of the postseason. Bradley, though, was better that its seed. The Braves, who would advance to the Sweet 16, were a veteran team with a lottery pick (Patrick O'Bryant) at center.

9. No. 7 Wichita State 78, No. 2 Kansas 65 (2015, Round of 32): The Shockers were clearly the better team, so the loss itself wasn't as bad as the manner in which it occurred. The Jayhawks were simply out-toughed and out-hustled by Fred VanVleet, Tekele Cotton, Ron Baker and the rest of the Shockers. Cotton had 19 points and held Wayne Selden scoreless.

10. No. 2 Michigan State 67, No. 3 Kansas 62 (2009, Sweet 16): Kansas led by 10 points in the first half but floundered after intermission, as the Spartans ended the game on a 10-2 run. Sherron Collins scored 20 points and Cole Aldrich had 17 points and 14 rebounds for a KU squad that exceeded expectations after losing seven of its top eight players from the 2008 NCAA championship team.

One play that stood out to VanVleet occurred when KU's Oubre lazily jogged to retrieve a loose ball. Just before Oubre corralled it, Wichita State reserve forward Zach Brown raced by, picked it up and went down the court for an easy layup.

Fred VanVleet: You take a guy who has been a first-round pick, a guy who turned into a great NBA player, and you put him against Zach Brown, a guy who no one knows who the hell he is, and they're going against each other for a loose ball, and Zach Brown tries harder and gets it. That kind of stuff was the difference in the game. Those kind of things are the reason we won. We weren't worried about careers or who was going to be the better player. For those 40 minutes, that was the kind of effort it took, and we had more of it.

Wichita State won the game 78-65 and advanced to play Notre Dame the following weekend in the Sweet 16. Kansas ended its season 27-9. Oubre scored nine points on 3-of-9 shooting. A few weeks later he announced he was leaving KU after one season to enter the NBA draft, where he was the 15th overall pick.

Evan Wessel: After we beat them, Fred said, "Well, he has all the time in the world to nap now." It was kind of funny.

Fred VanVleet: It was surprising. We thought it was going to be a tougher game. We expected it to be a dogfight, and it was for a little bit. But we were more physical. I don't know if we were more prepared, but I think we were hungrier. We were the bigger, stronger, tougher team that game. Once the second half started, we were on cruise control from there. I don't know of too many teams that could've beat us that night.

I will say this: I think their guys grew up in that game. They had some young guys out there, along with Perry. It was an experience for them and they definitely got better after that. It was a learning experience for them. Not to take anything away from them, but that day, we were just the better team.

VanVleet was likely referring to Devonte' Graham. The freshman scored 17 points off the bench and also recorded five steals. Mason (17 points) and Ellis (16) also scored in double figures for the Jayhawks, who shot just 35.1 percent from the field. Wichita State made 49 percent of its shots, including 59 percent in the decisive second half.

Devonte' Graham: I was just trying to do what I always did, which was come off the bench and bring some energy. It was a rough game for some of us on the squad that day. I was just trying to make some plays and get some shots.

After that I was definitely more motivated. I remember about a month later, I was working out one day in the gym by myself, and Coach came in and said, "Keep working hard. You should never not start another game as long as you're here." That just motivated me even more, just him having that confidence in me.

Fred VanVleet: The weirdest thing about that game is that those KU guys have never been anything but cool to us. We worked camps with them in the summer. Guys like

Selden, Mason, Traylor, Perry ... we weren't best friends or anything, but we all were cool. The players were cool but the fanbases hated each other, so it was a weird dynamic.

Everyone was cool in the handshake line. We respected one another. I wanted to make sure I got in front of Jerrance Howard to shake his hand. He was at Illinois when I was in high school in Rockford. He recruited me, but not hard enough (laughing).

A little more from ...

Wayne Selden: I had to deal with a lot that year. One night, Jamari and I were eating at Quinton's and we searched our name on Twitter. A tweet pops up that says "Wayne and Jamari just chilling" and under it was a picture of two trash bags. That's a lot to deal with for a 19-year-old. We were like, "Damn man, this is real." What made it worse was that the tweet was from a Kansas fan. Back then I probably favorited it, but eventually I learned to ignore that stuff.

You can't do anything about what people are saying. It's just part of being in that environment. When things were great there, things were fantastic. But my sophomore year, even off the court, it was like a cloud was over us. We lost nine games—which would be a solid year for most teams in the country. But that's unacceptable at KU. Even though I was mad most of the time, that year really helped me as a player. I started looking at some numbers and some things that were hurting me, and I realized I was taking way too many long twos, way too many 17- and 18-foot jump shots. Those killed me. I don't know why I was doing that. Maybe I was just trying to change my game or find an identity, but I decided to put a stop to it.

If I would've left after my freshman year, who knows what would've happened. But after the sophomore year I had, there's no chance I could've entered the draft. I had no choice but to come back.

Considered one of the top recruiters in the country, Jerrance Howard—who played for Self at Illinois and then coached there under Bruce Weber—arrived at Kansas in May of 2013. Since the recruiting cycle was already finished for that year's class, Howard's first contribution to KU as a recruiter was the 2014 haul that consisted of Alexander, Oubre, Graham and Mykhailiuk.

Jerrance Howard: I didn't come in here cocky, but I was pretty confident when I got the job at Kansas. I was at one of the best programs in America with the best coach in America, who was also a great recruiter. We had a great staff. I thought I was going to be able to go out and get everybody. I had been recruiting Jahlil Okafor since he was in the seventh grade. I was going to his junior high school games. I had a good relationship with his dad. They were like family. Not long after I got here, I was on the phone with Jahlil and he said, "Hold on, Coach. I've gotta take this call real quick." He clicked back over and said, "Let me call you right back. Coach K is on the other line." That's when it hit me. I was like, "OK, this is the real deal."

People always think you're supposed to get guys easily when you're at Kansas. But what they forget is that the competition level increases, and all of a sudden you're going against Duke and Kentucky and Arizona for players, so you've got to work harder than ever. That was the time where I said, "I've got to roll up my sleeves and get to work."

Cliff Alexander was our main big man target in that class. There were some rumors that some third parties had gotten to Tia, his mom. I was in the airport and Coach Self was doing a home visit out east. He was supposed to meet me in Chicago, and then we'd go to Cliff's for a visit. I'm on the plane about to take off and Cliff's mom calls and says, "Coach, I think we're going somewhere else. I'm not feeling Kansas. I'm not feeling Kansas at all. I just heard that y'all want Jahlil more than y'all want Cliff." Someone had put that rumor in her head. So Coach is in the air, coming to meet me in Chicago, and we don't even know if we can get in Cliff's front door. The flight attendant was telling me to get off the phone and I was like, "Ma'am, you're going to have to kick me off of this plane, because I can't get off this phone." She came back to me three times and told me to get off the phone. I told Cliff's mom that I wasn't hanging up until she promised me we could still come visit. She finally said OK, and we ended up going and having a great time. We won her over and we ended up getting Cliff.

Although he wasn't highly-ranked at the time, the jewel of that class ended up being Graham, who had originally signed to play at Appalachian State and then was forced to go to prep school when he decided he wanted out of his commitment and Appalachian State coach Jason Capel would not comply.

Devonte' Graham: It was definitely tough. I just didn't know if I was going to be able play college ball or where I was going to go. I knew teams wanted me, I just couldn't talk to them because I was still tied by that letter-of-intent to Appalachian State. There were a lot of stressful nights.

I definitely had some anger inside. The coaching staff at Appalachian State had always told me they wanted what was best for me, but that changed once I told them I wanted to reopen my recruitment. So I was mad at the fact that they really *didn't* want what was best for me. At my high school games, a lot of people were wearing "Free D-Tae" shirts in the stands.

I had committed and signed early, in November, before the season had started my senior year. I started playing really well and I started realizing I could go to a bigger school than App State. But when I told their coach I wanted to reopen my recruitment, he wouldn't let me do it.

I was at the barbershop about to get a haircut when my coach at Brewster Academy called and told me the App State coach (Jason Capel) had been fired and that I was getting my release. My mom called, everyone called to congratulate me. Twitter blew up and my phone started blowing up with coaches. My phone wouldn't stop ringing. I set up a visit to Kansas. I went to NC State and Virginia, too.

I ended up signing with Kansas and came in with Kelly and Cliff and Svi. One thing Coach Self always says is, "Faces change, expectations don't." Each year, we're going to lose people, but other guys come in. Every year, we're excited. We know we've always got that target on us, because of what is on the front of our chest.

I think I had an OK freshman year. I battled through some injuries. It was definitely a big step up from Brewster. The weight room was the biggest obstacle for me. On the court, I adapted to stuff pretty well. But the weight room was tough. I had lifted before, but Coach Hudy does things so much differently. She does a lot of Olympic-type stuff, where it's all about technique. I was just used to doing basic stuff like bench press and squats. Now I was having to do snatches and cleans. It wasn't just about how much you can lift, it was about doing it with the right form and not getting hurt. It only takes two or three weeks to notice how much it's helping. Udoka (Azubuike) lost about 30 pounds his first three months. Hudy knows what she's doing.

I didn't feel any pressure freshman year. I wasn't a top-tier recruit, so a lot of people didn't know who I was. It didn't matter, I just wanted to be on the court.

Svi and I really bonded. He came in and really couldn't speak English. I was always telling him how to pronounce certain words. He didn't know what a spoon was or how to say "spoon." I taught him all about our lingo and how we talk. Even before he came over here, he loved hip-hop. His favorite artist is DMX.

Naz Mitrou-Long: We definitely thought we were going to win the league that year. We really, really believed we were going to break KU's streak. The problem was that they never got upset. They never lost a game they weren't supposed to lose—and we did. We dropped a game at Texas Tech, and that was kind of the difference-maker. We still had an opportunity after that, but we lost at Kansas State and then we couldn't beat Baylor at home. We shot ourselves in the foot.

Although it may have seemed like it at the time, the Baylor loss wasn't all of that big of an upset. The Bears got off to a 3-4 start in the Big 12 before battling back to finish 11-7. The impressive turnaround prompted a phone call from Self to Scott Drew.

Bill Self: I thought Scott did as good of a job as anyone in our league that year. When you get off to a start like that it's easy to lose your team. But he clearly got their attention and they were able to change their season. They were playing as well as anyone during that last month.

Scott Drew: Bill and I came into the league together, and a lot of times people will worry only about themselves or their program. Bill has always been about the entire league. He wants what's best for the conference. There have been times when he's called me and said, "You're doing a great job, hang in there!" He knows success by any school in the league benefits the entire conference.

He's on the college basketball committee. That takes a lot of time. I respect him for doing that. He's a great ambassador for college basketball. He gets along with people. He finds a common ground with everyone he meets. I joke with him about it, but I honestly think he'd be a heck of a governor.

Gary Browne: Beating Kansas at home my last two years created a new rivalry. It's good for college. It's good for us. I would have loved to have won at Kansas, just one time. Unfortunately, it didn't happen. And I missed that great (2015) game with an injury. That would have been my last game there and me and Juwan couldn't play that game because we were hurt. It was sad, because it's like missing out on playing at Madison Square Garden or the Carrier Dome at Syracuse. It's always a great atmosphere. But I'll take the two wins at West Virginia. I'll remember those forever.

Anytime we beat Kansas, Coach Huggins got a bonus. I knew about the bonus because I'm a little bit more mature. I try to know what's going on around me. I don't think nobody thought about the bonus. And he doesn't ever talk about it because he doesn't care about it.

I still ask him for some of that bonus money. He always laughs and says "I gave you a scholarship." We won the last two years I was there. That's $50,000. I know he can give me something. *Give me something!* I'm still going to ask Coach for that bonus every time I see him. I promise you that.

ESPN commentator Fran Fraschilla: The Florida game at Allen Fieldhouse in 2015 was one of the best games I've called. KU was down by about 20 and then Wayne Selden went crazy and they came back and won. The thing about Kansas fans is that they never let the team lose. On the rare occasions that they do lose at home, time may have run out, but it's not because every single person in that building hadn't given it their all.

There are a lot of places where a team gets down 15 with 8 minutes to go and people head for the exits. By and large, Kansas fans have had the ability to will their team back into the game when it was necessary. That's rare around the country.

2014-15 Season Summary

Results (27-9, 13-5)

November

14	UC Santa Barbara	W, 69 - 59
18	vs. Kentucky	L, 72 - 40
24	Rider	W, 87 - 60
27	vs. Rhode Island	W, 60 - 76
28	vs. Tennessee	W, 82 - 67
30	vs. Michigan State	W, 56 - 61

December

5	Florida	W, 71 - 65
10	@ Georgetown	W, 70 - 75
13	vs. Utah	W, 63 - 60
20	Lafayette	W, 96 - 69
22	@ Temple	L, 77 - 52
30	Kent State	W, 78 - 62

January

4	UNLV	W, 76 - 61
7	@ Baylor	W, 55 - 56
10	Texas Tech	W, 86 - 54
13	Oklahoma State	W, 67 - 57
17	@ Iowa State	L, 86 - 81
19	Oklahoma	W, 85 - 78
24	@ Texas	W, 62 - 75
28	@ TCU	W, 61 - 64
31	Kansas State	W, 68 - 57

February

2	Iowa State	W, 89 - 76
7	@ Oklahoma State	L, 67 - 62
10	@ Texas Tech	W, 51 - 73
14	Baylor	W, 74 - 64
16	@ West Virginia	L, 62 - 61
21	TCU	W, 81 - 72
23	@ Kansas State	L, 70 - 63
28	Texas	W, 69 - 64

March

3	West Virginia	W, 76 - 69
7	@ Oklahoma	L, 75 - 73
12	vs. TCU	W, 64 - 59
13	vs. Baylor	W, 62 - 52
14	vs. Iowa State	L, 66 - 70
20	vs. New Mexico State	W, 75 - 56
22	vs. Wichita State	L, 65 - 78

All-Big 12 Team

Player of the Year:
Buddy Hield, Oklahoma, Jr., G

Defensive Player of the Year:
Jameel McKay, Iowa State, Jr., F

Newcomer of the Year:
TaShawn Thomas, Oklahoma, Jr., F

Freshman of the Year:
Myles Turner, Texas, Fr., F

Sixth Man of the Year:
Taurean Prince, Baylor, Jr., F

Coach of the Year:
Bob Huggins, West Virginia

First Team
Rico Gathers, Baylor, Jr., F
Georges Niang, Iowa State, Jr., F
Perry Ellis, Kansas, Jr., F
Buddy Hield, Oklahoma, Jr., G
Juwan Staten, West Virginia, Sr., G

Second Team
Kenny Chery, Baylor, Sr., G
Taurean Prince, Baylor, Jr., F
Monté Morris, Iowa State, So., G
Frank Mason III, Kansas, So., G
Le'Bryant Nash, Oklahoma State, Sr., F

Third Team
Jameel McKay, Iowa State, Jr., F
TaShawn Thomas, Oklahoma, Sr., F
Phil Forte, Oklahoma State, Jr., G
Isaiah Taylor, Texas, So., G
Myles Turner, Texas, Fr., F

Honorable Mention
Dustin Hogue, Iowa State, Sr., F
Kelly Oubre, Kansas, Fr., G
Wayne Selden, Kansas, So., G
Marcus Foster, Kansas State, So., G
Thomas Gipson, Kansas State, Sr., F
Nino Williams, Kansas State, Sr., F
Isaiah Cousins, Oklahoma, Jr., G
Ryan Spangler, Oklahoma, Jr., F
Kyan Anderson, TCU, Sr., G
Jonathan Holmes, Texas, Sr., F
Devin Williams, West Virginia, Jr., F

All-Defensive Team
Rico Gathers, Baylor, Jr., F
Jameel McKay, Iowa State, Jr., F
Michael Cobbins, Oklahoma State, Sr., F
Anthony Hickey, Oklahoma State, Sr., G
Myles Turner, Texas, Fr., F
Jevon Carter, West Virginia, Fr., G

All-Newcomer Team
Jameel McKay, Iowa State, Jr., F**
Kelly Oubre, Kansas, Fr., G
TaShawn Thomas, Oklahoma, Sr., F
Anthony Hickey, Oklahoma State, Sr., G
Myles Turner, Texas, Fr., F

** Unanimous selection

Kansas Awards

Perry Ellis
NABC All-District (8) First Team
Orlando Classic MVP

Frank Mason
NABC All-District (8) Second Team
Orlando Classic All-Tournament

Wayne Selden
Big 12 Championship All-Tournament

Season Stats

#	Player	CL	POS	HT	Hometown	G	GS	FG%	3P%	FT%	R	A	S	B	PTS
34	Perry Ellis	JR	F	6-8	Wichita, KS	34	34	.457	.391	.730	6.9	1.2	0.8	0.7	13.8
0	Frank Mason	SO	G	5-11	Petersburg, VA	36	36	.441	.429	.786	3.9	3.9	1.4	0.1	12.6
1	Wayne Selden	SO	G	6-5	Roxbury, MA	36	36	.382	.365	.657	2.8	2.6	0.6	0.5	9.4
12	Kelly Oubre	FR	G	6-7	Henderson, NV	36	27	.444	.358	.718	5.0	0.8	1.1	0.4	9.3
2	Cliff Alexander	FR	F	6-8	Chicago, IL	28	6	.566		.671	5.3	0.4	0.2	1.3	7.1
4	Devonte' Graham	FR	G	6-2	Raleigh, NC	29	0	.393	.425	.724	1.5	2.1	0.9	0.0	5.7
14	Brannen Greene	SO	G	6-7	Juliette, GA	35	2	.422	.404	.917	2.1	0.8	0.3	0.1	5.7
31	Jamari Traylor	JR	F	6-8	Chicago, IL	35	18	.486		.600	3.7	0.9	0.8	1.1	4.8
33	Landen Lucas	SO	F	6-10	Portland, OR	32	14	.532		.667	4.3	0.4	0.3	0.6	3.5
10	Svi Mykhailiuk	FR	G	6-8	Ukraine	26	6	.306	.288	.833	1.2	0.7	0.3	0.0	2.8
42	Hunter Mickelson	JR	F	6-10	Jonesboro, AR	19	0	.500		.867	1.8	0.1	0.4	1.0	2.4
5	Evan Manning	JR	G	6-3	Lawrence, KS	9	0	.400	.333		0.2	0.2	0.3	0.0	0.6
22	Josh Pollard	FR	G	6-4	Orem, UT	7	0	.250			0.3	0.1	0.1	0.0	0.3
11	Tyler Self	SO	G	6-2	Lawrence, KS	7	0	.250	.000		0.1	0.1	0.0	0.0	0.3
15	Christian Garrett	SR	G	6-3	Los Angeles, CA	9	1	.200	.000		0.2	0.1	0.0	0.0	0.2
23	Chris Huey	SR	F	6-7	Kansas City, KS	1	0	.000			0.0	0.0	0.0	0.0	0.0

## CHAPTER 12

2015-16
A BETTER FIT

Kansas didn't have to wait long to get back to work after what was a down year by KU standards in 2014-15. The Jayhawks were selected to represent the United States at the World University Games in Gwangju, South Korea in July.

Other than Kelly Oubre and Cliff Alexander—both of whom entered the NBA draft—Kansas returned all of its key pieces from the previous season. Bill Self had also made a decision to return to a two-point guard look—similar to the 2006-2010 teams—with Frank Mason playing alongside sophomore Devonte' Graham in the backcourt. This allowed Wayne Selden to move from shooting guard to small forward after a subpar sophomore season.

Graham suffered a partially torn quadricep tendon during a practice leading up to the overseas event and was replaced by SMU point guard Nic Moore, allowing Selden to stay on the wing. Kansas rolled through the bracket and won gold with Selden shining in his new role, averaging 19.3 points per game. He was named the MVP of the tournament less than four months after going scoreless in the postseason loss to Wichita State.

Wayne Selden: I needed that. After my sophomore year, I was so happy that we only had to wait a few months to get back on the court, because I was really messed up mentally after that season. My whole mindset from that point on was "let's go get it."

At the World University Games, I was really depended on heavily because we were so short on guards. It was just *"Go score!"* which was exactly what I needed to hear. It gave me the confidence to say, "I've still got this. It's still in there. I've still got what it takes."

Bill Self: The World University Games came along at just the right time, especially for Wayne. It gave him so much confidence. He was by far the best player there. Frank had a good tournament. Perry didn't have a great tournament—he was decent. The pieces on that team just fit better than they had the previous year.

We won that tournament and Devonte' didn't even play. To win that deal the way we did, it was cool. It was a lot of fun. I thought it was good for us. There was no pressure. It was just, "Hey, let's have fun and enjoy each other." We didn't have curfews. We didn't need to eat together and didn't do scouting reports. We just went over there and had fun and played. They responded well to it.

First Cliff, Now Diallo

The drama of Cliff Alexander's suspension late in 2015 had been a huge distraction for the Jayhawks—and now they were forced to deal with it again at the start of the 2015-16 season.

Five-star freshman Cheick Diallo, a McDonald's All-American originally from Mali, could travel with the team but was unable to play as the NCAA looked into his past coursework to deem whether he was academically ineligible. KU's own research determined there should not be an issue, and the school went on the defensive.

Bill Self: It was so exhausting. I was spending more time on Cheick's situation than I was coaching the team. If I hadn't of known what I'd known, I'm sure we wouldn't have spent as much time on it, because you have no idea where the NCAA is getting their information, and we'd have just assumed they were right. A lot of times you assume what they say is 100 percent accurate. In this situation, we went, "Nooooo! No, we know that he didn't do that. We know that's not right. We know this."

On Nov. 25, the NCAA ruled Diallo eligible and determined he had received a limited amount of impermissible benefits, which resulted in a five-game suspension. Since he had already missed five games, he was allowed to play in KU's sixth contest—a Dec. 1 tilt against Loyola (MD). Diallo scored 13 points in his debut, but he would only score in double figures one more time all season.

Bill Self: We talked about it beforehand, because we loved Cheick, but it was going to be hard for him to play a lot even if he did get eligible. He'd just missed so much time—he couldn't practice until that point—and was so far behind. But it was best for his life that he got eligible. So I was real happy with our administration. They said, "Hey, if he deserves to be eligible, we've got to do whatever we can to make sure he is." It didn't work out great for him from a playing time standpoint, but we also had a lot of big guys.

On the court, the Jayhawks didn't seem distracted at all by the Diallo controversy. They finished non-conference play with an 11-1 record and won the championship of the Maui Invitational.

Wayne Selden: Dealing with what happened to Cheick our junior year wasn't as difficult as the year before with Cliff, because Cheick wasn't really going to play that much no matter what, and we knew that.

That was a season where we pretty much had everything figured out. Me and Perry and Frank and Devonte' … by then we had all been together for a while. We felt like we were the best team in the country. It just all came together. We had all developed leadership qualities by that point in our careers. Instead of just looking for one leader, we had three or four.

Whoa Buddy!

Kansas opened the Big 12 with an impressive 102-74 win over No. 23 Baylor. Two days later on Monday, Jan. 4, the Jayhawks moved up to No. 1 in the USA Today Coaches' poll. Undefeated Oklahoma (12-0) was No. 1 in the Associated Press poll. The timing was perfect, as the debate over who the "real" No. 1 team in the country would be settled that night when the Jayhawks and Sooners squared off at Allen Fieldhouse. Oklahoma was led by Buddy Hield, the early National Player of the Year favorite who had averaged 28.5 points in his previous six contests.

Jamari Traylor: People were saying it was one of the biggest games in the history of college basketball because we had two No. 1 teams going at it.

Devonte' Graham: There was so much hype before the game. We were bouncing around in practice. We had so much energy. The fans were lining up outside and Buddy Hield was gonna be here.

Kansas 109, Oklahoma 106
January 4, 2016 · Lawrence, Kan.

Kansas (13-1)

Player	MP	FG	3FG	FT	R	A	F	S	TO	B	TP
Perry Ellis*	53	11-28	2-3	3-4	13	3	2	0	1	1	27
Devonte' Graham*	46	6-12	2-2	8-9	7	3	4	1	4	0	22
Frank Mason*	53	5-20	1-5	4-5	7	6	4	3	4	0	15
Hunter Mickelson*	9	1-4	0-0	0-0	3	0	0	0	0	0	2
Wayne Selden*	43	9-17	3-7	0-1	5	2	3	1	0	0	21
Carlton Bragg	3	1-2	0-0	0-0	1	0	0	1	1	0	2
Cheick Diallo	5	0-0	0-0	0-0	1	0	1	0	0	0	0
Brannen Greene	17	2-3	2-3	0-0	5	2	1	1	1	0	6
Landen Lucas	25	1-3	0-0	3-4	8	1	1	1	0	1	5
Svi Mykhailiuk	6	1-2	1-2	0-0	0	0	3	0	0	0	3
Jamari Traylor	15	3-3	0-0	0-0	4	0	3	1	2	3	6
Team					6				1		
Totals	275	40-94	11-22	18-23	60	17	22	9	14	5	109

Oklahoma (12-1)

Player	MP	FG	3FG	FT	R	A	F	S	TO	B	TP
Isaiah Cousins*	39	2-14	0-3	0-0	2	4	2	1	1	1	4
Buddy Hield*	54	13-23	8-15	12-14	8	7	4	0	5	0	46
Khadeem Lattin*	46	5-9	0-0	0-1	14	2	3	1	2	6	10
Ryan Spangler*	51	6-11	2-4	0-0	18	0	4	2	3	2	14
Jordan Woodard*	50	9-20	6-9	3-4	4	7	5	2	2	1	27
Dante Buford	10	0-4	0-1	1-2	1	1	1	0	0	2	1
Christian James	6	0-1	0-0	1-2	1	0	0	2	0	0	1
Akolda Manyang	3	0-1	0-0	0-0	1	0	1	0	1	0	0
Dinjiyl Walker	16	1-5	0-1	1-1	4	0	2	0	1	0	3
Team					2				1		
Totals	275	36-88	16-33	18-24	55	21	22	8	16	12	106

	1st	2nd	OT	2OT	3OT	Total	FG%	3FG%	FT%
Kansas	40	37	9	8	15	109	42.6	50.0	78.3
Oklahoma	44	33	9	8	12	106	40.9	48.5	75.0

Officials: John Higgins, Kelly Self, Steve Olson
Technicals: Oklahoma (0), Kansas (1 Bench)

Landen Lucas: It was just crazy. That was one of the biggest games I'd been a part of at Kansas. I remember all day hearing 1 vs. 1. Usually when games get hyped up that much, they don't live up to expectations. But you could kind of tell going into the game that it was going to be something special. It wasn't going to be a deal where one team was overrated. They were really, really good—and we were, too.

Oklahoma assistant coach Chris Crutchfield: I remember Brent Musburger at shootaround talking about, "We'll get a chance to see who the real No. 1 is." Our guys were fired up. They were anxious and very confident. We were undefeated. It was a great atmosphere leading up to it because of the way ESPN portrayed the game.

Oklahoma guard Jordan Woodard: It was a championship game atmosphere. We hadn't won at KU since 1993, so we wanted to be the ones to end that streak. We felt like we had the team to do it.

Coach (Lon) Kruger wanted us to go in with that championship mentality that we couldn't lose that game. We treated it as a championship game and wanted to go all out, play our hardest and execute.

Oklahoma forward Ryan Spangler: Me and Buddy and Isaiah (Cousins) were seniors at that point, and Jordan was a junior. We were a little tired of KU beating us. We'd been starting together for three years, and entering that season we knew it was going to be our year. We went undefeated in the non-conference and were playing really well. That Saturday we played Iowa State, another Top 10 team, and beat them. Two days later we had to go to KU and knew we couldn't be tired. We had to be ready to go. It was going to be one of the biggest games of our careers.

Jordan Woodard: Our game plan was just to push the ball and take good shots. Obviously we needed to defend, but we had rim protectors with Khadeem Lattin and Ryan Spangler. On the offensive end, we wanted to use our guards' quickness to really speed up the tempo and not let them get the momentum because they were at home.

Oklahoma coach Lon Kruger: We liked to push the pace and liked attacking and certainly KU did, as well. The result was a high-paced game in which a lot of players made a lot of really good plays.

Oklahoma and Kansas traded leads throughout the opening half. With 3:02 left before intermission, Jayhawks guard Svi Mykhailiuk nailed a 3-pointer right in front of OU's bench to put KU ahead 37-26. The Sooners, though, closed the half on an 18-3 run and led 44-40 at the break. Hield had 22 points.

Jamari Traylor: He came out scorching. I always knew he was a good player but his senior year he came out on a whole new level.

Wayne Selden: The game plan was for me to come out and guard Buddy, but I picked up two early fouls.

Frank Mason: I wanted to guard Buddy. I said something to Coach, because I felt like I was going to be able to guard him the best.

Wayne Selden: Frank wanted to guard him, of course. Frank did a good job. But Buddy put on a performance.

Perry Ellis: They were getting rebounds and getting the ball right to him. He was putting shots up so quick. Frank was on him, but it didn't matter. He was on fire, hitting everything. It seemed like he couldn't miss.

Bill Self: I loved Buddy. We had them down by 11 in the first half, but then he got on a roll and they came back to take the lead. He made a shot and looked right at me and smiled and clapped his hands. He said, "Looks like we've got a ballgame." (Laughing). I love stuff like that.

Chris Crutchfield: He was never quiet. It was constant. He was talking s**t. He was saying, "I got this s**t. I got it." He started getting that swagger.

Jordan Woodard: There was talking but it wasn't to the point that anyone lost focus. I felt like each player was so locked in, it was hard to talk because if you started jawing, you'd lose focus and lose sight of your man. They left me open a couple times, and if you leave me open, I'm going to make you pay.

Assistant coach Kurtis Townsend: We told our guys, "Guard him and don't let him catch the ball. Play him before he catches it." He was feeling so good. He was a kid I'd recruited since he was a sophomore in high school. I knew him well, to the point where we still communicated even when he was playing for Oklahoma. He'd text me after a good game, or vice versa.

That night he ran by our bench after he made a 3, looked at us and smiled with his buck teeth, and started clapping. He was like, "We got us a ball game, guys! We got us a ball game!" He was in a zone. It's great to see. He's the nicest kid in the world. If you knew him, you knew he wasn't cocky. He just wanted to compete. That's why it didn't bother us.

Oklahoma maintained its lead for most of the second half—the Sooners were up by as many as 10—but Kansas refused to fold.

Ryan Spangler: Playing at KU is tough. You can get up by 20 or 30 and it's still not over. That game was proof.

Chris Crutchfield: As the game played out, it became an all-time classic. No one knew Buddy was going to play the way he played in an environment like that. It's a hard place to play. It's so intimidating walking into the place, for one, and if you have a team who is not secure and not talented and mature, you can get blown out really easy just because the effect the crowd has on you—and on Kansas. It's going to take a very secure and veteran team to go in there and beat those guys. Not many people do it.

Jordan Woodard: After Buddy got hot (in the first half), we felt like we had the game. I remember during a timeout, Coach Kruger said that it's not over yet. He was basically reminding us that we're the road team and we're still the underdog.

Chris Crutchfield: Coming out in the second half, we just went on a run and made shots. During timeouts, the first thing we told our guys was, "Calm down, calm down. They're going to make a run. They're a good team. They're going to make a run." We kept stressing it. Sure enough, Perry went to work.

Ellis scored nine second-half points to help Kansas remain close. The Jayhawks finally tied the game when Mason got a steal and found Selden for a layup with 5:45 left.

OU dribbled the ball up the floor and called timeout. With the decibel level at The Fieldhouse reaching deafening heights, ESPN's Dick Vitale declared on the broadcast: "This is the loudest I have ever heard an arena in my 37 years."

Chris Crutchfield: The bad thing about that place is you can't hear anything and you can't call a play. You can't yell anything onto the court, because you just can't hear. I know it's like that for both teams, but it's harder on the opposing team because most of the time they're on a run when it gets that loud, and you're trying to calm your team down by calling a set, but you can't get it in. Guys are looking over at the bench trying to lip read.

Perry Ellis: The game could've gone either way. They'd make a big play and then we'd make one. Everyone was so tired. Coach was like, "I know you guys are exhausted, but you've got to dig deep. This is a game you'll never forget."

Oklahoma came out of the timeout and regained the lead when senior guard Isaiah Cousins, who was 0-for-9, finally made a jump shot to put his team ahead 70-68.

Chris Crutchfield: It was a mid-range pull up. We were reeling at that time. I remember telling Coach Kruger, "Isaiah needs to give us a bucket." He finally hit one. *Damn, about time. Maybe he could get another one and help close this thing out.* Of course, he didn't and Buddy just decided, "I'm going to take this thing over."

Kansas tied the game again with 3:31 left when Graham got a steal and scored on a fastbreak layup. He was fouled and made a free throw to put KU ahead 73-72. Oklahoma would go right back on top, 75-73, when Woodard buried his fourth 3 of the game with 1:43 remaining.

Jordan Woodard: I had some good looks throughout the game. I started off slow and Isaiah did, too. Buddy picked up a lot of the slack. Then Buddy started to get hot and they focused their attention on him so I was able to get some open looks.

Lon Kruger: He made a lot of big shots. Buddy set the tone but other guys stepped up and made good plays, and Jordan certainly shot the ball well that night, as he did on many nights.

Self called timeout after Woodard's 3 and drew up a set to go to Ellis in the post. Ellis missed a hook shot and then scored on a putback with his left hand to tie the game at 75. After Woodard missed a 3, Kansas went back to Ellis and he nailed a turnaround hook shot over Spangler to give his team a

77-75 lead with 43.2 seconds left.

Ryan Spangler: I always guarded Perry Ellis. He was a tough player to defend. He can do a little bit of everything. He can spread you out and take you inside. The three years I played there, he and I went at it every game. We're two different players, but kind of knew each other's games pretty well. He was their leader. When they needed a basket, they went to him.

Lon Kruger: Perry was tough. He was a really tough matchup, especially when he knocks down a few jumpers. He was very good in the paint and a good finisher around the rim. He became a really good perimeter shooter as well. In that game, he was outstanding.

Trailing by two, Oklahoma went back to Hield in isolation against Mason. Hield tried to shake him but couldn't, so he pulled up for a mid-range jumper and was fouled with 21.3 seconds left. Hield made both free throws to knot the game at 77. Milking the clock for the last shot, Kansas spread the floor for Mason.

Wayne Selden: I always had confidence because we had Frank and Devonte'. I knew that we weren't going to make a dumb mistake. Even if we messed up, it wasn't going to be something dumb, something out of our control.

Rare as those instances may be, that's exactly what happened. Mason missed a contested layup and Oklahoma's Lattin snared the rebound. Instead of letting the clock run out to force overtime, official John Higgins blew his whistle from the left sideline, behind the play, and called a foul on Lucas, who had tried to get the ball from Lattin after Mason's miss. With the Sooners in the bonus, Lattin went to the line with 2.1 seconds left and the score tied at 77.

Bill Self: First of all, it was a terrible no-call. Frank got the crap fouled out of him on the drive and then they called the slap on the rebound.

Landen Lucas: It was kind of a natural play for me to go after the rebound. Usually at the end of games you would hope that they'd just let you play. I still should've been a little smarter.

Wayne Selden: It was a terrible over-the-back call, especially at that point in the game. I think I was saying something like, "You can't call that! If he makes it, game over." As we were going back to the bench, Lattin was screaming, "I got this! I got this!"

Chris Crutchfield: Everybody was talking to him telling him to calm down, because he was fired up. *He was fired up!*

Jordan Woodard: We were all talking to Khadeem, just telling him to stay focused. *Just go up there like you do in practice and follow through.* He was saying, "I got this. I got this." I believed in him. I trusted him.

Landen Lucas: We got to the huddle, and Coach Self said, "He's going to miss this and we're going to play in overtime." He was calming everybody down. He wasn't angry or mad at all.

Kurtis Townsend: I knew Lattin wasn't a great free throw shooter. We fouled him and you heard him going, "We got this guys. It's over." Deep down in his mind, I don't think he really believed that. He was trying to psyche himself out. So when Coach called a timeout to ice him, he was probably over there saying, "Oh my God! Oh my God!" That was a lot of pressure.

Lon Kruger: In those situations, you want guys to take their mind off it a little bit, so you talk about blocking out and not getting in the lane. You're talking to other players more than you're talking to Khadeem, but wanting him to just go through his routine and trust himself and shoot it with confidence.

Perry Ellis: When he went to the free throw line, I was sick. I was like, "Man, don't let it end like this."

Landen Lucas: The place got loud and that probably took his percentage down quite a bit.

Lon Kruger: He shot it up there pretty well, but it just went off the heel.

Jordan Woodard: I feel like seven times out of 10 he'd make that shot, that just happened to be one of the times he didn't.

Wayne Selden: Looking back on it, it's funny how he's yelling "I got this!" and he shoots it off the backboard too hard. I was like, "Phheewww!" A huge sigh of relief.

Chris Crutchfield: Of course, he *didn't* have it. It was a moment that he wasn't quite ready for, but at the same time, that's a very intimidating environment to have to go shoot free throws with 2.1 seconds left on the clock. That's intimidating for a young, unproven sophomore. He might have been a little bit overconfident, but the atmosphere was hard. I remember thinking, "If he makes these, I'll see him in a whole new light."

Bill Self: Even though we got lucky that he missed the free throw, he should have never been shooting. Frank should have been shooting them to win it.

Jamari Traylor: I wasn't surprised. I never feel like a game is over in Allen Fieldhouse until that final horn sounds. Crazy things happen in there. You always feel like you've got a chance.

Devonte' Graham: At the end of regulation, we were like, "Man, we've got to get this done. We're at home. The crowd is behind us." Every time we made a play, they made a play, and vice versa. Khadeem missing that free throw gave us new life. That got us real energized. We were in the huddle, locked in and focused.

Kansas made the first basket of overtime, but Oklahoma would eventually take a five-point lead when Hield scored back-to-back buckets. The first was a spin move around Mason on the left side of the basket, and then he followed that with a quick, catch-and-release 3. At that point, he had 38 points and the Sooners led 86-81.

Chris Crutchfield: It was surreal because as the game played out, I realized there wasn't a bunch of plays being called. It just became a free-flowing game, and you see guys getting into those zones like he was in, you just leave them alone. You set one ball screen, space the floor and play.

Devonte' Graham: Buddy definitely played his tail off. That was our first game against him that year. We didn't know he was that good and could shoot like that. He'd always been a volume shooter, but that year he was making more of them than he had in the past.

It was frustrating, but you can't let it get to you. He was getting a lot of second-chance points and kick-outs for 3s before we could really get to him. In those situations there's nothing you can do.

Ryan Spangler: Oh man, I got used to those kind of performances from him. It was just another day for ol' Buddy. It's what he did every day. We saw him put in work every morning and every night, getting up shots. You don't expect him to do anything less than that every game.

The previous summer, he'd thought about leaving to go pro. I think for a time he questioned whether he made the right decision to come back for his senior year, and in that game he kind of sold it to himself. *"Hey, I'm going to be the best player in college and I'm going to make myself a bigger name and go even higher in the draft because I stayed an extra year."*

I don't think he regretted staying, but in the back of his mind, I'm sure he was thinking, "Man, I could be making a lot of money right now." But we had a good group of guys and he didn't want to leave us and also he wanted to better himself.

Jordan Woodard: Buddy was incredible, man. It's something that we saw him do every day in practice, but to see him do it on that stage against a rival, it was amazing. He almost surprised me and I saw him do it every day. The shots he hit were incredible. They were challenged and he was shooting over the top. It was amazing. He was a true professional. He didn't do a lot of jawing. He was making shots that I'd see him make every day, but to see him do it on a bigger stage was just amazing.

Landen Lucas: Frank had asked to guard him, which he had done before. It wasn't anything new for him to step up and want a challenge. To see Buddy go out there and still score like he did was definitely impressive, because Frank was getting after him, and even if the shots went in, they were tough shots. With Frank playing so hard, the least we could do is match his intensity and help him out.

Kansas responded to Hield's heroics with a 5-0 run to tie the game. The Jayhawks had the ball on the final possession of overtime with a chance to win. Ellis airballed a jumper, but the ball grazed off Hield's hand and went out of bounds with 2.4 seconds left. Mason threw the ball into Selden, who had come off a double screen and had an open look from the right wing.

Wayne Selden: I could have made the shot to win the game, but I shot it short. It was on line. At the buzzer, right wing ... front-rimmed it. I wanted that one bad.

The Jayhawks and Sooners went back and forth throughout the first portion of the second overtime. And after a pair of free throws by Woodard forced a 94-94 tie with 2:34 remaining, fatigue set in. Neither team scored again and the game went to triple OT.

Landen Lucas: At that point, it started feeling like something big, like something special, like something different than what we were used to.

Jordan Woodard: We were just locked in on the game. Obviously you can hear the crowd, but for the most part you're so tuned in and focused on each possession like it's the last one. The crowd played a factor, but for the most part it came down to each play.

Ryan Spangler: It was tough. That's why it's one of the hardest places to play in college basketball. Their fans are great. Their student section, right there by the bench, is great. Those speakers that are down there by the court … they make sure to turn those up pretty high. But a veteran team like us was used to being put in situations like that. We'd played 100 games so far together at that time. We were ready for it.

Chris Crutchfield: We had three seniors on the floor and one junior. That kept us levelheaded when a lot of teams would've fallen apart. We had enough security and enough maturity and talent to withstand the first overtime. You get through the first overtime and Kansas is looking at themselves like, "Can we win it?" Now they have some self-doubt, and we had all the confidence. It was a heavyweight match, just blow after blow after blow.

Lon Kruger: I was impressed with players on both teams. It was a very fast-paced game and everyone was tired, but yet they kept making good plays. It wasn't a case of guys making bad plays and staying close down the stretch. It was a case of players answering each other's good plays despite fatigue. It was really impressive how players on both teams really stepped up.

Jordan Woodard: I don't remember sitting down in the second half. I was pretty tired, but at the same time you're so locked in on the game and you've got teammates telling you to keep going and you don't want to disappoint your coach. But I'm not going to lie, I was tired. That's the longest game I've ever played in.

Ryan Spangler: We were used to playing the whole 40 minutes, but in a game like that you do get exhausted because of the adrenaline and the energy you're putting out.

Landen Lucas: I can only imagine how some of those guys who had played 40-plus minutes felt because it's draining being out there. When you are playing that kind of basketball, where each detail matters in such a big game, it can just be exhausting. It's one thing for me, who was probably the freshest out there, but I can only imagine what it was like for Frank or Buddy, who'd been through the game at full speed.

The third overtime was more of the same. Selden opened with a 3 but Hield answered with another acrobatic layup. Kansas surged ahead four but the Sooners responded when Lattin found Hield at the top of the key for a 3 that gave him 46 points.

Chris Crutchfield: He was catching it at 30 feet from the rim. They wouldn't allow him to get off screens. They pushed him off screens. He had to catch it at 30 feet and then go to try to make individual one-on-one plays. If you look at his last three or four buckets, they all came off of one-on-one stuff. That's when he showed the nation that he was a pro who could just go get buckets. Frank Mason and Devonte' Graham are good defenders, and he was able to go get buckets with those guys hanging on him.

Lattin followed Hield's 3 with a layup to put OU ahead by one. The teams traded leads five times in the third OT. Ahead by one with the shot clock winding down, Hield again went to work on Mason, but this time Mason stripped him and Graham grabbed the ball and raced toward the rim. Graham attempted a fast-break layup and was fouled by Woodard with 15.2 seconds left. It was the fifth foul for Woodard, who had 27 points. Graham made both free throws, and OU dribbled into the frontcourt and called timeout with 11.9 ticks remaining.

Chris Crutchfield: They turned their defense up to a point where they were swarming you, and that happens a lot, because they tend to be a little bit more aggressive defensively because they kind of know that the officials aren't going to make that call at Allen Fieldhouse.

I will tell you this, and you've probably heard this before when you've talked to other coaches, there's always a questionable call in The Fieldhouse. (Laughing) You know that, right? There's always a questionable call in The Fieldhouse down the stretch that decides the game.

That moment—at least in the Sooners' eyes—occurred when Hield attempted to inbound the ball with Mason crowding him.

Frank Mason: The official might have told me to step back, but I knew once he handed him the ball, it's live and whatever happens happens.

Chris Crutchfield: It was right in front of our bench. You can only fit a size 15 shoe between the out of bounds line and the scorer's table. Frank Mason was all over him. The referee blew the whistle and told him to step back, which he did. But then the official handed Buddy the ball and Mason stepped right back where he had been in the first place. Legally, we all know, it should have been a technical foul. We saw the video.

We should have been going to the free-throw line shooting free throws.

Ryan Spangler: I don't think it was legal, but at the same time if you play well enough and take care of what you're supposed to take care of, you won't be in that situation.

Lon Kruger: The whole issue of the defender crowding the inbound passer is talked about a lot, and there's not that much room at Kansas. But in the moment, you don't think about that too much. You think about trying to get the ball in bounds, and obviously we turned it over and didn't get the shot up. We needed to be a little stronger and make stronger plays at that moment.

Assistant coach Jerrance Howard: As special as Buddy was, that turnover lost the game for them. Frank made Buddy earn everything he got in that second half. I think he was exhausted by the time he turned it over on that inbounds pass.

Mason deflected Hield's pass intended for Cousins and then grabbed the ball. He dribbled into the frontcourt where he was fouled with 7.9 seconds left.

Wayne Selden: I was just so happy. I was just hoping they didn't call anything, because it's so loud you can't really hear anything. When he stole it and they blew the whistle and they fouled Frank, I knew... once I saw the call, I wasn't worried. I knew he was going to make the free throws.

Mason made both free throws to put Kansas ahead 109-106. OU would have one last chance to send the game to a fourth overtime. OU set up a play that called for Cousins to dribble past the 3-point line and then pass to a trailing Spangler.

Lon Kruger: In that situation, we try to push the pace and get into the lane and maybe kick it out to the guy who is trailing the play.

It appeared that Spangler tried to shoot, but he was stripped by Ellis. Running toward the play from the right wing, Hield caught the ball and, with Mason attached to his hip, threw up a double-clutch shot that went off the backboard and over the rim.

Chris Crutchfield: I just remember them walking off the floor like they'd been in a heavyweight fight. They were just drained and they were dejected, because you don't get many opportunities in Allen Fieldhouse to win a game, especially a game of that magnitude and a game at that level. Bill shook my hand, smiled and laughed, like, "Wow! I've just been a part of something special," and everybody knew it. We knew that was special.

Lon Kruger: There was tremendous buildup going into the game, and it was one of those that didn't disappoint by any means. A lot of those games don't live up to the billing, and that one did. A lot of players on both sides made good plays.

Ryan Spangler: I think we knew right then how special it was. The handshake line was just respect from both teams and realizing it was early in the year, and we'd see each other again.

Jordan Woodard: We'd just lost. Once Coach got to the locker room, he told us that was a hell of a game. You kind of realize it. And once you get home, you start to get all these text messages and tweets and you really start to realize you were part of something special.

Buddy Hield: I just wanted to win (there). As a kid, I grew up watching that place in the Bahamas. I always said I wanted to play there and win there. And I came up short. I'll have to go through the rest of my life saying I never won at Allen Fieldhouse.

Hield returned to the court after the game with his shoes off and did an interview via satellite with ESPN's Scott Van Pelt. The Kansas fans still in attendance gave him a warm ovation when he finished.

Lon Kruger: He was fantastic, obviously the key to our team. He's a guy that can make shots and gave players around him confidence. Scoring 46 in there is not easy to do, and he was fantastic.

Bill Self: Thank God Frank was guarding him or he would have gotten 56.

Buddy Hield: It's going to hurt my heart forever. It was a tough matchup (with Mason). He's quicker. He was all over me. He made everything tough for me. It was a tough 46 points.

Jordan Woodard: Buddy had 46, so I can't say too much about Frank. He did a pretty good job and he stayed locked in to him, but Buddy was able to shoot over the top and use his height against him. Frank challenged him. Buddy will tell you the same. Like I said, he still had 46. He might have won that matchup.

Chris Crutchfield: Frank did a great job on him. I went back and watched it—I've watched it three times since—and he made some tough step-back 3s with Frank right in his face. A couple times Devonte' Graham is touching him while he's shooting it, and he made some tough shots. He had a drive where he changes and reverses at the last minute and Landen Lucas is about ready to block it, and he sticks it on the other side of the rim where no one could get it and finishes. Sometimes guys have an out-of-body experience, and he did that night. He made shots—all various types of shots.

Frank Mason: What I thought of Buddy didn't really change. I knew how good of a player he was coming into that game, and he showed how special he was and how good he can shoot it. He had a really special night.

Assistant coach Norm Roberts: Our players really respected Buddy as a good player. They loved to play against him. It was different than the way they looked at Georges Niang or a Monte Morris. They thought Buddy was a volume guy who would shoot it, shoot it, shoot it. After that game their respect level for him grew. In games before that, Buddy would play well but we'd find a way to get to him at the end. That game, we were like, "Yo, he's taken things to a new level." That game was a lot of fun, exhausting.

Bill Self: Both teams played great. I thought that we actually played better than OU. It was just that Buddy was so good, he made every hard play. OU was so good, though. Jordan Woodard had a great game. They were *good*. Spangler made some 3s. It all set the stage for a great game down in Norman.

Lon Kruger: I thought players on both sides really appreciated the battle. I know KU felt great about winning. Their comments and the way they showed respect for our guys was something our guys appreciated.

Devonte' Graham: We didn't go out and celebrate. We were exhausted after that. I definitely watched the full game a few times.

Landen Lucas: The only reason we've had this streak for so long is we take care of business in big games at home more times than not. We knew going into that game that would be huge, knowing we'd have to go back to their place and play them.

For me, it was an up and down game and it was still part of the season where I was figuring out where I stood. To be a part of all three overtimes and get all my points inside a minute of one of the overtimes, it felt awesome to be a part of something like that. It was just special. We went on and on for 30 minutes to an hour in those overtimes where each possession and each second felt like the final possession. It was fun to be a part of and something none of us will ever forget.

Buddy Hield: I'll look back on it 10 years from now and realize it was one of the greatest games I ever played in.

Not No. 1 For Long

The victory over Oklahoma catapulted Kansas from No. 2 to No. 1 in the Associated Press poll, but the Jayhawks didn't maintain their perch for long. The very next day, on Jan. 12, Self's squad lost at West Virginia for the third straight season. The Jayhawks had a season-high 22 turnovers in the 74-63 defeat.

Perry Ellis: West Virginia is one of the toughest teams to play. They speed you up. You feel rushed. Every time I got the ball I felt like someone was right behind me. You've got to be in crazy shape to do that, to press on every single play. A lot of players wouldn't want to go somewhere where they play that way, but at West Virginia they embrace it. Their players are all bought in.

The environment in Morgantown is very good. Well, good for them. Not for us. Their fans really get after you. They have these little bulletins they pass around the stands talking trash about our starting five. A copy or two usually finds its way into our locker room. We read that sometimes before the games.

Welcome Home ... or Not

Kansas bounced back from the WVU loss with a win over TCU at Allen Fieldhouse, but the next road trip was to a place that had haunted Self: Oklahoma State. Self's alma mater was just 1-4 in conference play, but they knocked off Kansas at home for the third straight year, 86-67.

Wayne Selden: It sucked because that was Coach's school and he always wanted to win there.

It's hard to say whether he treated that game any different because we did lose every time, and usually when he's different, we would play better.

We Want Landen

At Oklahoma State, Self had inserted Diallo into the starting lineup for the first time all season. The results were poor, as Diallo scored four points and grabbed just two rebounds in 13 minutes. A few days after the loss, Self brought his other four starters—Mason, Graham, Selden and Ellis—into his office to ask their opinion about who the fifth starter should be. Their answers were all the same: Landen Lucas.

Devonte' Graham: Landen did all the little things. He knew what his role was and his IQ on the court was as good as anyone's on the team. He was a veteran who knew the plays. His toughness inside, rebounding and blocking shots, he did things to make us better.

Landen Lucas: It gave me a lot of confidence when the guys told Coach Self they wanted me to start. Wayne came up to me that afternoon when we were walking to practice and told me they had met. He didn't give me many details about the meeting. He just told me to go out there and do my best and that the team would be better for it. Then I walked onto the practice floor and Coach Self came over and basically told me the same things. He just said to make sure my focus stays on doing what's best for the team, and that's what I did.

That whole situation helped me reset and remember the things that had gotten me there. I realized the best way to help myself out was to help the team out. The next game was against Texas, and I got the start and had double-digit rebounds. I was kinda bummed that I didn't score, but I did some good work on the boards. We came out with a win and everybody was happy. That showed me that's really all I needed to focus on, just making the team good. We already had such good players around me that if I went out there and handled those small things, they'd handle the rest.

Bill Self: Anybody would say that it was disappointing that (Diallo) didn't play more, but I think deep down even he understood for our team to have the best chance, Landen was probably better.

Lucas started every game but one (Senior Night) the rest of the season, and over those final 20 contests, he averaged 6.6 points and 8.5 rebounds. KU's defense also improved with him on the floor, leaving no doubt he was the right choice.

Iowa State forward Georges Niang: I never liked Landen Lucas. He was a good dude off the floor but on the floor, he'd go up for a rebound and put an elbow in your chest. I thought he was dirty, but he did what he had to do to get stuff done. I can't fault anybody for that.

Time for Panic?

Kansas traveled to No. 14 Iowa State on Jan. 25 for a Big Monday matchup with important conference ramifications. The Big 12 was top-heavy with three teams (KU, OU and West Virginia) ranked in the top 10 nationally and another two (ISU and Baylor) ranked in the top 20.

Georges Niang: With the group of guys we had, we were pretty confident going into that game. We had a lot of seniors and more experienced guys. I just felt real confident with them because I felt like KU hadn't really established a go-to guy. We ended up beating them pretty handily.

I just remember Hilton being crazy and you see the ESPN playback of the Kansas fans looking all sad, and then Bill Self's face. That stuff is just funny.

The Jayhawks were in unfamiliar territory after the 85-72 loss in Ames. At 5-3 in the Big 12, Kansas now trailed Oklahoma, Baylor and West Virginia—all 5-2—in the standings. All three would win that week to move to 6-2. Iowa State was also 5-3.

Perry Ellis: We were down and everyone said, "This is the team that isn't going to do it. This is the year the streak is going to end."

Georges Niang: I thought KU was vulnerable that year. The rest of us just blew it.

Bill Self: I was worried, too, but one of the losses was in Ames. Those were tough places to play. I thought we got tired during the season in large part because we practiced for like five weeks for the World University Games. Still, when we finally figured out how we should play—and it took us a while to figure it out— we got so confident and so good and everybody knew their roles. We were a dangerous team from that point forward.

Round 2 Against OU and Buddy

Instead of dwelling on the Iowa State loss, the Jayhawks bounced back in spectacular fashion. Selden scored 33 points to spark KU to an overtime win over Kentucky in the Big 12-SEC showdown at Allen Fieldhouse. And then Self's squad beat Kansas State, TCU and West Virginia. At 8-3 in league play, KU was in a three-way tie for first place with the Sooners and Mountaineers.

On Feb. 13, the college basketball world turned its eyes to Norman, Oklahoma for the Jayhawks' battle with Oklahoma—a rematch from that epic triple-overtime thriller back in January.

Bill Self: Our guys were so ready to play that game. So ready. So excited. I could sense it at dinner the night before, how in tuned everybody was. They were asking all sorts of questions during scouting report. You can just tell when a team is all in, and they were all in.

Devonte' Graham: That was one of the wildest games. I knew I'd be guarding Buddy. I was locked on him days before the game. They gave me a sheet detailing where he liked to shoot, where his hot spots were and whether he liked to go this way or that way. I was just really locked in on playing defense. I remember watching GameDay the morning of the game. All they were talking about was Buddy and how he was going to be unstoppable. That fueled me.

Frank had guarded him the first time we played them; he was exhausted. We needed Frank to be able to make plays on offense, as well. Buddy got a lot of second-chance possessions that game. This time, every time the shot went up and they missed, I had to run straight to Buddy. *Don't even watch the shot to see if they make it. Just pay attention to what Buddy is doing.* I also knew he liked to go left, with one- or two-dribble pull-ups.

Lon Kruger: Graham was great. It was a really good game. It almost got overlooked because it wasn't triple overtime, but it was a game that went down to the wire and both teams played really well. That game seems almost... not a disappointment, but I think people were reliving the first game so much.

Chris Crutchfield: College GameDay was there and it was a big hoo-ha. We didn't play well. We were out for revenge as opposed to just playing the game the way it should have been played. We had a slow start, but we did a great job of guarding everybody—except Devonte' Graham. He went off on us. He had a game where he was hitting step-back, off-the-dribble pull-up 3s that we couldn't do anything about. He had the ability to go by you, and then he starts making quick, step-back crossover jump shots. You feel helpless on those plays, because you do everything you can as a defender, but the shot still goes in.

We were down by 12 early in that game, but we finally got back in contention and made a run to take the lead. Then it was a battle down the stretch to close the game out. Of course, Graham hit two big 3s, and then again, there was a questionable call in the last minute and a half. Perry Ellis set an illegal screen on Jordan Woodard to allow Graham to get a 3 in the corner, and that popped the game open. He had a big night.

Graham hit six 3s and scored 27 points to carry the Jayhawks to a 76-72 win. Hield still managed to score 24, but he needed 16 shots to get it done and also had four turnovers.

Jerrance Howard: I called it the Devonte' Graham coming out party. He took off. He locked up Buddy that day and he made big shots late to win the game.

We went down there with a chip on our shoulder. That's what Coach Self is so great at and what he doesn't get enough credit for. You look at his record on the road. He programs his players like this: You're supposed to win at home, but on the road is where you're going to win the title. It's 25 against 14,000 or 18,000. Our players, our staff, Hudy, Cheddar … everyone in our travel party. It's just us. The huddle is tight. We have that mindset where going on the road is the fun part. We look forward to it. There's nothing like going into an area when it's just you and your guys with your backs against the wall. The bigger the challenge, the more he wants to go get it.

Kansas 76, Oklahoma 72
February 13, 2016 · Norman, Okla.

Kansas (21-4)

Player	MP	FG	3FG	FT	R	A	F	S	TO	B	TP
Perry Ellis*	29	4-12	2-3	0-0	7	2	2	0	2	1	10
Devonte' Graham*	39	8-13	6-9	5-6	3	2	1	0	2	0	27
Landen Lucas*	28	2-3	0-0	3-4	10	0	2	0	2	1	7
Frank Mason*	26	4-7	1-4	5-6	5	3	5	1	1	0	14
Wayne Selden*	32	2-9	1-5	1-2	2	1	2	1	1	0	6
Carlton Bragg	3	1-1	0-0	0-0	0	0	2	0	1	0	2
Cheick Diallo	7	0-0	0-0	0-0	4	0	3	1	1	1	0
Brannen Greene	25	4-8	1-5	0-0	4	2	4	0	3	0	9
Jamari Traylor	11	0-1	0-0	1-2	3	1	3	0	1	0	1
Team											
Totals	200	25-54	11-26	15-20	38	11	24	3	14	3	76

Oklahoma (20-4)

Player	MP	FG	3FG	FT	R	A	F	S	TO	B	TP
Isaiah Cousins*	37	8-19	3-9	2-2	5	5	1	3	4	0	21
Buddy Hield*	37	5-15	5-11	9-10	4	1	4	0	4	0	24
Khadeem Lattin*	30	1-3	0-0	4-4	5	0	4	0	0	1	6
Ryan Spangler*	33	1-4	0-3	1-2	7	1	4	1	0	0	3
Jordan Woodard*	30	3-12	1-6	3-3	6	4	3	0	1	0	10
Dante Buford	14	1-4	0-1	0-0	1	1	1	0	0	0	2
Christian James	11	1-1	1-1	3-4	3	0	1	1	2	0	6
Jamuni McNeace	3	0-0	0-0	0-2	1	0	0	0	0	0	0
Dinjiyl Walker	5	0-2	0-1	0-0	1	0	1	0	0	0	0
Team					3						
Totals	200	20-60	10-32	22-27	36	12	19	5	11	1	72

	1st	2nd	Total	FG%	3FG%	FT%
Kansas	38	38	76	46.3	42.3	75.0
Oklahoma	33	39	72	33.3	31.3	81.5

Officials: Mark Whitehead, Gerry Pollard, Don Dailey

Technicals: None

Bill Self: Those were two great games, two tough wins. That's the difference between winning and not winning the league. If those games go the other way, OU wins the league.

Ryan Spangler: We knew we didn't play as well as we wanted to and that hurt us down the stretch in the Big 12, but hey, we went to the Final Four, so it's all good.

Senior Night for the Champs

While the Big 12's other top teams took some lumps, the Jayhawks kept rolling after beating Oklahoma. By Senior Night, Kansas had already secured the league title outright thanks to nine straight Big 12 wins. Motivation was not a problem, though, as Iowa State—the last team to beat KU—was in town.

The Cyclones pushed the Jayhawks and led by three with 5:09 remaining after two free throws from Niang, but Iowa State went scoreless over the next 4 minutes, 27 seconds, and the Jayhawks went on to win 85-78. Ellis and Niang, who battled each other for four years, each scored 22 points in their final meeting.

Perry Ellis: Georges and I were in the same class, so we played against each other tons of times. We knew the ins and outs of each other's games, yet it seemed like we still scored on each other every time we touched the ball. He's so skilled. You look at him and think he's slow, but he just knows how to move efficiently. He's crafty.

Georges Niang: As much as I hate saying this, I hated Perry Ellis ... but I respected him. He's just one of those dudes who didn't talk smack, played his game and was tough. Those are the worst guys to play against, ones where you can't throw them off their game by talking smack. He just brought it every night. He didn't say anything! He was like a mute. Just like you thought he was off the court, that's how he was on the court. He didn't say *anything.*

If he wasn't starting off the game good, I'd say something like "not today Perry." Just try to get in his head, because he was obviously a good player. I definitely have respect for Perry Ellis.

Kansas fans apparently respected Niang, as well. Most of the KU faithful had remained in the stands for Senior Night speeches, and as Niang was finishing a courtside interview with Iowa State's radio crew, Bob Davis—who was MC-ing the postgame festivities—acknowledged him to the crowd. Seconds later, Niang joined Kevin Durant and Buddy Hield as the only opponents during "the streak" to receive a standing ovation in Lawrence.

Georges Niang: I was pretty shocked when that happened, to be honest with you. If you watch the video, I didn't know how to take it. You think a place hates you and then they're giving a standing ovation. I can't explain what it was like. It was weird—but I appreciated it at the same time.

Kansas has shown nothing but love to me as a competitor. As much as I hate them when I'm playing them, I have nothing but respect for their program.

Bill Self: (laughing) Tell Georges that I said he didn't deserve that. Georges was one of the most fun kids to compete against. He is such a good kid. I loved playing against him and Monte (Morris) and Naz (Mitrou-Long) and those guys.

The Jayhawks finished 15-3 in league play after starting 5-3. In a season when everyone had pegged them to be vulnerable, the Jayhawks were dominant. Again.

Lon Kruger: I think every year teams go in thinking they can be the one to end KU's streak, and it hasn't happened. Kansas has been able to survive a lot of really good teams. Over 13 years, there have been a lot of really good teams in the league and that's what makes Kansas' streak even more remarkable.

Georges Niang: I thought that was the year for sure. The rest of the league just didn't close out games. You have to give Kansas credit. They win the games they're supposed to win. They may drop one to a Texas Tech or a TCU or lose one at K-State when they're not supposed to, but those guys usually find ways to win the games they're supposed to win.

Continued Domination at the Big 12 Tournament

The Jayhawks' surge continued in the Big 12 Tournament in Kansas City, where they made easy work of K-State in the quarterfinals, 85-63, behind 21 points from Ellis. The senior stayed hot in the semis, scoring 20 points in a 70-66 win over Baylor. It was KU's eighth straight win against the Bears.

Perry Ellis: Baylor was always one of the most-talented teams we played, and also one of the longest. They frustrate a lot of people with their zone defense, but we just attacked their bigs. We'd get the ball into the middle of that zone and just attack from there. After a couple of successful possessions, they'd lose confidence and things would snowball on them from there.

Baylor forward Rico Gathers: We didn't want to go man with them. We wanted to play zone as much as possible. If you go man they're going to run you out of the gym. With our zone, if we're rotating the way we're supposed to, it can cause problems.

To me, the Kansas game was just another game. I never got fazed when we played them. We hadn't had much success against them, but that didn't mean we were scared. For a long time, before I got there, Baylor had a reputation of being soft. I tried my best to set a tone that would change that. You couldn't put anyone on the floor with me and expect me to be frightened, or to play soft. That doesn't run in my bloodline. You can't go out there and be soft. Me having that mindset … I didn't care who we were playing, even if it was Kentucky. I knew what I brought to the table. I knew I was going to go out there and rebound the ball. That's how my opportunities were going to come.

I think that mindset rubbed off on our players. Guys like Jonathan Motley and Taurean Prince, those guys usually played well against Kansas, and that's because they weren't soft either. I didn't mind taking a cheap shot on someone, just to let them know, "This is how it's going to be." If you've got enough courage to come down in the paint and bang with me, then I've got to let you know who is running things. I had to show who the paint belonged to.

Most of the talk following KU's victory over the Bears was not about the game itself, but rather a monster dunk that Selden had over Baylor's Ishmail Wainright as the forward attempted to take a charge. Selden jumped from outside the charge circle, cocked the ball back in his right hand and threw down a monster jam that made his Uncle Anthony go nuts in the stands. Within hours, the celebration—and the dunk—had gone viral.

Jerrance Howard: When I think of Wayne Selden, I'll forever remember that dunk he had against Baylor.

Fans at the Sprint Center were hoping to see Round 3 of Kansas-Oklahoma in the Big 12 Tournament title game. But the Sooners lost to West Virginia 69-67 in the semifinals. (Hield banked in what appeared to be a game-winning, half-court 3-pointer at the buzzer, but he got off the shot a second too late and it didn't count).

Lon Kruger: Anytime you don't advance you're disappointed. Obviously the West Virginia game came down to the last shot and it came after the buzzer. But yeah, we were disappointed that we didn't get to play Kansas again.

The Jayhawks beat the Mountaineers, 81-71, in the championship game. Graham was named the tournament's Most Outstanding Player after tallying 27 points, five rebounds and three assists. Selden chipped in 21 points and Ellis added 17.

Landen Lucas: Devonte' was awesome for us during that stretch. He always brought life and energy to any situation. Whether it was in shootaround or pregame, he was always the one who kept things fun and lively. Even if it was right before a big game and people are feeling tight, he was shooting half court shots and dancing around. It put you at ease.

Devonte' Graham: Someone has to be that spark plug, whether it's off the bench or as a starter. I've got that personality that can get people going and get people excited. People say that me smiling and raising my arms energizes the arena and gets people going.

Perry Ellis: Devonte' is a people person. Everyone loves Devonte' around campus and around school. He's someone who is always smiling and encouraging everyone. If you're down, seeing him will get you excited.

The Favorite

Now on a 14-game winning streak, Kansas was slotted as the No. 1 overall seed in the NCAA Tournament, and it more than justified that billing in its first two games: a 105-79 thumping of Austin Peay and a 73-61 win over Connecticut. Up next was a Sweet 16 matchup with fourth-seeded Maryland, coached by former Jayhawk and Kansas native Mark Turgeon. Another Kansas native, though, sent Turgeon and the Terps home, as Wichita's Ellis erupted for 27 points in a 79-63 victory.

Landen Lucas: Perry never showed much emotion. Against Maryland in the Sweet 16, he was killing it and we kept going back to him every possession. I remember after he got this one bucket, he kept a straight face at first. He was coming back down the court with a normal Perry expression, and then he looked over at a couple of us and shot a quick little grin, like he knew his guy has no chance of stopping him.

I remember all of us started cracking up, because Perry rarely showed much of anything, and that little smile was the equivalent of somebody jumping up on the scorer's table and screaming at everybody. We all enjoyed that.

Wayne Selden: We all came together perfect at the end of that year. Everybody was really striking on all cylinders. I had terrible NCAA Tournaments my first two years, so I'm thinking, "This is it. I've got to go make it happen." So then you started to see the confidence come out of us. We were so connected. It was easy for us.

Easy, that is, until it was time to play Villanova.

Once again, the Jayhawks were back in the Elite Eight. Once again, things just didn't feel right. Villanova concentrated on stopping Ellis and held him to four points. Mason and Selden both scored 16 points but combined to shoot just 1-of-12 from beyond the arc. Graham made five 3s, but it wasn't enough. As a team, KU shot just 6-of-22 from deep, and the eventual national champion Wildcats advanced to the Final Four with a 64-59 win.

Wayne Selden: I felt like if I made a shot… if we made one of those 3s—if one of them goes in— it changes the whole game. I can't remember too much from that night. I just remember the small things. I knew they were triple-teaming Perry and I knew that if one of us made a shot, if somebody made a shot other than Devonte', we'd get going and win. But me and Frank couldn't buy a 3. We couldn't swing the momentum.

Bill Self: We tried hard. I don't know if I'd say it went south. Villanova was just so good.

We played bad the first half, but we came back after intermission and got the lead immediately. Then we traded baskets for a while. They kind of controlled it late, and (Ryan) Arcidiacono made a 3 at the end of the shot clock that was unbelievable. Then we got the call on Devonte' on the offensive foul.

The things that I remember most are that we didn't attack the little 1-2-2 halfcourt press worth a crap, and then we didn't get the ball inside against their zone. Perry didn't have it. They did a good job on him after Perry was so good against Maryland.

Kansas 59, Villanova 64
March 26, 2016 · Louisville, Ky.

Kansas (33-5)

Player	MP	FG	3FG	FT	R	A	F	S	TO	B	TP
Perry Ellis*	34	1-5	0-0	2-3	5	1	3	1	4	0	4
Devonte' Graham*	35	6-13	5-9	0-0	7	0	5	1	3	0	17
Landen Lucas*	35	3-3	0-0	0-1	12	2	2	0	0	0	6
Frank Mason*	40	7-14	1-6	1-2	3	4	3	1	4	1	16
Wayne Selden*	38	6-14	0-6	4-5	2	3	3	1	3	1	16
Carlton Bragg	6	0-0	0-0	0-0	0	1	0	0	1	0	0
Svi Mykhailiuk	7	0-1	0-1	0-0	0	0	1	0	0	0	0
Jamari Traylor	5	0-0	0-0	0-0	0	0	2	1	1	0	0
Team					3						
Totals	200	23-50	6-22	7-11	32	11	19	5	16	2	59

Villanova (33-5)

Player	MP	FG	3FG	FT	R	A	F	S	TO	B	TP
Ryan Arcidiacono*	33	3-6	1-3	6-7	3	1	3	1	1	0	13
Jalen Brunson*	22	2-6	1-2	2-2	1	0	1	0	1	0	7
Josh Hart*	38	6-17	1-4	0-0	4	0	3	2	2	0	13
Kris Jenkins*	28	3-10	1-7	6-6	4	3	4	1	2	0	13
Daniel Ochefu*	29	5-8	0-0	0-0	8	2	3	1	0	1	10
Phil Booth	12	0-1	0-1	0-0	0	0	0	0	0	0	0
Mikal Bridges	26	2-4	0-1	2-2	3	1	2	5	2	0	6
Darryl Reynolds	12	0-0	0-0	2-2	4	0	0	1	1	1	2
Team					1						
Totals	200	21-52	4-18	18-19	28	7	16	11	9	2	64

	1st	2nd	Total	FG%	3FG%	FT%
Kansas	25	34	59	46.0	27.3	63.6
Villanova	32	32	64	40.4	22.2	94.7

Officials: Jeff Clark, Terry Wymer, Chris Rastatter
Technicals: None

It was just a game with no rhythm.

You go back to the games that we've lost and it's usually because something's happened during the course of the game to make sure that we didn't have rhythm, whether it be the big kid from Northern Iowa (Jordan Eglseder) making those 3s or Josh Jackson getting two fouls in the first four minutes against Oregon. Something has taken us out of it, and that's what happened against Villanova, too.

A litte more on Perry, Wayne and Jamari ...

With 1,798 points, Ellis finished eighth on KU's all-time scoring list. He was a second-team All-American as a senior, and his workmanlike approach made him one of the most-respected Jayhawks in recent years.

Bill Self: He'll go down as one of the most consistent Jayhawks ever. He'll be appreciated more the longer he's gone. He scored 1,800 points. He did a lot of things that were just unbelievably good. But he never called attention to himself and was just a good dude.

Wayne Selden: Perry was a true professional, even in college. He came in and got his work done. People say he's not that talkative, but Perry would talk in the locker room. He's not as quiet as people think. He was one of my favorite teammates ever, because it was so easy to throw it in the post and get out of the way so he could do his thing.

Devonte' Graham: Perry was a killer, a quiet assassin. He made stuff easier for everyone because so much attention was on him. He could score in so many different ways. He never talked, though, which was kind of weird at first. But once you see that that's his personality, it was cool. When he did say something, everyone was so shocked that they'd listen.

Perry Ellis: I never really had another player trash-talk me. People would give a lot of my teammates a hard time. But they'd come up to me and say, "Man, I respect you. I'm not going to say anything to you."

Fans were a different story. They said what they wanted, and they had a lot to say about me. "Perry Ellis is the oldest guy alive playing basketball," was the main theme ... just stuff about me being in college forever. At first I was frustrated. I was like, "Man, I can't help the way I look." But then I just started embracing it. I'd even crack on myself sometimes and it'd make the fans laugh, and then they'd just move on.

Jamari Traylor: I respected his work ethic. Coach Self would always get onto him. He didn't get on him nearly as much as a freshman as he did his senior year, when he really demanded things from him. He always rose to that occasion. Perry never changed from when I first met him. That's one thing I can say about him. He was very mild-mannered and didn't disrespect anyone. I can't think of anyone that would have anything bad to say about Perry.

He just had such a great touch around the rim. He finished everything. There was a point when whenever his shot went up, I felt like it was going in. We competed every day. He was one of the first guys to practice every day. He was always getting extra shots up. His work ethic was one of the main reasons for his success.

Ryan Spangler: Perry Ellis is the KU player I most respect. He did his business and didn't say anything or try to start anything, but knew he was going to play great every night.

Baylor coach Scott Drew: Perry Ellis is a guy that we were happy to see graduate. I know some people criticize different parts of his game, but he was always effective against us. They've had so many great players, but the ones that are one-and-done don't hurt you as much as the ones who are there three or four years and beat you repeatedly.

Selden, who averaged 13.8 points and shot a respectable 39.2 percent from 3-point range, declared for the draft after his junior year. He went undrafted but has caught on with the Memphis Grizzlies and has had a successful start to his NBA career.

Perry Ellis: Wayne played with a level of confidence his junior year that I hadn't seen. He was so confident in taking the big shots. He was always knocking them down. He was just having fun. His freshman and sophomore years he was putting too much pressure on himself. People were probably saying, "Wayne is one-and-out." It gets to you sometimes. It's hard not to think about the stuff that people say. His junior year he just let go and had some fun.

Bill Self: Wayne was great to coach. He was a little inconsistent shooting the ball, and I thought he fell in love with the jumper too much. But the game against Florida (his sophomore year) when he put us on his back (14 second-half points and 21 for the game) and then the game against Kentucky (as a junior when he scored 33 points) ... those are two of the best performances anybody's had for us since I've been here.

Jerrance Howard: Wayne kind of took a backseat to all of those guys and got caught up into Kansas and winning. He wanted to go to the NBA, but he eventually realized his best chance to make a name for himself and get there was by winning in college. He did a good job of keeping a positive attitude and still wanting to be here. He loved Kansas. He was one of our best hosts for recruits.

His career was up and down. We had to really monitor his health, but he was tough and competitive. He didn't want to miss any practices. We'd tell him to take a day off, but he never would. He's going to take off in the NBA. He's got a little chip on his shoulder. A lot of people don't want to go to the D-League when they don't get drafted. They just head straight overseas. Wayne went the hard route because he has so much confidence in himself.

Wayne Selden: My junior year was one of the best years of my life. I came into my own and played my role to the best of my ability. Even if somebody says we weren't the

BEST OF THE STREAK

BEST DUNKS

1. Wayne Selden vs. Baylor, March 11, 2016: In transition, Selden stuck his knee into Ish Wainright's chest, lifting himself higher for a one-handed tomahawk slam that sent Uncle Anthony into hysterics in the stands.

2. Tarik Black vs. Texas, Feb. 22, 2014: Black used Texas' Cameron Ridley for a boost, taking off outside the lane before throwing the ball into the hoop for a "Mozgof" slam; it sent teammate Wayne Selden hopping over teammates on the KU bench in celebration.

3. Thomas Robinson vs. Baylor, Jan. 16, 2012: Though Tyshawn Taylor's alley-oop pass was a little behind Robinson, that didn't end up mattering, as KU forward caught the ball with his one hand behind his head and threw it down emphatically in one ferocious motion.

4. Julian Wright vs. Texas, March 12, 2006: Wright finished off KU's Big 12 championship victory in style, spinning for a 360 dunk with his left hand before popping his jersey on the way back down the court.

5. Jamari Traylor vs. Texas, Feb. 29, 2016: Traylor, with a boost from Eric Davis, elevated so high for the emphatic alley-oop slam that he hit his elbow on the backboard and rim — an injury that required four stitches.

6. Jeff Withey vs. Kansas State, Feb. 11, 2013: Withey received a pass in the lane from Thomas Robinson, threw down a vicious one-handed dunk over Jordan Henriquez with a foul, screamed out in satisfaction, then tugged at his jersey like Superman.

7. Julian Wright vs. Missouri, Feb. 10, 2007: On the right baseline, Wright leaped to the right of defender Kalen Grimes — he was trying to take a charge — and contorted his body to extend with both arms for a jam with a foul.

8. Andrew Wiggins vs. Kansas State, Jan. 11, 2014: The future No. 1 pick scooped up a loose ball, took one dribble, then took off with two feet between two K-State defenders for a right-handed flush before stomping toward the baseline with a look to the crowd.

9. Ben McLemore vs. Oregon State, Nov. 30, 2012: After a steal at midcourt, the Sprint Center crowd watched in awe as McLemore soared so high into the air that his right armpit was parallel to the rim as he cocked back for a tomahawk flush.

10. Josh Jackson vs. UAB, Nov. 21, 2016: Jackson picked up a head of steam from halfcourt at Sprint Center, taking two dribbles and two steps before throwing down a one-handed slam over Tosin Mehinti with a foul.

best team, we were the best team we could be.

Going into my junior year, my goal was to leave after the season. When we lost, I was like, "Damn, this is over." I was messed up for a little while, just not knowing what was going to happen. When I first left Kansas, I was like, "Dammmn." I was so accustomed to living at KU and waking up and everything being right there. I had to adapt to a new lifestyle.

I don't have any regrets about leaving a year early. Even though I didn't get drafted, I think it was a great decision, because it gave me in an opportunity to be here in Memphis. When I left, I was fully sold, fully bought in. There was no going back.

Traylor is one of Self's all-time favorites. During his redshirt sophomore season, Self encouraged him to tell his backstory, which included a time when he was homeless and living in an abandoned car in Chicago.

Jamari Traylor: Coach Self knew that having the opportunity to play at Kansas really meant something to me. He knew I'd run through walls if it would help us win. He'd say, "If we're down by two and we need a stop, I know Jamari will do whatever it takes to make it happen." Guys like me and the Morris twins and Thomas and Tyshawn—guys who had a tough upbringing—we had a little bit of an edge to us. In big moments we wouldn't fold or back down from anyone, because we had that grit to us. If you're not tough, I don't think you can play for Coach Self. Mentally, you have to be tough.

As far as the tough things I've been through off the court, he really embraced me for that.

When my story was first coming out ... initially I didn't really want to let anyone know about it. He was the one who thought it would be a good idea for me to share my story with people. At the time, I was a little bit embarrassed about it and I didn't want to tell anyone. It was his idea for me to share it with the world. I think it was a good decision. It helped people understand where I came from. It let them know about me. I feel like that's another reason why I get so much love when I'm in Kansas. People there know everything about me and they still accept me. They've made me feel like I'm always going to have a home there.

Bill Self: Jamari is always going to be one of my favorite players, just because he'd been through more than what maybe all the other ones had been through combined. He's seen a lot of things and he's had his heart broken. We've all had our heart broken in our

own mind. But he's had his ripped apart.

I loved how he always hung in there and had a great attitude and always had energy and bounce. He was ornery, but he's definitely our kind of guy. I think he was very grateful to be playing at KU. What those two attorneys in Topeka did for him out of the blue after hearing his story ... they got with Jamari and his family and asked for clemency for his father Jessie (who was serving a life sentence) ... and it actually worked. That was all done because of Jamari and his story and how he carried himself. His family will have a chance to be reunited pretty soon. I love that kid.

Perry Ellis: The most underrated guy in our program was Jamari Traylor. The way he competed in practice ... he made me a better player. He just went so hard on every play, trying to block everything and steal everything. A lot of people don't do that in practice. His effort was even better in games and it helped us win. The play he made at Texas (in 2015), where he dove out of bounds to save a ball and then raced to the other end of the court to make a play ... he did stuff like that in practice all the time.

He had a very inspiring story. We heard it a lot. Every time you hear it, you realize how fortunate you are. For him to get out of that situation in Chicago and make it as far as he did is inspiring. He loved Coach Self for all he did for his game and for all he did for him as a person. He appreciated and relished every minute he spent in the program, and it showed.

2015-16
Season Summary

Results (33-5, 15-3)

November

13	Northern Colorado	W, 109 - 72
17	vs. Michigan State	L, 79 - 73
23	vs. Chaminade	W, 72 - 123
24	vs. UCLA	W, 73 - 92
25	vs. Vanderbilt	W, 70 - 63

December

1	Loyola (MD)	W, 94 - 61
5	Harvard	W, 75 - 69
9	Holy Cross	W, 92 - 59
12	vs. Oregon State	W, 82 - 67
19	Montana	W, 88 - 46
22	@ San Diego State	W, 57 - 70
29	UC Irvine	W, 78 - 53

January

2	Baylor	W, 102 - 74
4	Oklahoma	W, 109 - 106
9	@ Texas Tech	W, 59 - 69
12	@ West Virginia	L, 74 - 63
16	TCU	W, 70 - 63
19	@ Oklahoma State	L, 86 - 67
23	Texas	W, 76 - 67
25	@ Iowa State	L, 85 - 72
30	Kentucky	W, 90 - 84

February

3	Kansas State	W, 77 - 59
6	@ TCU	W, 56 - 75
9	West Virginia	W, 75 - 65
13	@ Oklahoma	W, 72 - 76
15	Oklahoma State	W, 94 - 67
20	@ Kansas State	W, 63 - 72
23	@ Baylor	W, 60 - 66
27	Texas Tech	W, 67 - 58
29	@ Texas	W, 56 - 86

March

5	Iowa State	W, 85 - 78
10	vs. Kansas State	W, 85 - 63
11	vs. Baylor	W, 70 - 66
12	vs. West Virginia	W, 81 - 71
17	vs. Austin Peay	W, 105 - 79
19	vs. Connecticut	W, 73 - 61
24	vs. Maryland	W, 79 - 63
26	vs. Villanova	L, 59 - 64

All-Big 12 Team

Player of the Year:
Buddy Hield, Oklahoma, Sr., G

Defensive Player of the Year:
Prince Ibeh, Texas, Sr., C

Newcomer of the Year:
Deonte Burton, Iowa State, Jr., G

Freshman of the Year:
Jawun Evans, Oklahoma State, Fr., G

Sixth Man of the Year:
Jaysean Paige, West Virginia, Sr., G

Coach of the Year:
Tubby Smith, Texas Tech

First Team
Taurean Prince, Baylor, Sr., F
Georges Niang, Iowa State, Sr., F**
Perry Ellis, Kansas, Sr., F**
Buddy Hield, Oklahoma, Sr., G**
Isaiah Taylor, Texas, Jr., G

Second Team
Monté Morris, Iowa State, Jr., G
Frank Mason III, Kansas, Jr., G
Wayne Selden Jr., Kansas, Jr., G
Jaysean Paige, West Virginia, Sr., G
Devin Williams, West Virginia, Jr., F

Third Team
Rico Gathers, Baylor, Sr., F
Johnathan Motley, Baylor, So., F
Wesley Iwundu, Kansas State, Jr., F
Isaiah Cousins, Oklahoma, Sr., G
Ryan Spangler, Oklahoma, Sr., F

Honorable Mention
Lester Medford, Baylor, Sr., G
Jameel McKay, Iowa State, Sr., F
Abdel Nader, Iowa State, Sr., F
Matt Thomas, Iowa State, Jr., G
Devonte' Graham, Kansas, So., G
Landen Lucas, Kansas, Jr., F
Jordan Woodard, Oklahoma, Jr., G
Jawun Evans, Oklahoma State, Fr., G
Jeff Newberry, Oklahoma State, Sr., G
Javan Felix, Texas, Sr., G
Toddrick Gotcher, Texas Tech, Jr., G
Aaron Ross, Texas Tech, Jr., F
Zach Smith, Texas Tech, So., F

All-Defensive Team
Devonté Graham, Kansas, So., G
Frank Mason III, Kansas, Jr., G
Wesley Iwundu, Kansas State, Jr., F
Khadeem Lattin, Oklahoma, So., F
Prince Ibeh, Texas, Sr., C **
Jevon Carter, West Virginia, So., G

All-Newcomer Team
Deonte Burton, Iowa State, Jr., G**
Barry Brown, Kansas State, Fr., G
Dean Wade, Kansas State, Fr., F
Jawun Evans, Oklahoma State, Fr., G
Eric Davis Jr., Texas, Fr., G
Kerwin Roach Jr., Texas, Fr., G

** Unanimous selection

Kansas Awards

Perry Ellis
Consensus All-American Second Team
NABC All-American Second Team
AP All-American Second Team
Sporting News All-American Third Team
Big 12 All-Tournament Team
Maui Invitational All-Tournament

Frank Mason
NABC All-District (8) Second Team
Maui Invitational MVP

Wayne Selden
NABC All-District (8) Second Team
Maui Invitational MVP

Devonté Graham
Big 12 Tournament MOP

Season Stats

#	Player	CL	POS	HT	Hometown	G	GS	FG%	3P%	FT%	R	A	S	B	PTS
34	Perry Ellis	SR	F	6-8	Wichita, KS	38	38	.531	.438	.785	5.8	1.3	0.5	0.5	16.9
1	Wayne Selden	JR	G	6-5	Roxbury, MA	38	37	.474	.392	.612	3.4	2.6	0.7	0.3	13.8
0	Frank Mason	JR	G	5-11	Petersburg, VA	38	38	.434	.381	.739	4.3	4.6	1.3	0.1	12.9
4	Devonte' Graham	SO	G	6-2	Raleigh, NC	38	36	.460	.441	.744	3.3	3.7	1.4	0.1	11.3
33	Landen Lucas	JR	F	6-10	Portland, OR	36	19	.643	.000	.663	6.8	0.6	0.4	0.8	5.8
10	Svi Mykhailiuk	SO	G	6-8	Ukraine	35	0	.450	.402	.680	1.3	0.9	0.3	0.1	5.4
14	Brannen Greene	JR	G	6-7	Juliette, GA	30	1	.524	.492	.840	2.1	0.8	0.3	0.0	5.4
15	Carlton Bragg Jr.	FR	F	6-9	Cleveland, OH	38	0	.561	.571	.667	2.5	0.4	0.4	0.2	3.8
13	Cheick Diallo	FR	F	6-9	Centereach, NY	27	1	.569		.556	2.5	0.0	0.3	0.9	3.0
31	Jamari Traylor	SR	F	6-8	Chicago, IL	37	8	.532		.675	3.2	0.5	0.6	0.9	2.9
42	Hunter Mickelson	SR	F	6-10	Jonesboro, AR	26	11	.439	.000	.688	2.3	0.5	0.5	0.9	2.3
2	Lagerald Vick	FR	G	6-5	Memphis, TN	19	0	.560	.471	.500	0.3	0.4	0.2	0.1	2.1
5	Evan Manning	SR	G	6-3	Lawrence, KS	15	1	.500	.500		0.3	0.1	0.3	0.0	0.6
21	Clay Young	SO	F	6-5	Lansing, KS	9	0	1.000		.500	0.3	0.0	0.0	0.0	0.4
11	Tyler Self	JR	G	6-2	Lawrence, KS	14	0	.167	.200	.000	0.1	0.3	0.1	0.0	0.2

## CHAPTER 13

2016-17

MAKING HISTORY

The eighth-leading scorer in school history graduated and their three-year starter at wing bolted school a year early for the NBA. Still, even after the departures of Perry Ellis and Wayne Selden, no one in Lawrence predicted the Jayhawks would take a step backward in 2016-17.

In fact, the belief was just the opposite.

"That's the perfect example of Kansas math," Bill Self chuckled. "Lose two of your three best players, and people expect you to get better."

Granted, a certain late addition to the 2016 recruiting class had a little to do with the optimism. Detroit native Josh Jackson—the No. 1-ranked prospect in the nation by Rivals.com—pledged to Kansas on April 11, choosing the Jayhawks over Michigan State and Arizona. A 6-8 small forward, Jackson spent just one season in Lawrence, but the impact he made during his brief stint there will never be forgotten.

"Josh Jackson," assistant coach Norm Roberts said, "is the best one-and-done we've ever had here."

Bill Self: Josh was really easy to recruit. I'm not saying it was easy to get him. I'm just saying we didn't have to work as hard on him as we have other guys. Josh was a lot like Wiggs in that he didn't need to talk to you every day. That's something I've learned about those top, top, top guys—the elite guys. They don't have to be told how good they are every day. You don't have to keep reminding them about how awesome you think they are or about how bad you want them. Josh was like, "Coach, you just told me that last week. You don't have to tell me again. I know your opinion hasn't changed in seven days."

Josh Jackson: I had always liked Kansas quite a bit, but I was really sold after I took my visit. I was there for the Texas game (a 76-67 KU win in January of 2016; Ellis and Selden combined for 45 points). Just being in that loud gym around all those crazy fans … they loved their team, and they treated the players so well. I thought, "This is the place for me." I didn't want to be anywhere else after that.

I hung out a lot with Frank and Jamari on that trip, and we went over to Coach Self's house. They had caterers there, cooking a big meal. The whole team was there with the coaches and their wives and kids. It just felt like a big family. I felt so much love from everyone, and it got even stronger those next few months.

When Coach Townsend and I talked or texted, it was never about basketball. Same with Coach Self. We talked about my family and my dreams beyond basketball. It was a tough decision, but I don't regret anything. I feel like I made the right choice.

Assistant coach Kurtis Townsend: Getting Josh was really rewarding. He kept things really close to the vest. Everybody was telling us that we'd never get him and that his mom was crazy, but that was so far from the truth. She wasn't that way at all.

We battled Arizona and Michigan State really hard. In his heart, I think he wanted to go to Michigan State, because Miles Bridges is a good friend and he was there. And that was his hometown school. But I think his mom convinced him that this was the best place. A lady that worked in her organization—Josh's mom has an AAU program—is my wife's cousin. So she was always in there with her, telling her, "They're good people. They'll look out for Josh. He'll have a home away from home." I think we won the mom over more than the kid.

Josh is a real extroverted guy. He loves hanging out and being with people. He liked the attention he received here. He was great with the media. They loved him. And he liked being the best player on one of the best teams in the country. He also liked that he could be away from the limelight by being sheltered in the athletic dorm when he needed some privacy. It made us feel good that the kid trusted us, because he was one of the best players we've ever had here.

Bill Self: Josh was a big get for us. Biiiiggggg get. He's the most prepared freshman we've ever had. He had the talent, he knew how to compete at a high level and how to make others better, how to be a teammate … he was great.

Devonte' Graham: I respect the fact that Josh came in and listened to the coaching staff. A lot of guys, especially McDonald's All-Americans, come into school thinking they know it all. But that transition from high school to college is tough. Josh realized that and he came in and listened. He struggled at first, like any other freshman. But once he got it down, he started playing almost every position, one through four. He was guarding four men, playing out of position, doing anything he could to help us win.

Josh is a fierce competitor. He'd get so mad, even in practice. Most freshmen don't dare say anything to the older guys when the older guys mess up, but Josh didn't care. He would definitely call us out. He'd say "D'Tae, that was your fault!" And usually he was right. He knew the game and he competed.

Josh Jackson: I may have been a freshman, but I didn't mind jumping on someone at practice if they weren't working hard. I think I earned their respect pretty quickly. Sometimes, when guys are older, it can be kind of dangerous because you don't know

how they're going to receive it. But when I was at practice and saw someone not giving the same effort as I was, I was on them. I didn't care if it was Frank or Devonte' or Udoka (Azubuike). Some days we would go back and forth and argue, but at the end of the day, we all remembered that we were on the same team and that we all had the same goal.

Landen Lucas: I haven't seen a freshman with the mentality and mindset that he had. After a few months he was carrying himself like he'd been with us for three years. And the thing was, everyone was fine with it because everyone respected him.

If we were doing extra running or people were late, a senior would usually step up and say something. But Josh would jump in and voice his opinion, as well. If we were having team meetings and there was something that needed to be said or things needed to be changed, he would state his opinion.

Assistant coach Kurtis Townsend: Josh was completely different than Wiggins. With Wiggs … I think one of his main goals was not to get hurt. His whole deal was, "Let me make sure I don't get a serious injury that will keep me from being the No. 1 pick." Whereas with Josh … he was a guy that absolutely hated to lose. Even though he knew he was going to the NBA, he wasn't looking that far ahead. While he was here he was focused on winning, and he attacked every game and every practice that way. His approach was really good.

Bill Self: Josh could not have handled a group of teammates better than he did, especially considering he knew he was the alpha dog, the one that leads verbally, the one that leads by example. He realized, "I'm a great competitor, but these other guys around here ... they compete just as hard as I do." He's a winner, and he respected the other guys because he knew they were winners, too.

Another thing Josh realized after he got here was that No. 0 (Frank Mason) was pretty strong-minded himself. I think Josh thought he'd come in here and say, "I'll just make this my team." Well, you had some pretty strong-minded dudes that had done quite a bit. Josh was able to respect that and still impose his own will on things at the right time.

By the time he was a senior, Mason's story had been told countless times. He was supposed to attend Towson, did not have the test scores to qualify, went to prep school and landed at Kansas after Townsend discovered him in the back gym of an AAU tournament in Las Vegas.

The initial hope from Kansas coaches was that Mason would one day be an All-Big 12-caliber player. But as the years progressed, expectations elevated. Entering his senior season, people close to KU's program sensed an even greater hunger in Mason, a desire to surpass expectations even further than he already had.

Lagerald Vick: That whole summer, he was always in the gym—every day and every night. Just being a leader and showing that he wanted it more than others. He had that dog in him.

Devonte' Graham: In the offseason he was in the gym every day working out on his own, not to mention our team workouts. His confidence in his jump shot went way up. It's hard to guard someone who not only can shoot, but is also super-quick and can finish around the rim. He knew that he was our leader and what he had to do in order for us to be successful. He came out and did it. He made a conscious effort to be more of a leader. Compared to what he was when I first got here, he definitely got more vocal on the court.

Landen Lucas: His development was outstanding, not just as a player but as a person. Even his text messages changed. When he was younger he'd text a certain way, but as a senior his wording was different, more mature. He was using periods and commas and that kind of stuff. He was trying to be a leader. Then, on the court, you just saw him work and work, and next thing you know, it was paying off on the court.

Josh Jackson: Frank impressed me in so many ways. He went so hard every day in practice. We fed off of him, energywise. I really respected him because he had so much responsibility. He was the face of the team, but he still kept us together and kept us strong throughout it all.

I remember getting off of planes after we got back to Kansas from away games. We'd bus back to Allen Fieldhouse. It'd be 11 at night and everyone was going home. But Frank walked inside and went on the court and started putting up shots. I saw so much from him. He's a hard worker and a really good guy.

Frank Mason: The previous years I had worked really hard, too. But I worked differently. That was the difference. It was the amount of reps I was putting in. It was a lot of work. I was in the gym a lot. I was working on all areas of my game instead of just focusing on certain areas.

Luke Cooper, Mason's personal trainer: I was with Frank the summer before his senior year. The first time we worked out it was, like, 6 p.m. one night. We got done and I left to go home. Then around 8:30, I get a text: *"Hey man, can you come back for another workout?"*

That was his mindset. He always wanted to make sure everything was perfect. I was always conscious about his legs and wearing him out, so I never wanted to make the workouts too long. I wanted to get him in and out pretty quickly. But that was tough, because we'd be doing a drill, and I'd say, "All right, do you wanna move on to the next thing?" and he was always like, "No, I gotta get it right." He'd say that over and over, to the point where I don't even think he realized he was still saying it. He'd just mumble under his breath. "I gotta get it right. I gotta get it right. I gotta get it right." He had a constant desire to be perfect. He'd make eight shots in a row, and he was still like, "Did I do it right? Was the footwork right? Was the angle right?" His attention to detail was huge.

There were times in the preseason where he'd have weights and then a team workout and then we would work out on our own. And then, after all of that, he'd want to work out *again* later that night, a third time. Sometimes he'd do that on Friday nights.

Frank's decision to sacrifice for his long-term goals has made him who he is. Also, if you listened to his senior speech, he said, "If I could play at KU for four more years, I would." Trust me, he meant every word of that sentence.

I remember the second time we worked out, I said, "Hey man, are you ready to get out of here and go to the NBA?" He was like, "No, dude. I owe everything I have to this place, to this university. I love these people. I love this place." He told me that day that if he could play at KU four more years, he would. He took the responsibility of the school on his shoulders, and you could see it in the way he played.

There'd be two minutes left in a game, and he'd played 30 minutes and locked up their best player. To find that kind of energy ... his "why" stemmed from a bigger reason. It was, "KU is my school, and I'm going to do this for KU."

Mason's story and his makeup made him a favorite of Self, but the coach challenged him at every turn.

Frank Mason: We had a pretty good relationship when I first got to Kansas. He loved the intensity I brought on the defensive end. He loved my toughness. It just carried along each year and the relationship grew. It changed from year to year—as freshman to sophomore, sophomore to junior and junior to senior. I just got better every summer and gained more trust each and every year. Coach Self is hard on everybody that first year. He was hard on me, especially as the point guard, and that helped me become the player I am today. He'd say typical stuff coaches say, just trying to get under your skin and make you better.

Wayne Selden: Frank would go back and forth with Coach Self. Most guys would just say "Yes, yes…" and agree with Coach Self whenever he said something. If Frank didn't agree, he's not going to say yes. Coach would be like, "Frank, you were a little soft today, right bud?" Frank would shake his head and say, "No!" Coach would say he was soft again, and Frank would be like, "I wasn't soft today, Coach. I don't know what you're talking about." He was stubborn, and that's what made him so good.

Assistant coach Norm Roberts: Coach would only get mad at Frank when he wasn't aggressive. Coach would just yell, "Frank … goooooo!" Frank's like, "Man, Coach, I just drove it hard on three straight possessions." But Coach would bark back, "Go again! Stop playing passive." When someone has that much confidence in you, it makes you play better.

Frank's Team

With the return of Mason and Graham in the backcourt and addition of Jackson, the Jayhawks carried a No. 3 ranking into the 2016-17 season. They were tested right away, as No. 11 Indiana and No. 1 Duke were the first two opponents on the schedule.

In the opener against the Hoosiers—the game was part of the Armed Forces Classic in Honolulu—Mason had 30 points, but KU lost in overtime 103-99. Jackson struggled in his college debut with nine points on 3-of-11 shooting.

Four days later, Kansas was in New York for a meeting with Duke in the Champions Classic at Madison Square Garden. Jackson fared better—15 points on 6-of-9 shooting—but he fouled out in just 18 minutes. Mason was there to save the day, burying a pull-up jumper from the elbow in the final seconds to give KU a 77-75 win. He finished with 21 points and five assists.

Bill Self: We knew Frank had improved his stroke so much. After those first two games, his feeling was, "I'm as good as anybody."

Frank Mason: That shot against Duke did a little bit for me, but honestly it did more for KU. The history Duke and Kansas have … you're talking about arguably the top two programs ever in college basketball. We took a lot of pride in competing and wanting to beat those guys. So I've done more for the Kansas and Duke tradition than I've done for myself.

Josh Jackson: In the beginning, I got a lot of tongue-lashings from Coach Self. The middle of the season, too. But the beginning was particularly tough. I knew he was going to be hard on me. I wasn't sure what he wanted from me. I didn't know whether he wanted me to be one of the main guys on the team, because we had already had so many veterans and guys who could do so many things.

Those first two games I was still trying to figure out my role. *Am I the guy who is supposed to score? Am I the guy who is supposed to be our defensive stopper? Am I the guy who is supposed to focus on rebounding?*

He ended up telling me, "I want you to come out and be yourself. I want you to bring us energy and score and be aggressive. Do everything that you've always done so well." Eventually I realized I was the guy that was supposed to be doing all of those things. Not just one of them.

Small Ball

Self was already asking a lot from Jackson, and shortly after the beginning of the season, he decided to put another challenge on the freshman's plate: a position change.

Sophomore forward Carlton Bragg was expected to replace Ellis and have a breakout year. Self, however, was not pleased with Bragg's progression in preseason practices. He gave him a shot to prove himself in games, but after five contests, he decided to bench Bragg and instead use an extra wing —either Sviatoslav Mykhailiuk or Lagerald Vick. The change in offense meant Jackson would move to the four position. Suddenly, Self found himself embracing something he'd hardly experimented with before: small ball.

Josh Jackson: When I signed with Kansas, the plan was not for me to be playing the four. But I did what they asked to help our team win. I don't think there are a lot of guys, especially today, who were ranked really high in high school, who would come in and sacrifice their game for another group of guys on the team. But that's exactly what I did. I sacrificed that whole year.

I wanted to win. I knew I had to do that and sacrifice my game to help our team win. I couldn't be the face of the team playing alongside the National Player of the Year. But I *loved* playing with Frank Mason. I took a backseat to him and we won games. I think everyone was happy at the end of the day.

Landen Lucas: Freshmen can make impact plays, but it's not often that a freshman takes over and changes a whole team's mentality. There were times when Josh would do that, and it wasn't just scoring. Sometimes it was, "Oh, I need to hustle extra hard right now, because we're kind of dead, and I've gotta get my teammates going." It was stuff seniors usually think of—not freshmen.

Bragg's final game as a starter was Nov. 22 against Georgia in the championship game of the CBE Classic. He played just 10 minutes, as Jackson spent most of his time at power forward. He excelled and won tournament MVP, averaging 18.5 points, 9.0 rebounds and 3.0 assists over two nights at the Sprint Center.

Josh Jackson: Right around the CBE Classic in Kansas City, I started to become really confident and believe in myself a little more. I thought I had a chance to do something special.

Down Goes Udoka

Bragg wasn't the only player to lose his starting spot after the CBE Classic. Self promoted freshman Udoka Azubuike to the starting center spot after Lucas, who was battling some nagging injuries, had struggled early.

Landen Lucas: It was a combination of a few things. I came out with a mindset that I was going to be a big-time offensive scorer, and that changed up the way I thought. I was trying to figure out what I could do to improve from the year before. I felt pretty confident that I'd reached a peak in rebounding toward the end of my junior year, and I was happy with the defensive side. And honestly, I was happy with how I was scoring toward the end of the year, too. But I thought if there was one thing I could improve on, it was that area. It wasn't to the point where it was selfish. I wasn't like, "I'm going to catch the ball every time, make a move and try to score." But I was definitely more offensive-minded, and it hurt everything else and made me think about the wrong things.

So that hurt me, and on top of that, I was battling some leg injuries. I was walking around in a boot, which mentally affected me more than anything. Whenever you walk to a game in a boot, regardless of how serious it is—even if it's just a precautionary thing—it can play a small factor in your mindset. It was tough because I didn't get off to the good start I wanted.

Based on preseason expectations, Azubuike—who'd been pegged by recruiting analysts as a "project player"—looked to be ahead of schedule. He scored 17 points against UNC Asheville in his first start. Mostly, his role was to rebound and block shots, and he was doing both at a high level. But during a practice on Dec. 20, Azubuike tore ligaments in his wrist and was forced to undergo surgery, knocking him out for the season.

Udoka Azubuike: I was really grasping everything. I was feeling really confident about my game. The injury came at a time where I was starting to understand every bit of what Coach was talking about. It was very frustrating for me. But sometimes stuff happens for a reason.

Bill Self: Losing Udoka really hurt. Who knows if Udoka would have kept starting or if Landen would have ended up being our starter, but just playing with one big last year, that put too much pressure on certain guys. Dwight Coleby ended up coming in and doing some good things late, but the reality was that we had to completely change how we played.

Throughout his career, Lucas had always played better when he didn't have to look over his shoulder and knew what his role was going to be. In his first start following Azubuike's injury, he had four points and 12 rebounds in a 71-53 win at UNLV. He followed that up with 15 points and 17 rebounds in the Big 12 opener against TCU.

Landen Lucas: I finally got to a point where I sat down and realized I just needed to get back to the right mindset in order for things to start changing.

Bill Self: He was our glue—one of the smartest players we've had here, hands down. He improved so much. We recruited him to be a rotation guy eventually, and all he did was basically start the last 2-plus years, and he was great. He's a great low-post defender, so tough. He had a great year. *Great* year.

A Running Start

After beating TCU in the league opener, Kansas was 12-1 and clearly in a groove. Even though Kansas State boasted an identical record, no one expected them to hang with the Jayhawks on Jan. 3 at Allen Fieldhouse, where the Wildcats were rarely competitive.

Josh Jackson: Playing in the Big 12, everyone wants to beat Kansas so bad. No matter who you're playing, you're going to get their best shot. No matter how the team had performed before, we were going to get their best, so we better be prepared. We had to give them our best, too. Playing against Kansas State, it was a different type of game that night, a different type of feeling. It was really exciting.

K-State forward Dean Wade: You've got to treat it like any other game. You can't hype yourself up too much. It's still just a basketball game. A lot of people overthink it. It's definitely a great environment. It's so loud and it can be intimidating. But you've still got to treat it like any other basketball game. It's still five versus five.

K-State coach Bruce Weber: If you go back to the year before at their place, we battled with them and it was a two-point game midway through the second half, and then we missed a couple plays and they went on a run and grabbed control of the game. Still, I thought that gave our guys some confidence going into the game the following year. It was early in the season, but they were already so good offensively. Probably not as good defensively, but really good offensively. And if they got running and Frank got going, it was tough to stop them. We got off to a great start and our guys played well.

The Wildcats came out on fire, burying nine of their first 13 shots to take a 24-15 lead.

K-State guard Barry Brown: There are always a lot of emotions when you play KU. Their fans start shouting insults as soon as we get there, but I love all of that. It's fun. It just motivates me to do something good. I love when the crowd goes silent. There's nothing better than when that happens at Allen Fieldhouse.

The Jayhawks responded to K-State's early success with a run of their own, outscoring K-State

37-16 to end the half with a 52-42 lead.

Bruce Weber: They went on a run, and I thought, "Ahhh, here we go again at their place." But this time we sustained it.

Wade helped the Wildcats charge back in the second half, scoring 13 of his 20 points after halftime. His jumper with 8:34 left tied the game at 75.

Dean Wade: I've always played well against good teams. Strong competition brings out the best in me. It's been that way since I was little.

The score remained close the rest of the way. With 20 seconds left and the score tied at 88, K-State called timeout and drew up a play for Wade.

Dean Wade: I had a wide open 3 at the end that I swore was going in. Somehow, I missed it. It felt good when I released it. It was online and I was like, "Oh, that's good!" But then it didn't go in. I wish I could have that shot back. I set a screen. I remember catching it on the right side and being open. You've got to be confident as a basketball player. You've got to think it's going in, and that's what I was thinking. It happens. You miss shots in basketball.

Bruce Weber: Obviously we had the shot to beat them. You can't get a better shot than Dean's shot. We had two guys go to grab the rebound and kind of knock it out of each other's hands. We had a chance to win.

The ball went out of bounds with 5.6 seconds left and KU called timeout. Mykhailiuk was the inbounder and tried to get the ball to Mason, who K-State double-teamed. Mykhailiuk passed to Graham instead. Graham fired the ball back to Mykhailiuk as he streaked down the court. The Ukrainian guard went coast-to-coast and made a finger roll over Wade as the buzzer sounded.

Sviatoslav Mykhailiuk: I just got a bucket. That's it. And we won.

Well, not exactly. If you watch Mykhailiuk's feet as he approached the basket, he appears to take an extra step. Maybe even two.

K-State guard Barry Brown: I saw that he traveled immediately. As soon as it happened I was literally looking at the ref, rolling my hands over one another, making the travel signal. But he didn't call it. It's the Big 12. Things happen.

Bill Self: He didn't walk. He ran! It would have gone overtime if they had called it.

Josh Jackson: We gave Svi a hard time about it. Over the summer I was at the rookie transition program with all of the NBA rookies. Me and (former K-State guard) Wesley Iwundu were laughing about Svi's travel.

Sviatoslav Mykhailiuk: After I saw video, I saw that it might have been a travel, but in the game, I didn't really realize it because I didn't hold the ball. In the video, I was like, "Yeahhhh, it might have been like three steps."

Bruce Weber: You can't help but think, "What the heck?" Our players were going nuts, yelling at the refs. I was like, "Come on guys. We don't need a problem." And they didn't want to get in the handshake line. I didn't know as much as they knew. We're on the other end, but obviously when we got to the locker room, our guys were just going crazy. *"This is wrong, Coach!"* I was trying to calm them down and kept saying, "Hey, we had the shot to win it. We gave ourselves the opportunity and didn't do it. You can't let a call affect you."

I was already trying to get ready for the next game, more than anything. Then I went back to the coach's locker room and my phone was going crazy. I walked out to do radio and even their fans were apologizing. *"Hey Coach, great game. Really sorry that the game ended on a controversial no-call."* Then I got to our radio people and they showed it to me on the replay, and there was no doubt. They were fuming. Then I went to the press conference and the Kansas writers were making fun of it. The thing that got me when I watched the video was that the officials were so adamant that the basket counted that they didn't see the walk.

But afterward, I was more worried about my team. I'd been involved in plenty of games that ended on controversial plays, and the thing I've learned is that, if I make a big deal about it, it's going to kill the kids for the next game. That was the main thing, that we respond from it and come back and play well.

Dean Wade: The ref didn't call a travel, so it wasn't a travel. Whatever they say goes and you can't change it. There was no reason to dwell on it.

Barry Brown: We didn't sulk about it. We had another game two days later. You can't live in the past in this league or you're going to keep losing.

More Trouble in Morgantown

After narrowly escaping against Kansas State, the Jayhawks didn't leave much room for doubt in winning their next five contests, the highlight of which came when KU shot 54.8 percent in a victory against Iowa State in Ames.

At 18-2 overall and 7-0 in the Big 12, the Jayhawks were atop the league standings when they traveled to play West Virginia on Jan. 24. Self's team had lost its last three games in Morgantown.

Devonte' Graham: I definitely like playing them because it's a good test, personally, to go up against those guards. But before the game, when you're sitting around at the hotel or whatever, you're definitely thinking, "Man, tonight is going to be tough. I'm about to get pressed for 40 minutes. I've got to make sure I don't turn the ball over."

Josh Jackson: The Big 12 was tough as a whole, but our toughest competition was West

Virginia. Every time we played them it was a tough game. I liked how physical they were. They played together. They had experienced guys. In some ways they were like us.

You can't take any plays off against West Virginia. They come after you non-stop. They want to be the team that establishes the pace of the game. They want to set the tone in terms of toughness. They want to be the aggressors, the ones who throw the first punch.

The Jayhawks didn't give the ball away a ton—only 13 turnovers—but they struggled defensively, and the Mountaineers rolled to an 85-69 win. It was the second year in a row KU had lost at West Virginia by double digits.

Bill Self: I don't think we've played well in the five years we've been going out there. We're 1-4 there and I don't even think we played well the time we won. But I do think their style keeps us from playing well. Bob Huggins gets a lot of credit for being a really good coach, and I still don't think he gets enough. He's really, really good.

Battle for First Place

After losing at West Virginia, Kansas was tied with Baylor for first place in the league at 7-1. Absent from Top 25 polls in the preseason, the Bears had opened with 15 straight wins—including three against Top-10 opponents—and achieved their first No. 1 ranking in school history.

When they took the court at Allen Fieldhouse on Feb. 1, the Bears were 20-1 overall. Like the Jayhawks, Baylor's lone loss was against West Virginia in Morgantown.

Baylor guard Manu Lecomte: Kansas was a great environment to play in, very special. It was the loudest environment I've ever been in—and remember, I started my career in the ACC, at Miami. So I'd played at Duke and North Carolina and Syracuse and Louisville. Allen Fieldhouse was better than all of them. I loved it. It gives us extra motivation.

We were really hyped. We went in there convinced we were going to win the game. We knew we could win. We had a special team, a very balanced team with some seniors mixed in with the underclassmen. J-Mot (Johnathan Motley) was a killer inside. Ish Wainright was a great leader who didn't really score much, but he did all of the little things.

Baylor led 34-28 at intermission before Kansas opened the second half on a 14-2 run to surge ahead 42-36. The score was close the rest of the way, and the Bears still had a chance when Lecomte swished a jumper with 53 seconds remaining to pull his team within a basket, 70-68.

Mykhailiuk split a pair of free throws to give Kansas a 71-68 lead with 18 ticks left, meaning Baylor would have one last chance to tie the game and force overtime. The Bears, though, never got off a shot, as Mason's suffocating defense on Lecomte forced the guard into a turnover.

Two free throws by Mason rounded out the scoring in KU's 73-68 victory. Mason scored 19 points and Josh Jackson had 23 points and 10 boards. Motley and Lecomte netted 16 each for the Bears.

Manu Lecomte: Frank is a great guard. He wasn't talking any trash. He was just hooping. There was a mutual respect between the two teams. At that point we were both ranked in the top five in the country. We knew it was going to be a great matchup. Even though we lost, we recognized they were a great team and they played a great game. Somehow, they always pull it off at the end.

Three'd to Death

Three days after beating No. 2 Baylor, KU hosted a downtrodden Iowa State squad. The Cyclones arrived at Allen Fieldhouse having lost back-to-back games against Vanderbilt and West Virginia and had dropped four of their previous six contests overall.

Still, Iowa State seniors Monte Morris, Naz Mitrou-Long, Matt Thomas and Deonte Burton had been a part of some epic battles with Kansas in the past, and they were determined to make their final visit to Lawrence a memorable one.

Iowa State guard Naz Mitrou-Long: Quick flashback to my freshman year in 2013: I was able to get in for, like, 25 seconds at the end of the game, and as the clock was winding down I told Korie Lucious, "One of my years at Iowa State we're going to get a win in here and I'm going to play really, really well. I promise you that." Now it was my last year, my senior year, and I was one of the main scorers now. I was no longer a role player. I remember telling the guys, "Look, if we take care of business and take every possession seriously, we can do it. We can win." Kansas played great the first half. They were hooping. They were balling, man.

The Jayhawks shot 70.4 percent in the opening stanza and led 52-38 at the break. KU maintained its advantage until the 6:32 mark of the second half, when back-to-back 3-pointers by Burton capped a 20-8 run that gave the Cyclones a 75-73 lead.

Naz Mitrou-Long: Guys didn't let up. Deonte started going bonkers.

Iowa State guard Donovan Jackson: I think my greatest memory from that game is Deonte coming down in transition, stopping at the 3-point line right by Coach Prohm and shooting a contested 3. That gave us our first lead of the second half and put us up two. That really got us going.

Naz Mitrou-Long: We were feeling amazing. If you really look at the game and you really break down myself, Deonte's and Monte's performances, at various points in the game, there were segments where each of us just took over. We were playing solid the whole time. The scoring was balanced. When you get in a zone like that—when you get enough shots and reps and touches where you feel like you could throw a rock in the ocean—that's a good feeling. All three of us felt like that at some point that night.

Deonte got hot and brought us back. Then it was my turn to exploit anybody who was guarding me. That's no shot at them. I've had rough games against them, those same KU players. But once you get in that zone, you feel like any shot you take is going to fall. I shot a couple that were on the beak of the Jayhawk, and they fell. At that moment I felt like I couldn't be stopped and I was just thankful that they dropped.

Kansas trailed by one when Mason split a pair of free throws to force an 82-82 tie with 50 seconds remaining. And it was Mason who ended up with the ball again, moments later, as the final seconds ticked away in regulation, but his attempt at a game-winning jump shot was off the mark, and the two teams headed for overtime.

Naz Mitrou-Long: My respect for Frank is as high as anybody in the country. I got assigned to guard Frank my junior year (2015) when he was a sophomore. From that moment on, anytime someone asked me to name the toughest guys I've ever had to defend, I would always say Frank Mason. He was so crafty with the ball and he's explosive and athletic. People didn't give him a lot of love for that. Everyone talked about him being small, but I knew how talented he was. That night he showed it. He didn't miss a shot until I guarded him on that last possession. He got to the right elbow and pulled-up—the same shot he hit to beat Duke, although that time he went to the left. This time he went to the right and it rimmed out. He hits that shot and it's ballgame.

The Cyclones hit a school-record 18 threes to win 92-89 in overtime. Burton scored 29 points, Morris had 25 and Mitrou-Long added 22.

But it was juco transfer Donovan Jackson, playing in his first game at Allen Fieldhouse, who sealed the win. Jackson scored 10 points and swished the dagger 3 with 26.7 seconds left in overtime.

Naz Mitrou-Long: Coach Prohm said something I won't forget. He told Donovan and Solomon (Young) that they didn't realize the significance of what they'd just accomplished by winning there, and he was right. They were 1-0 in that gym, but I was 1-3. I knew how hard it was to win at Allen Fieldhouse and how much it meant when we finally did.

Donovan Jackson: It was a great moment, hitting that final 3. It was dope playing there, just because where I come from I'm used to watching it on TV—me and my homies. It was a blessing to be out there and be a part of that win.

I wasn't scared to take the shots I made. I don't run from nobody. I'm not afraid to play anybody. I'm just a confident dude when it comes to playing basketball. Naz told us never give up and always believe. That was his thing all year long, whenever we were down. *Just keep believing*, and we did.

Everybody was amped up jumping around in the locker room. It was a cool opportunity. Georges Niang didn't get to win in The Fieldhouse, so he called us when we got back to Ames and talked to a couple of the guys. I told him that was for him.

The Jayhawks lost despite getting 32 points from Mason on 9-of-11 shooting. He also made 10-of-12 free throws to go along with six rebounds and five assists.

Naz Mitrou-Long: We've got the utmost respect for Frank, and I know he has the same respect for our program. I've talked to him a bunch. I played with him on the

Sacramento Kings summer league team. He's a good dude. He deserved that night. I know he wishes he would have got that win, especially with the performance he had, but he's one of the toughest guys I've ever seen play and ever had to personally guard. The respect for him is high.

Devonte' Graham: We had a lot of respect for those guys. Monte Morris was someone I liked playing against. He's a friend, but he's a heck of a player, too.

Norm Roberts: It's kind of cool ... last year (2017) when we went to Iowa State and we beat them up there, it was Monte's senior year and also Burton's and the kid, Naz. We'd had so many good battles. Monte comes up to me before the game and says, "Man, Coach, I love these games. I love these games, Coach. I'm going to miss these games. Playing against y'all, man, it's always competitive. It's always a war, but we respect each other. It's cool, Coach. It will never be like this again."

Frank and Devonte' and Landen felt the same way. They felt like it was a war, but it was always something special when you played against them. The younger kids don't feel it during that first year. For Josh and Wiggs and Joel or Kelly Oubre, they didn't get a feeling like that. Somebody like Frank ... he'll always talk about Kansas and those games and those wars, because he was in them for three or four years.

Octagon of Doom

The schedule did the Jayhawks no favors after losing to the Cyclones. Next up was a trip to Bramlage Coliseum, where the Wildcats were hungry after losing in the Big 12 opener on Mykhailiuk's controversial game-winner.

Devonte' Graham: K-State and Iowa State are the two toughest road arenas in the Big 12. For K-State, when we play there, it's definitely the loudest it ever gets.

K-State fans ... I don't listen to them. I don't know how I do it, but I've got a good way of blocking people out and ignoring them. When I'm on the court I don't really pay attention to the fans. But during shootaround about an hour-and-a-half before the game ... that's when I listen and pay attention a little bit.

Norm Roberts: It's great for our guys because it's always a huge challenge. We let our guys know that it's going to be one of the most hyped, negative, aggressive atmospheres they'll face all year. West Virginia can be like that, but not at the feverish pitch Kansas State is. We know they'll have their biggest crowd of the year when they play us. We know it's the only game where the kids are going to be lining up two hours in the cold before the game. We warn our guys that they're going to say things before the game and during it. We tell them what their No. 1 chant is, and they're going to play that song and do it all day.

Coach will say, "Go enjoy it! It's *so* much fun. It's a war when we go in there. Bring it on! Don't shy away. *Bring it on!*" It's never a deal where we're like, "We've got to beat K-State!" What helps us is that we've already played at Iowa State or West Virginia or

Oklahoma. We've already played in tough atmospheres. They may not be as feverish as K-State, but at least your guys come out of the locker room focused.

Frank was so into enjoying everything and relishing every moment as a senior. He said, "There are things I want to make sure I accomplish as a senior, and one of them is winning at Kansas State."

Mason delivered, scoring 21 points in 74-71 win. The Jayhawks followed that up with a one-point win at Texas Tech and then returned home to face ninth-ranked West Virginia.

No Way

The Mountaineers came into Lawrence on Big Monday more determined than ever to beat Kansas in its own gym. Two years earlier, they'd taken the Jayhawks to overtime at Allen Fieldhouse. And they had whipped Self's squad four straight times in Morgantown, including that 85-69 beatdown just three weeks earlier.

Sure enough, with 2:58 left in regulation, it appeared the Mountaineers would finally get the signature road win for which they'd long strived, as Tarik Phillip's basket put West Virginia up 64-50. Kansas had made just three field goals the entire second half, and at that point, the advanced statistics website KenPom.com gave KU a 0.3 percent chance of winning.

Landen Lucas: If there was ever a game where I felt like it might be slipping away from us at home, that was definitely it. I remember when they went on that run to put us down 14 toward the end of the game, I was already starting to think about the route we'd have to take after that night to make sure we still won the Big 12 championship. It was tough. I was trying to keep my mind right and focused on what we needed to do on the court, but at the same time, you see people leaving and doubt starts creeping in for everybody.

Lagerald Vick: I was kneeling down at the scorer's table, waiting to check in, and I looked up into the stands and people were walking out. I glanced at the time and there were still 2 minutes left on the clock.

Bill Self: They totally dominated the game. We're shooting 29 percent from the field *at home* with like three minutes left. Unbelievable. We couldn't score. We ran bad offense. Guys were pressing. It was just a beat down. And then I don't know how it happened, but somehow it happened.

Mason made two free throws with 2:43 left, but fans continued to flock toward the exits—which is almost unheard of at Allen Fieldhouse. At the 2:19 mark, Mason made a 3, and KU called timeout.

Bill Self: Most of the time as a coach, in that type of situation, you stay positive. Sometimes if you just know that it's not gonna go your way, you may not be quite as positive. I've always felt like the first 30 minutes of a game, you coach it different than the last 10. You can get on guys or whatever in the first 30, but the last 10 you've got to win the game. Also, you can't get mad at guys for trying too hard and pressing. I think

BEST KU PASSERS

1. Aaron Miles: The school's all-time leader in assists was incredibly unselfish and was the table-setter for some of the best offenses in school history. He helped make three big men (Gooden, Collison and Simien) first-team All-Americans.

2. Devonte' Graham: One of the most pure point guards Self has coached played off the ball his first three seasons to allow Frank Mason to be the lead guard. Still, his passing ability has been evident. Graham is especially gifted at throwing lobs.

3. Brady Morningstar: Bill Self wants the ball to swing in his high-low offense, and no one has been a better ball-mover than Morningstar. He was also adept at feeding the post. Cole Aldrich and the Morris twins benefitted greatly from that skill.

4. Julian Wright: He arrived before his time, because Wright would have been ideal playing in a role like Self had Josh Jackson fill as the small-ball four. Wright had awesome vision and imagination. He could see (and complete) passes no one else would even try.

5. Josh Jackson: One reason Kansas was so difficult to defend in 2016-17 is that Jackson was like a third point guard on the floor. He had great vision and could complete difficult one-handed lasers with ease.

6. Sherron Collins: Few people could keep the powerful Collins in front of them off the dribble, and when he broke down a defense, he was savvy at identifying where the defense sent help and then finding his teammates.

7. Tyshawn Taylor: Similar to Collins, Taylor was a master at breaking down a defense off the dribble. He struggled with turnovers at times, but he regularly got his teammates open shots off penetration.

8. Frank Mason: Mason came to KU not knowing how to play point guard and left with the sixth-most assists in school history. He averaged a career-best 5.2 assists per game in his National Player of the Year senior season.

9. Russell Robinson: He wasn't flashy but he got the ball where it was supposed to go in KU's offense. He ranks 10th in school history for most assists.

10. Marcus Morris: He didn't put up big assist numbers, but Morris had a great feel for the game, and that included finding open teammates when he drew double teams. He also had a knack for setting up his twin brother.

that's what we were doing.

Josh Jackson: We had already lost to West Virginia in Morgantown and we weren't very happy about it. We *did not* want to lose again. It was a night when things weren't going right the entire game until the very end. Then stuff just started clicking for us. In our huddles down the stretch, we kept believing. We believed that we were going to win. We talked about getting stops, securing the rebound and taking smart shots on offense. That's exactly what we did.

If one guy in our huddle had looked at the scoreboard down the stretch and thought, "Uh-oh ..." we would have lost that game. But no one did that. We always believed we were going to win.

Devonte' Graham: Coach Self had this look on his face, like we could still do it. And none of us looked defeated. We still had fight left in us. He told us it was now or never. We had to get up and press them and make some plays. He kept telling us that we were going to make shots, we just needed to get stops. That's really what we started doing.

Frank Mason: I never doubted that we could win. I kept telling the guys that we could do it—just one stop at a time. No matter how late it was. Right when it got to under three minutes, I knew we had to have a stop every time, and then good possessions on the offensive end. I believed.

Landen Lucas: All of a sudden the momentum started to switch. The doubt disappeared. Even when it got to a 9-point game, it was an, "OK, let's just see what happens" kind of thing.

Lagerald Vick: We stayed together as a team. Two minutes was still a long time to us. We couldn't take that loss at home.

Twenty-three seconds after Mason's 3-pointer, Graham buried another 3, and a 14-point lead had quickly shrunk to six with 1:56 seconds still remaining. With Kansas pressing, West Virginia was unable to inbound the ball and got called for a five-second violation.

West Virginia coach Bob Huggins: We had a five-second call that was three, and it's on the tape. You can see the guy. You can see him count to three, but he got caught up in the hype, in the atmosphere. Crazy things happen in that building. It's kind of like Boston Garden used to be. Crazy things happen.

But could this seriously happen? After the five-second violation, the Jayhawks failed to capitalize. Graham drove toward the basket and forgot to take the ball with him. Turnover.

A few possessions later, Mykhailiuk barreled into the lane and charged over Jevon Carter. With 1:15 left, the Mountaineers had the ball and a seven-point lead.

Bill Self: When we won it all in '08, it seemed like everything went right down the stretch. In this situation, we had a lot of things not go right.

After each team traded a pair of free throws, Graham was fouled with 52.4 seconds left. He swished both charities. West Virginia inbounded the ball to Phillip, but he passed the ball right into the hands of Mason, who caught it in stride for a layup, but missed. Lucas was there for the offensive rebound and dunk to pull KU within three.

West Virginia guard Jevon Carter: There were stupid mistakes on our part—turning the ball over, panicking. Everything went downhill quick.

Landen Lucas: I think it was kind of ironic. They were acting like they hadn't been pressed before. But since they run Press Virginia I'm assuming they were going against it every day in practice. We were actually out there running stuff we'd learned by watching their film. When Coach said, "Get on the ball and pressure the inbounder and pressure behind that," I was thinking, "That's the same thing they do."

Next thing you know, we started coming back. I almost knew what was going to happen just because you're in The Fieldhouse and you can kind of see them start to panic.

Frank Mason: Reading their body language and hearing the West Virginia guys complaining and yelling at each other about who is doing what wrong, and Coach Huggins' body language—mad and kind of fussing at himself—I knew it was all going downhill for them.

Devonte' Graham: Sometimes they couldn't even hear what their coach was calling out. When the crowd gets into it, the momentum starts to shift. You can look at the man you're guarding and tell he's thinking, "It's way too loud in here."

Landen Lucas: The funny part is seeing people try to convince themselves that they're fine and knowing that they're not. I could see it in some of the younger guys; they were showing their emotions and then you would see the older guys going, "It's fine. It's fine." You know in their head, they're going "Oh crap. This is not going well."

Jevon Carter: You've got to play against them, the crowd, everything. That gym gets hot, too. With the crowd, it gets real hot. That was as hot as it's ever got there. And then they broke the record with the loudest crowd ever. I guess all that played a factor.

Bob Huggins: They set a record for the decibel level that game—Ripley's Believe it or Not. You couldn't hear anything.

After the dunk by Lucas, there was enough time left (44 seconds) that Kansas could defend without fouling and hope to get a stop and have a shot to tie the game. Self tried to yell at his players not to foul, but they also couldn't hear anything, and freshman Mitch Lightfoot fouled West Virginia's Esa Ahmad. The forward made both free throws to put West Virginia ahead by five, 71-66

Mason brought the ball back down the floor, dribbled into the corner and picked up the ball.

After a couple precious seconds ticked off the clock, he found Graham at the right elbow. Graham pump-faked, turned his back to the rim and dribbled out to the 3-point line and then turned and hit a contested fadeaway 3 over Carter. It went in with 33.1 seconds left and KU trailed 71-69.

Bob Huggins: He makes every shot against us, and it just pisses me off. He makes *every* shot against us. I don't know why he doesn't make them against everybody else the way he does against us. He just makes shot after shot against us.

Kansas called timeout and set up its press again. The Mountaineers inbounded the ball to Phillip in the corner, and he was trapped. With a timeout still remaining, Phillip opted to flip a wild, one-handed pass to teammate James Bolden along the opposite sideline. Bolden caught the ball falling out of bounds and tried to call timeout, but the officials didn't give it to him, and KU had the ball with 26.5 seconds left.

The Jayhawks gave the ball to Mason, who drove and got fouled. He made both free throws to tie the game and Phillip missed a 3 at the buzzer. Overtime.

Kansas 84, West Virginia 80
February 13, 2017 · Lawrence, Kan.

Kansas (23-3)

Player	MP	FG	3FG	FT	R	A	F	S	TO	B	TP
Devonte' Graham*	42	5-14	5-12	3-4	2	1	1	2	2	1	18
Josh Jackson*	41	4-13	0-2	6-8	11	3	3	5	6	0	14
Landen Lucas*	32	3-6	0-0	2-7	13	0	4	2	1	2	8
Frank Mason*	43	3-13	2-6	16-18	4	5	3	1	3	0	24
Svi Mykhailiuk	21	1-4	0-2	2-2	3	1	5	0	2	0	4
Carlton Bragg	18	0-1	0-0	0-0	1	0	5	0	0	0	0
Dwight Coleby	2	1-1	0-0	0-0	1	0	0	0	0	0	2
Mitchell Lightfoot	8	0-1	0-0	0-0	3	0	1	0	0	2	0
Lagerald Vick	18	4-8	2-4	4-5	2	2	5	1	1	0	14
Team					2						
Totals	225	21-61	9-26	33-44	42	12	27	11	15	5	84

West Virginia (20-6)

Player	MP	FG	3FG	FT	R	A	F	S	TO	B	TP
Nathan Adrian*	39	3-10	2-5	2-2	7	6	1	2	3	0	10
Esa Ahmad*	32	6-11	1-2	7-7	7	1	5	0	3	0	20
Jevon Carter*	32	3-6	2-2	3-4	5	1	4	3	2	0	11
Elijah Macon*	21	4-5	0-0	0-0	8	0	3	0	4	1	8
Tarik Phillip*	21	5-10	1-2	7-9	3	2	5	6	3	0	18
James Bolden	14	1-5	1-4	1-2	2	2	1	0	0	0	4
Sagaba Konate	13	1-4	0-0	0-1	4	0	2	0	0	1	2
Daxter Miles, Jr.	24	2-5	0-2	0-2	3	0	3	0	1	0	4
Teyvon Myers	6	1-2	1-1	0-2	1	0	1	0	0	0	3
Brandon Watkins	7	0-1	0-0	0-0	1	0	2	0	2	1	0
Lamont West	16	0-4	0-3	0-0	1	0	4	0	0	0	0
Team					2				3		
Totals	225	26-63	8-21	20-29	44	12	31	11	21	3	80

	1st	2nd	OT	Total	FG%	3FG%	FT%
Kansas	32	39	13	84	34.4	34.6	75.0
West Virginia	39	32	9	80	41.3	38.1	69.0

Officials: Patrick Adams, Ray Natili, Doug Sirmons
Technicals: None

Bob Huggins: I think everybody in the arena got caught up in the comeback, but they still had to make shots and they made shots. We panicked. And they made shots. They made some huge 3s to get back in the game. We just panicked. We just weren't thinking. We thought we had it and let it slip away.

Landen Lucas: We went ahead and completed the comeback. I always feel like, with an overtime game in The Fieldhouse, we have a pretty good chance of winning, so I think we all felt pretty confident.

Not surprisingly, the Jayhawks went on to win the game in overtime, 84-80. The hero in the extra period was Graham, who buried two more 3s and finished with 18 points. In the first 38 minutes of the game, he scored four points. Mason finished with a game-high 24 points.

Frank Mason: It was one of the top wins for me ever.

Devonte' Graham: I didn't know until after the game that people were leaving with two minutes left. That was crazy. But the people that stayed made it loud enough for us to win.

The ones who left definitely missed out.

West Virginia guard Daxter Miles: That loss hurt. It was a bit of a surreal feeling in the locker room, like "Wow, we seriously just lost that?" We were shell-shocked.

Bob Huggins: Somebody called me and asked what makes Kansas so good. I said, "Well, they've got a Hall of Fame coach and the best players in the league." It's not that hard to figure out, really. The best players make plays. It's not that hard.

They're the best team because they don't lose at home. ... People have got to start winning there. We've got to start winning there. We had chances. We just didn't do it.

Landen Lucas: I would talk to my friends on other teams and they would talk smack, "We're going to come in there and win" and this and that. And I'm like, "You can say all you want but I know in the back of your head, you know that's not the case." That's kind of how we felt as we were coming back in that game. No matter how confident they tried to say they were, it wasn't going to be enough.

Finishing off No. 13

Kansas followed the epic overtime win over West Virginia with a trip to No. 4 Baylor. The Bears (9-4) trailed the Jayhawks (11-2) by two games in the Big 12 standings. A Baylor win would make the race interesting. Kansas, though, pulled out a 67-65 win to push their lead to three games. With four games left on the regular-season schedule, Kansas winning a 13th consecutive Big 12 title was a foregone conclusion.

Josh Jackson: Baylor gave us some really tough games. They were so versatile. They were a lot bigger than us. They were different than any team we played. Every game in the Big 12, we had to prepare for in a different way. For Baylor, we'd set our second team up in their 1-3-1 zone. They'd use these long pads that they'd stick up in the air or out to their side to bother our passes. The goal was to simulate Baylor's length, because guys like Motley and Jo Lual-Acuil and (Nuni) Omot had such long arms.

We had so many close games and we were almost always able to get over the hump. We had great energy at the end because we were in such good shape because of Hudy. And we all wanted to win, so our focus was good. Down the stretch, we'd be up or down and, depending on where we were in that game, we knew what we had to do, whether it meant focusing really hard on defense to get stops or focusing really hard on offense and making sure we executed. Being in those situations so many times and in so many close games, it helps you to be more and more focused. We didn't panic.

One week later, Kansas clinched the Big 12 title outright by defeating Texas 77-67 in Austin.

BEST KU SHOOTERS

1. Brandon Rush: Ranks third on the Jayhawks for career 3-point field goal accuracy (43.5 percent); went 13-of-22 from beyond the arc in the 2008 Big 12 tournament.

2. Ben McLemore: Boasts one of the smoothest strokes of the Bill Self era; led KU in average 3-pointers made per game (1.97) and accuracy (42 percent) in 2013; banked in a 3 to force overtime in a home win over Iowa State.

3. Tyrel Reed: Led the Jayhawks in 3-point field goal percentage (47.3) in 2010 and average makes per game (1.89) in 2011; had at least four 3s in 15 games as a senior in 2011.

4. Devonte' Graham: On pace to finish in the top three for all-time 3-pointers made at KU; has 186 after three seasons; a career 41.2 percent long-range shooter; swished six 3s at Oklahoma in 2015.

5. Brannen Greene: Was arguably the best pure shooter on the team from 2013-16, but attitude issues and lack of intensity on defense limited his minutes; made 31 of his 63 attempts from distance in 2015-16.

6. Frank Mason: Shot 42 percent from three for his career, a mark that ranks sixth all time. Made 47.1 percent of his 3s as a senior in 2017, which was up from 38.1 percent the previous season.

7. Sherron Collins: The Chicago native made 232 3-pointers during his KU career, the fourth-most in school history. No shot was bigger than the corner 3 he hit during the Jayhawks come-from-behind win over Memphis.

8. Mario Chalmers: Made the biggest three-pointer in KU history in the 2008 national title game against Memphis; made eight 3-pointers that same year against Texas in the Big 12 tournament championship.

9. Jeremy Case: His teammates from 2003-08 swear he'd beat any Jayhawk in a pure shooting contest; rarely got opportunities in games to show what he could do; made three 3s against Texas Tech on Senior Night.

10. Jeff Hawkins: The Jayhawks' defensive stopper off the bench was underrated as a shooter; made four 3-pointers in the championship game of the 2006 Big 12 tournament; went 5-for-5 against Baylor.

Mason and Jackson combined for 34 points. With 13 straight conference crowns, Kansas was now tied with UCLA for the longest streak of league championships in college basketball history. The Bruins won 13 in a row from 1967-79. The legendary John Wooden was the coach for the first nine of those titles.

Devonte' Graham: I don't want to sound cocky, but no, I don't think we had any doubt that we would be the team that breaks the streak.

Senior Night

All Senior Nights at Kansas are special, but some more so than others. The 2017 edition ranks high on the list for Self, and not just because his son, Tyler, a walk-on, was in uniform for the final time.

Hours after KU propelled to No. 1 in the Associated Press poll, Frank Mason—who in four seasons went from the least-heralded member of the 2013 recruiting class to the AP National Player of the Year—played his last game on the Allen Fieldhouse court where he'd honed his craft, before the fans who'd watched him grow up.

Kansas (which also honored Lucas) has not lost on Senior Night since 1983. But the Sooners, who were just 4-12 in conference play, threw a scare in the Jayhawks. With 10 minutes remaining, the Jayhawks trailed by 12.

Bill Self: Frank played awful. That was one of the worst games he had. He was pressing. Everyone was. There's a lot of emotion on Senior Night. Guys are nervous about their speeches afterward.

But that was one of my favorite Senior Nights, because we played so good down the stretch. That was one of the great comebacks we've had. It took 30 minutes to get the lid off the basket and play worth a flip. They had us down 12 with about 10 minutes left, and next thing you know, it happened that fast (snaps fingers). In like three minutes, it was a tie game. And Frank got his.

The Jayhawks took the lead 59-58 on a Graham 3-pointer with just under 4 minutes to play. Kansas finished the game on a 31-9 run to win 73-63. Mason had a poor shooting night—8-of-17—but he finished with a solid line of 23 points, six assists and three steals.

Oklahoma coach Lon Kruger: Mason was fantastic. A great competitor. He was very good in late-game situations and competed like crazy to get the result, especially in late-game situations. You really respect that.

"Naw, Coach! I'm playing every minute!"

With the pressure of winning the Big 12 title—not to mention Senior Night—now behind them, the Jayhawks entered their regular-season finale at Oklahoma State as loose as they'd been all season. Even Self, who was just 3-6 in road games against his alma mater, seemed more relaxed than usual when Kansas took the court March 4 at Gallagher-Iba Arena.

Kansas would be facing one of the hottest teams in the country in Oklahoma State. Led by first-

year coach Brad Underwood, the Cowboys had won 10 of their last 12 games after opening Big 12 play 0-6. The backcourt of Phil Forte and Jawun Evans was regarded as one of the nation's best.

Norm Roberts: One of the coolest games I've been a part of was the Oklahoma State game this year in Stillwater. We had already won the league, but we had lost at Oklahoma State three years in a row. People always talked about how we struggled to win there, and about how it was coach's alma mater. They had a really good team, too. At that time—the last game of the regular season—they were playing as well as anyone in the league, next to us.

Coach knew our guys were fatigued by that point in the season, especially since we really only played about eight guys. We were in meetings talking about, "Should we rest Frank and Josh and some of those guys? They're tired as hell and they're beat up." Coach even told Frank, "Hey, we may not play you as much. We've got to worry about the Big 12 Tournament and the postseason." Frank wasn't having it. He was like, "Naw, Coach. I'm playing! I'm playing every minute! I'm not tired! I'm playing!"

Devonte' said the same thing. "We're going down there to win!" Coach's whole mantra was like, "OK, but just go down there and play with a free mind. Just go play. We're going to play faster than we've ever played. Play fast! Shoot it! Let it fly! I ain't going to say one word to you. All I'm asking you to do is play hard. If you do that, I won't say one word to you. I want you to play fast. I want you to have fun. I want you not to worry about winning or losing or whatever. We've got the Big 12 title. We've done our job. I want you guys to go down there and have as much fun as you can have."

We went out there and we were flying. Now, Oklahoma State was flying, too. After the first 10 minutes, we were like, "Good God!" But even in the huddle, Coach was like, "Isn't this fun? How about this atmosphere?" Our guys were so loose and relaxed, but also so focused. It was a really cool thing to watch. To see Frank and Jawun Evans go at each other … Coach was like, "Who's the best point guard in the league, Frank? Is it you or Jawun? Devonte' … let's see who has the best backcourt?"

It was a battle. The crowd was on us. It was one of the best games I've ever been a part of. Our guys were coming into the huddle coaching themselves.

The battle between Mason (27 points, nine assists) and Evans (22 and 15) was epic, but Mason walked away with the stat that mattered most: a 90-85 win that gave Kansas a 28-3 record to end the regular season.

At 16-2 in the Big 12, Kansas finished four games ahead of Baylor, West Virginia and Iowa State in the standings. Each of those teams went 12-6. The four-game separation between first and second place matched the largest of any season during KU's 13-year streak. In 2010, the Sherron Collins-led Jayhawks went 15-1 and won the Big 12 by four games.

No Jackson, No Chance

As good as the Jayhawks were feeling after the win in Stillwater, the mood soured a few days later when Self announced Jackson would miss the first game of the Big 12 Tournament against TCU.

Earlier that week, Jackson—whose name had previously been attached to some unrelated off-court drama involving the vandalism of a KU women's basketball player's car—informed Self he'd been issued a ticket for leaving the scene of an accident after backing into a parked vehicle on Feb. 2. When Kansas took the court at the Sprint Center, Jackson was in street clothes.

TCU coach Jamie Dixon: That didn't really change things for us. The first game we played them he got in foul trouble and Vick came off the bench and was the guy that killed us. (Vick scored 17 points; Jackson had four.) We'd have won the game if Jackson had played and Vick hadn't played. He's the one that hurt us.

We had already played them close twice before and had been ahead most of the game at our place and all of the first half at their place, so it wasn't like we felt like we couldn't play with them. Both games were close. Both games came down to the end. But at the same time, we hadn't won either of those games, and we felt like we should've.

The thing that stood out to me was the home-court advantage they have in Kansas City with that Big 12 Tournament. It's like a party before the game, and the party has already started before the championship's won. It's like a foregone conclusion.

In 2017, the party never truly got started, as the Horned Frogs went on a 9-2, game-ending run to upset Kansas 85-82. The pivotal moment came when Mykhailiuk fouled TCU's Desmond Bane as he attempted a 3-pointer with 2.5 seconds remaining. Bane made all three free throws to give the Horned Frogs the win. Mason had 29 points and six assists in a losing effort for KU.

TCU forward Kenrich Williams: Mason was a great player. He deserved that Player of the Year award. He came in here and hit some big shots, and I thought it was over with but we were resilient.

Williams, who Jackson would have guarded, was the star for the Horned Frogs. He dominated across the board with 18 points, eight rebounds, five assists and four steals.

Kenrich Williams: Every game there's people in the crowd yelling at you… that game they were yelling that I've got a lunch lady haircut.

All the Kansas fans here were just sick because we beat them. We upset them. It's great. It's one of the best feelings. You can't compare that to winning at home. It's different when you spoil everybody's bracket. It definitely put us on the map around the nation. People took us more seriously and we carried that momentum onto the NIT and won the NIT championship.

While the loss was disappointing for KU, it didn't affect their NCAA Tournament seeding. It also gave the Jayhawks a few extra days to rest before opening NCAA Tournament play in Tulsa as the No. 1 seed in the Midwest region.

Postseason Poundings

After thumping UC-Davis 100-62 in the opening round, the Jayhawks prepared for a showdown with No. 9 seed Michigan State in the round of 32. The game was especially meaningful to Jackson, a Detroit native who almost signed with the Spartans before deciding to attend KU. Jackson's close friend, Miles Bridges, was a forward for Tom Izzo's squad.

Josh Jackson: After I picked Kansas, I had a lot of Spartans fans who were mad at me and saying some crazy things. A lot of people from back home were upset, too. In my mind, coming into that game, there was no possible way I was going to let us lose.

I was probably a little too excited to start the game. I'd played against Miles a bunch of times. It's always a great game between us. His stats are always good. My stats are always good. I win most of the time. It's always a good game, especially since I'm going against a guy who is competitive just like I am. He's very athletic and skilled and versatile. It's a challenge. Anybody who knows me knows I love a challenge. Playing against Miles Bridges is always a challenge.

History held true. Bridges put up a good stat line (22 points and eight rebounds) and so did Jackson (23 points, two blocks and two steals) as Kansas won 90-70.

The Jayhawks headed back to Kansas City to face No. 4 seed Purdue at the Sprint Center. Led by All-American forward Caleb Swanigan and 7-footer Isaac Haas, the Boilermakers touted one of the best (and biggest) frontlines in the country. Basketball pundits questioned how KU's four-guard lineup would fare against Purdue's size.

Kansas forward Dwight Coleby: People kept asking that question: "Can we handle them?" To me, the question should've been, "Can they handle us? Can they handle our speed and quickness?"

The answer, emphatically, was no. After a back-and-forth game early, the Jayhawks ran away from the Boilermakers to win 98-66. Mason and Graham poured in 26 points apiece.

Kurtis Townsend: Oh my god, they were unbelievable. We kept emphasizing that, 90 percent of the time, speed beats size.

Kansas led 47-40 at intermission before outscoring Purdue 51-26 in the second half. The Jayhawks went 15-of-28 from beyond the arc and became the first team since Connecticut in 1995 to score 90 or more points in its first three NCAA Tournament games.

Bill Self: That was one of the best games we played all year. The second half was as complete as we'd played.

Homecourt (Dis)advantage

The Jayhawks entered their Elite Eight matchup with Oregon with an average victory margin of 30 points—the third-highest in the last 10 seasons—through the first three rounds.

Playing at such a high level in front of a hometown crowd, Kansas seemed destined to return to the Final Four for the first time since 2012. The Ducks, led by former Creighton and K-State coach Dana

Altman, were the last remaining hurdle.

Assistant coach Jerrance Howard: Oregon was super hungry. They were in the same position as us, having lost the year before in the Elite Eight to Oklahoma. They had that same fire and bitter taste. For the first time, I thought playing at home in Kansas City was a disadvantage. I remember ironing my shirt in the hotel before the game. I told my wife, "Turn off that TV." The news was on and there were damn near 30,000 KU fans swarming throughout Power & Light. They were so hyped and excited. The atmosphere was crazy. It almost seemed too perfect. I was like, "Man, I hope our players aren't watching this. This may be too much." Of course, on the flip side I'm thinking, "How can we lose with all of this support?"

Bill Self: It should be an advantage, but I think when you're playing at home in a game that you're supposed to win, I think it definitely adds to the pressure. If you're playing well, it's great. But when you start pressing a little bit and every fan is on edge and nervous with every shot you miss, I think it adds some pressure to it.

Oregon set the tone early when Jordan Bell blocked Jackson's layup attempt on the game's opening play. Less than three minutes later, Jackson was forced to the bench after picking up his second foul—an iffy call on a hand check that infuriated everyone from Jackson to Self to the 18,000-plus in the Sprint Center stands.

Josh Jackson: My second foul, no, I don't feel like I fouled him at all. It's just an opinion. Refs, they're all just people out there and they make mistakes too. But I definitely think those calls impacted the game. I was a pretty big piece of the puzzle and, for most of the first half, I couldn't contribute because I was sitting on the bench. It was definitely hard for me. And then, once I came back into the game, I couldn't be as aggressive as I normally am. That's a huge part of my game that was taken away. I couldn't be myself because I was scared to pick up another foul.

Bill Self: It hurt us. I think Jordan Bell (eight blocks, 13 rebounds) hurt us just as bad. He controlled everything within seven feet of the basket.

Oregon guard Tyler Dorsey was also a pest with four 3s in the first half. Two of those bombs came in the final 42 seconds before intermission, when Oregon uncorked an 8-0 scoring run that gave the Ducks a 44-33 lead and, more importantly, a ton of momentum.

Bill Self: We puttered around and cut it to three with about a minute-and-a-half left in the first half, and then (Dorsey) banks in a 3 and then throws in another late. Tough, tough, tough.

The score would've been worse if not for Mason, who scored 17 points in the first half. Jackson played just 10 minutes and was scoreless at the break.

Josh Jackson: We were slightly unprepared. They came out from left field. They were in a matchup zone. Leading into that game, our practices were against a man-to-man defense. No one expected them to come out in that zone. Especially since they were kind of identical to us. They had athleticism and four guards just like we did. It seemed to make sense that they'd play man to man, so they surprised us.

Jerrance Howard: We were pressing when we got down. We got out of our game and couldn't get into our flow. The crowd was trying to get going.

Eventually, a few things started to go right for the Jayhawks. Jackson found his rhythm and scored 10 second-half points. Mykhailiuk also heated up and hit a huge 3 with 2:49 left in regulation that pulled Kansas within reach, 66-60. Moments later, Kansas appeared to get a key defensive stop. With the shot clock about to expire, Dorsey intentionally threw the ball at the rim to prevent a violation.

Kansas 60, Oregon 74
March 25, 2017 · Kansas City, Mo.

Kansas (31-5)

Player	MP	FG	3FG	FT	R	A	F	S	TO	B	TP
Devonte' Graham*	38	0-7	0-6	3-4	2	2	2	0	1	0	3
Josh Jackson*	30	3-8	0-2	4-6	12	5	4	1	5	0	10
Landen Lucas*	33	4-9	0-0	1-2	3	1	2	0	1	1	9
Frank Mason*	40	8-20	2-8	3-3	4	4	2	1	1	0	21
Svi Mykhailiuk*	28	4-7	2-4	0-0	0	0	3	2	0	0	10
Dwight Coleby	4	0-1	0-0	0-0	1	0	0	0	0	0	0
Lagerald Vick	27	2-8	1-5	2-2	3	2	0	0	0	0	7
Team					7						
Totals	200	21-60	5-25	13-17	32	14	13	4	8	1	60

Oregon (33-5)

Player	MP	FG	3FG	FT	R	A	F	S	TO	B	TP
Jordan Bell*	34	5-6	0-0	1-1	13	4	1	0	4	8	11
Dillon Brooks*	37	7-18	3-8	0-0	5	4	2	1	2	0	17
Tyler Dorsey*	35	9-13	6-10	3-4	5	1	3	1	3	0	27
Dylan Ennis*	39	5-8	2-4	0-0	2	0	2	2	0	0	12
Payton Pritchard*	25	1-5	0-2	0-0	5	2	3	1	0	0	2
Casey Benson	21	2-5	0-1	0-0	2	0	1	0	1	0	4
Kavell Bigby-Williams	8	0-2	0-0	1-2	1	1	1	0	0	0	1
Keith Smith	1	0-0	0-0	0-0	0	0	0	0	0	0	0
Team					3				3		
Totals	200	29-57	11-25	5-7	36	12	13	5	13	8	74

	1st	2nd	Total	FG%	3FG%	FT%
Kansas	33	27	60	35.0	20.0	76.5
Oregon	44	30	74	50.9	44.0	71.4

Officials: Ted Valentine, Randy McCall, Terry Oglesby
Technicals: None

Josh Jackson: I got a hand on the ball but just couldn't pull it in with two hands. They had been grabbing offensive rebounds the whole night. After I tipped the ball, I looked and Frank was right there to get it. If I had never touched the ball, we probably would have had the possession.

Frank Mason: I felt like that could have turned the game. That was a big point of the game when we didn't grab that ball. We were down six with two-and-a-half minutes left. If we could have got that stop there, we could have had a good possession and cut it to three or four points.

Instead, Bell snagged the offensive rebound. Oregon milked 30 more seconds off the clock and then Dorsey crushed KU's spirits with another 3-pointer—his sixth of the game—to give the Ducks a 69-60 cushion. They cruised from there to a 74-60 win. Dorsey scored 27 for Oregon on 9-of-13 shooting. Mason led KU with 21.

Graham entered the game averaging 20 points in the NCAA Tournament and had made 13 of his 22 shots from beyond the arc in the Jayhawks' first three wins. He was 0-of-7 from distance against Oregon and finished with three points, all on free throws.

Josh Jackson: That night, stuff just didn't fall for us. Shots that Svi normally makes, shots that Devonte' normally makes, just didn't go in that night. If two or three of those 3s go in, it'd be a whole different game. We'd have energy and swagger and the crowd on our side. But shots just didn't fall.

Bill Self: We played good in the tournament. With all the distractions that we had, we played good in the tournament. But we didn't play good against Oregon at all.

Jerrance Howard: I've lost in the Elite Eight as a player under Coach Self when Arizona beat us at Illinois in 2001 to go to the Final Four. That game still stings. But to have back-to-back years at Kansas, when we thought both groups were special, when we thought we had the right pieces and that everything was in place … it's always going to sting. That's the bad part about coaching. We were blessed to get to the Elite Eight, but when you get that close and don't finish it off, there are so many mixed emotions. It's extremely painful. You've just got to keep kicking on that door.

Player of the Year

As difficult as it was to make the trip without his teammates, Mason traveled to the Final Four in Phoenix the following week. He had to collect some hardware. Mason swept the various National Player of the Year awards. The Associated Press trophy was particularly meaningful, as Mason became the first player in KU history to be named AP National Player of the Year.

Landen Lucas: I thought the goal going into his senior year would be to win Big 12 Player of the Year. That's what we thought was realistic for him. But as soon as he had that good game against Indiana, and then the game against Duke, we started to realize he might have a case for something a little bit more than the Big 12 award.

Tarik Black: I watched Frank's Senior Night speech, and to hear Coach Self say he was the best player that ever played for him, that's a huge accolade. He used to tell us all the time that Sherron Collins was the best. He'd say, "Sherron is the only guy who ever played for me that could do whatever he wanted with the ball. All you other guys need to pass it around. You're not like Sherron."

But now that Frank has that label, that's amazing for a kid that came in who was committed to Towson. He came in and everyone was talking about Andrew Wiggins and Joel Embiid and Wayne Selden and Brannen Greene. They were talking about everyone but the little Virginia kid. Now the little Virginia kid has the title of the best player to ever play for Coach Self. That's amazing.

Sherron Collins: I don't really get into the comparisons to Frank, but I didn't have the players around me my junior and senior year like Frank had around him. It was basically just me and Cole. Tyshawn and the twins were great, but they were just coming along. They were young. Either way, no matter what order you put Frank and I in, we're still No. 1 and No. 2. And if people say he's No. 1, I'm fine with that. Almost anytime someone sets a bar, it gets broken.

I told Coach Self before Frank's sophomore year that he'd be one of the best guards to ever play here, and Coach told me I was crazy.

Wayne Selden: Frank's a warrior. He's really like my brother. There isn't anyone more competitive. If you tell him he can't run through a wall, he's going to run through a wall. He's a warrior.

Perry Ellis: Some people were surprised by Frank's senior season and that he won National Player of the Year. I wasn't. From the moment Frank came into the program, I knew he was a dog. He was a competitor. When he lost in practice, he'd get so mad. He'd start yelling at everyone, like, "What are y'all doing?" And that's when he was a freshman! So, no, I wasn't surprised with how he played as a senior, because he really wanted it. He'd put in the work and waited his turn. It was his time and he took full advantage of it.

Jamari Traylor: Going into his junior year, Coach was saying some things about how Frank was going to score the ball a little more. He let him off the leash a little bit and we got to see a little of what he could do. His senior year he took over. The offense was so different because they didn't have a traditional big like Thomas or Perry or JoJo. The timing of it was perfect for Frank.

Naadir Tharpe: The more games he played and the more reps he got, you could just see as the years went on how easy it was becoming for him. It just became easier and easier as the years progressed.

It definitely feels good to see Frank have that success. We had a relationship. We hung out every day. Even to this day, if I hit him up, it's the same type of genuine friendship that existed before he even committed. To see him grow and eventually win Player of the Year, it feels good to know I was able to help him out.

ESPN commentator Fran Fraschilla: Frank Mason understood—probably more than any player Bill ever coached—what it meant to be a Kansas Jayhawk and how important it was to uphold the legacy. With his personality and athletic ability and talent, he allowed himself to be coached. Even when he became a star, he never stopped allowing himself to be coached.

I don't know that there's a player that epitomizes what Kansas basketball has meant under Bill Self more than Frank Mason. He came in as a nondescript, backup point guard and left as the National Player of the Year. He poured his heart and soul into that program and spilled his blood and guts, night in and night out.

Norm Roberts: With our atmosphere and what you go against every day … my son was a walk-on here. He couldn't play dead and I knew it, but he wanted to come to Kansas. But by the time he left here, he was actually competing in practice, where guys had to respect his energy level and his competitiveness. He'd make it hard on our guys.

I sat back there as a dad thinking, "Wow! My son has gotten this much better?" It's a day-to-day thing. Get better. Challenge yourself.

Frank is going to challenge Devonte'. Devonte' is going to challenge Malik (Newman). Malik is going to challenge Charlie (Moore). Challenge, challenge, challenge. In practice, Coach is all about being competitive. A guy may think he's playing good, but then Coach will blow the whistle and say, "You're not competing at all. You made a couple of shots. Who gives a s**t? You're not competing at all. In fact, you're getting your ass kicked. Even though you made two shots here, that was because Frank got into the lane, drew your defender and gave you an easy shot. But four other times you could've had a rebound near the basket and you never went for the damn ball. There was a loose ball and you didn't go after it. You didn't dive. You're not competing!"

Coach says, "Frank, people think you can't shoot. You've got to improve your shooting." The next day Frank would be in there shooting. If you're a bad shooter you should be in the gym after practice working on your shot. Don't complain about how bad of a shooter you are when the shooting gun is right there, or coaches are lingering around waiting to work with you.

Our young guys see the veterans going to the gym every night to work and to shoot. And they almost feel like an outcast if they're not making the same effort.

People will say all the time, "How come Kansas hasn't signed an elite point guard? That's because Frank was here. Recruits came in and saw him and said, "This dude is really good." We had a recruit say the same thing about Devonte' even after Frank left.

A little more from ...

Bill Self: Devonte' is probably the most popular kid on campus. And he's a terrific player and a better guy and a better personality. We've had some guys that could be the face of the program. I don't think anybody's going to be a better face than him. Thomas was for his stretch, and you could say the twins were and Sherron was and Mario was, but I don't think anybody has the total package like Devonte'—as far as being a really good player and so competitive, but also having a smile and a personality that people are just drawn to.

Frank Mason: Devonte' was great to play with. I loved playing with Devonte'. He's an unselfish guy and can do a little bit of everything—guard, score the ball and share it. Not only that, he's a good guy and has good character. He brought a lot of positive energy.

Josh Jackson: Devonte' ... I loved playing with him because he's such a smart player. Me and him had this thing where we'd make eye contact and we'd automatically be on the same page. You can probably look back at our highlights this year and find tons of plays where Devonte' would be driving to the basket, and you see me cut out of the corner from nowhere. Devonte' isn't even looking at me, but he knows I'm there and he'd pass me the ball for two points.

He was loved by everyone on the team. He's a guy that really kept us together. There would be times when we'd be out there arguing and getting on each other, but he was the guy that calmed everyone down and kept us together.

Svi is one of the best shooters I've ever played with. He's another guy who we expected a lot out of. He brought it. There were times when he slipped up a little bit because he wasn't always super-good on defense. But he took on that challenge and, by the end of the year, he took pride in playing defense. Winning mattered to him and you could see it in the way he competed.

Landen, being our only center, did a phenomenal job the entire year. Another very, very smart player. He did so many things that didn't show up in the stat book. He was like another coach out there for us. We were lucky to have him because he was so experienced and knew so much about the college game. Sometimes he'd tell me things before they ever happened.

One thing Coach Self used to say to me was, "Be who you are all the time." At first I didn't understand what that meant, but I ended up getting it. Basically he was just telling me to play the way I play all the time. Sometimes I'd be a little tired, so I'd take a possession off. Sometimes I'd be out there trying to do things that I'm not as good at. I really appreciate that advice from him, because after I took what he said to heart and started being who I was the entire game … that's when I really started to get better and better and progress.

I got so close to everyone there. All of the players there, I still talk to each of them. Same with all of the coaches. I went through some tough times, some tough situations, and they never turned on me. They always supported me and had my back. They're all just really good people. You get your fair share of players in any program who may not be your ideal player or ideal teammate. But no matter what at Kansas, you're part of the family. They love you no matter what.

TOP 10 QUOTES

1. "I feel like someone put a meat necklace around my neck and threw me into a lion's den." – Texas Tech coach Pat Knight, after his team's 109-51 loss to KU on March 3, 2008

2. "It's the worst team Kansas has ever put on the floor since Dr. Naismith was here. I think he had some bad teams when he lost to Topeka YMCA in his first couple years." – Bill Self after his team's 62-55 loss to TCU on Feb. 6, 2013

3. "I was hoping that was vodka." – Bill Self, after drinking a sip of water following his team's 72-40 loss to Kentucky on Nov. 18, 2014

4. "He can make plays you can't coach, then he can make plays you wonder if he's ever been coached." – Bill Self on guard Tyshawn Taylor

5. "That's the only time my wife has been excited when I answered the phone." – Bill Self talking about his wife Cindy, who called to make sure he was alive after Bruce Weber held a "mock funeral" for Self at Illinois in 2004

6. "We're going to beat Kansas at home. We're going to beat them at their house. We're going to beat them in Africa. Wherever we play, we're going to beat them." – Kansas State forward Michael Beasley, predicting victory before his team's 84-75 victory on Jan. 30, 2008 in Manhattan

7. "A bowel movement would be nice." – Bill Self, when asked for a health update on an ailing Keith Langford heading into the 2005 NCAA tournament.

8. "Because the club was crackin'!" – KU's Brandon Rush, who answered Self honestly before a practice when asked why he missed curfew the night before

9. "I saw the USA Today coaches poll came out today and we were third. If you watched us practice you would think third in your county, let alone country." – Bill Self, talking about his team looked during early practices before the 2017-18 season

10. "Most every day — if not every day — for the rest of your life, you will be reminded or think of this night. And I want to thank you in advance right now for the great memories it's going to be." – Bill Self, talking to his team with CBS cameras rolling before the 2008 national championship against Memphis

2016-17 Season Summary

Results (31-5, 16-2)

November

11	vs. Indiana	L, 99 - 103
15	vs. Duke	W, 77 - 75
18	Siena	W, 86 - 65
21	vs. UAB	W, 63 - 83
22	vs. Georgia	W, 54 - 65
25	UNC Asheville	W, 95 - 57
29	Long Beach State	W, 91 - 61

December

3	Stanford	W, 89 - 74
6	UMKC	W, 105 - 62
10	Nebraska	W, 89 - 72
17	vs. Davidson	W, 89 - 71
22	@ UNLV	W, 53 - 71
30	@ TCU	W, 80 - 86

January

3	Kansas State	W, 90 - 88
7	Texas Tech	W, 85 - 68
10	@ Oklahoma	W, 70 - 81
14	Oklahoma State	W, 87 - 80
16	@ Iowa State	W, 72 - 76
21	Texas	W, 79 - 67
24	@ West Virginia	L, 85 - 69
28	@ Kentucky	W, 73 - 79

February

1	Baylor	W, 73 - 68
4	Iowa State	L, 89 - 92
6	@ Kansas State	W, 71 - 74
11	@ Texas Tech	W, 79 - 80
13	West Virginia	W, 84 - 80
18	@ Baylor	W, 65 - 67
22	TCU	W, 87 - 68
25	@ Texas	W, 67 - 77
27	Oklahoma	W, 73 - 63

March

4	@ Oklahoma State	W, 85 - 90
9	vs. TCU	L, 82 - 85
17	vs. UC Davis	W, 100 - 62
19	vs. Michigan State	W, 90 - 70
23	vs. Purdue	W, 98 - 66
25	vs. Oregon	L, 60 - 74

All-Big 12 Team

Player of the Year:
Frank Mason III, Kansas, Sr., G

Defensive Player of the Year:
Jevon Carter, West Virginia, Jr., G

Newcomer of the Year:
Manu Lecomte, Baylor, Jr., G

Freshman of the Year:
Josh Jackson, Kansas, Fr., G

Sixth Man of the Year:
Tarick Phillip, West Virginia, Jr., G

Coach of the Year:
Bill Self, Kansas

First Team
Johnathan Motley, Baylor, Jr. F**
Monté Morris, Iowa State, Sr. G**
Josh Jackson, Kansas, Fr. G
Frank Mason III, Kansas, Sr. G**
Jawun Evans, Oklahoma State, So. G

Second Team
Nazareth Mitrou-Long, Iowa State, Sr., G
Devonte' Graham, Kansas, Jr., G
Jeffrey Carroll, Oklahoma State, Jr., F
Vladimir Brodziansky, TCU, So., F
Jevon Carter, West Virginia, Jr., G

Third Team
Manu Lecomte, Baylor, Jr., G
Deonte Burton, Iowa State, Sr., G
Wesley Iwundu, Kansas State, Sr., F
Keenan Evans, Texas Tech, Jr., G
Nathan Adrian, West Virginia, Sr., F

Honorable Mention
Ishmail Wainwright, Baylor, Sr., G
Matt Thomas, Iowa State, Sr., G
Landen Lucas, Kansas, Sr., F
D.J. Johnson, Kansas State, Sr., F
Kameron McGusty, Oklahoma, Fr., G
Phil Forte, Oklahoma State, Sr., G
Jaylen Fisher, TCU, Fr., G
Kenrich Williams, TCU, So., F
Zach Smith, Texas Tech, Jr. F

All-Defensive Team
Jo Lual-Acuil, Baylor, Jr., F
Ishmail Wainwright, Baylor, Sr., G
Vladimir Brodziansky, TCU, Jr., F
Nathan Adrian, West Virginia, Sr., F
Jevon Carter, West Virginia, Jr., G

All-Newcomer Team
Manu Lecomte, Baylor, Jr., G
Jo Lual-Acuil, Baylor, Jr., F
Josh Jackson, Kansas, Fr., G**
Kameron McGusty, Oklahoma, Fr., G
Alex Robinson, TCU, Jr., G
Jarrett Allen, Texas, Fr., F

** Unanimous selection

Kansas Awards

Frank Mason
Consensus All-American First Team
John R. Wooden Award
Naismith College Player of the Year
NABC Player of the Year
AP Player of the Year
Oscar Robertson Trophy (USBWA POY)
Sporting News Player of the Year
CBE Classic All-Tournament

Josh Jackson
NABC All-American Third Team
AP All-American Third Team
Sporting News All-American Second Team
CBE Classic MVP

Devonté Graham
CBE Classic All-Tournament

Season Stats

#	Player	CL	POS	HT	Hometown	G	GS	FG%	3P%	FT%	R	A	S	B	PTS
0	Frank Mason	SR	G	5-11	Petersburg, VA	36	36	.490	.471	.794	4.2	5.2	1.3	0.1	20.9
11	Josh Jackson	FR	G	6-8	Detroit, MI	35	35	.513	.378	.566	7.4	3.0	1.7	1.1	16.3
4	Devonte' Graham	JR	G	6-2	Raleigh, NC	36	36	.428	.388	.793	3.1	4.1	1.5	0.2	13.4
10	Svi Mykhailiuk	JR	G	6-8	Ukraine	36	25	.443	.398	.702	3.0	1.3	0.9	0.3	9.8
33	Landen Lucas	SR	F	6-10	Portland, OR	35	30	.631		.624	8.3	1.1	0.5	1.0	8.0
2	Lagerald Vick	SO	G	6-5	Memphis, TN	36	6	.443	.370	.826	3.5	0.9	0.6	0.4	7.4
15	Carlton Bragg Jr.	SO	F	6-9	Cleveland, OH	31	5	.508	.000	.643	4.1	0.5	0.4	0.5	5.2
35	Udoka Azubuike	FR	C	7-0	Nigeria	11	6	.629		.379	4.4	0.2	0.2	1.6	5.0
22	Dwight Coleby	JR	F	6-9	Bahamas	24	0	.567		.389	1.8	0.1	0.2	0.5	1.7
44	Mitch Lightfoot	FR	F	6-8	Gilbert, AZ	25	0	.556	.667	.167	1.0	0.0	0.1	0.4	1.0
20	Tyler Self	SR	G	6-2	Lawrence, KS	13	1	.300	.333	1.000	0.2	0.4	0.0	0.0	0.8
21	Clay Young	JR	G	6-5	Lansing, KS	10	0	.000		.400	0.7	0.1	0.0	0.0	0.2
12	Tucker Vang	JR	G	6-2	Goddard, KS	10	0	.000			0.1	0.1	0.0	0.0	0.0
55	Evan Maxwell	JR	C	6-10	Clarks Summit, PA	Redshirt									
14	Malik Newman	SO	G	6-3	Jackson, MS	Redshirt									

THE STREAK, EXPLAINED

Kansas has won 13 straight Big 12 regular-season championships and counting. If the Jayhawks make it 14 straight in 2017-18, they'll hold the NCAA record for most consecutive conference titles in college basketball history. During interviews for this book, Jayhawk players and coaches—and even their opponents—were asked to give their thoughts on one of the most impressive streaks in the history of sport at any level.

Bill Self: There's a big sense of pride. I took a picture today with all of the hardware we've won since we've been here. It's just amazing. Just amazing how many trophies are out there. It's just a great sense of pride—although I'd rather go to five Final Fours than win 13 straight league championships. But I don't think they allow you to think about it like that.

Norm Roberts: One thing that Coach Self is great about is ... we don't talk about the streak. We talk about getting better every day and this team making its legacy and this team doing what it has to do. Forget about what's happened in the past. This is a different team.

If we lose, if we get beat, it's never the end of the world. That's not how Coach does it. He doesn't treat it that way. He'll be like, "This is why we got beat. I saw this coming. But it's not the end of the world." Then we attack those problems and deficiencies right away. Was our ball screen defense bad? Was our transition defense bad? Was our ball movement not good? Are we not getting the ball inside enough? Coach is very good at looking at the specific things that hurt our team. He'll warn our guys that we're living on the edge and that it's going to come back and bite us. He doesn't want it to bite us. But when it does, it's like, "OK, now we can get in the room and I can really tell them. I can really show them." Our guys respond to that.

When we get to the middle of the conference schedule, then our guys start to think, "Hey, let's go. We've got to win this deal. We can't lose at home. We're going to Texas Tech and they're on a six-game winning streak. We've got to get after them." They find different motivations for each game. If TCU has lost three in a row, it's "They can't wait for us to come in there. They want us bad. They lost their last game by one point. They're on the cusp of being really good." We find a motivation somewhere along the line to prepare them. Guys like Devonte' Graham, guys that have been here a while... they'll say to the new guys, "We're going to Iowa State, man. We've got to be focused, man. It ain't nothing like you've ever played against. You just don't know. It's different. They're going to come at us." They get them to understand. They don't want them to fear it. We embrace challenges.

If and when the streak ends ... it ends. There will be media cameras around and everyone will be freaking out. "Oh my God, the streak is over." Coach will just shrug his shoulders and say, "Oh well, that's fine. We're just going to move on and keep playing basketball."

Jerrance Howard: If you come to our practices in November and come see us in March, it's the same practice. Coach believes in repetition. If you do something every day, at the pace and with the energy we demand, you don't have any choice but to get better. He prides himself in that. We steal an extra practice on the day of the games, because our shootarounds are not shootarounds. You add on 30 more practices that no one else gets ... it's huge. Plus, he's not scared to coach and push guys to the limits, especially with his best players. It's a culture, where our guys know that we play hard and you've got to be a good teammate.

Coach has spoiled college basketball fans to where it's expected for Kansas to win the Big 12 every year. But when you look at it, there's always turnover. It's always a different group. He always has to plug in different pieces. That's coaching. Lots of schools have talent and good athletes. But you have to fit the pieces together to make it all work. I think it's one of the most impressive accomplishments in all of sports.

It's never really talked about. There are no meetings to say, "Hey, guys. This is the 11th one. We've gotta go get No. 12." We just try to stay tough and guard and let everything fall into place.

You've got to credit Coach for creating a culture where we don't worry about the streak. We don't worry about winning it the next year. We just worry about getting better and being tough.

Kurtis Townsend: One key element is how close our staff is. That's all because of Coach and his wife, Cindy. Before I even came here, he called my wife to make sure she was OK with moving to Lawrence. Almost every chance he gets, he stops in every assistant's office around lunchtime to see if they want to go eat. We do stuff that's not always centered on basketball. We go to the casino to gamble and have some drinks. We've rented a house in Cabo before that was about $1,800 a night. We chipped in a little bit but Coach paid for most of it. We get out on the golf course and talk s**t and drink beers. To me, that kind of stuff makes you closer than just working with someone. It's so good here, you don't want to leave.

Wayne Simien: People want to focus on the players when they're talking about the streak. One thing I appreciate about Coach Self is how he says, "There's no one player or coach that's bigger than Kansas basketball."

When you think about how you create a culture in anything, whether it's in basketball or in your own home, it's about consistency, not only in your core values but in your personnel. Kurtis Townsend has been here almost the whole time. Norm has been here a long time. Same with Hudy and Scooter and Cheddar. Being able to have a core group of staff members—in addition to sticking to your core principles and foundations—ensures the culture doesn't change. It's helped foster the type of consistency that has defined the streak.

Aaron Miles: Coach Self is in the Hall of Fame for a reason. He has a great understanding of the game and of people. He pushes everyone and gets the most out of them. There's a culture of toughness and resiliency that he instills in his teams. It's a mindset: We're going to protect our house, and then we're going to go on the road, into these hostile environments, and pull off some Ws. It's a culture he works to instill every day. His practices are so intense that it makes games seem easy. It helps to have some talented players, but the biggest thing is the preparation on a daily basis.

Mike Lee: For the streak to have gone on this long, you've got to point to the leader. You've got to point to the head of the horse. That's Coach Self. A part of that, too, is the culture. At Kansas, the expectations never waver. It's not about you. If you can't figure it out, there's not a problem with Kansas. The problem is with you.

Coach Self is so smart. You don't have any level of success in a conference as big as the Big 12 without being able to recruit. He's a proven recruiter. He's proven that he can develop guys. A great example of that is Russell Robinson. I know what it was like for him on the front end. It was hard for Russell. He was a tough kid from New York. A prideful, strong-minded dude. But Coach Self doesn't have any back-down. He's not going to budge. He pushed Russell and eventually he responded.

For Russell to finish at Kansas as the starting point guard on the national championship team, that's not just development. That's genius. That story right there epitomizes Coach Self's genius, because he breaks you down and builds you back up. And once he builds you back up, he loves you. He loves you forever, and once you realize what he's done for you, you love that man right back.

Stephen Vinson: Don't think that the former players aren't following every game and every moment to try to keep this thing alive, because it really does kind of connect all of the classes that have come before this year's current team. It's cool to be a part of the Kansas fraternity of basketball players and basketball teams, but it's really cool to be a part of this time frame as well, too.

Russell Robinson: Even though we rarely discussed it out loud, the importance of winning the Big 12 title was something the coaches were always trying to stress.

There was a big board in our video room where the team managers updated the league standings every day. Each team had a nameplate, and every morning the managers would slide the nameplates up or down depending on what had happened in the Big 12 the night before. So we always knew where we stood.

Obviously, the goal was also to win a national title. But the way Coach Self presented it, in order to win a national title, you needed to win your conference. Because winning your conference—especially a conference like the Big 12—gives you a great chance to get a No. 1 seed. And we knew how important that was.

Coach Self has the recipe. He adds some new spices to it every season, but the main ingredients remain the same. He's got the rhythm and the recipe. Now it's about sticking to it. Coach Self and his staff have the experience now. They know how the league works. They know how to prepare for each game. They know how to get through that Saturday-Big Monday gauntlet. Knowing how to prepare your team to win both of those big, nationally-televised games in 48 hours ... that isn't easy. Most teams can't do that.

Then we have Allen Fieldhouse. Most teams aren't disciplined enough to come in and handle the Fieldhouse. That's why, when I see 52- and 53-game home-winning streaks, I'm not surprised. I feel sorry for teams having to play there. Guys need to pay heed. The West Virginia game this past year (2017), there's no way we should've won that game. Those guys made wonderful plays, those guys did everything they could, but The Fieldhouse won that game. You've just got to pay heed. It's Phog Allen's house. That's a huge factor in this streak. The gym definitely wins them some games.

Darnell Jackson: We won four Big 12 titles when I was here. But to win 13 straight? C'mon, man. I didn't know that was even possible.

Basketball has changed. Kids are developing faster. You go to camp games and watch these guys jump and run. They're so much more athletic than we were back then. The players are getting better all over the country but it hasn't changed what's happening at KU.

Darrell Arthur: No matter how much talent Coach Self has, he's always going to have them playing the right way. Playing hard, playing for each other, playing good defense ... it doesn't matter if he has the best recruits or not, they're always going to be in position to be good because of how he coaches. He's a great motivational coach. His speeches get you ready to go. Any team with him on the sidelines is going to have a chance to win.

Sasha Kaun: In the last 10 years, how many times have you heard people talking about how it's going to be a down year, and about how we're not going to be any good? Then somehow, throughout the season, the team gets better and better and better, and we're winning the Big 12 championship once again. A couple of years ago (in 2015) we lost four or five games in the Big 12 and then we ended up being good. Somehow he always figures out a way to do it.

Jeremy Case: The key to winning the Big 12 is to win on the road—and the key to doing that is toughness. You can't be soft to win on the road. You've got to be tough. You've got to be able to take the crowd. You've got to be able to take some punches. I think that's what Coach Self instills in everybody. We're going to go in somebody else's house and we're going to win.

Each group passes that mentality on to the next group. We felt like we instilled it in Sherron and Cole, and those guys passed it to Tyshawn and the Morris twins, and so on.

Sherron Collins: I never thought the streak would get to 13. S**t, it was in jeopardy when we were playing. The impressive thing is that it's not one group doing it. So many different guys have come in, and we continue to win. That just shows the type of coach Bill Self is. He hasn't changed too much. It just shows that if you buy into what he tells you, it's going to happen.

Brady Morningstar: The streak is cool. It just goes back to the man that's the head of it all. He prepares all of us to get ready for it. That's hard to do. Every year he's got a bunch of knuckleheads that he has to bring together and prepare to play together. The Big 12 is a good league. It's hard to put into words, because 13 years is a long freaking time. People are like, "How are you doing this?" Number one, our home court advantage is crazy. The Fieldhouse has to be a top-two venue in the world to play basketball in, pro or college. Our game days are crazy. Our home-court advantage is the best in the country. People that haven't been to a game there don't understand that. But when they come to a game there and see how it is and what's going on, they'll see that it's just different.

Good players go to other schools, too. Not just Kansas. There's good basketball everywhere. It's harder and harder to stay consistent. But Coach Self doesn't coddle anyone. He doesn't give a s**t if you're a one-and-done. He's going to coach you just like he'd coach a walk-on. He might expect more out of you because you've got more skill and he's seen it before. But he's not going to treat you like a princess or a little baby because he doesn't want you to transfer. He doesn't give a s**t.

Tyrel Reed: I almost forget about the streak. They've won so many times in a row that I don't even think about it anymore. I know it's hanging out there. I think that's why we've been able to maintain it. We don't put too much pressure on ourselves to win it. It's one of those things.

It's definitely a big deal and an honor, but at the same time, hey, if we're going to position ourselves to win at the end of the year, we have to do well in the Big 12.

Marcus Morris: I'm not surprised by the streak. Coach Self... the way he puts teams together, the way he masterminds games, he's going to go down as one of the greatest coaches ever. His basketball mind is off the charts, his system is off the charts, he's successful every single year, and not because he gets top guys. My recruiting class didn't have any McDonald's All-Americans and he turned us into great players. Every year, it's like watching the same thing over and over and over.

Thomas Robinson: The key to the streak is preparation. No one else conditioned like us. And if they did, they didn't condition under the pressure that we were under. We went a whole three weeks without touching a ball. It started at 6 in the morning every day, and then it was on to weights, and that was intense. We were in shape. That's all it comes down to. Even if you're not that good, if you're in better shape than someone, you can at least hold your own until it comes down to it. People can't think as well when they're not in shape. At that age not everyone is mature yet. You're talking about 18- and 19-year-olds that don't always know the importance of being in shape and making sure your body is OK. At first, we were eating pizza every night and going out and partying. We got it instilled in us early that the season was going to be about which teams were in the best shape.

Tyshawn Taylor: It's the system. Coach can get good players to play with each other. He can get one-and-dones to play with walk-ons and to buy into the system. He can get a four-year guy like myself to be efficient each year and improve each year. It's crazy. That being said, the man runs the same stuff. He'll tweak some things every now and then. But the primary offenses and the way we guard ... it's the same. And year in and year out, with different players, it works the same way. That's what so impressive. Every coach in the Big 12 knows what they're about to guard, and they still can't stop it.

A lot of my friends went to school in the Big East. After my career, we'd watch college basketball and we'd talk about winning conference titles. They'd say, "It's easier to win in the Big 12." These people don't know how it feels to get everyone's best shot every night. Every single day we had to be on our game. We couldn't have a bad day or we'd lose—and when we'd lose, it was a big deal. A huge deal!

The Dooleys and Mannings and Townsends and Hudys and Cheddars and Scooters

... the whole atmosphere surrounding this program is professional. It's run the right way and that's why we win.

Kevin Young: You've got to give most of the credit to Coach Self when it comes to the streak. He finds a way to win every year. It's not just about recruiting talent. It's about getting those talented players to play well with each other. Think about it: in one class, he had Joel Embiid, Andrew Wiggins, Wayne Selden and Frank Mason. Earlier in his career he had the twins at the same time as Sherron and Elijah and Tyshawn. To have all of those guys and keep their egos in check and continue to win ... it's amazing.

Elijah Johnson: It's to a point now where this has taken on its own identity. There's pressure now. The only thing is that you don't want to be that team at this point. That's just not fair.

This is how crazy KU's system is. If everyone stayed four years, this past season, the seniors would've been Frank Mason, Brennan Greene, Andrew Wiggins, Wayne Selden and Joel Embiid. We get people in and out so fast that you didn't really think about that class.

Coach Self is 96.3 percent the reason this is happening. He picks the lotto numbers. He tells you who he wants here. He tells them what to do. He puts the game plan together. He doesn't always get the guys he wants and the ones he gets don't always do what he wants them to do. But he still figures it out every year.

Naadir Tharpe: It's the dedication that Coach Self has. There were several times we'd get back from the road and he'd be right up in his office watching film and sleeping in his office. There were plenty of times he did that. It just shows how much time and commitment that he put into it.

Perry Ellis: There was a huge emphasis on the streak. That's what was right in front of us. Sure, you want to win the national title, but you get all of your momentum and confidence during the conference season. That's what we'd say in huddles: "Big 12 Champs!"

We had a board in the video room with the standings on it, and there was a time my senior year when we weren't in first place. It was hard to look at it. We all had so much pride.

Josh Jackson: The pressure came a lot more from the outside than it did from the inside. In practice, we never talked about the streak. We never worried about it. We just knew that, if we took it game by game, we would get there. We knew we had to be focused when we were going over scouting report, eat healthy and making sure we were going hard in practice. We knew it'd transfer over to game day. Fans would talk about the streak and media would talk about it, but actually inside practice or when we were all together, we never talked about it. We just knew we would get there.

Landen Lucas: When you first come in, you quickly realize how big it is. As far as the pressure of winning it, I think the pressure is there. Everybody handles it really well. The only time it would start creeping up is each year—and I feel like I went through this every year—there's a time where doubt creeps in and you wonder whether you'll be able to maintain the streak. It gets really stressful. *Will it happen or will it not?* Somehow it always seems to work out.

By my last year I had learned that there's no reason to panic. We went through a tough stretch, but guys like Frank and Devonte' and myself had been there before. We would have team meetings and we would always start and end with, "This is nothing that we haven't been through before. It's going to work out fine."

Devonte' Graham: You've definitely got to list coaching first, because of the countless hours and film and recruiting and practices and overall time they put in. Then there's the tradition and the guys that were here before us who started the streak. We're playing for them, too. It's not easy to win a conference championship, much less 13 straight.

As soon as you step on campus, you hear about it. When we break down the huddle, we say, "Big 12 Champs!" It's installed in your head as soon as you get here. We don't really spend a lot of time talking about "we've got to win the Big 12 championship." You already know. Before players ever get here, they've already heard about it. It's always talked about on TV. You walk in and see the trophies and the rings on the wall before you come into the locker room. It's ingrained in you. Plus, you don't want to be the team to end it.

The fans deserve a lot of credit, too. There are games we definitely wouldn't have won if it wasn't for them. Even during exhibition games, our fans come and sell out The Fieldhouse. They're excited just to see us play. During conference play it amps up even more. It means so much to so many people, and it should.

Michigan State coach Tom Izzo: When you do it 13 times, that's more than consistency.

The transfers and the one-and-dones make it more difficult. But what he's been lucky on … his rosters don't look like the ones at Duke and Kentucky. He's got that perfect mix. He's got a bunch of three- and four-year guys and that helps.

They don't lose at home. When you're guaranteed to win nine games … it's going to get a little harder. TCU and Kansas State and Baylor have all gotten so much better. You're also going to get some calls at home that you might not get on the road. You think Duke wins all of those home games because they're the best? If that gets you a couple of games in the conference … a couple of games is going to win you the league.

He stays to his principles and his system. They're a very solid basketball team. They've always got pretty good bigs because his system mandates that. They're always tough. That's what I think he has going. He's been consistent. He plays to his system, he's solid defensively and he's got a great home court advantage. Those are good things to have going in your favor.

Former Iowa State coach Fred Hoiberg: It's one of the most impressive streaks in the history of college basketball. To do it in today's era of the power conferences, it's just an unbelievable accomplishment. Bill obviously deserves a heck of a lot of credit for it.

He was great to me. When I came into the conference, he was always willing to talk. It was my first year in the business and he was always willing to give advice. He'd talk about things that helped him be successful.

We still maintain a close relationship to this day. My daughter actually works for him in the KU basketball office. I think we're coming to a family weekend football game. One thing I didn't tell her is I'll never wear a KU piece of clothing. I'll just wear a neutral white.

K-State coach Bruce Weber: There's no doubt it's impressive. Even though the league was divided into two divisions at one time, to just continually do that is really impressive. To be that consistent ... it's one of the better runs ever in NCAA college basketball.

Baylor coach Scott Drew: I never thought something like this could happen in the modern era. To win as long as he has, with as many different players and teams ... it means he's adjusted to the personnel he's had. It shows you he's continued to bring in good personnel, as well. That's why he's in the Hall of Fame. It's well-deserved.

South Carolina coach Frank Martin: When I got hired, I came under the gun. I was attacked personally. The school was attacked. No one thought I deserved to have that job. Whether it was right or wrong, it's irrelevant. That's just the way it was reported. Bill and I knew each other, but not great. He called and he was unbelievable in offering me help and advice and guidance and opening his door to help me during my first year. Bill and Rick Barnes were the senior statesmen that ran the Big 12. They both called me and treated me like I was one of their former assistants who had just gotten their first head job. For them to do that—especially with Bill being at KU—you don't forget those things. That's why I've always had the kind of respect I have for both of those guys.

Now that we were playing against each other two or three times a year ... I always took a lot of pride in our team defense, and I always said that KU was the hardest team to defend that I coached against. And Bill always said that we were the hardest team to play offense against. When I got hired at South Carolina, we all got together and shared offensive and defensive ideas. I know I incorporated and used a lot of the things he taught me when I got to South Carolina. Just spending time around him gave me a new appreciation for him and the job he does. That streak is as impressive as anything you'll ever see in sports, but the more you get to know Bill, nothing he accomplishes comes as a surprise.

Wichita State coach Gregg Marshall: I think the Big 12 needs to step up. KU is obviously the flagship team in that league. I don't think since I've been here, it's been really close. One year (2013) K-State tied them. You'd think at least one year someone would step up and give them a run for the money, but it doesn't seem to be the case. They're just so consistently good, especially at home, that other teams can't compete, I guess.

Saint Louis coach Travis Ford: Bill is one of my favorite coaches. I've got a lot of admiration and respect for him. I study him quite a bit. The thing that stands out is his consistency. He doesn't change much. He'll implement some certain plays for certain players at times. He's so good at what he does. I've always been a coach that changes a lot. I change from year to year. I look at someone like that and try to be a little more like that at times. Not long after I left Oklahoma State, Bill called and invited me to Lawrence to hang out for a day. I went to their practice, spent time with them watching film and talking ball in his office. That's something Bill did for me that I'll always appreciate.

Notre Dame coach Mike Brey: Their streak is as powerful as anything that's happened in college basketball in the last two decades. To be able to have that kind of run of winning your league … it's just not human. Duke and Carolina haven't come anywhere close to doing it, and they're in a position to get players that a lot of us aren't. As a coach, you look at that consistency and just shake your head.

Bill has done a great job of adapting too … it's very interesting how he's now gone the transfer route. He may be tired of the one-and-done world. He's picked off really good transfers, and that keeps you old. He's got the Lawson brothers and Malik Newman. I give him credit. He's adapted. Recruiting against Duke and Kentucky … those are hard battles. He's won a couple of them. I think he's said, "You know what? I don't know if we can do that long term." He's really adjusted.

I think the biggest thing is how he gets them to defend. What has sustained these 13 league titles has been big-time defensive belief. He gets them to believe that they have to guard. They do it willingly. He gets gifted offensive guys to relish playing defense. They know it's their identity. That's a hard sell these days. It's a harder sell to get guys to want to guard together. But now he's got it as part of their culture. The new guys come in, and the older guys tell them, "Hey, one thing we do here is we freaking guard. So get down in your stance or you're not going to make it." The culture builds itself when he's not around. When you have older guys helping you run your program, it's pretty powerful.

Iowa State coach Steve Prohm: I think it's a couple things. It starts with Coach Self. Obviously, he's a Hall of Fame coach and one of the elite and top coaches in the country. Then it goes to he has a great staff that's brought in tremendous, tremendous players who understand Kansas, their history, their tradition and how they want to play. And then Allen Fieldhouse is one of the toughest places to play, if not the toughest place to play—I'm a little biased because of Hilton—in the country.

I've been in the league only the last two years, but over three of the last four years, our league has been No. 1 in the RPI. The other year it was No. 2. When you take the No. 1 league and you take a streak like Coach Self and his program has, it's even more impressive. Obviously it speaks volumes about them as coaches, and within their program, they've done an incredible job.

Illinois coach Brad Underwood: They're simple, and yet they're so well-drilled. They execute so well. There's going to be three or four different things thrown at you throughout the course of the game, and he's great at reacting to what you do. He's a Hall of Fame coach. He's not just doing that with his ability to recruit players. He's doing that on the sidelines. You better be prepared when you play one of his teams. He's going to counter it.

We have a great relationship. I've known Bill since high school. He took me on my recruiting visit to Oklahoma State. Our staffs were very close when I was at Kansas State with Frank. As soon as we got the job at South Carolina, that summer, Kansas going on a foreign tour, Bill brought in our whole staff and we watched three days of practice and then went out at night and talked ball. Those are things that we respected. It was fun. We were trying to knock them off the perch when we were at K-State, but when we left there was mutual respect and friendship.

Colorado coach Tad Boyle: What Bill has done with the 13 straight conference championships … I don't think the average person—or even someone that follows college basketball religiously—understands what an accomplishment that is. To me, it's mind-boggling. It's worthy of him being in the Hall of Fame, I can tell you that. It's harder to maintain that stability of greatness, knowing people are gunning for you. You've got that target on your back. Part of that just comes from being at Kansas, but the fact that they've won 13 straight, every road game they go to, it's like that team's Super Bowl. Allen Fieldhouse is instrumental in that streak, as well. That building and those fans have a lot to do with it.

ESPN commentator Fran Fraschilla: The main thing that comes to mind every time I call a game at Allen Fieldhouse is, "How do they ever lose with this incredible home court—and a coach that continues to drive them at such a high level?" Bill never settles for anything less than complete effort.

The losses are more memorable than the wins, because they don't happen as frequently.

Whether it's a top-five recruit like Andrew Wiggins or a guy like Brady Morningstar, who just wanted to give his left arm to be a part of Kansas basketball, you sense from every one of those guys that they're part of a legacy that they don't want to tarnish.

Playing at Kansas is like a religious experience. Allen Fieldhouse is the St. Patrick's Cathedral of college basketball. It's a religious experience in there, not just for the players, but for the fans. The players, as they come to KU, whether they're role players or stars, whether they're NBA players like Josh Jackson or physical therapists like Tyrel Reed, they all understand the sense of importance of upholding the incredible tradition. That's won them some games through the years.

Kansas fans understand, just like the coaches and the players, the legacy of what Kansas basketball means. There's something that hangs in the air that's bigger than any one person. It's a mystique that can't be explained unless you experience it.

I did a Missouri game one year and it was a 6 p.m. tip. There was a blizzard that night. I remember telling someone at the hotel around 3 that afternoon, "Oh, man. It's going to be brutal. It's going to be a late-arriving crowd. I wonder how many people will be there." At 5:45, the place was packed, blizzard be damned.

When you decide that you're going to play at Kansas, you know before you get there that Bill Self is going to coach you the same as if you were a top 300 player or even a walk-on. I've seen Bill work with Andrew Wiggins and Joel Embiid and the Morris twins and Josh Jackson. He coaches his best players as hard as he coaches his role players. That's why a lot of those guys go to KU. They realize that, even though they're only going to be there one year, Bill is going to get them ready for the NBA. He's not going to let them skate by. I've seen him crush guys in a practice because they weren't going hard with no fear that they'd call their AAU guy or pack up their stuff in the dorm and leave. You go to KU and there are so many great, extraneous parts of being a player there, but part of the agreement is that Bill Self is going to coach you like you're a freshman walk-on.

For every top 10 recruit that has played for Bill Self at Kansas—Simien, Embiid, Wiggins, Jackson—the unsung reason for the incredible streak is the development of players who have shown up at Kansas without a lot of accolades.

The misconception is that every player Bill signs is a McDonald's All-American. If you look at the history of the Kansas program under Bill … from Devonte Graham to Frank Mason to Tyshawn Taylor to Tyrel Reed to Jeff Withey, who couldn't have played dead in a cowboy movie when he showed up in Lawrence … the beauty of Bill Self's run at Kansas is that it's been done with a lot of guys we'd describe as role players. They showed up at Kansas not having the same accolades as the top guys that show up at Kentucky and Duke. But they became great players because of Bill's ability to push every button correctly. They understood the pride that came with being a KU player, so they gave it all they had. Travis Releford hardly played as a freshman but he was an incredible team player by the time he graduated.

In many ways, those four-year guys contribute more than the one-and-done guys, because they stayed longer. Joel Embiid was in and out the door. Frank Mason's blood and guts were on that floor by the time he left. Tyshawn Taylor and Brady Morningstar and Darnell Jackson can say the same thing.

Bill has carved out a Hall of Fame career by getting every ounce out of the players he coaches. He did the same thing at Oral Roberts and Tulsa and Illinois.

Jay Bilas: I was a big fan of (Travis) Releford when he was there, just because of the way he went about things. He was an everyday, utility winner. He was a high school star but then he played whatever role was necessary for his team to win. He went through the trials of being a big-time star in high school, but then took a backseat to some other guys at Kansas. But he was a star. He was a star in his role. That's the type of guy you can point to when you're talking about the title streak. This streak didn't happen because of their stars. Their stars were instrumental, but they won the 13 because of the Relefords and the Russell Robinsons and the Brady Morningstars and the Kevin Youngs.

I grew up in Los Angeles. When I was a kid, the Pac-12 was called the Pac-8. UCLA absolutely dominated it. The rest of the league never got credit for being good, because it was UCLA and everybody else. One year, when I was a kid, USC won every game they played except the games they played against UCLA. Arizona State was unbelievable in the early 80s. They had so many pros. But UCLA was better.

It's kind of the same way right now in the Big 12. The sustained excellence over time that Kansas has exhibited has really taken away from some of the accomplishments of the other programs in the league. It's hard to claim you're really, really good when you're not the best team in your conference.

I had a similar experience as a player. When I got to Duke, North Carolina was the dominate force in the ACC. There were other programs who did well, but it wasn't close as far as who the dominate program was. You had to fight through that. Until you broke through it, you weren't going to get any respect outside of your league until you won your league. You had to take it.

You get a "here-we-go-again" feeling with teams like Kansas. I'm sure Oklahoma got it in 2016. They were as good as anyone that year. They went to the Final Four. But they still couldn't beat Kansas.

Allen Fieldhouse helps, but I don't think it helps anymore than Hilton helps Iowa State or Cameron Indoor helps Duke. There's never been a time where Bill Self or Mike Krzyzewski walked into a press conference after a loss and said, "Our crowd just wasn't good enough tonight." The crowds don't take any blame. It's the team that does it. It's the players that do it. Nobody is afraid of Allen Fieldhouse, they're afraid of the product on the floor.

The places in the league where people say, "Those places aren't that tough to play ..." well, they are when Kansas goes there. Kansas plays the best crowd in the league every game they play. It's sold out. People camp out. The teams you see on film from game to game ... those aren't the teams that Kansas gets. Kansas gets everyone's best. Watching film of an opponent's prior games doesn't give them any indication of what they're going to face. None.

In my years in the game, the only thing that's comparable is UCLA and Gonzaga.

As far as taking care of your backyard, no one else has done it. It's crazy. It's hard to wrap your head around. I think people will only feel it when Kansas doesn't win one. Everyone will really feel it then. You intellectually know it now, but you can't feel it. It's like the sun coming up. You know it's going to come up.

When media members do their preseason picks to generate interest, they should just write "Ditto" each year for the Big 12 champion. The answer should be "What do you think?"

EPILOGUE

When speaking with recruits and their families, Bill Self has a phrase he often uses to describe the effect Kansas basketball can have on someone's future.

"If you give it a chance," Self says, "it will change your life."

The line may sound corny—but you'll realize it's not after reading these parting comments from the Jayhawks stars interviewed for this book. Yes, Self and his staff helped them improve their game during their time in Lawrence. Yet in almost every heartfelt response, players say their appreciation for Kansas basketball stems not from the success they had on the court, but from the growth experienced off of it.

Wayne Simien

Life after Kansas: The Miami Heat selected Simien in the first round (30th overall pick) of the 2005 NBA draft. Simien played two seasons with the Heat—averaging 3.3 points in 51 games—and then briefly in Spain before dedicating his life to ministry. These days Simien is back in Lawrence working for the KU chapter of Called to Greatness, a campus ministry and mentoring program.

The impact of being a Jayhawk: Being a part of Kansas basketball is like having another family. It gives you relationships, purpose, joy, accountability, a little bit of dysfunction … all of the things that you'd experience in a traditional family setting is multiplied in a program like this. It's a lot of fun.

Aaron Miles

Life after Kansas: Miles suited up for 19 games with the NBA's Golden State Warriors before being waived in January of 2006. From there he embarked on a successful career overseas, winning a French Cup and two Russian Cups. In 2013, he was the Russian Cup MVP.

Miles entered the coaching ranks in 2015 and spent a year on the staff at Kansas. He worked under former KU assistant Joe Dooley at Florida Gulf Coast in 2016-17 and is now the head coach of the Santa Cruz Warriors, the NBA G League affiliate for Golden State.

Impact of being a Jayhawk: There's obviously a connection. It's a brotherhood, a family. It's just special to be a part of that family. My four years of playing and living there, it was always love. You don't get that everywhere else. I was under the assumption that all schools were like that. But then you get out and play professionally and you meet guys from other schools. I'm telling my stories about the way I was treated at KU and none of them can relate. They don't go back and visit their schools. J.R. Giddens and C.J. Giles … they saw it when they transferred. They didn't have that sense of family like they had at Kansas. I can reach out to Danny Manning and Jacque Vaughn and Billy Thomas and Nick Bradford—not to mention Kirk (Hinrich) and Nick (Collison) and Drew (Gooden)—any time I want and bounce stuff off of them.

When I became a part of the staff, I saw the other side of it. The program operates like a well-oiled machine. I realized how much work was being done behind the scenes to help our team. It all goes together. Hudy, Scooter, Cheddar...

Coach Self walks into a room and it feels like you've known him forever. It's funny. When I was out on the road recruiting for Florida Gulf Coast, I'd watch Coach K walk into a gym. He'd go off and sit by himself with his assistants. He might say "Hi" to one or two people. Coach (Roy) Williams comes in and speaks to a few people and then focuses in on the players he's there to watch. He has this wholesome, fatherly approach to things. Then Coach Self walks in, and everyone is like, "What's up, Bill? What's up?" He'll have 10 to 15 conversations with people—head coaches, assistants, fans, tournament organizers, janitors, whoever—before he ever gets to his seat. He might not even get to watch the game. Everyone wants to talk to him. He treats people so well. He never looks down upon people. He makes people feel good. He's so down to earth.

Keith Langford

Life after Kansas: Langford is in first season with the Shenzhen Leopards in the Chinese Basketball Association. He's been one of the top players in Europe over the last decade, winning several championships, MVP trophies and scoring titles. At one point he was the highest-paid American player in overseas basketball. Langford—who appeared in two games for the San Antonio Spurs in 2007-08—has had multiple opportunities to play in the NBA, but he's continued to opt for more lucrative offers from foreign teams. In December of 2015, Langford and his wife, Brittany, opened a Wingstop restaurant in Lawrence.

Impact of being a Jayhawk: Being a KU basketball player has impacted me in the same way it would anyone who has ever put on a Jayhawks uniform. Notoriety, great nights, great laughs, memories and fanfare. Some have enjoyed more of those things than others, but as Jayhawks, we've all had our fair share.

That being said, after 12 years as a professional, I've developed a deeper perspective and appreciation about the time I spent at KU. Playing at Kansas means instant credibility when you're in a room of basketball contemporaries. It means living up to the type of player others have always seen you as—even if their memory stems from watching you in the Final Four more than a decade earlier. It means having haters because you went to a blue-blood school. It means forever being linked with the likes of Wilt Chamberlain and Roy Williams. Most of all, it means being remembered. In the end, that's all any of us can ask for.

Michael Lee

Life after Kansas: After leaving KU in 2005, Lee played briefly overseas and then for the Harlem Globetrotters. He worked as a graduate student manager for KU's 2008 national title team and then spent two years as an assistant at Gardner-Webb and three under former KU guard Rex Walters at San Francisco. In June of 2015, Lee became the head coach at Portland (Ore.) Roosevelt High, but he left that position in the September of 2017 to join Aaron Miles staff with the Santa Cruz Warriors of the NBA G-League.

Impact of being a Jayhawk: I tell people all the time that I was fortunate to have great teammates and great coaches. Each year, as I get older, that four-year window of my life becomes more and more special. My youngest daughter is 5 years-old. She's starting to understand things. She knows what a Jayhawk looks like. She's a Jayhawk through and through.

Being a Jayhawk is like being in a fraternity, a brotherhood. Each year that passes, I realize how fortunate I was to have the opportunity to play and coach at KU. Kansas taught me the value of discipline and of being the best version of myself everyday, on and off the court. The relationships I built with players have extended to my family, and the lessons I learned provide constant guidance for me far beyond the court. I'm honored beyond belief to say that I played for the University of Kansas.

Christian Moody

Life after Kansas: Christian Moody, a graduate of the KU School of Medicine, is a fifth-year chief orthopedic resident at Greenville Health System in Greenville, S.C.

Impact of being a Jayhawk: Not a day goes by where I'm not reminded about everything that happened to me as a KU basketball player, about how great my experience was. That can be from talking to somebody and having a friendship, or building a work relationship over conversations about sports and about KU basketball. There are just so many things that I give Coach Self and Roy Williams credit for that make my life what it is today. To be a part of that tradition, and to be included among the names of the players that have been there is just a dream. I love watching the current players. I love feeling a part of their success. I love the staff. You feel so connected to them after sharing such a huge life experience that not many people get to have.

Jeff Hawkins

Life after Kansas: Hawkins graduated in 2006 and played professionally in Germany. He was the head coach at Perry-Lecompton High School from 2010-14 and now serves as the Recreation Programmer at the Sports Pavilion in Lawrence. Hawkins also runs his own basketball skills academy and a non-profit youth basketball program in Lawrence. He and his wife, Heather, have three children: Mavrick, Sienna and Atticus.

Impact of being a Jayhawk: All of the blessings I've received from being a Jayhawk, it's mind-blowing how much support there is for the players. It's played a role in everything I'm doing now. Just being involved with that program puts you in an elite group, an elite fraternity. It's not just the immediate basketball family. It's the fans. They're in that fraternity, too. It's a huge community. There are Jayhawks everywhere. I've been blessed to come across a lot of incredible, influential individuals that are Jayhawks, people that bleed crimson blue. It's changed my life.

Stephen Vinson

Where is he now: Vinson is an investment consultant for New York Life in Overland Park. He married his high school sweetheart, Anna Vinson, and they have four children.

Impact of being a Jayhawk: I grew up a Kansas fan long before I played, so to be a part of the program was incredible. It's affected my adult life as much as you can imagine, as far as my closest friends and the people I was associated with. They helped me get into the line of work that I'm in. There are few parts of my life that it hasn't affected.

Darnell Jackson

Life after Kansas: The Miami Heat selected Jackson with the 52nd pick in the 2008 NBA draft and immediately traded him to Cleveland. He spent close to two seasons with the Cavs and finished his second year with the Milwaukee Bucks. He was then traded to the Sacramento Kings, where he played one season in 2010-11.

Since then, Jackson has traveled the world, playing in China, the Ukraine, Turkey, Poland, Dominican Republic and Venezuela. "The last time I was in NBA was 2010-11," he said. "I thought about trying to go back, but I don't want to go through that grind anymore."Jackson currently plays for the French club Boulazac Basket Dordogne.

Impact of being a Jayhawk: The things I went through at Kansas ... sometimes I get emotional just thinking about them. The guys knew what I was going through. The coaches knew what I was going through. Even the fans knew certain things. For everyone to embrace me and keep me here during those tough times ... they saved me, because I was going to leave. I was like, "I'm done. I don't want to play basketball anymore." Now I wish I could come back and do it all over again. I don't miss going to class, but I miss playing and traveling and getting on planes and winning games. That's the impact it had on me. Those were the best times of my life. It gave me an identity. I don't know what would've happend to me if not for Kansas basketball.

Mario Chalmers

Life after Kansas: The Minnesota Timberwolves selected Chalmers with the 34th pick in the 2008 draft and immediately traded him to Miami, where he won two NBA titles starting alongside LeBron James, Dwyane Wade and Chris Bosh. He was traded to Memphis in November of 2015 and tore his Achilles the following March. After sitting out the 2016-17 season to rehab, Chalmers re-signed with the Grizzlies over the summer and opened the 2017-18 season as the team's sixth-man.

Impact of being a Jayhawk: All around the league, every time I see a (KU player), they're like, "What's up, Jayhawk?" We've got a connection like that. Whether we played with each other or not, it's a brotherhood, a family. It's a good feeling to be remembered, not just for what the team did, but for what I did. Not to be selfish, but it's nice to get recognition for what you did. Who wouldn't want that?

Russell Robinson

Life after Kansas: Robinson plays for KK Rabotnički in the Macedonian First League. He's spent a majority of his career overseas, winning a Polish League championship and Polish Cup in 2015.

Impact of being a Jayhawk: Playing at KU has impacted my life in many ways. My experiences as a college student, my achievements in athletics and all the people I've come to meet along the way have helped inspire my future. When I looked in the mirror my senior year after graduation, I was proud of the man I had become. Fear was gone, replaced with positive expectations and confidence that I can accomplish anything I set out to do. Winning the national championship was an honor. For me it took some sacrifice, the calming of my ego, a lot of smart work and some patience. All qualities that have allowed me to have success playing basketball all over the world for the past 10 years. Playing at KU showed me the power of a community when everyone is doing their job and pulling in the same direction. It taught me how me how showing love and support can lift up young men and women, and keep them inspired through life's life struggles. It's more than a game. Winning is a powerful thing and takes more than just the players and coaches to do it. It literally takes everybody.

Brandon Rush

Where is he now: The 13th pick in the 2008 NBA draft has played for four different teams in the NBA, most recently with the Minnesota Timberwolves in 2016-17. He entered the 2017-18 season as an unsigned free agent. Rush won an NBA title with the Golden State Warriors in 2015. Much like at KU, Rush has been a consistent 3-point shooter in the league. His 40.2 career 3-point percentage ranks 36th-best all-time in the NBA.

Impact of being a Jayhawk: The day I was kicked out of Westport High School in Kansas City, the principal there told my AAU coach that I'd never amount to s**t. The principal said that. I was a 15-year-old sophomore then, and for years that comment was in the back of my mind. I actually thought about it the night we won the title. Part of me wanted to drive around KC until I found that lady. I pictured myself holding the trophy in her face to show her what I'd accomplished.

Signing with Kansas was one of the best decisions I'd ever made, and not just because of basketball. I became a man at Kansas. I did a lot of growing up in the three years I spent there. It's nice to know that I'll always be able to go back to Lawrence and feel welcomed.

Sasha Kaun

Life after Kansas: The Seattle SuperSonics drafted Kaun with the 56th pick in the 2008 draft and then traded him to Cleveland. Kaun, though, decided to return to his native Russia to play for CSKA Moscow. He won five championships in the VTB United League—the top tier of Russian basketball)—along with five Russian League championships and a Russian Cup. In 2014, Kaun was the VTB United League Defensive Player of the Year.

Kaun played his final season of competitive basketball in the NBA as a seldom-used reserve for the 2016 NBA champion Cleveland Cavaliers. During a speech following team's victory parade through downtown Cleveland, LeBron James recognized Kaun for his behind-the-scenes contributions to the Cavs' championship. "A good friend texted me the other day, by the name of Mario Chalmers," James said. "He said, 'You know you can't win a championship without a Jayhawk on your team.' Sasha, everything that you did this year, that no one ever saw … you worked out every single day with no one from the coaching staff saying, 'You're going to play. You're going to get minutes.' You had no (sense of) entitlement all year. You've got to be an unbelievable person and an unbelievable professional to be able to take that and still come to work every single day and give it your all. Thank you, Sasha!" Kaun retired after the season and now lives in Denver with his wife, Taylor.

Impact of being a Jayhawk: The best part about going to KU was that I met my wife there. You can't ask for much more than that. I love Kansas. I always go back with pride. I played with a lot of guys that played for big schools, and they don't ever go back. To me, the desire that so many guys have to go back and visit says a lot about the program and the way that it's run. Going there was one of the best decisions I've ever made.

The stuff LeBron said about me at the victory parade after we won the title was really nice. It meant a lot. I retired after that season and, the next year (2017) Cleveland lost to Golden State in the finals. I thought about calling LeBron and saying, "Hey, you needed a Jayhawk." Seriously, they couldn't win the year before, I got there and they won, and then I left and they lost. There has to be something to that, right?

Darrell Arthur

Life after Kansas: Now in his fifth year with the Denver Nuggets, Arthur has established himself as one of the best second-unit big men in the NBA. The 27th pick in the 2008 draft spent his first five years with the Memphis Grizzlies. Arthur has averaged 6.7 points in his NBA career. He and his wife, Chariote, welcomed their first child, a baby girl, in the summer of 2017.

Impact of being a Jayhawk: Going to Kansas made my game so much better. A lot of players from different programs come into the league and they don't know the game. It takes them a while to adjust. Learning under Coach Self and Danny Manning gave me such an advantage going into the league. I was a step ahead of almost all of the other rookies in terms of knowledge and work ethic. I was prepared, and that earned me a chance to play right away.

Defensive positioning, showing on screens, footwork on offense … a lot of rookies that come in don't understand that kind of stuff.

Coach pushed us every day and made us work. The day I got there, he told my mom and my grandma that he was going to work me into the dirt and that's exactly what he did. Hudy got me in shape and had me physically ready, and then he got me mentally ready to go out there and play. Everything he did for me in college got me ready for the NBA.

There are so many Jayhawks fans in Denver. They love me out there. I'm always hearing Rock Chalk Jayhawk and people are always asking me to sign KU stuff. I see KU fans everywhere I go.

I've torn my Achilles, I've torn my pec muscle and I'm playing with a torn labrum right now. I've had two scopes and a stress fracture in my left knee. I've dealt with a lot since I've been in the league but I'm not going to give up. I'm going to keep going.

Jeremy Case

Life after Kansas: Case was hired at KU's video coordinator in August of 2016. Prior to that he spent four seasons as an assistant coach at Houston Baptist and three seasons at Southeast Missouri State.

Impact of being a Jayhawk: The Kansas basketball program shaped me into the person I am today. Playing at Allen Fieldhouse is an experience I will cherish for the rest of my life. Being a former Jayhawk gives you instant credibility in the coaching profession.

But with that comes the responsibility of upholding the tradition and the culture of the program wherever you go. For the rest of your life, you're representing everyone that's ever played or coached at Kansas. Once you graduate and move forward with your life, the memories and the relationships you made are magnified. You appreciate them more as the years pass, and it starts to sink in just how fortunate you were to be a part of something so special. The pride you have grows and grows, because you're a part of a fraternity—a family—that only a select few ever have the honor of joining.

Matt Kleinmann

Life after Kansas: Kleinmann is currently working on his doctorate degree in architecture at KU with a focus on public health. He's also the co-director of the Dotte Agency in Kansas City, Kan. Kleinmann has had a successful career in architecture that included a stint as an adjunct professor in architecture and urban design at KU.

Impact of being a Jayhawk: If you had asked me what it means to be a Jayhawk 10 years ago, I would have talked about how great it was to be on the basketball team and the tradition and the culture, but the more I reflect on it now, it feels less important. I've realized there's so much more to this world than basketball. That's a hard thing to acknowledge. I've experienced KU as both a fan and a player, and now I have a lot more insight into how things go.

Every year people get so worked up about KU basketball—a bunch of 18- to 21-year-olds who are pushed together into an environment where it's extremely stressful trying to win games on national television and without getting any compensation. They're doing it because they want to be there. OK, maybe some of them don't want to be there, but they've got to somehow show up every day, six days a week, four hours a day and compete. That's a grueling experience.

What I appreciate the most now is how much it means to everyone else outside of it. We just came back from our reunion that Brian Hanni puts on, and it was so fun seeing Christian Moody and his kids and seeing Darnell and talking about his family and seeing Sasha and his wife and hearing about his two daughters. That's what I take away: the family part of it. But then you see thousands of people lined up for autographs because it means something. The fact that a bunch of 18- to 21-year-olds can have that kind of impact is what I really feel blessed to be a part of. Every now and again you'll hear about somebody's nephew who has terminal cancer and it's their last wish to go spend a day with the basketball team. You hear that and think, yes, at some level, all we're doing is playing basketball, but what's really fascinating to me, looking in from the outside, is how much significance and importance it has to other people's lives. You never quite grasp it as you're going through it. Years later you look back and think, wow, there's an entire city of Lawrence built around this. People's jobs built around this, people who spend their entire lives writing about it. It means a lot. When you're an 18- and 21-year-old, you just want to win a game and go out to a bar and meet a cute girl and have a good semester.

Sherron Collins

Life after Kansas: Collins went undrafted in 2010 and signed as a free agent with the Charlotte Bobcats. He played 20 games with the Bobcats as a rookie before eventually getting waived. Collins recently moved back to Lawrence with his 7-year-old daughter, infant son and girlfriend.

Impact of being a Jayhawk: When I showed up at Kansas I didn't trust anyone. I had a wall up. I had grown up in rough, predominantly black neighborhoods in Chicago. Gangs, drugs, shootings, prostitution … it was all right there in my apartment courtyard. When I got to Lawrence I was in culture shock. But after just five or six months, my eyes had opened. The people in Lawrence made me feel so welcomed. It was odd at first. I had never felt that kind of love before, at least not from strangers. The fans, the players, the coaches and their wives and children … they all opened their arms and took me in, and because of that I started to grow in the way I viewed different types of people and races. Being around that diversity was good for me. It changed me, and because of that I eventually became a better man, a better father. I wasn't perfect. I made some mistakes, but when I did, people didn't turn their back on me. They supported me and helped me. Being on that basketball team helped me form relationships with guys that I'll call brothers forever. Even the guys that came after me, guys I never played with, I feel like they're my brothers, too—my little brothers. We migrate to each other and ask each other questions. For the rest of my life, I'll be tied to Kansas basketball. My plan is to always be around and always find some sort of way to be involved. The best decision I ever made was the decision to come to Kansas. It didn't just change my life. It saved it.

Brady Morningstar

Life after Kansas: Morningstar's playing days were far from over after graduating from KU in 2011. There were overseas stints in Greece, Argentina and Finland and stops with Tulsa and Canton of the NBDL. Finding a team was rarely a problem for the defensive standout. Eventually, Morningstar star retired and dabbled as a trainer, working with former KU stars such as Brandon Rush and Travis Releford in the offseason. In September of 2017, Morningstar landed his first college coaching gig as an assistant at Texas Wesleyan, the reigning NAIA Division I national champion.

Impact of being a Jayhawk: I grew up more quickly at KU than I probably would've at another school—even though I did make some dumb decisions while I was in college. Being from Lawrence and going to games with my dad when I was younger and seeing how cool it was and how important it was to people, and then having an opportunity to play on the same court and having fans watching me do it … when I was playing I wasn't thinking about that, but after my career was over, I was like, "Wow, that was fast." It was the best time of my life. It really was. It meant a lot to my family, because my dad went to Kansas and has a lot of Kansas ties. It meant a lot to him that I was able to exceed the expectations of a lot of people and actually be competitive and get on the court and help us win games.

Tyrel Reed

Life after Kansas: Reed played briefly in Belgium before returning home and enrolling in graduate school at the University of Kansas Medical Center. In 2015 he received his Doctorate in physical therapy. Reed and his wife, Jessica, recently moved to Lawrence, where he works as a physical therapist at OrthoKansas, LLC.

Impact of being a Jayhawk: For me it was just a dream come true. I grew up idolizing those players. I was the biggest Kirk Hinrich fan a kid could ever be. Once I started playing well in high school I felt lucky to have a chance to go to North Carolina or Stanford—and, of course, to have KU offer me a scholarship. When they did, it was an easy choice for me.

The tradition and the brotherhood of KU basketball is what drew me back to Lawrence to live and work. It's just something that, once you've been a part of ... it's hard to put into words. There's people who still remember and still look back. I guess it will always be that way. The streak is a big reason for that. Since 2005, we're all kind of lumped together because we've all been doing the same thing. That's pretty cool that's been able to be carried on for so long. I hope it goes on a lot longer.

Marcus Morris

Life after Kansas: Morris was selected by the Houston Rockets with the 14th overall pick in the 2011 NBA draft. (His brother, Markieff, was picked one spot ahead at No. 13 by Phoenix). Marcus spent two seasons each with the Rockets, Suns and Detroit Pistons before signing with the Boston Celtics during the 2017 offseason. In his first six NBA seasons, Marcus earned just under $18 million. Markieff, who is now with the Washington Wizards, has earned just over $24 million.

Impact of being a Jayhawk: I grew up a lot at Kansas. I had to. We showed up there as two immature guys coming from so much poverty and so much crime in Philly. Getting out there and seeing so much love ... it was kind of hard to adjust to, if that makes any sense. It was hard to adjust to people loving you so much, because you're coming from a place where there's a lot of crime, a lot of hate. When I first came, we'd be walking down the street and people would pull over and say, "Do you guys need a ride?" At first I wouldn't accept an offer like that. It just didn't seem real, because where I'm from, that just doesn't happen. If someone is pulling up on you, you better take off running. It was a culture shock. But as I got accustomed to how things went around there—and the love that was everywhere—it became a lot easier. I'm glad I had the opportunity to go there. God works in mysterious ways.

Tyshawn Taylor

Life after Kansas: The Portland Trailblazers selected Taylor with the 41st overall pick in the 2012 NBA draft and immediately traded him to the New Jersey Nets. Taylor spent nearly two years with the organization before being traded to New Orleans, which waived him two days later. Since then, Taylor's talent has landed him roster spots in Puerto Rico, Venezuela, Israel, Turkey and Russia. He makes frequent visits to Lawrence during the offseason.

Impact of being a Jayhawk: Kansas impacted my life tremendously. I graduated from college, became a father and was able to live my dream of playing in the NBA—all because of the great coaches and people in Lawrence who helped mold me into the person I am today. Some of my closest friends are my college teammates. I loved everything about my time at Kansas.

Thomas Robinson

Life after Kansas: Despite being the fifth overall pick in the 2012 NBA draft, Robinson struggled to find stability in the NBA, as he played for six different teams in his first five seasons before opting to go the overseas route in the fall of 2017. Robinson is off to a strong start in his first year with Khimki of the VTB United League in Europe and hopes to be back in the NBA soon.

Impact of being a Jayhawk: It's been pretty frustrating the last few years, with things not going as well for me in the NBA. But it's not like I haven't dealt with adversity before. If anything, it's motivating—just like getting killed by Cole in practice every day was motivating; just like losing my mom fueled me; just like trying to get out of D.C. drove me. I've been doing this my whole life. The stage I'm at now is nothing new. I'm at peace with where I am in my life.

I'm not saying it's been easy, or that I've always been at peace. There was a time not long ago when I was like, "You know what? I'm done. I'm going to take the money I've made, invest in a couple of businesses and just live my life." I was struggling and I didn't have the support system I had at Kansas. I needed someone to believe in me and to give me a chance—just like Coach Self did. When you fight so hard to get that chance, and it never comes … it hurts. Especially when you give your all in everything you do. I don't half-ass anything.

Luckily for me, the Morris twins have always been there, just like they promised they would back in the Towers that night my mom died. Sometimes it's tough love, which is exactly what I need in certain moments. When I told them I was thinking about giving up, they told me I was acting like a girl. They were like, "You're crying and complaining too much. You need to get back in the gym and keep working. Get your mind right so teams will want to sign you." They don't sugarcoat anything. Coach Self was the same way. They don't tell me what I want to hear. They tell me what I need to hear. It's the straight truth. I'm glad I went to Kansas because, otherwise, I wouldn't have them in my life.

Conner Teahan

Life after Kansas: Teahan was recently promoted to Senior Vice President of Merrill Lynch Wealth Management in Kansas City. His client list includes several former KU teammates.

Impact of being a Jayhawk: I wouldn't be nearly as successful or in the spot I'm in—in terms of what it has meant for my professional career—without the structure that was provided for me at Kansas, the hard work and the work ethic instilled in me and also just the support of KU fans and the university.

Travis Releford

Life after Kansas: Releford has had a successful career playing overseas, most recently for the Promitheas Patras B.C. in the Greek League.

Impact of being a Jayhawk: Coming into KU, I didn't think anything of the streak until I had maybe three rings and saw the guys before me had four or more. To be a part of that—and to have it continue it while I was there—was a blessing. I have so many stories and memories my teammates and I shared on and off the court. It's something I will always remember.

Jeff Withey

Life after Kansas: Withey is in the first year of a two-year deal with the Dallas Mavericks. He was originally drafted 39th by the Portland Trail Blazers in 2013 and then traded to the New Orleans Pelicans later that summer. He spent two seasons with New Orleans and two with the Utah Jazz before landing in Dallas.

Impact of being a Jayhawk: Some of my best friends are from Kansas. Justin Wesley is a like a brother to me. He's my roommate. Tyler Self and Evan (Manning) and I still talk. I grew so much as a person there. I've gone through a lot of hardship but I came out a lot stronger because of it. That's because of Coach Self. He's a great college coach.

He turns us into men and gets us mentally stronger and ready for the real world. I grew up during my time at KU. I made great relationships. There are Jayhawks alumni everywhere. They love their school. In Dallas I'll be walking down the street and people are screaming Rock Chalk all over the place. Whenever that happens, I get a smile on my face. It was definitely a time in my life that I'll cherish forever.

Elijah Johnson

Life after Kansas: Johnson's basketball career hasn't slowed down a bit since his graduation from Kansas in 2012. He's played for teams in Turkey, Greece, Germany, Croatia and Poland. In October of 2017 he signed a contract with Galil Gilboa, a professional team in Jerusalem. In the offseason he returns to Lawrence often.

Impact of being a Jayhawk: Being a Jayhawk has changed my life in so many ways. I was able to accomplish goals no one in my family had ever been able to achieve. I graduated from college, played basketball on live, national television more times than I could ever dream of and had a chance to compete for an NCAA title. Through the process I met many famous, important, blessed individuals. Becoming a Jayhawk was both a gift and a curse. The gift was being a part of something so special that it's bigger than you. The curse is that, once you leave Kansas, you realize there's nowhere else like it in the world.

Kevin Young

Life after Kansas: Young has played professionally in Mexico, Puerto Rico, Canada and the NBA G League. In 2015, he was named the NBL Canada Defensive Player of the Year. In September of 2017, Young signed a pro contract with Keflavik, a professional team in Iceland.

Impact of being a Jayhawk: The people at KU are amazing. Even now, years after my last game, there is still so much support. You can walk into the coaching offices whenever you want and ask for advice, or you can go work out with Hudy whenever you're back in town. It's truly a family here. That's what makes it great.

My mom (Alicia) and my little brother, Donovan, moved to Lawrence my senior year. They're both still there. Donovan just graduated from Free State High School (May of 2017). Me coming to KU changed our lives in a lot of ways.

Ben McLemore

Life after Kansas: McLemore signed a multi-year contract with the Memphis Grizzlies in July 2017, joining former Jayhawks Mario Chalmers and Wayne Selden.

The seventh pick of the 2013 draft spent his first four years in the league with the Sacramento Kings.

Impact of being a Jayhawk: Being a Jayhawk turned me into the man I am today. I told Coach Self the same thing when he got into the Hall of Fame. Everyone there helped me become the person that I am. Being there for two years, developing my game, developing my lifestyle and social skills ... it's bittersweet. I miss it. Everything was so family-oriented there. I'm big on family. That's what brought us together. They saw the lifestyle and the poverty I was living in. They saw a kid that came from nothing, a kid that never had anything, but wanted to fight to get to that next level. They wanted to help me. They wanted me to be a part of their family. I'm grateful for that. I'm forever going to be a Jayhawk. I'm always going to go back and show love.

Joel Embiid

Life after Kansas: Embiid likely would've been the No. 1 overall pick in 2014 if not for a foot injury that required surgery a few weeks before the NBA draft. Instead he was picked at No. 3 by the Philadelphia 76ers. Embiid missed what were supposed to be his first two NBA seasons before debuting in 2016-17, when he averaged 20.2 points and 7.8 rebounds in 31 games. Already established as one of the best big men in the NBA, Embiid's potential will be limitless if he can stay healthy. In October he signed a five-year, $148 million contract with the 76ers.

Impact of being a Jayhawk: Kansas is a basketball town. They love basketball so much. The love I got when I was there prepared me for the love I get when I'm in Philly. The fans are crazy over there, too. They're literally insane. Being at Kansas helped me embrace who I am—a guy with a fun personality who loves being around everybody. People like to call me, "The Man of the People." It seems like I am that.

Even though I was only at Kansas for one season, I feel the connection to the program. It's not like I'm never going to go back there, or pretend like college didn't happen. I loved it there. Sometimes I miss it. Every chance I get to represent KU, I always do. I still wear the same colors in Philly so it worked out pretty well. Every time they play and I don't have a game, I make sure to watch. Every chance I get to support them, I do what I can. I send texts to Devonte' or Udoka or whoever. KU will always be a big part of my life.

Tarik Black

Life after Kansas: Black is back with the Houston Rockets, who signed him as an undrafted free agent out of college in 2014. He spent half of his rookie season with Houston and half with the Los Angeles Lakers, who then inked him for two more years. The Lakers waived Black in July of 2017, which allowed him to become a free agent and sign with Houston.

Impact of being a Jayhawk: The way the program was run ... it was so family-oriented. The coaches cared so much, and we were around them so much. If we needed anything we could go talk to them. If there was something that was going on with our families, we could go talk to them. It was truly like a second family—or a first family, for some guys. Plus, we were playing for a coach that was so experienced. He doesn't beat around the bush. He shoots you straight.

Naadir Tharpe

Life after Kansas: Tharpe considered transferring to another school after leaving KU, but he chose to turn pro instead. In 2014-15 he played 14 games for the NBDL's South Bay Lakers but was waived after three months. And in November of 2016 he was waived after just one game with the Delaware 87ers.

Impact of being a Jayhawk: For me, Kansas was a beginning stage of getting into the real world. There are no fans like Jayhawk fans. They'll love you in a second and they'll let you know in a second how bad you are. That's just how life is, truthfully. You have bad times in life and you have good times in life, and you're going to have people that are going to be down on you and you're going to have people that try to uplift you, but if I could say one thing about Kansas Jayhawks fans, it's that they always kept it real at all time. They always showed love. And that's a place I'm always going to have love for, and I'm always going to want to go back for sure.

Perry Ellis

Where is he now: Undrafted in 2016, Ellis averaged 9.8 points for the NBDL's Greensboro Swarm in 2016-17. In the summer of 2017 he signed with the Sydney Kings of the Australian Basketball League.

Impact of being a Jayhawk: Being a KU basketball player taught me the importance of taking no days for granted and of giving your best in whatever you're doing. It's something our coaches talked about on a regular basis, and it helped me become the player and person I am today. The lessons I learned as a Kansas Jayhawk are ones I'll carry with me for the rest of my life.

Wayne Selden

Life after Kansas: Selden went undrafted in 2016 and eventually signed with the Memphis Grizzlies. He started his rookie year in the G League and eventually was signed to a 10-day contract by the New Orleans Pelicans. After his contract in New Orleans was up, he got scooped back up by the Grizzlies and finished the season there, eventually starting five regular season games, including two playoff starts. After his successful rookie season, he signed a multi-year contract with the Grizz.

Impact of being a Jayhawk: My time at Kansas did a lot for me. Even though people might think while I was there I didn't get much better, I think I got so much better mentally. My mind became so much stronger there. I had to put up with a lot of stuff. As an 18-year-old I had to deal with fans telling me I sucked.

I'm in a different state right now, for sure. I feel like I've grown up, come into my own and figured things out. It's been great. Going undrafted, I was like, "Damn man. I might have to go overseas." I just tried to stick with it and play basketball. I was so mad going undrafted and then getting cut and having to go to the D-League when I felt like I should have been here. Going through the D-League, I was playing mad, but it was so much fun, honestly, being on the D-League court. Being in the D-League might not be the most fun, but it was fun to just be able to spread my wings and come into my own. All of the experiences, good and bad, got me to where I am today.

Jamari Traylor

Life after Kansas: After graduating from KU in 2016, Traylor played the 2016-17 season with the Oberwart Gunners in Austria. In the fall of 2017, he joined Kymis Seajets, a Greek professional team.

Impact of being a Jayhawk: More than anything, I'm proud of myself for getting a degree from a distinguished school like Kansas. I'd never participated in any sort of graduation ceremony. That was really emotional for me that day. Of all the fun and amazing things that happened on the court, that was the highlight for me, being able to get my degree and seeing my mom so happy, knowing I'll always have something to fall back on. When I first started playing basketball, I didn't know where it would take me. I was doing it for fun and to pass time. I'm so happy that it took me to that place and that I met the people I was able to meet.

I was a long shot based on the cards that were dealt to me. But I made something spectacular happen. To see where I'm at now, I feel blessed every day.

Frank Mason

Life after Kansas: The 2017 National Player of the Year was drafted 34th overall by the Sacramento Kings. He signed a guaranteed deal with the Kings in July of 2017.

Impact of being a Jayhawk: Being a Jayhawk means everything to me. It helped changed my life on and off the court. I love the KU tradition, and not only basketball, but the entire school. They helped me get my degree and gave me so many opportunities for me and my family as a young man. It's one of the best schools, and I'm just happy to be a part of it.

Landen Lucas

Life after Kansas: Lucas followed in his father's footsteps, heading to Japan to play professionally. He signed with the Toyota Alvark Tokyo in Japan in the summer of 2017.

Impact of being a Jayhawk: I chose to play at KU because I knew I'd regret it if I didn't try to be the best player possible at the highest level program. I learned toughness and grit beyond what I could've imagined. I was mentored by Wayne Simien and baptized by him when I decided to renew my faith in God. My time at KU taught me that life will throw extreme ups and downs at me, but I can get through anything with mental toughness and continual trust in God. I appreciate the incredible fan support and all that I learned from my coaches. I'm grateful for the experience and will forever be a Jayhawk.

ACKNOWLEDGEMENTS

A few days after embarking on this project in June of 2017, I came to a realization: there was no way I could do it alone.

I wanted "Beyond the Streak" to include perspective not only from Kansas players—both the stars and the scrubs—but also from dozens of high-profile opponents who had tried, unsuccessfully, to halt what has become the most impressive run in all of sports.

The goal was ambitious—yet attainable. But only if I enlisted help. Thus, it's only fitting that my first "thank you" goes out to C.J. Moore, my former Bleacher Report colleague who ensured my vision for this book came to fruition. As riveting as his conversations were with former Jayhawks such as Wayne Selden, Travis Releford and Tyrel Reed, C.J.'s biggest impact on this project can be found in the reflections and anecdotes he coaxed from former KU foes such as Jacob Pullen, Georges Niang and Acie Law and coaches like Fred Hoiberg, Bob Huggins and Lon Kruger. Their unique perspective on Kansas' title streak is every bit as gripping as the tales we gleaned from the Jayhawks themselves. So thank you, C.J., for attacking those interviews like a Baylor zone—and, more importantly, for being a sounding board and friend throughout a stressful five months.

I'd also like to pass along my gratitude to Beau White, the former KU media relations czar and graphics wizard who designed the 512-page encyclopedia you're holding. Impressive as his efforts were on "Beyond the Phog," Beau outdid himself with the cover design for "Beyond the Streak." Mix in the masterful way he laid out all of the words and pictures, and it's clear that I was working with a talented individual with a Marcus Morris-like skill set in terms of its versatility. I'd also like to thank photographer Steve Puppe—a yearly fixture on the Allen Fieldhouse baseline—for providing all the pictures, just as he did for my first two books.

Equally important are the proof-readers who did their best to make sure this 200,000-plus-word manuscript contained absolutely zero typographical errors, or at least somewhere within 100 of that number. Jennifer King, Dow Tate, Jayne Quimby, Joey Berlin, Thor Nystrom, Jonathan Cooley, Mike Fitzgerald and Susan Fitzgerald, Piotr Zygmunt, Justin Weigel and Mark Zeligman ... 'preciate y'all! And you, too, *Kansas City Star* beat writer extraordinaire Jesse Newell, for compiling so many of the Top 10 lists that will certainly lead to numerous e-mails questioning whether my parents built my swing set facing a brick wall. Brad Witherspoon is WAY too low on the Top 10 Walk-ons list, dammit!

And finally—along with, Ben, the manager at the Overland Park Corner Bakery who let me office out of the back booth, the one by the power outlet, for five months—I'd like to thank my wife, Jennifer, and my kids, Carson (8) and Kacie (6). I'm sorry for the five-month hiatus I took from bath-and-bedtime duties, and I apologize for missing a gymnastics practice or four (I had to work, I swear) but hopefully I'll make up for lost time soon. I love you all. And no, Carson, you can't text Russell Robinson—again—to tell him about the touchdown you scored in flag football, or that you wear No. 3. You've already informed him. Twice.

–Jason King

I could not have worked on this project without the support of my wife, Kirsten. Parenting is a team endeavor. She often had to play a one-woman zone the last few months. Thank you to my mom, Jayne Quimby, who has always been my biggest fan. You are my hero, and I'm so proud to be your son. Thank you to my dad, Curt Moore, who took me to my first game at Allen Fieldhouse. I fell in love with basketball watching the Jayhawks growing up, and it was a blast going down memory lane to tell this story.

– C.J. Moore